1986

ABORTION:
The Continuing Controversy

ABORTION:
The Continuing Controversy

AN EDITORIALS ON FILE BOOK

Editor: Carol C. Collins

Assistant Editor: Oliver Trager

Facts On File Publications
New York, New York • Oxford, England

ABORTION:
The Continuing Controversy

Published by Facts on File, Inc.
460 Park Avenue South, New York, N.Y. 10016
© Copyright 1984 by Facts On File, Inc.

Library of Congress Cataloging-in-Publication Data
Main entry under title:

Abortion: The Continuing Controversy.

  (An Editorials On File book)
  Includes index.
  1. Abortion—United States—Addresses, essays, lectures. 2. Abortion—Law and legislation—United States—Addresses, essays, lectures. I. Collins, Carol Chambers. II. Series. [DNLM: 1. Abortion, Induced—United States—legislation. 2. Ethics, Medical. HQ 767.5.U5 A1544]
HQ767.5.U5A275 1986   363.4'6'0973   85-27601
ISBN 0-87196-994-7

International Standard Book Number: 0-87196-817-7
Library of Congress Catalog Card Number: 84-5943
9 8 7 6 5 4 3 2 1
PRINTED IN THE UNITED STATES OF AMERICA

TABLE OF CONTENTS

Preface

Abortion has been called the single most important issue in politics today, the one most likely to decisively turn a voter for or against a particular candidate. Certainly, it is one of the most emotional issues ever to become a dominant part of the American political scene. But it is not only a political issue, involving as it does the most private of decisions. This is why it is so difficult to resolve. A question that involves so many factors—medical, religious, moral, legal—is one that is ill-designed for public mediation. It pits one against the other two groups with irreconcilable differences, each of whom seeks governmental protection for what they consider to be a fundamental right. 'Pro-choice' advocates feel that the decision about whether to carry a pregnancy to term should be left to each woman's conscience; 'pro-life' supporters believe that every child conceived should be born. (In this highly volatile controversy, even the names the two groups have chosen for themselves are at issue, and thus are apostrophized throughout this book.)

Abortion is a debate which is impatient of compromise or gray terminology; just as it is impossible to be a little bit pregnant, it is impossible for a fetus to be a little bit aborted. Thus the debate, far from being quelled by the Supreme Court's landmark 1973 ruling legalizing abortion, has grown in proportion and intensity in the intervening years. Medical advances that have made it possible for the fetus to survive outside the womb at an earlier stage of development have tended to bolster a view of the fetus as a 'little person,' but have not provided any means of establishing when human life as we know it actually begins. And the continuing legal battles over various aspects of the abortion question—from Medicaid funding obligations to the permissible restrictions placed on abortions by state and local governments—have avoided this fundamental uncertainty. The protests of those who believe that full human life begins with conception have spilled over from marches and demonstrations into violence directed at clinics where abortions are performed, while the courts have steadfastly held that a woman's right to privacy includes the right to choose an abortion. The current national ferment over abortion shows no sign of abating.

Abortion: The Continuing Controversy explores the meaning and possible repercussions of this explosive issue through the commentary of the nation's newspaper editors. Their perceptions of the events and arguments surrounding the tangled abortion debate provide a unique documentary record of one of the most searing issues ever to divide the American public. The editorials reprinted here, a representative sample, have been selected only with the intent of including the widest possible variety of newspaper reaction nationwide; no attempt has been made either to evenly balance viewpoints or to give weight to one opinion over another.

April, 1986

Carol C. Collins

Abortion, Public Opinion and the "Silent Majority"

It is difficult, with the strong rhetoric used on both sides of the question, to gauge exactly where the American public stands on the question of abortion. A Washington Post-ABC News poll conducted in February 1986 indicated that 54% of Americans agreed with the statement that a woman should have the legal right to an abortion "if she decides she wants one, no matter what the reason," and 34% "only under certain circumstances"; 10% of those polled thought abortion should be illegal in all cases. By contrast, a Newsweek poll conducted in January 1985 found that 21% of respondents thought abortions should be legal under all circumstances, 55% only under certain circumstances, and 21% thought that abortion should be illegal in all circumstances. The general current trend, according to most experts, is that a solid majority of the American public supports a woman's legal right to have an abortion at least under certain circumstances—a phrase which is usually taken to include cases of rape, incest or medical necessity—and that only a minority, less than a fourth of the public, favor an absolute ban on abortions.

One interesting result of the Newsweek poll was that 38% of the respondents indicated that they had doubts about whether their own position on abortion was "right." This uncertainty may be the most important legacy of the current public debate over abortion; caught in the crossfire of rhetoric between radical feminists and die-hard antiabortionists, most thoughtful observers find it difficult to adopt either position wholeheartedly or, on the other hand, to simply dismiss the arguments that support it. For many men and women, the legal right to an abortion is a separate matter from the "moral" choice that must be made in each individual case about whether to terminate or proceed with an unplanned pregnancy, when trying to weigh the consequences of each choice not only for the parent(s) but for the unwanted child. Another indication in the Newsweek poll of the mixed feelings held by most of the public was that even among those who support a ban on abortions in most circumstances, the majority recognize the serious social consequences that might occur as a result: illegal and unsafe abortions, many more unwanted children and higher welfare costs to pay for the unwanted children of the poor. It may be that the often-cited "silent majority" on the issue of abortion are less silent than they are ambivalent about their own position.

THE MILWAUKEE JOURNAL
Milwaukee, WI, August 20, 1981

Abortion and the silent majority

It's time for the great majority to speak up in the public debate on abortion.

In a recent Journal series, Barbara Dembski reported that the small faction most zealously opposed to abortion is well organized, well funded and determined to rally voters district by district to defeat lawmakers who do not share the minority view on abortion.

A Journal poll published after the series confirmed what national polls have long revealed. The majority of people surveyed (57%) believed that abortion should be legal under certain circumstances. Only a minority (20%) believed that abortion should be flatly illegal, just as only a minority (21%) believed it should be legal under all circumstances.

If the majority would break its general silence, politicians would be less easily cowed by the single-issue minority. Citizens should be aware of the dangers of single-issue politics. Simply put: You're less likely to get the best overall person in elective office.

Furthermore, if the majority would speak up, the public debate on abortion might be more rational and lead to a clearer consensus on the issue. While many citizens find abortion a personally repugnant way of coping with unwanted pregnancy, they are hesitant to restrict the right of women in general to have an abortion — particularly when the life of the mother is in danger, when rape or incest is involved, when the child is likely to be born severely retarded, when the mother's mental or physical health is genuinely jeopardized by continued pregnancy. However, even this degree of legal flexibility could be lost if the majority does not make its voice heard.

St. Louis ⚞ Review
St. Louis, MO, March 21, 1980

Too Few Impelled to Try

Over the centuries, men have recognized that human laws and justice are not synonymous. In fact, human laws and interpretations of law can be biased, vicious, and sometimes evil. To cite instances from the past, we can recall the discriminatory laws against Catholics in Northern Ireland, laws proscribing the Catholic religion in England, the vicious laws of Nazi Germany and the Communist Soviet Union. In the United States, we recall with deep regret our constitutional acceptance of slavery and our slow retreat from that infamous institution.

Where laws have been unjust or been interpreted unjustly, men have had recourse to various remedies. Traditionally these have included efforts to change unjust laws through new legislation as well as judicial litigation. In recent American history this has been the course pursued by those seeking vindication of civil rights and an end to the Vietnam conflict. It is questionable, however, whether the enactment of civil rights legislation or the American withdrawal from Vietnam would have been accomplished without the massive demonstrations and instances of civil disobedience having sensitized those in power to the urgency of the problems.

Until Jan. 22, 1973, human life was regarded as sacred in most of these United States. On that date, the U.S. Supreme Court, after refusing to hear the medical evidence, declared war on the unborn and discounted the value of all human life. Despite repeated efforts of legislators in many states, the U.S. Supreme Court has continued its unconstitutional role of judicial legislation and social engineering. One bizarre ruling after another has manifested the determination of the judiciary to preside over the American holocaust.

In the face of the continuing American slaughter of the innocent and the insistence of the courts that all Americans must support abortion with tax monies, some pro-lifers have undertaken a campaign of civil disobedience. Non-violent civil disobedience arises from a conviction that injustice must be confronted even at extreme personal cost. It is an honorable course of action which is sometimes extremely effective. It requires purity of motive, a willingness to undergo extreme physical and psychological hardship and the conviction that the existing injustice is such that it justifies such conduct. Civil disobedience must always be a matter of personal decision, after an intense examination of the existing situation and of one's own capacity to endure.

We don't know if massive civil disobedience might have stemmed the carnage in the Nazi death camps. The tragedy of modern German history is that so few felt impelled to try.

The Detroit News

Detroit, MI, March 18, 1981

Abortion in America

An authoritative report from the Alan Guttmacher Institute, a private research agency named for a former president of Planned Parenthood, states that 30 percent of all pregnancies in America now end in abortion.

Abortion is the single most common medical "procedure" in the United States, more common than episiotomies and biopsies, and three times as frequent as tonsillectomies.

This suggests the kind of binge that should give pause to many who identify themselves as "prochoice." We refer to those who justify abortion as a rarely used backstop for contraceptive failure, in cases of rape and incest, when the mother's health is threatened, and when there is a genetic disorder present in the unborn.

Some other troubling statistics:
● Ten percent of all abortions are done in the second trimester of pregnancy, when there is a possibility the aborted fetus might be born alive.
● Thirty percent of the women seeking an abortion are repeaters.
● One-third of all abortions are performed on teen-agers.

Instead of pushing for more clinics to accommodate the queue, shouldn't we be asking why so many American women are seeking abortions, and how many fetuses will have to perish to guarantee the "right" to abortion on demand?

Detroit Free Press

Detroit, MI, June 9, 1981

WOMEN : Hard-won rights are being challenged on many fronts

FEMINISTS AND their allies are alarmed over what they consider a Reagan administration drive to scuttle hard-won women's rights. Actually, the administration may have something much worse in mind. During last year's Republican Convention, Sen. Jesse Helms, R-N.C., thundered against "the permissiveness, the pornography, the drugs, abortion, living together, divorce." Now he and other spokesmen for the New Right seem bent not just on keeping women barefoot and pregnant but on setting moral standards for everybody.

The attack on women's rights has been both blunt and subtle. In its broader sense, it involves calling for cuts in programs vital to women's survival, including food stamps and affirmative action. Households headed by women are the fastest-growing family group in the country and, partly because of traditionally lower salaries for females, two-thirds of such households receive welfare payments.

To make matters worse, a proposed plan would dilute enforcement of an executive order requiring employers doing business with the government not to discriminate. This would eliminate awards of back pay to victims of sex bias and remove any incentive for avoiding bias.

The congressmen working to make abortions illegal would impose further hardships on women. Women would be forced to bear unwanted children, including children fathered by relatives or rapists. And the escalating number of teenagers becoming pregnant every year would no longer have legal abortion as an option. But more of them than ever would probably become pregnant, since Mr. Reagan's secretary of health and human services, Richard S. Schweiker, wants to end his department's support of sex education and family-planning information for minors and indigents. For far too many women, especially the young, the only options left would be living in poverty or practicing chastity.

But that is just what the New Right and the so-called Moral Majority want. "Deep down, the New Right is nothing if not a movement in reaction to the sexual revolution of the 20th Century, especially the liberation of women," writes Peter Ross Range, in a recent edition of Playboy. "The abortion issue brings the conservative extremists together on the things that stir them most: fear of sex, religious fundamentalism, racist hostility to minorities with 'loose morals,' the independence of young people."

Fortunately, the public, despite its supposed shift to the right, isn't likely to support such drastic attempts to turn back the clock. According to a national opinion survey conducted for Time magazine this month, most Americans favor the Equal Rights Amendment and oppose making abortions illegal. Americans worry about the moral standards of their children, but they worry just as much about the government's intrusion into their private lives. They are no more likely to condone attempts to regulate their sex lives than they are to support the losses in family income that some of the rollbacks contemplated in Washington would cause.

This is not the sort of conservatism cherished by the far right and the Moral Majority. It is good old American pragmatism and individualism heated up in the cauldron of rapid social change. Plain common sense, coupled with self-interest, ought to make most Americans see that the feminists' fight for women's rights is everyone's fight.

The Evening Gazette

Worcester, MA, June 12, 1981

Abortion: No Consensus

The newest poll on abortion shows the impossibility of translating this emotional moral issue into an effective political consensus against abortion.

The nationwide survey, commissioned by The Washington Post and ABC News, says that 74 percent of Americans condone abortion either on demand or in most circumstances. Only 26 percent disapprove abortion in most or all cases.

More specifically, the poll shows that 88 percent favor legal abortions to save a woman's life, 82 percent in cases of rape and incest and 84 percent in cases where the woman might suffer severe health damage.

At the same time, other questions in the poll show that many people have a deep moral repugnance to abortion. And 72 percent said they believed life begins either at conception or during the first three months of pregnancy. Also, 54 percent of those polled disapprove of using public money to pay for abortions for poor women.

But those feelings do not override the strong majority conviction that abortion is a necessary medical procedure in some cases and should not be prohibited by the government. After 40 years of ever-increasing government intrusion into private matters, it is perhaps not surprising that most people feel the government should keep its hands off such individual and personal decisions.

In moral matters, laws do more harm than good unless they are based on a strong popular consensus. It is clear that no such consensus exists in regard to outlawing or restricting abortions.

"WHY DO THE POLITICAL AND FOOTBALL SEASONS COME AT THE SAME TIME?"

THE ⬛ SUN
Baltimore, MD, September 21, 1982

Law, Logic and Abortion

Washington County Circuit Court Judge Daniel W. Moylan issued an injunction last week to prevent a Boonsboro woman who was less than three months pregnant from having an abortion. Her husband asked that she be prevented from taking such action. Judge Moylan preceded his order with remarks that included quoting a 1976 U.S. Supreme Court decision in which concern for a father's feelings was expressed. Justice Harry Blackmun wrote in that case: "We are not unaware of the deep and proper concern and interest that a devoted and protective husband has in his wife's pregnancy and in the growth and development of the fetus she is carrying."

But the Supreme Court ruled in that case a Missouri law giving a husband a right to prevent his wife from having a first-trimester abortion was absolutely, unequivocally unconstitutional. The husband's interest had to give way totally to the wife's. The Supreme Court had earlier ruled that a woman has a constitutional right to an abortion—and the state may not interfere.

Given this clear Supreme Court command, which has not been weakened or modified in any way since 1976, and given the clear and unambiguous declaration in the Maryland Constitution to the effect that the U.S. Constitution is "supreme" over state law, we do not see how Judge Moylan could have made his ruling.

Judge Moylan appears to have based his decision on two arguments. We understand him to say that the husband and wife have conflicting *private* rights. No state action is involved. Thus the Supreme Court ruling is inapplicable. But he also says the husband's rights are derived from the common law and the Equal Rights Amendment to the state's constitution. In this context, both are certainly state acts, just as in the Missouri case.

Judge Moylan says the decision to have an abortion "requires the consent of two people." But when two people disagree, "the view of only one of the two marriage partners can prevail," as Justice Blackmun put it. And there can be do doubt in law or logic which one it has to be. As Justice Blackmun said, "Inasmuch as it is the woman who physically bears the child and who is the more immediately and directly affected by the pregnancy, as between the two, the balance weighs in her favor."

The Union Leader
Manchester, NH, March 21, 1981

A Word for Doctors

"I will give no deadly medicine to anyone if asked, nor suggest any such counsel; furthermore, I will not give to a woman an instrument to produce abortion."

——Excerpt from the Oath of Hippocrates, named for the father of modern medicine whose principles of medical science, laid down 400 years before the birth of Christ, gave the medical profession a sense of duty to mankind that it was never supposed to lose.

One wonders how many graduating medical students today take the oath, which includes rules for the relationship between a doctor and his patients. Specifically, one wonders how it can be taken in good conscience by medical practitioners of abortion.

That same thought may have occurred to that intellectually courageous and unrelenting foe of abortion, Dr. Mildred F. Jefferson, the first black woman to be graduated from Harvard Medical School, as she addressed three groups of Kennett High School seniors recently.

Dr. Jefferson minced no words as she defined for her North Conway audiences the most apparent result of the U.S. Supreme Court's intellectually corrupt refusal to decide when life begins while at the same time fixing a timetable for its destruction:

"This leaves my profession with an unlimited right to kill. And I do not intend to use my medical skill to destroy life. I became a doctor to try and save lives, not to destroy them."

Commenting on the doctors in Germany before World War II who went along with Adolf Hitler's plan to remove "undesirables" and create a "master race," Dr. Jefferson added:

"I see the same thing when the Supreme Court gives to my profession the means of aiding those who want to control the social order by doing away with those thought likely to be a burden. I cannot accept the philosophical view that there are some lives that are less valuable than others. That the lives of the unborn . . . of a child . . . of the elderly . . . must be balanced against what they are going to cost or how much they are going to produce."

Strong words? Yes, as strong as the dehumanizing practice of exterminating more than 1,000,000 innocent lives annually through abortion in America warrants. What a happier world this would be if the doctors of pre-war Germany had been equally outspoken!

The Charlotte Observer
Charlotte, NC, January 22, 1982

Legal Abortion
It's Not Holocaust Revisited

Increasingly in their propaganda, Right-to-Lifers are equating women who choose to have abortions with the Nazis who exterminated 6 million Jews. Right-to-Lifers passed out anti-abortion booklets in the N.C. legislature last year that were stamped with the Nazi swastika, and they talked about living in the midst of a Holocaust. Closer to home, the Charlotte Right-to-Life organization plans to raise the issue tonight as it marches from the offices of Planned Parenthood to Holocaust Square.

The implication that legal abortion is only a first step toward compulsory murder of "undesirables" has no basis in fact and slanders women who have had to make the anguished decision to have an abortion.

No one has been able to say for sure, at least within the first three months following conception, when human life begins. Thus, no one can say for sure when an abortion becomes the taking of human life. That has to be an individual decision, at least within those first three months.

There is a world of difference between an individual having the right to make that decision, which is what the pro-choice people believe in, and a government that dictated who should live and who should die. In Nazi Germany, the government was more important than the individual; in the United States, the individual is more important than the government.

Some aspects of the Right-to-Life movement are, in fact, closer to Nazi policy than the freedom of choice policies they oppose. In talking about the Holocaust, what they're really trying to do is drum up support for legislation which would make abortion illegal — thus imposing the will of the state over the rights of individuals. That is exactly what the Nazis did when they made abortion illegal.

None of this is to say that the Right-to-Lifers do not raise questions about human life and the taking of life that ought to be discussed. But we do not hear them raising questions about the life of the mother, which may be threatened by the baby she's carrying, or the life of the convict on Death Row, or the lives of people who would be destroyed in a nuclear "holocaust."

As the anti-abortion National Catholic Reporter said in an editorial, "There is something wrong in a movement which . . . can value life in just one stage of development." And, one might add, which does so in a mean-spirited, irrational manner.

Chicago Defender
Chicago, IL, February 18, 1982

Abortion — sick society

"May men and women know how to embrace every human life as a precious gift to be guarded, respected and promoted in a climate of authentic love," said Pope John Paul II last week during a speech in Vatican Square. "Abortion is the product of a society that is sick with selfishness and death."

Those strong words did not sit well with the advocates of abortion on demand, pro-choicers and radical feminists. What does the Pope, with millions of dollars at his disposal, know about the anguish of unwanted pregnancies? — they ask. How dare he interfere in the lives of others!

Yet, the words should be taken at face value. Do they make sense? And do they actually describe the situation in the U. S. today? Indeed, the vehemence with which abortion advocates attack such warnings indicates a deep unwillingness to think about the reality of abortion. It's just too painful to hear the unvarnished truth.

As a people, Blacks have not bought into the abortion mentality as have so many other segments of American society. We have tried to cling to the old-fashioned ways; we still want to 'embrace every human life as a precious gift." Yet, there is evidence we are weakening in the 1980s, losing our hold, conforming more and more to a society that is "sick with selfishness." To do so would be tragic. We must resist glib slogans and pro-choice and face the ugly facts about abortion without flinching. The stakes are too high for compromise.

the Charleston Gazette
Charleston, WV, May 30, 1981

The moral policemen

ABORTION is an issue about which thoughtful persons hesitate to offer unqualified opinion. The argument that a fetus is a human being cannot be dismissed out of hand. But it is difficult to accept the argument that a woman may not exercise control over her own body, especially in circumstances in which her own health and mental stability are at stake.

Without demanding any specific conduct of women, we find ourselves recoiling from the idea of casual abortions, with women being sped through clinics like cars through a car wash. But we are forced to acknowledge that in our view there are circumstances in which termination of a pregnancy should be acceptable.

In this we probably are at odds with the assistant secretary of Health, Dr. Edward N. Brandt Jr., who said Wednesday that unless the mother's life is endangered, abortion should be denied a woman who learns that the fetus she is carrying is that of an abnormal child. Here we would stop and think for a long, long time before offering moral preachments — not only out of concern for the parents but also out of concern for the child.

The abortion issue looms large today mostly because of the heavy influence of the Moral Majority on the Reagan administration. It does not seem inconsistent to the Moral Majority to uphold the sanctity of life while endorsing as God's will an overabundance of lethal weapons and state executions. It should be noted, as it was in a Charleston church publication this week, that troopers of the Moral Majority regard Sen. Jesse Helms as a hero of the movement because he is opposed to abortion. They are not disturbed by his role in retaining government support for tobacco, a cancer-causing substance which takes many lives.

We do not suggest that abortion is a subject not worth discussion. But we cannot assign it the priority given it by administration ideologues. Because it is an issue to which simplistic pronouncements cannot be applied, it can be debated forever. Our fear is that the debate will prevent action on the many, many other problems facing our nation.

It seems doubtful to us that abortion is a subject of compelling interest in America. It seems dangerously likely to us that government, and hence the people, will suffer from the single-mindedness of the moral policemen who speak for the administration.

DAYTON DAILY NEWS
Dayton, OH, January 25, 1982

Abortion political issue pits lobby vs. national will

It is time to stop referring to the anti-abortion "movement." There are only anti-abortion organizations. If there is any "movement," it is pro-abortion.

If that message doesn't get through to Congress, the nation will be burdened with the kind of law whose policing inevitably is capricious, arbitrary and, finally, cruel because it is out of sync with the way most people feel and act. Congress is to take up proposals this year to outlaw abortion.

The annual anti-abortion march in Washington Friday was designed to rev up the push for abortion prohibition. It was given added political oomph when the leaders were welcomed by President Reagan, who reversed his earlier tolerance of abortion after right-wing political groups at the core of his constituency took up the issue.

The supposed anti-abortion "movement," however, is only a collection of a rather small number of organizations that lobby full time to bend the political system contrary to the wishes of an overwhelming majority of Americans. The groups can produce letters, telegrams, phone calls and delegations on demand, but their apparent numbers are an illusion.

That is made clear once again by the new Associated Press-NBC News poll, which shows that three-fourths of Americans oppose a ban on abortions.

For years now, independent polls have found that a large majority favors the basic outline of the 1973 U.S. Supreme Court ruling that established abortion as a private, personal decision. Charted for nearly a decade, this support obviously is durable.

Americans have heard and considered every possible argument on the issue. Their general support of a free-choice policy has survived intense political and persuasive efforts from abortion opponents.

The Supreme Court ruling has its lobbyists, too, but mainly from organizations interested in a wide range of social issues; they do not concentrate on abortion as the be-all of politics, the single focusing lens of their political view. They speak for the majority, but they are, frankly, no match for the anti-abortion lobby.

And that, politically, is what this issue finally comes down to: A contest between a single-issue lobby and the obvious but vague national will.

The AP-NBC poll found that only 19 percent of us want to outlaw abortions; 6 percent were undecided.

The decision will not be made by the sincere opponents of abortion in Congress or the sincere supporters of it. It will be made by the in-between members. They will judge whether that 19 percent, relentless and unforgiving, could cost them re-election, or whether the majority has become so enlivened that they, too, will be at the polls in force if a prohibition they oppose is fastened on them.

The State
Columbia, SC, July 18, 1983

Anti-Abortion Effort Has Run Its Course

NOT SO many years ago, the word "abortion" was only whispered, for the most part, in polite society. And the not-so-polite press generally confined its discussions of the subject to articles on dangerous and illegal "abortion mills" run clandestinely by non-professionals.

But this changed abruptly in the middle 1960s, partly as a result of the births of a number of deformed babies due to pre-natal disease or drug use and partly as a result of looser lifestyles.

While abortions in the early stages of pregnancy were condoned by the English Common Law, the danger to the mothers in the days before modern medicine was so great that all states in this country banned them. As the state of medicine improved, most states began to loosen their restrictions to allow the procedure to save or reduce the danger to the life of the woman. By 1972, four states had gone so far as to permit a woman to have an abortion after consultation with her physician.

Then came 1973, the watershed year in this field. The U.S. Supreme Court, wisely or unwisely, waded deeply into this medical arena. In a detailed decision (*Roe v. Wade*) that determined what was permissible in each trimester of a pregnancy, the justices made abortion legal nationwide. They concluded that the Constitution's implied right of privacy encompasses a woman's right to decide whether to end her pregnancy.

That did not end the debate; it poured fuel on it. Anti-abortion, "Right to Life" groups organized to find ways to overturn the decision or to lessen its impact. Pro-abortion groups, in turn, fought hard to preserve their gains. Both of these single-issue segments seemed determined to convince the nation that abortion was about the only subject worthy of consideration. For a decade, the country has been subjected to endless arguments on legal, moral, religious, medical and other grounds. Most of us in the middle tried to stay clear of an issue that so stirred the emotions of other sincere people. But many political candidates couldn't; in some areas victory or defeat hinged on it.

Over the decade, numerous bills cropped up in Congress and state legislatures to regulate abortions. At the same time, information was gathered that indicated, not surprisingly, that the legalization of abortions had made them safer for women. If we can rely on statistics compiled by an affiliate of Planned Parenthood, a pro-abortion organization, the death rate per 100,000 abortions dropped from 4.1 in 1973 to 0.5 in 1978.

June turned out to be a very bleak month for the anti-abortion forces. First, the Supreme Court took up a case testing an Akron, Ohio, ordinance that tended to curb abortions and two companion cases from other states, and shot down every restriction these jurisdictions had imposed. In a 6-3 decision, Associate Justice Lewis Powell wrote, "the doctrine of *stare decisis* (precedent) ... is a doctrine that demands respect in a society governed by the rule of law. We respect it today and reaffirm *Roe v. Wade*." Associate Justice Sandra O'Connor wrote the dissent.

Then on June 28, the U.S. Senate easily defeated a proposed constitutional amendment that would have overturned the Supreme Court ruling by stating simply, "A right to abortion is not secured by this Constitution." That would have allowed the states to curb them. The vote was 49-50, 18 short of the two-thirds needed to approve an amendment.

These actions would seem to bring the issue to an end. The court's ruling will make it extremely difficult, if not impossible, for Congress and the local governments to significantly alter women's freedom of choice by statute, and Congress has demonstrated that it is not ready to submit an amendment on the subject to the states. The "pro-life" forces, however, vow to fight on.

While we feel somewhat uncomfortable with figures that indicate there have been 13 million legal abortions in this country in the past decade, we must conclude that the practice has been widely accepted. The matter has been thoroughly argued, adjudicated, and legislated. Let it rest.

The Boston Herald
Boston, MA, April 5, 1984

The sacred gift we must protect

ABORTION is an issue that involves a collision of rights — the right of a woman to choose whether to bear or abort a fetus, and the right of that fetus to the precious gift of life.

The Herald, as a matter of conscience and conviction, stands on the side of life. The Globe has chosen the other side.

We've made our decision because we believe that no right, however cherished, can be absolute.

In an enlightened, civilized, and compassionate society, it must be limited whenever the exercise of it would do violence to the rights of another.

That violence occurs every time a woman carrying the beginnings of a child in her womb chooses to cast it out.

In 1982, the last year for which the State Public Health Department has figures, it happened 40,394 times.

Every time it did, a life was ended.

The kind of life we are talking about begins with the union of a man's seed and a woman's egg — with conception. It is the act of two human beings, sheltered and nourished in a human body.

And it should be considered a human life, as much entitled to the whole range of human rights as a full-grown child — or a mother.

To choose deliberately to destroy a fetus in the womb, or to expel it forcibly before it is viable enough to exist outside it, is an irreparable violation of its most basic right — to live.

There are those who believe that the opposition to abortion or, if you prefer, the right to choose, is a "Catholic" issue — as if the laity and clergy of that particular faith were alone in the position they hold.

The truth is that it transcends — and to varying degrees — divides members of all faiths.

It is not a sectarian issue, it is a moral one — the sacredness of life.

It happens to have been a Catholic newcomer to Boston, Archbishop Bernard F. Law, who put the question in its proper context when, in his first sermon in this city, he said:

"Jesus came that we might have life and have it more abundantly. Yet we deal out death through abortion to the most innocent of human beings. This is, I believe, the primordial darkness of our time; this is the cloud that shrouds the conscience of our world.

"Having made our peace with the death of the most innocent among us, it is small wonder that we are so ineffective in dealing with hunger, with injustice, with the threat of nuclear war.

"In naming the darkness, we must speak the truth in love ... The truths of faith must illumine all our decisions; we cannot tolerate the false notion that it can be 'yes' in some aspects of life and 'no' in others."

The Globe professed to be puzzled by that. "Supporting a woman's right to choose a safe, legal abortion in no way conflicts with supporting an end to the nuclear arms race," it said.

The Globe completely missed the prelate's point — which was that if we can practice or condone the basic evil of deliberately ending helpless human life before it has hardly had a chance to develop, then we cannot hope to make progress against lesser ones — including nuclear war.

To repeat his words: "We cannot tolerate the false notion that it can be 'yes' in some aspects of life and 'no' in others."

The Legislature will soon meet in joint convention to vote on a proposed amendment to the state Constitution against both abortion and "private or public funding of abortion or the provision of services or facilities thereof."

It has already been approved once, and if it passes again it will go on the November ballot for action by the voters.

Its effect, given the U.S. Supreme Court's 1973 ruling that the constitutional right to privacy extends to a woman's decision about whether to have an abortion, is debatable.

But the principle on which it is based — that human life in all its forms and stages is sacred — is clear and firm.

We believe it. We support it. We stand on the side of life.

THE TAMPA TRIBUNE

Tampa, FL, December 23, 1985

Toward an Agonizing Consensus on Abortion

The abortion controversy in the United States continues, and while it continues some 1.5 million fetuses are killed every year. Whatever their general views on the subject, we don't think many people hail that awful fact.

Basically, the argument can be reduced to two strongly held attitudes. The pro-lifers stress that a developing, unborn human organism, if it is not subjected to mayhem, will absolutely grow into a human baby. Therefore, to destroy that organism is murder.

Abortion's defenders say that although the "procedure" is regrettable, every woman has a right to control her own body, to decide if her baby will or will not be born.

★ ★ ★

At the extremes, plausible cases can be made on both sides.

Tom Braden, a syndicated newspaper columnist, tells a story about his daughter being gang-raped. After the crime she became pregnant. Braden fully supported his daughter's decision to have an abortion, a decision that few other fathers would be quick to condemn.

Or consider the Tampa woman who told us she was generally hostile to the idea of abortion but who posed this hypothetical predicament: "I am married and have three children. What if one day I was raped and became pregnant because of that rape. Should I carry that baby to term? If I did, what would be the effect on my husband and my children? Would the situation destroy my family? I think it very likely would."

Now let's look at the other side. Biologists tell us that life begins at conception. There is no argument about that. The argument emerges over the question of the humanity of that life. Is the unborn organism human from the instant it is conceived or is it non-human for a few weeks or months?

Scientists say it is human from conception. It is human just as the tiniest sprout from a tomato seed is a tomato plant, even though that sprout is extremely fragile and to-tally invisible to the gardener who awaits its appearance above the soil. There is no question about the biological identity of the tomato sprout. There is no question about the biological identity of the developing unborn baby, however new, however small.

So, the problem stands. A woman becomes pregnant by rape and so grievous would be the burden of carrying and then birthing the issue of a rape that her decision to abort would raise few protests among any but absolutist pro-lifers. And yet the human nature of the fetus is in no way mitigated by the circumstances of conception. It's not the fault of the fetus that it came into being because of a terrible crime. The fetus is innocent and innocent absolutely. Must society sanction its death?

All of us can see there is a moral dilemma here that defies an altogether humane solution. But such hard cases aren't the part of the problem that chiefly concerns us. We are much more concerned about the huge majority of abortions that involve neither rape nor other extraordinary circumstances. We are concerned about the present system of abortion on demand. We are concerned about abortion taking on the color of just one more means of birth control.

We are concerned about the slaughter.

Most women who have abortions do so because having a baby would be inconvenient. No more. Very inconvenient, perhaps, but still only inconvenient. The woman might have to drop out of high school or college for a time. She might have to interrupt a business or professional career. She might think her family is already large enough.

We once discussed family size with a man who had a wife and two children. How did you decide upon two? we asked. "Well," he said, "I observed long ago that in restaurants most tables seat four. I thought we should take that into consideration."

Most decisions to have a small rather than a large family spring from more substantial concerns, and they are usually economic. Those decisions deserve our respect. But, it seems to us, there is an immense difference between controlling family size through pre-conception measures and controlling it by killing a fetus.

Still, we hear that women should have the right to control their own bodies. It's obvious, however, that the women who exercise that right before the fact, the women who intelligently control their bodies in such a way as to avoid pregnancy, have no need to contemplate the destruction of a baby that is developing in their womb.

Even Planned Parenthood, which (out of the best of motives) has contributed so much to the slaughter, agrees that preventive action is far more desirable than abortion.

That being so, would it be possible to reach a new consensus in the United States about the right to abortion? Would it be possible to agree that abortion should be reserved for victims of rape and other women whose pregnancies involve extraordinary circumstances? Couldn't we then reasonably deny abortions to women for whom pregnancy is only hugely or somewhat inconvenient?

★ ★ ★

Such a solution would require legal definitions for all those terms. And it would do nothing to eliminate the basic moral question so many people have about *any* abortion. Such a compromise to a dispute apparently not susceptible to compromise would probably put society in the position of saying: We agree to permit abortions in certain, relatively rare circumstances. While we recognize a moral contradiction here, we agree to accept an odor of wrongfulness, or at least moral ambiguity, in order to reduce a far greater wrong — the slaughter of 1.5 million human fetuses every year.

If in so doing we could save the large majority of those babies, our pragmatism, while offering small solace to ethical purists, would yield a grand net gain for humanity.

Part I: Abortion & the Supreme Court

More than a decade ago, in 1973, the Supreme Court issued its landmark decision legalizing abortions. The 7-2 ruling, in *Roe v. Wade,* divided the nine-month term of a normal pregnancy into three trimesters, narrowing the choices of the pregnant woman as she moves nearer to full term. The majority opinion, authored by Justice Harry Blackmun, found that "a woman's decision whether or not to terminate her pregnancy" was guaranteed, during the first trimester, by the right to privacy granted by the Fourteenth Amendment. During the final trimester, however, when the fetus "presumably has the capability of meaningful life outside the mother's womb," Blackmun wrote, the state may protect its legitimate interests in "protecting potential life" by banning abortions "except when it is necessary to preserve the life or health of the mother." In between, during the second trimester, the state could intervene to protect the health of the woman, regulating the procedure through licensing and procedural measures, but the woman's right to choose remained. This highly controversial ruling overturned restrictive abortion statutes in 44 states; in more than half the states, abortion had been a crime.

Ninety percent of the abortions now performed in the United States—at the rate of roughly 4,000 a day—take place before the 13th week of pregnancy, or during the first trimester. But recent developments in neonatal care have moved the time when a fetus can be expected to survive outside the womb, known as viability, earlier into the second trimester than ever before. Critics of the *Roe v. Wade* ruling argue that these developments have placed the reasoning behind the 1973 ruling, largely dependent upon then-current medical technology, on shaky ground. These critics include President Reagan's 1981 appointee to the Supreme Court, Justice Sandra Day O'Connor, who wrote in 1983: "It is certainly reasonable to believe that fetal viability in the first trimester of pregnancy may be possible in the not-too-distant future. The *Roe [v. Wade]* framework is clearly on a collision course with itself." O'Connor's remarks were part of a dissent from a 1983 decision in which a majority of six justices strongly reaffirmed *Roe v. Wade* by overturning a host of states' procedural restrictions on abortion. (The Justices have in recent years approved some state limits on abortion, but have adhered to the fundamental view that women have a constitutional right to obtain abortions.)

In light of that 1983 decision, the Reagan Administration's efforts to have the Court itself abandon *Roe v. Wade* seem doomed to failure, at least while the present roster of Justices remain. But five of the Justices are now over 75 years old; it appears likely that if any replacements are appointed during Reagan's second term, they will be abortion foes. The Justice Department has appealed to the Court to overturn the 1973 decision and return the responsibility for setting abortion policy to individual states, arguing both that the ruling was flawed in its logic and that it concerns an issue better dealt with in the legislative than in the judicial sphere.

Annual Protests Continue to Mark Date of 1973 Supreme Court Ruling

More than a decade after the Supreme Court ruling in *Roe v. Wade*, which made abortion legal during the first trimester of pregnancy, the issue of abortion refuses to lie dormant. There is perhaps no clearer indication of the continuing national ferment than the marches and demonstrations held each year on the anniversary of the January 1973 ruling. For the largest of these, the annual March for Life in Washington, D.C., opponents of the Supreme Court decision rally in the thousands to protest the decision and call for its reversal.

President Reagan spoke by loudspeaker Jan. 22, 1985 to more than 70,000 people who had gathered in the nation's capital for the March for Life. The marchers were the first to be addressed by a President in the 12-year history of the event. "I feel a great solidarity with all of you," Reagan told the demonstrators. He predicted that the antiabortion movement's "momentum" would end "the terrible national tragedy of abortion."

The State
Columbia, SC, February 7, 1981

A CROWD, estimated by police at 50,000, descended on Washington to mark the eighth anniversary of the Supreme Court's decision permitting abortions and to demand additional legislation restricting the practice.

New Health and Human Services Secretary Richard S. Schweiker appeared before the group and offered them his support. President Reagan also opposes abortion. N.C. Sen. Jesse Helms has been pushing for a "pro-life" amendment to the U.S. Constitution.

Senator Helms, the new head of the Senate Agriculture Committee, has also been busy working on plans to whittle down the food stamp programs. There are proposals to broaden the federal statutes on capital punishment.

These were just a handful of the emotionally charged issues on hand as the new administration took over. In each case, opposition is loud and strong. On issues such as these, both sides sometimes let rhetoric drown out reason.

Such matters mean a great deal to some people, but, as Washington columnist Jack Germond reminds us, they are not issues that have much direct affect on how most voters live. They are not the kind of things that will help Mr. Reagan build a political majority and keep his ideology in the ascendency.

Two overriding issues brought Jimmy Carter down and caused the voters to turn with hope to Mr. Reagan — the economy and national defense.

Mr. Germond, writing for *Enterprise* magazine, gives Mr. Reagan about two years — before the voters begin to turn against him — to show some progress in these areas. The new President must manage to convey a "subjective impression to the electorate that the United States is both consistent and competent in world affairs," Germond says. That will require sound decisions in defense and foreign policy.

On economic matters, Mr. Reagan will be judged by more objective standards, standards that relate to the pocketbook, such as interest and inflation rates, unemployment, personal income, corporate profits, etc.

The great danger for the new administration and the new Congress is that they will be distracted by the high-decibel lesser issues and waste time and energy that should be devoted in these early months to matters of overriding concern.

The Reagan team indicated during the transition that it knows the difference and has its priorities in order. Indeed, its early actions so indicate. But it will have to take care that pressures from highly vocal minorities do not cause it to lose sight of the main course.

The Washington Star
Washington, DC, January 22, 1981

Today, the eighth anniversary of the Supreme Court decision lifting the bans on abortion, finds the issue as much a call to battle as it ever was. Perhaps more, since the accession of Ronald Reagan to the presidency.

Both before he was elected and since, President Reagan has been the major American politician least given to hedging on abortion. Rather than being merely "personally opposed," he is against it and, in spite of the desire of some of his advisers to have him play it down, he has said so.

Thanks to the unabrasive manner we are beginning to recognize as salient in the Reagan political style, the controversy has stayed fairly civilized at the official level. Among the advocacy groups, pro and con, however, there has been a stepping up of activity. Today's "pro-life" march and "pro-choice" counter-gestures are only the latest skirmishes in what promises to be a long war.

There has been a change of strategy among the anti-abortion forces. The problems of mobilizing a two-thirds majority in Congress being what they are, the focus of effort has shifted from the Human Life Amendment to a new bill introduced earlier this week by Rep. Henry Hyde and Sen. Jesse Helms. This measure would not bar all abortions, but would enjoin the states from supporting them, either by direct funding or through contributions to state medical facilities. The proposed legislation attempts to get around the Supreme Court's 1973 edict via the 14th Amendment and the right of the Congress to make the decisions on political questions. In *Roe vs Wade*, the case through which the Supreme Court struck down so many state legal barriers to abortion, the justification was the uncertainty of determining when life begins. Backers of the new bill use this presumed ambiguity of fact as reason for calling the question political and relegating it to Congress.

Meanwhile, the rhetoric has been heating up on both sides. Some anti-abortion people make it a shorter step than psychology, morals or logic would suggest it is from voluntary abortions for 16-year-olds to involuntary euthanasia for their slightly senile grandmothers. Certain of their opponents see any curb on abortion as a shortcut to a nightmare future of murder trials for the use of contraceptives and government-enforced monthly pregnancy tests for all women of fecund age.

"Stop HLA Before it Takes Your Life," says a brochure put out by the National Organization for Women. And, while there have been no recent episodes involving violence against abortion clinics, efforts to keep women out of abortion clinics by physically standing in the way still occur.

It is tragic that so grave an issue should bring out such intellectual distortions and incivilities of behavior. But if controversies over human life did not arouse major passions, we would have to recognize ourselves as deeper in depravity than we do now.

THE ANN ARBOR NEWS
Ann Arbor, MI, January 25, 1983

It is, as one of many columnists and reporters who have addressed the issue in recent days noted, the kind of anniversary one does not quite know how to mark — Jan. 22, the 10th anniversary of *Wade v. Roe*, the U.S. Supreme Court decision that legalized abortion in the United States. Steadfast opponents of abortion have marked it a black day, a reminder of a moral and ethical scourge they must battle to eliminate. Strong advocates have marked it as a victorious recognition of a woman's rights to privacy, to control her own body.

Yet there are very few, even among the staunchest supporters of a woman's right to choose it, who have no qualms about abortion. As a member of the local affiliate of Planned Parenthood put it in a News story this past weekend: "We know that abortion is not the best answer — only the last."

The News' position on abortion remains today as it has been throughout most of the years-old debate on the issue:

TO CONSIDER ABORTION as a means of birth control, even of last resort, is an overwhelming tragedy. Still, it cannot be the province of government to force upon its citizens a choice for which they, individually, must bear the consequences and responsibilities. In that sense, we count ourselves among the staunch defenders of *Wade v. Roe*. But like the vast middle of American society, we also count ourselves among those who fervently wish abortion would go away.

And in that sense, it seems appropriate to mark this anniversary with a tribute to those among us who have not settled for wishing it away, but have worked with courage and purpose to make it go away. They have operated not from a rigid yes-no, right-wrong position, but have sought instead to address those problems which lead to the need for abortion.

We refer to the Washtenaw County League for Planned Parenthood, which for many years has sought to promote, encourage and provide the means for responsible family planning. Planned Parenthood is a volunteer organization, and it, and this community as a result, has been blessed through those years with a large number of prominent members of the business, medical and religious communities who have leant their energy, money and sometimes most importantly their good names to that effort.

THERE IS A CERTAIN IRONY in the fact that in the wake of *Wade v. Roe*, Planned Parenthood became the major provider of abortion in this community. It was a burden accepted with great reluctance. They have shuddered under it more than once in this decade, but ultimately have sought to turn it to their higher purpose. They have used it in individual cases to provide the counseling and contraceptive services that can prevent its recurrence. And they have invested income from the fees charged to fund educational programs to further the same goal. For the last several years, the demand for abortion in Washtenaw County has declined. "We would like to think," said Executive Director Joanne Peterson, "that the decline in demand for abortion is the result of educational programs."

It is perhaps too early to draw such a conclusion, but it reflects a similar trend being noted nationwide. And that's promising.

IF THE DAY COMES that the distressing incidence of abortion declines to some irreducible minimum, it will be, we suspect, the result of the kinds of enlightened effort put forth by people like these:

William Bott, Eleanor Cross, William Dobson, Margaret Cameron, Betty Anne Duff, Wendell Lyons, Lana Ursprung, Sally Fleming, Nancy Margolis, Mary Sexton, Mrs. R.C. Eldersfeld, Anneke Overseth, Marilyn Lindenauer, John Dobson, the Rev. Douglas Evett, Ethel Nesbitt, Mary Warner, Jane Schmidt, Nedra Otis, Harriet Arnow, Darli Mayerson, Margo MacInnes, Peter Heydon, Trudy Huebner, Sue Van Appledorn, William Sturgis, Judie Wood, Ann Andrews, Ann Rubin, Phyllis Wright, Judie Morris, Fanny Haber, Margaret Towsley, Jerry Lax, Mildred Sergeant, Alysse Weeks, Trudy Bergemann, Molly Prendergast, Starry Leutheuser, Charles Kinney, Joy Bartell, Richard Fry, Taffy Larcom, Dona Lurie, Jane Mack, Deborah Oakley, David Pollack, Sadye Power, Eugene B. Power, Sylvia Price, Susan Sayre, Beverly Ware, David Williams, Marilyn Poulter, Dennis Pearsall, the Rev. Bennie Smith, Dorothy Bauer, Robert Weeks, Ferol Brinkman Decker, Mary Palmer, Ida Pettiford, Elvira Vogel, Dora Craycraft, Richard Chesbrough, Jacqueline Hoop, Mary Rinne, Clifford Sheldon, Marcy Westerman, Miriam Wolf, Elizabeth Dexter, Barbara Seaburg, Lolagene Coombs, the Rev. Henry Lewis; and the late Eleanor O'Brien, Nancy Bates, Margaret Gray, Mrs. Bradley Patten and Mrs. Charles Noble.

Among the members of the local medical community who have leant support through service on the agency's medical advisory committee are Drs. J. Robert Willson, Leslie Corsa, Johan W. Eliot, John W. Atwater, John Konnak, Joseph Pearson, Edwin Peterson, Roger Postmus, Rhoda Powsner, William VanderYacht, David Anderson, F. Wallace Jeffries, George Sayre, Thomas Bass, William Coon, Wm. P. Edmunds, Parvitz Meghnot, Alan Menge, Donald Rucknagel, John R.G. Gosling, George Marlis and Otto K. Engelke.

St. Louis Globe-Democrat
St. Louis, MO, January 24, 1981

"I hope that future Marches for Life will be addressed by a President of the United States who shares the historic respect for life embodied in the Hippocratic oath.

"More importantly, I hope that enactment of the Helms-Dornan Human Life Amendment will obviate the need for such tragic anniversaries."

Ronald Reagan, who spoke the above words on Feb. 7, 1980, got his wish.

As President of the United States Ronald Reagan invited Pro-Life leaders into the Oval Office on Jan. 22, the day marked annually in protest of the Supreme Court's 1973 decision legalizing abortion.

With President Reagan were Sen. Jesse Helms, R-N.C., and Rep. Robert K. Dornan, R-Calif., sponsors of the constitutional amendment which, if adopted, would protect the lives of unborn children.

In contrast Jimmy Carter would not give Pro-Life delegates the courtesy of recognition when he was in office.

With Mr. Reagan in the White House and increased numbers of conservatives in Congress, the possibility of adopting a Human Life Amendment for submission to the states has been enhanced considerably. There is definite progress on the Pro-Life front.

BUFFALO EVENING NEWS
Buffalo, NY, January 22, 1983

That the abortion issue remains intensely controversial a full decade after the Supreme Court's landmark decision in Roe v. Wade on Jan. 22, 1973, testifies to the deep and continuing divisions among the American people over the morality of abortion.

The high court's 7-2 decision, written by Justice Harry A. Blackmun, held that women had a constitutional right to abortion during the early stages of pregnancy. The ruling overturned or liberalized anti-abortion laws in 46 states, provoking agreement among some Americans and shock and dismay among others. One religious leader branded it "an unspeakable tragedy for this nation."

Many persons continue to hold that view. President Reagan, among many others, strongly favors a government ban on abortions. But public opinion surveys indicate that a majority of Americans agree with the Supreme Court decision, feeling that abortion should be a private matter between a woman and her doctor.

This week, after years of avoiding a stand on the abortion issue, the League of Women Voters declared that "public policy in a pluralistic society must affirm the constitutional right of privacy of the individual to make reproductive choices." A league official emphasized that the organization was not endorsing abortion itself and that its statement did not imply moral approval or disapproval of abortion.

While we respect the views of those who oppose abortion as the killing of the unborn, The News has supported the Supreme Court decision. As the league indicated, it is not necessary to take a stand on abortion itself to believe that Americans are too deeply divided on the personal morality and ethics of terminating a pregnancy for the government to intrude into these decisions beyond the limits imposed by the court ruling.

Even if the 1973 decision were to be overturned by a constitutional amendment, few can doubt that countless women would continue to obtain illegal abortions, as they did before the Supreme Court decision. Some matters are best left to the individual consciences of those most directly involved, and we believe with the court that this should continue to apply to the difficult question of abortion.

THE MILWAUKEE JOURNAL
Milwaukee, WI, January 27, 1983

A woman's decision to have an abortion will never be easy, but in the last 10 years the decision has become less hazardous for America's women.

We note this positive development while acknowledging that, in the decade since the Supreme Court's landmark decision legalizing abortion, conscientious voices in the pro-life movement have been a consistent reminder that abortion must not be taken lightly. Partly through the efforts of pro-life activists, abortion in this country is not considered simply a convenient method of birth control. That is important.

Yet while the pro-life movement has served a useful purpose, a new ban on abortion would be both unjust and unwise. The reasons are several and among them is the need to protect women's health. To envisage what would happen if abortion were once again driven underground, consider the health benefits for pregnant women that have occurred since the procedure was legalized:

First, since 1973, women have been obtaining abortions earlier in pregnancy when the health risks to women are at the lowest. In 1973, fewer than 40% of all women obtaining abortions did so before nine weeks of pregnancy. By 1978, more than half of all abortions were performed before nine weeks and more than 9 in 10 abortions were performed during the first 12 weeks.

Second, health complications and deaths occurring to women as a result of abortions have decreased significantly. In the 1960s, complications from abortions accounted for almost 20% of all pregnancy-related admissions to municipal hospitals in New York and California. In 1965, 235 women's deaths were attributed to abortion. In 1978, there were 11 deaths from legally induced abortions and 7 from illegal abortions.

The 10th anniversary of the abortion ruling finds the nation still torn by the issue. Amid the many considerations, it is well to remember the reality of abortion before 1973 when the procedure was illegal and exceedingly hazardous to its desperate seekers. Yes, abortion is an ugly choice, but abortion would become all the more ugly if it were once again banned and pushed into back alleys.

THE ATLANTA CONSTITUTION
Atlanta, GA, January 21, 1983

The decision of the national League of Women Voters to support legal abortion is another strong demonstration that, whatever the feelings of some, the clock on this issue simply cannot be wrenched back without springing the social works.

The bipartisan league, which is well regarded as a careful student of policy issues, takes positions on such flash-point political controversies slowly and reluctantly — and then only if the position is overwhelmingly endorsed by its members.

Its declaration that "public policy in a pluralistic society must affirm the constitutional right of privacy of the individual to make reproductive choices" was supported by 92 percent of the 985 chapters involved in the deliberation.

This near-unanimous finding matches opinion polls, which steadily have logged about 75-percent approval for the Supreme Court ruling 10 years ago that permitted abortion. The unavoidable fact is that despite all the heat generated by anti-abortion organizers and politicians, lawful abortion is now a well-established and widely supported custom — and laws can't be effectively enforced without the general concurrence of the population.

Abortion is an intensely moral question, and the League takes no position on that. But while a few Americans hold abortion to be immoral in any circumstances, most consider it a moral choice in one situation or another. And those situations vary so widely, from person to person, that it is impossible to draft a law that could contain and accommodate them reasonably.

In short, the League has gotten the issue just right. There is no practical alternative to the Supreme Court's judgment that the moral decisions must be left to individuals.

The Hartford Courant
Hartford, CT, January 23, 1983

Did you ever imagine 10 years ago, when the U.S. Supreme Court legalized abortion, that one of every four pregnancies would be terminated voluntarily in the 1980s?

No, that is a shocking statistic, painful even to the most militant protectors of women's constitutional right to choose. But one question raises another: Did you know that as many as 1.2 million illegal abortions were performed annually before the Roe vs. Wade decision? Imagine the deaths and injuries if government again forbids women to seek these medical procedures in safe, accredited clinics and hospitals.

Can you deny, however, the objectionable consequences of the court decision?

The methods of some clinics, competing for business, are revolting. So is the tendency to confuse abortion with birth control. We have yet to practice fully what we know — it's better to prevent a pregnancy than to terminate it. Moreover, the emergence of so-called single-issue campaigns, triggered to some extent by the controversy over abortion, is detrimental to the body politic.

What, then, are the desirable consequences of Roe vs. Wade?

The immediate answer is found in the reduced number of women terminating unwanted pregnancies in the proverbial back alleys. The more compelling argument, however, lies in the belated recognition of a fundamental right. Opponents of abortion claim that Americans must strictly adhere to the codes inherited from past generations. That argument fails to make sufficient allowance for the inevitable changes in dynamic societies. A government that doesn't take such change into account is a government that will fail its people. Roe vs. Wade was emancipating in asserting that individual values in this matter should not be subordinated to the codes of government.

These arguments may sound valid in the abstract. In reality, we are talking about terminating human life, about murder, about subordinating the rights of a fetus to the rights of its mother.

That's what opponents of abortion say. Undoubtedly, a fetus is life, but can't you see a difference between conception and birth? Is there no meaningful difference between human life after birth and the fetus in the early stages of pregnancy? Can you show me any society, past or present, that treated a 1-day-old baby equally with a fertilized egg in the uterus?

If there was no equal treatment, shouldn't there have been?

By what standards and whose definitions? There is no agreement, even among the clergy, let alone scientists, judges, philosophers and politicians, about when life begins. Aristotle theorized that life did not begin until "quickening" — until the mother felt life in the womb. That took nearly three months, he said, and his theory was codified and dominated European abortion laws for centuries. The distinction between an abortion before and after quickening was maintained until the early 19th century. Church and state laws shift. They are not unchangeable.

Isn't that obvious?

Not to those who want to return to societal codes holding that to cause "unlawful" interruption in pregnancy is murder. To them, that rule is immutable. Indeed, the use of any birth control device will be impermissible, if the absolutists had their way.

That's harsh criticism of the anti-abortion movement, isn't it?

The movement's drive to set up problem pregnancy centers and to educate teenagers about responsible sexuality is encouraging. But at the core is the determination to pass what's called a Human Life Amendment to the Constitution — to subordinate everyone's rights to the moral and religious beliefs of others. And there is that single-minded determination that tempts the use of any means to achieve the goal.

Can't you say the same of the pro-choice movement?

Here, you find some zealots on the edges, not at the core. If the polls are accurate, most Americans support the extension of civil rights brought about by Roe vs. Wade.

And what of the future?

There will be some fine-tuning of the 1973 decision, some of it through law but much of it through the promotion of self-awareness and informed choice — the development of an attitude that says, it is not only better to prevent than to terminate a pregnancy. It is your individual moral imperative to do so.

DESERET NEWS
Salt Lake City, UT, January 22, 1983

Ten years ago Saturday, the U.S. Supreme Court committed one of its most tragic blunders ever, one that created a continuing source of controversy.

We're referring, of course, to the court's landmark ruling legalizing abortion.

Since then, as physicians developed safer techniques and more expertise, there has been a marked decline in deaths and medical complications associated with abortion.

But when that much has been said in its favor, the benefits resulting from the Supreme Court's action have just about been exhausted.

On the other side of the ledger is the added impetus the abortion ruling has given to the trend toward looser morals and cheapening the value that society places on human life.

If that assessment of the situation sounds excessively harsh and puritanical, consider a few fundamental facts:

● Since it was legalized in 1973, abortion has become one of the most frequently performed surgical procedures in the nation. In fact, on this score it rivals the tonsilectomy.

● Specifically, more than 1.5 million legal abortions were performed in the United States in 1980, the most recent year for which complete statistics are available. This means that one-fourth of all pregnancies that year were terminated by abortion.

● As time goes by, some scientists are uncovering potential health problems related to abortion.

First, there is some evidence that women who obtain more than one abortion run an increased risk of having a miscarriage, a premature birth, or other complications in future desired pregnancies.

Second, there is preliminary, tentative evidence that some women run a much higher risk of developing breast cancer if they have had an abortion.

In any case, there's room for suspecting that abortion is being used not so much as a means of safeguarding the life or health of the mother, but more as a method of birth control.

That's inexcusable in light of the well-known shortage of children being sought for adoption.

No wonder that foes of abortion have tried in every session of Congress since 1973 to pass a constitutional amendment to ban the procedure. No wonder, too, that they intend to keep trying this year despite repeated disappointments.

Last year, for example, Congress cold-shouldered two major anti-abortion measures: a constitutional amendment sponsored by Sen. Orrin G. Hatch of Utah that would give Congress and the states joint authority to restrict abortions, and a measure sponsored by Sen. Jesse Helms of North Carolina declaring that life begins at conception and the states can pass laws to protect the unborn.

But when Sen. Hatch withdrew his amendment last September because its prospects were bleak, he was given public assurance by the majority leader of the Senate that he could bring it up early in 1983.

An issue that has been around as long as the abortion controversy won't go away just because of a few setbacks and disappointments. Plenty of determined Americans are prepared to keep fighting as long as it takes to start correcting the monumental blunder the U.S. Supreme Court committed a decade ago.

The Providence Journal
Providence, RI, January 22, 1983

The struggle began 10 years ago, when the U.S. Supreme Court ruled that the decision whether to terminate a pregnancy prematurely should be made by the woman and her physician. Since that time, both sides have been vigorous in promoting their views.

Today, a group of about 100 Rhode Islanders, including Governor and Mrs. Garrahy, will participate in a Washington demonstration marking the 10th anniversary of the Supreme Court ruling. They will be asking, as is their right, that legalized abortion be ended. If their views prevailed and either the high court reversed itself or Congress exerted its authority in accord with the anti-abortionists' wishes, the clock would be turned back.

A ban on abortion would return this country to a period in which all too frequently the life of the mother was sacrificed in the cause of saving the fetus. It was a time when the wealthy traveled abroad for safe abortions, but the poor turned in desperation to the life-threatening

Both sides have been vigorous in promoting their views

illegal abortionists — the medical frauds who exploited the suffering of women for their own material gain

Understandably, the controversy arouses deep emotions. Fundamental rights relative to the quality of human life do not give way readily to impassioned argument, no matter how well reasoned or on which side it comes down. Is it to hope in vain that over the next decade the bitterness will gradually subside and the disputants will concede that all life is precious and that while abortion is never a desirable end in itself, the woman's right to privacy and sovereignty over her own body must be respected by law, by religion and by the people of the United States?

Minneapolis Star and Tribune
Minneapolis, MN, January 22, 1983

When the U.S. Supreme Court issued its ruling in Roe vs. Wade 10 years ago today, it confirmed that a woman's decision about abortion is a private matter. No other action in the high court's history has made as much difference in women's lives.

The court correctly placed the right of women to choose abortion alongside other familial rights protected against government interference. This protection has helped both individuals and society. It has decreased abortion-related deaths by 73 percent since 1973. And it has granted to millions of women a crucial freedom by allowing them to run their own lives — to choose whether and when they will have children.

Opinion polls show most Americans favor legalized abortion and understand its benefits. But those who hold the opposing view keep trying to undo the 1973 decision. Abortion opponents in Congress have worked in vain to amend the Constitution to prohibit abortion, to pass a federal statute that grants "personhood" to fetuses, to deny the federal courts jurisdiction over abortion cases. And although the supreme court has consistently defended a woman's right to choose abortion, it has sometimes let stand laws that make exercising the right more difficult, especially for the poor and the young.

This term, the court will rule on another handful of state laws restricting abortion. One requires a 24-hour "cooling off" period following an abortion request; another forces doctors to tell patients that a fetus is a person.

If Roe vs. Wade brought an important breakthrough in privacy rights, it also spurred this decade's most anguishing social dispute. Justice Harry Blackmun, the conservative Minnesotan who wrote the Roe opinion, anticipated it. Views on abortion, he wrote, are influenced by "one's philosophy, experiences, exposures to the raw edges of human existence, religious training and moral standards." Those differing views create an inevitable struggle, pitting an important civil right against the value of potential life.

Individual citizens will continue to differ on abortion's rightness or wrongness. Few would deny that the moral question is difficult and deep. But Roe vs. Wade decided a constitutional issue, not a moral one. The court ruled that the constitutional right to privacy included the right to end an unwanted pregnancy. It declared that, in this troublesome corner of a woman's private life, the government must not interfere. Ten years later, that is still the right decision.

St. Louis Review

St. Louis, MO, January 20, 1984

It is the eleventh anniversary of the Supreme Court's decision allowing women the right to abortion on demand. As such, it is also the eleventh year of anti-abortion efforts by a dedicated, yet often divided, group of believers in the child's right to life.

This past year was notable for the defeat of the Hatch amendment in the U.S. Senate. This proposed constitutional amendment had been the focus of the majority of the pro-life movement's efforts in recent years. It was brought to nought by legislative mishandling and also by internal disagreement among the pro-lifers themselves.

In some critical areas the pro-life forces have lost a bigger battle. Women's right to abortion has become part of the philosophical canon taken up by the national television industry and women's magazines. The Columbia Journalism Review, a highly respected media commentator, in its January/February issue recounts an eye-opening example. The Public Broadcasting Service funded a projected TV series on "unpopular viewpoints." These topics were ones which most stations would never dare broadcast. The series included programs on choosing suicide, the "curing" of homosexuals' orientations, a story of romance with considerable nudity, and a film equating abortion with infanticide. The film, "Slaughter of the Innocents" is a visual essay on abortion narrated by Dr. C. Everett Koop, the surgeon-general of the U.S.

So we conclude from this magazine article that to speak out against abortion on public-funded television is so countercultural that it takes a fool or potential martyr to do it. The series was "tabled" because of lack of member-station consultation in its planning. The pro-life movement has had other martyrs this year. Four people committed to the pro-life movement have been jailed in St. Louis County for their dedication in protesting abortion.

It is amazing that in our rapidly aging society we, the living, are so determined to eradicate our own race. There are fewer and fewer children born each year to inherit the future. Currently one-third of all pregnancies are aborted each year in the United States. We spend so much time and effort in proclaiming and defending our rights that we seldom stop to realize that every right which a person enjoys bears with it a responsibility to protect others' rights. The unborn have rights, too, but few people stand up to proclaim them or protect them.

Detroit Free Press

Detroit, MI, January 19, 1983

SATURDAY is the 10th anniversary of Roe vs. Wade, the Supreme Court decision that legalized abortion in the United States. That ruling did not end the debate over abortion. What it did do was to bring public policy into line with what a majority of Americans believe and practice: When abortions were illegal, women still sought and obtained them. And despite the controversy over Medicaid funding, most Americans seem to consider abortion a private matter, or an option that should remain available to pregnant women in at least some circumstances.

Roe v. Wade did end the scandal of back-alley abortions and the double standard that said the well-to-do could obtain a safely performed abortion, but the poor could not. It recognized the fallibility of humans and of contraceptive methods; it tried to find a middle way between the right of private decision in the early stages of pregnancy and the interest of the state in protecting the unborn child in the later stages.

The decision was not a moral or ethical absolute, but a political compromise. It may have been imperfect. Advances in pre-natal and neonatal medicine may rapidly outdate it, and the medical and legal professions are already grappling with the implications of that. But at the moment it is the most workable legal doctrine on the subject that we have.

The court has left it for us to address the ignorance or alienation in which unwanted babies are conceived, the neglect and abuse of living infants, the privation and hopelessness in which so many children in this country still grow up to perpetuate a cycle of unwanted pregnancies and unloved children. Roe v. Wade only acknowledged reality. The great unfinished business of society is to improve upon it.

ST. LOUIS POST-DISPATCH

St. Louis, MO, January 21, 1983

Ten years ago tomorrow, the Supreme Court handed down one of the most divisive — and necessary — rulings in its history. We refer, of course, to *Roe v. Wade,* in which the high tribunal declared that the constitutional right to privacy extends to a woman's decision, in consultation with her physician, to terminate her pregnancy.

In so deciding, the court did not grant women an unrestricted right to abortion. It held that to preserve the health of the woman such procedures could be prohibited in the second trimester; and that to save a viable fetus abortions could be proscribed in the final three months of pregnancy. Even so, the ruling in one quick stroke delineated the legal landscape in which abortion statutes would henceforth have to exist. After Jan. 22 1973 no government — municipal, state or federal — could place obstacles in the way of a woman's decision in her first trimester to secure an abortion.

At every level, government has attempted to circumvent the Supreme Court's guidelines, and few states have worked more energetically to undermine them than Missouri. One early effort at sabotage reached the court in 1976, when most of a Missouri statute requiring a husband's consent for abortion and prohibiting the most commonly used abortion method was thrown out as unconstitutional. (The husband's consent provision was overturned on the obvious ground that the state could not delegate to a third party an absolute veto power that it itself did not possess.) Even now, the court is deliberating a Missouri statute that would require parental consent or a court order for abortions for women under 18 and that second trimester abortions be performed in hospitals.

In Congress, opponents of abortion have worked tirelessly to restrict women's access to the procedure. Their most notable achievement has been to prohibit the use of Medicaid funds for abortion — a law that affects only poor women. Although the Supreme Court has held that government has no positive obligation to provide money for abortions, it has steadfastly resisted any efforts to modify the principles laid down in *Roe v. Wade.* Indeed, many opponents of abortion now conclude that the only certain way of outlawing it is through a constitutional amendment.

The debate over abortion involves far more than legal questions. Some who oppose abortion do so in accordance with their religious doctrines; others see the sanctioning of abortion as a profound moral challenge to the nation. Those who support a woman's right to choose abortion find in the issue a contest over what may well be her most fundamental right — that of deciding whether to bear children.

The polls consistently find that most Americans decidedly support the principle of free choice in reproductive matters. Medical statistics repeatedly underscore the safety of abortion as against carrying pregnancies to term. Women, in fact, are more than seven times as likely to die from childbirth as from abortion. In the final analysis, however, neither opinion polls nor medical statistics provide a compelling argument for legalized abortion.

That argument is to be found in the concept of privacy, which underpins the entire notion of freedom and liberty. For if the state can intrude into the most intimate sphere of a woman's life, then there can be no such thing as privacy — then no area of personal decision-making can be free from the threat of government interference.

The Birmingham News

Birmingham, AL, January 26, 1984

The 11th anniversary of the U.S. Supreme Court's abortion decision has come and gone. But controversy over the ruling still seems far from subsiding. On the contrary, both pro-abortion and anti-abortion groups seem to have grown stronger and better organized as the country has experienced the effects of the law.

Because no broad consensus has been reached throughout the country, one is disposed to believe that some modification of the ruling may lie in the future. This feeling is reinforced by the alarming statistic that as many as 17 million unborn have been killed or destroyed through abortions since the court's ruling. Doubtless, neither the Supreme Court nor the country as a whole foresaw that abortions would reach such proportions.

The jury is still out on another aspect — the possible psychological and spiritual damage done to prospective mothers and fathers who are made aware of the abortions.

Since the ruling in 1973, abortion has emerged as both a legal and a moral dilemma. Anti-abortion forces argue that the protections of the Constitution extend to the unborn infant and that abortions are legalized murder of innocent and helpless human beings.

It is even more difficult to ignore the moral issues: Should anyone have the blessings of the highest court in the land in the destruction of human life? And why should the law sanction assaults on the female psyche and spirit and exempt males? Does not the wholesale destruction of such beings scar the national psyche and render it less sensitive to the sanctity of human life?

Of course there are impassioned arguments on the other side of the issue: That no one has a right to force a woman to have an unwanted child; that only women have the right to decide what happens to their bodies, including their reproductive systems. But does not that right also include controlling their bodies *before* they become pregnant or in order *not* to become pregnant? Then there is the practical argument that abortions for the poor and the extremely young prevent millions of additional poor from being added to welfare rolls.

The latter argument is subject to debate. Statistics are not at all clear on the matter. Some say that despite the liberal abortion law, young, single women are adding substantially each year to welfare problems. In fact, some feel that the abortion law itself has so altered sexual mores that it is itself stimulating increased pregnancies out of wedlock.

Going beyond the individual who chooses abortion for whatever reason, does the society as a whole have a stake in the practice? Do wholesale abortions affect the national psyche in a negative manner? Do they tend to weaken the social fabric by creating a callousness toward sex in marriage and toward the sanctity of human life? Do they not prepare the psychological ground for legalizing euthanasia and disposal of the terminally ill and the helpless aged?

Few of these questions have been answered authoritatively. In fact, a consensus on when a human life actually begins (or, for that matter, ends) is still absent. The Supreme Court says it doesn't know. Religious organizations seem generally to agree that abortions for reasons other than to protect the life of the mother are immoral and that abortions are contrary to scripture. Doctors, confronted by the physical evidence, seem no closer to agreement on the moment when a fetus becomes a human being.

All of which says that the country has by no means settled the issue. But regardless of how strong anti-abortion forces become, one should not expect to see any great changes in either the law or the practice overnight. Abortions, to be straightforward about it, have created a lucrative business for thousands of persons, including doctors, nurses and technicians. And closely allied are many family planning groups and a wide variety of "sexologists" and social workers. Many very well may see their personal welfare tied to legalized abortions and resist modifications in the law.

But it is an issue that is not going to disappear unless the country finds a better way, a more humane and a more moral way, to deal with it. The national conscience will not tolerate indefinitely what it conceives to be the destruction of a million and a half to two million fragile beings every year.

Birmingham, AL, January 22, 1985

The 12th anniversary of the U.S. Supreme Court ruling which legalized abortions has come and gone without an upsurge of violence and without signs of compromise between pro-abortion and pro-life forces.

In reality, in the 12 years of legalized abortion, the two positions have become set in concrete, with neither side showing any inclination to modify its stands. That being so, the debate in the private sector as well as in the political arena is likely to continue into the foreseeable future with neither side retreating.

In the meantime, some estimates place the number of abortions at about 1.5 million per year or 18 million to 20 million since the high court ruled and abortion clinics sprang up across the country.

Questions about abortion remain and are still hotly debated. Pro-lifers claim unlimited abortions are infanticide — murder of unborn children Pro-abortion adherents claim abortions are simply a medical procedure to terminate a pregnancy.

Pro-lifers claim, and with good reason, that society and the state — civilization itself — has an historic interest in preserving human life, despite the high court's ruling, and that unlimited abortions are gradually eroding the ancient belief in the sanctity of human life.

Some feel that humankind is now on a "slippery slope" and sliding toward other rationalizations for terminating a life which society does not feel it can support or that is inconvenient or considered to be unfulfilling.

They fear that in the future euthanasia and even genocide could be rationalized and perhaps legalized. Some feel that sexual abuse of children, rape, withholding medical aid for severely handicapped babies and such deviant behavior are related to the pro-abortion mentality and are evidence of being on the "slippery slope."

Some of the promises held out by pro-abortion adherents have not been delivered. Despite the relatively inexpensive medical procedure, the past 12 years have seen sharp increases in illegitimate births and teenage pregnancies. Unlimited abortions, even when some are subsidized, have not appreciably reduced the number of unmarried mothers applying for welfare. Some researchers say the number has increased substantially over the past 12 years.

However, regardless of how strongly pro-lifers feel, resorting to bombings and other forms of destruction are not reasonable or productive ways to go about opposing abortions any more than bombings are an effective and proper way to oppose nuclear arms, nuclear power plants or U.S. foreign policy.

The proper way is patient presentation of statistical as well as of individual evidence of harm, evidence that is necessary to change opinions, and then follow with the legislative process. No doubt the issue will come before the 99th Congress and will be debated fully again. And that is the proper method, the only effective way to obtain lasting changes in a democratic society.

The Burlington Free Press

Burlington, Vt., January 13, 1985

That misguided people have resorted to violence in efforts to shut down abortion clinics should not be surprising in light of the rising crescendo of heated rhetoric from opponents of abortion.

Certainly the passions of the gullible **Editorial** must be inflamed when pro-life advocates compare abortion to Nazi genocidal policies and display photographs of aborted fetuses being torn from their mothers' wombs. It is little wonder then that individuals with strong convictions resort to violence to destroy those facilities where abortions are performed. Such actions are inexcusable and were properly condemned by President Reagan. The guilty should be severely punished for their reckless disregard for the law and for endangering the lives of people who live near the clinics.

At the same time, pro-life organizations are stepping up their demonstrations against the clinics and using questionable tactics to harass doctors and employees. In some cases, demonstrators have splashed paint in waiting rooms, dropped stink bombs or chained themselves to examining tables. In others, they have traced license plate numbers and annoyed patients at home. Homes of clinic operators have been picketed on a number of occasions.

Abortion thus has become one of the most volatile issues of the 1980s and the effects of the demonstrations are being felt in communities, state capitals, Congress and the White House. At the community level, many doctors are refusing to perform abortions for ethical reasons. Pressure is being exerted on legislators to prepare measures to ban abortions should the Supreme Court reverse itself on the issue. Some congressmen have expressed concern about the influence of right-to-life groups on elections and fear that they may lose their seats if they continue to support abortion. Such organizations as the Moral Majority are demanding that President Reagan fulfill a four-year-old commitment to them to put an end to abortions.

The response of "pro-choice" groups to the bombing and picketing of abortion clinics has been equally emotional. They contend that the bombings are either orchestrated by right-to-life groups or have their blessing. While there seems to be little that can be done to prevent such bombings, abortion proponents have focused their attention on picketers and have called for changes in the law which would allow police to prevent such actions. But if steps were taken to prevent peaceful demonstrations against the clinics the measures would collide with those rights which are granted by the First Amendment of the Constitution. The precedent easily could be applied in other cases where advocates of causes take to the streets to plead their cases to the public. Trespassing or vandalism cannot be condoned. But abortion opponents should not be prevented from picketing the facilities.

That abortion simply is an issue which is too complex to be easily dismissed is evidenced by the fact that 12 years since the U.S. Supreme Court legalized the procedure in Roe vs. Wade it is still the subject of heated controversy. While there is merit to the argument that women should be permitted to make choices in cases of unwanted pregnancies, there is equal merit to the conviction that killing of the unborn clashes with beliefs that are based on an innate respect for life. Because people on both sides are unwilling to make compromises, it appears that the debate between the opposing groups will continue for years.

In the meantime, the public can only hope that proponents and opponents will make an effort to dampen their emotions and discuss the issue on a reasonable basis.

Even though right-to-life groups are not involved in the bombings of abortion clinics, violence can only do incalculable damage to their cause.

The Kansas City Times

Kansas City, Mo., January 22, 1985

The two camps are more polarized over the issue of abortion than ever since the Supreme Court legalized the medical procedure 12 years ago. The Congress and the courts still uphold that basic right, but across the country intimidation, scare tactics, bombings and harassment take place in defiance of law.

To date, more than 20 family planning clinics have been bombed. National Right-to-Life Committee officials have condemned the bombings. Yet those who believe that abortion is wrong have proceeded with other tactics: harassment of women who enter the clinics, and intimidation of workers, even in their homes and neighborhoods. Anti-abortion leaders cannot say such lawlessness is "understandable," and wave the bloody shirt of "murder!" at conventions and in literature, and expect not to overturn unstable minds.

Agencies such as Planned Parenthood do not promote abortion as the way to resolve problems of teen-age motherhood, too-large families or unwanted pregnancies, despite what their critics say. They advocate family planning. They promote contraception, which is what those who truly abhor abortion should do if they are sincere in wanting to reduce it.

Under the present administration, family planning aid has been cut back for undeveloped countries, birth control clinics have had to fight for every penny in the federal budget at home, and the infamous 'squeal rule' was promulgated. If it had been left to stand, it would have discouraged thousands of youngsters from seeking birth control help.

The state does not tell people when to have sex, and it should not tell them when to have children. That decision still must be made by those involved, not by meddlers seeking to impose their beliefs on others. No one is forced to get an abortion. It is a personal, medical decision.

With greater access to contraceptives, and better education about birth control, there will be far fewer abortions. Family planning is the goal that all should work for — together and peacefully.

The Washington Times

Washington, D.C., January 22, 1985

Thousands of Americans are not marching today to protest a "surgical procedure," or to put pressure on "providers," or to rail against the "termination" of pregnancy. If abortion were merely a technique, if its target were something so worthless as tonsils, today's rally would also have been cancelled due to the weather — indeed, it would never have been scheduled. But then there's a lot more to abortion than the euphemists admit, and so the columns in the cold.

Since *Roe vs. Wade* was decided 12 years ago, more than 15 million human lives have been destroyed in the womb at various stages of development. The rate now hovers around 4,000 abortions a day. At the same time, doctors have been able to perform life-saving operations closer and closer to conception, making it more difficult for the euphemists to deny personhood to an abortion victim while granting it to the unborn beneficiary of a friendly scalpel. That line drawn in time has always been arbitrary; now it seems not a great deal less sinister than the arbitrary hand signal from the official greeter at a concentration camp that determined who lived or died.

This is not an exaggeration. The people in the street today can cheer the fact that abortion is becoming more widely accepted as a life-and-death issue. In Torrington, Conn., a televised abortion drew praise from people on both sides of the issue, and among callers, three women said they would not have had abortions if they had known what was really involved. Pro-life leaders know this, and so do the people who run abortion "clinics" (a euphemism whose equal would be calling Josef Stalin, who filled the ground with nutrient-rich corpses, an "agrarian reformer," or "a friend of the Earth.")

That such a tremendous decision was made by unelected men is not a grand endorsement of democracy. (And just think how the feminists would rage if those men had decided otherwise.) That President Reagan might find himself in the position to alter the court's makeup, perhaps leading to a revision, would be the proper remedy, especially since the Democrats warned that he might do such a thing if reelected.

It isn't pleasant marching in the cold or maintaining a vigil outside the various "women's health centers," but then the fight for civil liberties has never been easy. Those who march today have many good reasons to believe that they toil not in vain. Our voice is with theirs.

Post-Tribune

Gary, Ind., January 27, 1985

As another anniversary of the Supreme Court's ruling on abortion passed, it became clear that the stridency level of the debate has increased dangerously.

President Reagan, addressing the March for Life demonstrators the other day, reiterated his support, his opposition to abortion. His is a powerful voice.

Our opinions

Fortunately he called for "a complete rejection of violence as a means of settling this issue."

He and other leaders should continue that stand, but they should do more. They should emphasize that tolerance is the bedrock of a free society, and that this emotional issue demands more tolerance than some people have shown in this ongoing debate.

Ridiculing, intimidating, even threatening women who go to abortion clinics is despicable. People who do that have crossed into the netherland of zealous extremism. They hurt their cause. Most anti-abortion activists abhor such behavior, but some of it continues.

There is a stark, disturbing revelation in this continuing debate. It is that some pro-life people, probably only a few, seem so sure that their morality is the ultimate truth that they consider those who disagree as immoral, devoid of consciences. That is the ugly side of extremism. It is intolerance. It is intolerable.

There is, as the president said, some new scientific, medical evidence that could add strong arguments to the anti-abortion cause. What the country also needs are new, compassionate, instructive ways to deal with the circumstances, the emotion, the trauma, the fear, the uncertainty that leads some women to awesome decisions about abortion. Until that is accomplished, this debate will continue on a plane that dodges some very personal realities that are not touched by religious or moral verities.

No legislation, no constitutional amendment will change that reality.

The Supreme Court's historic decision seemed to endorse tolerance and rights more than it endorsed abortion. That is what some of the debaters overlook.

Extremists on the side of individual rights are wrong in arguing that abortion is none of a government's business. Its medical nature requires some government regulation and concern.

But there is a tolerable limit to a government's power over personal, moral matters, and that limit is what is involved now.

Abortion is not a modern issue, and it has always divided societies. It will continue to do that. The test of this civilized democratic society is to keep the divisiveness on a tolerable plane. That requires restraint on all sides.

THE CHRISTIAN SCIENCE MONITOR

Boston, Mass., January 24, 1985

ANTAGONISTS on both sides of the American abortion issue are deeply disturbed by the recent turn to abortion clinic bombings — a form of urban terrorism that has no place in a society governed by law. There have been more than 20 such incidents across the country. President Reagan rightly called for an end to such acts in his unprecedented Oval Office address to the Washington March for Life demonstrators Tuesday, the 12th anniversary of the 1973 Supreme Court decision legalizing abortions: "We cannot condone the threatening or taking of human life to protest the taking of human life by way of abortion," he said.

The need to maintain civility in the abortion debate, which touches on deep emotional and moral issues, is almost universally recognized by Americans. Only a handful — 5 percent by one survey — see any usefulness in the bombings as a form of political protest, and then only so long as no one is injured. Many who oppose abortions fear a backlash.

The public debate appears headed for more intense emotional appeals as it is, with video documentaries and other techniques intended to make the anti-abortion case more graphic. This trend too can hardly be welcomed.

The public, despite a decade of controversy over abortion, has maintained a consistent view. About one-fifth oppose abortion under all circumstances, about one-fifth approve a woman's right to abortion under all circumstances, and half would approve it in certain cases such as rape, incest, or when the mother's life is in danger, in a new Gallup survey for Newsweek. Somewhat more than half say they do not question their own position on abortion, but about 2 in 5 admit to doubts.

Perhaps more to the point is how the public views what would happen if the nation returned to the pre-1973 conditions and abortions were made illegal under just about all circumstances.

Nearly 90 percent think that women would again break the law by getting illegal abortions and that many women would be physically harmed in abortions performed by unqualified people. Eighty-one percent think wealthy women would still be able to get safe abortions. Seven in 10 think more women would end up with unwanted children and that welfare costs would rise to pay for unwanted children of the poor. Six in 10 think the moral tone of America would not improve.

It has proved difficult to weigh the moral concerns about abortion — among them, the assuming of responsibility for conception in cases where a pregnancy was not imposed upon the woman, and respect for evidences of life — against other moral concerns, such as the woman's right to privacy and conscience.

The debate becomes more difficult yet when these concerns are set against the practical public issues of making abortion illegal, which was the public's experience before 1973: An extensive resort to illegal abortion that was unsafe for the poor, readily available for the better off, and which encouraged, as did prohibition, an unhealthy flouting of the law.

Individuals must come to grips themselves with this issue, both for their own sake and society as a whole. President Reagan no doubt is acting out of his own conscience as a citizen and as a political leader. The Supreme Court in 1973 had the difficult choice of weighing the rights of the unborn, the mother, and the social context. It decided 6 to 3 to legalize abortion in the early stages of pregnancy. Congress has since decided to exclude public funds for abortions for the poor. A differently composed Supreme Court, looking at other cases, could alter the previous decision.

It does not help, with so difficult a private and public issue, for the antagonists to resort to highly charged condemnations, physical violence, or intimidation. Legal change, if it is to come about, must be approached with civility, respect for the orderly system, and regard for the rights of those holding different views.

AKRON BEACON JOURNAL

Akron, Ohio, January 24, 1985

THE 12th anniversary of the Supreme Court's abortion decision has come and gone. Fortunately, it was not marred by the violence that many people had feared would occur.

Akron had special reason to feel tense. The city was thrust into the limelight two years ago when the Supreme Court struck down its ordinance regulating abortion procedures.

Akron thus holds a special place in the national controversy surrounding abortion. And as the anniversary of *Roe v. Wade* approached, federal officials warned area abortion clinics to be on the alert.

Calm prevailed this week. For that, everyone should be grateful. Yet it is troubling that widespread fear existed in this country at all.

Twelve years after the Supreme Court decision, the nation is still wrestling with a difficult and painful moral issue. Emotions have always run high among sincere and well-intentioned people on both sides of the debate.

But during the past year, protests against abortion took on an especially frightening character.

More than 20 abortion clinics and medical offices were torched or bombed, sometimes repeatedly. This violence marked a dreadful new escalation of the battle touched off by the historic 1973 ruling.

In his message to pro-life marchers in Washington Tuesday, President Reagan correctly condemned the violence. He also repeated his support for legislation banning abortion, an effort that has met with repeated failure in Congress and is not expected to succeed this year either.

In recent years, anti-abortion groups have become more politically sophisticated. They know where to focus their energies: at Capitol Hill and the White House.

During his second term, the President may have an opportunity to make several appointments to the Supreme Court. Pro-life groups hope that will be the case, for a new court represents the best chance for reversing the 1973 decision.

But so far the court has unwaveringly stood by its ruling that legalized abortion. We support that ruling as a strong statement in defense of the constitutionally guaranteed right to privacy.

Under the law of this land, a woman can make a very difficult, very personal decision according to her own conscience and beliefs — not someone else's, not the government's. So it should be, for that woman is the one who will live with the decision for the rest of her life.

Regardless of how people feel about *Roe v. Wade*, or a woman's right to control her body, the spreading violence and intimidation show the abortion debate has reached a new level of intolerance. If the law is to change, there are peaceful ways to change it. Extremist tactics are a danger to democracy and the rights of us all.

Pittsburgh Post-Gazette

Pittsburgh, Pa., January 30, 1985

Twelve years ago this month, the U.S. Supreme Court rendered a sweeping decision striking down state laws against abortion. In his majority opinion in the case of Roe. vs. Wade, Justice Harry Blackmun laid down a legal formula based on the division of pregnancy into trimesters:

In the first trimester, a pregnant woman's right to choose abortion (derived from a constitutional guarantee of privacy) was paramount; in the second trimester, that right could be restricted only by the state's interest in protecting a woman's health; but in the final three months — when the fetus is "viable" and thus presumably capable of "meaningful" life outside the mother's womb — the woman's right of choice could be overridden by the state's "legitimate interest in protecting the potentiality of human life."

•

The 12 years since Roe vs. Wade have been marked by two antagonistic developments. One is the entrenchment of legal abortion in America and its enshrinement in some circles as the consummate symbol of female emancipation. The other is the galvanizing of a "pro-life" movement for which the termination of even the earliest pregnancy is an abomination.

The blood feud between "pro-life" and "pro-choice" forces has been made even more bitter by the fact that it has become a kind of proxy war between opposing views of sexuality, motherhood and the role of women. In such a battle there is precious little middle ground, and much of the commentary on last week's 12th anniversary of Roe vs. Wade predicted a continuation of the present dialogue of the deaf.

•

But that view may reckon without another series of developments since the 1973 decision. We refer to advances in medicine that challenge the analysis of Roe vs. Wade and also point the way to a refinement of the decision — one that would prevent the late-term abortions that constitute the anti-abortion movement's most affecting argument.

Such abortions, it needs to be said, are very much the exception. In 1980, the last year for which comprehensive figures are available, fully 91 percent of the 1.6 million abortions in the United States were performed during the first 12 weeks of pregnancy. Of the remaining abortions, 4.7 percent were performed on women 13-15 weeks pregnant, 3.2 percent on women 16-20 weeks pregnant,

and a minuscule 0.8 percent on women pregnant 21 weeks or more.

•

Yet it is late abortions that have provided the pro-life movement with its most powerful propaganda — those disquieting photographs of the fetuses aborted in such procedures. And, however few in number they may be, such late abortions are a problem that cannot be wished away.

Nor can an even more disturbing phenomenon: abortions that "go wrong" and produce a live infant. The New York Times reported last year that, of more than 160,000 abortions performed in that city in 1982, 18 resulted in the accident of a live birth. "We have to warn the families," said Dr. Hugh Barber, chief of obstetrics and gynecology at Lenox Hill Hospital. "You have to tell them there is a slight possibility the fetus may live."

Dr. Barber's hospital performs abortions up to the 24th week of pregnancy — the legal limit in New York State and the cutoff point established by the Supreme Court in Roe vs. Wade, which noted that "viability is usually placed at about seven months (28 weeks) but may occur earlier, even at 24 weeks."

But medical advances since 1973 have made it possible to sustain the lives of infants born as early as 23 weeks. Such advances pose a problem for the "viability" framework of Roe vs. Wade. Just this observation was made by Justice Sandra Day O'Connor in a dissenting opinion in a 1983 decision reaffirming Roe vs. Wade and striking down a variety of local restrictions on legal abortion, including a requirement that second-trimester abortions be performed in hospitals.

"Just as improvements in medical technology inevitably will move forward the point at which the state may regulate for reasons of maternal health," Justice O'Connor wrote, "different technological improvements will move backward the point of viability at which the state may proscribe abortions except when necessary to save the health and life of the mother . . . The Roe framework, then, is clearly on a collision course with itself."

Justice O'Connor's concerns aside, viability is arguably no more arbitrary than another popular line of demarcation — quickening in the womb (16-18 weeks). What is not arbitrary is the underlying insight of the original Roe vs. Wade decision: that, while fetal development is a continuum, at some point the fetus reaches a stage of delineation at which abortion raises moral questions

that properly engage the attention of society.

•

Reacting to the concerns expressed by Justice O'Connor, some constitutional lawyers have proposed a revision of the Roe vs. Wade "schedule" that, while probably anathema to both extremes in the abortion debate, has much to recommend it.

One version offered by Ohio State University law professor Nancy K. Rhoden would establish a new cutoff point for abortion of 20-22 weeks into a pregnancy. Exceptions after the cutoff point would be allowed only in cases in which a mother's health was threatened or the fetus suffered from serious genetic defects. (Amniocentesis, a procedure used to diagnose fetal abnormalities, cannot be performed until the 14th-17th week and results may not be available until the 21st week or later.)

An exception for even later abortions on the grounds of fetal defects raises troubling questions. Chief among them is the fear that a "quality of life" evaluation of a fetus' worth might spill over into public attitudes toward the handicapped and the retarded generally. Still, it is notable that, from the beginning of the modern debate over legalized abortion in the 1960s, a birth-defects exception has been supported by physicians and others who otherwise opposed abortion.

Rough as the justice might be, such an exception would probably have to be part of any revision of Roe vs. Wade. But so would another refinement: a significant narrowing of the definition of the dangers to maternal "health" that justify a late abortion. Vague threats to a woman's psychological "well-being" should not qualify.

This newspaper welcomed the Roe vs. Wade decision and still believes that its basic holding was correct. Abortions during the first trimester of pregnancy — which, as we noted above, represent the overwhelming majority of those now being performed — should remain a private matter between a woman and her doctor, free of intervention or harassment by government.

But we also believe that an important element of the 1973 decision, its recognition that the state has a "legitimate interest in protecting the potentiality of human life," has suffered from an unforeseen and undesirable erosion. A future Supreme Court ruling that recognized that fact would be no defeat for women's rights.

THE ARIZONA REPUBLIC
Phoenix, AZ, January 22, 1986

AS the nation marks the anniversary of the U.S. Supreme Court's 1973 landmark ruling on abortion, the sharp divisions between the so-called "pro-choice" and "pro-life" positions remain basically unchanged.

It's been 13 years since the *Roe vs. Wade* decision, but the central issue to the abortion debate, both legally and morally — when "life" begins — remains subject to question.

However, even more complicated questions are now being raised over a new drug — RU-486 — which, according to *The New Republic* magazine, ". . . could well transform, if not end, the abortion debate."

Developed by the French drug company Roussel-Uclaf, and currently being tested in Paris, Stockholm and at the University of Southern California, RU 486 prevents a fertilized ovum from attaching to the uterine wall.

Although some define "life" as beginning at conception, studies show that 40 percent to 60 percent of all fertilized ova fail to implant naturally. Federal courts and the American College of Obstetrics and Gynecology define "conception" as implantation.

By blocking the cells in the lining of the uterus from receiving progesterone, a hormone that allows a fertilized ovum to implant and mature in the womb, RU-486 prompts a breaking down of the wall of the uterus, just as in a normal monthly female cycle.

The drug could be used at any time an early pregnancy was suspected, prompting a menstrual cycle, or it could be used on a regular monthly basis, taken on the three days before a normal female cycle, much like a contraceptive.

Ironically, the advances of medical science that have sharpened the debate over abortion — making longer-term abortions "safer" and providing evidence of earlier fetal viability — may actually serve to blur the issue.

While some anti-abortionists also oppose contraception, most do not. If the new drug is used on a regular basis a woman would never know if she was "pregnant."

If used in the first weeks of a suspected pregnancy, the drug-induced "abortion" could be performed at home, diluting the objections to government funding and abortion clinics.

While the drug remains at least five years away from the commercial market, tests indicate that RU-486 produces fewer and less severe side effects than birth-control pills or the IUD.

If the drug is marketed, medical concerns will be raised, as they should. And until long-term studies are completed, users of RU-486 will be risking unknown medical complications to their lives, and the lives of any children born after discontinuing the drug.

To some, abortion is a black-or-white issue; to others, it's a moral vs. medical question; and others perceive abortion as the rights of the unborn vs. the living.

One thing is certain though: If RU-486 proves safe — whether perceived as "contraception" or "abortion" — personal responsibility will become the deciding factor.

The Union Leader
Manchester, NH, January 22, 1986

"I'm here because innocent human beings are being killed right here in Concord and across our state and nation. The offspring of human beings are not cows or pigs or chickens . . . abortion kills human beings."

— *U.S. Sen. Gordon Humphrey*

It took time, too long, but the world finally reacted with shock and horror to the atrocities committed against Jews by Hitler's Nazi Germany — and the sense of revulsion in the civilized world remains undiminished these many years later.

Yet in that same ostensibly civilized world, millions of unborn babies are being murdered — no other word will do — every year in abortion mills and the majority of Americans remain silent.

In this country, the highest court ruled in one of its darkest moments — Jan. 22, 1973 in Roe vs. Wade — that abortion was legal, in essence that unborn children have no rights protected under the Constitution, that they can be denied life, liberty and the pursuit of happiness, at the whim of the mother.

The court ruled that the unborn children, indeed, are no different from cows or pigs or chickens, and can be slaughtered as mercilessly as Hitler slaughtered the Jews — only this time with the full protection of law.

The Catholic Church, which claims to stand opposed to abortion without qualification, has been shockingly slow and unconvincing in rallying to the pro-life banner. Indeed, Odore J. Gendron, bishop of the diocese of Manchester, participated in the annual March for Life protest against the U.S. Supreme Court ruling in Roe vs. Wade for the first time Saturday in Concord.

The bishop should be applauded for rallying to the cause, but the public cannot be blamed for wondering aloud what has taken so long, why the church here has so qualified its stand on wholesale murder, why the abhorrence of the Pope in distant Rome has been downplayed among the faithful by the church's clergy in the United States?

And yet despite that, the Catholic Church has been light years ahead of most other organized religions in recognizing the repugnance of the wholesale slaughter of the unborn.

Abortion is murder, pure and simple. There can be no qualification simply because the unborn infant is dependent upon its mother — the child is no less capable of surviving if left totally alone after its birth than it is of surviving without the mother before its birth.

Abortion is murder, and as U.S. Rep. Robert C. Smith says, "The tragic anniversary of the Roe vs. Wade decision serves to remind us of how urgent it is that we stand as one to end this oppressive chapter in American history."

THE PLAIN DEALER
Cleveland, OH, January 19, 1986

Today is National Sanctity of Human Life Day, as proclaimed by President Reagan. In his proclamation, the president again criticized the 1973 Supreme Court ruling that supported the right of choice, saying: "There were those who predicted confidently that in time Americans would come to accept the court's decison and the 'new ethic' that it reflects. History has proved them wrong." What "new ethic"? What "history"? Indeed, what prediction? We recall no forecasts that the nation would become insensitive to abortion.

What we do recall is a genuine optimism that the nation would come to understand the 1973 court ruling. It said that the *decision* about whether to have an abortion was a private and personal matter upon which the federal government could not intrude. No supporter of the court's ruling believes abortion is an excuse, an escape, a painless and non-tragic solution. Instead, they believe in the right of individuals to make the decision—one way or the other—free from federal or state interference.

There is no "new ethic" surrounding abortion. Supreme Court rulings regarding privacy do not alter the fundamental questions that, for thousands of years, have been addressed by potential parents. Nor is there any recent history that indicates majority disquiet with the 1973 court. In a Harris Poll conducted last November, 50% supported the court's decision, 47% opposed it. On the question of a constitutional ban on abortions—which the president supports—55% opposed the provision; only 35% favored it.

Support for the ruling and opposition to the constitutional ban has slipped slightly. But in both cases, the declines can be attributed to issue distortion by anti-choice campaigners. The court did not condone abortion, as some strident opponents would contend. It only established the right of choice through the right of privacy. Thus on Sanctity of Human Life Day, we also remember the sanctity of freedom and of self-determination, both of which require sometimes painful and always essential protections.

Local Restrictions Struck Down in 1983; Parental Notification a Major Issue

The Supreme Court voted 8-1 in July 1979 to strike down a Massachusetts law that required an unmarried minor to obtain the permission of both parents or a judge before having an abortion. The cases, consolidated for judgement, were *Bellotti v. Baird* and *Huerwadel v. Baird*. In a March 1981 abortion case, *H.L. v. Matheson*, however, the court upheld a Utah parental notification law that applied only to girls who were unmarried, under 18 and dependent on their parents. Three other states had similar laws. The law had been challenged by a pregnant 15-year-old who claimed that it violated her constitutional right to privacy and failed to distinguish between mature and immature teenagers. Writing for the majority, Chief Justice Warren Burger said the law "plainly serves the important considerations of family integrity and protecting adolescents."

Parental notification was one of many issues affected by three major Supreme Court rulings on five cases in June 1983 that curbed the power of state and local governments to limit access to legal abortions. Taken together, these decisions strongly reaffirmed the court's landmark 1973 ruling in *Roe v. Wade*, which gave women an unrestricted right to abortions in their first three months of pregnancy. The overturned restrictions included an Akron, Ohio ruling requiring parental consent for abortions performed on girls under 16 years of age. But the justices voted, 5-4, to uphold a provision of a Missouri law that required parental consent for abortions on "unemancipated" girls under 18 years old. The justices upheld parental notification in Missouri because that law, unlike the Akron restriction, took into account previous high court decisions requiring states to differentiate between teenage girls who were mature enough to make their own abortion decisions and those who were not.

In addition, the 1983 decision eliminated several other restrictions including a mandatory 24-hour waiting period for all abortions, hospitalization for all abortions after the first trimester of pregnancy, and a procedure under which doctors were required to inform pre-abortion patients of the dangers of abortion and to state that the fetus was a human being from the moment of conception.

The Miami Herald
Miami, Fla., July 9, 1979

IT WAS only a matter of time before the U.S. Supreme Court extended to unmarried adolescents its 1973 ruling that an adult woman has a Constitutional right to have an abortion. Except for one "if," that time has now arrived.

The High Court on Monday struck down, 8 to 1, a Massachusetts law that permitted girls under 18 to have abortions only with approval of their parents or a court. Those restrictions made the law unconstitutional, the Court ruled.

But the ruling was not a clear-cut victory for those who would extend to "mature" teenagers the absolute right to an abortion. Four of the Justices outlined modifications that they said would make the Massachusetts law Constitutional while still requiring the teenager to have a court's approval for an abortion.

The suggested modifications seem reasonable enough. First of all, the Justices said no law could require that parents be notified or that they have veto power over their daughter's abortion. The Massachusetts law contained both provisos, although the parents' refusal could be overridden by a judge.

To be Constitutional, the Justices said, an abortion law may require only that the teenager "go discreetly to a court without first consulting or notifying her parents." If the court finds that the teenager "is mature and well-informed enough to make intelligently the abortion decision on her own, the court must authorize her to act without parental consultation or consent." If the court finds the teenager incompetent to act on her own. it still must approve the abortion if it concludes that abortion would be in her best interests.

The Justices' "advisory" opinion will satisfy neither those who would remove all restrictions from abortion nor those who believe that parents have a right to participate in so fundamental a decision affecting their daughters. But the opinion goes as far as the Court could — or should — go in an area in which the rights of the teenager and of her parents are so inextricably intertwined.

In any matter involving juveniles, a court's first interest is to protect their welfare. The Court's decision does that, for it recognizes that some teenagers are "mature" enough to decide on an abortion and some are not. Those who are not require guidance even if their individual rights permit them to obtain that guidance from a judge rather than from their parents.

The debate over abortion, like that over capital punishment, is fundamentally irresolvable. It pits concepts of life and of individual rights that always have been, and always will be, diametrically opposed. So the Court's decision, while not a clear "victory" for either side, was as sound as the issues themselves permit.

THE LOUISVILLE TIMES
Louisville, Ky., July 9, 1979

If judges across the nation are feeling put upon by the Supreme Court, they have cause. Not only are they now responsible for determining whether or not criminal court proceedings can be open to the public, they also are going to be deciding whether or not pregnant minors can obtain abortions.

A decision handed down by the high court last Monday shakes the very heart of the 1973 Supreme Court ruling on abortion. Weakened is the right of some women to decide whether they will seek an abortion after consultation with a doctor. The high court has allowed judges, not doctors, to ultimately determine whether a pregnant woman under 18 is mature enough to make the decision.

It was the first time in six years that the Supreme Court had wobbled on its position that the right of privacy protects the woman's decision to abort. Inevitably, legislatures across the nation will follow the court's lead.

At issue was a Massachusetts statute which required parental consent in cases where minors wanted to obtain abortions. The high court wisely rejected the mandatory provisions of the consent law, but at the same time it permitted judges to horn into determinations that are medical, not legal.

The majority decision, written by Justice Lewis Powell, said there are three reasons why the constitutional rights of minors cannot be equated with those of adults: children are especially vulnerable to others' influence; they are in many cases unable to make decisions in an informed, mature manner; and the importance of the guiding role of parents in childrens' upbringing.

With abortions, reliance on parental supervision seems particularly shaky, especially when young women are so apt to incur their parents' wrath for becoming pregnant. To safeguard her against such intimidation, the high court ruled unconstitutional the parental consent section of the Massachusetts law.

That squares with a 1976 ruling that voided a Missouri law requiring parental consent forms prior to abortion from the parents of minors. At that time, the court reiterated its 1973 statement that "the abortion decision and its effectuation must be left to the medical judgment of the pregnant woman's a tending physician."

Now, however, consent comes from a judge.

"Every minor must have the opportunity — if she so desires — to go directly to a court without first consulting or notifying her parents. If she satisfies the court that she is mature and well-informed enough to make intelligently the abortion decision on her own, the court must authorize her to act," wrote Justice Powell.

If the judge finds the young woman mature, she and her doctor can make the decision. If he finds her immature, the judge makes the decision.

The potential for chaos under this standard is frightening. There will be candidacies for judgeships by "pro-life" advocates. Racist judges who eye the high rates of unwed pregnancies among minorities may delight in ordering abortions.

In either case, it is not a welcome prospect.

The Philadelphia Inquirer
Philadelphia, PA, June 23, 1979

It is reasonable, as well as constitutionally permissible, for a state to set regulations in the second trimester of pregnancy to protect the health of women undergoing abortions. So said the U.S. Supreme Court in its landmark 1973 ruling on abortion. It is not reasonable and most likely not constitutional, however, for states to set regulations that effectively interfere with a woman's right to have an abortion.

But that's exactly what New Jersey would be doing if a bill that has passed the State Assembly becomes law. The Senate should defeat the bill; barring that, Governor Brendan Byrne should veto it.

At first the New Jersey proposal sounds innocuous enough: Under it doctors would be required to inform patients of possible ill effects from abortions. They would have to tell women seeking abortions that the state considers the fetus a living human being, and they would have to describe the physical characteristics of the fetus at that stage. Doctors would be required to inform the parent or guardian of a girl under 18 before the girl could have an abortion. A woman would have to consent in writing before having an abortion and would have to wait 48 hours before getting it.

If such rules would simply promote sober consideration of a serious decision, they would be acceptable. But that is not their real purpose, nor would it be their effect. They are designed to make it more difficult for women to exercise rights defined by the Supreme Court in 1973, and that would be their result. To be specific:

• For a doctor to tell a woman about potential ill effects of having an abortion is well and good, but would he or she also describe the possible ill effects of carrying a pregnancy to term? Would the patient be told that complications from abortion are rare and that many experts consider abortions in the first trimester less risky than giving birth?

• What purpose, other than psychological coercion, would be served by a doctor's telling a woman the state considers a fetus a living human being? This could not possibly be construed as an effort to protect maternal health, which is the only right the Supreme Court gives a state in regulating abortions in the second trimester. And in the first three months of pregnancy it would be an unwarranted interference in what the Supreme Court has said is a private decision between patient and doctor. Further, doesn't this view of fetal life mean the state is promulgating the beliefs of some religious denominations but not others, so as to violate separation of church and state?

• Informing the parents of a minor girl before she can get an abortion could be tantamount to giving those parents veto power, which the Supreme Court has already ruled unconstitutional. What about the young woman's right to privacy, established in case law?

• Waiting 48 hours to get an abortion would not be a problem in most cases, but mightn't it be an onerous burden for a low-income woman who had to travel some distance to her doctor or clinic, who had to take time off from work and arrange day care for her children?

There are other provisions in the New Jersey bill that amount to harassment of women seeking to exercise their constitutional right to choose abortion. Bills like this have been enacted in several other jurisdictions but have never gone into effect pending federal court challenges. So far those challenges have been successful and similar regulations have been struck down. That's what would probably happen in New Jersey. But the Senate would save the state a great deal of trouble if it refused to pass this politically popular but probably unconstitutional proposal.

THE SACRAMENTO BEE
Sacramento, CA, June 7, 1980

Since 1976, the U.S. Supreme Court has held that an unmarried minor female has a right to an abortion without parental consent. California law properly conforms to that standard. Yet, the state Senate recently passed a bill that clearly violates those guidelines.

The measure, SB 1814, labeled a "parents' rights" bill by its author, Sen. John Schmitz, would require an unmarried girl to obtain either parental permission or a court order declaring she is mature enough to make an abortion decision before she can get such an operation. Schmitz was at least candid about the Senate's action: "In an election·year, some legislators may be looking for an opportunity to cast a pro-life vote."

But Schmitz's SB 1814 contains real dangers. The measure would create serious obstacles for those youngsters least able to surmount them, leading to unwanted births, possible health complications for both mothers and babies, or illegal and dangerous abortions. For the fact is that medical risks in obstructing teen-agers' access to abortions are high. Babies born to teen-agers, for example, are two to three times more likely to die in their first year than those born to women in their early 20s. And teens who give birth are twice as likely to die from hemorrhage and miscarriage.

The Supreme Court has struck down laws in other states containing blanket requirements for parental consent or permitting a minor to seek a court order only after being denied parents' permission. Schmitz tries to dodge judicial hurdles with a provision that a minor may go directly to a judge without first seeking parental consent. That unrealistically assumes, however, that a minor will possess the sophistication and knowledge to initiate a court proceeding.

This bill's underlying purpose, as Schmitz admits, is to discourage abortions. But he tries to have it both ways; a girl too immature to decide for herself whether to have an abortion must also be too immature to become a good mother.

Given the court's clear direction, the Senate acted irresponsibly in approving the measure. It remains for the Assembly to take a more sensible course by rejecting this bill.

CHICAGO Sun-Times
Chicago, IL, August 2, 1980

Illinois lawmakers had plenty of warning last year that they were passing a severely defective piece of legislation: the 1979 act regulating abortion.

Legal scholars tried to tell them their punitive, guilt-engendering methods to deter abortion weren't legal. They passed it overwhelmingly. Gov. Thompson tried to tell them—by vetoing the bill. They overrode him.

Then U.S. District Court Judge Joel M. Flaum struck down many key provisions, but left many others standing. And now the U.S. Court of Appeals has upheld Flaum—and expanded on his ruling, throwing out almost all the rest of the flawed sections of the law.

This week the appeals court ruled against the 24-hour waiting period the Legislature imposed, against the requirement that the same physician perform a pregnancy test and the abortion, against the particularly cruel requirement that women seeking abortions view pictures of fetuses in various developmental phases and against vague homicide provisions for the doctor.

The message to the Legislature is clear, in this case and in those of the other restrictive abortion·laws this one was designed to supplant: Regulation of abortions is a legitimate government concern, but those regulations must not be drawn to harass either the woman seeking an abortion or her doctor. That's obviously a hard lesson for lawmakers to learn, but they'd better start trying.

• • •

After the Supreme Court's decision upholding the Hyde Amendment, abortion foes challenged their opponents to come up with money to pay for abortions for the poor in Medicaid's absence. The Eleanor Roosevelt Institute has responded with a $100,000 donation to the Planned Parenthood of America Justice Fund. Others are giving, too.

It's a worthwhile cause—but a pity that private funds have to undo public injustice.

THE COMMERCIAL APPEAL
Memphis, TN, July 5, 1979

THE SUPREME COURT seems to be under the delusion that only the courts know best, and nothing could better illustrate this misguided sense of self-importance than two of its latest rulings. One is on abortion, the other on pretrial hearings, but together they suggest that this nation's justices think judges have a monopoly on sense when it comes to running the country.

THE FIRST DECISION struck down a Massachusetts law requiring the consent of both parents or of a judge for an unmarried girl under 18 years old to have an abortion. While the justices ruled that a minor is constitutionally entitled to choose, they qualified her right to do so. Her parents need not be informed or consulted, but she may have to convince a judge that she is mature enough to make that decision. If the judge is not satisfied that an abortion is in her "best interest," she can be denied it.

This is dangerous business. It institutionalizes the notion that courts — not parents — have an inherent right to be concerned with a child's welfare. We make no brief for the belief that parents are automatically imbued with knowledge, wisdom and compassion at the instant of birth, but since when have our courts become so Solomon-like that they can cloak themselves in authority and set themselves up as the sole judge of family matters?

Parents may not have the right of "absolute veto" over a daughter's abortion, and we agree that a requirement of parental notification would pose a particularly difficult problem in cases of incest.

But parents are responsible under the law for their child's behavior, and their importance goes beyond questions of legality. This nation is rooted in the family, and the courts have no business further undercutting its strengths.

THE HIGH COURT used reasoning just as convoluted in its decision to allow the public to be kept out of pretrial hearings in criminal cases. The majority held 5-4 that a judge can close the doors when "all parties" have agreed to closed proceedings, but it had to turn the Constitution on its head to conclude that the public is not a party to the judicial process.

In his dissent, Associate Justice Harry A. Blackmun put the public's role in proper perspective: "Open trials enable the public to scrutinize the performance of police and prosecutors in the conduct of public judicial business."

In a nation where some 90 per cent of all criminal cases are disposed of before trial, Blackmun continued, pretrial proceedings are "the only opportunity the public has to learn about police and prosecutorial conduct and about allegations that those responsible to the public for the enforcement of (the) law themselves are breaking it."

He concluded that the public's interest in open courts is so "fundamental" that it cannot be waived by individual parties to a trial.

THAT INTEREST goes beyond seeing to it that public servants are on the job. It goes to the heart of the fair-trial concept.

For all the talk about the possibility that pretrial publicity may deny a person's right "to a speedy and public trial by an impartial jury," there is also the possibility that defendants' rights may be abridged in star-chamber proceedings.

They may not understand what is being asked of them, they may not be adequately represented by counsel, they may stand before a judge who doesn't know his law as well as his political cronies.

The Constitution guarantees against such abuses, but a public presence helps guarantee its protection in courtrooms each day.

The Supreme Court has done the nation an injustice by letting the public be locked out of what is rightly its business.

DAYTON DAILY NEWS
Dayton, OH, August 25, 1979

The morality of abortion/anti-abortion politics is tangled at best, and the tangle is thick in the Akron abortion ordinance a federal court has now substantially upheld.

The judge ruled against two provisions — one requiring parental consent for teenagers, another requiring that physicians impress the details of fetal development on women requesting abortions. As a result, pro-choice groups call the ruling a victory, but the anti-abortionists are more nearly right when they claim the victory for themselves. The court upheld 17 major points in the ordinance.

Those include written consent by the woman, a 24-hour waiting period, counsel by a physician outlining all the risks involved, detailed medical reporting, attendence by a second physician who would try to save the life of the fetus in any circumstance where it is possible the fetus would be viable, and a ban on fetal experimentation.

The last point is an especially chaotic bit of moralizing. Fetal experimentation sounds gruesome, but it has been key in the development of diagnostic and treatment techniques that are making it possible to bring more troubled pregnancies to full term with healthy babies.

The ordinance is not, as is claimed with broad winks, protection for women. It is meant to confuse and frighten women who already are in physically and emotionally trying circumstances. And given the cases in which the ordinance most often will be applied, it is hard not to suspect that a large part of the impulse behind it is a self-righteous attempt to terrorize and punish teenage girls for having been "bad."

In any event, the purpose of the ordinance is to harry women and physicians in the exercise of a decision that is perfectly legal. If that is moral, it is morality of a very subtle kind.

THE BLADE
Toledo, OH, December 3, 1980

DESPITE some modifications, an "informed-consent" abortion-control bill passed by the Ohio Senate remains as defective as a similar measure which bogged down in a House committee last May. Much like a proposed Toledo ordinance that was resoundingly rejected by voters last year, the new legislation would simply make abortions more difficult in the guise of "protecting" the health of pregnant women.

One reason for opposing this bill is that there is no demonstrated need for it; the push has come from well-organized anti-abortion groups attempting to impose their narrow interpretations of moral and biological considerations on society.

As in other such efforts, the present measure includes a change in the legal definition of a fetus to term it an "unborn child," a highly debatable point which has not been settled even by the nation's highest court. It also would mandate a waiting period and detailed information to be given pregnant women, requirements designed more to delay the procedure and frighten them than to be helpful.

The present bill, in fact, is little different from the one which died in committee earlier despite the addition of some amendments sponsored by Sen. Marigene Valiquette of Toledo. They do nothing to make the proposal any more acceptable. And, in spite of her professed reluctance to vote for the measure, it is little wonder that at least one Toledo pro-abortion group expressed puzzlement over Senator Valiquette's support for it in view of the defeat of the proposed Toledo ordinance in 1980.

As pointed out previously, The Blade does not take lightly the matter of abortion with all the complex factors that are involved. But it is a choice that should be available to a pregnant woman as a matter between herself and her physician. Sen. Michael Schwartzwalder was right in terming the Senate bill "an unconstitutional infringement on a woman's right to make that critical personal choice," and it should go no further in the General Assembly.

The Providence Journal

Providence, RI, January 20, 1980

The General Assembly should not waste the public's time trying to write an acceptable version of the "Informed Consent for Abortion" law now ruled unconstitutional by Chief Judge Raymond J. Pettine in U.S. District Court.

As might be expected, the director of Planned Parenthood of Rhode Island, Maryann Sorrentino Ciullo, said the judge's ruling is "a message to the state legislature to let it stop here . . . the courts have spoken."

Judge Pettine said a few parts of the 1980 law are innocuous and appropriate: for example, requiring that the patient be told an abortion is a medical procedure to terminate pregnancy and is irreversible. But most of the statute, he said, goes beyond the constitutional limits on a state's right to interfere with an abortion decision.

What is left intact, assuming Judge Pettine's dissection of the statute is not overturned on appeal, is an unnecessary bit of law-making. Why? Because a basic obligation for informed consent is implicit in any ethical practice of medicine.

A patient facing a hernia repair or a coronary artery bypass has to give consent after being told: what the surgeon is going to do, what benefit is being sought and what risks are present if the procedure takes place — or if it does *not* take place. A physician performing an abortion should make sure that the same degree of informed consent exists.

Instead of stopping there, the General Assembly lengthened a simple, common-sense relationship between doctor and patient into a whole *megillah* of requirements in order to achieve "truly informed consent" to an abortion.

Without recounting Judge Pettine's entire ruling in detail, he found "totally inappropriate," extravagant and coercive a requirement that the patient be told that the Department of Health could make available reading matter describing characteristics of the fetus at the various times at which an abortion might be performed.

The 1980 measure was one in the legislature's endless series of attempts to interfere with women's constitutional rights and promote a particular doctrinal view. Sen. Robert J. McKenna, D-Newport, principal sponsor of the enactment, said he wants to see if acceptable portions of the stricken statute can now be revived and implemented.

The senator is perfectly at liberty to seek such a revival; his fellow legislators are free to adopt any measure they please. However, to use a phrase from Judge Pettine's decision, what "compelling interest" on the part of the public can be satisfied by such an exercise? At best, the General Assembly could only reinforce and restate the type of informed consent already existing in a doctor-patient relationship.

The Charlotte Observer

Charlotte, NC, October 2, 1980

News of "more sex, more contraception, but more pregnancies" among teenagers, reported last week by Johns Hopkins University researchers, underscores the importance of a case the U.S. Supreme Court has agreed to decide during its current term. The case involves a teenager who sought an abortion under a Utah law that required her parents to be notified before a doctor could operate.

The court has already ruled that women have a right to abortions and that minors don't need permission from their parents to get an abortion. This case touches new ground: The Utah law says simply that parents must be *notified* before the abortion.

Attorneys for the 15-year-old involved in this case argue such a requirement is a chilling obstacle to a minor's right to an abortion; they say such a law encourages many teenagers to avoid dealing with a pregnancy until it's obvious and an abortion is a more difficult, even dangerous, choice. They argue that some parents might abuse a child or physically restrain her to prevent the abortion, even when it would be best for the teenager's health.

Utah officials argue that the state has an interest in encouraging minors to consult their parents on such an important decision. In fact, parents may have information about a minor's health, information a teenager might not reveal or perhaps understand, that would bear on a doctor's decision to perform an abortion.

The court must reconcile parental responsibilities and rights with an individual's right. It won't be easy.

It reminds us that abortion is *not* birth control. Yet current birth-control methods clearly are not adequate — either because people won't use them or because they fear the side effects. (The Johns Hopkins report, for example, found that girls who know about birth-control pills now are rejecting them more frequently because they fear health problems.)

The abortion issue will not subside unless adults work to help teenagers understand the consequences of sexual acts and to speed birth-control research. Failing to act, as the Johns Hopkins report shows, results in more pregnancies and more abortions.

The Boston Globe

Boston, MA, June 9, 1980

The governor would like to believe he has helped put some beneficial abortion legislation on the books. As King said last Thursday, when he signed the controversial bill, "It is appropriate that the Commonwealth of Massachusetts is leading the way in enacting model legislation which will bring our families closer together." The legislation is not a model and does anything but hold families together.

The new law requires any woman seeking an abortion to sign a consent form that describes fetal development, possible medical complications and alternatives to abortion; it also requires a 24-hour waiting period between the time a woman signs the form and the time of her abortion. Further, a minor must have the consent of both parents or a Superior Court judge before she can get an abortion, a provision that is similar to a statute declared unconstitutional by the Supreme Court in 1976. The consent form must also carry a rather odd disclaimer stating that a woman's refusal to undergo abortion is not grounds for denial of public assistance.

Anti-abortion activists in other states have pushed for and passed this so-called model legislation and watched it fail court test after court test. Judges in Missouri, Louisiana, Nebraska, New York and Maine have struck down assorted statutes requiring consent forms or delay times, and just last week a federal court judge in Kentucky issued a temporary restraining order against legislation requiring a 24-hour waiting period. The Civil Liberties Union of Massachusetts has filed suit here charging that the new state law — which won't go into effect until September — is unconstitutional as well because it places an unfair burden on women and minors by wrongfully restricting abortions and discriminating against a woman's decision to terminate a pregnancy.

Proponents of consent and delay laws, Gov. King included, would apparently like to believe that this kind of legislation strengthens the family. Hardly. Such measures are written and passed purely to intimidate and harass women who want or need abortions. The reasoning behind them is transparent: women who want or need abortions must be punished, they must overcome obstacles designed to elevate anxiety and pain during an already anxious and painful time. Proponents of consent and delay laws, Gov. King included, are only fooling themselves if they argue otherwise.

THE SAGINAW NEWS
Saginaw, Mich., March 20, 1981

In a pair of cases from the touchy realm of youth behavior, the U.S. Supreme Court rendered a split decision this week.

We applaud its ruling allowing states to require that doctors notify parents when a minor child, living at home and supported by her parents, seeks an abortion.

It has upheld, in our view, a parental role in guiding the conduct of children.

Too many parental rights have been slowly lost to the misplaced theory that constitutional guarantees — even in the case of life-and-death decisions — belong equally, in every instance, to youngsters, no matter how immature.

The court majority carefully did not insist on parental notification in every case where a minor woman requests an abortion. It drew a distinction, as we do, between fully dependent children — remembering they become biological adults at 11, 12 or 13 — and independent young women who may not even be living at home.

The court also wisely did not assert a parental veto power over a decison that may be recommended by a physician as in the best interests of the patient. That indeed would violate the right of medical privacy.

But privacy and secrecy are not the same. The one is healthy. The other can be deadly to a family unit whose strength depends on keeping mutual trust alive. The state should play no role in eroding that trust by excluding parents from even the awareness of a child's errant behavior.

While the decision firmly supports the strong social purpose of upholding family integrity, it is good law as well. It simply declares that minors do not always have the same rights as adults. To rule otherwise would stretch the Constitution out of shape besides damaging the parent-child relationship, and the parental responsibilities that are a cornerstone of society.

In the other case, the court's conservative wing delivered a setback to the movement toward equality in a separate set of rights: Those of males and females.

The decision that males may be subject to statutory rape laws, while their partners are subject to no criminal penalty, violates the basic legal premise of equal protection under the law.

That conservative Justice William Rehnquist wrote the majority opinion is not surprising. But his reasoning is. The argument that discrimination is all right if it serves a good purpose — preventing teenage preganancies — is based on the same kind of social engineering for which conservatives long criticized the activist Warren Court.

The ruling, in a California case, may have little impact because 37 states already have gender-neutral rape laws. But it's disappointing to see the court sanction a men-only morals law that has proved to be of little use, and to sometimes cause grave injustice, in the first place.

Arkansas Gazette.
Little Rock, Ark., March 27, 1981

It hasn't worked a second time – the privacy argument on which the Supreme Court based its constitutionalization of abortion. A teenage girl who pleaded her privacy in challenging a Utah law requiring parental notice of abortions for the underaged found the high Justices 6-3 in favor of such notice.

That's not only a victory for family authority, it's also a discouragement of teenage sex. If a girl can't keep her pregnancy secret from her mother and father she's more likely to think twice about careless sex.

Though the decision was only 6-3, it does show that the majority of Justices takes a negative view of the worst effect of the court's abortion-for-all doctrine – teenage pregnancy. The ruling also means that any states that care to can follow Utah in requiring doctors to notify parents when a dependent, unemancipated (still at home) girl below 18 requests an abortion.

The notification requirement isn't absolute. Aside from applying only to dependent, unemancipated girls under 18, it appears to leave major determinations to the doctor. He isn't required to notify parents unless he judges a girl too immature to make the abortion decision for herself. He can also skip notice if he believes that notification wouldn't seriously alter her relationship with her parents.

Obviously, the ruling means that young women 18 and over, whether away from home or not, are free to have abortions on demand without parental notice – and that those below 18 who impress the doctor as mature or of broadminded or alienated parents can do the same. But a great many teenagers won't qualify for these exemptions and the thought that Daddy and Mother will know it if they seek an abortion is a deterrent.

The court decision is sound public policy. Arkansas should pass a similar law at first opportunity if for no other reason than that teenage pregnancy is rife in this state.

The Wichita
Eagle-Beacon

Wichita, Kans., March 26, 1981

The narrowly drawn Supreme Court decision upholding the right of states to require that parents be notified of their dependent minor child's plans to obtain an abortion is grounded firmly in law and common sense.

As the ruling implies, such a notification requirement may not be sustainable in cases involving a child who legally has been declared emancipated, or where the underaged person seeking an abortion reasonably can be considered a mature, independent person capable of making such important decisions alone.

It would be logical, in those less frequently encountered cases, where such a choice could be expected to have little, if any, deleterious impact on a parent-child relationship, that notification might be waived. But in cases where a minor still is living at home or is otherwise clearly dependent on a parent, such major decisions shouldn't, with the state's backing, kept from the parent.

Clearly, the most basic concepts of law hold that a minor is not accorded the full rights and responsibilities of adult citizenship until he or she reaches the age of majority. In lieu of that the young person is afforded the protection, guidance and support of what is hoped will be a responsible adult — most often, his or her parents.

The thing that argues most persuasively for notifying parents of a dependent child's intentions to undergo an abortion, in the more common family context, is that parents are expected to bear a large legal and moral responsibility for their children's health, behavior and welfare, until they are adults. So long as those responsibilities exist, parents also have the right to know about such potentially dangerous, harmful matters as abortions obtained by their children.

Sentinel Star

Orlando, Fla., March 25, 1981

THE abortion issue has always had the power to polarize the emotions of Americans. And Monday's U. S. Supreme Court decision, upholding a Utah law requiring that parents be notified of a minor daughter's decision to have an abortion, simply highlights that division again.

The Utah law required a blanket notification of parents "if possible." The court, by a 6-3 vote, upheld the rights of states to make such stipulations, but went a step further by trying to balance the rights of parents with the needs of the child.

In Florida, for instance, many parents are aghast when they learn they will not be notified if their child has an abortion, yet they are required to sign a medical release if the child requires medical treatment of any other kind.

On the other hand, a minor child, terrified that she may be the victim of physical abuse if her parents learn she is pregnant, could attempt to abort herself or even commit suicide. With those conflicts in mind, the court:

● Recognized parental responsibility for minor children by permitting mandatory notification laws in those cases involving a minor girl living with and dependent upon her parents.

● Upheld the individual rights of the minor girl by eliminating notification in cases where she is either married or living as an "emancipated" minor on her own.

● Eliminated the notification requirement if the girl can show she is mature enough to make the decision herself or that her relationship with her parents would be seriously affected as a result.

It is unclear how much such a ruling will change things. Abortion clinic officials in Orlando say about three-fourths of the minors coming to them now do so with parental permission.

The court appears to have given states the go-ahead to enact such laws, but has recognized the realities of parent-child relations and the failures on both sides. For that there is no blanket answer; you have to go case by case.

The Hartford Courant

Hartford, Conn., March 26, 1981

The Supreme Court declared in 1976 and 1979 that states may not demand the consent of parents before a minor receives an abortion.

Yet, the court this week upheld a Utah statute requiring doctors to notify parents before performing an abortion on their minor daughters. The decision should not be shrugged off as a small setback or a temporary aberration in an otherwise consistent court. The court already has effectively barred poor women from obtaining abortions by allowing Congress to withhold Medicaid payments for that purpose.

The newest ruling affecting young women is all the more alarming in the aftermath of President Reagan's comments last week that he will stand "shoulder-to-shoulder" with the anti-abortion lobby and with a serious Senate drive to enact a bill establishing that life begins at conception. (Abortion then would be considered murder.)

Nearly a third of the abortions today are performed on teen-age women, many of them minors. Forcing doctors to notify parents of an impending abortion will deny many such women the right to decide privately with their doctor, how to handle their pregnancy.

The long-term consequences of the pregnancy fall primarily on the young woman, not her parents. In many instances, she may choose to discuss those consequences with them. But a state cannot expect to legislate harmonious family relations. A young woman may have good reason to be afraid to tell her parents that she is pregnant and considering an abortion. No state law can mandate a cooperative resolution of her dilemma with her parents.

The doctor in the Utah case which reached the Supreme Court agreed with the young woman that her best interests would not be served if her parents were informed of her decision. He, however, would have been held criminally liable under the Utah statute if he performed the abortion without telling her parents.

The court did not rule whether a state may force notification of the parents of an emancipated minor (a minor who has obtained court permission to be treated as an adult) or a mature minor (who is deemed legally capable of deciding for herself).

The serious, almost insurmountable, problem arising from the latest decision will not disappear if the justices decide in the future that states may not require notification of parents of "mature" or "emancipated" young women.

Consider just one scenario: A young woman goes to a physician, discovers she is pregnant, decides to have an abortion and then is forced to go to court to be legally emancipated from her parents. But by then so much time may have elapsed that it is medically unsafe to have an abortion.

A pregnant young woman deserves the same constitutional protection as any other pregnant woman, not paternalistic oversight by the state. By allowing states to interpose themselves in family relationships, the Supreme Court unwittingly may be contributing to family breakdown.

AKRON BEACON JOURNAL
Akron, OH, March 1, 1981

OHIO LAW states that abortion "is the practice of medicine or surgery," and that "No person shall perform or induce an abortion without the informed consent of the pregnant woman."

But that doesn't keep legislators, prodded by Right-to-Life groups, from coming back with repeated efforts to greatly expand Ohio's abortion laws, with the intent, they say, to require "informed consent" — no matter that it is already required.

The issue of payment for abortions was fought in the Ohio Assembly in 1979. A bill was introduced in 1980 that would have made it more difficult for a woman to get an abortion, even though the U. S. Supreme Court has clearly upheld a woman's right to make that decision.

Three similar bills have been introduced so far in 1981 and two hearings already have been held by the House State Government Committee on a bill submitted by Rep. Kenneth Rocco, D-Parma. Supporters were heard at those hearings; opponents will appear before the committee on the next two Tuesdays.

Rep. Vernon Cook, D Cuyahoga Falls, has been named to head a subcommittee that will study the Rocco bill. He, Rep. William Batchelder, R-Medina, and Richard Maier, R-Massillon, are among the co-sponsors.

Rep. Cook says he believes such a bill is needed, though he adds that it is designed to "put into legislation what the federal court has ruled."

If that were so, it would be hard to justify spending so many hours on reaffirming the work of the court when so much other work is waiting for legislative consideration.

Typical of bills pushed by anti-abortion groups, this one includes what Mr. Cook refers to as a "laundry list" of information physicians would be required to give a woman considering abortion and conditions for performing the surgery.

One of the provisions, requiring anyone under 16 to get juvenile court permission in lieu of parental consent for an abortion, is not part of the major 1973 Supreme Court ruling. Many of the other items sound much like those in the Akron ordinance struck down in part in a court test.

A physician would be required to give the woman a description of the unborn child at the time of abortion, and tell of complications — physical and emotional — that could occur, what alternatives to abortion are available, and so on. The woman would be obliged to wait until 48 hours after being counseled before the abortion could be performed.

Rep. Cook, whose performance into this area is disappointing, says informed consent is required for every other surgical procedure — ignoring the fact that it already is also required in law for abortion. The law does not list specific information a physician is to provide someone facing even the most critical other type of elective surgery, and it should not do so for abortion.

Again this year, as in 1978 and 1979, the proposed legislation will provoke angry, emotional arguments. And, again, when all is said and done, the case remains the same:

Abortion is an intensely personal issue, to be decided by the pregnant woman in consultation with her physician. That is her constitutional right, and the legislators ought not to spend their time trying to rewrite the Constitution or practice medicine.

TULSA WORLD
Tulsa, OK, March 4, 1982

THE STATE House passed a bill Tuesday which would require, in most circumstances, the consent of parents before their minor child can have an abortion.

The bill, sponsored by Rep. David Riggs, D-Sand Springs, attempts to deal with a frustrating problem — a decline of parental authority over teen-age children. Few would argue that parents should not have a voice in such an important decision as an abortion. But it isn't that simple.

It is a tragic reality of American life that many teen-age children are, for practical purposes, separated from their parents, estranged and beyond parental control.

In such a case, the main effect of this bill would be to frustrate a girl seeking a legal abortion. Fearful or distrustful of her parents, she would either refuse to seek their consent or ignore their decision if she disagreed with it. A likely result: an illegal abortion with grave dangers to the girl's life and health.

The bill addresses this problem, but only in part. Under certain circumstances — if the parents refused their approval or the girl did not want them contacted — the girl could petition district court which could grant approval if a judge determined the girl was sufficiently mature and competent to give informed consent to the operation. But even this procedure would not always prevent a girl from seeking an illegal abortion. She would be tempted to avoid the hassle of a court action or she could simply ignore any decision made for her by her parents or a court and head for the nearest medical butcher shop.

The bill could strike a blow for parental guidance by requiring doctors to consult parents where practicable, but leaving the final decision to the prospective young mother. She is the one, after all, who is facing the prospect of having an unwanted child and who will be responsible for the infant when it arrives.

Perhaps such a change could be made in the bill in the Senate.

Parents have constitutional rights — as yet not fully defined — over the care and raising of their children. Riggs' bill seeks to accommodate those parental rights without offending the legal rights of the child.

The author of the bill quite correctly tries to draw a valid distinction between the rights and responsiblities afforded adults and those which can be exercised unilaterally by minor children. But the line is misplaced.

Restoring parental guidance and control is a worthy goal. But in this case, the risk of reviving back-alley abortions makes the price too high.

Portland Press Herald
Portland, ME, September 3, 1983

Members of the Maine Legislature can learn an important lesson from the U.S. Supreme Court's June rulings on abortion: Passing laws which appeal to popular interests may be easy, but due regard must be given to basic constitutional protections.

Four years ago, legislators approved two restrictive abortion laws which the court rulings appear to have struck down. One would have required parental notification whenever a pregnant minor seeks an abortion; the other would have established a 48-hour waiting period before an abortion was performed and required doctors to counsel women on alternatives.

However well-meaning the laws, they stood in clear violation of earlier Supreme Court decisions that—at least during the first trimester of pregnancy—a woman must be allowed to have an abortion "free from interference by the state."

The court reaffirmed its interpretation in June, ruling on similar laws passed by other states. The U.S. District Court in Maine—which enjoined the Maine laws against being put into effect shortly after their passage in 1979—is expected to follow the Supreme Court's lead and formally strike down the Maine laws following a hearing next week.

Even anti-abortion lawyers concede that the Maine laws are essentially moot and will confine their arguments to preserving language in one of the laws which calls upon physicians to certify that a woman has consented to an abortion "freely and without coercion."

That, at least, has the virtue of being constitutional. Legislators, take note.

The Birmingham News
Birmingham, AL, June 20, 1983

The U.S. Supreme Court's rulings knocking down a number of state laws relating to abortions vividly demonstrate the widespread confusion regarding female rights, parental responsibilities and the public interest.

Among other powers, the court ruled states do not have the Constitutional power to require girls under age 15 to obtain parental consent or a judge's approval before getting an abortion.

Yet, no one would seriously challenge the states' powers to deny girls drivers' licenses before age 16, require parental consent for marriage licenses to be issued to minor girls or set the legal drinking age at 21.

Furthermore, a 15-year-old girl in a hospital for an abortion would have to get her parents to sign a statement giving consent for the girl to have such minor surgery as removing a mole or wart. And before a boy or girl under 18 can enter military service, he or she must also have parental consent.

If people and institutions are confused about state and federal powers, about parental responsibilities for the welfare of minor children and about legal versus moral issues, they have every right to be

The Burlington Free Press
Burlington, VT, March 21, 1982

Let's review the editorial positions of the Free Press on abortion.

On March 8, we encouraged the Vermont Legislature to approve a bill that would require that parents be told before an under-18 girl receives an abortion. The same editorial endorsed a Reagan administration proposal that federally funded health clinics be required to notify parents before minors receive birth control prescriptions.

Yet, on March 13, the Free Press said the U.S. Senate should reject a constitutional amendment that would enable Congress and the states to adopt laws banning abortions.

Some have suggested we are inconsistent on the subject. We think not; hence this editorial.

On the second issue — the banning of abortion or passing laws that would limit a woman's right to have an abortion — we make no moral judgment. Although we respect both the arguments for and against abortion, our view is that the decision whether or not to have an abortion properly rests with the persons who must live with whatever decision they make. For some women, abortion is wrong; but it should be wrong because they consider it wrong, not because the government considers it wrong. For other women, abortion presents no moral dilemma. For them, abortion should remain an option which if chosen will not place them outside the law.

On the former issue, however, the child's rights must come second to the rights of the parents who are ultimately responsible for the welfare of their children until they reach 18.

Parents should consider the fact that public schools can not even administer an aspirin to your child without your consent. If your child is in need of emergency treatment at a hospital, only a court order makes it possible without your approval. Yet abortions — and the prescribing of possibly harmful birth control paraphernalia — can be done without your knowledge.

Yet, it will be you — the parent — who must cope with the consequences of the decision if it is a mistake. No one suggests that some women don't live to regret having an abortion. If an under-18 youngster requires psychological help after opting for an abortion, it is mom and dad who will bear the cost of that help. And, hopefully, it will be mom and dad who provide the moral support the child will need to get on with the rest of her life.

Representatives of Planned Parenthood, Inc., and other federally funded health clinics argue that lack of communication in the home is the main reason so many youngsters turn to them for help. And they say that girls, if required to consult with their parents before receiving a birth control prescription — or abortion — would turn elsewhere for help rather than confront their parents. That, unfortunately, is probably true.

But if any government-funded agency is allowed to disregard the wishes of parents, we believe the government is dangerously close to establishment of a state religion. Religion, after all, really only helps us establish moral values. If the religious views of parents can be set aside by any government agency, we have Big Brother government at its ugly worst.

Before continuing with this editorial, it is appropriate that we say a few words in support of Planned Parenthood and other federally funded health agencies. They provide invaluable service to many Americans, but particularly to those young people who turn to them for help.

We reject the notion of some anti-abortion groups that Planned Parenthood promotes sexual promiscuity. We believe Planned Parenthood is right when it states that the overwhelming majority of young people seeking birth control devices do so only after they have become sexually active.

Nor will we quarrel with Planned Parenthood's contention that a young woman is encouraged to consult with her parents before birth control paraphernalia is prescribed or she receives an abortion.

Yet we only have their word for that. Just as we would not attest to the ethics of every journalist, no one can convince us that every member of Planned Parenthood operates ethically.

And, frankly, we are disturbed when representatives of federally funded health clinics suggest, as was the case last week in a meeting with the editorial board of this newspaper, that some parents who feel abortion or pre-marital sex is wrong are "stupid or ignorant." And, for that reason, they argue it is all right for them to approve a child's request for a birth control prescription — or an abortion — without knowledge of the parents. Again, we hear Big Brother's footsteps.

Here we are not talking of cases involving parents who abuse their children, but those parents who for moral reasons object to sex before marriage or abortion.

In those special cases where the parents are known to have abused their child, the courts should decide whether an abortion is in the best interest of the child.

We do not attempt to minimize the enormous problem in this country today because of unwanted pregnancies involving young women. And we sincerely hope that every parent today will sit down with their sons and daughters to honestly discuss sex and the enormous responsibilities that come with it.

Poor communication, however, is not the only reason young people don't turn to their parents for help. We suspect some young women opt for abortion out of love for their parents. Perhaps because a parent is ill or unemployed — or because they wish to spare the parents the hardship of knowing they are pregnant — they turn elsewhere for help.

Hopefully, professional help always will be available. But mom and dad have a right — and a responsibility — to share in that help. That's why we support legislation to maintain their rights as parents.

Finally, a few words in support of anti-abortion organizations and those religions opposed to abortion.

Sometimes, we feel, those Americans who opposed the Vietnam war forget their own experiences when attacking anti-abortion groups. Because they viewed the war as immoral, they marched in protest, encouraged ministers to leave the pulpit to demonstrate against the war, and voted for candidates who expressed opposition to U.S. involvement in Vietnam.

Yet many of these same Americans (and we suspect the majority of the anti-war protesters take a pro-choice stance on abortion) object to use of the same tactics by those who see abortion as morally wrong.

Both sides in the debate need to cool the rhetoric.

The Virginian-Pilot

Norfolk, Va., June 17, 1983

In striking down selected state and local restrictions on abortion, the U.S. Supreme Court has again affirmed the right of a woman to terminate her pregnancy subject to *some* state and local regulation.

The high court first proclaimed the right to abortion in its *Roe v. Wade* decision a decade ago. That pronouncement ignited explosive controversy between those who champion the absolute right of women to choose abortion and those who demand protection of the fetus at every stage.

The controversy is unlikely to be dispelled by Associate Justice Lewis F. Powell Jr.'s forthright opinions for the court majority in the cases decided this week. If anything, Associate Justice Sandra Day O'Connor's equally forthright dissent provides fresh fuel for the right-to-life movement.

Abortion is an unhappy subject. Throughout much of American history abortion was outlawed. The United States was hardly unique in this regard: Laws restricting the termination of pregnancy existed in nearly all countries. Which doesn't mean that induced abortions were rare. On the contrary. Many women died from "criminal" abortions.

The easing of anti-abortion attitudes and laws was proceeding in the United States and elsewhere even before the Supreme Court spoke in *Roe v. Wade*. Some state codes permitting abortion to protect the health of women virtually sanctioned abortion on demand. As the '60s faded into the '70s, more and more American women could obtain relatively inexpensive abortions in safe settings. No longer was it necessary to seek out the abortion underground or fly to foreign lands where legal abortions were available — traveling from one state to another would do.

Abortion wasn't much in the news back then. *Roe v. Wade*, which anti-abortionists (including Associate Justice O'Connor) assail as bad law, changed all that. Suddenly there was a national "right-to-life" movement that sought to forbid all, or nearly all, abortions despite widespread approval of liberalization.

Associate Justice Powell made it clear that the court's stance on *Roe v. Wade* is unchanged: States and localities may not place gratuitous obstacles between women and abortion. Of course, *Roe v. Wade* permits reasonable regulation to protect the women undergoing abortion in the fourth, fifth and sixth months of pregnancy and the interests of "viable" fetuses in the seventh, eighth and ninth months. But the portions of the Akron, Ohio and the Missouri laws on abortion were invalidated as unreasonable.

Five of the 17 provisions that constituted the Akron ordinance were declared unconstitutional: those mandating second-trimester abortions in hospitals; parental consent for all abortions involving unmarried minors; specific statements by attending physicians to assure "informed consent" to abortions; a 24-hour waiting period between signing a consent form and performance of an abortion; and decent burial of fetuses. The court declared but one provision in the Missouri law unconstitutional, the requirement that second-trimester abortions be done in hospitals. That declaration struck similar provisions in more than a score of states.

These were states that had good reason to believe they had legislated properly, because *Roe v. Wade* expressly affirmed states' right to require second-trimester abortions in hospitals. But the court has now accepted medical evidence that such operations may be performed safely in adequately equipped clinics. Further medical advances could cause it to strengthen protection of "viable" fetuses.

In *Roe v. Wade*, and in subsequent abortion decisions, the court has tried to find a balance between the rights of the pregnant woman and the state's interest in protecting the unborn. In the cases decided this week, the court further defined that balance. The court majority recognizes that abortion poses a complex challenge to both public policy and personal conscience. In this week's rebuffs to Akron and Missouri, the court was both consistent and responsible.

THE ATLANTA CONSTITUTION

Atlanta, Ga., June 28, 1983

The Supreme Court earlier this month delivered itself of a ringing affirmation of the government's responsibility to protect a woman's constitutionally guaranteed right to abortion. But President Reagan refuses to take no for an answer.

Reagan will not merely support a politically perilous effort in Congress to overrule the high court; he will lead it, in a head-to-head confrontation with the judicial branch of government.

"Our society is confronted with a great moral issue, the taking of the life of an unborn child," he has declared in a statement calling on Congress to "make its voice heard against abortion on demand" — as if that were the only "moral" position in this terribly complex matter.

The president looked for support to Supreme Court Justice Sandra O'Connor's minority opinion, which called the legislative branch an appropriate forum for abortion regulation. But this rigidly ideological opposition to abortion flies in the face not only of the landmark 1973 Supreme Court ruling, which legalized abortions, but of overwhelming public support for keeping abortion a private matter, to be decided by a woman and her doctor.

In striking down several state laws that attempted to restrict access to abortion, the court deliberately reaffirmed its earlier finding that the constitutional right to privacy "encompasses a woman's right to decide whether to terminate her pregnancy."

As repeated surveys and polls have found, about two-thirds of the public supports the Supreme Court ruling. Most of the political organization around this issue has been on the opposition side, but an increasing number of citizens are growing resentful of blatantly ideological, and often shamelessly political, meddling in their private lives.

In a matter of such terrible intimacy, where the circumstances of every case are different, the president of the United States would be wisest to trust Americans to make their own personal decisions.

THE ARIZONA REPUBLIC

Phoenix, Ariz., June 17, 1983

ANTI-ABORTIONISTS may be aghast over the U.S. Supreme Court's decision against most state restrictions on abortion, but their worst fears about Justice Sandra O'Connor weren't realized.

What the nation saw once again in the first woman member of its highest court was a jurist true to her principles.

Justice O'Connor dissented from the triple-case ruling.

Although she refused to condemn abortion, she came down on the side of local government and its right to decide whether to impose some regulations on a practice fraught with social and emotional problems.

In the process, she remained firm in her faith in government closest to the people it touches.

The abortion issue is a politically delicate one, she and Justices Byron White and William Rehnquist said, and local legislatures should have to face it.

The court's majority decided that Akron, Ohio, had gone overboard with its 24-hour waiting period and "informed consent" impediments to abortion — impediments which prompt women to seek often-dangerous "underground" operations.

A major issue in the cases was the requirement that second-trimester abortions be performed in hospitals.

That makes little medical sense — and no economic sense at all with hospital costs already out of control.

Sensibly enough, the court majority left states with the right to determine when a minor may have an abortion.

But Justice Lewis Powell and the Supreme Court's majority clearly confirmed — and even broadened — their 1973 commitment to women's privacy rights.

The Detroit News
Detroit, Mich., June 19, 1983

Ten years after *Roe v. Wade*, a majority of the U.S. Supreme Court has acknowledged that advancing medical technology has rendered obsolete that decision's quaint distinctions between trimesters of pregnancy.

Roe, as you may remember, held that the state's compelling interest in the health and welfare of the mother and fetus was a kind of sliding scale conforming to questions of patient safety and fetal viability. During the first trimester, the state has no interest in the matter. Beginning in the second trimester, the state "may regulate the abortion procedure" to protect maternal health. After viability, during the third trimester, the state may proscribe abortion except when necessary to protect the life and "health" of the mother. The "health" qualifier, of course, is broad enough to grant a constitutionally protected "right" to abortion from conception to virtually the onset of labor.

New medical technology, today's court majority declares in an opinion written by Justice Lewis F. Powell, Jr., makes abortion "safer" during the second trimester. Thus, the state — in this case Akron, Ohio — may not require that second-trimester abortions be performed in a hospital.

In a dissenting opinion, Justice Sandra Day O'Connor points up the obvious flaw in the majority's reasoning:

"Just as improvements in medical technology inevitably will move *forward* the point at which the state may regulate for reasons of maternal health, different technological improvements will move *backward* the point of viability at which the state may proscribe abortions except when necessary to preserve the life and health of the mother.

"In 1973, viability before 28 weeks was considered unusual. . . . It is certainly reasonable to believe that fetal viability in

the first trimester may be possible in the not too distant future.

"The *Roe* framework, then, is clearly on a collision course with itself."

But is it really?

Justice O'Connor has more faith in her colleagues' fidelity to widely accepted principles of law than we do.

Roe was a legal fiction fabricated by men convinced that elective abortions are a social good. Some of the nation's most prominent legal scholars, who support current abortion policy, admit as much. There is no guarantee of the abortion "right" in the Constitution. That asserted right was invented in 1973.

The decisions handed down the other day are nothing more nor less than an elaborate wink in the same direction. Justice O'Connor's concern for intellectual consistency is alarmist, given the court's present membership. There isn't a thing in the majority's opinions that suggests the majority will ever acknowledge an internal contradiction in the concept of abortion "rights."

Here are some of the nonfiction implications of the majority's opinion:

There are 530 abortion clinics in the United States, and their future viability has been assured by the nation's highest court.

The law is a teacher, and the nation's most important legal forum is straining mightily to teach this culture that abortion is a socially acceptable form of birth control.

The re-election of Ronald Reagan (who would probably have the opportunity to appoint several new justices) is the best hope — perhaps the only hope for the short term — of those who are concerned about the continued assault by a large class of American elites on traditional moral values, especially on the value of innocent, developing human life.

THE PLAIN DEALER
Cleveland, Ohio, June 17, 1983

Take a stand: Pro-abortion or anti-abortion. Go ahead, make your choice, and then realize that no matter how you have chosen, you are wrong. Because the question is not one of medical procedure or pregnancy. The question is, fundamentally, whether people should be allowed to choose between the two.

We have made the case before for the right to choose. And so now we address a different issue: the *ability* to choose. And along these lines, we must emphatically agree with the Supreme Court, which ruled recently that women do have an ability to choose (sad to say there was ever any doubt) and that local laws which attempt to influence that choice are wrong.

Hence an Akron ordinance requiring specific, pre-abortion counselling was struck down, along with a law requiring those who chose abortion to wait 24 hours before having the procedure performed. Contrary to the arguments of pro-life groups, those laws (and others) were not "pro-women." Rather, they implied that women are so emotional that they are unable to make clear decisions for themselves.

Obviously, they were rules well-worth overturning.

So was another ordinance — also struck down — that required hospitalization for abortions performed during the second trimester. Science and technology are not static; the abortion procedure is becoming safer every day, even for those as far along as 24 weeks. There is no reason, therefore, why the procedure should be performed in hospitals during the second trimester, except that it was an obvious disincentive. The laws were mandated not out of concern for a woman's medical safety, but because the extra cost and inconvenience are inhibiting influences on the underlying abortion decision.

We are not here to say that those who are pro-abortion are correct. Nor will we contend the opposite. But we do wish to reaffirm the right to choose; to reiterate our belief that women — and men, too — are capable of making that decision without intrusion; and to emphasize our belief that such laws insult the intelligence and integrity of all those touched by unwanted pregnancy and the controversy it engenders.

BUFFALO EVENING NEWS
Buffalo, N.Y., June 24, 1983

The Supreme Court has reaffirmed its 1973 decision legalizing abortion in clear, explicit terms that rule out any prospect of a court reversal on this emotionally charged issue in the foreseeable future.

Justice Lewis F. Powell, writing for the majority, stressed that "the court repeatedly and consistently has accepted and applied the basic principle that a woman has the fundamental right to make the highly personal choice whether or not to terminate her pregnancy."

The court restated its abortion stand in striking down a series of state and local regulations that restricted access to an abortion. One ordinance voided by the court required that all abortions in the second trimester must be performed in a hospital; as the court noted, certain procedures can be carried out safely in a clinic. Also rejected was language prescribing what a physician must tell a woman seeking an abortion; this seemed designed, in the court's words, "not to inform the woman's consent but rather to persuade her to withhold it altogether."

But the high court displayed flexibility in upholding other legislative restrictions as consistent with its general abortion guidelines. Thus, states may mandate the attendance of a second physician at emergency abortions in the later stages of pregnancy. And while parental or judicial consent may not be required for all minors seeking an abortion, it may be required if the minor can't demonstrate maturity within strictly defined processes.

The new rulings, which drew a dissent from the court's only woman justice, Sandra Day O'Connor, will not end the debate on abortion. With the possibility of a Supreme Court reversal now all but precluded, abortion opponents will undoubtedly intensify their efforts to prohibit abortion through a constitutional amendment.

Getting such a measure approved, however, is likely to be difficult in a nation where polls indicate that the majority of citizens agree in effect with the high court that abortion should be a private matter, at least in early pregnancy.

Clearly, there is no simple way to resolve the deep and sincerely held differences among the American people concerning the morality of abortion and the proper role of the state and federal governments in dealing with abortion.

That in itself argues for leaving decisions on abortion where the court has left them — not with government but rather with the individual consciences of the persons directly involved, subject to appropriate regulation based on medical considerations and concerns relating to minors.

The Chattanooga Times
Chattanooga, Tenn., June 18, 1983

It has been 10 years since the Supreme Court declared, in *Roe vs. Wade,* that the concept of personal privacy, guaranteed by the Constitution, encompasses a woman's right to decide whether to obtain an abortion. Since then, numerous efforts have been made to restrict access to abortions; but with the court's ruling on Wednesday, the time may have come for abortion opponents to focus primarily on the moral aspects of the issue, including alternatives for women contemplating abortion, rather than trying to legislate the problem away.

By a 6 to 3 vote, the court struck down several state and local restrictions that restrict access to abortions. While the logic of the 1973 ruling may now seem questionable in light of medical developments which the court itself acknowledged Wednesday, the fact remains that the court is not about to overrule *Roe vs. Wade.* And Sen. Orrin Hatch, R-Utah, acknowledges that a constitutional amendment to reverse the 1973 ruling is unlikely to pass the Senate.

It should be clear by now that abortion is less a social or political problem than a moral one. To that end, those to whom abortion is an abhorrent quenching of life, whether actual or potential, have a responsibility to keep the morality of this issue before the public. The responsibility, essentially educational, is not fulfilled by shrill denunciations of proponents of abortion, waving pictures of aborted fetuses or urban guerrilla warfare against clinics and hospitals that provide abortions. It will be more valuable if, for example, anti-abortion organizations expand their efforts to counsel women to consider having their babies and giving them up for adoption, thus avoiding the guilt that often follows the act of having an abortion.

That responsibility is all the more important in the wake of the court's *Akron* decision, for it effectively invalidated restrictions in 21 states, including Tennessee, that, for example, limited second trimester abortions to hospitals. It is difficult to imagine any restriction that can stand against the court's latest decision.

In her dissent, Justice Sandra O'Connor drew attention to the court's recent cases which "indicate that a regulation imposed on 'a lawful abortion is not unconstitutional unless it unduly burdens the right to seek an abortion.'" That is a reasonable restriction — but it could hardly be said that the voided Akron ordinance imposed an undue burden on women seeking an abortion. It required that all abortions after the first trimester be performed in a hospital; set out rules for notification of and consent by parents of unmarried minors before they obtained abortions; required doctors to ensure that a woman's "informed consent" was just that, and stipulated a 24-hour waiting period between the time the consent form is signed and the abortion is actually performed.

But the court held that the second trimester restriction placed a significant obstacle in the path of a woman seeking an abortion, primarily because of the added cost; that Akron could not make the "blanket determination that *all* minors under the age of 15 are too immature" to opt for an abortion without their parents' consent; that the informed consent procedure was intended to persuade the woman to withhold it altogether, and that the 24-hour waiting period was inflexible and arbitrary.

But it is the court that has demonstrated arbitrariness. As Justice O'Connor observed, quoting from a previous ruling, "No other [medical] procedure involves the purposeful termination of a potential life." And she added: The waiting period is surely a small cost to impose to insure that the woman's decision is well-considered in light of its certain and irreparable consequences on fetal life, and the possible effects on her own." Given those consequences, and the reasonableness of the restrictions that Akron and other jurisdictions sought to impose, it is proper to wonder at the majority's apparent willingness to invalidate *all* obstacles to abortion.

THE LINCOLN STAR
Lincoln, Neb., June 17, 1983

This writer is a male and is religiously out of tune with abortion, so will not seek to make any heavy comments about the U.S. Supreme Court opinion which reinforced women's rights to an abortion. It seems that the court left virtually untouched the right of women to have an abortion within the first six months of their pregnancy.

Only in the last three months of a pregnancy can states require two doctors to be present for an abortion. And news accounts did not give any further enlightenment on the subject concerning final trimester of a pregnancy. Whether doctors must make an effort or not to save a fetus aborted in the final trimester, we do not know, but such could be one of the reasons for the presence of two doctors, the safety of the woman being the other reason.

While the court opinion sets broad public policy, it does nothing to remove abortion as an issue on the national scene. The matter will continue as one of significance in debate between opposing interest groups and as the focus of an anti-abortion amendment to the U.S. Constitution.

But in fixing the current law of the land on the matter, the court has laid a heavy responsibility on groups and individuals. Church groups will now find it even more imperative to inform their members as to the moral questions involved in this issue and public health officials may find themselves with added problems due to the consequences of any increase in abortions.

Individuals will have to look, not to the law for guidance, but within their own consciences. Certainly, it is fair to express the hope that women might seek to avoid unwanted pregnancies and, thus, not have to face the question of an abortion. And it seems fair to offer the observation that the court did not sanction abortions; it simply fixed free choice on the part of women as the prevailing law.

But whatever the law, the subject will remain an issue of heated public debate because large numbers of people will not let it fade into oblivion. Life-and-death choices are not the kind easily swept under the rug.

The Honolulu Advertiser
Honolulu, Ha., June 20, 1983

The effort to restrict or deny abortion has been set back again. Citing "fundamental" guarantees of personal liberty and privacy, the U.S. Supreme Court has wisely affirmed its ruling that women have the right to end a pregnancy.

Last year the Senate shelved an anti-abortion bill, and prospects of its approving a so-called "human life amendment" this year appear remote. Further, a misguided attempt last year to remove a sensitive social issue from the Supreme Court's purview (specifically school prayer) was beaten back, closing another avenue to those who would again outlaw abortion.

THE COURT "built upon" the landmark Roe vs. Wade decision of ten years ago that made abortion legal but acknowledged the states' interest in protecting the health of the mother and of the fetus when it can survive on its own.

The new ruling threw out state laws clearly designed to erect obstacles to abortion through extra cost, delay and by leading women through a verbal "parade of horribles" in the name of informed consent.

The newest justice, Sandra Day O'Connor, led three dissenters in challenging the basic assumptions of Roe vs. Wade. She called differing conditions for abortion in each trimester of pregnancy "arbitrary" and "unworkable," saying: "Potential life is no less potential in the first weeks of pregnancy than it is at viability or afterward."

But writing for the majority, Justice Lewis F. Powell (a generally conservative Nixon appointee) noted that the 7-to-2 decision in 1973, having been argued twice before the court, was carefully considered and ought to stand. Further, he said, the effect of O'Connor's views "would be to drive the performance of many abortions back underground, free of effective regulation and often without the attendance of a physician."

THAT IS the basic reality of the million abortions performed in the U.S. each year. Were they outlawed, we would revert to the times when those with enough money paid for secrecy or travel to countries with abortion and those without were left to quacks, self-remedies or unwanted — and often unloved — children they could not afford. If anything, after a decade of availability, things would be worse today.

While opinion polls find that most Americans believe abortion ought not to be denied women, no one promotes it as a favored alternative for birth control. It is a difficult and at times painful last resort that some women will take, as is their right.

The court was correct to uphold this view against the entreaties of the Reagan administration (which couches its argument in terms of states' rights) and others who would legislate their own sincerely held moral beliefs upon others, but do not have to live with the effects.

Richmond Times-Dispatch

Richmond, Va., June 28, 1983

It would be vain to hope that this nation could formulate an abortion policy that would be acceptable to all Americans. No issue is more deeply entangled in conflicting social, ethical and moral codes. Attitudes toward abortion range from the view that it is the unrestricted right of every woman to the view that it can never be justified for any reason.

When confronted by opposite extremes on controversial issues, society often finds it desirable and even necessary to compromise, to develop a solution that is the most acceptable to the most people. This is the democratic way, and it is the procedure that should be followed on the abortion question.

Our own view is that there is a middle ground, that abortion can be justified, and should be legally sanctioned, under certain circumstances: to protect the health of the mother, for example, or to terminate, in the very early stages, a pregnancy that had resulted from rape or incest. But the notion that a woman has absolute freedom to decide whether to have an abortion, a notion that has been strengthened by the Supreme Court's latest abortion ruling, is abhorrent.

This concept is irreconcilable with civilized society's traditional view that human life is endowed with a sanctity that can be violated only for very good reasons. That the human fetus becomes a human life at some stage is undeniable; and it is now possible for a fetus to be aborted even after it has become viable. This, as columnist George Will recently noted, can result in some fascinating contradictions: In California, for example, a policeman has been accused of murder in the death of a fetus in a woman he shot and wounded; the woman, however, could not have been charged with murder had she elected to "kill" the fetus by abortion.

The increasingly cavalier attitude toward abortion has had a corrosive effect on respect for human life. Allowing handicapped babies to starve to death is a practice that has been gaining acceptability. Will snuffing out the lives of old people who are inconveniences be the next practice to be condoned?

In the opening debate yesterday on a proposed constitutional amendment that would restore the right of individual states to establish abortion policies, Republican Sen. Bob Packwood of Oregon complained that it is the effort of people whose "personal or religious or other deeply held views" have been offended by abortion. They are trying, he said, "to impose their morality" on others.

Technically, he is wrong, for the amendment, sponsored by Utah Republican Sen. Orrin G. Hatch, would not establish any kind of policy on abortion. It would merely state that "A right to abortion is not secured by this Constitution." Each state would be free to decide for itself what to do on this issue, and it is possible, though unlikely, that all 50 states would adopt rules as liberal as the policy that prevails today.

But even if Sen. Packwood were correct, so what? In a democratic society, groups that are motivated by "personal or religious or other deeply held views" are always trying to impose their standards on society. This is the way the system works. Polygamy was outlawed because it conflicted with the "morality" of most Americans. So was child labor. Many actions are considered crimes because they clash with the standards observed by most citizens.

Sen. Packwood argues, too, that a woman's right to "bodily integrity" and the right of all women to "control their bodies" make abortion an inalienable female right. But abortion does not involve merely the body of the woman. It involves, too, the body of the human being she is carrying. It involves the interests of the father of that child. (Only yesterday the Supreme Court threw out the appeal of a Maryland man who had attempted to prevent his wife from having an abortion.) And when abortion becomes epidemic, it involves the interests and welfare of society.

Abortion, then, is a public issue on which the American people have the right to speak. Congress is not likely to approve the Hatch amendment, but its intent is commendable; and by ensuring a major legislative discussion of abortion it will serve a most useful purpose. The debate could be the first important step in a retreat from the callous direction in which this nation has been rapidly moving.

Post-Tribune

Gary, Ind., June 22, 1983

The Supreme Court has stopped a sneak attack on its 1973 decision legalizing abortion nationwide. In the process, it re-affirmed that a women's right to seek an abortion is basically a private matter.

Anti-abortion forces, rather than challenging the basic right directly, asked the court to rule on a few "rules" in effect in some states and cities. These laws were aimed at denying access to abortion and not at health concerns, the purported intentions behind the laws.

Our opinions

The court last week struck down such state and local regulations as those that forced women to have second-trimester abortions in hospitals, where costs average twice as high as in competently run clinics; forced teen-agers to seek parental consent for abortion, regardless of the young woman's maturity or family circumstances; forced all women to wait 24 hours between the request for an abortion and having the abortion, with no consideration for the added cost and hardship; forced doctors, under threat of criminal charges, to tell each patient that the fetus "is a human life from the moment of conception" and that the operation is "a major surgical procedure."

Although state and local control traditionally limits constitutional freedoms to a degree, it seldom squelches the right itself. It wasn't working that way in this case. The beliefs involved are too divergent and emotional. The result was fast becoming a hodge-podge of laws making a right depend on where you live. Consistency is needed to keep one belief from overpowering others.

The laws requiring some abortions be done in hospitals and the 24-hour wait did nothing but keep low-income women from having abortions, at least safe legal ones. Money should not preclude a right.

All the aforementioned laws are demeaning to the medical profession. Where and how any medical procedure is done should be a medical decision, based on accepted medical practice. Any doctor deserving of a license to practice can judge a person's physical and emotional conditions; this is what should determine recommending waiting periods, more counseling and such.

The doctor-statement law simply uses doctors, who may or may not agree, to expound state-composed theories, thus letting the state accomplish indirectly what it can't do directly. A doctor can, and should, tell a woman what in his professional opinion are the risks, in all aspects, of abortion. Then an informed decision can be made.

The law does not force any doctor to perform an abortion; that is decided by professional judgment.

Teen-age abortions pose a major dilemma in the moral realm of abortion. Constitutionally abortion rights include all women. But it is traditionally the parents' right to know and approve of medical care of their children. The real problem here isn't medical. It partially involves moral beliefs on abortion itself; but, most often, the sexual implications are the hang-up.

This society has never come to grips with the fact that women can conceive children at a much younger age than it is generally accepted to do so. It is also an age when males and females are most questioning of traditional beliefs, when they are developing their morals. Men get away with growing up. Women sometimes don't. If, as is often the case, there already is an unstable family relationship, should a young girl be plunged further into turmoil? Surely this, too, is a medical decision.

The court is being realistic; regulation of abortions can go only so far. When they start to infringe on the fundamental right, it will stand firm.

Constitutionally, the court spoke in 1973. Morally, abortion is a matter of belief. Ramifications can go in every direction. No law can cover every possible situation.

So the court says it is the woman's choice. Her beliefs, as formed through religion, family, society, and her situation, as only she knows it, determines her final decision. That decision is not the business of the state.

Meese Criticizes High Court, Asks Roe v. Wade Reversal

When Attorney General Edwin Meese 3rd in July 1985 criticized the Supreme Court for what he called "policy choices" instead of decisions "based on constitutional principle," he was in part continuing efforts by the Reagan Administration to undermine existing abortion legislation. In a speech to the American Bar Association convention in Washington, D.C., Meese condemned the court's recent major decisions involving school prayer, government aid to religious schools, and the upholding of the 1973 abortion ruling. (See pp. 20-31.)

Within a week, acting U.S. Solicitor General Charles Fried filed a brief with the Supreme Court asking that the court overturn its own landmark 1973 decision establishing abortion as a constitutional right. Fried filed the brief on behalf of the Reagan Administration. The asked-for reversal would allow states and localities to curb or ban abortions. The brief assailed the decision in *Roe v. Wade* as "such a source of instability in the law that the court...should abandon it." Justice Department officials said the action marked the first time since 1954 that an Administration had asked the court to reverse itself on a key decision. Observers felt that, in light of the 1983 Supreme Court decision upholding *Roe v. Wade*, it was unlikely that the court would now reverse itself on the same issue.

When asked by Newsweek magazine why the Justice Department was re-examining the abortion ruling, Meese replied that the Supreme Court had become involved in matters that previously had been left primarily to the legislative branch, including legislative branches of states. "That's why we have a problem with *Roe v. Wade*," he said. "Even if it did not relate to abortion at all, the case, we feel, was wrongly decided because it usurped both a legislative function and a function that had traditionally been handled by the states."

AKRON BEACON JOURNAL
Akron, OH, July 17, 1985

EVEN the most ardent right-to-life groups admit the odds are pretty slim for the Supreme Court reversing its historic 1973 abortion ruling anytime soon.

But the new attorney general, Edwin Meese 3d, doesn't seem to be concerned about the odds. Instead, he appears intent on pushing the Reagan administration's social agenda with a disturbing new aggressiveness. The Meese assault now extends to the steps of America's highest court.

So for the first time in more than 30 years, a presidential administration has directly asked that a Supreme Court ruling be overturned.

The Justice Department filed a friend-of-the-court brief Monday to strike down *Roe v. Wade,* the landmark case that legalized abortion 12 years ago. It argues that the ruling has proved to be flawed and unworkable and that it infringes upon the right of a state to limit abortion.

With Mr. Reagan's blessing, the department is urging the court to uphold laws in Pennsylvania and Illinois that restrict access to abortion. Both laws have been declared unconstitutional by lower courts.

Those courts based their rulings on the 1973 abortion decision, plus subsequent Supreme Court decisions that reaffirmed principles found in *Roe.* One of the most important was the strongly worded ruling that struck down Akron's restrictive abortion ordinance just two years ago.

For more than a decade, there has been virtually no sign the high court is prepared to back away from its historic ruling. The right of a woman to make the difficult and personal decision to terminate her pregnancy — without a host of restrictions imposed by the government — has been consistently preserved, despite the fact that some of the faces on the Supreme Court bench have changed since 1973.

There is slim reason to believe the pattern of decisions will be broken soon. Both opponents and supporters of abortion admit that the makeup of the current court will have to change before the Reagan arguments sway a majority of the justices.

At this juncture, then, Mr. Meese appears more interested in scoring political points with conservative groups than in winning an unlikely legal victory. Even in the Akron case, when the Reagan administration sided with the city, it stopped far short of seeking to overturn the 1973 ruling.

The new attorney general has embarked on a disturbing course as he searches for new ways to inject the Reagan social philosophy into the law. The tone was set last week, before the American Bar Association, when he accused the Supreme Court of making political decisions instead of constitutionally based ones.

He told his audience: "We hope for a day when the court returns to the basic principles of the Constitution." On the subject of abortion, the court has rarely strayed from those principles. The hope seems better applied to the attorney general of the United States.

St. Petersburg Times
St. Petersburg, FL, July 17, 1985

In a landmark 1973 decision, the Supreme Court guaranteed a woman's constitutional right to an abortion. That ruling was reaffirmed — by the same nine justices now serving on the court — in a 6-3 opinion two years ago. The issue should be closed: Laws that attempt to ban abortions in the early stages of pregnancy violate women's 14th Amendment right of privacy.

Yet for reasons that appear increasingly cynical and partisan, the Justice Department and some congressional ideologues continue their efforts to make a political issue out of what is ultimately an intensely personal, moral decision.

IN A VIRTUALLY unprecedented action, the Justice Department has asked the Supreme Court to overrule its 12-year-old Roe vs. Wade decision establishing the present national guidelines for women's rights to an abortion. Apparently following the political lead of Attorney General Edwin Meese, whose ill-founded partisan attacks on the court are well documented, the Justice Department brief is an executive-branch intrusion into a matter of constitutional law properly left to the judiciary. The action amounts to an admission that the administration cannot summon the political support to overturn Roe vs. Wade through the appropriate channel — a constitutional amendment.

The last such Justice Department intrusion came in 1954, when the government asked the court to overturn a 19th century ruling that affirmed the constitutionality of racially "separate but equal" education. That executive action hastened the granting of basic rights to millions of Americans; this week's action seeks to take away a basic constitutional right from more than half of our population.

But the Justice Department's violation of constitutional precedent is less troubling than its politicization of what should be a personal, religious and moral question. Perhaps no other issue is as complex and troubling as abortion. No sane person can be said to be "for" abortion: It can never be more than a painful choice among several agonizing options for a woman with an unwanted pregnancy.

THE SUPREME COURT recognized that reality in its 1973 opinion. Roe vs. Wade in no way mandated abortion, nor did it even legitimize abortion as a moral option. The decision merely affirmed the legal right of each woman, with the help of her loved ones, to make that intensely personal decision without governmental intrusion.

But many cynical politicians want to hold women hostage to the cause of a narrow social agenda. The true motives of many high-profile opponents of abortion were brought into focus by a recent study by Catholics for a Free Choice. That report showed that members of Congress who oppose abortion are also likely to oppose financing for programs that offer women an alternative to abortion. These self-appointed moralists would damn low-income pregnant women who do seek an abortion, and damn those who don't.

The sincere opponents of abortion should be working for programs that provide child care facilities for low-income mothers, that offer adequate sex education and birth control information for young adults, that expand Medicaid benefits for poor pregnant women. Those kinds of efforts — not further federal intrusion into personal morality — can help to create an environment in which abortion becomes an unnecessary option.

ustice Department—33

THE PLAIN DEALER
Cleveland, OH, July 17, 1985

Nowhere is it written that a law must be easy to interpret and apply. That would be a foolish test of legal wisdom, especially with regard to the U.S. Constitution. Yet for some reason, the Justice Department suddenly is advocating legal simplicity. In doing so, it displays a rather less flattering form of the same thing.

Under the leadership of Edwin Meese, the Justice Department has filed a "friend of the court" brief with the U.S. Supreme Court in which it argues that the court should retreat from *Roe vs. Wade.* That 1973 decision, based on expansions of the 14th Amendment, established the right of women to make their own decision about abortion.

The Justice Department claims that the ruling is "so far flawed" and "such a source of instability within the law" that it should be abandoned. Thereafter comes almost 30 pages of argument about the "textual, doctrinal and historical" bases that *Roe vs. Wade* allegedly violates.

Advocates of uncomplicated legal reasoning probably should start with their own briefs, but that's not the point. Rather, the point is: (a) that the law inevitably will conflict with the morals and politics of some people; (b) that those conflicts will create confusion and differing interpretations, and (c) that the courts will have to remedy that confusion over time. Complicated laws are not bad, they are only complicated. Helping to interpret them is a main function of the appeals process.

Why is the Justice Department lecturing the Supreme Court about the Constitution and politics? Because if the Constitution is above politics the

Justice Department is not. For the administration to complain about politicizing the Constitution—and for the Justice Department to complain about the politics of the law after adopting a new, dogma-based activism—is, well, you know what it is.

No one expects the court to abandon *Roe vs. Wade*, especially since that ruling was strongly reaffirmed a scant two years ago. This makes the Justice Department's brief all the more unsubtle. Because Justice cannot expect to have any impact on the Supreme Court's 1973 decision, the purpose of the brief becomes entirely political. It is a deliberate herald of how a new, juiced-up Justice has redefined itself. And it is an appeasement of the anti-abortion crowd, which has been waiting since January for President Reagan to make good on his promise to help overturn the abortion laws.

□

An argument can be made that so-called "soft" executive agencies—Justice, Education, the Civil Rights Commission, the EPA—be distinguished from "hard" agencies such as the departments of State and Defense. The latter are inextricably bound to the politics of the administration.

The former, however, have different, non-political mandates. For Justice, those responsibilities include law enforcement, the provision of legal counsel in federal cases, and the interpretation of the law for other agencies. Using its tremendous power to advance a specific set of ethical and political considerations is conspicuously absent from the list

Birmingham Post-Herald
Birmingham, AL, July 18, 1985

In a misguided effort to turn back the clock, the Reagan administration has urged the Supreme Court to overturn its landmark 1973 decision that legalized abortion.

Filing a "friend of the court" brief in cases involving Pennsylvania and Illinois attempts to restrict abortion, the Justice Department called on the high court to return the law to where it stood 12 years ago.

Before the court established in Roe v. Wade a constitutional right to abortion, many state laws made it a crime for a woman to seek to end an unwanted pregnancy and for a doctor to help her.

If the court accepts the administration's argument that no constitutional right to abortion exists, states will be free to ban the procedure and numerous ones will do so. Then, as before 1973, well-to-do women will be able to travel to states where abortions are legal and safe. Poor women will have the choice of carrying to term or risking "back-alley" abortions.

Fortunately for women who wish to make for themselves the most personal decision of whether or not to have a child, the justices rarely reverse themselves quickly on constitutional rulings.

Two years ago the court strongly reaffirmed Roe v. Wade in a 6-3 decision against abortion restrictions imposed by the Akron, Ohio, city council. The court's membership has not changed since then, and thus it is likely that the administration's latest attack on women's right to make their own reproductive decisions will fail.

Nevertheless, it is disappointing that President Reagan, who preaches about getting government off people's backs, personally approved his solicitor general's intrusion into private choices that should be made by women and their doctors.

In a country as diverse as the United States, there are persons whose religious beliefs reject abortion under any circumstances. There are those whose religious beliefs permit abortion under most circumstances. And there are those who stand somewhere in between.

And in a country undergirded by democracy and pluralism, it is unseemly and lacking in tolerance for a government and a president to select one set of religious values and attempt to impose them on all.

Roanoke Times & World-News
Roanoke, VA, July 19, 1985

TWELVE years ago, when Justice Harry Blackmun, with remarkable hindsight, discovered a constitutional right to abortion, the U.S. Supreme Court made bad law.

It took away from the states the right to regulate the termination of a biological process that leads, ultimately, to an adult human. It arbitrarily divided the prenatal stages of human existence into trimesters, and decided that the fetus was entitled to full state protection only during the third trimester, when it is presumed to be sufficiently developed to survive outside the womb.

Blackmun inferred a constitutional right to privacy, then maintained that this right took precedence over the right of survival for a developing fetus during the first six months. A majority of the Supreme Court agreed with him. The historic *Roe vs. Wade* decision resulted.

That decision didn't sit well with the millions of Americans who regard a developing fetus as a separate human life and who regard human life as something too precious to be terminated for any but the most urgent reasons.

The Reagan administration has been hostile toward this decision from the outset. It has looked favorably upon a constitutional amendment that would state, simply, that nothing in the Constitution secures a right to abortion.

More recently, it has asked the Supreme Court to reverse *Roe vs. Wade.*

Both proposals make constitutional sense. Both are exercises in futility.

The present Supreme Court two years ago upheld the principle behind *Roe vs. Wade* on a 6-3 vote. No new arguments have been advanced since. The Supreme Court is not going to reverse itself.

Neither would passage of a constitutional amendment return the nation to the *status quo ante* 1973. While most Americans seem to decry abortion as a method of birth control, a substantial number believe it to be a personal decision between a woman and her doctor. There is no guarantee that, after 12 years of relatively easy access to abortion, the states would rush to shut off this access. It's more likely that liberalized abortion laws would survive in enough states to make stricter abortion laws about as effective as local gun-control laws now are.

The incidence of abortion is unlikely to yield to either political or legislative remedies until a national concensus has formed against prenatal termination of life. The 1973 Supreme Court released a genie that can't be rebottled as easily as the classic Coke.

While a reversal of *Roe vs. Wade* would bring the law of the land closer to the original Constitution, the real battleground on abortion is in the conscience of the public. It must be fought by reasoned appeals to Americans of all religious and political persuasions. Once the nation is ready to reach a moral verdict, the courts and the legislatures will follow.

Los Angeles, CA, July 16, 1985

Three years ago, former Solicitor General Rex Lee argued before the U.S. Supreme Court that the courts' authority over abortion be reduced. When Justice Harry A. Blackmun, who wrote the 1973 *Roe* v. *Wade* decision establishing a constitutional right to abortion, asked Lee if he sought to overturn that decision or the 1803 decision delineating the high court's powers, Lee replied, "Neither, neither." It is clear this time around, however, that overturning *Roe* v. *Wade* is precisely what the Reagan administration wants to do.

Yesterday, the Justice Department filed a friend-of-the court brief in two cases involving abortion laws in Pennsylvania and Illinois which, state courts ruled, limited women's right to abortion. The DOJ asked the court to undo that right by overturning *Roe* v. *Wade*, saying the 1973 decision "is so far flawed and ... is a source of such instability in the law that this court should ... abandon it."

This criticism is misplaced. The real source of "instability" on the abortion issue is not the Supreme Court, but rather those who refuse to accept that *Roe* v. *Wade* is the law of the land. As the high court clearly established in 1982, the ruling does not prevent states from regulating the circumstances under which abortions may be performed, as long as they do not limit the right to privacy (that a woman has over her own body) that flows from the Constitution's due-process clause.

If *Roe* v. *Wade* were overturned, states could ban abortion except in cases where the mother's life is in danger. The result: Some states would enact more restrictive laws than others. Women in those states who could not afford to travel to more lenient states would unfairly be denied their right to choose an abortion.

Though the administration's intent is clear, its chance of prevailing is far from certain, given the current composition of the court. But the direction is set. Undoubtedly, when there are vacancies on the court we can expect the administration to select judges who will go along with the effort to undo the decision which gives women the constitutional right to seek abortion.

THE ATLANTA CONSTITUTION
Atlanta, GA, July 17, 1985

The Reagan administration's direct legal assault on the constitutional right of women to chose abortion early in a pregnancy may be just politics as usual, as pro-abortion groups say and even some anti-abortion advocates suspect; it is certainly a legal long shot. But make no mistake. It is not litigation as usual. This is a radical step.

The position itself is no surprise. Although a supporter of abortion until opposition became a touchstone issue of the right, Ronald Reagan has opposed abortion since well before his election to the presidency. He has led the Republican Party into making opposition to abortion a measurement for appointment to the federal judiciary, and his administration has acted to undermine international birth-control programs where the governments or agencies allow abortion.

Even so, the approach the government is now making to the court is breathtaking. At issue are Illinois and Pennsylvania laws designed to throw procedural barriers in the way of abortions. Appellate courts firmly disallowed the laws, but the White House now argues, not that the laws are permissible under the 1973 decision that legalized abortion nationally, but that the '73 ruling itself should be overturned.

The filing is nervy even within the limits of the disputed state laws, for in an Ohio case just two years ago the justices ruled 6-3 against laws of the same sort, reaffirming the original ruling as well. They have given no hint they welcome a new challenge.

Just how striking a departure from custom this intervention is can be measured by two milestones. This is the first time since 1954 that the government has asked the Supreme Court to reverse itself on a basic constitutional issue. (That was when the government prevailed against the court's 1896 indulgence of separate-but-equal segregation laws, a reversal that had been prepared by 20 years of case law.) And apparently this is the first time in history the government has asked the court to withdraw a grant of constitutional rights.

Pernaps the White House is just cementing itself with anti-abortion allies and taking a shot as long as one is open, with no real expectations. But its action leaves no doubt that the administration's ambitions don't end at placing limitations on abortion, the extent of its previous filings, but extend to the criminalization of women who have abortions and of physicians who perform them.

THE LOUISVILLE TIMES
Louisville, KY, July 16, 1985

Since the Reagan administration has repeatedly failed in its effort to gain congressional approval of a constitutional amendment banning abortions, it was only a matter of time before the effort switched back to where it all began: the U. S. Supreme Court.

Consequently, the "friend" of the court brief filed yesterday by the Reagan Justice Department is not a surprise. It is filed in connection with cases that would expand the power of states to regulate abortions. But the brief is anything but friendly to the court's line of precedents that consistently have upheld a woman's right of choice in abortion decisions.

A dozen years after the landmark decision, *Roe v. Wade*, a majority of the American people consistently tell pollsters that it supports the right of a woman, during the early months of pregnancy, to choose — in consultation with her doctor — whether to obtain an abortion. As recently as 1982, a 6-3 majority of the justices reaffirmed that doctrine. It's difficult to understand why the administration, led by Attorney General Edwin Meese III, is making a big push to obtain a change now, since the same nine justices who decided the 1983 case are still sitting.

The most plausible explanation is that the White House is counting on a change in the court's membership. You don't have to be particularly ghoulish to realize that the actuarial tables aren't on the side of some of the justices. Five of the six justices who constituted that majority are past 70. The sixth, John Paul Stevens, has reached the customary retirement age of 65, although he's the third youngest member of the current court. And the author of the 1983 abortion decision, Justice Lewis Powell, 77, has been treated for cancer and is said to be considering retirement. So perhaps Mr. Meese and the President, who approved release of the friend of the court brief from his hospital bed, think that the time may be ripe for a new attack. The two cases come from Illinois and Pennsylvania, and arguments are not expected before December.

But anyone as politically astute as the President must realize that even if he were able to name a justice or two by the time this case is argued — and it's highly unlikely that he could — an outright reversal of *Roe v. Wade* is even less likely. It takes time for the court to alter its decisions.

What's more, history shows that it's impossible to predict how justices will behave once they join the high court. Dwight Eisenhower was distressed by progressive attitudes of Earl Warren and William Brennan, two justices he had hoped would turn out to be conservative. Richard Nixon's strict constructionists — Warren Burger, Harry Blackmun and Lewis Powell — supported the abortion decision.

The fact is that now as in 1973, the abortion decision makes great sense. It brought from the alleys and the backrooms into the open a medical procedure that had been widely used, but illegal. While it offered women and their doctors certain rights, it also left states a great deal of latitude in setting standards for safety and cleanliness.

So while the subject of abortion still polarizes many Americans — often as a result of sincere moral and religious convictions — it's hard to imagine that the court will give the disreputable illegal abortionist a new lease on life.

Since the administration's well-known opposition to abortion has failed so far to provoke any change at the congressional level, Mr. Meese had no choice but to go to court. The justices owe his brief a polite reading — and then they should spike it.

THE SACRAMENTO BEE

Sacramento, CA, July 24, 1985

One would think that Ed Meese, having struggled through a year of hearings and often embarrassing disclosures to become attorney general, would try to behave like one once he was confirmed. But the signs are quite otherwise. Earlier this month, he used his chance to address the American Bar Association for a clumsy, heavy-handed political attack on the U.S. Supreme Court because it chose to regard the Constitution as a living document, particularly on church-state issues, not the dead letter that the administration would like it to be.

The other day, Meese went all the way to London to repeat the attack before the same organization, accusing American judges of "chronological snobbery" because they interpreted the Constitution in terms of contemporary conditions rather than freezing it, as Meese seems to prefer, in the 18th century. What particularly upsets Meese is that the justices don't think it's constitutionally proper for the taxpayers to pay the salaries of people who teach in parochial schools.

Meanwhile, back in Cleveland, a grand jury investigating the doings of Teamsters' boss Jackie Presser, an honored member of Ronald Reagan's inaugural committee and the only major labor leader to endorse Reagan in

1984, is so restive with Justice Department inaction that it has complained to two federal judges about it. The grand jurors are wondering why Justice has not sought to indict Presser in connection with alleged payroll padding in Presser's hometown local. Six months ago, members of the federal strike force in Cleveland recommended an indictment, but senior Justice officials have continued to block it. Senior Justice officials in this case means Ed Meese.

When Meese was going through the difficult process of explaining all those loans and favors from people who subsequently got federal jobs and appointments, he acknowledged that he might have been less than fully sensitive to the finer implications of those relationships, and he promised the members of the Senate Judiciary Committee that he would try to mend his ways. But the political attacks on the court — attacks thought to be unprecedented for an attorney general — and the endless foot-dragging in the Presser case make it clearer than ever that the administration's tolerance of embarrassment on behalf of its friends and cronies is as bountiful as ever and that Meese is still the political hack he always was.

THE SUN

Baltimore, MD, July 22, 1985

The Justice Department has formally called on the Supreme Court to reverse itself on the abortion issue. This is a very unusual move. But we are not surprised. The administration is getting desperate.

From campaign days on, President Reagan and Attorney General Edwin Meese have made it clear they oppose the 1973 Supreme Court decision, Roe vs. Wade, which said a woman has a constitutional right to have an abortion. The Reagan administration thought it could convince the court to narrow its interpretation of women's abortion rights, but its pleas in behalf of state and local ordinances related to abortions failed to convince the court. It tried to get Congress to enact a constitutional amendment overturning the court, and that got nowhere.

So now, in desperation, Mr. Meese's department has filed a friend-of-the-court brief arguing that the 1973 ruling "is such a source of instability in the law that this court should reconsider it and on reconsideration abandon it." In fact, this ruling has been a source of stability, not instability, legally speaking, and that's what the administration really objects to. As recently as 1983, the court ruled 6-3 that Roe vs. Wade still applied with full force. It did so in such clear-cut language that we can't believe Mr. Meese has any hopes of being taken seriously now.

The court said then, "[A]rguments continue to be made . . . that we erred in interpreting the Constitution. Nonetheless, the doctrine of *stare decisis*, while perhaps never entirely persuasive on a constitutional question, is a doctrine that demands respect in a society governed by the rule of law. We respect it today and reaffirm Roe v Wade." *Stare decisis* is the doctrine that the court is bound by its previous decisions. We wish the attorney general, the nation's chief legal officer, would respect that doctrine, too.

We believe that women have a qualified right to have an abortion without state interference. We would hate to see the court reverse itself. But it is possible that the author of the 1983 decision, Lewis Powell, may retire this summer, or after one or two more terms at most.

The author of the 1983 dissent, Sandra O'Connor, didn't argue that Roe vs. Wade should be overruled, but her argument, as Justice Powell noted, "for all practical purposes would accomplish precisely that result." So if Mr. Powell retires, and if Chief Justice Warren Burger retires or changes his mind on abortion, new justices nominated by Mr. Reagan on the advice of Attorney General Meese could prove decisive in overturning Roe vs. Wade. What today appears to be an act of desperation could in the future achieve the results sought by both the administration and its anti-abortion supporters.

San Francisco Chronicle

San Francisco, CA, July 17, 1985

IN SEEKING TO overturn the decade-old Supreme Court decision legalizing abortion, the Reagan administration is satisfying a debt to some of its most fervent fundamentalist supporters. Nothing in the recent record of the court indicates that the effort will succeed. The decision in the historic case of Wade v. Roe was a good one and it must be sustained.

One fact which made it such a good decision is never stressed by those who seek to turn the clock back. We would remind anti-abortionists that outlawing abortion does not mean that they will no longer occur. What outlawing would guarantee, however, is that the quality of current medical care would be diminished with a revival of abortion "mills" which flourished well into the 1970s.

Quackery prospered when abortions could be obtained only outside of the law. Women were victims and not patients. Deaths and maiming injuries were commonplace; those harmed could not sue for damages for they were co-conspirators in felonies and faced the threat of prosecution if they made any allegations against abortioners.

SIMULTANEOUSLY, safe abortions were available to those who were affluent enough to travel abroad. This basic unfairness was, in fact, a product of a law that was, on its face, unenforceable, a further reason for supporting the Supreme Court decision.

We have long supported the right of women to free choice. We believe that this freedom is basic and should not be subject to state intrusion. These are reasons enough to support the 1973 decision of the highest court. Knowing the consequences and tragedy involved in illegal abortions adds another convincing argument supporting the court's wisdom.

DESERET NEWS

Salt Lake City, UT, July 17/18, 1985

In filing a friend-of-the-court brief this week asking the Supreme Court to overturn its controversial 1973 decision on abortion, the Reagan administration is taking what can only be described as a long shot.

Unfortunately, barring an historic change of heart, the court is likely to uphold the 12-year-old ruling, although it's possible the vote might be as close as 5-4 for the first time.

In its 7-2 vote in 1973, the high court essentially struck down any limits on abortion, particularly in the early stages of pregnancy. While that has been the law of the land for a dozen years, the abortion rule has drawn fierce criticism and shows little sign of general acceptance.

This is not the first time that challenges to the abortion ruling have made it back to the Supreme Court. Two years ago, the court upheld the 1973 verdict by a 6-3 vote; membership of the justices has not changed since.

However, support of four of the justices is necessary to grant a Supreme Court review, and since the cases are scheduled, those four votes must have been obtained — although that's no guarantee of anything when it comes to making the final decision.

The 1973 decision held that states may not interfere in a woman's decision to have an abortion in the first three months of pregnancy, may interfere only in the second three months to protect a woman's health, and may take steps to protect fetal life only in the final three months, when the fetus has become "viable" and possibly able to live outside the womb.

The case advanced this time by the government does not raise the profound moral issues associated with abortion, but argues that advances in medicine and technology have made such arbitrary divisions meaningless. In addition, the brief says the 1973 ruling was too broad and stripped powers from the states to set even minor limits on abortions.

The brief is associated with two cases now on the Supreme Court docket. In both cases — in Illinois and Pennsylvania — federal appeals courts struck down state laws that sought to place some limits on abortions.

For example, the Pennsylvania law required that women seeking an abortion be provided with information on possible physical and emotional effects of abortion; that they be provided with alternative information about public assistance benefits for pre-natal care and childbirth; and that a second doctor be present at an abortion to attempt to save a viable fetus.

Such restrictions do not appear to deny abortions, but simply surround them with certain delays and safeguards.

The government brief is asking the Supreme Court to overturn its 1973 ruling — in effect leaving the states free to impose whatever limits they choose.

This obviously would result in a patchwork pattern where what is legal in one state would be illegal in another, and a woman denied an abortion in one state could simply travel to another. But uniformity is not a virtue by itself. Many laws vary from state to state.

One thing is certain: If the states were allowed to establish their own abortion laws, the results would undoubtedly be closer to what the people in those states really want.

St. Louis Review
St. Louis, MO, July 19, 1985

On Jan. 22, 1973, the U.S. Supreme Court shocked the nation with its decision that abortion is a right protected by the Constitution. The majority opinion chose to ignore the medical and scientific evidence and chose to discover a constitutional right to privacy which was used to justify the right to an abortion. The Supreme Court decision has since been applied to invalidate the explicity anti-abortion legislation of most of our 50 states.

For years, the Right to Life Movement has sought ways to persuade the U.S. Supreme Court to reconsider the landmark Roe vs. Wade decision. During these years, many prominent jurists have criticized the tenuous judicial basis for the majority ruling and have pointed to the myriad factual, technical, legal and practical flaws in the decision.

Against this background, the Supreme Court has agreed to hear arguments on recent state laws affecting abortion passed by the legislatures of Illinois and Pennsylvania.

The Reagan administration's Justice Department has entered a friend-of-the-court brief in these cases, arguing that the Constitution itself contains no language guaranteeing abortion rights and urging that the 1973 abortion ruling "is so far flawed that this court should overrule it and return the law to the condition in which it was before that case was decided."

The last time the Justice Department sought such an historic overruling was in 1954 when the department successfully asked the court to throw out the 1896 ruling permitting racially "separate but equal" schools.

The Justice Department's brief is supported by many prominent members of Congress, but pro-life groups should seek to enlist the wholehearted support of those congressmen who have not as yet taken their stand in behalf of innocent life.

The 1973 ruling was truly a "fatally" flawed decision in that it resulted in the deliberate taking of some 18 million lives of pre-born children. The Supreme Court will hear arguments on the Illinois and Pennsylvania cases during its 1985-1986 term. We pray that the justices will act to stop the holocaust for which the court provided a cloak of legality.

The Des Moines Register
Des Moines, IA, July 18, 1985

Again, abortion.

Surely, the destruction of an embryo or a fetus presents a grave moral dilemma, for no destruction of life can be taken lightly by a principled people.

Yet a pregnancy is an intensely private thing. It is a matter of love and legacy — or perhaps of violence, despair or purposelessness. It is a matter of faith and health and joy and fear, of physical and material resources, of commitment and competence. A pregnancy is not a piece of the public domain.

Finding the balance between a woman's private right to control her own destiny and the public responsibility to protect life is a challenge of rare proportions. It was the Supreme Court's attempt to do it that resulted in the 1973 decision called Roe v. Wade.

No one is wholly satisfied with Roe v. Wade. Its opponents feel so deeply about it that abortion has remained a painfully divisive issue in the nation ever since the decision.

Ronald Reagan is among those opponents. The Reagan administration has now taken an opportunity to urge the Supreme Court to reverse itself, and thus to permit state or local governments once again to ban abortions.

The opportunity came when the Supreme Court agreed to consider two state laws, setting up restrictions on abortions, which have been struck down as unconstitutional by federal appeals courts.

Given this court's 6-to-3 vote two years ago reaffirming a woman's "fundamental right" to abortion, it is unlikely that the Justice Department expects the court now to overturn Roe v. Wade. The department's brief, instead, seems to represent the more activist approach of the new attorney general in advancing the administration's social agenda in the courts.

Rights cannot be turned on and off like a faucet. The administration should recognize that, and should appreciate that the proper course for its goal is a constitutional amendment — the very course the president has publicly advocated.

Pursuing the goal in court is a lamentable change of approach. Although the initiative has little chance of judicial success, it will contribute fuel to the fire of controversy that keeps the nation from moving beyond this question, to which the court has given a careful and responsible answer, to the pressing public-policy questions related to it.

Sex education and contraceptives, family-planning counseling and support for teen parents, strengthened adoption services and assurances that those children who have been born of unwanted pregnancies will have decent lives: These are the issues that cry out for the national attention that is diverted instead to Roe v. Wade.

Abortion presents a grave moral dilemma, but — beyond the guidelines laid down by the court — it is not the nation's dilemma. It is a private dilemma. Unwanted children, child neglect, child abuse, poverty, malnutrition, ruined lives: These are the public-policy questions.

By seeking yet again to fight the old fight, the Reagan administration saps the nation's energy for the real challenge.

The Burlington Free Press
Burlington, VT, July 21, 1985

Neither the federal government nor anyone else should be able to deprive women of the fundamental right to make those choices which can affect their physical or mental well being.

What is essentially a matter between women and their consciences should concern no one but themselves. It is a question of privacy that is as basic as the right of law-abiding citizens to do what they wish in their homes. Yet there are groups in the nation who wish to deny women the opportunity to make those decisions which should be reserved to them. Morally outraged by the idea of abortion, several organizations have been fighting for a decade to persuade first Congress and now the Supreme Court to overturn a court ruling that a woman's right to end a pregnancy is a right that is protected by the 14th Amendment. They argue that the decision opened the floodgates for indiscriminate abortions.

Joining the debate have been women's rights advocates who sometimes have been as strident in their defense of abortion as their opponents. The result has been a heated debate on the issue that has periodically grown in intensity. Both sides have made little or no attempt to work out a compromise.

Even so, the arguments that women have a right to choose are consistent with the basic principles of the Constitution. No matter how effectively their opponents' case may appear to be, they cannot escape the fact that they would interfere in matters that properly belong in the realm of privacy. Contending that a fetus is a human being from the time of fertilization, they maintain that abortion is murder. There is, however, no persuasive scientific evidence to prove their point.

That the Reagan administration has filed a brief with the Supreme Court asking the justices to overturn their 1973 ruling is an indication that the White House is under considerable political pressure from right-to-life organizations. The court should negate its decision and return the law to the condition that preceded the Roe vs. Wade case. The jurists in that instance held that a woman's right to abortion is protected by the 14th Amendment. Should the decision be overturned, abortions doubtlessly would be illegal in many states. Women and doctors then could face criminal penalties if abortions were performed.

The administration's brief, filed with the approval of President Reagan, appears to be an effort to fulfill a campaign promise. He considers abortion a "horror" and a "tragedy." Speaking to a right-to-life rally in Washington in January, he said the "momentum" is with those who oppose abortion.

However that may be, the court should refuse to reverse the ruling on the grounds that doing so would deprive women of a fundamental right of privacy which would contravene constitutional principles.

Minneapolis Star and Tribune

Minneapolis, MN, July 17, 1985

When the U.S. Supreme Court issued its landmark ruling in Roe v. Wade, it declared that a woman's decision about abortion is inherently private. A dozen years later, the Reagan administration is urging the high court to abandon that sound principle. The court should not be swayed.

The 1973 ruling held that women have a constitutional right to choose abortion and limited states' power to abridge that right. A decade later the court reaffirmed its ruling by striking down several local regulations designed to make abortion less accessible and more expensive. As Justice Lewis Powell noted in the 1983 decision, the court "repeatedly and consistently has accepted and applied the basic principle that a woman has a fundamental right to make the highly personal choice whether or not to terminate her pregnancy."

Justice Department lawyers hope to use two pending cases to undermine the tradition and the right. In a brief filed Monday, the administration argued that the 1973 decision unreasonably prevents states from regulating the circumstances under which abortions are performed. It criticized appellate court decisions which struck down statutes in Illinois and Pennsylvania — statutes that, among other things, required doctors to give women seeking abortions a detailed description of the fetus, to warn that abortions might cause psychological harm and to urge patients to contact agencies offering aid after childbirth.

The administration defends these rules as "modest and reasonable" state regulation of abortion. But their approval could imperil the abortion right itself. Like many of the rules struck down in 1983, they intrude on doctor-patient relationships. They seek to accomplish indirectly what the state is forbidden to do openly: persuade a woman not to exercise her right to abortion under the guise of "informed consent."

At least the administration is being forthright about its purpose in filing Monday's brief: It wants to topple a high-court decision that has granted crucial privacy and freedom to millions of women. The moral questions surrounding abortion are difficult, but reversing Roe v. Wade is the wrong way to resolve them. We hope the court reaffirms its 1973 pronouncement: that in this deeply personal decision, the government must not interfere.

The Houston Post

Houston, TX, July 18, 1985

The question of legal abortions is one of the thorniest, most divisive and most hotly argued that faces our society on a continuing basis. It is thus especially disheartening to see the administration drag it forcibly back into the U.S. Supreme Court again at a time when any reasonable person on either side must admit that nothing is going to change.

In 1973, the high court overturned the abortion laws in Texas and 30 other states. The justices ruled 7 to 2 that no state's interest is sufficient to interfere with an abortion decision between that woman and her doctor, provided the fetus is not yet viable. Two years ago, the court affirmed the precedent by a vote of 6 to 3.

The makeup of the court has not changed since then, nor are the arguments much different. The Supreme Court is historically extremely loath to overturn its own precedents. This is the first time in more than 30 years that the government has asked it to do so. Indeed, of the two states whose laws were recently overturned at the appellate level — Illinois and Pennsylvania — the former did not even file a brief in defense of its own law.

Given that the chance for actually overturning the 1973 decision is almost nil, we are forced to conclude that the adminstration is simply using the court as an ideological billboard to advertise its already well-understood position on the subject.

In this instance, it does not matter how one views the abortion question itself. It is simply sad to see an overburdened branch of government thus misused and our society further divided.

Maine Sunday Telegram

Portland, ME, July 21, 1985

☐ Even as women from around the world met last week in Kenya to observe the end of the U.N.'s "Decade for Women," the Reagan administration asked the Supreme Court to take from American women a constitutional right they've held since 1973.

It was that year the court legalized abortion. The case was Roe vs. Wade, and the court's 7-2 decision established that pregnancy is part of a fundamental "right of privacy" protected by the 14th Amendment.

The administration, supported by abortion opponents, has been determined to change that decision. It has fought it in election campaigns, at rallies and in a "friend of the court" brief filed with the court last week. The brief scores Roe vs. Wade as "inherent unworkable" and "so far flawed that this court should overrule it."

But is it?

No.

With sensitivity and clarity, the 1973 decision brought volatile conflicting claims into legal balance. Steering clear of any ruling on the moral question of when life begins, Justice Harry Blackmun balanced the life of a mother against a fetus' growing *potential* for life.

For the first three months of pregnancy, abortion is a decision the law leaves to a woman and her doctor. In the second trimester limitations begin and strengthen as the fetus grows toward viability—able to survive outside the womb.

The 1973 decision is sound, workable constitutional law. The court should ringingly reaffirm it.

To do otherwise would return the United States to a time when laws governing abortion varied considerably from one state to another. It was a time when only those aware of their options and rich enough to afford them were assured clinically safe abortions. Other women had only torturous home remedies and the back streets.

That was a bleak era which the court has shown no inclination to revive. Two years ago, in a case from Akron, Ohio, the court reaffirmed Roe vs. Wade by a vote of 6-3. It should do the same with the pending cases from Illinois and Pennsylvania.

In 1983, Justice Lewis Powell, writing for the majority, praised the U.S. system of legal precedents as "a doctrine that demands respect in a society governed by the rule of law."

The court should demonstrate its respect again.

The Seattle Times

Seattle, WA, July 18, 1985

APART from appeasing ultraconservatives within his constituency, it's hard to see any practical purpose in President Reagan's new attempt to undo the U.S. Supreme Court's historic ruling in 1973 that most anti-abortion laws are unconstitutional.

Even the most ardent foes of legalized abortion concede the administration strategy unveiled this week — filing "friend of the court" briefs in two cases due for hearings in the court's fall term — is not likely to change any minds on the nation's highest bench.

There may be a retirement or two coming up, but the court's makeup has changed little since the landmark decision in Roe vs. Wade a dozen years ago, reaffirmed in several subsequent cases, most recently in 1983. The gist of those findings is that criminal penalties for abortions violate privacy and due-process-of-law guarantees in the federal Constitution's Fifth and 14th Amendments.

Legal scholars say Roe vs. Wade was in harmony with a succession of interpretations dating back to the 1890s, in which court majorities have proclaimed, as Justice Brennan put it in one case, a right "to be free from unwarranted governmental intrusion into matters so fundamentally affecting a person as the decision whether to bear or beget a child."

Despite professing a belief in getting government "off the backs of the people," the president and his conservative followers long have argued against the court's majority view. Moving for direct Justice Department intervention in the pending cases is noteworthy because it's the administration's strongest attack yet on legalized abortions except where necessary to save a woman's life.

Thus, the unusual new strategy has greater political than legal significance. Unfortunately, it also will stir fresh emotions among lunatic elements on the fringe of the anti-abortion movement against which the Justice Department has been disgracefully slow to move in cases involving arson attacks and other criminal violence.

The Detroit News
Detroit, MI, July 17, 1985

The Reagan administration has asked the U.S. Supreme Court to reverse its landmark 1973 Roe vs. Wade abortion ruling. That ruling effectively overturned state laws that regulated or prohibited abortions during the first trimester of pregnancy.

President Reagan's views on abortion are well-known. But it is important to remember that in filing its brief, the U.S. Justice Department is not seeking to outlaw abortion. Rather, it is attempting to return the issue to the political process in the 50 states — which is exactly where it belongs.

The administration has filed a friend of the court brief in cases pending before the U.S. Supreme Court from Pennsylvania and Illinois. In those cases, state laws controlling access to abortions have come under legal challenge. Those states, and the Justice Department, argue that the Roe ruling's doctrine of a constitutional "right" to abortion is so broad that it limits legitimate state regulation of abortions.

In fact, the Roe case is breathtaking in its sweeping declaration of a constitutional "right to privacy," which is not discussed in the Constitution. The ruling, written by Justice Harry Blackmun, acknowledged this fact: "The Constitution does not explicitly mention any right of privacy." Nevertheless, Justice Blackmun proceeded to "infer" this right, and by extension, a right to abortions in the first trimester unhindered by the regulatory powers of the state, in the 14th Amendment's "concept of personal liberty and restrictions upon state action."

But Mr. Blackmun could not point to any words in the Constitution to support his new-found discovery of this constitutional right. The Justice Department, in its brief, said the Roe decision "is so far flawed and . . . is such a source of instability in the law, that this court should reconsider that decision, and on reconsideration, abandon it."

One need not be a prolife advocate to share the Justice Department's view of the Roe ruling. Professor Harvey Cox of the Harvard Law School observed that the opinion failed to "articulate a precept of sufficient abstractness to lift the ruling above the level of a political judgment . . ." Stanford University Law School's John Hart Ely said the constitutional right to abortion is "not inferable from the language of the Constitution. . . . It [Roe] is not constitutional law and gives almost no sense of an obligation to try to be."

The ruling was sheer legislation, which is precisely the term applied to it by Justice William Rehnquist in his dissent: "The decision here to break pregnancy into three distinct terms, and to outline the permissible restrictions the state may impose in each one, for example, partakes more of judicial legislation than it does of a determination of the intent of the drafters of the 14th Amendment." By such judicial legislation, the court in Roe usurped the powers of the Texas Legislature, whose law it specifically addressed, and every other state legislature affected by the ruling — which was almost every one in the nation.

Such a bald usurpation violates the basic understanding upon which our government is founded: that political questions will be decided not by the most arbitrary and politically inaccessible branch of government — the courts — but rather by the most politically responsive branch of government, the legislature. Abortion is an emotionally charged issue.

But it is, at its very essence, a political issue. To remove the most emotion-tinged issue of our time from the political arena is to deny to our political institutions their ability to function. Such a usurpation corrodes the trust of the people that their basic concerns will be dealt with by persons who will be accountable to them.

THE COMMERCIAL APPEAL
Memphis, TN, July 18, 1985

IN A misguided effort to turn back the clock, the Reagan administration has urged the Supreme Court to overturn its landmark 1973 decision that legalized abortion.

Filing a "friend of the court" brief in cases involving Pennsylvania and Illinois attempts to restrict abortion, the Justice Department called on the high court to return the law to where it stood 12 years ago.

Before the court established in Roe vs. Wade a constitutional right to abortion, many state laws made it a crime for a woman to seek to end an unwanted pregnancy and for a doctor to help her.

If the court accepts the administration's argument that no constitutional right to abortion exists, states will be free to ban the procedure and many will do so. Then, as before 1973, well-to-do women will be able to travel to states where abortions are legal and safe. Poor women will have the choice of carrying to term or risking "back-alley" abortions.

Fortunately for women who wish to make for themselves the most personal decision of whether or not to have a child, the justices rarely reverse themselves quickly on constitutional rulings.

Two years ago the court strongly reaffirmed Roe vs. Wade in a 6-3 decision against abortion restrictions imposed by the Akron, Ohio, city council. The court's membership has not changed since then, and thus it is likely that the administration's latest attack on women's right to make their own reproductive decisions will fail.

Nevertheless, it is disappointing that President Reagan, who preaches about getting government off people's backs, personally approved his solicitor general's intrusion into private choices that should be made by women and their doctors.

IN A COUNTRY as diverse as the United States, there are persons whose religious beliefs reject abortion under any circumstances. There are those whose religious beliefs permit abortion under most circumstances. And there are those who stand somewhere in between.

And in a country undergirded by democracy and pluralism, it is unseemly and lacking in tolerance for a government and a president to select one set of religious values and attempt to impose them on all.

ST. LOUIS POST-DISPATCH
St. Louis, MO, July 17, 1985

So far the Reagan administration has been trying in the Supreme Court to nibble away at established civil rights and civil liberties. Now, for the first time, it is asking the high court to overturn a major decision — this one in the 1973 case of *Roe vs. Wade,* which made a woman's choice of abortion a constitutional right.

The administration has attempted, without much success, to get the courts to move closer to its ideas about school busing, school prayer, affirmative action employment programs and public aid to parochial schools. But the last time the Justice Department flatly urged the Supreme Court to reverse a decision was in 1954, when the court did abandon its "separate but equal" policy of racial segregation. That at least put the department and the court on the side of expanding freedom. Not so with the department's idea of reversing the abortion case, which suggests states' rights should take precedence over individual rights.

The Justice Department is contending that the 1973 Roe decision denies state control over abortion. By and large it does, and that was a purpose of the decision: to assert a national right to abortions with which the states could not interfere. Just two years ago the court voted 6-3 to reaffirm this right against state restrictions.

Why a "national" right? For decades now the Supreme Court has been applying much of the Constitution's Bill of Rights to the states under terms of the 14th Amendment's requirement for due process. The court has recognized that free speech and freedom of religion or freedom from arbitrary police procedures are rights that should belong to every citizen and not be dependent upon the preferences of the individual states. So it is with abortion. So it will be unless the administration can persuade the court to turn its back on itself and allow 50 states to create their own varied ideas of women's rights.

The Hartford Courant
Hartford, CT, July 19, 1985

Ronald Reagan has never made a secret of his hatred of abortion, nor of his intention to give aid and comfort to those who want it made criminal once again. The mystery is why the president waited so long to act to overturn the 12-year-old U.S. Supreme Court ruling legalizing the procedure.

Last winter, Mr. Reagan told a right-to-life rally he would do all he could to overturn the landmark Roe vs. Wade decision. He made good on the promise this week by personally approving the Justice Department's filing of a friend-of-the-court brief in connection with two pending abortion rights cases. The department argued that states must be allowed to place restrictions on abortion and asked that Roe vs. Wade be overturned.

Mr. Reagan has sent a powerful — and chilling — message that he has no intention of leaving the abortion issue on the back burner.

His move may, of course, be only a political sop to his administration's anti-abortion constituency. But it should be noted that it is highly unusual — if not unprecedented — for an administration to call for elimination of a constitutional right recognized by the Supreme Court.

The Roe vs. Wade decision was based on a fundamental right of privacy protected by the 14th Amendment. But the Justice Department's brief argues that the basis for the decision was "so far flawed and . . . is a source of such instability in the law that this court should reconsider that decision and on reconsideration abandon it."

The brief said states have an interest in regulating abortion, saying appellate court decisions striking down statutes in Illinois and Pennsylvania that controlled abortions were "multiply flawed. . . . The courts of appeal betrayed unabashed hostility to state regulation of abortion and ill-disguised suspicion of state legislators' motives."

The Justice Department's states'-rights arguments aren't expected to change the high court's mind. The court emphatically reaffirmed Roe vs. Wade in a 6-to-3 decision in 1982 that struck down abortion restrictions imposed by the City Council in Akron, Ohio. The membership of the court hasn't changed since then.

But even if the reproductive rights of American women are safe — for the moment, at least — the administration's heating up of the issue is distressingly cynical.

In a major policy speech last week, Attorney General Edwin Meese III accused the Supreme Court of making political decisions rather than decisions based on the Constitution. It is ironic that the administration he serves would, for political reasons, now urge the high court to deprive citizens of a basic constitutional right.

The Oregonian
Portland, OR, July 23, 1985

Why would the Department of Justice submit an unsolicited friend-of-the-court brief to the Supreme Court defending a Pennsylvania abortion-counseling law when a similar law was struck down by the same court two years ago? Because a government victory in this case might become the wedge to reverse the most despised Supreme Court ruling of all for the pro-life movement, Roe vs. Wade.

In that 1973 decision, the court granted a woman's right to have an abortion free of undue state interference. The 1973 decision was vigorously endorsed in a 6-3 decision in 1983, Akron vs. Akron Center for Reproductive Health, when Justice Lewis F. Powell appealed to the 1973 precedent as "a doctrine that demands respect in a society governed by the rule of law." In the Akron decision the court curbed the powers of state and local government to limit access for legal abortions.

The Reagan administration is banking on a change of heart or of members in the Supreme Court between the 1982-83 term and the 1985-86 term. Chief Justice Warren E. Burger is said to be reconsidering his position on the issues posed by abortion-related cases, and Powell's health after two major operations within seven months makes his future presence on the court uncertain. Both Burger and Powell voted with the majority in the Akron case.

The administration thinks that a reversal of the decision from Pennsylvania, which requires that women be warned that an abortion may have unforeseen and detrimental physical and psychological effects, would open the door for a reconsideration of Roe vs. Wade.

A reversal of Roe vs. Wade might produce the prior situation, where each state had its own abortion laws, or it could be a prelude to federal legislation that would limit the conditions under which abortions could be performed. When the Senate considered a constitutional amendment to ban abortion in 1983, it lacked 18 votes for a two-thirds majority but only one vote for an absolute majority. A majority is all that is needed for statutory changes.

Thus, the fight is just beginning — again.

The Washington Times
Washington, DC, July 16, 1985

It is more than 30 years since an administration asked the Supreme Court to overturn one of its rulings. That was in *Brown* vs. *the Board* , which reversed *Plessy* vs. *Ferguson,* which established the doctrine of "separate but equal." Now the Justice Department is supporting Pennsylvania and Illinois, which are challenging a Third Circuit Court decision striking down abortion-related laws in those states. The Justice Department's brief takes a further step, asking the court to declare *Roe* excessively broad.

To see the poisoned post-*Roe* judicial atmosphere, it is only necessary to examine some of the provisions the Third Circuit struck down: requirements that the doctor inform the mother of available child-care benefits; that, in cases approaching term, the doctor choose the method most likely to allow the fetus to survive except where the mother's health might be endangered; that insurance companies offer no-abortion policies at lower cost; that doctors prescribing a morning-after contraceptive explain that its method of action is abortifacient.

The Justice Department recognizes that, while it can be argued that the Pennsylvania and Illinois statutes are constitutional even under *Roe*, accepting *Roe* as permanent is to give that decision more respect than it deserves. *Roe* is open policy-making in place of interpretation. It uses "scientific" categories (the "trimester" system) that have been rendered meaningless by advances in fetology. It plays word games with the Constitution so as to make up a "right" that would have shocked and sickened the Framers. It is time for 20th century *Dred Scott* to go.

The Record

Hackensack, NJ, July 18, 1985

The Reagan administration wants to do in court what it can't do in Congress: outlaw abortions. In an extraordinary move this week, the Justice Department asked the Supreme Court to overturn its 1973 *Roe v. Wade* decision — in which it held that a woman has a constitutional right to an abortion in the first three months of pregnancy for any reason, and during the second three months to protect her health.

The government's lawyers now argue that this decision is vague, flawed, and "the source of ... instability in the law." They also say it's outdated. In 1973, the court allowed states to ban abortions in the third trimester — the final three months of pregnancy — on the ground that a fetus could survive outside the womb at that age. Advances in medical technology now make survival possible for younger fetuses as well.

The court must reject these arguments. A reversal of Roe would invite legal chaos, since it would then be up to the states to decide the conditions for an abortion, such as allowing them in cases of incest and rape. State legislatures would be clogged with debate for years — and would probably enact a variety of statutes or restrictions. A woman's right to have an abortion, then, would depend on where she lived.

Nor would such state laws end abortion, any more than they did in the days before *Roe v.*

Wade. Many women would simply get illegal abortions — which, it will be remembered, were often murderously unsafe. They were expensive, too; if abortion is outlawed, many poor women will be forced to bear children they don't want and can't afford to raise.

The best argument against overturning the Roe decision is also the most simple. The court would be revoking a basic right to privacy. Even before 1973, the justices barred the government from interfering in private decisions about raising families. In 1965, striking down a Connecticut ban on the sale of contraceptives, Justice William J. Brennan Jr. wrote, "If the right of privacy means anything, it is the right of the individual, married or single, to be free from unwarranted governmental intrusion into matters so fundamentally affecting a person as the decision whether to bear or beget a child."

President Reagan and his antiabortion allies believe that the fetus, at no matter what stage of development, is a person. They have every right to that view, but they must recognize it for what it is: an opinion, not a scientific fact. Doctors, theologians, and legal scholars disagree furiously on when a fetus becomes a person. The Supreme Court did not to attempt answer that unanswerable question in 1973, and it should not do so now.

The Philadelphia Inquirer

Philadelphia, PA, July 18, 1985

In 1983 the Reagan administration asked the U.S. Supreme Court to back away from the court's 1973 landmark decision affirming a woman's right to abortion. By a 6-3 majority, the court rejected the administration's position and reaffirmed its 1973 stand.

The membership of the Supreme Court has not changed since 1983, and there is no reason to presume that the justices' thinking has reversed. Yet the Justice Department announced Monday that next term it would insist before the court that the same justices must overturn the 1973 ruling.

No credible chance of that exists. Doing it would undermine the bedrock of all judicial authority — the consistency of precedent as the guiding rule of legal interpretation. It was precisely that rule of settled precedent that Justice Lewis F. Powell Jr. rested his opinion upon when writing for the majority in the 1983 case.

"The doctrine of *stare decisis* ... demands respect in a society governed by the rule of law," he said. In a lengthy footnote, Justice Powell emphasized that "especially compelling reasons" dictated adherence to precedent in reviewing the controversial 1973 abortion decision in *Roe vs. Wade.* "That case was decided with special care," he said.

Given these facts, why now would the administration insist that the Supreme Court must proclaim itself absolutely wrong? Such a frontal assault on the court risks erosion of its authority and inflammatory division of the public to no good purpose. How could any administration disregard such concerns so cavalierly?

The answer lies more in the realm of politics than law. Since the court's 1983 decision, Mr. Reagan swept 49 states in winning re-election. If ever the forces of the New Right are to be repaid, if ever their agenda is to be nailed into America's code of law, now must be the time.

That is not to denigrate those who truly believe that abortion should be outlawed. Their position usually is based upon deep moral conviction. The Supreme Court acknowledged as much in its painstaking 1973 decision, *Roe vs. Wade.* But in that case a 7-2 majority of the justices concluded that the Constitution requires that a decision on abortion fall within a woman's right to privacy. Only when the fetus has evolved to a point where it "has the capability of meaningful life outside the mother's womb" — that is, in the third trimester of pregnancy — does the state's interest in protecting potential life then permit state regulation or prohibition of abortion.

That is the law, reaffirmed in unmistakable terms only two years ago by the same jurists who still are entrusted by the Constitution with being the final arbiters of law.

In these circumstances, for the administration to assail the court, undermine its authority and stir public passions anew is nothing more than irresponsible political posturing.

The Grand Rapids Press

Grand Rapids, MI, July 21, 1985

Miraculous progress in neonatal medicine has created ethical and medical predicaments well beyond the vision of even a Supreme Court justice.

The high court 12 years ago ruled that abortions were legal. The decision stands as a landmark while medicine has been in motion. As doctors grow increasingly able to save younger and younger premature infants, the performance of abortions becomes correspondingly difficult.

Those complications threaten to antiquate the Supreme Court's decision's to divide pregnancy into trimesters. They aren't, however, sufficient reason to toss aside the basic premise of the Roe vs. Wade decision. The ruling was fundamental: A woman's decision to end a pregnancy *is* guaranteed by a "right of privacy" protected by the 14th Amendment. Scientific advances do not refute that reasoning.

In a brief filed last week before the Supreme Court, the Reagan administration asked the nation's highest court to repudiate the Roe vs. Wade decision and permit states and localities to control the procedure.

The Justice Department — acting with the support of Mr. Reagan — contends that the court's definitions of viability of a fetus, trimesters and the right to terminate one's pregnancy have no solid foundation in constitutional doctrine.

On the first two points, the government may have legitimate complaints. When Roe vs. Wade was shaped, the justices based their formula on the assumption that fetuses under six months of age weren't viable. The justices were correct — then. Ten years ago, babies born weighing less than 3.3 pounds and less than 30 weeks along in pregnancy usually didn't survive. Today, thanks to the development of sophisticated neonatal units, increased knowledge of infant lung problems, and improved monitors, babies weighing as little as 1.1 pound and born even before the 25th week

of pregnancy have a chance for survival, albeit small.

According to the law of the land as established a dozen years ago, a woman's decision to have an abortion during the first three months of her pregnancy must be left to her. States may interfere in the woman's abortion decision during the second trimester only to protect the woman's health, and may take steps to protect the fetus only in the third trimester.

Medical progress has blurred those distinctions. The lines need to be redrawn based upon the most recent medical accomplishments. There remains an inherent right to private choice for women, and that should not be eliminated in the process.

In pushing for "state's rights" on abortion, the Reagan administration overlooks the fact that Roe vs. Wade did not create the constitutionally guaranteed right to privacy. That warranty was based on a series of decisions, which began 94 years ago, establishing individual rights in a free society, including the right to make one's own decision on giving birth.

There is little reason to fear the justices will overturn that well-established right, particularly in light of a 6-3 decision two years ago which strongly reaffirmed a woman's "fundamental right" to abortion.

The administration's strategy, in an effort to fulfill an election promise to ban abortion, appears to be chipping away at the Roe vs. Wade decision. Two years ago, the Justice Department stopped short of asking the court to overturn itself. This time, the administration took a no-holds-barred approach.

The Justice Department is wrong. State and local regulation or banning of abortion would return this nation to the days before 1973. Abortion has become one of the most frequently performed surgical procedures in the nation. Women seeking the operation once again would be forced to sneak across borders or worse, to take their chances in dark alleys with makeshift operating rooms and doctors.

Part II: Abortion & Politics

When the Supreme Court in 1973 considered the case of Jane Roe, an unmarried Texas woman who sought a safe abortion but was denied one under state law because her life was not threatened by her pregnancy, the Justices eschewed the question of whether a human life actually begins at the moment egg and sperm are united. "We need not resolve the difficult question of when life begins," wrote Justice Harry Blackmun. "When those trained in the respective disciplines of medicine, philosophy, and theology are unable to arrive at any consensus, the judiciary, at this point in the development of man's knowledge, is not in a position to speculate as to the answer." Many members of Congress, however, have felt no similar compunction about attempting to translate their beliefs on the matter into legislation. The Reagan Administration, frustrated in its efforts to change the body of abortion law through individual court cases, and chafing under the criticism of conservative supporters, has supported proposals before Congress to override *Roe v. Wade* and subsequent Supreme Court rulings on abortion through passage of a constitutional amendment. (Under Article V of the Constitution, a constitutional amendment—the only means of overturning a Supreme Court ruling—can be initiated if approved by two-thirds of both houses of Congress, and then ratified by three-quarters of the states.) The most highly publicized of these amendments, sponsored by Rep. Henry J. Hyde of Illinois and Sen. Jesse Helms of North Carolina, simply declared that life begins at conception; the fetus' life would thus be entitled to full protection under the law, and abortion at any point during pregnancy would become murder.

The relentless stance reflected in such a measure, which ignores any claim by the pregnant woman to rights of her own, is one that has set the tone of the abortion debate in the national political sphere. Politicians who have attempted to separate their personal beliefs about abortion from their political platform on the issue—including 1984 vice presidential candidate Geraldine Ferraro—have found it difficult to combat the black-and-white representation of this complicated issue by fervent antiabortionists, including prominent members of the Roman Catholic Church. Likewise, clinics and hospitals which perform abortions, as well as individual medical practictioners, have suffered from the violent measures, including arson and bombing incidents, which are encouraged by such a single-minded viewpoint—though these acts themselves are not espoused by the majority of antiabortionists. Increasingly, however, the 'pro-choice' movement has been able to garner similar levels of emotional—and financial—support for its side of the debate. Just as the 'pro-life' movement had been galvanized by the *Roe v. Wade* decision, the 'pro-choice' movement reacted to the results of the 1980 election with an increased attention to campaign politics on the state and national level. The growing effectiveness of its defense of women's rights found expression in January 1986 in the turnout of 80,000 demonstrators for the "March for Women's Lives" in Washington D.C. Organized by the National Organization for Women in response to the annual antiabortion march on the Capitol, the event constituted a dramatic show of public support for the right of women to make their own decisions about bearing children.

Two 'Human Life' Amendments Introduced, Debated, Defeated

The Senate opened hearings in April 1981 on a proposed statute that would define human life as beginning at conception, thus making abortion equivalent to murder under United States criminal law. The legislation, sponsored by Rep. Henry J. Hyde (R, Ill.) and Sen. Jesse Helms (R, N.C.), was the focus of intense controversy. The Senate Judiciary subcommittee on the Separation of Powers first heard testimony from five doctors, all of whom opposed abortion and believed that life began at conception. When the hearings resumed in May, however, eight eminent physicians criticized efforts in Congress to pinpoint the moment a human life began. These physicians assailed the bill as scientifically unjustifiable. After the final impassioned arguments ended the third round of subcommittee hearings in June, still no conclusions had been reached. The issues that provoked the strongest disagreement were those of the constitutionality of the bill, its potential to create complicated legal tangles in cases where the interests of the mother would conflict with those of the unborn child, and its possible application to matters beyond abortion, including some birth control methods. Intrauterine devices (IUDs), for example, function not by preventing conception but by preventing implantation of the fertilized ovum, thus destroying life under the definition of the Helms bill. Debate on the bill continued a year later when liberal senators began a filibuster after Sen. Jesse Helms reintroduced the antiabortion amendment, attaching it to a bill that proposed a federal debt ceiling. After three unsuccessful motions for cloture to end the filibuster in September 1982, the Senate finally voted to table the antiabortion amendment Sept. 15. The defeat came in spite of the fact that President Reagan had announced his support for the Helms proposal.

In September 1981, Sen. Orrin Hatch (R, Utah) had introduced another type of antiabortion amendment. The Hatch amendment would give federal and state governments "concurrent power to restrict and prohibit abortion," and, in cases where the federal and state laws differed, would give precedence to the more restrictive legislation. The Senate Judiciary Committee's Constitution subcommittee in December approved the so-called "human life federalism" amendment 4 to 0 only an hour after hearings on it, chaired by Hatch, ended; and in 1982 the full Judiciary Committee approved the proposal. But in June 1983 the full Senate rejected, 50-49, the proposed amendment. Sen. Helms declined to vote for or against the Hatch amendment, reflecting a split within the antiabortion movement that had persisted for more than two years. Helms said in a brief speech before the vote that he could not support the Hatch proposal because "it does not advance the principle that human life is inviolable."

The Miami Herald
Miami, FL, November 11, 1980

ONE OF the more-ominous implications of Ronald Reagan's decisive victory was the impetus it gave to those who seek to legislate private morality. Any lingering doubt on that point was dispelled Sunday when John Quinn, president of the National Conference of Catholic Bishops, hailed the President-elect's promise to support a Constitutional amendment to ban abortions.

Although the Roman Catholic Church does not necessarily identify with the evangelical Protestants of the Moral Majority organization, the two groups seem to agree on the issue of abortion. Together they represent a powerful political force that now threatens seriously to deny the right of religious conscience to those millions of Americans who disagree with them.

Public-opinion polls consistently show that most Americans, including a majority of Roman Catholics, believe that abortion should be permitted at least under certain circumstances. Many Jewish and Protestant religious leaders teach that the right of an individual to decide whether to terminate her pregnancy is a matter in which the Government should not interfere. That is the sound Constitutional view.

Clergymen who believe that abortion is immoral ought to preach against it. They rightly can exhort their flock to detest that act or any other they believe to be unacceptable. But they have no right to impose that belief on other Americans whose own religious convictions lead them to different conclusions.

A conservative Administration should be dedicated to keeping Government out of people's private lives as much as possible. True conservatives will be guided by the nation's unhappy experience with a previous effort to govern private morality through an amendment to the Constitution. In 1919 the Eighteenth Amendment outlawed the sale, manufacture, or transportation of alcoholic beverages. In 1933 the Eighteenth Amendment was repealed by the Twenty-first.

Abortion, like alcohol and myriad other subjects, is an issue about which Americans of different religious convictions are bound to disagree. Each individual therefore must be free to follow his own conscience. None should seek to impose his will on others.

The Federal Government already is strained beyond its capabilities by the challenges of inflation, energy, and international relations. It should not seek to legislate the religious conscience of the American people.

THE PLAIN DEALER
Cleveland, OH, July 14, 1981

Abortion is beyond doubt one of the most emotional issues in America. It is an issue in which the attitudes of people toward sex and life itself are caught in conflict. Among the questions of religious, philosophical and scientific significance is when life begins. Is there life at the moment of conception? Or does life begin at the moment of birth? Or is it somewhere in between?

We do not presume to have the answer. And we suggest that a political body is the wrong place to look for it, either. Yet, while as august an assembly as the Supreme Court failed to find an answer in its controversial 1973 abortion decision, five men in a subcommittee of the Senate have decided, 3-2, that they know best. Last week they passed a bill that, if ever enacted by Congress, would overturn the Supreme Court decision, define life as beginning at conception, grant from that moment 14th Amendment due process rights to a fetus and make all abortion murder.

How easy. How tidy. How ridiculous. We hope the full Senate Judiciary Committee recognizes the legislation for what it is and disposes of it.

Chicago Defender

Chicago, IL, May 4, 1981

"At two months of age, the human being is less than one thumb's length from head to rump. He would fit at ease in a nutshell. But everything is there: Hands, feet, head, organs, brain — all are in place. His heart has been beating for a month already. Looking closely, you would see the palm creases ... With a good magnifier, the fingerprints could be detected ..."

So testified Dr. Jerome Lejeune, a world renowned geneticist, who spoke last week before a U. S. Senate subcommittee considering an anti-abortion bill. "The human nature of the human being from conception to old age is ... plain, experimental evidence," concluded Lejeune.

For a variety of reasons, Blacks have refused to jump on the pro-abortion bandwagon. And we suspect one of them is because we have always recognized in the depths of our being the truth of what Professor Lejeune is talking about.

Human life begins at conception. We can rationalize about the rights of women over their bodies or the shame of bringing unwanted babies into the world. But until we learn otherwise, life begins at conception — and abortionists ignore or ridicule that fearful truth at their own peril.

Richmond Times-Dispatch

Richmond, VA, May 11, 1981

Sen. John P. East, R-N.C., tried to get away with holding perhaps the most stacked and one-sided public hearing on record April 23 and 24 on the question of when life begins. But criticism was so heavy that the senator agreed to allow other viewpoints a chance to be heard in a new series of hearings beginning May 20.

Sen. East holds to the view that life begins at conception, so he invited to his April Judiciary subcommittee hearings seven doctors who agreed with that view and one who disagreed. No one else was allowed to speak. Even some foes of abortion — which would be outlawed by the bill on which the hearings were held — criticized the stacking of the hearing, so the panel chairman gave in and promised to hear all sides.

The bill at issue, sponsored by Republican Sen. Jesse Helms of North Carolina and Republican Rep. Henry J. Hyde of Illinois, would say that "present day scientific evidence indicates a significant likelihood that actual human life exists from conception" and that therefore the word "person" in the Fourteenth Amendment covers embryos and fetuses from moment one. If the bill became law, abortions would be murder, no matter at what stage of the pregnancy they were performed, and even if the pregnancy resulted from rape or incest.

Some forms of birth control might be made illegal by such a law, according to opponents of the measure. For example, one theory is that the IUD works by preventing the fertilized egg from being implanted on the lining of the uterus. Conception, in such cases, has taken place, and halting the pregnancy at that point would be murder. Some low-dose birth control pills are believed to work the same way.

The purpose of the bill is to override the U.S. Supreme Court's 1973 opinion that, with certain exceptions, legalized abortions. The court majority said that it was persuaded "that the word 'person' as used in the Fourteenth Amendment does not include the unborn." It also said:

"We need not resolve the difficult question of when life begins. When those trained in the respective disciplines of medicine, philosophy and theology are unable to arrive at any consensus, the judiciary, at this point in the development of man's knowledge, is not in a position to speculate as to the answer."

The lone dissenter during the congressional hearings, Dr. Leon E. Rosenberg, chairman of the department of human genetics at the Yale University School of Medicine, told the committee:

"Some people argue that life begins at conception, but others say that life begins when the brain function appears, or when the heart beats, or when a recognizable human form exists in miniature, or when a fetus can survive outside the uterus, or when natural birth occurs. There is no single simple answer."

But the bill would attempt to provide a simple answer. A so-called "pro-life" constitutional amendment banning abortions would require a two-thirds majority vote in each house of Congress and ratification by three-fourths of the states. The bill in question, designed to achieve much the same goal, would require only a majority vote of each house of Congress and signing by the president, with no state approval necessary.

We frequently disagree with the American Civil Liberties Union, but we believe the ACLU is right in warning that adoption of the bill "would create a law enforcement nightmare." The measure is not in the public interest and should go down in defeat.

The Des Moines Register

Des Moines, IA, March 11, 1981

President Reagan's closing comments at his press conference last week were encouraging words to anti-abortion groups backing a "human-life" bill in Congress. The bill would declare that human life begins at conception.

If the bill passes, abortion would be an action that takes human life, thus a crime. This would open the way for state legislatures to prohibit abortions and possibly even to ban some contraceptive devices, such as the intrauterine device, or IUD.

The bill has two aims: avoid the drawn-out wrangling over a proposed anti-abortion amendment to the Constitution, which would require a two-thirds majority in Congress in order to submit the proposition to the states; circumvent the 1973 abortion ruling by the U.S. Supreme Court, which didn't try to define when individual life begins.

Asked about the bill, Reagan reiterated his belief that "in abortion we are taking a human life." Once it is decided when life begins, he continued, there is no need for a constitutional amendment because "the Constitution already protects the right of human life [in the 14th Amendment]."

There was refreshing intellectual humility in the Supreme Court opinion on abortion, in which Justice Harry Blackmun acknowledged, "When those trained in the respective disciplines of medicine, philosophy and theology are unable to arrive at any consensus [on when life begins], the judiciary, at this point in the development of man's knowledge, is not in a position to speculate as to the answers." The law, the court said in effect, could live with a mystery.

Reagan said he expects "testimony by medical authorities, theologians, possibly legal authorities" before the bill is put to a vote. That is no assurance, however, that the legislators will respect the differing opinions of authorities in the learned professions.

In the emotion-charged atmosphere usually surrounding the abortion issue, push and shove usually trample reason. Legislators are easily tempted to "settle things" by letting the vote of the majority decide. Majority votes don't decide the human verities. So the prospect of watching Congress declare, by majority vote, that human life begins at the moment of conception is frightening.

TULSA WORLD

Tulsa, OK, September 30, 1981

THERE ARE two positions in the abortion debate that offer the clearest logic, start to finish. However, most Americans believe the logic weaves its way to cruel results.

The question, as it is framed in the current debate, is when does life begin?

Opponents of abortion argue that life starts at the moment of conception. Therefore, abortion at any time, for any reason — except, perhaps to save the life of the mother — is murder. Given the underlying assumption, no one could deny the logical thread of that argument.

Others, however, believe that life does not begin until the child is born. They argue that abortion should be allowed up until the time of birth. Again, given the underlying assumption, that is an entirely logical, though repugnant, conclusion.

The nice thing about both of these conclusions is that they are simple. No more soul-searching is required. The trouble is that the majority of Americans find neither an acceptable answer to a very complex question. According to national polls, Americans reject both positions.

Few, for example, contend that abortion should be permitted right up until the time the child is born. And most would not hold that abortion should be prohibited regardless of the circumstances of conception of the stage of pregnancy.

The issue arises again in the case of an Oklahoma City girl seeking an abortion. Twelve years old, she became pregnant when raped by three older teenagers. Putting aside the corollary issue involving parental consent, the state Supreme Court was correct in allowing an abortion.

Most Americans would be hard pressed to argue that the girl should not be allowed an abortion in the first trimester of her pregnancy.

Hard cases, it has been said, make bad law. So, too, does hard logic.

The Hartford Courant
Hartford, CT, July 20, 1981

The nation learned a new bit of abortion-related theology this month in the Senate. Not only are the scientific and moral questions of when life begins best decided by a show-of-hands, but life also begins at different times, depending on whether the definition has Democratic or Republican roots.

The three Republicans on the Senate Judiciary Subcommittee on the Separation of Powers voted for a bill that stated, "The life of each human being starts at conception." The two Democrats on the subcommittee voted against the proposition.

A 60 percent-40 percent split on such an issue does not suggest a bedrock of reassuring public policy. This defective effort by some members of Congress to force mothers, doctors and clergy to conform to theology-by-majority-vote, is untenable — and unconstitutional.

Mothers who, with the advice of their doctors and spiritual leaders, have abortions, are not murderers, or accomplices to murder, and no vote on Capitol Hill can force a disbelieving society to accept the premise.

St. Petersburg Times
St. Petersburg, FL, January 25, 1981

Even people who oppose abortion ought to be against the so-called "human life" amendment introduced in Congress last week by Sen. Jesse Helms, R-N.C., and Rep. Robert K. Dornan, R-Calif. Certainly, no thoughtful conservative could support it.

This is what it says: "The paramount right to life is vested in each human being from the moment of fertilization without regard to age, health or condition of dependency." Congress and the states would be empowered to enforce it "with appropriate legislation."

IT WOULD, obviously, repeal the 1973 Supreme Court decision that said abortion isn't the government's business. But what else might it do?

From the moment of fertilization . . .

Some birth-control methods, such as the intra-uterine device, the "morning-after pill" and the low-estrogen contraceptive pill, function by preventing the implantation in the uterus of a fertilized ovum. Would this be illegal? Specifically, does the Congress mean to make it a crime for a rape victim to prevent the rapist's seed from taking root in her body?

From the moment of fertilization . . . without regard to . . . health . . .

Constitutional amendments create constitutional rights. Will the government be required to take active steps to preserve those with which the amendment might endow even the tiniest human embryo? Would pregnant women, and their doctors, be required to take heroic measures to prevent the spontaneous abortions (commonly called miscarriages) that occur in a significant number of pregnancies? Many occur so early that the women don't know they're pregnant. It is often nature's way of purging grossly deformed fetuses. Under the Helms amendment, would a woman to whom this happened be subject to prosecution for failing to protect her embryo? Would her physician be obliged to inform the government? Will pregnant women be subject to government supervision to insure that they protect the civil rights of their fetuses?

GEORGE ORWELL, the author of the prophetic novel *1984*, was not so far off in his anticipation of a ruthless government intruding into the most intimate aspects of human life. The Helms amendment's unlimited implications for the violation of privacy speak volumes about the radical foolishness of tampering with the Constitution in this regard.

The Cleveland Press
Cleveland, OH, May 1, 1981

A parade of medical witnesses went before a Senate subcommittee to prove what we thought everybody learned in seventh-grade biology — that human life begins with a fertilized egg.

So does fish life and bird life and every other form of animal life. In the beginning, the eggs are indistinguishable from each other.

Indeed, the developing human embryo recapitulates the evolutionary history of its species, briefly sporting breathing gills and a rudimentary tail.

It is one thing to acknowledge that a certain fertilized egg has the potential of developing into a human being. It is quite another thing to declare that it IS a human being, a person, and accord to it the full protection of the laws.

But that was the purpose of the hearings held by Sen. John East, R-N.C. — to lay the ground for hearings next month on a "human life statute" which would declare, for the purpose of the 14th Amendment's guarantee of due process of law, that "human life shall be deemed to exist from conception."

This would permit states to ban abortions, and thus get around the Supreme Court's 1973 decision legalizing abortion.

It could also outlaw intrauterine devices and other forms of contraception which interfere with the fertilized egg. According to one witness, the only one not outspokenly anti-abortion, it could end all prenatal tests to determine the health of a fetus.

Paradoxically, such a statute ultimately would undermine the anti-abortionists' very arguments about the sanctity of life.

Law enforcement authorities would have to prosecute every woman who used an IUD or who willfully aborted a fetus with the same vigor as they do any other murderer. Spontaneous miscarriages would have to be investigated as involuntary manslaughter.

Unless anti-abortionists demanded that this be done — and obviously it would be impossible — they would be admitting that some forms of human life (the fertilized egg or fetus) are qualitatively different from other forms (the already born), and that "humanness" is often a matter of definition.

A "human life statute" would be a mockery if enacted and a nightmare if enforced.

The Charlotte Observer
Charlotte, NC, June 16, 1981

As congressional hearings on anti-abortion legislation continue, it's becoming clear that the bills don't enjoy much support, especially the so-called "Human Life Bill." Scientists dispute that bill's assumptions. Constitutional lawyers raise serious legal questions about its provisions. And two recent polls show that most Americans simply don't agree with its intent.

The majority of Americans polled by Louis Harris and the Washington Post-ABC News organizations said they support legalized abortion and oppose efforts to outlaw it. The pro-choice sentiments cut across political, class, regional, age and religious lines.

Fifty-six percent of Harris's respondents said the decision to have an abortion during the first trimester of pregnancy should be a private matter between a woman and her doctor. Even among those calling themselves conservative, 53% favored legal abortions; among Southerners, 52% did.

The Washington Post-ABC News poll found that 40% of those surveyed approve of abortion on demand and another 34% approve of it in most circumstances. More than two of every three respondents opposed any law making abortion murder.

The "Human Life Bill," sponsored in the Senate by North Carolina Republicans Jesse Helms and John East, declares that human life begins at conception and that the word "person" in the 14th Amendment includes all human life. Though it doesn't prohibit abortion, it would probably force the states to do so by passing anti-abortion laws or applying existing murder laws to abortion.

Six former attorneys general oppose the bill. So do the American Medical Association, National Academy of Sciences, American Public Health Association and a Boston group including several hundred scientists and six Nobel laureates.

The Boston group declares that "the attempt to reach a scientific resolution of (when life begins) represents a misuse and misunderstanding of science." The AMA says the notion that life begins at conception means two legal persons exist in the same body, raising questions about the legality of giving a pregnant woman any medical treatment that might entail risk to the fetus.

So far, however, there's little indication Congress is listening. The Senate recently followed the House in restricting poor women's right to federally paid abortions. Both houses have decided that women who become pregnant as a result of rape or incest are no longer eligible.

Perhaps there's some consolation in the N.C. legislature's refusal to follow Congress's example. Last week anti-abortion forces attempting to restrict state money for poor women's abortions lost a crucial vote. Such action, coming from the state whose two U.S. senators are among Washington's most ardent right-to-lifers, indicates that good sense may prevail closer to the people.

Sentinel Star
Orlando, FL, February 14, 1981

OVER THE past seven years, millions of American women have exercised their right to terminate an unwanted pregnancy by abortion.

They have done so with relative safety, in hospital or clinic settings, with qualified doctors present. Gone are the days of furtive inquiries about back-alley abortionists, some qualified and some not, who charged outrageous fees to perform the formerly illegal procedure. Almost wiped out are the tragic cases of deaths from botched abortions.

The Supreme Court's famous, and controversial, 1973 ruling on abortion was indeed a landmark decision. It granted women the right to an abortion during the first three months of pregnancy. Further, it allowed the states to regulate the medical aspects of abortion during the second trimester. Perhaps most importantly, it left to the woman the right to decide for herself, measured in her own values, what she wanted to do.

During the final trimester, the high court ruled, states could forbid all abortions, except those performed to save the mother's life.

Today, the majority of Americans have come to accept this ruling. In 1964, 41 percent of the people polled nationally by the National Opinion Research Center at the University of Chicago believed legal abortions should be available. In a new poll last year, the center found that 67 percent favored the availability of abortion under certain circumstances. Many who favor the idea of available abortion, however, say they would not necessarily choose it for themselves.

Now, Congress is being asked to take on a bill which would render abortion at any stage of pregnancy illegal. The law would stipulate that a fetus becomes a viable human being at conception and, thus, any abortion — and possibly some birth control devices — would constitute murder.

There are two things wrong with the bill. Not only is Congress attempting to override what appears to be the majority opinion in this country, it is attempting to referee an unsolvable dispute. It is trying to define when a fetus becomes a viable human being and then set that instance at some arbitrary point. That is a moral, philosophical and medical question that has been debated through the centuries and remains unanswered.

The move to abolish abortion through a constitutional amendment is similarly without solid foundation. In this case there is one other point: The U. S. Constitution was designed as a flexible legal framework for judicial and legislative action, not as a vehicle to legislate social behavior or something to be changed with every legislative majority and every shift in public opinion.

The Supreme Court produced an equitable ruling on an issue that will probably remain unresolved. That ruling, which offers a choice, not a mandate, should be left untouched.

Oregon Journal

Portland, OR, April 29, 1981

Fighting over the same ground is disheartening work, but it must be done from time to time in a democracy.

But there are so many things that the people of a democracy must decide — or help their elected representatives to decide on their behalf — that it seems wrong to quarrel continually over issues that pertain to individual belief and morality.

The United States was founded on the principle that religion and government must be separate. The Founding Fathers had had enough of the Established Church and the religious wars that had tortured England and Europe over the centuries.

The divisiveness that comes from differences of religious belief, with the one trying to enforce itself upon the other, has been carefully avoided. Shall we say, until now?

For years now, we have witnessed the agony of Northern Ireland, where economics, politics and religion have become inextricably intertwined. Yet both factions accept the most basic of Christian principles, "Do unto others as ye would have them do unto you."

The doing has turned to killing, bombing, destroying and hating. It seems more like the antique justice, "An eye for an eye, a tooth for a tooth."

We cannot let our nation be torn by such abominable strife.

Yet the hearings before the Senate sub-committee on the abortion bill have been stacked to allow the bulk of the testimony reflecting the pro-life, admittedly Catholic, point of view. Many of the groups gathered under the Moral Majority banner share this view.

But the fact remains that there are millions who do not subscribe to the idea that abortion equates with killing a human being. It is, in fact, often as natural a process as conception. For one reason or another, nature causes a fetus to be rejected by the mother's body.

The state has no business to interfere, for reasons of religious belief of some of its citizens, with the most intimate aspect of a woman's life. The bearing of a child is unique to women, and no male senator or pastor or priest or pope can fully experience the process.

This is an imperfect world, as all of us would admit. Legal, medically safe abortion is needed as a procedure to correct pregnancies that never should have happened. The decision should be only in the hands of the woman and her doctor.

It is unlikely that the Senate committee will have the courage to reject the abortion bill. The political threat of the religiously oriented pressure groups is very strong.

Yet, if the committee acceeds to the protestations of the groups, it will have rejected the greatest principle of the American Constitution: separation of government and religion.

The present threat of wrath from the religious know-it-alls will be as nothing to the wrath of the generality of American citizens betrayed.

THE EMPORIA GAZETTE

Emporia, KS, July 11, 1981

SOME few Senators made the news Thursday by approving in a Senate sub-committee legislation defining life as beginning at conception. Perhaps now they will attack the question of how many angels a pinhead will hold.

Certainly the state has the duty to protect the lives of its citizens. But the Senators who will later consider this legislation should be warned that the bill, which extends full Constitutional rights to the unborn, would deprive some women of the right to their own lives.

—

Consider the mother who becomes pregnant and then discovers she has a medical problem that would make that pregnancy fatal; think about the other children she might leave motherless. Consider a young victim of incest, something that does occur even though society wishes it did not. Consider the rape victim who would be forced to bear the child of her attacker or be accused of murder.

And then consider the audacity of would-be philosophers who take precious time away from their legislative business to dispute a question that philosophers and theologians have battled with for centuries. As individuals, they have every right to come to such a decision. As legislators, they are wasting their time and the time of their constituents.

—

The abortion issue is a difficult one. It is proper for a legislature to enact rules regulating the practice of abortion, which has been legal in this country for the last eight years. But it is not proper for legislators to base their laws on generalized moral decisions.

Amending the Constitution or drafting Federal legislation is not the way to settle moral arguments. — V.A.R.

Roanoke Times & World-News

Roanoke, VA, July 14, 1981

The battle against abortions of convenience won't be won or lost in the legislative halls or in the court chambers. It will be won or lost in the hearts and minds of Americans. And hearts and minds of thoughtful people are not to be won over by suppressing evidence.

So foes of easy abortion should wince painfully at news of the suppression of an 11-page statement detailing the purported favorable effects of abortion. The statement was prepared by Dr. Willard Cates Jr., chief of abortion surveillance at the National Center for Disease Control.

He was to testify before a Senate Judiciary subcommittee last May. But his superiors, including Health and Human Services Secretary Richard S. Schweiker, replaced him at the hearing with another CDC official, who gave a three-page report omitting most of the information. Schweiker opposes abortion and favors a constitutional amendment to ban it. The Judiciary subcommittee voted in favor of a bill to define the moment of conception as the beginning of human life—thus establishing the fetus as a "person" with rights protected by the Constitution.

Cates' statement said that legal abortions have produced a dramatic decline in abortion-related illnesses. They have cut back on the number of abortion-related deaths and dramatically reduced the number of hospital beds occupied by women suffering complications of abortion.

Advances in surgical methods, Cates maintained, have made abortion safer than childbirth (for the mother, that is; abortion means death to the fetus). Legal abortion has helped reduce the number of high-risk teen-age marriages. And amniocentesis, permitting doctors to identify and abort abnormal fetuses, has led to 10 percent more childbearing in families with genetic risks.

None of these findings undermines the basic premise of those who oppose easy abortions: that the aborting of a fetus represents the taking of a human life. Instead of rebutting the findings, Schweiker and his anti-abortion allies chose to suppress them. They thereby reinforced the widely held belief that foes of abortion are a group of narrow-minded zealots eager to enforce their morality on the rest of the nation.

The Senate's attempt to define the beginning of life is as misguided as the Supreme Court's attempt to establish the moment of viability for a fetus. The court chose to speak boldly where the Constitution remained silent. The Senate is attempting to amend the constitution by statute.

If the Senate action finds its way into the lawbooks, it will be another noble experiment doomed to failure. Until the preponderance of American public opinion holds casual sex to be immoral and abortion to be repugnant, laws and court rulings will not stop the practice. They may indeed multiply its evils.

Political hit lists and one-sided congressional hearings will not bring about that change in the moral climate. Neither will suppressing of evidence from the other side. Millions of reasonable prople need to be convinced, and they will not be convinced by gagging opposing witnesses.

CHICAGO Sun-Times
Chicago, IL, September 22, 1981

As we mentioned Tuesday, a Senate sub-committee headed by Sen. John East (R-N.C.) is taking medical testimony this week on the question of when human life begins.

East and his anti-abortion crowd have unfortunately stacked the deck to fit their own narrow view: that life legally begins at the very moment of conception, so every protection of U.S. law ought to extend to a fertilized egg. That, of course, would ban abortion, as well as many conventional forms of birth control and many widely needed medical procedures for pregnancies that go awry.

But East and his panel are unlikely to hear that. They've ruled it out, and their dealings with the obstetrics-gynecology faculty of Northwestern University Medical School and Northwestern Memorial Hospital show how.

Its Prentice pavilion is one of the foremost women's facilities in the country, its faculty, staff and students among the most respected.

Members of its obstetrics-gynecology department asked to testify: "There is no medical and/or scientific evidence to document when life begins" and "the question ... must remain in the area of philosophical discourse because of the absence of accurate medical or scientific documentation."

No thanks, said the committee. Dr. Louis Keith would not be allowed to speak on behalf of the department. Why? Because the "hearings will address only the question of when human life begins." Which is *precisely* what Keith addressed, but the "wrong" way.

At last count, 31 Prentice staff members, 15 residents, 78 medical students and 34 nurses indicated their agreement with the statement—and their fury that the panel ignored it. Others didn't agree with the statement, but are still irate that it was not given a fair hearing. But then, who can expect fairness when ideology's the issue, not facts?

The News and Courier
Charleston, SC, August 12, 1981

Life begins when it begins.

Neither philosphers nor medical practitioners have been able to reach a consensus as to exact timing. Maybe they never will. The fear that they won't seems to a principal factor behind an effort to push through Congress a law which defines the start of life as the moment of conception.

The S.C. Board of Health and Environmental Control recently passed a resolution opposing that move. That took some courage. The board may draw criticism but it was nonetheless the right thing to do.

As the board sought to point out, the debate between abortionists and anti-abortionists about when life begins is primarily personal, religious, and moral. We should have had our fill by now of trying to legislate such questions. The Board of Health and Environmental Control has set a good example for us all by refusing to get mixed up with a misguided effort to rush to conclusions which may have to await the judgment of the ages.

San Francisco Chronicle
San Francisco, CA, June 4, 1981

THE UNITED STATES CONGRESS is not, and we believe never could be, a competent tribunal for deciding the question of when human life begins, which is partly a philosophical question, partly theological and partly scientific.

The current Senate hearings on the proposed anti-abortion bill show that the question probably cannot be resolved rationally to the general satisfaction. Apart from its competence to decide the issue, which is altogether doubtful, Congress would necessarily have to decide it in terms of only one of these intellectual disciplines, to the exclusion of the others from consideration. That would be satisfactory to practically no one.

In 1973, the U. S. Supreme Court came to a definition of when life begins which was broadly satisfying because it was a negative one. The court concluded that it could not determine when human life begins, and therefore could not reach a finding as to whether abortion amounted to the taking of a human life.

THE WISDOM OF THE COURT in confessing an inability to decide comes through strongly to us when we listen to the passionate arguments in the Senate, wherein the exponents of one view or another fulminate in helpless anger. There are some issues about which people feel so passionately and with such variations of conviction that a democratic state simply should not attempt to impose its judgment. The Gallup poll consistently reveals how completely and agonizingly divided on the subject of abortion people are.

When we pass to other abortion deliberations currently going on in Congress, we come to the question of taking away the right of abortion from poor women who cannot prove that the choice for them is their baby's or their own life. The reasoning of the legislators seems utterly indefensible. They are proposing to invoke restrictions allowing for payment by Medicaid only if the poor mother's life is at stake. This malignant discrimination against the poor on the irrelevant question of ability to pay is a cause for real despair.

THE CONFERENCE COMMITTEE sitting in judgment of the matter has done one thing, however, that we welcome. It has refused to extend restrictions on the right of abortion to female federal employees who contribute to a government health plan and who look to the plan to cover the cost.

Pittsburgh Post-Gazette
Pittsburgh, PA, June 6, 1981

To some extent it was a media event, the genial joint appearance of Archibald Cox and Robert Bork this week at a Senate hearing on anti-abortion legislation. For what attracted the cameras was not the fact that these two lawyers both served as solicitor general of the United States. The "angle" was that in 1973, in what soon became known as the Saturday Night Massacre, Mr. Bork, Richard Nixon's acting attorney general, fired then-Special Prosecutor Cox for seeking incriminating Watergate tapes.

But while their long-ago differences over Watergate made them sensationally strange witness-table fellows, it was the two scholars' philosophical differences that made their appearance together significant.

Mr. Cox, a longtime Harvard professor and current head of Common Cause, is one of the nation's best-known liberal constitutionalists. Mr. Bork, who teaches at Yale, is one of its foremost "strict constructionists." Their political as well as their legal philosophies place the two scholars more than a few ideological gradations apart.

Yet both men spoke up in the Senate against a proposed effort by right-wing senators to overrule the Supreme Court's abortion rulings with a simple statute proclaiming that a fetus is a "person" under the Fourteenth Amendment from the moment of conception. Mr. Bork joined with Mr. Cox in denouncing that end-run as an unconstitutional attack on the independence of the judiciary.

In their view — and in that of six former attorneys general — those intent on overruling the court's abortion decisions must do so through the deliberately laborious process of amending the Constitution. Additionally, Mr. Bork, who has disagreed with the high court's abortion rulings, argued that "the deformation of the Constitution is not properly cured by former deformations."

Attempting to substitute Congress' view of the Fourteenth Amendment for the high court's is the most objectionable feature of the proposed "human life statute." But the bill also would attempt to circumvent pro-abortion rulings by denying lower federal courts — but not the Supreme Court — jurisdiction over abortion-related cases. Overruling unpopular decisions by tinkering with federal courts' jurisdiction is a strategem that is also being pursued by congressmen unhappy with rulings on school prayer and busing.

There is marginally more support among legal experts for this approach than for the proposal to define fetuses as constitutionally protected "persons." But many constitutional scholars have been critical of that provision as well — and for good reasons. Congress' constitutional power to define the jurisdiction of the courts is essentially a neutral housekeeping function. To turn it into a mechanism for overruling specific decisions Congress happens to dislike is to distort its purpose, and to set the stage for wholesale amendment of the Constitution through the back door of simple legislation. This approach is also an attack on the discretion of the Supreme Court, which, after all, is at present free to strike down lower-court rulings on abortion it finds unsound.

Abortion is obviously a controversial and an emotional issue. Opponents of abortion have the right to challenge its legalization — but not by an attack on the separation of powers that has served the nation well through all sorts of controversies.

ARKANSAS DEMOCRAT
Little Rock, AR, May 27, 1981

Hearings have resumed on Sen. Jesse Helms' "life definition" bill, and the opposition is out in force against it. No wonder. If the bill should become law – and if the Supreme Court should let it stand – abortions would just about cease in this country.

For the Helms bill defines life as beginning at conception. Its strategy is to fill a vacuum left by the high court which, in its 1973 abortion decision, declined to define the beginning point of life. That being so, it's argued, a congressional definition would withstand review by that court.

That might or might not prove to be the case. But, meanwhile, the arguments against the Helms definition are remarkable for their evasiveness. They either (1) concern themselves with the bad consequences of defining the beginning of life in such terms or (2) try to turn the question into one of whether a "human" exists from the point of conception.

Of all the supposed bad consequences, only one is persuasive. Some doctors testify that if a fetus had a right to life from the moment of conception, they could no longer diagnose, treat and cure various diseases in pregnant women with the freedom they do now. The point is well taken – though the basic definition of life's beginning could be supplemented, for medical purposes, to give a mother's life the primacy over the unborn it has always had.

Apart from the medical question, though, arguments against the evil consequences of the Helms' definition are less than weighty. There are warnings of a revival of the backroom butchery of illegal abortions, of the poor prospects unwanted babies of the poor will face, of the inability of the teenaged pregnant to recoup their mistakes, of the definition's being an attack on women and women's rights – and even of its imposing a sectarian religious view on a whole population.

Granted, undoubted social and economic problems do flow from bearing unwanted children. But that's been true since the human race began. Society can't guarantee ideal postnatal conditions for unwanted children or any other children. The question is simply one of whether society owes everybody the constitutional right of life from the beginning, the beginning being constitutionally defined.

In their 1973 decision, the Supreme Court justices shirked any such definition – declaring that it wasn't a concern of judges. They did so because they wanted to legalize abortion – and went on from there to define a "viable" human being as one a few months advanced in pre-natal life.

Helms goes back to the beginning, arguing uncompromisingly that "viable" isn't the issue, that the human being is implicit in the union of sperm and egg. That's a facer for the opposition; for that definition of life's beginning is so baldly and exactly factual as to be unarguable.

If the same showing of cause and effect could be made for, say, evolution, as for the beginning of life, those people who argue so absolutely for evolution (and many will be found in the anti-Helms camp) would have the conclusive proof for the world's beginning that they don't now have.

Yet, even Helms' definition can be improved on. For life never stops and starts; life is continuous. Conception simply bridges and extends the generations – instantaneously recreating in a new combination the common force that animates all mankind.

Whatever the cautionary social and medical arguments in favor of abortion and against giving the unborn a pre-natal guarantee of life, they're irrelevant to any definition of life. The foes of the definition that Helms so uncompromisingly supplies know that is the case. What they say proves it; so does what they don't say.

THE BLADE
Toledo, OH, June 12, 1981

PRESIDENT Reagan has forged a remarkable consensus on Capitol Hill and, it appears, in the country at large for his economic programs in Congress. But the ill-timed and ill-advised efforts by right-wing members of Congress to enact a statute defining when human life begins is a time bomb that the Administration should do its best to defuse.

On the face of it, as Sen. John East of North Carolina puts it, this is merely legislation that would declare, for legal and constitutional purposes, that "human life shall be deemed to exist from conception." But its ramifications extend far beyond that seemingly simple and limited objective.

If it became law, it would set up conflicting legal rights between a mother and her unborn child. It could raise questions as to the legality of intrauterine contraceptive devices or prenatal tests to determine the health of a fetus. It could result in the prosecution for murder of one who performs or submits to an abortion. And even miscarriages might result in investigations for involuntary manslaughter.

The American Medical Association has become sufficiently alarmed about the tenor of Senator East's hearings to announce that it will send spokesmen to testify against the human-life measure. The AMA position is that there is no consensus on the question of when human life begins and that the legislation would set up two legal persons in the same body, thus posing real problems for doctors attempting to treat pregnant women.

Senator East has attempted to soft-pedal the matter himself by saying that his proposal is "a gentle prodding" of the U.S. Supreme Court to reconsider its 1973 abortion decision. But the proposal is more than gentle prodding. One section, for example, would deprive federal courts other than the Supreme Court of the power to interfere with the operation of state anti-abortion laws. This means that a pregnant woman might have no legal recourse if she felt her constitutional rights were being violated.

Congress already has acted on a bill imposing the strictest limits ever imposed on federal financing of abortions for the poor, including banning federal medical payments for abortions unless the mother's life is in danger. The new restrictions specifically remove rape and incest as grounds for women to qualify for medicaid funds for ending pregnancies.

This seems heartless enough, but it is at least within the scope of Congress' power of the purse. And it is in accord with recent surveys showing that while the public widely condones the right of personal choice for abortion, there is considerable opposition to using public funds to pay for abortions.

The human-life legislation, however, is basically unenforceable unless police could be installed in every gynecology ward or physician's office. A recent survey of 1,533 Americans showed that almost three-fourths of the respondents had little confidence that a flat ban on abortions — which the proposal before Senator East's subcommittee amounts to — would work.

It is little short of amazing that in the face of such overwhelming public acceptance or tolerance of abortions — including tests at the ballot box — that efforts to end them have become the primary social goal of the resurgent right wing in Congress. One suspects that abortions are seen as a symbol of everything these forces view as wrong and permissive in our society.

Mr. Reagan, despite his avowed opposition to abortions, should not lend his name and prestige to the misnamed human-life bill.

THE ARIZONA REPUBLIC
Phoenix, AZ, March 30, 1981

ABORTION — the issue which the U.S. Supreme Court thought it settled in 1973 — is as alive and controversial as ever.

Anti-abortionists have embarked on a new legislative approach — known as the "Human Life Bill" — introduced in both houses of Congress.

Congress would declare in the legislation that human life begins at conception and the fetus is a "person" under terms of the 14th Amendment.

Thus, both the mother and doctor involved in the recent Phoenix hospital case in which an infant survived an abortion attempt might have been deterred by such congressional action.

The Congress would be supporting state statutes banning or restricting abortion. This would set the stage for another constitutional showdown with the Supreme Court on the issue.

Supporters believe the bill has a chance of enactment in the current Congress. However, whether it does or not, the arguments of "pro-life" groups appear certain to receive considerable public exposure.

The bill indicates a new strategy by the anti-abortionists — placing less emphasis on a long-term constitutional anti-abortion amendment requiring two-thirds approval of the Congress and focusing on a more immediate showdown.

Those who support the legislation also continue to spotlight the issue as a reminder to President Reagan that he campaigned on the promise to appoint "pro-life jurists" to the Supreme Court. One or more pro-abortion justices may step down in the new few years because of health or age.

Terrifying examples, such as the recent Phoenix hospital case, continue to plague the abortion movement.

However, events seem to indicate that the moral determination and political tenacity of the pro-life groups will remain the focus of keeping the controversy alive for years to come.

THE ☼ SUN

Baltimore, MD, September 5, 1981

The so-called "human life" bill in the Senate says, among other things, that "Congress finds that present day scientific evidence indicates a significant likelihood that actual human life exists from conception."

Most scientists would say that scientific evidence doesn't indicate *anything* about when human life starts, and can't. Some of them are upset with the bill —which would extend constitutional protections to fetuses and thereby overturn the Supreme Court's 1973 decision allowing abortions—for including this reference at all. Whatever the merits of other arguments for the bill, it starts off with a false step by invoking a scientific imprimatur for its authors' beliefs where none exists, or could ever exist.

The problem is not that scientists lack scientific evidence, but rather that they lack *moral authority*, to say that human life starts at a particular point. Some sort of creature lives in the womb immediately following conception, all scientists would agree. But as Dr. Leon Rosenberg of the Yale Medical School testified at hearings, why should scientists have any more right than anyone else to presume to say what that creature's moral status is? "Ask your conscience, your minister, your priest, your rabbi—or even your God— because it is in their domain that this matter resides," Dr. Rosenberg told the legislators. In other words, some scientists might vote for the bill, and others vote against it, but most would say their choice had nothing whatever to do with science.

The authors of the human life bill often style themselves as leaders of a movement to return to religious values. But in this case they have invoked not only religious authority but also what they apparently regard as the leading secular authority, science. In so doing, they have betrayed their lack of understanding of what science is all about.

THE LOUISVILLE TIMES

Louisville, KY, September 28, 1981

With increasing good sense, legal scholars are showing why Congress must not do what wiser heads have been unable to do since the dawn of time — define when life begins.

An intensive movement is being mounted to pass a bill which states that life begins at the moment of conception. The measure is a reaction to the 1973 Supreme Court decision which struck down most state laws prohibiting abortions at least during a woman's first three months of pregnancy.

A definition of when life begins was impossible, the high court declared. Under the 14th Amendment, however, Justice Blackmun noted that government must protect every person's right to enjoy life, liberty and property. "When those trained in the respective disciplines of medicine, philosophy and theology are unable to arrive at any consensus," he wrote, "the judiciary, at this point in the development of man's knowledge, is not in a position to speculate as to the answer."

Until the fetus was capable of life outside the mother's womb, the court concluded, the woman's right to obtain an abortion transcended the right of the government to protect the life of the unborn child.

In the current issue of the *American Bar Association Journal*, Washington lawyer Charles E. M. Kolb, argues that a law defining when life begins would create "a social problem of immense practical significance." However, it is less difficult, he says, to define what is a person, entitled to the rights granted by the Constitution.

Traditional Western philosophy, he writes, defines "person" as "the simultaneous functioning of mind and body, working together in the same organism." Those functions occur sometime after a certain stage of pregnancy [which differs in every woman's case] and "until this point, freedom to abort must prevail," he states.

The beauty of the Supreme Court's decision is that it protects the rights of all. Those who sincerely believe, as many people do, that life is sacred from the moment of conception are under no compulsion to obtain abortions. And those who don't agree are entitled — during at least the initial period of pregnancy — to abort.

Among the difficulties with a law defining when life begins is that it would also make illegal many commonly used forms of contraception. Again, support or opposition to birth control varies according to religious faiths or social mores — but its use is something that must be determined by those who use it, not by the state.

Another problem that Mr. Kolb notes is that if Congress creates its own definition of when life begins, despite the Supreme Court's refusal to do so, it would be an "unconstitutional step in violation of the separation of powers.

"The proposed ... statute is in effect a bold attempt by some members of Congress to usurp the role of the judiciary," which Mr. Kolb fears would be "one of the most Draconian and potentially divisive legislation exercises since Prohibition."

Just last week, a coalition of 72 anti-abortion organizations urged President Reagan to drop his support for a constitutional amendment that would outlaw abortion and to get behind the push for the bill instead. They contend that it would be faster and achieve the same purpose as an amendment.

What these groups refuse to accept is that their opposition to abortion, like their beliefs on subjects ranging from the Transfiguration of Christ to the seven-day creation, are not shared by all. Our system protects the right of every citizen to worship as he chooses or to believe whatever he will as long as he does not endanger the rights of others to do the same.

Passage of a bill defining human life embraces but one set of beliefs. And that means no individual could be sure that additional laws won't be passed limiting his freedom to act in other areas as well.

☼ The Knickerbocker News

Albany, NY, September 10, 1981

There is much to be said for persistence: sometimes it pays off against overwhelming odds. But this is hardly a comforting thought as Congress returns to face new issues, such as further budget cuts and a brake on military spending, and old issues that won't go away — abortion, busing and school prayer.

Although it seems like a long time since the Supreme Court ruled on the latter issues, opponents of the court's rulings, led by Sen. Jesse Helms, R-N.C., have been devising ways to overturn them on Capitol Hill. Regardless of where one stands on the issues themselves, the idea of Congress as an appellate division of the Supreme Court would not serve well either the judicial or the legislative branch.

To nullify the court's ruling on abortion, Sen. Helms would bypass the route of a constitutional amendment, which most legal experts view as the correct method for overturning a high court decision. But Sen. Helms is pushing a law to erase the Supreme Court's view that a fetus is not a person and stipulate instead that life begins at conception. This law would be used as a stop-gap until a constitutional amendment is enacted. Any action on the bill, however, is pending until the Senate completes hearings this fall on a constitutional amendment banning abortion.

On the issue of school prayer, Helms contends that the Supreme Court rulings in 1962-63, in effect, established a religion of secularism, and he has proposed a statute to correct this "judicial usurpation of power." The bill has come close to passing previous congresses.

The school busing issue has set off a Senate filibuster this year that has held up action on a Justice Department authorization bill. An amendment sponsored by Sen. Bennett Johnston, D-La., would forbid federal judges from ordering busing if students were to be taken more than five miles from their homes.

The opponents of these bypass attempts are formidable, however, and their reasoning exposes the sophistry.

For example, the American Bar Association has long, and rightly, maintained: "It is difficult to conceive of an independent judiciary if it must decide cases with constant apprehension that if a decision is unpopular with a temporary majority in Congress, the court's judicial review may be withdrawn."

As strong as the opponents' arguments are, however, the persistence of Sen. Helms and his supporters may well pay off in a Congress that is sure to be entangled in economic issues, and perhaps even vulnerable to swapping its previous opposition to old proposals in exchange for support on matters more at hand.

Before Congress gets to work on these new issues, it ought to check first to see if the back door has been bolted.

THE COMMERCIAL APPEAL
Memphis, TN, March 17, 1981

FRUSTRATED BY their failure to get a constitutional amendment to end abortion, the so-called "pro-life" forces are trying a new tactic on Capitol Hill. Sen. Jesse Helms (R-N.C.) and Rep. Henry Hyde (R-Ill.) have introduced identical bills declaring a "significant likelihood" that life begins at conception.

This legislation, its supporters contend, would let the states end abortion without subjecting an absolute ban to the prolonged and uncertain process of constitutional ratification.

Other people on both sides of the issue rightly wonder whether that is the real purpose.

If the majority in Congress were to adopt this national definition of when life begins, more would be at stake than freedom of choice for a woman and her doctor. Our nation's legislators would effectively hold that abortion is an unacceptable medical alternative in cases of rape and incest and when pregnancy places a mother's health in jeopardy.

That, however, is only the start:

• Birth control methods such as intra-uterine devices, or IUDs, morning-after pills and some varieties of the Pill, itself, would clearly violate the letter of the law despite supporters' protests to the contrary. Thus, women unable or unwilling to take the Pill because of associated health risks could use contraceptive barriers or rhythm — the two least effective means to prevent pregnancy — or they could abstain from sex altogether until they decide to have a child. Or they could choose to be sterilized.

• A woman who wants a child but miscarries would face possible court action if a government official or the fetus' legal guardian suspects she was criminally liable or merely negligent in her diet or exercise or medical care.

If these limits don't go far enough, the bills go on to deny any federal court but the U.S. Supreme Court power over these questions of life and liberty once conception has occurred. Whether Congress can restrict court business this way is a fundamental challenge to our form of government and the foundation it rests on.

GIVEN THE WAY this legislation is drawn, it could not be supported by members of Congress acting in good conscience or in behalf of all but those few constituents not content to control their own lives unless they dictate everyone else's. And therein lies the real objective.

With this legislation the radical right thinks it's found a way to embarrass and defeat those who would oppose it on abortion or the other issues on its "moral" agenda. Anyone against this measure is for abortion — right? Wrong. But don't think legislators who oppose these bills will be allowed to explain their vote when it's read and reread and reread in the 1982 campaign or in 1984. By then, their stand will be cast as an "us-or-them" roll call by that oh-so-moral minority.

THE SACRAMENTO BEE
Sacramento, CA, December 27, 1981

Sen. Orrin Hatch of Utah is the chief sponsor of an amendment to the U.S. Constitution that would permit Congress or individual states to pass laws restricting or outlawing abortion. Sen. Jesse Helms of North Carolina is the sponsor of legislation declaring that life begins at conception, thus making all abortion (and some forms of contraception) tantamount to murder. The Hatch amendment, if it secures the necessary two-thirds majority in each house of Congress, would also have to be ratified by 38 states. The Helms bill would require only a simple majority in each house and the president's signature to become law.

Sens. Hatch and Helms are at odds about the best way to proceed and about any agreement they might have had regarding the way Hatch, who heads a key Senate committee, would handle the two measures. The hardliners among the pro-life forces say the Hatch amendment, because it's permissive, is only half a loaf, a compromise with murder. Those among the pro-lifers who respect constitutional due process say the Helms bill is a dangerous evasion that is almost certainly unconstitutional but which nonetheless would cause considerable mischief, even if the courts quickly overturned it. If nothing else, it would be used to justify still more attacks on the courts for thwarting "the will of the people."

Both sides are generally correct. Whatever the substantive merits of his proposal, Sen. Hatch is taking far and away the more responsible route toward his objective. He doesn't propose to make an end run around the Constitution. Helms, on the other hand, wants, in effect, to amend the Constitution by congressional action, something which, were it ever to succeed, would make Congress, not the Constitution, the supreme law of the land.

In the final analysis, however, either choice is bad. Both proposals represent dangerous extensions of the power of government to impose the moral views of a minority on everyone else. Before the Supreme Court held, in *Roe v. Wade*, that restrictions on abortions in the early months of pregnancy are unconstitutional, there were an estimated 2 million illegal abortions in this country every year, some of them performed under the most dangerous and demeaning conditions. If abortion were once again to become illegal, that situation would undoubtedly recur: The rich, who could afford it, would go abroad to get legal abortions. The poor, who could not, would go to butchers.

For the sake of the Constitution, the Hatch route is much to be preferred over Helms' evasion, a measure whose dangers reflect in the most extreme form the legal hazards generated by an uncompromising attempt to legislate true belief. But if one judges by the standards of good sense and wise social policy, both are bad bills. The best course is for the Senate to pass neither.

Democrat and Chronicle
Rochester, NY, March 19, 1981

FOR THE MOMENT, economic issues are occupying most of the attention of Congress. But the abortion question, forever delicate, emotional and controversial, is prominent in the background and is likely to become a priority item before too long.

This time, however, the threat to legal abortion is less likely to be a constitutional amendment than a legislative action.

The constitutional change which anti-abortion forces have pressed for almost every year since 1973 is not considered to have a very good chance of passage. It would have to be approved by a two-thirds vote of both House and Senate and then ratified by 38 state legislatures.

By contrast, a legislative act would need only a simple majority of each chamber before being signed by the president. So in what is essentially an end run around the Constitution, Sen. Jesse Helms (R-N.C.) and Rep. Henry J. Hyde (R-Ill.) have introduced identical bills they say will lead to banning abortion without invoking the Constitution.

The legislation (usually called the Human Life bill) would declare as a national policy that human life begins with conception and would, according to the sponsors, allow states to pass laws outlawing abortion to protect the lives of the unborn.

If such legislation were approved, abortion would be the taking of a human life and thus a crime. Since neither rape nor incest is mentioned in the legislation, presumably the victims of such acts would have to carry out their pregnancies.

It's also being pointed out by those who favor abortion that the legislation could make illegal such birth control methods as the intrauterine (IUD) device and the pill, which prevent a fertilized egg from growing.

Although Hyde denies any such extreme intention, the fact remains that the protection of life from fertilization would prevent the use of the pill and the IUD.

Karen Mulhauser, executive director of the National Abortion Rights group, is right when she says that the legislation is a "back-door" attempt to infringe constitutional rights and to circumvent the 1973 Supreme Court ruling that voided most laws against abortion.

If, as they should, American women are to keep the right to make their own choices, they'll need to make sure that their lobbying efforts are as effective as those of the well-organized abortion forces.

The Virginian-Pilot

Norfolk, VA, November 16, 1981

For nearly a year, pro-lifers have squandered an opportunity to reduce the incidence of abortion in the United States. While a potentially friendly Senate has waited for a sound anti-abortion approach, pro-life forces have quibbled about whether Congress should define "life," whether a mother's right to life ever outweighs an infant's right to birth, and, whether victims of rape and incest might have legitimate reasons for aborting their fetuses.

Instead of debating these hard cases, they should be concentrating on the one conviction they all share—that the Supreme Court exceeded its power by granting abortion a privileged status that no state or court had recognized previously. In effect, it wrote the "reserved powers" clause—that all powers not explicitly listed in the Constitution are reserved for the people or the states—out of the Constitution.

An amendment recently proposed by Sen. Orrin Hatch would correct this error. It says: "A right to abortion is not secured by this Constitution. The Congress and the several States shall have the concurrent power to restrict and prohibit abortion: Provided that a law of a state which is more restrictive than a law of Congress shall govern."

This simple amendment has several virtues. First, it would eliminate the court's almost categorical endorsement of abortion at a time when medical technology has begun to undermine conventional views about the fetus. Physicians continue to find new ways to correct before birth abnormalities and diseases that once were considered legitimate reasons for aborting a fetus, and thus to push "viability" back toward the moment of conception. As these changes in science occur, the amendment would enable citizens through their legislatures to approach the issue of abortion anew—with a mind open to science, freed from the court's dogma.

Second, the amendment would not enter the thickets of argument where pro-lifers have been quibbling. Instead, it would give those generally opposed to abortion the opportunity to turn their shared convictions into constructive change.

Third, the amendment tacitly would discredit the "fundamental rights" theory upon which the abortion decisions rest, and provide a reasonable method for correcting judicial excesses without tampering with the courts' powers and independence. This would satisfy most constitutional law scholars, including many who support abortion, who believe that the court's abortion decisions were unsoundly based and yet who also reject the current efforts in Washington to restrict the federal courts' jurisdiction.

In one respect, the amendment could be improved. Senator Hatch should delete the "more restrictive" proviso and give states the final authority to write abortion regulations. This would permit disputants on both sides of the issue to fight for the hearts and minds of citizens in each jurisdiction.

While we have general reservations about the wisdom of amending the Constitution, the Senate should give the Hatch Amendment a close look. Politically and theoretically, it seems more marketable than other pro-life legislation because it offers something that other proposed abortion laws do not: a promising way to reduce or outlaw abortion in America without contaminating the federal Constitution. At the same time, it is a fundamentally fair approach in that it would allow pro-abortionists to have their say. Pro-lifers should seize this opportunity to build a potent political consensus while they can.

The Oregonian

Portland, OR, August 7, 1981

Congress, in asking science to determine when life begins, is asking the wrong question. Laws deal with rights and protections, so the issue here is at what stage of human development shall a biological entity be assigned all the rights and protections of the law as prescribed by a faction-ridden body of lawmakers?

Science might say it finds life that will eventually become a human being in a single zygote, or it may delve deeper and find it in a portion of a cell or virus, or even a molecule, atom or particle. But are these vital elements alive? In a biological sense? Legal sense? Religious? Moral? Human?

Science should not be required to set frontiers for life that will satisfy only clergymen or legislators bent on passing laws regulating abortions. Science should stick to learning how things work and attempting to understand biological events. Drawing fine legal lines is the business of lawmakers and the courts.

Science need not concern itself with helping Congress write a legal code of conduct that might be the product of many religious beliefs, historic events, personal views, social and political attitudes and a garden of morality forms nurtured by a variety of cultures. Or it might be the product of any one of these forces with the loudest voice.

That the laws of man disagree on how to treat homicide and murder, whether premeditated, accidental, or ordered up by the state, as in an execution or war, or conceived privately in blind rage and hatred, makes it more obvious this cannot be an arena for precise, scientific judgments. Nor should it be.

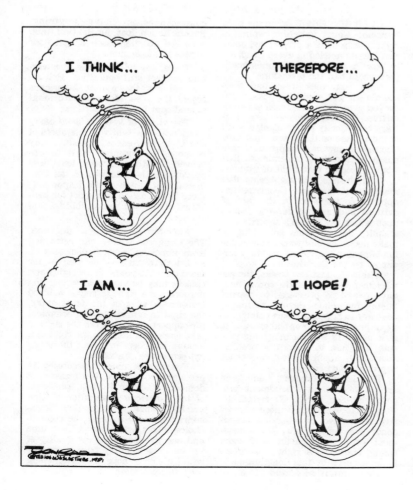

Los Angeles Times

Los Angeles, Calif., March 12, 1982

The proposed constitutional amendment to allow either the states or Congress to restrict abortions will probably die in the U.S. Senate this year, as well it should. But its proponents seek constantly to deny the right of a woman to choose an abortion, and these forces must just as constantly be resisted.

Although the opponents of abortion are warring among themselves, they still had the strength to move the amendment, sponsored by Sen. Orrin G. Hatch (R-Utah), out of the Senate Judiciary Committee on a 10-7 vote. As a constitutional amendment, Hatch's bill will need a two-thirds vote to pass the Senate. Fortunately, many senators are aware that Americans have said repeatedly in public-opinion polls that they do not favor any amendment restricting abortions.

Hatch's amendment represents a clear attempt by people holding a minority opinion to overturn a U.S. Supreme Court decision that they do not like. There has been far too much talk of late about tinkering with the Constitution to undermine the court's authority; rejection of the Hatch amendment would be as good a place as any to draw the line.

There will be a move on the Senate floor to alter the amendment to remove Congress from the picture and let states govern abortion themselves. That will make the amendment very tempting to those in Congress who either favor state's rights or just want to be clear of the issue themselves. It's another bad idea.

Sen. Alan K. Simpson (R-Wyo.) commented: "I would like to see this leave us. It is tedious to me." It is tedious to us, too, and to all Americans who think that the Supreme Court ruled appropriately in 1973 when it said that abortion was a woman's private decision.

AKRON BEACON JOURNAL

Akron, Ohio, March 17, 1982

EVER SINCE 1973, when the U.S. Supreme Court upheld a woman's right to terminate a pregnancy, abortion foes have tried in every Congress to pass a constitutional amendment that would ban the procedure.

Until last week, they had been unable to get their proposals approved even by a congressional committee. Unfortunately — and contrary to majority public opinion — 10 of the 17 men on the Senate Judiciary Committee now have approved a proposed constitutional amendment that would abrogate that right of women.

It is strange and frightening that members of the same Congress that appears so impotent in the face of critical budget and defense issues upon which the nation's security and stability depend seem so willing to make decisions that would undermine fundamental individual rights guaranteed by the Constitution.

Within the last few weeks, the administration and Senate committees have bowed to pressures to restrict busing for school desegregation — contrary to Supreme Court rulings; to deny prescription contraceptives to girls under 18 without informing parents; and now to restrict or prohibit abortion — again contrary to earlier Supreme Court rulings.

The Senate Judiciary Committee action was on an amendment proposed by Sen. Orrin G. Hatch, R-Utah, that would give more restrictive state laws on abortion precedence over federal law. The amendment would overturn the 1973 court ruling, stating: "A right to abortion is not secured by this Constitution."

The committee action alone, of course, does not change anything. But the action does, for the first time, open the abortion issue to full floor debate in the Senate.

There, and in the House, it is certain to meet stiff opposition. Poll after poll has shown that Americans reject the idea of a constitutional amendment banning abortion.

The views of voters *should* carry considerable weight with members of the Congress, especially since any proposed amendment must be approved in 38 states after two-thirds approval in both houses of the Congress. But, even more important, there is a question of respect for individual rights and responsibilities and opinions.

Abortion is a medical decision. The Congress wisely has refrained from imposing medical decisions on American women — or men — for more than 200 years. Some rights and choices may be viewed as wrong and immoral: the right to refuse a blood transfusion when a life is at stake, the right to refuse use of mechanical life-support systems, even the right to take one's own life, and the right of a woman to accept or reject the medical procedure of abortion.

Freedom of choice, according to one's own conscience, is a treasure of democracy. Mary Purcell, president of the American Association of University Women, suggests that "legislators who wish to deny the right to choice might better spend their time and energy improving the quality of life for those children born every day with little or no hope of ever reaching their full potential."

Newsday

Long Island, N.Y., March 16, 1982

Conservatives in Congress are pushing hard for action on three so-called "social issues" this year: abortion and school busing, which they oppose, and school prayer, which they favor.

So far, their campaign against abortion has stood out from the others. Instead of trying to override court rulings with legislation, which would probably be unconstitutional and would certainly be unwise, some opponents of abortion are pushing to make room for their views by changing the Constitution itself.

We think their objective is wrong. Abortion, in our view, should remain the province of individual conscience. But at least these opponents have resolved to take the high road in pursuing their goal.

It's unlikely, however, that the proposed amendment being pushed by Sen. Orrin Hatch of Utah will make it through Congress this year.

The Hatch amendment would overturn a 1973 U.S. Supreme Court decision that confirmed the legality of abortion. It would do so by declaring the issue to be beyond the scope of the Constitution. That would permit either the states or Congress to write more restrictive abortion laws.

More hawkish opponents of abortion, such as Sen. Jesse Helms of North Carolina, seek a simpler but constitutionally shakier law that would define life as beginning at the moment of conception. In effect, that would make an end run around the Constitution to cancel out the high court's finding that abortion in the first three months of pregnancy is legal.

The split between supporters of these two legislative efforts may be crucial to their fate. That split, and the opposition of people who favor current abortion law, could be enough to block either change.

We hope neither approach prevails in Congress this year. The Helms bill is simply unacceptable to the majority of Americans, who favor present abortion standards. And even though the Hatch amendment would put the issue to a series of subsequent votes—first to win passage of the constitutional amendment, then to change the law—the single-minded militancy of abortion foes could stampede Congress and state legislatures into voting for the minority view, out of sheer political fear.

Congress should leave matters of conscience to those who must live with the consequences.

THE KANSAS CITY STAR

Kansas City, Mo., March 12, 1982

Anti-abortion forces have succeeded in getting to the Senate floor for debate a constitutional amendment which seems fraught with more difficulties than solutions for their cause. Some of the congressmen who voted to send the amendment out of the judiciary committee have raised serious doubts about what it would accomplish.

Sponsored by a long-time abortion foe, Sen. Orrin Hatch of Utah, the amendment would give Congress and the states "concurrent power to restrict and prohibit abortions." The 50 states, however, could enact laws which are more restrictive in abortion rights than a federal one enacted by Congress.

The result of this amendment, if adopted by Congress and ratified by the states, undoubtedly would be a potpourri of new abortion laws across the nation. The abortion issue would be fought over and over again in the 50 state capitals, as pro- and anti-abortion forces each attempted to make inroads with their legislative bodies to get state laws on the books which reflected their respective viewpoints.

The zeal which anti-abortion activists have displayed so far makes it appear unlikely that many of them would be satisfied allowing some states to adopt laws less stringent than the federal rule. If they lost the battle in state capitals, undoubtedly they would return to Congress, again seeking more restrictive federal legislation.

Some staunch supporters of the right-to-life cause have been lukewarm about the Hatch proposal all along, seeing it as falling short of their goal of outlawing abortion altogether through the so-called "human life amendment," which has been introduced in the Senate. Other legislators would like to leave the matter entirely in the states' hands, including Sen. Strom Thurmond, Republican chairman of the judicial committee from South Carolina.

One who questioned his vote even as he agreed to pass the amendment out of committee was Sen. Alan Simpson, a Wyoming Republican, who contends that "abortion meccas" would spring up in some states. Women would travel to states with less stringent laws to end their pregnancies legally, he predicted. Left unsaid was what would happen to women in states with strict laws who could not afford to go elsewhere, but who would seek closer to home abortions which would be illegal and much more risky to their health.

The Hatch amendment would have to pass three-fourths of the state legislatures before it became part of the Constitution. But the first step is a two-thirds vote in the Senate. The predictable long and heated debate later this spring will come not only from the two sides of the central issue but from anti-abortion senators who believe the proposal is not the right answer.

Judging from the congressional reaction so far, the proposal which came out of the Senate Judiciary Committee faces a long battle among people who are convinced they have the right answer to an old problem.

The Chattanooga Times

Chattanooga, Tenn., March 24, 1982

Its zeal to do something, anything, about abortion has led the Senate Judiciary Committee to approve a dishonest and potentially dangerous constitutional amendment under which both the states and the federal government could outlaw abortion. The amendment, sponsored by Sen. Orrin Hatch, R-Utah, states there is no constitutional protection for abortion. It would allow state laws more restrictive than federal ones on this issue to prevail.

There's a catch, however. The amendment itself would not outlaw abortion. That would be done by future state or federal legislation; the amendment would merely make such laws easier by forbidding court review of constitutional issues. Congressmen, therefore, could vote for the amendment by asserting glibly that the legality of abortions remained undecided.

In a sense, then, the Hatch amendment is intellectually dishonest. Two other measures, the Right to Life Amendment and legislation by Sen. Jesse Helms, R-N.C., both of which would prohibit all abortions, at least address the issue directly. And despite laws banning the use of federal funds to pay for abortions for poor women, several states still fund the procedure. That's likely to continue even under the Hatch amendment. Wealthy women living in states with restrictive laws, moreover, could travel to other states to obtain abortions. Amazingly, the anti-abortion movement — including the National Right to Life Committee and the National Council of Catholic Bishops — support the Hatch amendment.

By far the most dangerous aspect of the amendment, however, is its elimination of constitutional protection for a procedure now legal in all states — and likely to remain so in some states even if the amendment is ratified. Under the amendment, states could enact whatever laws they chose governing abortion and yet citizens would have no legal recourse whatsoever. That's wrong.

The Detroit News
Detroit, MI, April 11, 1982

The first sentence in a discussion of the Hatch amendment, which would permit Congress and the individual states to proscribe abortions, should probably recognize the inconvenience, and indeed severe hardship, that can be caused by an unwanted pregnancy.

A woman who invites a man into her bed may, understandably, decide that the consequences are infinitely less agreeable than the cause. And, in that case, we can hardly blame her, if she is not disposed to be pregnant, for resenting the biological arrangement that forces her to bear the burden of conception while her partner can, at least physically, trot off unencumbered.

Even so, abortion is not in the strictest sense a "woman's issue." It is a human issue. Many feminists, while prepared to hurl paving stones to advance the Equal Rights Amendment, are nevertheless opposed to abortion unless the life of the mother is at serious risk, a situation that today is rare.

(Also rare are pregnancies resulting from rape or incest, which disqualifies those crimes from central consideration in the construction of a general law.)

Until only a few years ago, there was a consensus about destroying unborn children. Such a "procedure" was regarded as immoral and properly illegal. But times change, and in the 1960s a new evaluation of human behavior began to attract wide support: Please yourself, above all. Implicit in the advice was the reassuring message that people need not accept responsibility for their acts.

Ironically, insofar as this attitude was applied to sex and abortion, it appeared at a time when a wide variety of new birth-control chemicals and devices were flowing into the marketplace. In other words, just when it was becoming easier than ever to copulate without risking pregnancy, it was becoming more "enlightened" to argue for the right to kill the unborn.

By 1973, the U.S. Supreme Court had caught the spirit. In Roe vs. Wade, the justices legalized abortion.

They said that because there is less maternal mortality from an abortion in the first three months of pregnancy, states are barred from pretending to protect the mother's health by outlawing abortions. In addition, states can't claim a right to protect the unborn child in that first trimester, because the fetus then is not viable (it couldn't survive outside the womb). Thus, during the first three months following conception, the pregnant woman has an absolute right to abort.

The Supreme Court then said that during the second and third trimesters, because an abortion is somewhat more dangerous to the mother, states have the option of regulating abortions to guard maternal health. This might include establishing qualifications for abortionists and their facilities.

At the same time, said the court, states are free to prohibit abortions when the fetus is viable, which, according to the justices, "is usually placed at about seven months but may occur earlier."

In Wade, the court made clear its disinclination to place value on fetal life. It said,

for instance, that it could not resolve "the difficult question of when human life begins."

But biologists, along with anybody else who looks conscientiously at the human reproductive system, are quick to say that human life begins at conception, when sperm and egg combine to form the *beginning* of a new person. How could it be otherwise?

Still, the justices said no, that conception is "a 'process' over time, rather than an event." Yet in another part of the opinion, the court accepted the reality of a "normal 266-day human gestation period."

Isn't some kind of "event" required to start the gestation period?

To support its attitude toward conception, the court cited "new medical techniques such as menstrual extraction, the 'morning-after' pill, implantation of embryos, artificial insemination, and even artificial wombs."

How, one wonders, do those matters support the court's decision?

Artificial insemination is a technique for conceiving life. Implantation of embryos and artificial wombs are used to sustain life outside the mother's womb. Menstrual extraction and the morning-after pill are designed to destroy life.

Thus the "new medical techniques" referred to by the Supreme Court assume that life begins at conception.

No wonder the abortion issue won't go away. No matter how often we hear tales of "back-alley butchers" or plaints of better-dead-than-poor, we — as a society that values all human life, no matter how young or old or handicapped or impoverished — can never live in peace with the idea that because of the mother's difficult circumstances (if they are difficult), her developing child must be denied the right of birth.

For that reason, two measures have been introduced in the U.S. Senate to guard the unborn.

One is a bill, sponsored by North Carolina Republican Jesse Helms, declaring human life begins at conception and that fetuses are therefore protected by the Constitution. The legislation would allow the states to enact anti-abortion laws and bar lower federal courts from striking them down.

The other measure is a constitutional amendment, offered by Utah Republican Orrin Hatch, stating the Constitution does not guarantee the right to an abortion and authorizing Congress and the states to restrict abortions.

The major problem with the Helms bill, it seems to us, is that it's unlikely to pass. And, indeed, it appears flawed precisely because it is a bill and not a proposed amendment. As Sen. Hatch notes, federal court decisions permitting abortions "can only be overturned by an amendment to the Constitution, not simply by a statute."

Many pro-lifers are opposing the Hatch amendment because, they say, if Congress passes a weak anti-abortion law, or no law at all, some states would quickly become "abortion havens."

So they probably would. No act of Con-

gress is likely to eliminate all abortions, any more than laws against bank robbery have eliminated that enterprise. But the Hatch amendment would save millions of children — save them to be born, to be seen and held, to be loved (by somebody, if not by their mothers), to be part of the mysterious, awful, gratifying drama of existence.

And it would do more. It would say to the world that, even in this era of self-solicitude and ethical torpor, Americans still retain the natural sensibilities of the human race.

THE ATLANTA CONSTITUTION
Atlanta, GA, September 17, 1982

The political arena hasn't heard the last of the abortion issue, of course, but the Senate vote Wednesday muted the issue for the rest of this year — and encouragingly suggested that Congress, when it's pushed to the wall by absolutist proposals, remembers that Americans overwhelmingly oppose re-criminalization of abortion.

The politics of this issue had been all the other way until recent Senate voting, which finally tabled strident anti-abortion measures by Sens. Jesse Helms, R-N.C., and Orrin Hatch, R-Utah.

Pressured and panicked by the demands of the hyperactive anti-abortion lobby, Congress has been happy to sacrifice the powerless or unpopular. Hence such unfair bills as the ones to deny funding to poor women for abortions and to remove abortion from the health-insurance coverage of federal workers.

But anti-abortion organizations have taken about all the inches Congress has to give. They want the whole mile now. Bills such as Helms' and Hatch's could make criminals even of raped women and girls who ended a resulting pregnancy. They could imprison physicians who ignored — as many would — political demands that they sustain a pregnancy in medically desperate circumstances.

Since the 1973 Supreme Court ruling which freed women and doctors to make abortion decisions on their best personal and medical judgments, opinion polls have shown that about 75 percent of Americans oppose revival of the old abortion laws. A decade's vigorous and sensational effort by anti-abortion groups has been unable to persuade the majority otherwise.

That large and obviously durable majority ought to make Congress balk for more than political reasons. It's virtually impossible to enforce a law that would be so widely unwelcome. That's how the nation got itself into the Prohibition mess. If abortion were outlawed again, the law almost surely would collapse under the weight of its own inequities and the accumulating personal tragedies.

It took political gumption for the Senate to deflect Helms and Hatch, especially in an election year; abortion opponents are swearing revenge. The Senate has taken a tentative but promising step toward freeing itself from its recent thrall to a demanding splinter group.

Minneapolis Star and Tribune
Minneapolis, MN, September 18, 1982

By tabling Sen. Jesse Helms's anti-abortion legislation, the Senate has wisely declined to mount an attack on the U.S. Supreme Court and on a woman's legal right to an abortion. That most likely means that the abortion debate is over for the year — as it should be.

The Helms legislation was an attempt to circumvent the supreme court by congressional fiat. It included a pronouncement that life begins at conception and a congressional "finding" that the high court erred in its 1973 ruling that a woman has a right to terminate a pregnancy. It would ban all federal support of abortion.

Oregon's Bob Packwood, leader of the successful Senate filibuster against Helms's proposal, correctly observed that the measure was an attempt to reverse the supreme court by statute. In their zeal, congressional opponents of abortion aspired to do what the court prohibited in its landmark ruling: They sought to override a pregnant woman's rights merely by adopting one theory of life over another. By voting to redefine life, Helms and his supporters hoped to change the high court's reading of the Constitution and rescue an otherwise unconstitutional law.

But leading lawyers say that a law meant to circumvent a supreme court ruling is unconstitutional. The only appropriate way to alter the court's interpretation of the Constitution is to change the Constitution. And in that pursuit, the anti-abortion campaign has failed. A constitutional amendment to ban abortions, proposed by Sen. Orrin Hatch, R-Utah, has almost no chance of attracting the two-thirds vote needed in both the House and Senate. Faced with certain defeat on that hard path, abortion foes sought what President Reagan called the "moderate approach": legislation that requires only a majority vote in Congress — and no ratification by the states.

In reality, that approach was immoderate and reckless. It was as much an attack on the Constitution and the political process as on a woman's right to choose abortion. It would have undermined the capacity of the supreme court to protect individual rights from the whims of the majority. And it might have opened the door to other congressional attempts to redefine the Constitution, with worrisome implications beyond the abortion controversy.

Though Helms lost, abortion opponents vow to pursue the same tactics next year. In doing so, they would not only be working to deny women a basic right, but would also violate constitutional principles. The supreme court has said that abortion is a matter between a woman and her doctor. Abortion foes may wish it weren't so, but they can't get around it just by passing a law.

The Burlington Free Press
Burlington, VT, March 13, 1982

The stage is set for the U.S. Senate to debate a constitutional amendment that would enable Congress and the states to approve laws banning abortions.

A bitter fight is expected, perhaps reflecting the often irrational verbal battles between pro- and anti-abortion factions on all levels of society. Ironically, some anti-abortion Senate members may cloud the issue further because they feel the so-called Hatch amendment — its sponsor is Sen. Orrin Hatch, R-Utah — doesn't go far enough.

What the Hatch amendment would do if it were to be approved by a two-thirds majority of each house of Congress and state legislatures, is allow Congress and the states to ignore the 1973 Supreme Court decision that permits abortions. If a state passed a measure that was more strict than one passed in Congress, the state law would prevail.

Abortion rights groups, a majority of Americans and this newspaper argue that abortion is a decision that a woman, not the government, should make.

Faye Wattleton, president of Planned Parenthood, views the issue in a wider context. "We see this as enlarging the battle over individual and civil rights...as part of a broader agenda of repression by extremists, by those who are attempting to define morality and to enact laws that reflect their narrow interpretation of what is moral," she said.

Anti-abortion groups obviously disagree, asserting the unborn have a right to live and hail the amendment's emergence from the Judiciary Committee "as an auspicious event for the cause of the unborn."

The lines are drawn in the Senate as they have been in the rest of the nation for years on an issue that appears will never be settled. We reassert our position that the amendment should be defeated because it conflicts with other rights that are guaranteed to individuals under the Constitution and that it denies the right of free choice to the citizenry.

Detroit Free Press
Detroit, MI, February 13, 1982

ONE CONSIDERATION that tends to be underplayed in the abortion debate is that, despite the frequently passionate rhetoric, most Americans do regard abortion as a matter to be decided according to circumstances and individual conscience.

Some may be troubled over what they regard as abuse of the right of choice. Some may oppose public funding of abortions out of a feeling that the poor ought to pay for their "sins" or out of sympathy for the conscientious objections of other taxpayers. For that reason, we have periodic showdowns such as the one last week in the Legislature, which fortunately ended in the continuation of Medicaid funding to assist low-income women. But every sampling of opinion shows that most people do approve the availability of safe, legal abortions in at least some circumstances.

And that is the chief reason for Congress to leave the issue alone, though not the only one. The various "human life" bills and resolutions on the right-wing social agenda are not only not supported by an American consensus, they also assume a unanimity of opinion that does not exist among scholars in law, medicine and theology.

Most people accept that there is a period of time during which a pregnancy may be terminated without doing violence to our sense of respect for life and the rule of law. Life may begin at conception, but what we think of as humanity or personhood does not; if we believed that it did, millions of women would not be using IUDs, nor would doctors prescribe them.

There is also a point after which nearly everyone concedes abortion is out of the question, not only because it endangers the mother but because it affects another viable or nearly viable human life. And in between, there lies a vastly uncertain middle ground whose boundaries change daily with advances in neonatal medicine.

We go through this review of the obvious to point out that although it is difficult to write a rule that takes all these uncertainties into account, nonetheless the Supreme Court did it in 1973 in Roe vs. Wade. That was a commonsense solution granting the widest possible latitude to conscience and the right of privacy in the early stages of pregnancy, while asserting the interest of society in protecting the health of a mother and the life of a soon-to-be-born infant in the later stages.

As it becomes possible for prematurely delivered infants to survive at ever earlier ages, the courts and the medical profession face a pressing ethical and practical responsibility to modify the rules we are now operating under. But for now, Roe vs. Wade is the best accommodation we have to what most Americans actually believe and do and want from their government.

The "human life" legislation would throw it out in favor of a rigid ban that could not be enforced, except harshly and selectively upon the most disadvantaged or luckless of women. The human life or "federalism" amendments are also nearly unprecedented in that they would alter the Constitution to limit rather than expand the scope of individual freedom. We have never tried that except in the case of Prohibition; an anti-abortion amendment would probably be met with the same response as the 18th Amendment, and for the same reasons.

What we should do, if we have any claim to be a wise and just society, is to make abortion the *unnecessary* option. If we supported education, job training, family services and medical research with the same passion with which we debate abortion, then unplanned pregnancies and unwanted children would be a rarity, not an epidemic. Someday that Eden may come about. What we need from Congress in the meantime is to let Roe vs. Wade stand.

'LIFE BEGINS AT FORTY.'

'LIFE BEGINS AT TWENTY ONE.'

'LIFE BEGINS AT CONCEPTION !'

'THIS IS LIFE ?'

ST. LOUIS POST-DISPATCH

St. Louis, Mo., September 9, 1982

The Senate today is scheduled to vote on a motion to limit debate on Sen. Jesse Helms' anti-abortion amendment to a bill to raise the public debt ceiling. In support of that motion, President Reagan has sent a letter to Capitol Hill urging the passage of the amendment.

The Helms amendment would ban forever federal funds or insurance coverage for abortions or abortion research. There are two things badly wrong with it. The first is that as long as abortion is a constitutionally protected medical procedure, the government ought not to intrude itself in a medical decision that legally and properly belongs to a pregnant woman and her doctor. A prohibition on federal assistance or federal insurance coverage for abortion is plainly and simply a slap at the poor. Women who can afford abortions will continue to have them; women who cannot will bear unwanted children.

The second thing wrong with the Helms amendment is that it is clearly irrelevant to the principal legislation, which concerns the national debt. Worse, it is one part of a parcel of irrelevant amendments, the others having to do with school prayer and court jurisdiction. By lumping them together, Mr. Helms obviously is trying to present a legislative package that touches all of the New Right bases.

Mr. Reagan's involvement in this mockery of the orderly legislative process puts him squarely in one of the bitterest controversies of the day. It will be interesting to see whether his influence on social issues is anywhere near as great as it is on economic ones. In the latter case, at least the country has been united on desiring better times. In the case of abortion and the other hot social issues, there is no consensus. Mr. Reagan is surely entitled to attempt to create one, but if he fails he will have to live with the political consequence of having stoked divisive fires.

The Boston Globe

Boston, Mass., September 14, 1982

President Reagan spoke out last week to encourage members of the Senate "to stand up and be counted" on abortion. He wrote nine senators and telephoned another six asking them to crack the filibuster that has prevented a vote on antiabortion legislation now before the Senate.

Reagan's personal initiatives may soothe conservatives frustrated by his Administration's failure to implement a social agenda, but they are disingenous and dangerous as well.

First of all, it's unlikely that the Reagan effort will help enact the legislation proposed by Sen. Jesse Helms. Many senators are reluctant to commit themselves on abortion so close to the November election. They don't particularly like Helms' approach. They can't delay action on the debt-ceiling measure carrying his amendment beyond an October 1 deadline. They'd rather not address the issue at all.

Last Thursday's Senate vote fell 19 short of the 60 needed to stop the filibuster and bring the bill to the floor. Yesterday's vote fell 15 short. Those aren't narrow margins. Even if Senate President Howard Baker rounds up the votes needed to invoke cloture later this week, opponents have moved to prolong the debate by introducing 700 additional amendments to the legislation. Letters and phone calls from the President can't change that. They aren't likely to move many senators to support Orrin Hatch's controversial constitutional amendment giving Congress and the states the power to ban abortions either.

Still Reagan's last-minute flurry of support may work to obscure the truly insidious nature of Helms' measure. In non-binding findings it declares that life begins at conception and asserts that the Supreme Court's 1973 decision legalizing abortion was wrong. It imposes permanent restrictions on the use of federal funds for abortion, abortion-related research and training.

The bill's least publicized provision strips the federal courts of jurisdiction and permits direct Supreme Court review of state court cases involving abortion restrictions. This isn't exactly how the Founding Fathers envisioned Congress and the courts at work.

It's disturbing that the President feels a greater obligation to the conservatives who elected him than to the Constitution he vowed to uphold. At this point the Senate must ignore his entreaties and fight cloture. That's the easiest way out of a bad situation.

The San Diego Union

San Diego, CA, September 17, 1982

Who can doubt that the cliffhanger 47-46 vote by which the Senate tabled anti-abortion legislation last week "sets the stage for next year" as its author, Sen. Jesse Helms, R-N.C., so confidently predicts?

Instead of waning with the passing years, the abortion issue waxes anew. Of the various anti-abortion measures submitted from time to time in Congress, none has come so close as the 1982 effort.

Abortion was within the province of the states to regulate during most of the first 200 years in the life of this country. Local control of abortion was overturned in 1973 by a stunning U.S. Supreme Court decision that denied the states authority to prohibit abortion in the early months of pregnancy.

Had the pro-abortion advocates been satisfied with their victory in excluding the government from the abortion decision and leaving this to the individual woman and her physician, the intense abortion debate might have subsided somewhat over the years. Instead, the proponents pulled the government back into the abortion issue by arranging for federal funding of abortion. Predictably, the use of tax money to promote abortion has played a large part in galvanizing anti-abortion forces into a national crusade.

After periodic and frustrated efforts to enact anti-abortion legislation in Congress and an anti-abortion amendment to the U.S. Constitution, the issue was fully joined for the first time in the Senate during recent days. President Reagan threw his administration's support behind anti-abortion legislation being sponsored by Senate conservatives. The Helms law would have prohibited funding for abortions and included a congressional finding that human life begins at conception. The legislation was in the form of an amendment attached to a "must-pass" bill required to raise the federal debt limit by Oct. 1.

"It is time to stand and be counted on this issue," Mr. Reagan said in a letter to key senators. He termed the anti-abortion legislation a "moderate approach" to "one of the most sensitive problems our society faces."

We think the President was not altogether wrong in this position but the legislation he supported was not altogether right either.

With its moral overtones and the passionate differences it generates, abortion is indeed "one of the most sensitive problems our society faces" and, therefore, ought not to be subsidized through tax funds. The pro-abortion activists cannot have abortion both ways — beyond government regulation but under government sponsorship. State and federal funding of abortions should be halted.

Nevertheless, we're not upset that the Helms amendment was defeated. We're troubled by its flaws. In the first place, we question the competence of Congress on both medical and theological grounds to pass a law defining precisely when a human life exists. And we are troubled at the tactic of the anti-abortion forces in attaching their legislation as an amendment to a bill to increase the federal debt limit, which must be enacted by Oct. 1 if the government is to pay its bills.

Surely, one of the most sensitive problems facing our society deserves legislation that can be considered on its merits without resort to parliamentary pressure or trickery. The Helms amendment is not likely to have set the stage for action on abortion in Congress next year unless its successor legislation avoids the 1982 pitfalls and sticks to the question of funding abortions with tax money.

Contrary to some court rulings that have upheld public funding of abortions, appropriation of public funds is a legislative and not a judicial prerogative. Moreover, the best way to defuse the gathering momentum for a constitutional amendment against abortion is for Congress to prohibit state and federal subsidization of abortion on demand. We question the wisdom of trying to engrave such a sensitive and moral issue into the Constitution of the United States.

THE WALL STREET JOURNAL

New York, NY, September 13, 1982

In a vote last week, the Senate refused to end a filibuster now being conducted on its floor against an anti-abortion measure. The vote does hot end matters, though. This week the anti-abortion forces are going to try ending the filibuster again, and yet again if necessary. The controversy, as so often in the past, has stirred passions on both sides in the Senate. It has drawn in President Reagan on the anti-abortion side. And it teaches a lesson not about whether abortion is good or bad, but why people should make every effort to keep issues like this one out of national politics.

Nearly a decade ago, pro-abortion or pro-choice advocates succeeded in radically changing the legal and political status of the abortion issue. The Supreme Court said that the matter was not just another policy area in which states had the discretion to legislate more or less as they wished. Instead, terminating a pregnancy must remain a decision for a woman and her doctor during the first three months, after which the state could interfere.

In the wake of this definition of where government must keep out, government stepped in—with federal funding of various sorts for abortion. And in the wake of all this action by the courts and the federal executive branch, Congress also got into the act. Anti-abortion activists began bringing pressure on the legislators to get rid of federal funding for abortions and somehow to nullify the Supreme Court's action.

The factions of the anti-abortion movement are truly luxuriant in their numbers and variety, so we've had quite a number of anti-abortion measures introduced in the Congress. Some have declared that human life begins at conception, and denied the lower federal courts jurisdiction over the matter. Some have proposed to amend the Constitution to declare abortion a non-right. Some would have denied federal funds for abortions except in life-or-death cases.

The version the Senate voted on last week was an amendment offered by Sen. Jesse Helms to a bill raising the debt ceiling. Its combination of provisions would permanently prohibit almost all federal funds for abortions, declare that life begins at conception and that the Supreme Court made a mistake in legalizing abortion, and set up a procedure to get the matter quickly before the Supreme Court once more.

It is not the most radical such proposal to have come before Congress. It tries to regulate the disbursal of federal funds for the purpose of abortion, which Congress has every right to do. It makes various pronouncements on the beginning of life, where the expertise of Congress is not so clear. It is a lopsided piece of legislation, but that is no great surprise.

The abortion issue in this country is stuck between the claims of two demanding visions of political morality. On the one side, pro-abortion activists insist that reproductive matters are among the very last place a government should be interfering. They are right, but would be more right if they were willing to forgo public financing for abortions. On the other side, anti-abortion people say that if we don't extend our aid to the most helpless and innocent among us—that is to say, unborn children—we lose our claim to be a decent society. They are right, too, but would be more right if they were willing to accept modifications of this principle that would reduce or eliminate the incentives for illegal abortions, which inflict greater damage than legal ones.

If we emerged from the current legislative struggles with abortion legal under the limits imposed in 1973 but unfunded, that would not be such a bad outcome. But more important is that we take a lesson from this debate about how we should deal with such controversial issues in the future.

It has seemed natural in the past for activists in liberal social causes to take their message to the national political arena—where the most publicity was possible and where officials from the courts to the bureaucracies and the press seemed the friendliest. Now they are learning that the passions they arouse by making these issues national ones may be antagonistic and strong. Maybe the best course of action where the sides of an issue are so unalterably opposed is to move cautiously and piece by piece, rather than going for the big, well-publicized victory. This might not be the most glamorous kind of politics, but would be safer for our political arrangement as a whole.

The Kansas City Times
Kansas City, MO, September 17, 1982

The lengthy, drawn-out Senate debate on a constitutional amendment to limit abortion is over for now. Senators voted to table the proposal by Sen. Jesse Helms, North Carolina conservative Republican. We hope the issue will not come up again this year.

It is unfortunate that the Senate considered this issue at all. The decision to terminate a pregnancy should be left to the woman who is pregnant in consultation with her physician.

Society, and its government, does have a legitimate role in curbing abortion through other means, however. Those means are programs which dispense information about and encourage the use of birth control to prevent unplanned pregnancies. The more of these pregnancies which do not occur, the less the need for women to seek abortion.

It is disturbing that the most vociferous anti-abortionists do not view this route as the most expedient to that ultimate goal. Unfortunately, those who will spend time and money to support a constitutional amendment on abortion often just as adamantly oppose the furthering of birth control availability. It is difficult to understand this type of thinking.

An example is in President Reagan's proposed rules change to require family planning clinics to inform parents when their teen-agers are given contraceptive devices. Many who oppose abortion under any circumstances are strongly in favor of this change. Yet the result of this new rule, if put into effect, would be to discourage youths from seeking the contraceptive information in the first place for fear that their parents will be told. More unwanted teen-age pregnancies, already frightfully high in number, would be the result. Likewise, public education programs to inform young persons about sex and what it can lead to are fought vehemently in some communities.

Government needs to look at resolving the abortion issue through programs which encourage people to exercise voluntary abstinence or use contraception. But the decision to terminate a pregnancy is no more a function of government than is the decision to have a child. The Senate has done the right thing in tabling this proposal.

DAYTON DAILY NEWS
Dayton, OH, July 3, 1983

The recent pro-abortion victories in the Supreme Court and U.S. Senate have upheld current standards but have not settled the issue; they have only focused the debate. It may not be possible to "settle" the issue, but the pain of the dilemma ought to be eased.

Though recent developments are victories for those who support a woman's right to decide whether or not to get an abortion in the early stages of a pregnancy, the victors should not feel satisfied or sanguine about how commonplace abortion has become. There are now one-and-a-half-million abortions a year in the United States.

The anguish over the unpleasant options and realities has been expressed repeatedly in these editorial columns. The preference here is for the woman's right to choose in certain limited circumstances, coupled with a reluctance to give governments the power to regulate the use of a woman's body.. Yet there must be a recognition that formative *human life* is being destroyed by these seemingly abstract policies.

Letters as well as columns on our opposite-editorial pages have debated the issue vigorously. A particularly well-balanced liberal commentary on the subject, reprinted from *The New Republic*, is offered today on the op-ed page. It presents some of the misgivings and conclusions that *The Daily News* editorials have expressed.

Usually those in the abortion debate get caught squarely on one side or the other. Some syndicated columnists, such as Joan Beck, valiantly have sought a middle ground (restrict abortions to first eight weeks of conception, before brain and nervous system is fully developed.)

Some middle ground ought to be available if the polarized sides would pursue it. That's a big if. At the least, seeking a closer consensus might get the sides to appreciate some of the valid points their opposites make.

Pro-abortionists ought to recognize that, even if it is counterproductive to legislate some forms of "morality," most thoughtful people have a moral basis for their political and social views. Liberal dissatisfaction with capital punishment and some arms issues come from a moral viewpoint — fundamental spiritual and ethical views of life. The sanctity of life is not an illiberal concept, and liberals should worry when they are backed into a corner where they have to deny human life, or dismiss it casually.

Anti-abortionists ought to acknowledge that prohibition can have severe medical and social repercussions, too. They should admit that there is something wrong when a government, say, can force a woman to have a child as a result of rape or incest. (Those instances may be rare, but they have to be allowed for.) They should consider the consequences of "punishment" against those who would have illegal abortions.

Not even a more "pro-life" Supreme Court would settle the issue; it would only change its dynamics. Most polls show the American public generally agrees with the high court's stance on this issue.

Unfortunately, it is unlikely that the sides will seek a narrower middle ground that might diminish abortion as an appallingly casual method of birth control. When some issues reach loggerheads, they sometimes are resolved not by head-on clashes but by unanticipated end-runs — by changes in the society itself, or the development of new options, or different views of life that take hold. This arena remains free.

Those who are disturbed by the extent and consequences of abortion — including consequences to women who choose it — have the greater work to do; those who feel satisfied with abortion-on-demand, the greater introspection.

Des Moines Tribune
Des Moines, IA, September 23, 1982

After the election of President Reagan and a conservative Congress in 1980, many people expected that the federal government would move quickly to restrict the right to obtain an abortion, but that hasn't happened. The effort to pass significant anti-abortion legislation has collapsed for the remainder of this session of Congress.

The Senate voted last week to kill an anti-abortion bill sponsored by Senator Jesse Helms (Rep., N.C.) that would have permanently prohibited the use of federal money for abortions and abortion research.

During the same week, Senator Orrin Hatch (Rep., Utah) announced the withdrawal, for this session, of his anti-abortion constitutional amendment in the hope that it may receive a fuller debate next year.

It seems increasingly clear that the anti-abortion effort is futile, and will remain futile as long as a substantial majority of the American people oppose severe restrictions on women's right to obtain abortions. But there is another approach that in the end both sides might find acceptable.

More than a million abortions are performed annually in the United States. That statistic should disturb many Americans who support freedom of choice to obtain an abortion. Only a minority favors prohibiting all abortions. A much larger percentage of the public probably would support efforts to reduce the number of abortions.

One strategy would be to reduce the number of unwanted pregnancies by teaching people how to use contraceptives more effectively, and by more aggressively promoting research into better contraceptives. Present educational efforts are pitifully inadequate, especially in the schools, where they are most needed.

Many of the same people who are active in the anti-abortion crusade oppose that common-sense strategy. Their opposition may be understandable, given their views on sexual morality and religion, but it makes no sense if they are interested in doing something practical to reduce the number of abortions.

It would be refreshing if the abortion debate in the next Congress focused first on such a less sweeping but more desirable and attainable goal.

The Miami Herald
Miami, FL, July 2, 1983

ABORTION'S opponents had their day in the U.S. Senate this week. They argued, they cajoled, and they pressured. And when it was over, they lost their effort to allow either Congress or the states to ban abortion.

The 50-49 vote failed even to muster a tie for the proposal. It fell 18 votes short of the two-thirds majority needed to approve a Constitutional amendment. The bitterly divisive issue now ought to be laid to rest.

It won't be, unfortunately. So strong are the emotions surrounding abortion that neither side's conscience will permit it to accept any setback. And so, having failed to push a Constitutional amendment through the Senate, which is far more amenable to their view than is the House, anti-abortionists vow now to press for a mere statute, which requires only a majority vote. That path is even less likely to succeed, however, because some senators who oppose abortion also oppose the principle of attempting to overturn a Supreme Court ruling by law.

Meanwhile, the Court's 1973 decision, recently reaffirmed, stands as the reasonable law of the land. For that, the American majority, which favors flexibility on the issue, can be grateful.

Floridians should share that gratitude, but they can take no comfort from their own senators' part in the drama. Both Democrat Lawton Chiles and Republican Paula Hawkins voted in favor of the failed amendment, which said, "A right to abortion is not secured by this Constitution." Both thus voted to allow states and possibly even local governments to supersede the judgments of women, their physicians, and their own religious counselors.

Fortunately, the Chiles-Hawkins position proved to be the minority as a bipartisan coalition of senators stood firm in favor of individual conscience on this most painful of questions. The issue may never go away completely, but perhaps now it at least will subside enough to let the Senate concentrate on its proper agenda.

WORCESTER TELEGRAM
Worcester, MA, July 1, 1983

The decisive vote in the Senate against Sen. Orrin G. Hatch's proposed constitutional amendment probably marks the effective end of the abortion issue on Capitol Hill.

Although the debate in Congress may continue intermittently, the opponents of abortion have little chance of changing the laws in any fundamental way. The Supreme Court only recently reiterated its 1973 *Roe vs. Wade* decision, and the failure of the Hatch proposal seems to block the constitutional amendment route.

There are several reasons for the failure of the anti-abortion movement, the chief one being the lack of any strong national consensus. Although various polls on abortion show different responses, there is nothing to indicate that the majority of the people are willing to take away a woman's right to make the decision.

St. Louis Review
St. Louis, MO, July 15, 1983

In recent weeks the United States Supreme Court handed down a decision which nullifies the laws of several states concerning the regulation of abortion. The majority opinion in these cases reaffirmed in effect the Court's original decision allowing free access to abortion first given 10 years ago. We are once again reminded that legal rightness says nothing about moral rightness or wrongness.

More recently the United States Senate debated a possible amendment to the constitution regarding the rights of states to regulate abortion within their own borders. The Eagleton-Hatch amendment under debate was defeated and once again we witnessed the sad spectacle of pro-life forces arguing among themselves over who should be blamed for this defeat. In this case it is interesting to note that something which has been public law for 10 years and which is so abhorrent to a substantial part of the electorate is just now for the first time debated in the national legislature. Up to now the Supreme

Court through their decision has acted as legislator in this life and death issue.

Those of our citizens who feel that a woman's right to decide what happens within her own body regardless of how it affects the life which it carries are jubilant at these developments. Some are saying that those who would protect the innocent life of the unborn are finally beaten and should give up this fight. Some advocates say that pro-life activities should center on motivating mothers of the unborn and abandon efforts to legally protect the unborn child.

We agree that there is room for educating mothers and developing the awareness of the life within them. Such efforts are very necessary, but are they adequate to protect the lives of our unborn in cases where women cannot be reached or where some refuse to listen to such pleas? We feel that such efforts are insufficient of their very nature. In some way the life of the unborn

must be legally protected.

Efforts at educating mothers must take into account the God-given right of women over their own bodies. However, this is not an absolute right, but rather a conditioned one. The mother's awareness of her dignity needs to include an increased awareness that her unborn child increases her personal dignity as well as her rights and responsibilities as a citizen. For all of human history women were respected and protected because as mothers they were important to the future life of the nation or people. Now within a few years the momentum of thousands of years is thrown into reverse and unborn lives have become disposable.

We do not advocate any lessening of efforts to protect the lives of the unborn. On the contrary our efforts need to increase and redouble. Legality is not morality. If some individuals take advantage of legal options, more individuals must realize the moral responsibilities of protecting all life and thus act in that direction.

Defining 'Personhood': The Legal Rights of the Fetus

Most current arguments about abortion turn on the status of the fetus. The defeated "Human Life Amendment," which would have equated the fetus with full human life from the moment of conception, has heightened awareness of the complicated question of when a fetus becomes entitled to legal protection of its interests. (See pp. 44-61.) Recent biomedical developments—such as the capability to perform surgery *in utero* on the fetus—have also encouraged a view of the fetus as a full human being. Such a view brings with it a complicated array of new questions. In-vitro fertilization—or the technique by which a woman's eggs are combined with her partner's sperm in a laboratory dish, and a fertilized egg then implanted in the woman's uterus—has raised the question of what happens to the fertilized eggs not chosen for implantation. If, as many abortion foes insist, life begins at conception, then the discarding of these fertilized eggs constitutes murder. One commonly suggested definition of 'personhood', or the point at which the fetus should be protected by law, is one that would make it simultaneous with the viability of the fetus. The Supreme Court in *Roe v. Wade* defined viability as the point at which the fetus is "potentially able to live outside the mother's womb, albeit with artificial aid"; this usually occurs about the twenty-eighth week of pregnancy. In other areas of the law, however, the fetus historically has been entitled to legal protection only from the moment of birth itself.

As applied to abortion, a definition of personhood as occurring before birth can pit the rights of the mother against those of the fetus. The extreme 'pro-life' view is that the rights of the fetus always supersede those of the mother, and that therefore abortion is always wrong, even when the pregnancy threatens the mother's own life. The extreme feminist 'pro-choice' position reverses these priorities, holding that the mother's right to control her own reproductive processes outweighs any consideration of the fetus' arguable status as a separate person. In some recent court cases, when the rights of the mother and fetus have appeared to conflict with one another, an attorney has volunteered or been appointed to represent the fetus.

The Des Moines Register

Des Moines, IA, June 22, 1980

The ordinary mortal will have to search beyond the customary limits of moral speculation to comprehend the "wrongful life" ruling of the California Court of Appeals. If this is a harbinger of judicial remodeling of first principles, then one should be prepared for a baffling wave of assaults on the "givens" of the human condition.

Life is one of those givens. So mankind has been taught since ancient times by prophets, scholars and even political revolutionaries. To this nation's founders, the promise of political freedom was encased in the phrase "life, liberty and the pursuit of happiness." Not contented life or healthful life or prosperous life — just life. Anxieties, ill health, poverty, even deformities are sometimes part of being alive.

Now we have the California appeals court telling a father that he can sue two medical laboratories for failing to detect that he or his wife was a carrier of Tay-Sachs disease, a genetic defect borne by some Jews. The couple's 2-year-old daughter has the defect, a degenerative disease of the nervous system.

"She had a right never to be brought into existence," said the father's lawyer. Extending legal "rights" to the unborn, apart from the rights of the pregnant woman, remains more of an abstract idea than a practical contingency. Now the lawyer speaks of a right of the non-existent, which translates into a legal and possibly even a social obligation to a life that should not be.

The court decided that the laboratories are to blame because they did not detect the possibility of Tay-Sachs disease. Had the parents been forewarned, they could have practiced birth control to prevent conception; or, if the defect had been discovered during pregnancy, the woman could have obtained an abortion. Now they have a little girl with a genetic defect, and they may have justifiable legal grounds for seeking some compensation from the laboratories.

What distresses us is the ruling's implication that physically imperfect persons might have been better off had they not been born. They are victims of wrongful life — human existence gone awry because they did not match some standard of normality. Only an arrogant cast of mind would insist that the gift of life must be perfect, risk-free and immune to human error.

DAYTON DAILY NEWS
Dayton, OH, May 15, 1981

It is a joyous event. A woman who had wanted children but had been unable to have them is pregnant. But if an anti-abortion bill pending in Congress becomes law, the procedure by which she became pregnant will be outlawed and physicians performing it will be felons.

This test-tube pregnancy is the first in the United States. It was announced by a clinic run by the Eastern Virginia Medical School. The woman's name is being kept confidential. Five such babies have been born in England and Australia.

In vitro fertilization — the real name for the method — removes a mature egg from the woman's ovary and fertilizes it in a laboratory with her husband's sperm. The developing embryo is then transferred to the woman's uterus. The Virginia clinic treats women whose Fallopian tubes, the normal conduit for the egg from ovary to uterus, are missing or irreparably blocked. This patient's tubes had been removed in an earlier surgery.

The procedure runs afoul of proposed legislation which defines the instant of fertilization as the beginning of life and extends full constitutional protections to that life. The in vitro procedure typically fertilizes several eggs in the laboratory, to increase the chances of success. Sometimes several "catch." The most robust is transferred to the woman's body. The rest are discarded. That, according to the proposed law, is "abortion."

There can be no doubt that this is technically so. Life indeed has begun in those dishes, though at such a tentative stage, with a mere chemical "click," that most of us would have difficulty recognizing the procedure as a crime in any authentic sense of the word.

Perhaps, as the anti-abortion militants in Congress and outside it imply, we Americans are such a wanton and heartless lot that we must be forced, through the medium of the abortion issue, to abide by an absolutist standard that in its cause would deny motherhood to women who are keen for it. You have to wonder, however, whether most Americans see themselves as requiring such a cruel discipline.

TULSA WORLD

Tulsa, OK, June 20, 1980

A RULING by a California Court of Appeal has injected a disturbing element into the issue of abortion. The court upheld a two-year-old girl's right to sue for damages because she was conceived with a severe genetic defect.

Shauna Curlender has Tay-Sachs disease, which usually results in death by the age of 3 or 4. Her parents, Hyram, 32, and Philis, 31, allege that two laboratories were negligent for assuring them that they were not carriers of the disease.

They are seeking to recover the costs of caring for Shauna, who is hospitalized, damages for emotional distress and $3 million in punitive damages.

But the Court of Appeal, reversing a lower court, referred to the suit as one of "wrongful life." The Curlenders' attorney contends that Shauna would not have been conceived had they not been assured by the labs that they were not Tay-Sachs carriers.

Mrs. Curlender had no tests during pregnancy which might have revealed the defect and, possibly, led her to seek an abortion.

So the Court of Appeal is saying that not only do the unborn, but also the unconceived, have rights.

But if a potentially defective child has the right not to be conceived, it follows that a potentially normal child has the equal right to be conceived, much less not be aborted.

So, can couples who don't carry genetic defects be forced to bring a child into the world through a court ruling?

Further appeals are likely and the validity of the "wrongful life" concept is far from being determined. But the outcome is sure to have wide repercussions in the continuing, emotional debate over abortion laws.

RENO EVENING GAZETTE
Reno, NV, January 23, 1980

There hardly seems room in our lives for yet another major issue.

Yet if test tube baby clinics multiply across the land, we will surely see angry Americans arguing pro and con. The debate may not be as bitter as the abortion fight, but it promises to be divisive nonetheless.

We already have witnessed a preview of the battle in Virginia, where the nation's first such clinic has been established at the Eastern Virginia Medical School in Norfolk. One couple selected to take part is complaining indignantly of harassment from persons who believe the clinic is violating moral laws.

The institute has been flooded with calls from women who want to be helped by the clinic, and a spokesman for a right-to-life group has been threatening a lawsuit to prevent the clinic from producing babies. The couple responds by saying no one is going to take away their right to have children.

So all the ingredients are there for another lengthy medicine-morals controversy, including passionate feelings on both sides.

At first glance, the opposition of right-to-life proponents would seem contradictory. On one hand, proponents want abortions banned, because life is sacred; on the other hand, they want to stop a process that gives life. The disparity is an illusion, however, because in both instances there appears to be a profound antipathy to tampering with the natural process of childbirth.

It is not just these right-to-life proponents who worry about test tube babies, of course. Other persons also look askance, and express concern about possible tampering with the genetic structure of the human race. They fear either a super race, which would be foreign to our conceptions of mankind, or disastrous failures which could lead to a generation of Frankenstein monsters.

These concerns over "genetic engineering" are valid. Many questions need to be answered before mankind begins artificially mutating himself. Those questions may never be answered satisfactorily, and self-induced mutations could well prove disastrous.

But when we talk of test tube babies, we are not talking of this type of massive intrusion into nature. In fact, if all goes well, there should be no genetic altering of any kind.

Quite simply, the female ovum and the male sperm are joined outside the human body and, after a child is conceived, it is placed inside the womb, there to mature naturally until birth.

The process obviously has its dangers, the chief one being unintentional damage to the ovum or sperm resulting in a deformed or retarded child. However, the process seems to be working well in England, with no harmful effects on the infant so produced.

This form of conception could aid the many couples who are fertile, but who cannot conceive because of blockage of the fallopian tubes or some similar reason which prevents sperm and ova from uniting. Some of these people want a child of their own very much, and it seems unfair to deprive them of such a child if medical science can aid them in producing one.

As long as the procedure is medically safe — as it seems to be — the decision to have a test tube baby should belong to the couple involved, without interference from the rest of us.

WORCESTER TELEGRAM.
Worcester, MA, January 22, 1980

Probably those most enthusiastic about the opening of this nation's first "in vitro" fertilization laboratory, already tagged as a test-tube baby clinic, are those childless couples who want their own son or daughter.

That is a large constituency. The clinic announced that there were 2,500 applications from women who have been unable to conceive naturally because of damage to their reproductive organs. The "in vitro" process is one that has been successful in England. Eggs are extracted from the prospective mother, fertilized with the husband's sperm in a sterilized glass dish, then implanted in the woman's body for natural development.

While the optimism of the 11 couples selected for the first "in vitro" implants is understandable, there are still many disappointments and unfortunate events which may occur and must be considered.

As with naturally conceived fetuses, the mother may not be able to carry the baby to term or complications may develop that cause birth defects. What then? Since doctors have already interfered with the natural conception patterns will they be bound to rectify mistakes by abortion or other means? And what if the child is born with physical characteristics different from the parents, will the doctors be accused of fertilizing or planting the wrong eggs?

Already many reliable medical authorities are concerned about the ethics and the possible complications concerning fertilized eggs which are surplus as well as those returned to the mother.

There has been so much dissension and controversy over birth control methods, abortion, artificial insemination and the so-called fertility drugs that "in vitro" fertilization becomes another of these medical, moral and ethical issues.

Future possibilities are awesome. Will the successes of "in vitro" fertilization lead to made-to-order babies? Will the failures of the same process lead to an introduction of damage to already fragile life processes?

It is difficult to tell eager couples they must remain childless. Still they are more fortunate than persons who are sentenced to die from terminal illnesses that medical research has not yet learned to suppress or cure. Does their right to a medical technique that may or may not end childlessness infringe on others who do not wish to see a medical Pandora's box of evils opened, with questionable results for society?

Those are very big questions. The answers will not be easy to find.

The Boston Globe
Boston, MA, January 16, 1980

Last week state health officials in Virginia gave final approval for the opening of the nation's first in vitro fertilization clinic at the Eastern Virginia Medical School in Norfolk. The decision will undoubtedly be welcomed by thousands of infertile American couples, particularly those who've been told they can't have children because the woman's Fallopian tubes are irreparably damaged. But it will also confuse and anger countless others who believe that medical science has no business "tampering" with the reproductive process.

The birth of the first so-called "test tube baby" in England a year and a half ago proved that it's possible to fertilize a woman's egg outside the womb and re-implant it for natural development. The ensuing debate over whether the technique marks the beginning of a brave new world has been muted, confined for the most part to professional circles. But the scheduled opening of the clinic in Virginia two months from now is bound to stir up more public discussion, particularly because members of the right-to-life movement plan to challenge the clinic's certification in court.

According to a survey of women taken by Parents' Magazine last year, 85 percent felt that in vitro fertilization should be available to married couples, but only 21 percent said they would try it themselves. Many simply view the technique as an advance that could help relieve human suffering. Others fear that some embryos conceived in the laboratory will be discarded because they are deemed unfit or that the procedure will ultimately lead to genetic engineering.

Right now the technology is still in the experimental stages. It's impossible to make such fine-line distinctions between embryos or to breed certain characteristics in the laboratory, according to Dr. Robert Murray, a member of the Ethics Advisory Board of the U.S. Dept. of Health, Education and Welfare. Defective embryos conceived and implanted naturally abort themselves and it's thought that the same thing will happen with those fertilized in the laboratory. The ethics board recently completed an 800-page study of the procedure and recommended that government fund in vitro research when certain strict guidelines were observed.

Clearly, this medical procedure has the potential to be abused like any other, but it also has the potential to alleviate the anguish of childlessness. Clearly, in vitro fertilization must be applied selectively in cases where physicians and patients fully understand the risks and benefits. Laboratory conception, like artificial insemination, raises some tough ethical questions, but some of those questions can't be answered fully until the medical profession refines and perfects the procedure. It's estimated that approximately 500,000 women are infertile because of tubal damage. One of them, a Providence woman who with her husband, has been selected as one of 11 candidates by the Norfolk clinic. As she put it, "This is our last chance." It's only a slim chance because the success rate for in vitro fertilization is still very low.

But to deny her and others like her the only opportunity they might have to bring a child into the world would be wrong. The procedure itself isn't inherently good or bad. What's at issue is how it's applied.

The Washington Post

Washington, DC, January 19, 1980

SINCE THE EXPLOSION of the Hiroshima bomb, scientists have been trying to anticipate the next scientific discovery that could affect the basic realities of life and death all over the world. Having been unprepared for the moral, ethical and even technical ramifications of atomic fission, they wanted to think through the next set of questions before, rather than after, the fact. Beginning with the discovery of the chemical structure of DNA—the genetic material— in the 1950s, and accelerating with the recent development of recombinant DNA techniques, which allow individual genes to be separated and manipulated, there has been little doubt that the next area in which scientific advance would shake the foundation of our social values would be reproductive biology.

That reality is already here. Two babies since Louise Brown have been born after *in vitro* fertilization, and last week the first medical clinic for carrying out the *in vitro* procedure in the United States was approved in Norfolk, Va. But while a few researchers, clinicians and philosophers have thought much about these social and ethical issues, society at large has not begun to grapple with them. If anything, the national debate over abortion has set back the level of clear thinking and understanding of the events of early human development.

During *in vitro* fertilization, a mature egg is removed from a donor just before it would normally be shed by the ovary, and is then mixed in a laboratory dish with sperm. After fertilization, the egg is observed through the first several cell divisions, and after several days—corresponding to the time normally required for the egg to traverse the Fallopian tubes—is reimplanted in the uterus of a woman. Under current conditions, the egg donor and the recipient of the developing embryo are the same woman, and the sperm must come from her husband—conditions imposed for social rather than biological reasons.

Opposition to the Norfolk clinic is fierce. Some opponents maintain the *in vitro* procedure is too manipulative of a biological process. But they ignore the fact that all of medicine is similarly intrusive. Others are concerned because developing embryos that are seen to be grossly abnormal will not be reimplanted. This, however, merely mimics nature: a very high proportion of eggs fertilized normally inside the body are never implanted in the uterus. Finally, there are those who oppose the procedure because it is still experimental—as all medical treatments are at first— or because embryos that cannot be reimplanted might be used for research. But why not? Nature routinely discards abnormal embryos, and use of this material could provide immensely valuable and otherwise unattainable understanding of the crucial and still largely unknown events of early human development. The possibility that some misguided doctor might sequester a normal embryo for research purposes, rather than implanting it, is highly remote.

There is a clear medical demand for the new clinic. Somewhere between 300,000 and 600,000 American women are infertile because of blocked Fallopian tubes, and for many of them the inability to bear children is a constant personal tragedy. For these people the procedure would be a godsend. The problem with the clinic has nothing in fact to do with them. Rather, the risks concern the road down which this procedure and the knowledge associated with it are taking society.

A good many steps down that road have already been taken. Research in mammalian genetics and embryology has gone way beyond what is ethically or technically feasible now in humans. For example, normal mice with as many as six parents have been produced in experiments using embryo fusion to reveal information on chromosome structure. The point is not that such things can or will happen soon in humans, but rather that the time for society to begin seriously thinking about these issues has long since come. *In vitro* fertilization is basically a surgical maneuver to get around blocked Fallopian tubes. In itself it raises few fundamental ethical questions. But other procedures and experiments, involving development of the fetus to full term in the laboratory or alterations of the genes (genetic engineering), *do* raise them with a great deal of immediacy.

The clinic should be built. But the trade-off for that should be some insistence on the part of medical authorities, religious leaders and others that we begin to get serious and systematic about exploring the ethical issues and setting real limits on the future directions of research and practice in genetic engineering and reproductive biology.

Nevada State Journal

Reno, NV, January 24, 1980

A Virginia medical school has initiated a project which at once brings new hope to infertile couples and calls to arms from a variety of groups disturbed by the ethics of it all.

Norfolk's Eastern Virginia Medical School announced earlier this month it will soon begin production of test tube babies - or more specifically, fetuses which are conceived in a laboratory dish, allowed to grow for a short period of time, and then emplanted in a mother's womb.

Such practices have been the realm of science fiction until only recently. Aldous Huxley, in his Brave New World, envisioned a human hatchery and fertilizing center in the middle of London.

But since Baby Louise was born in Britain a year and one half ago, the result of in vitero fertilization, thousands of American couples who cannot have children the "normal" way have yearned for the day it would become available to them. Since Louise's birth, two other "test tube babies" have come into the world.

But opposition to the Virginia clinic promised from the outset to be strong. The reason is best summed up by Journal columnist Ellen Goodman: "To some, this procedure is nothing more than a bridge to take the sperm and egg across a gap of broken fallopian tubes. To others, it is a social tunnel into the unknown."

Opponents are seriously concerned about what can happen once control of human reproduction is removed from nature and put into the hands of men. Like the development of atomic energy, it has potential for awesome destruction as well as great good.

Such persons look with horror to a day when "rent-a-womb" becomes acceptable: when women agree to accept an implanted embryo, carry the growing fetus and give birth, turning the baby over to the woman who hired her in exchange for a fat fee.

They shudder at the prospect of genetic engineering, conjuring up Hitlerian ideas about production of a super race, eliminating all fetuses which don't measure up.

Among the opponents are pro-life groups who are worried that a variety of eggs will be fertilized, and then extras and the abnormal will be discarded with no more thought than if they were caviar.

That appears to be the crux of the matter, to persons who regard a two-cell embryo as a human being. Thus, organizations which are adamantly opposed to abortion view this clinic not as a place where life can be made possible, but as a place where decisions will be made to destroy much of the life that has been created. Such decisions, they believe, must remain in the hands of God, not laboratory scientists.

In the end, what must be weighed are the rights of infertile couples to a technique which would give them a child, versus the value of every embryo produced in the laboratory.

In considering this question it must be remembered that nature has its own process of elimination, which the clinic will mirror. Only one egg at a time will be harvested, and then fertilized, the same way it happens normally. For every 1,000 pregnancies which occur today, only 400 result in full-term babies. Of the 600 which are lost - often, before the mother even realizes she is pregnant - about 450 have chromosomal damage. Of those born, only five to seven percent are abnormal. Thus, nature has its own way of discarding the majority of embryos.

We view in vitero fertilization as one step removed from articial insemination. Both techniques are life-affirming, bringing babies to couples who long for them and could not have them otherwise.

The ethical questions raised by the approval of the Virginia laboratory are valid, and deserve the attention of other states which may seek a similar clinic.

Such clinics may need guidelines, created with attention to the very valid concerns raised by opponents.

As for us, we will watch and wait, and be very glad infertile American couples have been given new hope.

Roanoke Times & World-News

Roanoke, VA, December 30, 1981

Roanoke, VA, February 8, 1981

ELIZABETH Jordan Carr — all five pounds, 12 ounces of her — was born Monday in Norfolk. That wouldn't be unusual, except that Miss Carr is America's first test-tube baby.

For some, that phrase has a frightening ring. It shouldn't. There's nothing scary about the in vitro process that set the conditions for tiny Elizabeth to come into being. She is the result neither of bizarre genetic tinkering nor of playing God in the laboratory.

To the contrary, her conception and birth is part of a story that by now should be familiar to most 20th-century Americans. It is the story of medical science using the intelligence with which mankind is endowed to assist the work of nature.

Certainly there is mystery about in vitro conception. But it's the same mystery that exists when the mother's body, rather than a clear plastic dish, is the place where egg and sperm join. We know that the union of egg and sperm can produce another life; the mystery is how and why. Ulti-

mately, those questions are not the sort for science to answer.

What science *can* do is help things along. In vitro conception gives nature a boost by removing egg cells from a prospective mother who could not bear children otherwise, putting the ova in a laboratory vessel with sperm from the father, and inserting the result — after it's grown to four or six cells — in the mother's womb. If all goes well, the embryonic infant implants itself in the womb: The mother is pregnant.

Laboratory fertilization is technologically complex. It is, like natural fertilization, mysterious. But at the same time, also like natural fertilization, it is profoundly simple.

For some anti-abortion groups trying to define the exact moment at which human life begins, the in vitro procedure is troubling. Is it right for doctors, rather than random chance, to determine which egg will have a chance to be fertilized? Is it murder when embryonic matter is returned to the

mother's body but does not implant itself in her womb?

The doctors in Norfolk have worked carefully, seeking to defuse their critics. But the central question remains: Is the procedure, however ethical its current practitioners, another step on the road toward knowledge that mankind would be better off not possessing?

The same question, however, could be asked of any scientific advance. The key consideration is the purpose to which such discoveries are put. The new knowledge itself is neutral and, given mankind's curiosity, probably inevitable.

Used properly, the in vitro technique promises to be life-affirming, not life-destroying. It will enable many parents to have children who otherwise could not.

Science didn't create Elizabeth Jordan Carr, but it has made her life possible. In that, in vitro fertilization is no different from insulin for diabetics or dialysis for kidney patients. Welcome to the world, Elizabeth.

A people at odds with each other over abortion law may be getting experience for a harder, more anguishing problem ahead. There is developing in California the legal doctrine of the "right not to be born." If this doctrine matures (as many strange ones do), it envisions a severely handicapped child suing somebody — his parents, doctors or a medical laboratory — for making the improper decision that permitted him to be born. It envisions the child or youth (or, even later, an adult) collecting damages for the pain and suffering thereby caused.

The right to go to trial seeking damages in a case like the one described above has been affirmed by the California Court of Appeals. The suit is styled *Curlender v. Bio-Science Laboratories* et al (1980). Essentially, it charges that the laboratory gave incorrect information on the probability that the unborn child might have the Tay-Sachs disease, a degenerative disorder of the nervous system. Because of the incorrect information, the suit alleges, the child was permitted to be born — with the Tay-Sachs disease — and now should receive money as damages.

Judge Bernard Jefferson, sending the case back to the lower courts for trial, said damage could not be claimed for a full 70-year life expectancy. It could be sought, however, for the four-year life span anticipated for one with such an impaired condition. His decision (the court's decision) did not firmly establish a "right not to born," but it came very close, saying:

If a case arose where, despite due care by the medical profession in transmitting the necessary warnings, parents made a conscious choice to proceed with a pregnancy, with full knowledge that a seriously impaired infant would be born ... we see no sound policy which would protect those parents from being answerable for the pain, suffering, and misery which they have brought upon their offspring.

That has all the ingredients of a horror story. But it is fully in accord with social and legal trends of the past two decades, and we expect to hear more of it. We have already read of children suing their parents for bad rearing. We have observed tremendous hindsight judgments rendered against obstreticians and pediatricians who used drugs and methods approved at the time they were used. The next step, claiming a "right not to be born," is not to be unexpected There seems to be no end to the philosophy that all of life — every aspect of it, from beginning to end — can be wrapped up in a lawsuit.

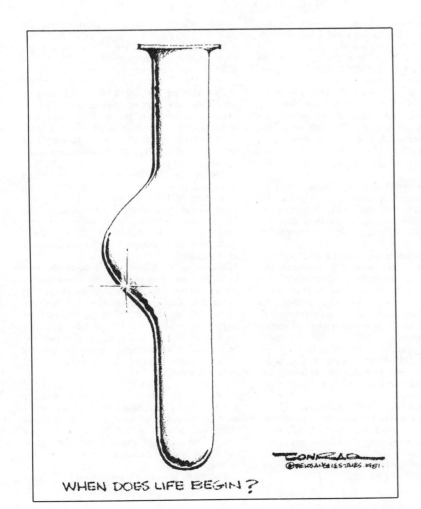

WHEN DOES LIFE BEGIN?

GASP ISN'T THAT YOUR SURROGATE MOTHER WITH MY TEST TUBE HUSBAND'S CLONE?

FUTURE SOAP OPERA

The Virginian-Pilot
Norfolk, VA, October 7, 1983

Some critics of Norfolk General Hospital's handling of a baby born during an abortion are letting their political views distort their judgment of the medical procedures used in the case.

The baby died two hours after birth on Sept. 20. The critics charge that the hospital did not provide proper treatment for the infant.

But an investigation by the Commonwealth's attorney's office — including an autopsy by the state medical examiner — turned up no evidence of improper care by the hospital. In fact, says Commonwealth's Attorney Joseph H. Campbell, the hospital "went beyond the requirements of the Virginia abortion statutes."

Is there any indication that Mr. Campbell and the medical examiner, Dr. Faruk B. Presswalla, have misled the public on this case? No. But anti-abortion leaders called a press conference Tuesday to request a further investigation. Why? Because they don't like abortion at all, and, as one of their leaders put it in an interview, the case provides a "dramatic illustration" for their side.

The anti-abortionists have raised legitimate questions about a public policy. They certainly may challenge that policy by attempting to change the state law or by bringing pressure for a change in hospitals' policies. (These issues are discussed in an appropriate manner in a letter published on this page today.)

But it is unfair to continue to imply misconduct or incompetence on the part of the hospital staff, the Commonwealth's attorney's office or the medical examiner's office when there is no evidence to substantiate such criticism.

There is a distinction between the politics of abortion and the procedures used by the hospital. Some of the Norfolk critics aren't making that distinction.

The Detroit News
Detroit, MI, May 19, 1981

A 17-year-old Chicagoan recently decided to have her 19-week-old fetus aborted. The fetus resisted the implements of its intended demise, and came out of the "operation" a tiny, but determined, little bundle of squawks and joys.

Now, the mother wants to keep her child. (Since the 1973 U.S. Supreme Court decision, a 19-week-old fetus outside the womb has legal protections as a "child" which are denied a fetus the same age, or even older, that is still in gestation.) Should she be allowed to keep the progeny she had willfully sought to destroy?

The court hasn't decided the case, and we wouldn't pretend to know what's best under these particular circumstances. But the story does raise some interesting questions that this country's militant pro-abortion party prefers to ignore.

Illinois law holds that when a fetus survives an abortion, "the irrefutable presumption" arises that the infant "was abandoned." Assistant state's attorney, John A. Dienner of Chicago, explains: "When the mother was intending fetal death through an abortion, she placed the child in a grievous medical condition. By intending to kill the fetus, the mother, in effect abandoned the child, and, by law, the child should become a ward of the state." Should the mother be judged fit in later hearings, she would normally be awarded custody, Mr. Dienner said.

The American Civil Liberties Union (ACLU), always ready to spot even an oblique challenge to a woman's absolute "right to choose," is representing the mother, and challenging the state law as a "patently flagrant and offensive" violation of the mother's constitutional "right of privacy."

While we prefer the state's position to the ACLU's, we find it almost preternaturally dim regarding the central issue. The state argument rests on the assumption that two different creatures are involved — the fetus, prior to the abortion, and the infant, immediately following the botch. By attempting to annihilate the former, the abortionist has placed the latter in a "grievous medical condition." This is roughly akin to saying it's all right to push a man off a cliff, but there'll be hell to pay if any injuries are sustained when he hits the rocks.

Don't blame the Illinois Legislature. Unlike Michigan, Illinois has tried to do what it can to protect fetal life in light of the Supreme Court decision. Elaborate legal fictions may be the only response to a court fiat that denies a 19-week-old fetus in the womb the legal protections accorded a 19-week-old born prematurely.

The ACLU's position in this case, however, is truly beneath contempt. By framing the issues around the woman's constitutional rights, the ACLU relegates even the newborn to second-class status. After all, the state is rightly concerned about the infant's "grievous medical condition," and that condition cannot be attributed to accidental causes. Surely, the state has some responsibility to judge the fitness of the mother.

But that, of course, is the rub. If the ACLU attorneys and other "pro-choice" partisans concede that an abortion calls into question a woman's fitness to be a mother — even of the child she initially didn't want — then an unwelcome moral dimension intrudes. Suddenly, the "tissue" in the womb takes unwanted shape.

And, then, the game is up, isn't it?

St. Louis ⚜ Review

St. Louis, MO, August 26, 1983

The infamous U.S. Supreme Court decision legalizing abortion was professedly an act of ignorance. The judges acknowledged that they did not know when human life was present in the unborn. Eschewing the prudence of seeking enlightenment, the august judges chose to ignore the accumulated scientific and medical evidence which clearly demonstrates that the fetus is a living human being. Instead, they opted to invent a novel concept of the right of privacy, which they claimed gives a mother the constitutional right to kill her unborn child.

The Supreme Court's action was yet another example of judicial legislation, since abortion was outlawed in most of our states, and there was a substantial body of judicial pronouncements in favor of the unborn in cases of legacies, and wrongful injury and death.

Now, the Missouri Supreme Court has ruled that under Missouri law a living fetus is legally a person. In an interpretation of Missouri's wrongful death law, the court said that a husband and wife have the right to sue for damages on behalf of their stillborn baby because of alleged negligence in medical care for the pregnant woman and her child. The special judge, James A. Pudlowski, wrote that: "Parents clearly have an interest in being protected against or compensated for the loss of a child they wished to have . . . the fetus itself has an interest in being protected from injury before birth."

While the attorney for the parents said that the decision had no relevance to the abortion issue, this is a logical, and hopefully legal, absurdity.

If the unborn child's right to life depends solely upon the wishes of its parents, then the court makes the unborn child, which it has declared to be a person, a chattel. This notion of the legal status of an unborn human being is a judicial re-introduction of slavery in its most vile form. The parents as owners of a human chattel have the right of life and death. If they want their child, he or she becomes a human being endowed with rights. If the mother doesn't want her child, he or she is reduced to the status of a legal non-person.

It is no wonder that the U.S. Supreme Court has overturned state laws calling for an informed decision on the part of a mother seeking abortion based on knowledge of her child's development and the abortion procedure. Even a few scraps of scientific information would make them more knowledgable than most of our courts.

Chicago Tribune

Chicago, IL, October 10, 1983

Surely when the Supreme Court decided more than a decade ago that women had an almost unrestricted right to abortion, the justices never foresaw the kind of tragedy that led, last week, to a physician being convicted of murder in connection with the termination of a pregnancy.

Dr. Raymond Showery was sentenced to 15 years in prison on charges that he drowned an infant in a bucket of water and dropped the body in a plastic bag after the baby survived a hysterotomy abortion. Although the mother was reported to be 24 weeks pregnant, witnesses described the newborn as weighing 3 to 5 pounds. The bag was apparently thrown away; the infant's body was not subsequently found.

Dozens of other infants have been born alive as the result of abortions. Most are too small and too damaged by the abortion process to survive for more than a few minutes or a few hours. Most states have laws requiring that such infants be treated as other premature babies and every effort made to keep them alive.

There have been other instances in which physicians have been tried on charges of killing a baby who survived abortion. Dr. William Waddill, accused of choking to death a 2 pound, 14 ounce girl following a saline abortion, went through two long trials, but charges were finally dismissed when neither jury could reach a verdict. Dr. Kenneth Edelin, who allegedly stalled in completing a hysterotomy abortion to make sure the baby was dead, was found guilty of manslaughter, but the Massachusetts Supreme Court reversed the decision.

It is a tragic irony that physicians can be charged—and in Dr. Showery's case, convicted—for murder in killing a baby outside his mother's womb just minutes after it is perfectly legal to kill the same infant inside his mother's body. It is even more ironic that the infant who can be killed legally is probably healthy and normal; the abortion survivor who must be kept alive no matter what is almost certainly damaged by the abortion process, may suffer serious, lifelong handicaps as a result of being born so prematurely and has parents who tried to end his life because they so intensely didn't want him.

The Supreme Court's 1973 decision legalizing abortion rested on assumptions about scientific facts that may have been dubious even at the time. Since then, new medical technology and new neonatal intensive care centers have made it possible for babies to survive after much shorter pregnancies than envisioned a decade ago. The inevitable result will be that more infants are going to survive abortion, although the odds are high that they will have serious handicaps as a result and taxpayers and health insurers will not only have to pay for expensive neonatal care for them, but perhaps lifelong institutionalization as well.

It is one thing for the law to uphold the right of a woman to have an abortion (that point won't be argued here). It is another matter to permit her to wait so long during the pregnancy that the baby could be born alive, yet faced with a lifetime of serious disabilities imposed by the unfortunate start in life.

The Supreme Court isn't likely to reverse the basic thrust of Roe v. Wade, the case that made abortion legal. The court has already overturned many state and federal laws that sought to put restrictions on the access to abortion. But cases like the Showery conviction make it clear that the court must revise its rulings to allow government to reduce the amount of time after conception that abortion is legal.

AKRON BEACON JOURNAL
Akron, OH, January 21, 1982

THE FIGHT over the right to abortion and the corollary dispute over the exact moment when life begins or a fertilized egg becomes a human being is a very serious matter, and has been treated that way by scientists and others with conflicting opinions.

President Reagan said in his press conference Tuesday that the inability of congressional hearings to resolve the question of when life begins was "a finding in and of itself," and added: "If we don't know, then shouldn't we morally opt on the side that it is life?"

But the President and members of the Congress disposed to accept the theory that a human egg becomes a person at the moment of fertilization should be prepared to answer practical questions that would arise out of any legislative attempt to confer all constitutional rights on a human embryo from the moment of conception.

Not the least of these will involve the omnipresent Internal Revenue Service. If a fetus, in the first or second month of development in November or December, reaches full term in, say, July or August of 1982, are the parents of the baby born then entitled to a deduction on their income tax for the child in 1981 because the Congress concluded that the fetus was a person then, entitled to equal rights under the Constitution?

Or might a fetus developed for even one month and then miscarried qualify the parents for an income tax deduction for the full year in which it existed?

The answer should not be the basis for passing or not passing laws, just as answers to questions of personal morality and religion should not be the province of Congress.

But the question of tax deductions is not a frivolous one. It is just one example of the trap Congress could set for itself if its members assume the role of philosophers rather than politicians.

Church/State Debate on Abortion Becomes Major 1984 Election Issue

In June 1984, Archbishop John J. O'Connor of New York said in a televised news conference: "I don't see how a Catholic in good conscience can vote for a candidate who explicitly supports abortion." This was the opening salvo in a series of verbal skirmishes involving representatives of the Roman Catholic Church and two prominent Catholic Democrats: Rep. Geraldine Ferraro (N.Y.), the Democratic vice presidential nominee, and Mario Cuomo, Democratic governor of New York. Both have stated that although they are personally opposed to abortion, they believe they have no right to use their elected position to force their view on the public.

Cuomo and O'Connor exchanged charges Aug. 3 on the issues of abortion and the role of the Roman Catholic Church in politics. In an interview reported in the New York Times, Cuomo accused the archbishop of telling Catholics they could not vote for Cuomo or any other politician "who disagrees with him on abortion." Cuomo said: "If you took literally what he's saying, he can only vote for a right-to-lifer." In response, O'Connor asserted that Cuomo had misinterpreted his statement. "My sole responsibility is to present as clearly as I can the formal, official teaching of the Catholic Church," O'Connor stated. "I leave to those interested in such teachings whether or not the public statements of officeholders and candidates accord with this teaching."

President Reagan brought the debate to a national level with his remarks during Republican National Convention week in August. Speaking to 10,000 people gathered in Dallas for an 'ecumenical prayer breakfast' Aug. 23, the President stated: "The truth is, politics and morality are inseparable, religion and politics are necessarily related." Reagan went on to reiterate his positions on abortion and school prayer, and said he was in favor of church leaders speaking out on political issues. Democratic presidential candidate Walter Mondale picked up on Reagan's remarks Sept. 6, while addressing a convention of the B'nai Brith Jewish service group in Washington, D.C. Stressing his belief that religious freedom was "not a passive tolerance, but an active celebration of our pluralism," Mondale characterized extreme Christian fundamentalist supporters of Reagan as a "determined band" that was "reaching for government power to impose their own beliefs on others."

The head of the nation's Roman Catholic bishops, Bishop James W. Malone, Aug. 9 released a statement asserting that it was "not logically tenable" for political candidates to say that they could separate their personal moral convictions from their public policy positions. "We reject the idea that candidates satisfy the requirements of rational analysis in saying their personal views should not influence their policy decisions," he wrote. Roman Catholic Archbishop Bernard F. Law of Boston Sept. 5 called abortion the central issue of the election campaign. "We are not saying you must vote" for a certain candidate, he said, "but we are saying that when you make up your mind, this is a critical issue." He also read a statement on the same theme signed by himself and 17 other Roman Catholic bishops from New England states. "To evade this issue of abortion under the pretext that it is a matter pertaining exclusively to private morality is obviously illogical," the statement concluded.

O'Connor returned to the attack in September, accusing Ferraro of having "said some things about abortion relative to Catholic teaching which were not true." He was referring to part of a letter, signed by Ferraro and sent to members of Congress in 1982, which had said that "the Catholic position on abortion is not monolithic" and that "there can be a range of personal and political responses to the issue." It was the first time that O'Connor, who had emerged as a leading antiabortion voice in the growing national debate on religion and politics, had used Ferraro's name and criticized her directly. Ferraro countered that her statement was referring to the beliefs of individual Catholics, and was not intended to imply that the official church position on the issue was divided, as O'Connor had charged. Ferraro, the Democratic candidate for vice president in the November election, continued to stress that she could separate her faith from her public duties.

Cuomo in September again disputed the idea that Roman Catholics in public office were morally bound to take a stand against abortion, in a lecture entitled "Religious Belief and Public Morality: A Catholic Governor's Perspective" and delivered at Indiana's University of Notre Dame. While he recognized the right of bishops to provide moral guidance to Catholics on such issues as abortion, contraception and divorce, Cuomo asserted that it was up to politicians to decide whether a consensus existed to translate such teachings into civil law. "What is ideally desirable isn't always feasible," he said.

The News and Courier
Charleston, SC, July 31, 1984

In a letter to the editor elsewhere on today's page, the bishop of the Diocese of Charleston, the Most Rev. Ernest L. Unterkoefler, addresses the question of whether a Catholic can subscribe to a double standard of morality. While not specifically mentioned by name, the center of the present controversy is the Democratic nominee for vice president, Geraldine Ferraro — a staunch Catholic.

The church, as the bishop points out in his letter, has condemned abortion as morally unjustifiable. He goes on to make the point that, as the Gospel says, Christians cannot serve two masters. Anyone (in this case, Ms. Ferraro) has double standards and is in error when she states "I am privately against abortion and I believe that it is evil for me; however I endorse abortion as public policy because I do not think it is evil for others."

On the other hand, Ms. Ferraro holds the position that, as a legislator, she feels women should not be forbidden by law to get an abortion. "I could never have an abortion, but I think you have to distinguish between imposing your religious beliefs on someone else and between setting priorities for yourself, and I think there's a difference between the two," she told Newsweek magazine in a recent interview.

There can be no doubt that, for Ms. Ferraro, the abortion issue is a political minefield. Those who raise doubts about the sincerity of her public stand on the issue versus her Catholic faith could very well have motivated her ill-timed and ill-conceived slap at President Reagan's practice of Christianity. Taken together, the two issues are related and both need to be put in perspective.

In many ways, especially for Catholics, the blueprint for separation of public responsibilities and private beliefs was laid down by John F. Kennedy in 1960 when he spoke before the Greater Houston Ministerial Association. If he were elected president, he said:

"Whatever issue may come before me as president — on birth control, divorce, censorship, gambling ... I will make my decision in accordance ... with what my conscience tells me to be the national interest, and without regard to outside religious pressures or dictates. And no power or threat of punishment could cause me to decide otherwise....

"I do not speak for my church on public matters and my church does not speak for me." In other words, he said he was running for president of the United States, not for pope.

There will be few, if any, positions taken by the Mondale-Ferraro ticket that could ever find the remotest empathy in this newspaper. But this is one. From a logical or theological point of view, nobody in high public office — Jewish, Muslim, Buddhist or Baptist — should be expected or allowed to impose his or her religious views on a pluralistic society.

Newsday

Long Island, NY, August 12, 1984

Even though Gov. Mario Cuomo obviously enjoys intellectual disputation, it was still a little surprising when he took on an issue that politicians have tended scrupulously to avoid: the relationship between religion and politics. As Cuomo himself observed, the subject is "hot stuff" that must be dealt with "very carefully."

Touchy though it may be, Cuomo was correct in raising the issue and responsible in the way he dealt with it. It's a legitimate subject for public discussion.

The occasion for Cuomo's comments on religion and politics was provided by Archbishop John J. O'Connor of New York, who said in an interview on June 24, "I don't see how a Catholic in good conscience can vote for a candidate who explicitly supports abortion."

The governor interpreted this to mean that O'Connor believes no Catholic "can vote for . . . anybody who disagrees with him on abortion."

Archbishop O'Connor later asserted that Cuomo had misunderstood him. He said, "It is neither my responsibility nor my desire to evaluate the qualifications" of any political leader. And he insisted that he had no intention of demanding "that everybody believe what we believe." Cuomo said he was "pleased" with the archbishop's clarification.

That may have ended the specific disputation between Cuomo and O'Connor, but it's far from the end of the debate about the role of religion in politics.

Even before the Cuomo-O'Connor exchange, Bishop John J. Malone, president of the National Conference of Catholic Bishops, had begun drafting a statement declaring that "it would be regrettable if religion as such were injected into a political campaign" but rejecting the idea that political leaders can separate their personal views from their public policies.

The statement appeared to challenge the positions of Cuomo, Democratic vice presidential candidate Geraldine Ferraro and other Catholic politicians who say that while they personally abhor abortion, they accept their responsibility as public officials to uphold the law and to avoid imposing their religious beliefs on others.

In responding to Archbishop O'Connor's June 24 remark, Cuomo also put his finger precisely on the issue raised by Bishop Malone's statement: Can a pluralistic secular democracy, firmly rooted in a tradition of church-state separation, function if religious leaders appear to be providing their followers with political as well as spiritual guidance?

The question obviously applies not only to Catholic bishops but to fundamentalist Protestant leaders, who have been much in evidence in the political sphere in recent years, and to any others who might be tempted to impose their religious beliefs on society as a whole.

Cuomo provided a good example of the dimensions of this problem. "I as a Catholic might be instructed by my church that birth control is wrong," he said. "If I choose to believe it, am I required to say that everyone must believe that birth control is bad and let's have a constitutional amendment to ban birth control? I don't think so."

Neither did John F. Kennedy when he was president. In a historic speech to a group of Texas Baptist ministers, Kennedy made it clear that as a public servant he placed his conscience and the Constitution before the teachings of his church.

That position — which Kennedy, a Catholic, and Jimmy Carter, a born-again Protestant, articulated and which Cuomo has now affirmed — is the proper one for a public official in this country. Those who cannot in good conscience embrace it shouldn't seek public office.

In an open society, everyone has a right to espouse moral positions, obviously including those that coincide with the teachings of one religion or another. But that right is accompanied by an obligation on the part of religious leaders not to attempt to impose their beliefs on others through the political process, and on the part of political leaders not to place the dictates of their personal religious beliefs ahead of their responsibilities to their broad and varied constituencies.

Any failure to carry out these obligations blurs the line that separates church and state and threatens this country's vital pluralistic character.

Pittsburgh Post-Gazette

Pittsburgh, PA, August 10, 1984

A brief but bracing debate over politics and religion has been brought to a close by the president of the National Conference of Catholic Bishops. In a letter to be circulated next week, Bishop James W. Malone of Youngstown, Ohio, reminds his fellow bishops that they should avoid acting "for or against political candidates."

Bishop Malone's letter is in response to a well-publicized controversy that began when the new archbishop of New York, the Most Rev. John J. O'Connor, was quoted as saying he couldn't see "how a Catholic in good conscience can vote for a candidate who explicitly supports abortion." New York's Catholic governor, Mario Cuomo, called the archbishop on his comments, concluding that they meant that "no Catholic can vote" for politicians who support the "pro-choice" position in their public lives — people like Mr. Cuomo himself, New York Mayor Ed Koch and U.S. Sen. Daniel P. Moynihan. (Gov. Cuomo might also have included on his list Democratic vice-presidential candidate Geraldine Ferraro, a Catholic whose voting record on abortion issues has been denounced by "pro-life" groups.)

At this point, Archbishop O'Connor clarified his position, stressing that "my sole responsibility is to present as clearly as I can the formal, official teaching of the Catholic Church. I leave to those interested in such teachings whether or not the public statements of officeholders and candidates accord with this teaching." Bishop Malone's statement would seem to soften even more the all-or-nothing impression left by Archbishop O'Connor's original comments. It is thus welcome in a political year that seems to have had more than the usual quotient of real and contrived religious issues.

That having been said, however, it is worth noting a couple of points about the O'Connor-Cuomo controversy.

The first is that the interrelationship of religious belief and political action is more complex than some of the archbishop's critics seem to believe — especially on the abortion issue. Opponents of legal abortion — not all of them Catholics — stress that their belief in the fetus' independent rights makes this issue different from others involving personal freedom of choice.

Where Archbishop O'Connor went wrong was in leaving the impression that a candidate's position on abortion is the only issue for a voter to weigh. That reckons without the possibility that an anti-abortion candidate might take unpalatable, or even immoral, positions on other "pro-life" issues of concern to the church — like capital punishment, nuclear war and peace and nutrition for poor children.

A few years ago, one might also be tempted to add that the archbishop erred in stirring up latent suspicions of the "authoritarian" Catholic Church, suspicions that dogged a Catholic presidential candidate as recently as 25 years ago. But the way the Cuomo-O'Connor colloquy developed suggests that that advice would be out of date, and rather patronizing.

For one thing, Gov. Cuomo is a Catholic himself, and by respectfully criticizing the archbishop he demonstrated a refreshing lack of concern about giving aid and comfort to diehard anti-Catholic bigots. His freeness with his thoughts reflects a savvy politician's recognition that America in general has matured a great deal in the past 25 years. It also reflects — as does Archbishop O'Connor's gracious participation in a dialogue with the governor — that the Catholic Church also has changed in that quarter-century.

BUFFALO EVENING NEWS
Buffalo, NY, August 14, 1984

THE STATEMENT issued by the National Conference of Catholic Bishops emphasizes a suitable distinction in supporting the role of the clergy in speaking out on important public issues but cautioning them to avoid positions "for or against political candidates."

The statement by Bishop James W. Malone, conference president, said this key distinction required emphasis lest "even what we say about issues be perceived as an expression of political partisanship."

It's a timely enunciation of policy because of the controversy stirred recently when Archbishop John O'Connor of New York said that he did not see "how a Catholic in good conscience can vote for a candidate who explicitly supports abortion." Gov. Mario Cuomo, a Catholic who personally opposes abortion but has said he would not impose his personal beliefs concerning this matter on public policy, said the archbishop should stay out of the political process. When Archbishop O'Connor denied trying to tell people how to vote, Gov. Cuomo responded that he had "misunderstood" and was "delighted to have the clarification."

The statement from the American bishops ranges beyond this one episode, touching broadly on church-state relations. Essentially, it holds that the Catholic clergy can instruct and influence with respect to public issues considered important but refrain from endorsing candidates or telling members of their denominations how to vote in partisan political contests. Members of the clergy retain every legal right, of course, to speak out on any issue and even recommend support for individual candidates. To endorse candidates, however, could plunge the church or a member of the clergy into the partisan political maelstrom.

There may be extreme circumstances in which such a mingling of church and state interests could be defended, but the distinction defined by the American bishops remains a sound one and conforms to widely held views in other religious denominations as well.

Another valid consideration raised by the bishops during this national election year is that just as the church should avoid positions on political candidates, so candidates should avoid temptations to appeal for votes on the basis of their religious affiliations. Such reciprocal restraints are prudent in preserving the delicate, appropriate relationship between church and state.

THE SUN
Baltimore, MD, August 12, 1984

American Catholic bishops have intervened vigorously into current political debate by contending there can be no disagreement "by Catholics and others who share our moral convictions" on two towering issues: abortion and nuclear war. Each is considered by the church to be an immoral threat to "innocent human life" and, as such, the touchstone on which to judge parties and politicians.

By a marvelous irony, these two issues cut right across the election battle between Ronald Reagan and Walter Mondale. Little over a year ago, the bishops were squabbling with the Republican administration on nuclear policy issues that have not really been resolved. Now they find themselves at odds on abortion questions with two of the nation's most prominent Catholic Democrats — vice presidential candidate Geraldine Ferraro and New York's Governor Mario Cuomo.

To Americans who advocate the strictest kind of separation of church and state, the present controversy represents a regression from John F. Kennedy's position that "no Catholic prelate would tell the president (should he be a Catholic) how to act." To others it seems a fulfillment of the Kennedy promise — a Catholic church no longer inhibited from full participation in the political life of the country. It is part of a global burst of religious political activism that has drawn mixed responses from the Vatican and is by no means limited to the Roman Catholic community.

The National Conference of Catholic Bishops insists it is not taking positions for or against political candidates by speaking out on public issues. But it also contends that there can be no dichotomy between the "personal morality and public policy" of a political figure. And there the trouble begins. For who is to define these terms?

Most politicians, of whatever faith, would say that their religion instructs them to be fair and honest and true to their oath to uphold the law. Both Mr. Cuomo and Ms. Ferraro say they are against abortion but will not impose their views on others in light of Supreme Court decisions permitting abortion early in pregnancy. The bishops hold that this position is "simply not logically tenable" on matters of life and death if it contradicts the "constant moral teachings of the Catholic Church."

In terms of pure and disembodied logic, the prelates may have a point. But they then have to deal with another syllogism — namely, that if a politician takes a stand on abortion that is intolerable to the church, the clergy would logically have to oppose that politician. And they also have to face up to the fact that their recent history on nuclear issues — which they equate with abortion in judging political morality — has been far from constant. Last year, the bishops softened their attacks on U.S. deterrent strategy after the White House complained of "fundamental misreadings of American policies." Nevertheless, it is fair to say that the bishops find themselves as opposed to Reagan nuclear policy as they are to the Mondale-Ferraro stand on abortion.

We do not believe the Catholic Church intends to be partisan, and this contrast reinforces the point. But in seeking to hold Catholic politicians to absolute positions which bring them into conflict with their public obligations, the bishops may be marring their otherwise healthy entry into the election-year debate. Let us contemplate.

The Kansas City Times
Kansas City MO, August 11, 1984

We had thought the whole business of a Catholic in the White House had been cleared up by John Kennedy who explained it all to the Protestant ministers in Houston on Sept. 12, 1960:

I do not speak for my church on public matters and the church does not speak for me.

Whatever issue may come before me as President — on birth control, divorce, censorship, gambling; or any other subject — I will make my decision . . . in accordance with what my conscience tells me to be the national interest, and without regard to outside religious pressures or dictates.

John Kennedy, the candidate, said bluntly that public officials should not request or accept instructions on public policy directly or indirectly from the Roman Catholic pope, from the National Council of Churches or any other ecclesiastical source seeking to impose its will on the general public. He said that no church power of excommunication held fear for him:

But if the time should ever come — I do not concede any conflict to be remotely possible — when my office would require me to either violate my conscience or violate the national interest, then I would resign the office and I hope any conscientious public servant would do the same.

So what is the current fuss about over Gov. Mario Cuomo of New York, Geraldine Ferraro and abortion? It started with a statement by Archbishop John J. O'Connor of New York to the effect that he could not see "how a Catholic in good conscience can vote for a candidate who explicitly supports abortion." Mr. Cuomo responded tartly that under the archbishop's instructions Catholics could not vote for Mayor Ed Koch, for Sen. Daniel Patrick Moynihan or Mario Cuomo, or any others who personally disavow abortion but would not try to restrict it legally — in other words, impose their personal view on others.

Now comes Bishop John W. Malone, president of the National Conference of Catholic Bishops, with a statement exhorting Catholics to "convince others of the rightness on our positions," but also telling the clergy to avoid supporting political candidates. Clear enough. But then the bishop muddled the issue with a statement apparently directed at Mr. Cuomo: "We reject the idea that candidates satisfy the requirement of rational analysis in saying their personal views should not influence their policy decisions."

But that is precisely the point. One can make a personal decision not to have an abortion or not to advise anyone to have an abortion without demanding a law saying that no one else can ever have an abortion. Isn't that what John Kennedy was talking about in 1960? Isn't that what Mario Cuomo and Geraldine Ferraro are saying in 1984?

The question of church-state sovereignty was settled centuries ago. The state has sovereignty. The churches have immense influence. Neither church nor state is a monolithic master in America. In a democracy the people will make their choices without fear of either.

Arkansas Democrat

Little Rock, AR, September 19, 1984

As columnist William F. Buckley says, the new doctrine that political candidates should not "impose" their religious views of a public issue on others is ridiculous in a government where everybody's free to politick as he or she chooses and in which the majority decides what view is to become law whether it happens to reflect a religious view or not.

Buckley is right. But there's another side to this argument against imposing one's religious views – the argument that church leaders shouldn't tell members of their churches how or how not to vote on political issues that happen also to involve religious beliefs.

Columnist Nicholas von Hoffman takes the view that Catholic Archbishop John O'Connor of New York ought not to be flogging Vice Presidential Candidate Geraldine Ferarro for supporting abortion in defiance of what O'Connor says is the church's stand against it. Von Hoffman calls O'Connor's stand political – and says that even though O'Connor is address-

ing only Catholics when he says he doesn't see how Catholics can vote for a pro-abortionist he is also attempting to "influence an election in which people of all faiths will vote."

Bull! He has as much right as anybody else. And as for his cracking down on Ferraro and saying Catholics shouldn't vote for anyone who supports abortion, that may be imposing a religious view on what many consider to be a mere political question but it's ex cathedra (official) so far as Catholics are concerned.

The Catholic Church has in fact done that immemorially when political issues touch faith or morals. For instance, it excommunicated the famous Louisiana segregationist Leander Perez for his views. And nobody, including Perez, argued that the church was wrongly or unconstitutionally imposing its religious views on him. The church can do the same to Ferraro if it sees fit – and tell the critics of "imposing" to think and say what they please about it.

SYRACUSE HERALD-JOURNAL

Syracuse, NY, September 17, 1984

How did we get into this debate, anyway?

Was it Geraldine Ferraro's claim that President Reagan is not a good Christian because of his policies toward the poor?

Did it start with Jimmy Carter's "born again" approach to the presidency.

Should we go back to 1960, when John Kennedy finally broke down the religious barriers and went to the White House in spite of his Roman Catholicism (and in spite of a deluge of bad jokes). Or was it 1928, when Catholic Al Smith lost, probably because of his Catholicism, to Herbert Hoover.

How about a century ago this year, when Samuel Dickinson Burchard, speaking for clergymen in support of James G. Blaine's candidacy against Grover Cleveland, said, "We are Republicans, and don't propose to leave our party and identify ourselves with the party whose antecedents have been Rum, Romanism and Rebellion"?

There has been more than a subtle relationship between politics and religion probably for as long as there has been politics, but never in our time have religious issues played such a dominant role in a presidential campaign as they have in recent weeks.

Blame the Republicans who have courted the fundamentalist faction on the right; blame the Democrats who have allowed themselves to become ambushed by questions of morality within a religious framework; or blame the religious leaders of Protestant fundamentalist and Roman Catholic persuasion who have pushed such issues as abortion onto the front burner.

⇨   ⇨

It's nothing new that Ronald Reagan is wooing the Bible Belt with its unique brand of God-fearing patriotism. What is new in the campaign is the Democrat candidates' willingness to be drawn into — perhaps even to have initiated — an "I'm a better Christian than you are" exchange.

For added flavor, we have the New York governor, Mario Cuomo, taking to the national secular pulpit to explain his own view of the separation of church and state, and the Catholic bishops who have chosen this election to test their political

clout. (Could this be at least subliminally a reaction to the power grab of four years ago by the Jerry Falwells of this land?)

The unsettling part of this exercise in "religitics" (or would it be "politigion"?) is that religion is *not* a valid issue in the current presidential campaign, if, indeed it were *ever* a valid issue in *any* race for the White House.

Certainly, the moral fibre of the man (or woman) seeking to occupy the highest office in the land should be required to stand the test of public scrutiny. That has absolutely nothing to do with endorsements, or the lack of them, from the church pulpit. For a politician to call upon celestial powers for support in his political pursuits is cynical, at best.

To seek, as Cuomo implied some are doing in his speech last week at Notre Dame University, the endorsement of God is to surpass the boundaries of good taste.

For some members of the clergy to tell the members of their flock — even if not directly — a certain politician is "chosen", not because he/she is a good person or a good leader, but because he/she marches in step with the church hierarchy on a single issue, falls into the same category.

⇨

Yes, there is a place for spiritual, certainly moral, leadership in government. Those who are most qualified to provide it should speak firmly and loudly when, in their eyes, the moral well-being of the nation or its people is at stake. If their beliefs are strong enough, and if they are shared with enough of the elected candidates' constituents, the message will get through.

If they think the proper approach is to dictate to the members of their congregations that they should not vote for politicians who refuse to impose their religious beliefs on others, not of their own faith, they are wrong.

Politicians who ignore the real issues of leadership in seeking office are equally wrong. If the debate among the candidates for the presidency of the United States centers on who is on better speaking terms with the Almighty — and doesn't touch on how the average citizen of this country is going to be able to feed his children for the next four years — we're being shortchanged.

THE ATLANTA CONSTITUTION

Atlanta, GA, September 10, 1984

As Gerald Ford sees it, Walter Mondale has no right to condemn Ronald Reagan for mixing politics and religion. "Who interjected religion the most in 1976?" Ford recently asked. "It was his running mate, Jimmy Carter."

It was? As a canard, this assertion ranks alongside the notion of a free and independent Poland. It seems that Mr. Ford has twisted the religion issue in more directions than a cyclone-struck weather vane. This time, that favorite Republican devil, Mr. Carter Mondale, is clearly innocent of all charges.

Religion *was* an issue in 1976, mainly because Carter openly professed his faith to anyone who asked about it on the campaign trail. Such direct and personal espousals of faith were (and still are) unusual in national politics. But Carter carefully emphasized that he stood for complete separation of church and state.

Carter did deliver one '76 campaign speech that amounted to a political altar call: He urged the nation's "men of faith" to get involved in government. But he explained: A separate church and state does not mean that public morality must be separated from private morality.

This stance contrasts vividly with Reagan's. While Carter approached religion as a personal matter, Reagan views it as a public one. Carter hoped religion would trickle up, from individuals into government. Reagan seems to want it to trickle down, from government to individuals.

Unlike Carter, President Reagan is a man who betrays little outward evidence of deep religious faith. Yet he wouldn't flinch from instituting public policy that is based on religious dogma. Carter would.

Reagan favors such proposals as prayer in public schools, tuition tax credits for parochial schools and outlawing abortion. Each would grant governmental favor to some religious group.

Ford could not be wronger as he casts stones at Carter and excuses Reagan's political sins. As a man of religion *and* politics, Carter knew the dangers of writing matters of faith into law. As a man chiefly of politics, Reagan doesn't seem to understand. And neither does Gerald Ford.

LOS ANGELES HERALD

*Los Angeles, CA,
September 16, 1984*

New York's Gov. Cuomo gave a thoughtful speech at Notre Dame Thursday night on the relationship between an official's religious beliefs and his public duty. (See today's Op-Ed page for excerpts.) Specifically, Cuomo discussed how a Catholic who accepts his church's teachings on abortion can support legislation that provides, say, public funds to an indigent woman seeking to abort an unwanted pregnancy. This is a profoundly complex subject — as is, indeed, the entire issue of abortion — and it is not necessary to agree with Cuomo's conclusions to applaud his seriousness, scholarship and, yes, his reverence.

Recent remarks by President Reagan and Vice President Bush on the same subject suffer by comparison. Bush, especially, has been all over the lot. In his unsuccessful 1980 presidential campaign, he said he favored federal funding of abortions in certain circumstances; now he says he does not. He does, however, currently approve of abortion in the case of rape or incest, or when the mother's life is in danger. At the same time, Bush denies he has any differences with Reagan, who says abortion is justified only to save a mother's life.

Meantime, the American people are left with the terrible task of reconciling morality and theology with the reality of their lives. How many families, on learning that a 13-year-old, unmarried daughter had become pregnant, for example, would protest her obtaining a safe, legal abortion? Not many, we think. Should the poor have access to the same services as the relatively well-to-do? Most people seem to think so.

The issue of whether a fetus constitutes life, legally and morally, at all stages of its development, is a religious one that may never be resolved. Certainly, most of us prefer to give the benefit of the doubt to the fetus precisely because we realize that *something* human — whether or not it is an actual human life — ends with an abortion. Still, in poll after poll, Americans indicate that, while they find abortion morally wrong, they nevertheless believe it is an issue to be decided by a woman and her doctor, not by the state.

As Cuomo said at Notre Dame: "The hard truth is that abortion isn't a failure of government. No agency or department of government forces women to have abortions....The failure here is not Caesar's. This failure is our failure, the failure of the entire people of God." ∎

The Evening Gazette

Worcester, MA, September 8, 1984

The 18 Roman Catholic bishops of Massachusetts, Maine, New Hampshire and Vermont have declared abortion the overriding issue of the 1984 campaign at all levels of political office.

In so doing, they have injected a distinctly religious element into local, state and national politics. Many, pleading separation of church and state, would reject their role. Many others who are of like mind with the bishops, and some who are not, welcome their contribution as a stimulus to the current political debate.

Informed and conscientious citizens must consider the bishops' contribution as they would a statement from any other responsible segment of our society. Catholics, like all others in our society, are free to make up their own minds.

The bishops, both in their statement and individually in press conferences after the statement was issued, stopped short of endorsing some candidates or condemning others. Their statement urges "all citizens to study the issues, form conscientious judgments concerning them and to vote their convictions." Surely there can be no more practical a formulation of the duties of citizenship.

The bishops have the right, and indeed the civic duty, of any who claim leadership in our society to speak out clearly and forthrightly on issues of public interest. It is no surprise that when they do speak out they attempt to do so in a way that will convince all citizens, not just Catholics.

Certainly the bishops are not so naive as to expect that everyone in our pluralistic society will agree with them, even on an issue that they themselves see as clearcut. Nor should those who disagree with them be so naive as to think the bishops, confronted with opposing views, will not push their own positions in forceful rebuttal.

The dilemma for the voter is whether he agrees that abortion is so overwhelming an issue that a candidate's stand on it should be the deciding factor in his or her election or defeat.

Some condemn such an approach as one-issue voting. They say that politics is practical, not ideal. They prefer to examine the totality of a candidate's stands and to evaluate a candidate on what he might be able to accomplish in a number of areas. The bishops themselves identified 14 crucial issues for the 1980s and named two of them — abortion and nuclear warfare — as the most important.

For those who agree with the bishops and the Catholic Church's stance that fetal life is totally human and that abortion is therefore murder, abortion may be so overriding an issue that candidates stand or fall on their positions and records. Others may not share that urgency and may in fact identify other issues, singly or in combination, as more important.

The bishops have demonstrated a welcome willingness to step to the fore for a cause they believe crucial to society. It is up to the voters to meet their challenge on this most important issue: to decide for themselves what role abortion should play in the decisions they make in the voting booth.

THE LOUISVILLE TIMES
Louisville, KY, August 15, 1984

America's Catholic bishops raised a tough issue the other day for public officials who also happen to be members of the Roman Catholic Church. Sad to say, they also revived the old suspicion, which sustained generations of bigots, that a Catholic in office would be a tool of the church hierarchy rather than the representative of a diverse cross-section of the public.

An officeholder or candidate, the bishops argued, cannot logically draw a line between "personal morality and public policy." And Catholics, presumably including politicians, should work vigorously "to convince others of the rightness of *our* positions."

The statement appears to have been aimed in part at New York Gov. Mario Cuomo and vice presidential nominee Geraldine Ferraro. Both say they oppose abortion as a matter of personal belief but won't impose what they consider a religious view on others. They argue that Americans have the right to decide according to their consciences and needs.

The church permits no flexibility on abortion, and many predominantly Catholic organizations want their doctrinal position to apply to everybody.

No one questions the right, or the duty, of individuals and institutions to seek majority support for their views. Churches have been instrumental in bringing to public attention the moral issues inherent in the civil rights struggle, human rights violations and the nuclear arms race.

The bishops are treading on treacherous ground, however, when they suggest that Catholic politicians cannot distinguish between their moral and religious beliefs and their public policy positions. Archbishop John J. O'Connor of New York went an unfortunate step farther — although he later retreated — when he suggested that Catholics could not in good conscience vote for a candidate who believes in freedom of choice on abortion.

Yet that sort of attitude is precisely what inflames the virulent anti-Catholic feeling that plagued John F. Kennedy and other candidates. The words of a Southern Baptist leader back in 1960 should not be too quickly forgotten. "All we ask," he declared, "is that Roman Catholicism lift its bloody hand from the throats of those that want to worship in the church of their choice."

One of Mr. Kennedy's achievements was to overcome the fears that lingered in many Protestant minds. In one of many statements on the issue, he said a president's religious views must be "his own private affair, neither imposed by him upon the nation nor imposed by the nation upon him as a condition to holding that office."

What matters, he said another time, is "not what kind of church I believe in, for that should be important only to me, but what kind of America I believe in."

Gov. Cuomo has been equally eloquent. ". . . The design of this country, its greatest strength," he said, "is that people are free to believe their own thing. . . . I want to be free to be Catholic, but that means you have to be free to be a Sikh or ethical humanist." Religious freedom would be in jeopardy, he went on, if he pushed "personal beliefs" on others.

While abortion remains deeply troubling for many citizens, law and science support the "choice" position. The objections are mostly based on religion. Candidates do not abandon logic, therefore, when they distinguish between their personal religious view and their public policy decision that others have a right to make choices on the basis of conscience.

Politicians of all faiths, including President Reagan, who wants to impose on us the attitudes of very conservative Christians, should heed the guidelines set forth by Messrs. Kennedy and Cuomo. That is the surest way to preserve that crucial boundary between church and state.

THE MILWAUKEE JOURNAL
Milwaukee, WI, August 9, 1984

New York Gov. Mario Cuomo and Roman Catholic Archbishop John O'Connor have conducted a useful dialog about the role of religion in politics. Already that issue has arisen in this year's campaign — in discussions of the religious fidelity of President Reagan and of Rep. Geraldine Ferraro, the Democratic vice presidential candidate. The debate deserves to be conducted without demagogy or religious bigotry.

The Cuomo-O'Connor clash stemmed from the archbishop's comment: "I don't see how a Catholic in good conscience can vote for a candidate who explicitly supports abortion."

Cuomo, who says he personally opposes abortion but must uphold its legality, suggested that the archbishop was, in effect, telling Catholics that they could not vote for politicians with Cuomo's views. O'Connor denied that he was instructing Catholics how to vote; he said he was merely setting forth the official church teachings on abortion.

To their credit, Cuomo and O'Connor then backed away from the potentially nasty brouhaha. O'Connor clarified his comment and Cuomo said he might have misunderstood O'Connor.

In our view, the archbishop has every right to express his church's doctrine and his own conviction on abortion, just as the Rev. Martin Luther King Jr. had the right to oppose racism on the ground that it contradicted Christian teachings on equality and justice. However, it would be a dangerous step for the archbishop — or any religious leader — to cross the line between religious or moral instruction and political endorsement.

Even so, religious values long have played a role in American political life. Religious ideas were appealed to as justification for the American Revolution, and used to oppose (and defend) slavery. More recently, religious leaders have cited religious ideas to support or oppose US foreign policy, especially with regard to military action in the Vietnam War and, now, in Central America.

This year, both the major parties invoke religious values to support their policies. Walter Mondale and Geraldine Ferraro stand in a religious tradition that is greatly concerned about social issues. President Reagan is the spokesman for those who view personal piety and morality as the source of national strength. Both are legitimate strands in the nation's religious fabric.

As politicians and religious leaders proclaim their competing views, however, they should remember that unrestrained zealotry and unwise attempts to wedge religious dogmas between citizens and the ballot box can undermine the nation's commitment to pluralism. It is that pluralism, after all, that ensures true religious freedom.

The Chattanooga Times
Chattanooga, TN, September 22, 1984

New York Gov. Mario Cuomo has good reason to challenge the Catholic prelates who condemn him for his views on abortion. The governor stands in defense, not so much of a woman's right to an abortion, but of a Catholic's right to exercise independence from the church hierarchy in discharging the duties of public office.

Like his fellow Catholic, vice presidential candidate Geraldine Ferraro, Gov. Cuomo accepts the church's teaching against abortion personally but does not favor imposing this religiously-grounded view on believers and non-believers alike through a legal ban on abortions. In a major address last week at Notre Dame University, the governor said the church is seeking to harness the power of the state to stop behavior it considers sinful when its more proper role is to seek an end to abortion through moral suasion.

The governor argued rightly that "public morality" in a pluralistic society must be based on consensus and that no such consensus exists on the issue of abortion. His position is buttressed by the *New York Times*-CBS News poll released this week which shows that Americans oppose a constitutional amendment to outlaw abortions by a margin of 63 percent to 28 percent and that even practicing Catholics are evenly split on the issue.

But Gov. Cuomo ventured beyond the narrow question of whether abortion should be legal to the broader questions of how society discharges its responsibilities to nurture and protect human life. In effect, the governor challenged those who call themselves "pro-life" and those who call themselves "pro-choice" to live up to those designations in their fullest sense.

To those who oppose abortion, he said, "If we want to prove our regard for life in the womb, for the helpless infant ... then there is work enough for all of us ... The work of creating a society where the right to life doesn't end at the moment of birth; where an infant isn't helped into a world that doesn't care if it's fed properly, housed decently, educated adequately; where the blind or retarded child isn't condemned to exist rather than empowered to live."

And those who support a woman's right to choose abortion, he said, should work to ensure that other choices are also available. He called for support for government programs to give the impoverished woman who finds herself pregnant "the full range of support she needs to bear and raise her children." Thus, he said, desperation and hopelessness will not make abortion seem to be the only choice.

The governor urged Catholics to do more than seek a legalistic solution. They should, he said, provide "funds and opportunity for young women to bring their child to term, knowing both of them will be taken care of if necessary." In that spirit, the governor offered the $1,500 honorarium he received for his speech at Notre Dame to the Nazareth Life Center, a Catholic-run home for unwed mothers in New York state. His gift was flatly refused.

The rebuff reflects the religious rigidity and intolerance which makes the mixing of church and state so dangerous in a free and pluralistic society. Gov. Cuomo's position, based in individual conscience and the principles of public representation, is correct. Those within the Catholic hierarchy who condemn him seek excessive control over the political process.

WORCESTER TELEGRAM.
Worcester, MA, August 12, 1984

American Roman Catholic bishops are trying to draw a fine line between politics and theology. A statement by the U.S. Catholic Conference urges American Catholics to support official church positions on public policy issues such as abortion and nuclear weapons. But the statement warned the clergy against endorsing specific office seekers.

Bishop James Malone, speaking for the bishops as president of the conference, issued the statement as a clarification for the clergy, Catholic laity and political candidates.

It followed a highly publicized exchange between New York Gov. Mario Cuomo and New York Archbishop John J. O'Connor over the abortion issue. The archbishop said that he did not see how any Catholic could vote for a candidate who "explicitly supports" abortion. The governor said that the archbishop was, in effect, telling voters not to vote for him or other politicians who are for freedom of choice. Cuomo said that while he personally is against abortion, he cannot impose that view on others through state policies.

Later Bishop O'Connor backed off somewhat and said he was only acting as a teacher of Catholic doctrine. Cuomo, on his part, said the archbishop may have been misunderstood.

The statement read by Bishop Malone cuts things even finer. It says: "We reject the idea that candidates satisfy the requirements of rational analysis in saying their personal views should not influence their policy decisions. The implied dichotomy — between personal morality and public policy — is simply not logically tenable in any adequate view of both." The bishop added that any candidate who expresses personal commitments as a qualification for office has to translate those commitments into public policies and programs.

Bishop Malone urged Catholic clergy and laity to take an aggressive role in trying to persuade candidates of "the rightness of our positions" on abortion, nuclear arms, human rights and other issues. However, he warned them against taking a stand on any candidate, pro or con.

The statement also warned against candidates who try to exploit religious views to partisan advantage. Some politicians have complained that President Reagan has tried to attract the Catholic vote by espousing its pro-life and other teachings.

The U.S. Catholic Conference may have been trying to take religion out of the political arena, but the result may be just the opposite. The Cuomo-O'Connor standoff has not been resolved. It is as difficult as it ever was to separate a candidate from his or her beliefs. In a pluralistic society, religion and politics can be an explosive mix.

The Founding Fathers understood all that from experience. That is why we have the First Amendment.

The Washington Times
Washington, DC, August 13, 1984

The National Conference of Catholic Bishops, headed by Bishop James W. Malone, has issued a statement on the church and political issues. Contrary to *The New York Times*'s premature story portraying the statement as a virtual reprimand of Archibishop John J. O'Connor for his tough stand on "pro-choice" politicians, the actual text is a ringing affirmation of the right and duty of the church to make its moral position clear on politically charged issues, especially abortion and nuclear war.

Some people did indeed come in for sharp, though implicit, criticism. Archbishop O'Connor wasn't one of them. After cautioning that bishops should avoid direct partisanship, the statement declared: "We reject the idea that candidates satisfy the requirements of rational analysis in saying their personal views should not influence their policy decisions; the implied dichotomy — between personal views and public policy — is simply not logically tenable in any adequate view of both."

The statement named no names. It didn't have to. This is precisely the position that Geraldine Ferraro and Mario Cuomo take on the issue of abortion — though not, of course, on social-welfare spending or disarmament. On these issues they put on their Sunday best and accuse President Reagan of being a bad Christian. Redistributionist liberalism, they aver, is the only admissible philosophy. Grave and judicious doubts about whether they can justly "impose their views on others"? These are for the abortion issue alone.

The bishops have declared — rightly — that the dichotomy between religion and politics is false on all issues, that thinking persons must make all decisions — religious and secular — in the light of the moral system to which they adhere. To do otherwise, it should have been unnecessary to observe, is to cast doubt on whether one has a moral system in the first place.

Los Angeles Times
Los Angeles, CA, August 13, 1984

Gov. Mario M. Cuomo of New York and John J. O'Connor, the Roman Catholic archbishop of New York, initiated in the pages of the New York Times an important discussion of the role of religion in politics. The issue is now joined nationally.

The initial exchange seems to have been provoked by a television news conference in June in which the new archbishop said: "I don't see how a Catholic in good conscience can vote for a candidate who explicitly supports abortion." By the governor's calculation, that would reduce the choice for Catholics of conscience to candidates supporting the so-called Right to Life movement, a situation that he found unsatisfactory. It is the more unsatisfactory for the governor because he regards himself as a faithful Roman Catholic personally opposed to abortion but, in respect to the law of the land, not prepared to impose his personal views on all whom he governs.

O'Connor has replied with a clarification that seems more in line with a recent pronouncement of the U.S. Catholic Conference. He has now said that he has no intention of telling anyone how to vote. The 28 bishops of the administrative board of the Catholic Conference, in an affirmation last March of principles of political responsibility for Catholics in an election year, had urged the faithful to base their choice of candidates on "the full range of issues as well as their integrity, philosophy and performance."

But the bishops, in subsequent communications to the platform committees of both the Republican and Democratic parties, have cited abortion as one of two pressing issues in this presidential election. The other is the prevention of nuclear war.

Now the president of the U.S. Catholic Conference, Bishop James Malone of Youngstown, has confronted Catholic politicians such as Cuomo and Geraldine A. Ferraro, the Democratic candidate for vice president, by asserting that it is "simply not logically tenable" to tolerate "the implied dichotomy between personal morality and public policy" that both have argued on the issue of abortion. He has not named them, but his challenge is no less clear.

This is disturbing. A persuasive case has been made by Cuomo, by other Catholics and by politicians of other religious persuasions for separation of their personal views from standards to be imposed by law on all citizens. The separation — call it "dichotomy" if you will — respects above all the pluralism of this nation that simply does not see the issues of abortion, contraception, divorce, nuclear disarmament, alcohol consumption and homosexuality from the same perspective.

Single-issue voting campaigns are not a monopoly of the foes of abortion. Many groups are seeking to provide their own quick and easy litmus tests for choosing candidates. That is their right. But voters will heed such advice at great peril to the republic, for they will be encouraging demagoguery.

Those who intrude their religious beliefs in the political arena bear a special responsibility. For many religiously inclined persons, their beliefs would be meaningless unless applied vigorously to the perfection of the society in which they live. It is not easy to draw a line between this legitimate application of principle and the unwarranted intrusion of one person's particular beliefs into the private thoughts and practices of another.

Abortion is a particularly inflammatory issue. The U.S. Supreme Court has ruled, correctly, that the right of a woman to interrupt pregnancy prevails over the right to life of the unborn child under certain circumstances. The effect of that ruling has been to rescue desperate women with unwanted pregnancies from the risks of illegal abortion clinics that still prevail where nations have withheld the sanction of this choice. Inflammatory as it is, however, abortion alone can in no way serve as a useful test of the virtue and competence of a candidate. This is true, if for no other reason, because no candidates are advocates of abortion; the only difference among candidates has to do with their respect for the law as it now stands or their determination to change that law.

Cuomo has invited a debate far deeper and more significant than this. He is questioning the habit of some candidates to cloak themselves in religious dress and of some religious bodies to play a more aggressive role in politics. Cuomo wants to redirect this situation, so easily abused by single-issue groups, to face the broader question of the way in which political parties and candidates address universal religious values, including the problems of poverty and peace.

But he recognizes the risks, the risks evident when Ferraro said, "I don't for one minute believe" that President Reagan is a "good Christian."

"I will encourage a debate as to values," Cuomo told the New York Times. "I'm not going to debate Ronald Reagan on whether he's a hypocrite."

Fair enough.

THE MILWAUKEE JOURNAL
Milwaukee, WI, October 13, 1984

US Rep. Henry Hyde (R-Ill.), speaking recently at the University of Notre Dame, made some points to keep in mind as the debate rages over religion and politics. He noted some too-often overlooked roots of the debate.

Although many will differ with Hyde's conservative views on issues such as abortion, the congressman did make the significant point that it is not wrong to appeal to traditional religious values to buttress arguments for or against social policies. The abolitionists did that in their attacks on slavery; the civil-rights marchers did that in their assaults on segregation; the peace activists of the 1960s did that in their dissent from American military action in Southeast Asia.

Of course, the narrow views on any one religion should not prevail — on abortion or on any other issue. Still, there must be room in the public debate for the expression of values that are grounded in religion.

It is also important to remember, as Hyde reminded his audience, that this debate has not sprung full-blown from the intervention of the Catholic hierarchy or evangelical Protestants. The growth of conservative forces, religious and political, is in large measure an attempt to hold on to traditional values and to restore those values to a once-honored place.

No one desires a triumph of theocracy. The notion is foreign to our system. Yet as the policy debate rages, it should be remembered that, in the democratic dialog, views that spring from traditional and religious values deserve a respectful hearing.

The Idaho STATESMAN
Boise, ID, September 12, 1984

This year's presidential race is noteworthy for its abuse of the religion issue. While the campaign will end in two months, the scars that are left could take longer to heal.

The debate about Geraldine Ferraro's stand on abortion as it relates to her status as a Catholic underscores the way religion inappropriately has become a key campaign issue.

One of the great things about America is that it has room for everyone: Catholics, Protestants, Jews, Methodists, Episcopalians, fundamentalists and those who adhere to no religion. The clear-cut separation of church and state has been a guarantee to religious minorities that, in this country at least, they won't suffer.

Those who are using this election to try to impose their conception of a Christian ethic on the rest of America run the risk of ending that spirit of live and let live and alienating a part of our society. In their zeal to make this country conform to its beliefs, the fundamentalist right is encouraging the very divisiveness and discrimination from which America has been a refuge.

Proponents of making our society "Christian" forget that not everyone practices a Christian religion, or any religion. The closer America comes to identifying politically with a particular religious philosophy, the greater the fear that those in the minority will find their rights diluted.

To be strong, any country must have a firm foundation of morals and ethics. America without its principles would not be America. But morals and ethics are not the domain of any one religious group. America's strength derives from its tolerance of diverse religions.

History shows that when religion and politics cross, chaos can be the result. Some of the world's bloodiest conflicts, from the Crusades on, have been over religion.

Religion is so fundamental and emotional an issue that it precludes any compromise, as the conflicts in Northern Ireland and the Middle East show.

No matter how politically expedient it may be to exploit the sincere concerns of some of this country's religious groups, America ultimately will lose if its guarantee of religious freedom for all is diluted in any way.

San Francisco Chronicle

San Francisco, Calif., September 14, 1984

THE APPARENT DECISION of some Catholic bishops to campaign against Geraldine Ferraro, the Democratic nominee for vice president, is an unfortunate and undesirable intrusion of religion into the nation's political arena.

It is right and proper that church groups and church leaders should take positions on issues that concern them. It is quite another matter for them to insist that officeholders of their faith hew to church dogma on every issue and for them to engage in what amounts to public debate with specific candidates.

Twice in the past few days, important Catholic bishops have gone out of their ways to rebuke Ferraro, by name, for taking the stand that, though, as a Catholic, she personally opposes abortion, she supports a woman's right to make her own decision on that subject and would not impose her views on others.

First it was New York Archbishop John J. O'Connor, who chastized Ferraro from the pulpit on Sunday. (Earlier, Archbishop O'Connor criticized Catholic officeholders who support freedom of choice on abortion. He contended that Catholic public officials have an obligation to act on the moral teachings of their church.)

Then it was Bishop James C. Timlin of Scranton, Pa., who called a press conference just 30 minutes after a campaign appearance there by Ferraro to denounce her stand on abortion as "absurd." He also constantly referred to the vice presidential nominee as "Geraldine," as if she were a child.

IT WAS IRONIC that the Scranton incident happened on September 12 — the 24th anniversary of John F. Kennedy's pledge in the 1960 presidential campaign that his Catholic religion would not interfere with his duties as a public official.

In a speech to the Ministerial Association in Houston, Texas that day, Kennedy said, "I am not the Catholic candidate for president. I am the Democratic Party's candidate for president who happens to be a Catholic. I do not speak for my church on public matters — and the church does not speak for me."

This week, in light of the current campaign by some Catholic bishops against Ferraro, Senator Edward Kennedy added his own views on the troubling question of religion's proper role in politics.

"Religious leaders may say anything they feel bound in conscience to say, but they may not ask government to do something which it cannot do under the Constitution or the social contract of a pluralistic society," he said.

"Where decisions are inherently individual ones or in cases where we are deeply divided about whether they are, people of faith should not invoke the power of the state to decide what everyone can believe or think or read or do. In such cases, cases like abortion or prayer or prohibition or sexual identity, the proper role of religion is to appeal to the free conscience of each person, not the coercive rule of secular law."

The Kennedy words, from 1960 and 1984, should be taken to heart by clergymen who may be thinking about behaving like some sort of moral truth squad.

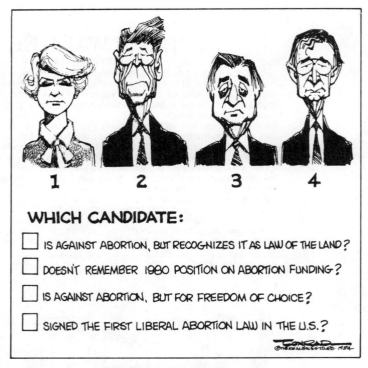

WHICH CANDIDATE:

☐ IS AGAINST ABORTION, BUT RECOGNIZES IT AS LAW OF THE LAND?

☐ DOESN'T REMEMBER 1980 POSITION ON ABORTION FUNDING?

☐ IS AGAINST ABORTION, BUT FOR FREEDOM OF CHOICE?

☐ SIGNED THE FIRST LIBERAL ABORTION LAW IN THE U.S.?

Post-Tribune

Gary, Ind., August 28, 1984

When John Kennedy ran for president 24 years ago, a prominent Protestant clergyman warned that a Catholic president "would be under extreme pressure from the hierarchy of his church" to support policies favored by the Vatican.

The Rev. Norman Vincent Peale was not an extremist looking for publicity. He was reflecting a strong, lingering public attitude.

Our opinions

Kennedy helped to defuse the issue by talking about it publicly. He told a group of Baptist ministers that "I do not speak for my church on public matters, and the church does not speak for me." That was, and still is, part of the debate over religion and politics — can a candidate be independent of official church stands? Should a candidate's religious preferences influence voters?

This year, Catholicism is being discussed in a surprising form. Several Catholic politicians, including Democratic vice presidential nominee Geraldine Ferraro, have had to answer charges that their official positions have betrayed their church teachings. And President Reagan, the favorite of many Protestant fundamentalist groups, often drops the name of Pope John Paul II in defending his policies.

There was little fuss this year when the president established diplomatic relations with the Vatican. And he has emphasized that his opposition to abortion and his support of tuition tax credits are examples of positions he shares with Catholics.

The religious issues are part of the campaign, but the lines are blurred.

A recent statement by Archbishop John J. O'Connor of New York indirectly criticized Mrs. Ferraro: "I don't see how a Catholic in good conscience can vote for a candidate who explicitly supports abortion." Mrs. Ferraro, like some other political figures, says she would not impose her religious beliefs on others. That, we believe, is a responsible approach to public life.

The abortion issue is one that has created some agreement among Catholics and Protestant fundamentalists. That is a significant development in debate about politics and religion.

The country has come many miles since the 1884 outburst of a Presbyterian minister who supported Republican presidential candidate James Blaine. He called the Democrats the party of "rum, Romanism and rebellion." Catholic immigrants and the Democratic Party moved together because of that.

Religion is almost sure to be an issue in 1984. It may be less intemperate than the 1884 slogan, but it also may be more insidious. There will be excesses on all sides. There is, unfortunately, a growing tendency of Americans to crusade on single-issue causes and to grade candidates completely on those issues. That is narrow, it is not democratic and it diminishes the process.

Mrs. Ferraro did not help matters by questioning the depth of the president's Christian commitment. The president does not help when he invokes the pope's name. Both of them can do better.

THE RICHMOND NEWS LEADER

Richmond, VA, October 5, 1984

The other day Catholic Bishop Walter Sullivan reportedly said:

"Moral, political, and economic responsibilities do not stop at the moment of birth. The right to life and the quality of life truly complement each other.

"Those who defend the right to life of the weakest among us must be equally concerned about supporting the quality of life of the powerless among us, the old and the young, the hungry and the homeless, the undocumented immigrant and the unemployed worker."

Casting doubt on the motives of certain anti-abortionists hardly seems bishoply fair.

Moreover, Bishop Sullivan implicitly says that those opposing abortion must support standard Leftist positions on welfare and political economy. In other words, it is wrong to oppose abortion and yet not support, say, increased funding for food stamps. A less rigid ideology would fail to find such illogical connections.

The bishop's statement contains more clichés than a spaghetti Western. And it recalls a reflection on intolerance from theologian Michael Novak's compelling *Confession of a Catholic*:

"It seems difficult for persons on the extreme religious Left to comprehend that there are serious persons who disagree with their views on political economy."

St. Louis Review

St. Louis, MO, October 12, 1984

It seems like only yesterday that supporters of abortion-on-demand would dismiss the pro-life movement as proponents of a Catholic point of view. Catholics may have been among the first to react to the legalization of abortion by the U.S. Supreme Court, but the pro-life movement today has far greater depth and breadth than the abortion lobby cares to concede.

The current political campaign reveals that abortion is a paramount issue among the electorate.

Although vigorous opposition to abortion is not merely a Catholic issue, it remains a vital issue for Catholics.

On Nov. 18, 1974, the Church's Doctrinal Congregation issued a statement on abortion. It insisted that: "it must be clearly understood that a Christian can never conform to a law which is itself immoral, and such is the case of a law which would admit in principle the licitness of abortion. Nor can a Christian take part in a propaganda campaign in favor of such a law, or vote for it. Moreover, he may not collaborate in its application."

The teaching and discipline of the Catholic Church is clear and unequivocal. Procuring an abortion is one of the very few transgressions which carries with it automatic excommunication from the Catholic Church. Under these circumstances, it is incomprehensible that a group of men and women styling themselves "Catholics For a Free Choice, Inc." have published an advertisement in the New York Sunday Times (Oct. 7, 1984) claiming legitimacy for dissenting opinions among Catholics on the subject of abortion.

It is not within the purview of any bishop or body of bishops to give explicit or tacit approval to this clearly heterodox position. The Times advertisement includes misleading statements about the Church's discipline on abortion, implying an uncertain tradition on the subject. The truth is that abortion has always been viewed as a grave sin. Canonical legislation has usually equated abortion with murder, although there are instances in which it has been treated as manslaughter. Neither designation leaves any doubt that the unborn child is regarded as a human being.

Those who call themselves Catholics for a free choice are wrong. There is no place within the Catholic Church for dissenting opinions on the evil of abortion.

Boston Sunday Globe

Boston, MA, September 9, 1984

The 18 Catholic bishops of New England, seizing "a splendid opportunity for clarifying some fundamental principles," issued a statement this week, urging "all citizens to study the issues, to form conscientious judgments concerning them and to vote their convictions."

"No one issue can be avoided," the bishops said, as they listed 14 issues varying "in complexity and urgency." The bishops' contribution to public dialogue is a healthy one.

The bishops are intelligent and sophisticated men of undoubted integrity. "Our prayer is for a deepened sense of public responsibility on the part of candidates and voters," the bishops said, "and our hope is that our words may help them both." Their letter is a far more profound and serious document than most of the statements made in recent weeks about religion and politics.

"There are ways to inject religion which are inappropriate" Archbishop Bernard F. Law of Boston said at a press conference. The bishops' letter is clearly not one of them. The genius of the Founding Fathers foresaw the occasion when forces hostile to religion would seek to deny freedom of speech to religious leaders.

The Constitution grants freedom of speech and prohibits "an establishment of religion," guaranteeing to all religious leaders the right to speak out. When religious leaders do speak, however, they become subject to the same rules as secular spokesmen. They cannot use dogma as a shortcut and must test their ideas in the marketplace of society.

Since the "splendid opportunity" to speak out occurs during a presidential campaign, it is worth noting that of the 14 issues isolated by the bishops, abortion is not only first alphabetically but also rhetorically.

"We believe that the enormity of this evil makes abortion the critical issue of the moment," the bishops said. That weighting of issues may explain the treatment of presidential candidates in The Pilot, Boston's archdiocesan newspaper. "Republicans Nominate Reagan on Platform of Moral Standards," said the lead headline Aug. 31, with the overline "Pro-Life, Prayer, Family." On July 27, with the overline "Democratic Nominee," the lead Pilot headline said, "Mondale's Record: For Social Justice, But Pro-Abortion."

Of the 14 issues chosen by the bishops, Reagan undoubtedly gets an A-plus on his report card for abortion but needs remedial work on other subjects: "arms control and disarmament, capital punishment, civil rights, the economy, education, energy, family life, food and agricultural policy, health, housing, human rights, mass media and regional conflict in the world."

Reagan's "pro-family" policies may be intensely spiritual, but in food, housing, education and health, they are anti-family. On arms control, the gap between the Reagan Administration and the Catholic bishops is wide and deep.

"While nuclear holocaust is a future possibility, the holocaust of abortion is a present reality," the New England bishops said, showing patience with Reagan. "The alarming fact is that during the past 11 years over 15 million human beings have been aggressively and willfully put to death in our nation with the sanction of the law," the letter states.

Before abortion had "the sanction of the law," that is, before the Supreme Court's Roe v. Wade decision in 1973, abortions were numerous, if illegal. According to federal statistics, 130,000 illegal abortions were performed in 1972. Who bore the moral responsibility for them? Surely not the state alone. The law's "sanction" should not and cannot be stronger than the power of right and wrong.

Religious leaders bear responsibility for the efficacy of their teaching. They bear responsibility, too, for the credibility of their teaching.

The 18 bishops of New England have little credibility on this subject of such importance to them and others. Outside the pulpit, in newspapers, on radio and television, they are stating a case that many of their fellow citizens reject. They are, after all, 18 males proclaiming certitude on an issue of profoundly female concern.

The bishops also represent an institution that for reasons of theology or historical inertia relegates women to a second-class status. How can women take seriously "fundamental principles" pronounced from such a fundamentally unfair and exclusionary platform?

The bishops must also take responsibility for the ineffectiveness of their preaching on artificial birth control. When the church rejected the humane and sensible invention of "the pill," it surrendered credibility, too.

Even minus that credibility, the bishops are welcome in the arena of politics. They are patriotic, thoughtful and responsible. So are citizens who do not share their priorities.

Violence, Harassment on Rise at Abortion Clinics

Since 1982 a disturbing trend has been the growing number of violent antiabortion protests directed against family planning centers and abortion clinics. According to federal figures, there were more than 150 cases of vandalism or harassment at abortion facilities throughout the country in 1984 alone, among them 20 bombing and arson incidents. In a November 1984 incident, for example, two bombs exploded within a quarter of an hour of each other at an abortion clinic and family planning center in Wheaton, Maryland, a suburb of Washington, D.C. No one was injured, but an estimated $400,000 in damages was caused by the blasts and ensuing fire. A few days after the explosions, an anonymous caller told a radio station that the "Army of God" claimed responsibility for the blasts and would continue to destroy abortion clinics. No abortions had been performed at the targeted Planned Parenthood office in Wheaton.

"The Army of God" was first heard from in 1982, following two Florida abortion clinic bombings, and has since become a familiar sobriquet, associated with many such violent incidents. But federal law-enforcement agencies now reportedly believe that the name is simply being used by different antiabortion extremists, and does not represent any organized group. The name was also implicated in a death threat received by Supreme Court Justice Harry A. Blackmun in October 1984. Blackmun had authored the high court's majority opinion in the 1973 ruling that legalized abortion in the first six months of pregnancy. (See pp. 9-19.) The rash of bombings and other incidents is as upsetting to many opponents of abortion as it is to abortion rights advocates, since they feel it discredits their efforts to ban abortions through legislation. It has been alleged by some clinic operators, however, that the connections between the perpetrators of such violence and mainstream antiabortion groups may go even further than tacit encouragement. Some individual demonstrators have apparently been arrested many times in different parts of the country. The constitutional right to demonstrate is defended by the abortion opponents, who claim they have been harassed by 'pro-choice' groups in return.

Many antiabortion activists bring a theatrical element to their protests, displaying bloody dolls, playing recordings of fetal heartbeats or videotaping would-be patients as an intimidation tactic. Protestors have pretended to be patients to gain entry to clinics before splashing red paint in waiting rooms, dropping stink bombs or chaining themselves to examining tables. Abortion clinic administrators have been picketed at their homes by protesters carrying defamatory signs. Other tactics have included telephone harassment of abortion patients at their homes as well as "counseling" meetings where they are propagandized by antiabortion extremists. One of the most highly publicized tactics employed by the antiabortionists was the production of "The Silent Scream," a sonogram videotape that graphically depicts a fetus being aborted. Although never shown on national television, "The Silent Scream" was distributed to every member of Congress and viewed by antiabortion groups at the White House. These tactics have had their effect. By February 1985, local doctors throughout the country were less likely to perform abortions at Planned Parenthood clinics for fear of backlash from the community. While some doctors now perform abortions only in their offices, others no longer perform them at all; office space has become hard to rent because of the insurance risk posed by the increase of violence. Indeed, a number of clinics have lost their insurance and leases after bombing attacks.

Many who defend a woman's right to choose abortion, thinking the battle was over with the Supreme Court's 1973 decision, were caught off guard by such tactics. Their naivete' was shaken with the dawn of the 'pro-life' Reagan Administration and buried with the violence directed against clinics. Support for the 'pro-choice' movement has increased as their publicity efforts have redoubled in the face of such highly organized opposition from antiabortion groups. Private contributions to National Planned Parenthood, for instance, increased from $2 million annually before Reagan's election in 1980 to nearly $12 million annually by 1985. And many 'pro-choice' activists have cited the need for emotional appeals, focusing on the plight of women faced with an unwanted or dangerous pregnancy and that of the children who are born in such circumstances, to match the appeals on behalf of the fetus made by 'pro-life' groups.

The Washington Times
Washington, DC, July 20, 1984

Supporters of abortion are attempting to maximize their publicity advantage from the recent bombings of abortion clinics and are demanding that President Reagan order a federal investigation of these outrages.

Federal investigators should become involved in these crimes, making available their special knowledge of explosives. On the other hand federal authorities should hardly be expected to drop everything else, simply because abortion is so highly charged emotionally.

Let us assume, for the nonce, that pro-life extremists *are* the culprits — even though the identity of the bombers has yet to be established. We may then address the larger question, which is whether violent tactics discredit a cause when they are rejected by reputable spokesmen for that cause.

The abortion lobby, just at the moment, probably would like to argue that they do, but few would want to apply that argument consistently. Did urban riots in the '60s discredit civil rights? Did the depradations of John Brown increase the moral prestige of slavery? All sensible persons will deplore these bombings, whoever the culprits, and will support efforts to bring the criminals to justice. All the same, the record of the leading pro-life organizations is clear on the question of violence, and they owe apologies to no one.

THE INDIANAPOLIS STAR
Indianapolis, IN, January 12, 1983

If you do much driving around the city, you've no doubt seen sidewalk picketing of abortion clinics. The demonstrations are usually small, peaceful, mostly silent, and identified only by placards proclaiming the right to life.

But they can get out of hand, according to a suit filed in Marion Circuit Court asking that picketing be barred at a clinic on East 38th Street. The suit alleged that two anti-abortion groups used bullhorns and yelled accusations to harass and intimidate customers and those escorting them into the clinic.

The case was a sticky one, mirroring the moral controversy and the emotional fervor that so often envelops the abortion issue. But Judge John M. Ryan's ruling at the end of a day-long hearing turned a strident confrontation into quiet good sense.

He recognized the right of peaceable demonstration under the First Amendment but emphasized "peaceable." He ordered pickets to limit their numbers, stay on public property, refrain from blocking entrances and exits and from accosting customers in groups. He also told the demonstrators to put away the bullhorn.

In essence, he counseled the clinic and the pickets to agree to disagree amicably, or at least with restraint and respect for each other's rights.

As long as abortion arouses passion and prods conscience, supporters and opponents must tread lightly, proceeding with as much good will and tolerance as they can muster. That was the gist of Judge Ryan's ruling and it is good advice for safeguarding not only personal freedom but a free society.

Birmingham Post-Herald
Birmingham, AL, July 12, 1984

Few would question the right of Father Edward Markley to abhor and to contest by every legal means the practice of abortion.

His strong sense of moral outrage is not unusual in a man of the cloth. But where most of us part ways with Father Markley is his taking the law into his own hands, even if his frustration after years of peaceful protest has led him to believe he has no alternative.

An orderly society simply cannot tolerate this kind of conduct. Before long somebody is bound to get hurt.

The priest was convicted in a Huntsville court Tuesday of assaulting two abortion clinic employees during the course of a "raid" on the clinic June 15.

One employee testifed she was injured when she attempted to prevent Father Markley from damaging clinic equipment.

The priest still faces a charge of criminal mischief because of red paint splattered in the clinic. In addition he also faces another charge of using a sledge hammer to damage equipment during the course of a raid on an abortion facility on Birmingham's Southside last May.

Father Markley's attorney says he will appeal the Huntsville conviction so that the priest may be tried by a jury. It's in a courtroom - or in other public forums — where the priest should have been fighting for acceptance of his views all along.

The Atlanta Journal
AND
THE ATLANTA CONSTITUTION
Atlanta, GA, September 22, 1984

The motives behind the firebombing Thursday night of Planned Parenthood's Cobb County clinic may never be altogether clear. Why anyone would want to destroy such a facility, or threaten the lives of its staff or clients, is a mystery.

But this much is known: It was not an isolated incident. It was the second attack on a suburban Atlanta family-planning facility since Sept. 13, when a northside clinic was firebombed. It may also come down, implausibly, to a case of misunderstanding.

Firebombings of abortion clinics and harassment of clients trying to enter them have more than tripled since President Reagan two years ago denounced as a "national tragedy" the 1973 U.S. Supreme Court ruling affirming a woman's right to terminate a pregnancy. Moral Majority, "right to life" and other anti-abortion groups have also stepped up their rhetoric since then, and there have been 177 reported incidents of "severe harassment," picketing or violence directed at clinics so far in 1984, compared with 40 in all of 1982.

But *no abortions* were performed or planned at the Cobb County clinic, which suffered some $20,000 worth of fire-and-smoke damage in the attack Thursday. In fact, faulty perceptions about the facility, which provides only birth-control services, may turn out to have had more bearing on the case than the facts.

Passersby could scarcely have been faulted for assuming abortions were performed there: Since it opened four months ago, it had been picketed almost daily by demonstrators bearing placards that decried abortion with such inflammatory messages as "Stop the Holocaust" and "Equal Rights for Unborn Children."

The pickets may have known that no abortions were performed there, and may have targeted Planned Parenthood, which does provide abortions at a few locations around the country, for symbolic reasons. But their signs carried no fine print. To suggest that the leaders of such protests are to blame for the firebombings would be stretching matters. None has even tacitly condoned such violence.

But it would be unwise to ignore the extent to which strident rhetoric can arouse explosive feelings in people several times removed. And the anti-abortion rhetoric of protesters, and some respected public figures, has escalated to the point where it's hard to remember abortion is not only legal, but protected by the U.S. Constitution and several strongly worded Supreme Court rulings.

Abortion, of course, remains a perfectly legitimate political issue. Vigorous debate is welcome and, in any case, inevitable. But the distinction between violent talk and violent action may be too subtle for someone who would even consider hurling a Molotov cocktail into a building where pregnant women are consulting with doctors.

It's time hotheads on both sides of the issue took responsibility for their inflammatory rhetoric, and cooled it.

Nationwide serious attacks against abortion facilities have come at an ever quicker rate.

At least 10 abortion clinics or offices of abortion-related organizations around the country have been bombed this year, including one within earshot of the Capitol building in Washington on July 4.

Others have been subjected to increases in telephone threats and harassment of personnel and patients.

Luckily, no one has been killed or injured in any of the bombing incidents. But if the pace of the attacks continues, a death or serious injury is bound to occur — and what will that say about the "right to life" ideology that apparently motivates the zealots?

A more pertinent question is whether the wave of bombings is part of a national conspiracy by frustrated anti-abortion extremists, as some abortion rights advocates believe.

"It is our sense that there are links between these incidents," says Nanette Falkenberg, director of the National Abortion Rights Action League. "We are more than willing to believe there is no conspiracy. But people don't teach themselves to build firebombs."

She and other "pro-choice" spokesmen have called on the Justice Department to investigate the possibility of a conspiracy by radical anti-abortionists to terrorize abortion clinics into shutting down.

Whether or not a conspiracy exists, something useful that could be done right now would be for responsible leaders of groups opposing abortion to denounce the use of violence and terrorism in their cause.

The place to fight abortion is in the courts and the legislatures. That abortion opponents have failed to prevail in these forums or to win over a majority of Americans cannot justify an abandonment of legal, democratic processes.

Bombings will not stop abortion. But they will stain and compromise the entire anti-abortion movement, even if they do not ultimately kill innocent people.

THE ☁ SUN
Baltimore, MD, July 9, 1984

The bombing of Planned Parenthood offices in Annapolis was a sick and deplorable act that can in no way be interpreted as a statement against abortion. No one was injured in that bombing early Saturday, but the act threatened the life of every person who worked in the targeted office building for either Planned Parenthood or other businesses located there, such as Air Cargo, Inc., where people were working at the time of the blast. It threatened the life of anyone who might have been walking or driving past the building when chunks of brick were blasted hundreds of feet into the street. No matter how one views abortion, this assault was intolerable.

What is most alarming about this incident is that it does not stand alone. It appears to be part of a pattern of violence directed against clinics that offer legal abortions or organizations that support them. Three days before the Annapolis explosion, a bomb went off at the headquarters of the National Abortion Federation in Washington. Officials there said that was the 10th attack on an abortion-related facility this year. In Baltimore, Planned Parenthood said there also have been threats of violence against its offices here.

Leaders of "pro-choice" groups have said they believe this to be a "national effort to put abortion clinics out of business." If that is true, what could such an effort hope to achieve? The termination of pregnancies did not begin with these clinics, and would not end even if anti-abortion bombers destroyed them completely.

Intelligent people who oppose abortion know that the moral and legal issues cannot be settled by planting explosives outside a clinic. The legal issues must be fought in the legislatures and the courts, which have upheld a woman's right to obtain an abortion. The moral issue is something that churches, families and individual women wrestle with every day. Meanwhile, the entire community must condemn the acts of crazies who plant bombs in the night. The authorities should make it a top priority to find the people responsible for these attacks around the country.

Abortion is a complex and difficult issue that will be the subject of heated debate for a long time. There is no place in that debate for terrorist bombings.

THE SACRAMENTO BEE
Sacramento, CA, June 15, 1984

The demonstrators at the Roseville City Council meeting Wednesday night were certainly angry when the council refused to pass a resolution condemning Planned Parenthood and declaring it unwelcome "now or ever" in Roseville. But the council, when it didn't come up with even a second to the motion to pass the resolution, was doing precisely what it should have. As Mayor Harry Cobb said, "We can't legislate morality. If they meet the zoning and other city criteria, they have a right to locate here."

There was a lot more he could have said: According to county records, there are about 4,000 women in the Roseville area in need of subsidized family-planning care, and that is a need Placer County sees no way to meet on its own. It was county health officials who invited Planned Parenthood to open a clinic in Roseville to provide low-cost gynecological and family-planning care, pregnancy testing, sexuality and contraceptive education.

One might get the impression from the demonstration Wednesday night that Planned Parenthood is widely despised in Roseville for the confidential contraceptive information and care it provides for teen-agers — its approach is, "We won't tell your parents, but we hope you will" — and, most important, for the abortion clinic the organization has in Sacramento. (There will be no abortion clinic in Roseville.)

But a broad network of church and medical groups in the area has supported the plan for a Roseville office. They know that the typical teen-aged patient to whom Planned Parenthood provides contraceptives has already been sexually active for six months to a year without using any birth-control method, and that the community as a whole is hardly helped by denying these teen-agers access to information and medical care.

Moreover, even those who oppose abortion for themselves can recognize that it is entirely legal for the Planned Parenthood clinic in Sacramento to perform abortions for women who choose them, and that its doing so does not reduce the value of the other services the organization provides.

The demonstrators, of course, have every right to hold their own opinions — and their own demonstrations at City Hall. But the City Council was right to refuse to endorse a divisive resolution that would have started it in the dangerous business of deciding what legal activities are welcome in the city and which are not.

THE COMMERCIAL APPEAL
Memphis, TN, November 25, 1984

THE abortion debate in this country is shrill enough without the addition of violence. Yet, misguided zealots seem intent upon substituting bombs and intimidation for political action, much to the discredit of their cause.

Last week an abortion clinic and a referral office in two Washington suburbs were bombed, raising the number of such facilities burned or blown up this year to at least 19. That compares with just three in 1983.

The tally of threats, break-ins and violent incidents on anti-abortion picket lines has mushroomed, too.

Apparently a fact of American life needs repeating: Violence, most especially when it threatens human life, cannot be justified on the basis of a presumed higher morality. This is not a police state, and there are ways to affect public opinion and policy short of picking up weapons.

Equally to the point, violence usually doesn't help a social movement. More often it breeds a backlash. Even the great civil rights legislation of the 1960s passed either before or in spite of the urban riots of that decade.

To their credit, most anti-abortion leaders have denounced the explosions. But more than that, they need to educate their followers to the dangers of a strategy of destruction. Based upon the reportedly positive reaction to the bombings on the part of a few, that warning will need frequent repeating.

Meanwhile, leaders of the pro-choice movement have another responsibility. They must stop implying complicity on the part of all anti-abortionists. The president of the National Organization for Women, Judy Goldsmith, has even gone so far as to charge President Reagan with giving "aid and comfort to these people."

Ms. Goldsmith's statement is a crass smear, the equivalent of calling all nuclear freeze advocates Communists because a few are and because Moscow supports the movement.

IT IS TIME both sides distinguished the violent from the nonviolent, and worked to make the former moral outcasts — not to mention identifying and prosecuting them.

The abortion debate is not about to go away, and it isn't about to stop fueling strong emotion, either. However, it need not produce civil strife. Now may be a critical time to stop the drift in that direction.

SYRACUSE HERALD-JOURNAL
Syracuse, NY, November 13, 1984

The anti-abortionists in Onondaga County have a new target — the Family Planning agency.

Family Planning is not a county unit but it occupies rent-free office space in the county's Civic Center. Free rent is not particularly unusual; several other organizations receive the same benefit in exchange for services to the county or its residents. With Family Planning, County Executive John Mulroy says, "It's an exchange of services. We give space and they give us different types of health counseling and health services."

The agency's problem, apparently, is it occasionally mentions the word that sends right-to-lifers into frenzies of hate: Abortion.

▽   ▽

Because of this, some county legislators want Family Planning's status reviewed. James Tormey III, chairman of the Legislature's Health Committee, said he will ask the committee to begin a review Wednesday.

It's healthy for any branch of government to make regular checks of its arrangements with outside groups or agencies. Healthy, that is, as long as the reviews aren't witch hunts to further a particular political point of view.

The issue came up when a mother complained that Family Planning had made an abortion referral for her 18-year-old pregnant daughter. Christian Action Council Director James Doupe complained to two legislators that Family Planning was involved in abortion counseling.

There's a big difference between "counseling" and "advocating." We presume Doupe and the mother are accusing the agency of advocating, but their proof is yet to be seen.

Family Planning says it is involved in "option counseling." One of the options is abortion. In fact, agency officials say, federal regulations governing grants require them to counsel clients on all options, including prenatal care and delivery, foster care, adoption and "pregnancy termination."

Legislator Gerald Mingolelli isn't satisfied. "The county should not be in the business of counseling on abortion," he said.

Mingolelli is parroting what anti-abortion groups want across the land — absolutely no government involvement in or recognition of abortion. They want it even though abortion is legal, and has at least the tacit support of a majority of Americans.

▽   ▽

The right-to-lifers aren't interested in what the law is or what public opinion says. They're intent on ending abortion, and look for every chance to further that cause. Rent-free use of Civic Center space gives them an opportunity for another skirmish.

Make no mistake, though. Free rent isn't the issue, and arguing the merits of it misses the point.

The focus should be on whether Family Planning provides useful service to the community. If legislators find the agency has been "pushing" abortions, that service can and should be questioned.

But if they find, and we believe they will, that Family Planning plays a key role in improving the maternal and child health of the county, they should vigorously defend it against the latest assault from anti-abortionists.

Richmond Times-Dispatch

Richmond, VA, November 24, 1984

"I am personally opposed to the destruction of property, but I respect the right of people who do it where babies are being slaughtered." So said a member of the Pro-Life Nonviolent Action Committee after the bombings of an abortion clinic and a Planned Parenthood office in Montgomery County, Md., last week.

So much for the "right" in righteous. So much for right and wrong. And so much for respecting moral and temporal law.

That attitude, echoed by several pro-life advocates in the Washington area and elsewhere, and the bombings that prompted them and are encouraged by them, are as grievous as the more than a million abortions performed in the United States each year.

Reducing that number ought to be high on the agenda of both pro-life and pro-choice advocates. But this is still the United States of America. It is a nation of, for and by the people, most of whom would prefer education and contraception as alternative methods of birth control but would not deny a woman an abortion under any and all circumstances. It is also a nation of laws, not men, in which acceptable procedures have been established for change, in which penalties are prescribed and opprobrium expected for those who operate outside them.

Any American who disagrees with the law as established in *Roe vs. Wade* is entitled to exercise moral suasion and political clout in an effort to change it. But until the law is amended, any woman is entitled to avail herself of it without being harassed or intimidated, and any reputable clinic to abide by it without being bombed.

"I was really angry [about the Maryland bombings]," said the president of the Pro-Life Nonviolent Committee, which had picketed the clinic the day before. "The work we're doing, it totally shoots it down. . . . There are a lot of minds and hearts to win over. Blowing up clinics only hardens hearts." He is but one of many prolifers cognizant of the damage done their cause.

But too many of those fail to acknowledge how thin the line between harassment and violence can become, how dangerously narrow some definitions of "pro-life" have become, how insufficient are disclaimers of direct involvement. For bombing not only hardens hearts; it also kills, sooner or later. And at that point, the bombers and their apologists both will have done the very thing for which they condemn others.

DESERET NEWS

Salt Lake City, UT, November 23, 1984

In the name of protecting the right to life, some foes of abortion are playing with possible death and destruction.

In the process, they are giving an undeservedly bad name to an otherwise important and constructive movement.

This week, for example, an abortion clinic and a referral office in two Washington suburbs were bombed.

These episodes, Scripps-Howard News Service reports, raises to 19 the number of such facilities burned or blown up this year, compared to three in 1983.

The figures, however, don't include the growing number of telephone-threats, break-ins, paint-throwing incidents, and other harassment at abortion offices.

To their credit, the leaders of the anti-abortion movement generally have denounced the use of violence. But they need to make their denounciations stronger and more frequent. Otherwise, if the violence keeps escalating, it may not be long before someone is killed or injured in one of these incidents.

The zealots need to be told that violence can boomerang by producing counter-violence. Or it can bring on heavy-handed government intervention.

For their part, leaders of the pro-choice movement should stop smearing their opponents by implying that violence by a few is the result of complicity on the part of all anti-abortionists.

The abortion movement has aroused some extremely strong emotions. But the way to fight that movement is not with bombs and threats but with persuasion and even with law suits. That's the way to fight the violence and bullying, too.

"I KNOW HOW TO STOP ABORTIONS... LET'S BOMB SOME BIRTH CONTROL CLINICS!"

Rockford Register Star

Rockford, IL, December 28, 1984

Even those Americans who abhor abortion should be shocked and dismayed at the recent spate of bombings and arson incidents at abortion facilities around the nation.

Three such facilities in Florida were bombed over the Christmas holiday, raising the number of attacks this year to at least 20.

Opponents of abortion might argue that the sanctity of human life takes precedence over property rights, and that property used for snuffing out the lives of the unborn merits no respect. We will neither concede nor dispute those positions here.

But, like most Americans, we must take exception to bombings and arson as legitimate tactics of protest against abortion or anything else. Such acts are both cowardly on the part of the perpetrators and perilous to innocent passersby. Nor do they prevent or even diminish abortions.

Numerous non-violent means of protest, both within and without traditional political channels, are available to opponents of the practice — passive civil disobedience, for example. Certainly, the great civil rights leaders of this century, Martin Luther King Jr. and Mohandas K. Gandhi, would have disapproved of bombings as a means of protest. It also is hard to imagine Jesus Christ lending assent to such violent tactics.

Abortion, as a political controversy, will not soon fade away. Nor should sincere, conscientious opponents give up their political fight against it. But neither should they lend silent assent to the reckless acts of violent fanatics in the movement.

No legal prohibition against abortion in this country will result from bombings.

The Chattanooga Times

Chattanooga, TN, October 15, 1984

If ever the name of God has been taken in vain, it has been by the violent anti-abortionists who dub themselves the Army of God. This despicable group of fanatics, who proclaim themselves righteous by virtue of their opposition to abortion, are believed to be the source of a menacing letter threatening the life of Supreme Court Justice Harry Blackmun. It was Justice Blackmun who wrote the majority opinion in the controversial decision which leagalized abortion in this country.

Three members of the Army of God were convicted last year in the kidnapping of an Illinois abortion clinic director, whom they had threatened with death. The group has also claimed responsibility for a number of attacks on abortion clinics around the nation. What extreme hypocrisy to indulge in criminal violence in the name of promoting respect for human life!

Abortion is an issue which automatically engages the emotions of those involved, and understandably so. But the terrorist tactics of the Army of God show where unrestrained fanaticism on this, or any other issue, can lead.

Soldiers in the Army of God may say, "But we are right and the pro-abortionists are wrong!" No doubt members of Islamic Holy War would respond similarly to condemnations of their attacks on U.S. installations in Beirut. A terrorist by any other name is a terrorist still.

FORT WORTH STAR-TELEGRAM

Fort Worth, TX, December 6, 1984

According to the National Abortion Federation, whose headquarters in Washington, D.C., were bombed last July 4, there have been 24 fires or bombing incidents at abortion-related offices, clinics and counseling centers this year.

One would be too many.

There have been no deaths or serious injuries in these attacks, but there easily could have been. A pipe bomb is indiscriminate. It doesn't care who is nearby when it explodes.

In some widely separated cases, an amorphous group calling itself the Army of God has claimed credit. It has established at least sufficient credibility that telephone calls purporting to be from the Army of God have been taken seriously by the FBI when they threaten attacks on abortion clinics in El Paso.

The Army of God, if it actually exists, is no different from Islamic Jihad, the terrorist outfit that takes responsibility for bombings and murders directed against a U.S. presence in the Middle East.

Terrorism is terrorism, whether it is in Northern Ireland, Lebanon or Maryland.

And there is certainly no place for terrorism in the United States. Not if it is committed by a group or merely by individual fanatics.

What terrorists have in common all over the world is a dedication to principle so single-minded that it obscures whatever validity there is in the cause being promoted. That has become true of the IRA bombers and assassins in the British Isles, of Islamic Jihad and of those who carry their opposition to abortion to violent extremes in this country.

Terrorist acts are self-defeating. But that does not keep them from endangering innocent lives.

Federal authorities do not believe that the incidents claimed to be the work of the Army of God are related to each other.

Those under attack, abortion rights advocates, are afraid the incidents are connected.

It doesn't really matter, though the authorities should be (and undoubtedly are) making efforts to establish for certain whether there is an organized terrorist conspiracy at work.

What does matter is putting a halt to such terrorism committed in the name of "pro-life" dedication. The place for the nation's attitudes toward abortion to be decided is in its legislatures, its courts and its homes and churches, not by outlaw bomb-builders.

Whatever the cause and its merits, America can not allow bombings and arson to replace reason and democratic solutions. And those who oppose abortion, from the smallest church to the White House, should be in the forefront of exerting their influence against terrorist acts.

Detroit Free Press

Detroit, MI, December 27, 1984

THE BOMBING of three abortion offices in Pensacola, Fla., is the latest in more than two dozen attacks on abortion clinics and family planning offices in 1984. The response of many pro-life groups has been complacent: It's too bad somebody's out there bombing, but at least there won't be any abortions performed in those places anymore. The response of the federal government has been non-existent; the FBI sees no evidence that an organized group or a federal crime is involved, although one is tempted to ask if anybody at headquarters has even looked.

It's hard to believe that if 24 churches — or 24 social agencies, or 24 fast-food franchises, or 24 of anything else — had been bombed in a single year, the FBI wouldn't have at least a teensy-weensy suspicion that a conspiracy existed or that a state line had been crossed. The clinic bombings, in contrast, are being shrugged off — hardly an attitude to discourage the bombers.

Two things come to mind: First, it's lucky that no one has been hurt yet, but if the attacks continue, it's only a matter of time until someone is. Secondly, the attacks are apparently being done in the name of a higher morality — somebody's belief that, despite the legalization of abortion by the Supreme Court more than a decade ago, it is acceptable to use violence and destruction to halt it. It's hard to decide which is the most dangerous: the dynamite, the bombers' self-proclaimed dispensation from the rule of law, or the fact that nobody in the federal law enforcement agencies seems to take either very seriously.

'IN THE NAME OF THE FATHER, AND OF THE SON...'

The Orlando Sentinel
Orlando, Fla., July 11, 1984

Last month a bomb exploded in a Pensacola abortion clinic. On July 7 a bomb went off outside a similar clinic in Maryland. Three days earlier a bomb had exploded at the National Abortion Federation offices in Washington. In May someone fired 42 shots at two Fort Lauderdale abortion clinics. In March a person representing The Army of God, an anti-abortion organization, claimed responsibility for setting a fire at a Maryland clinic.

There's room for debate about abortion but there's absolutely no defense for this violence in the anti-abortion campaign. And it is strange indeed coming from a campaign that has been based on the right to life. But consider what has been happening. There were 28 bombings and fires at abortion clinics nationwide in 1982, 43 in 1983 and 53 so far this year.

Harassment and violence at clinics offering abortions is not new. For example, employees at a clinic in Orlando have received death threats. There have been bomb scares and the clinic's windows have been shot out. Patients have been called "murderers" as they walked through the doors.

Some right-to-life groups have been urging members to intensify their fight by picketing and organizing sit-ins outside clinics. Sit-ins and picketing are harassment but they aren't violent and usually they aren't illegal. That distinction obviously has been lost on some within the right-to-life movement. Responsible leaders within that campaign should make the distinction clear. Such violence sounds all too much like a kind of fanaticism that pushes aside both law and reason.

There may never be a meeting of the minds between those who consider abortion a woman's right over her body and those who consider it murder. But for members of any group to use bombings and fires to drive home their point is criminal.

The News American
Baltimore, Md., July 10, 1984

Had the bombing of the Planned Parenthood building in Annapolis been just an isolated incident, one might be able to write it off as the cowardly act of one individual. But the Annapolis bombing occurred the same week someone or some group — perhaps the so-called (and obscenely misnamed) Army of God, which called a newspaper to claim "credit" — tried and failed to bomb the National Abortion Federation offices in Washington. So far this year nine abortion clinics across the country have been bombed.

Fragments of the bomb that went off in Annapolis are undergoing laboratory scrutiny, and you have to pray the technicians come up with clues that could lead to the culprits. What's going on is incredible as well as nauseating. The abortion issue is always going to be controversial, always going to be bitter. But it was inconceivable that anyone would resort to terrorism.

The leaders of Planned Parenthood are calling for federal intervention to end the bombing. They should get all the help the federal government can give them.

The Wichita Eagle-Beacon
Wichita, Kans., October 12, 1984

The death threat against Supreme Court Justice Harry Blackmun is the latest example of how the abortion debate is turning strident and ugly. It underscores the importance of mutual respect and civility in addressing such an emotional subject. The justice, who wrote the court's 1972 Roe vs. Wade majority opinion legalizing abortion in the first six months of pregnancy, received a threat by mail, purportedly from a radical group calling itself The Army of God. The group has taken responsibility for recent violent attacks on abortion clinics, attacks that have tripled in the past year.

Whether the organization is sizable or just a handful of zealots is unknown. What's clear is that those who resort to violence have no respect for life whatsoever. Recent violent attacks against abortion clinics seem symptomatic of, if not actually encouraged by, some of the more ugly protests and pickets that have followed the Democratic candidates in recent weeks.

Of course, abortion is a legitimate subject for public debate, and as both President Reagan and Walter Mondale showed in their first meeting, it can be discussed within civil guidelines, without resorting to invective and slander. Certainly the recent attacks have not had the backing of responsible pro-life groups.

Abortion is a complex issue about which moral and honest people can disagree. That's why the moral certainty sometimes found on both sides of the issue is troubling. But in searching for solutions to this problem, it is most important that passioned advocacy not descend into blind, dangerous fanaticism.

THE BILLINGS GAZETTE
Billings, Mont.. November 21, 1984

Abortion is a gut level issue. There are ayes and nays, but very few maybes.

And opponents are caught in a moral dilemma.

They believe that to remain silent is unforgiveable. Each day the practice continues, more babies die. Some 15 million have been aborted since the Supreme Court decision in 1973.

So protests and pickets have sprung up around the nation. That's the American way.

When the Supreme Court ruled in the Dred Scott case that Blacks weren't real people, northern protest boiled over into civil war.

In the 60s, Blacks took to the street to protest their second-class citizenship.

In the late 60s, campuses across the United States erupted. "Hell no, we won't go," was the focus of unrest among the nation's students over the Vietnam War.

And protest has been born of abortion.

It has been a quiet protest reflecting the fact that most of the protesters are quiet people — middle-class, middle-aged Americans. Parents, not children. Establishment, not anti-establishment.

But recently that has changed.

There is a lunatic fringe of people who consider themselves pro-lifers, and those people have begun bombing Planned Parenthood offices and abortion clinics around the nation.

This year there have been 21 incidents of bombing and arson, in 1983, three; in 1982, eight; 1981, one; and 1980, none.

Monday, twin bomb blasts ripped through a clinic in a suburb of Washington, D.C. The rear wall of an abortion clinic was blown away, and a nearby Planned Parenthood office was heavily damaged.

It was 6:15 a.m., a time when an early riser might well have been in his office, a paperboy sauntering down the street, an elderly woman walking her dog.

The point is that those bombs put people in danger.

And that fact should be as abhorent to anti-abortionists as abortion.

The second point these people might keep in mind is this: The pro-life movement in the United States is being heard.

Abortion was one of the key issues in the last presidential race. Voters were told their votes would put Reagan, an avowed anti-abortionist, or Mondale, a proponent of abortion, in a position to pick the next justices for the Supreme Court.

But the bombings may well change that. The backlash to the violence could hurt the cause these people apparently believe they are espousing.

It is time to put a stop to the bombings. It is time to reveal the bombers for what they are, terrorists, who apparently care more for their own ego gratification than they do for their cause.

They are certainly not part of the pro-life movement

The Providence Journal
Providence, R.I., October 11, 1984

Talk about a religious war in the United States is clearly excessive. Still, the fears of William Baird, a leader of pro-choice forces in the abortion controversy, positioned next to reports of abortion clinic fire-bombings, indicates the level to which this nation's emotional binge has sunk.

Firebombings do not just happen. They are carefully planned and executed by extremists engaged in a hate campaign, using violence as a symbol of love for the unborn. The bombings or attempted attacks have escalated from three in 1982 to four last year to 19 so far this year. Yesterday it was reported that an anti-abortion group called the Army of God two weeks ago sent a death threat to Supreme Court Justice Harry Blackmun, author of the court's legalized abortion ruling of more than a decade ago.

Mr. Baird's verbal excess notwithstanding, when justices lives are threatened, when abortion and pregnancy counseling clinics arm themselves and doctors begin carrying pistols for protection, the violent fanaticism of some anti-abortionists must be condemned.

On the whole, the so-called pro-life organizations do not condone violence. "It does our movement no good," said John C. Willke, president of the national Right To Life group. Why then does Mr. Willke give comfort to the perpetrators of these insane deeds by saying, "I don't think the external violence will ever stop until the internal violence ceases"?

Inflammatory rhetoric, no matter how heartfelt or intimately related to religious beliefs, fuels the attacks that have occurred in Virginia, Maryland, Delaware, Florida, Georgia, California and the District of Columbia. The presidential election campaign has stirred an outpouring of anti-abortion rhetoric unequaled in recent memory. The extent to which it has contributed to the violence is questionable but there is little doubt that the less stable individual may be incited to violence when exposed to terminology such as "baby killers" and unsubstantiated charges that aborted fetuses suffer a painful death.

This country cannot afford such social divisiveness. The clergy and public officials have a solemn responsibility to speak out on the side of reason rather than to further inflame passions when religious controversy reaches the point of violence. That time has come.

LEXINGTON HERALD-LEADER
Lexington, Ky., November 26, 1984

In a nation such as the United States, where the peaceful means for effecting needed change are a constant of our democratic system, violence as a method of promoting or defending a cause is indefensible.

That is one reason for deploring the recent bombings of an abortion clinic and a Planned Parenthood office in the suburbs of the nation's capital. If the wishes of those who oppose abortion are to be achieved, then the proper avenue is to change the prevailing law of the land through the existing system. To do so, they must change the opinion shared by a majority of Americans that abortions should be legal. Violence is hardly likely to bring about that change.

In this instance, there is another reason for abhoring violence for a cause. Those who oppose abortion label themselves as being "pro-life." No one was injured or killed in the two recent bombings, but someone easily could have been. Sooner or later, if this year's rash of violent attacks on abortion clinics and family-planning centers continues, death or injury will occur. That will be the ultimate irony in this controversy — a loss of life inflicted by some terrorist cloaked in the "pro-life" banner.

The vast majority of the pro-life movement would not consider, and do not condone, the use of violence. They oppose abortion on the basis of legitimately held moral beliefs, and their opposition is directed through equally legitimate channels for effecting change.

But that small fanatical fringe of their movement that does condone violence, that bombs and attacks clinics, deserves the terrorist label just as surely as does any fanatic who drives a truck bomb into a U.S. embassy. They should be treated as such by law enforcement agencies.

The fact that these attacks — five bombings in the Washington, D.C., area and 24 violent attacks of one type or another across the nation this year — are the work of terrorists makes what family planning groups call the Reagan administration's "thundering silence" on this problem all the more apparent. If 24 violent attacks had been mounted around the country in one year by a group championing some cause not espoused by the New Right, we wonder if the Reagan administration would not label it a conspiracy and commit the vast resources of the federal Justice Department to the investigation, apprehension and prosecution of the persons involved.

But the Reagan administration sees no "link" in 24 attacks on abortion clinics and family-planning centers. So, although the federal Bureau of Alcohol, Tobacco and Firearms is investigating the individual bombings (as it does with all bombings), the Justice Department and the FBI are ignoring this terroristic violence. Like the violence itself, that is indefensible.

The Morning News
Wilmington, DE, January 8, 1985

LAST JANUARY 14, Delaware had the dubious distinction of having to report the first abortion clinic arson of 1984. While the Dover Reproductive Care Center and the Wilmington-based Women's Health Organization were spared any further violence during 1984, nationwide 23 other clinics were subjected to bombings and arson, according to government figures.

This year, the criminal attacks on abortion clinics began on New Year's Day in the nation's capital.

To date, the bombings and arson have caused no physical injuries, though they have inflicted trauma on persons working in the clinics and those who wish to use the clinics' services. There is also the ever-present danger that an innocent passerby or a security guard could be injured. The cost of the property damage has been large. In Dover, the damage ran to $100,000, and the crime remains unsolved.

A recent Media General-Associated Press poll showed that 50 percent of the respondents did not wish to restrict legal abortions with a constitutional amendment, while 35 percent favored such an amendment. Those 35 percent of Americans who oppose abortions are fully entitled to their views and to any and all legal strategies for getting their views across.

Most of the abortion opponents make good and proper use of their rights. In elections, they support candidates who share their views; they demonstrate peacefully against abortion; they urge legislation, local and national, that embodies their point of view; they make available support services for pregnant women.

But, unfortunately, there are also a few misguided persons who believe that the end that they hold dear justifies criminal means. These are the folks who set fire to clinics and plant bombs. In doing so, they become criminals, pure and simple. Law enforcement officials must make every effort to apprehend these criminals, and our record on that is not too good. Of the 24 acts of violence against clinics last year, the alleged perpetrators for seven cases have been charged.

Now that President Reagan, a firm opponent of abortion, has spoken out against against the criminals who attack these clinics, the national effort to prosecute may be stepped up. And the welcome result may be a decline in these criminal acts.

Abortion opponents who employ violence should be mindful that violence besmirches their cause.

The TENNESSEAN
Nashville, TN, January 11, 1985

ELEVEN years after the U. S. Supreme Court ruled in the landmark case of Roe vs. Wade, abortion continues to be one of the most emotional and divisive issues in America.

Recently some abortion opponents have taken drastic and destructive measures to halt abortions. In 1984, at least 24 bombing and arson attacks were reported on abortion clinics around the nation. Three clinics in Pensacola, Fla., were bombed on Christmas Day. Many other facilities were vandalized.

But these violent acts accomplish nothing but cheap publicity. Bombing a clinic might disrupt service for a few days at a location, but that is certainly no justification for committing a criminal act.

There are thousands of people in this nation who adamantly oppose abortion and many others who are uncomfortable with it, but would not want to see it made illegal. But most of those people, whether they oppose abortion for religious, ethical, or moral reasons, realize that criminal acts committed in the name of a personal conviction are still criminal. And most of those people realize that there are other more rational, effective, and legal means of protest.

One local group, the Christian Action Council, has protested abortion for the past year by holding a vigil outside Nashville's Planned Parenthood offices. Although the action of the Christian Action Council might be irritating to the employees of Planned Parenthood and harassing to women entering the clinic, the group is carrying on its vigil in a peaceful and legal manner.

Just because abortion is legal now does not mean it will remain so. The country, the courts, and the Congress are more conservative now than in 1973. Roe vs. Wade could possibly be overturned by the Supreme Court, or could be superseded by a constitutional amendment.

But in the meanwhile, no matter how virulent one's opposition might be, abortion is legal. Blowing up buildings is not.

WORCESTER TELEGRAM
Worcester, MA, December 12, 1984

The Planned Parenthood Clinic on Main Street has been harassed almost from the beginning. It had to get a court order to protect the rights of its clients. Recently, its medical director resigned. Although he is not saying why, the executive director of the Planned Parenthood League of Massachusetts says it was because he received anonymous phone calls threatening violence against his Fitchburg office. Also, she says his children have been harassed in school.

Those who have been picketing his office are claiming credit for his resignation from Planned Parenthood but also say they had nothing to do with the threats of violence. However, it seems likely that the picketing and the publicity led to the threats. That has happened in other places. Worse things have happened too.

So far this year in this country, 24 clinics offering contraceptive and abortion services have been torched and bombed. More than 150 cases of harassment have been reported.

Abortion is one of the most emotional issues known. But it needs to be remembered that what Planned Parenthood and other abortion clinics are doing is legal and, some believe, humanitarian. Bombings and arson are neither.

Emotional or not, issues like abortion have to be discussed in a rational manner and within the bounds of the law. Threats, harassment and violence have no place in our system.

THE BISMARCK TRIBUNE
Bismarck, ND, December 5, 1984

March backward a step, you so-called Christian soldiers who belong to the "Army of God," or who sympathize with its actions.

Do you think threats of kidnapping, attacks on abortion clinics and other violent measures are really consistent with your goal of protecting human life?

Like dedicated believers in other, sometimes less holy causes, you condone violence after failing to resolve your differences with society through persuasion and other peaceful means.

So far this year, there have been 20 attacks on abortion clinics and family practice centers across the nation. Most antiabortionists have denounced them, but nationwide the trend toward violence seems to be growing fast. Apparently those who carry out or condone the attacks don't realize that extremism will only help to ensure the failure that they fear, by driving away public sympathy and potential support.

In recent years, the issue of abortion has come down to the definition of human life. "Right-to-life" groups contend that this definition includes the unborn fetus at some point in its development — possibly as early as conception. Stopping the development of this fetus they see as murder.

"Pro-choice" groups contend that the unborn fetus, certainly in the earliest stage of development, is no more than the germ of life to come. They claim that the mother's right to control her own body outweighs the right of a fetus to become a child.

If every seed in a woman's body has the absolute right to development and birth, they ask, why not every seed in a man's body? Should not birth control be banned, also?

But being pro-choice does not mean being pro-abortion. And many pro-choicers are increasingly uncomfortable with the idea of abortion on demand.

That means they may at least support more effective programs and policies that encourage alternatives to abortion.

Unfortunately, for the antiabortionists, that isn't enough. In their eyes, innocent lives will be taken with every abortion that is performed. The watching inspires anguish, which in some turns to anger.

But when the Army of God begins picking up weapons, it loses much of the moral force of its arguments. Terrorists are neither Christians nor soldiers.

The Birmingham News
Birmingham, AL, January 1, 1985

One trusts that the federal agents who arrested a suspect in Pensacola's Christmas Day bombings of three abortion clinics will pursue the cases relentlessly.

Regardless of the deep concern many may have for the life of the unborn, destroying abortion clinics with bombs is no solution to the issue. And bombing or otherwise damaging the clinics does not further the cause of pro-life adherents. The bombings, regardless of who instigates them, can only damage the pro-life movement.

One trusts that responsible pro-life groups and individuals who oppose abortions will just as strongly oppose the criminal use of force to intimidate those who perform abortions. Bombs are the last resort of individuals who lack the patience and insight to work for a cause within the framework of law. Bombings may appear to be a shortcut to obtain a political goal, but any gains are transitory and counterproductive in a democratic society.

One should remember that respect for life is confirmed by respect for the law. It is improbable that society can have one without the other.

The Philadelphia Inquirer
Philadelphia, PA, January 5, 1985

The increasing incidence of bombings of abortion clinics is a deadly game. Igniting bombs in the dark in the hope of shedding light on one of the most controversial and intensely emotional questions of our time is an act that obviously exceeds the bounds of lawful or justifiable protest. No stand, however just, on any issue can validate such action.

The Hillcrest Women's Surgi-Center in Washington was on New Year's Day the scene of the latest of several bombings at abortion centers across the nation. Even before the smoke and debris was cleared away, tempers among supporters and opponents of abortion rights flared. Public officials and religious leaders joined the fray as Washington Mayor Marion Barry and the Rev. Jerry Falwell, who heads up the Moral Majority, traded petty insults on national television. They should have used their time, energy and influence to issue clear warnings concerning the dangers of planting bombs rather than making arguments related to the longstanding abortion controversy.

Mr. Barry characterized the anti-abortion terrorists as "deranged" and called on the "Jerry Falwells of the world to condemn such activities." Many right-to-life groups have done so.

Mr. Falwell castigated the mayor for his "uninformed" statements. But he added fuel to the fire when he said he could "understand how deranged people can do those things when I think about what goes on in the back rooms of those clinics."

It hardly seems proper to use the background of a newly bombed-out clinic to slip into a fresh debate on the issue of abortion. Each new bombing heightens tension and elevates violence. Mayor Barry and Mr. Falwell should have had more to offer concerning the bombings than attacking each other.

On Thursday, President Reagan ordered the Justice Department "to see that all federal agencies with jurisdiction pursue the investigation [of clinic bombings] thoroughly." Though belated, it is an entirely proper emphasis.

On the other hand, unresponsive leadership such as that of Mayor Barry and Mr. Falwell may stoke the fires of frustration and unrest. Playing politics with such an incendiary issue is a luxury Americans — whatever their views are about abortions — cannot afford.

Roanoke Times & World-News
Roanoke, VA, April 6, 1985

BY NOW this editorial page has, we hope, established its credentials as an opponent of abortion on demand. We believe that it devalues life and treats the helpless being inside the mother as no better than inert tissue.

That said, we take strong exception to the plans announced by anti-abortion activist Judy Cline this week to begin offering "sidewalk Christian counseling" outside an abortion clinic in Roanoke's Old Southwest.

Street-corner or parkside preaching is a tradition in America. It makes no demands on people, who are free to listen or pass by, and as long as it leads to no disorder, it is within the bounds of free speech. What Judy Cline and Kathy Hayden are talking about sounds rather different.

Their group already has permission from the city to stand outside the clinic six days a week, 9 a.m. to 5 p.m., and hand out leaflets. That is one thing. It is quite another to proffer advice to those who have not sought it. The sidewalks belong to the public, and it is illegal and contrary to public order to obstruct them or try to prevent anyone from passing, or from entering the clinic. And prevention — deterrence, at least — obviously is a prime goal of the picketers.

Frankly, we shrink from the thought of what kind of "counseling" can be given under such circumstances: in broad daylight, perhaps on the move, and probably not in confidential tones. It smacks of harassment, and on the whole it does not sound very Christian, either. The women who approach the clinic for abortions may be misled, they may be mistaken, they may be downright wrong. But until they ask the picketers for their counseling, they should not be hindered from what is their right under the law.

The picketers are zealous people, and some of them may believe that if they take extraordinary measures to stop abortion, they are following a higher law. If so, they should be willing — as have been Christian non-conformists down through the ages — to pay whatever penalty man's law exacts from them.

'IT BECAME NECESSARY TO DESTROY LIFE TO SAVE IT.'

The Morning Union

Springfield, MA, January 3, 1985

Tuesday's bombing of another abortion clinic — this one in Washington, D.C. — was an ominous sign of rising violence in this country and the government's apparent sympathy with the cause behind it.

Is the long battle over abortion now shifting from the courts, the polling places and the picket lines to the bomb-maker's basement? The possibility is chilling.

So far, the bombings have produced only damage. But a blast like the latest one, which not only wrecked the Hillcrest Women's Surgi-Center but also broke hundreds of windows on the other side of the street, could have killed or maimed many innocent people.

The bomb went off at 2:45 a.m., when few people would be up and about. But did the person who placed it on the clinic's windowsill *know* that no one was inside? Did the bomber *know* that no one, infant or adult, was sleeping behind a window across the street?

□ □ □

The clinic bombings apparently are being carried out by radical individuals. We doubt that the responsible majority in the pro-life movement would advocate such violence; more dangerous is the lack of interest among authorities to treat it as terrorism.

For terrorism it is, even if the FBI says no conspiracy is involved. A bomb is a coward's weapon — a tool of anonymous terror planted by someone who fights from the shadows, and doesn't care who suffers or dies as a result.

Pro-life advocates, even those high in government, would serve their cause better by hunting down and condemning the bombers than by pretending that the growing violence is merely a form of protest.

As many nations have learned, it is only a short step from "protest" bombings to bloodshed on a massive scale, when terrorism has become established as a way of life.

Los Angeles, CA, March 10, 1985

Abortion is tragic, morally dubious and distasteful. Yet access to a legal abortion remains a woman's right — as it should. At the same time, people who gather outside abortion clinics and yell cruel insults at those who enter, hoping to dissuade them, are also exercising a right that is morally dubious and distasteful.

Indeed, as long as the protesters refrain from committing an outright crime, their right to protest also must be preserved. But testimony before a House Judiciary subcommittee suggests that they have sometimes overstepped those rights. The subcommittee has heard witnesses report that they have even been threatened with death and bombings — activities that some members of the panel have asked the Reagan administration to crack down on.

Such tactics are not just wrong. We strongly doubt that they will ever put an end to legal abortions. One does not instill a "pro-life" attitude in a woman by subjecting her to cruelty or hatred; firebombings of abortion clinics (a tactic that is condemned even by most anti-abortion groups, by the way) haven't made a significant dent in the number of abortions performed each year.

The anti-abortion movement operates from a moral premise — that unborn life is sacred from the very moment of conception; but a moral premise cannot be foisted on an unwilling subject, except by force, which then, frequently, brings the premise itself into doubt or disrepute.

In history, force *has* been used in moral causes (as during the American Civil War), but, more often than not, the results are the opposite of what were intended. In any case, calling someone a murderer as she enters an abortion clinic is unlikely to make her sympathize with her tormenters.

Like anti-abortion activists, we look forward to a day when abortion is never necessary under any circumstances. But, if that day ever arrives, it will be at least partly because there are better alternatives. We urge the "pro-life" movement to help develop them and to rely on *rational* argument. Intimidation isn't the answer.

F.B.I. Terrorism Definition Excludes Antiabortion Violence

There had been only 8 acts of terrorism in the United States in 1984, announced Federal Bureau of Investigation Director William Webster at a press conference in December 1984. That figure was down significantly from previous years, but the F.B.I. terrorism data were challenged because they did not include a recent rash of bombings at family planning and abortion clinics. Webster explained that the abortion clinic bombings had not been included in the data because they had not been attributable to organized groups and had not been directed against any government. According to a New York Times article dated Dec. 12, 1984, definitions of terrorism used by the F.B.I. in 1982 and 1983 (numbering 51 and 31 respectively) for its terrorist statistics had not included those criteria. The executive director of Planned Parenthood of Minneapolis, Thomas Webber, called Webster's statements on the terrorist data "about the dumbest thing I've ever heard." The Planned Parenthood abortion clinic in Minneapolis had been the target of arson four times. According to federal authorities of the Bureau of Alcohol, Tobacco and Firearms in December 1984, some 30 instances of bombings and arson directed against family planning clinics had occured since May 1982, 24 of them in 1984.

President Ronald Reagan, who had long been criticized for not speaking out against the violence, issued a statement in January 1985 denouncing the bombings: "I condemn, in the strongest possible terms, those individuals who perpetrate these and all such violent anarchist attacks." While pledging to do "all in his power" to bring the perpetrators to justice, the President did not say he would change the way the cases were being investigated. Some critics had pressed the President to have the Federal Bureau of Investigation lead the probe of the cases rather than the Treasury Department's Bureau of Alcohol, Tobacco and Firearms. The Treasury agency had jurisdiction over cases involving explosives, and had reportedly assigned 500 agents to the incidents.

On Jan. 5, 1985 the Reverend Jerry Falwell, leader of the fundamentalist Christian group Moral Majority Inc., also condemned the bombings, saying they were the work of "deranged" persons.

The Kansas City Times
Kansas City, MO, December 11, 1984

What do the fanatics want with their bombings of abortion clinics across the country? To stop abortion? It won't happen. Most Americans will recognize these acts for what what they are — terrorism against women and teen-agers — even if the federal administration at this point refuses to denounce the assaults as such.

So far the clinics have not reported a decrease in those seeking birth control help. However, women who are frightened to go to the facilities may turn elsewhere, and that doesn't mean they will not seek abortions. They are likely to go to the back alleys where abortion thrived before clean, legal facilities were available.

A number of clinics which have been hit with acts of irrationalism are not even abortion clinics, but offered birth control services. Without access to these services, teen-agers and others increase their chances of pregnancy. That leads to more abortions. Somehow, the right-to-lifers have never caught on to the fact that fewer abortions are linked to birth control.

Damage to property has been heavy. Although no one has been hurt so far, sooner or later someone will be. A terrorist-inspired propane gas explosion destroyed part of the National Abortion Federation building in Washington on July 4. But only a few minutes later, police found another bomb that could have destroyed the entire building, damaged others on the block and hurt or killed scores of people. The same story is told across the country in an estimated 25 or more violent happenings this year alone.

Those aren't the only hostile acts, either. Picketing, long a staple of the anti-choice crowd at some clinics, has been supplemented with harassment, threats of bodily harm against workers, and destructive acts.

Other clinics in various cities reportedly have been targeted by a misbegotten group calling itself the Army of God. The clinic staffs are attempting to protect themselves with assistance from federal authorities. Still, more should be done and that is to arouse public sentiment against this method of espousing right to birth by deathly violence. It can begin with a White House condemnation of these life-threatening acts. Those who perpetrate this type of terroristic violence at home should be given the same denunciation as others who practice it against Americans on foreign soil.

THE LOUISVILLE TIMES
Louisville, KY, December 28, 1984

The director of the FBI says it was not terrorism when a wave of bombings hit abortion clinics — most recently in Pensacola, Fla., early Christmas morning. A Baptist minister allows that the attacks were "deplorable," but that they may more effectively combat abortion than peaceful demonstrations.

And law enforcement authorities — following more than 29 abortion-related attacks in the past three years — have filed charges in only eight.

What we are seeing is a disturbing pattern emerging among those in positions of authority. When abortion is the target, they seem to be saying, tactics that are unacceptable in other contexts may be, if not appropriate, at least less offensive. Never mind that these are attacks on lawful operations — clinics, doctors' offices and other medical facilities.

A pre-Thanksgiving attack on abortion and family planning clinics in Maryland began the most recent spate that led to the three bombings Tuesday in Florida. A variety of threats have been made elsewhere.

In Florida, investigators for the federal Bureau of Alcohol, Tobacco and Firearms have offered a $10,000 reward for information leading to the arrest of those responsible. Unless law enforcement gets tough, the wave of violence is unlikely to be checked.

Columnist Ellen Goodman recently observed that there's no evidence that the violence directed at abortion clinics and their staffs is coordinated. Nor is there any proof that the well-known organizations that oppose abortion are involved or approve.

But what does seem clear, as Ms. Goodman noted, is that the episodes are "occurring in an atmosphere of general frustration, escalating anger and mounting pressure for action among anti-abortion activists."

Their frustrations have, if anything, been aggravated by the empty promises of political figures, whose rhetoric ignores the Constitution, as articulated by the highest court in the land. As the Rev. David Shofner of West Pensacola Baptist Church said, "Bombing and fire will certainly stop it (abortion); picketing doesn't."

He's wrong, though. History shows that abortions will occur, whether the law allows them or not. The difference is that instead of being conducted in unlawful chambers by sometimes disreputable personnel, they occur now in licensed, inspected hospitals and clinics.

The record shows that the Justice Department, state and local officials haven't done a very good job in apprehending the anti-abortion terrorists. That must change, and every law-abiding American, whatever he thinks of abortion, should encourage prompt arrests and convictions.

Lincoln Journal
Lincoln, NE, March 5, 1984

The lunatic fringe of the anti-woman's-choice crowd — and apparently it's a fairly substantial fringe — is getting rougher still.

Blowing up medical clinics or trying to intimidate women seeking abortions wasn't enough. Now they have tried to assassinate the Supreme Court member who wrote the 1973 abortion-rights decision. Doing so would allow President Reagan to make a "right" kind of replacement.

Whoever deliberately fired a 9mm bullet into the Arlington, Va., third-floor apartment living room of Associate Justice and Mrs. Harry Blackmun last Thursday night was following up on the stream of death threats mailed to the judge.

Federal agents ultimately arrested several men because of clinic bombings in the Washington, D.C., area. Let us hope the FBI is equally successful tracking down the potential killer of the 76-year-old Blackmun.

We can be absolutely sure that the leadership of the anti-abortion movement, and especially Catholic and some Protestant ministers, were just as shocked and sickened by the disclosure of the attempt on Justice Blackmun's life as everyone else.

But who can doubt that an incessant flow of the most violent rhetoric aimed against the reality of abortion, those women who elect it, those medical personnel who assist them and even those men and women from agencies which counsel birth control will not twist the minds of the susceptible, the irrational, the unbalanced?

Murderous words set loose can find lethal ways to targets. They end up trying to destroy presidents as well as judges.

In the trying, they also smash at the our common experiment of ordered liberty and self-government.

The Hartford Courant
Hartford, CT, December 31, 1984

William H. Webster, director of the Federal Bureau of Investigation, said earlier this month the FBI doesn't consider bombings of family planning and abortion clinics to be terrorism because they aren't "acts of violence committed in furtherance of an attack on a government."

But the FBI itself has included in its definition of terrorism incidents of violence that are directed against civilians for "political or social objectives" — a description that obviously applies if it's some anti-abortion activists who are behind the attacks on clinics.

There have been 29 of them in the past three years — 20 in 1984. No one has been injured, but the threat to patients and staff is clear.

Agents of the federal Bureau of Alcohol, Tobacco and Firearms, which investigates bombs and arson, have begun to look into the possibility that three Christmas Day bombings that destroyed one clinic and damaged two more may be linked to others in the Southeast.

Dan Conroy, head of ATF's Miami office, said there may be a connection among them and said the bureau will take "the forefront in investigating abortion-clinic-associated bombings across the country."

It's welcome news that someone will. Time wasted quibbling over definitions can only comfort those responsible for the violence. State and local police, even with the help of ATF agents, probably cannot conduct needed investigations alone.

Mr. Webster ought to re-read his agency's own materials and get cracking.

The Orlando Sentinel
Orlando, FL, December 27, 1984

It's probably only a matter of time before one of the nuts bombing abortion clinics blows up some people along with the brick and glass. The explosions at three Pensacola sites on Christmas morning are just the latest outrages. Such clinics have been bombed and torched at a record rate this year, and such crimes shame the anti-abortion movement.

When will "pro-life" activists drop their absurd ambivalence about this destruction — after it finally kills a guard or passer-by? Once that inevitable murder happens, the activists surely will distance themselves from this dangerous game of chance. But until then, too many of them absurdly claim that — while they wouldn't have done it themselves — they are happy with the result.

By condoning these violent acts, anti-abortion activists encourage more violence. That's outrageous — and it tarnishes the credibility of those who protest openly and peacefully. The "pro-life" people should be at the fore in denouncing these bombings and arson attacks instead of offering wimpy excuses.

This year's toll of attacks nationwide is 24, contrasted with a total of five during 1982 and 1983. If any of these potential murderers believe such crimes aren't taken seriously, they should wake up. A man convicted of multiple attacks in Washington state, for example, recently was sentenced to 20 years in prison. That was in line with other recent sentences.

People have been arrested and convicted in all of the 1982 and 1983 incidents, but 21 of this year's crimes remain unsolved. The Bureau of Alcohol, Tobacco and Firearms says it has the expertise to be Washington's lead agency handling these crimes but that solving them simply takes time. That sounds reasonable, but if months pass without progress, President Reagan should consider whether the FBI can do the job better.

Abortion is a legal option that will spark controversy and sear consciences for years to come. But it is a difficult choice to be made by potential parents, not by nighttime vigilantes.

Portland Press Herald
Portland, ME, December 17, 1984

The Federal Bureau of Investigation makes an inappropriate political judgment when it decrees that most bombs which destroy in the night are terrorism, but bombs which destroy abortion clinics are not.

Who's kidding who? The explosions and fires which have ravaged 20 to 25 abortion clinics have a single purpose: to discourage and interfere with women who are exercising a constitutionally guaranteed right to a legal medical procedure.

When night bombers interfere with the rights of others in Lebanon or Nicaragua, terrorism as the right name to describe it comes easily to mind. Just so, the FBI has no difficulty fitting its definition of terrorism to the lone man with a truck who died laying siege to the Washington Monument two years ago.

The FBI defines terrorism as "the unlawful use of force or violence against persons or property to intimidate or coerce a government, the civilian population or any segment thereof, in furtherance of political or social objectives."

OK. The bombing and burning of abortion clinics is unlawful. It is violent. It is directed against property. And its purpose is to discourage a segment of the population—women—from obtaining abortions. Anyone who thinks such discouragement does not serve a social objective has forgotten a good portion of Maine's recent state Equal Rights Amendment debate.

The FBI may draw praise for terrorism statistics that omit the abortion clinic attacks. Leaving them out enables the bureau to say there have been only eight terrorist attacks in the United States this year, as compared with 31 in 1983. Including them, of course, would erase the dramatic decline. But it would serve the truth.

As it is, those who have a right to expect full protection of their person and their property confront terrorism protected not by the FBI's anti-terrorism investigators, but by the Bureau of Alcohol, Tobacco and Firearms.

That may not be second class citizenship, but it smacks of second class protection.

The Kansas City Times
Kansas City, MO, January 8, 1985

President Reagan at last has spoken out against the growing number of frightful bombings at family planning clinics across the nation. The president's words were tough. Given that, it took him a long time to denounce these acts which have been going on since May 1982. In at least one of the bombings, the clinic which was hit performed no abortions.

Mr. Reagan said he will do all in the power of the presidency to make sure the perpetrators of these bombings are brought to justice. Despite his tough talk, the president did not say he was changing the method by which the bombings are being investigated by the federal government. The Bureau of Alcohol, Tobacco and Firearms of the Treasury Department is in charge of the investigations, but family planning advocates have sought a greater role for the Federal Bureau of Investigation. Mr. Reagan, although he called the acts "anarchist," declined to identify them as terroristic — which would put them under the FBI's jurisdiction.

It is difficult to visualize what more it would take for these acts to be considered terroristic in nature. They fit the dictionary definition of terrorism, which is "use of force or threats to demoralize, intimidate and subjugate, esp. such use as a political weapon or policy."

If all is as it seems, the president's statement will signal that the federal government is going to take a more active role in bringing a stop to the bombings. Mr. Reagan is to be commended for not adding the unctuous disclaimer — as have other anti-abortion advocates — that these acts never would have happened if abortions were not being performed. To say that the bombings are wrong but "understandable" is the sort of code that gives unstable minds all they need to unhinge completely.

Abortion is permitted by law. Violence will not deter those seeking to exercise their rights under the law, and it does nothing to add support to the anti-abortion zealots. The National Right to Life Committee and other so-called pro-life advocates have denounced the bombings, realizing that one does not gain respect for life by condoning deadly acts.

The Houston Post
Houston, TX, December 24, 1984

It is curious that the administration has vowed to "get tough" with terrorism abroad but seems willing to do little about terrorism here at home: the bombings of abortion clinics.

Just this week, three more such facilities were devastated by explosions in Florida. The fanatic fringe of those opposed to abortions, stymied for now in its efforts to make abortion illegal, has elected to try making it impossible.

Yet despite the ongoing rash of bombings and arson attacks, FBI Director William Webster says the incidents are not terrorism.

You could have fooled us. When people sneak around in the dark with gasoline cans and homemade explosives and use them against the property of those with whose moral choices they disagree, it *is* terrorism, and saying it isn't will not change that.

We offer neither a defense nor a condemnation of abortion itself. We simply observe that, currently at least, elective abortions are entirely legal in this country. Having or not having an abortion is perhaps the most wrenching moral decision a human being can make, and our sympathy goes out to anyone who is confronted by such a choice, no matter which path they take.

But there is no sympathy from this quarter for the night-stalkers. They are engaging in violence and extreme psychological terror against people who are acting entirely within the law.

They say they are against murder — that they are only damaging real estate. Sooner or later though, one of their bombs will malfunction and blow up at 3 p.m. instead of 3 a.m. How, we wonder, will they feel then?

But for now, they are not terrorists. Just ask William Webster.

The Washington Post

Washington, DC, January 4, 1985

PRESIDENT REAGAN has issued a strong statement, his first, condemning the bombing of abortion clinics and pledging that he will do all in his power to bring the guilty to justice. This unequivocal commitment from the top has been much needed. In two years, 30 facilities in the country have been bombed, and the rate of the attacks has recently accelerated. Until yesterday, the political leadership of the administration had been silent at a time when forceful moral leadership was required to combat a vicious series of crimes.

Fortunately, federal law enforcement officials have not been sitting on the sidelines. From the time of the first bombing in 1982, the Bureau of Alcohol, Tobacco and Firearms—an agency with expertise in crimes involving explosives—has been on these cases. Twelve cases have already been closed, and the bombers sent to prison. Five individuals are serving terms—some for as long as 20 years. Four arrests have been made already in the Christmas Day bombings in Florida. The kidnappers of an abortion clinic owner and his wife have been convicted and sent to prison.

Yet there has been confusion about the federal effort in the minds of many citizens. Would Washington's response have been stronger if the criminals had been called "terrorists" instead of "fanatics" or "crazies"? Would the investigations have been more thorough if the FBI, the federal law enforcement agency best known to the public, were running the show instead of the ATF?

At the heart of these semantic and organizational questions is a simple notion: The administration has a responsibility to take these bombings as an ominous threat to the exercise of citizens' constitutional rights, and to convey its seriousness to the public. Good investigative work and speedy prosecutions are vital and surely will continue. But the president's own voice has been needed not only to reassure those whose rights are threatened but also to condemn and isolate the individuals who have been resorting to violence.

Most right-to-life groups already have spoken out against the bombings. They have a particularly strong interest in making the distinction between orderly and protected forms of protest against abortion and the activities of those on the fringes of the movement who think they are doing "God's work" and helping the right-to-life cause by blowing up buildings.

The ugly pattern of violence must be broken before more destruction and the inevitable loss of life occur. People, like the president, who oppose abortion and abhor the bombings have a special role to play in this effort.

The State

Columbia, SC, December 16, 1984

RECENTLY nocturnal explosions rocked an abortion clinic and a Planned Parenthood office in Maryland. No one was hurt, but damage was heavy; the clinic in fact was destroyed.

If these were isolated incidences, they might be dismissed of the handiwork of some kind of kook. Unfortunately they were just the latest of a series of bombings and burnings on abortion and family planning facilities. Planned Parenthood says that 20 of its offices have been hit this year alone, up from four in 1983.

A group calling itself the "Army of God" has claimed responsibility for outrages in Virginia and Florida, but most are believed to be unrelated.

The targets suggest strongly that the perpetrators are anti-abortion and pro-life, violently so. How can people be so misdirected that they think they can advance a cause with such methods? This is terrorism, pure and simple.

Any time arson is committed or a bomb is detonated, someone, some innocent party, can be killed. How can any pro-lifer who professes a respect for all life take such a chance? Most anti-abortion groups, it must be pointed out, have denounced these wanton acts.

Arsonists and bombers who act stealthily under the cover of night are among the hardest criminals to catch. When one is nabbed, the book should be thrown at him.

Perhaps one way to reach these people is through public denunciations by prominant leaders in the anti-abortion movement. President Reagan, fundamentalists like the Rev. Jerry Falwell, and leading Catholic bishops could singly or in concert repudiate these dastardly and cowardly acts.

We are constantly amazed how the abortion issue so stirs passions among people on both sides that the thinking of some is warped and excesses are committed.

San Francisco Chronicle

San Francisco, CA, January 1, 1985

THE ARREST OF A SUSPECT in the Christmas Day bombings of three Florida clinics where abortions are performed is one of the first positive signs that the federal government is finally waking up to the seriousness of the attacks that have grown in number and ferocity over the last year.

In the latest attacks, the clinics were hit by powerful bomb blasts which did substantial damage and were potentially lethal had anyone been in the buildings.

These bombings brought to more than two dozen the number of serious bomb and arson attacks against family planning facilities in the United States this year. That figure does not include hundreds of other lawless acts against the clinics and their staffs, including death threats, vandalism and harassment.

AFTER THE ARREST, of a young man who is said to believe he was only following "God's law," investigators said they think the Florida bombings, and perhaps others, may be the work of a secret organization.

Despite all this, key voices in the federal government have treated these attacks as relatively minor police matters and have remained uncharacteristically silent in face of the campaign of terrorism now clearly being waged.

One official who has seemed oddly unconcerned is FBI Director William Webster, who didn't admit the seriousness of the attacks on abortion clinics until a few days ago. However, he still insists the bombings do not qualify for FBI investigation because he does not view them as terrorist attacks.

WEBSTER TRIED to slough off the dispute over his refusal to use the word terrorism as just "semantics," but the FBI concedes that listing the attacks as such would lead the Bureau to investigate them vigorously.

Instead, they are being investigated by the federal Bureau of Alcohol, Tobacco and Firearms, which made the Florida arrest despite the fact that it is much smaller and has far fewer investigative resources than the FBI.

Another silent official has been President Reagan, whose opposition to terrorism is usually as outspoken as his opposition to abortion. While he has denounced terrorist bombings in other parts of the world, he has been silent so far toward bombings in a dozen American cities.

IT SEEMS CLEAR that the bombers and arsonists are hoping to achieve through their acts what they have not been able to accomplish through civilized political and legal channels — ending abortion in the United States.

It is also clear that these are terrorist acts and should be treated as such. The bombers and arsonists may believe their terrorist acts against abortion clinics are holy, but so did the terrorists who blew up the U.S. Marines in Beirut.

So far, no one has been killed in the bombings and arson at family planning clinics. But it can only be a matter of time until a bomb goes off in the vicinity of a patient, a staff member, a child or even a bomber.

There have been a few prosecutions so far, and a Washington State anti-abortion leader was sentenced last month to 20 years in federal prison for fire-bombing an abortion clinic in Everett, Wash., but the latest bombings show that the situation is far from being under control.

BESIDES STEPPED-UP investigation of the bombings and arson attacks, we need public officials who are not afraid to condemn these terrorist acts, regardless of their feelings about abortion.

The Providence Journal
Providence, RI, January 5, 1985

To the extent that any of the abortion clinic bombers may have taken misplaced comfort in the administration's anti-abortion stand, President Reagan has clearly and emphatically set the record straight. His vigorous denunciation of the bombings as "violent anarchist activities" is a welcome reminder to extremists that they undertake their reprehensible missions without any form of public or private approval.

"I condemn, in the strongest terms," the President said, "those individuals who perpetrate these and all such violent, anarchist activities. As President of the United States, I will do all in my power to assure that the guilty are brought to justice."

Had Mr. Reagan spoken sooner he would have blunted criticism of his silence and avoided misunderstanding on that point. Understandably, women's groups are sensitive to any imbalance in the government's approach to terrorism. One group asked that the President condemn "the terrorist acts in the same strong terms you condemn the attacks of international terrorists upon American citizens." In his statement of Thursday he did just that.

Further, it seems the administration may be edging toward fuller involvement of the Federal Bureau of Investigation in this matter. Well it should. Mr. Reagan said he would tell Atty. Gen. William French Smith "to see that all federal agencies with jurisdiction pursue the investigation vigorously." An aide said, however, that this was not a call for change and that primary responsibility would remain with the Bureau of Alcohol, Tobacco and Firearms. Still, the FBI would appoint an agent liaison with BATF, he said.

Mr. Reagan should follow his strong statement with an order to William Webster, FBI director, to list the bombers officially as terrorists and to assume investigative authority from BATF. Further hesitancy to do so flies in the face of the FBI's own definition of terrorism which encompasses violence against civilians toward "political or societal objectives."

The nation is aroused over the 30 or so abortion clinic bombings since 1982. Bishop J. Keith Symons of Pensacola-Tallahassee, Fla. said, "We cannot in any way condone willful destruction of property as any sign of disapproval of abortion."

Mr. Reagan can fulfill his pledge to do all in his power to bring the bombers to justice by bringing to bear the full force of the FBI, which has the manpower, training and resources to do the job.

THE ARIZONA REPUBLIC
Phoenix, AZ, January 1, 1985

YOUNG Matthew J. Goldsby presumably will go to trial one day as the bomber of three abortion clinics in Pensacola, Fla., and presumably he will claim then what he's claiming now — that he felt "God's law was what he had to follow, not man's law."

This is what he told agents of the U.S. Bureau of Alcohol, Tobacco and Firearms when he was arrested for bombing the clinics with black-powder charges. A conviction could lead to a sentence of up to 100 years in federal prison.

Goldsby, a 21-year-old construction worker, will be hard pressed, of course, to find any of "God's laws" that commanded him to plant explosives under the cover of darkness to blow up someone else's property.

As detestable as abortion is to many people, using violence to try discouraging operators of abortion clinics is surely no answer.

Anti-abortionists who work through court cases, through boycotts, through picketing and through the political process would agree that violence is wrong.

But violence has become part and parcel of some anti-abortion efforts.

Federal agents report at least 24 abortion-clinic bombings in the past several years, a hint of the extreme behavior that can be anticipated from here on out.

Goldsby's belief that he was responding to a higher spiritual commandment in carrying out the bombings has a familiar ring to it. The world hears such claptrap from the mouths of crazed Moslem terrorists who want to hurry up their life in eternity by mad acts of murder and bombing.

Those who invoke God's name as justification for murder and mayhem commit the ultimate sacrilege.

The Washington Times
Washington, DC, January 7, 1985

Abortion-on-demand is a moral outrage, and public revulsion toward assembly-line abortion clinics is understandable. But violent assault on those clinics is morally indefensible, as well as illegal, and the president's condemnation of the deluded fanatics responsible for recent bombings is a welcome development.

The Bureau of Alcohol, Tobacco, and Firearms has jurisdiction in matters involving explosives and, despite criticism from pro-abortion zealots, has discharged its responsibilities well. Thirty bombings have occurred since May 1982. In 12 of these cases, arrests have been made, and five persons have been convicted. Last week, four arrests were made in connection with the Christmas Day bombing of three Florida clinics. Yet some find it odd that the FBI has played only an advisory role, offering the ATF technical assistance.

FBI Director William Webster says the clinic attacks don't require the bureau's attention, even though his own guidelines define terrorism — a prime FBI target — as violence committed by two or more persons to achieve social or political ends. Unless each of these bombings is the work of a single individual — highly unlikely — the destruction easily fits the bureau's definition.

As we say, the ATF is performing its duties well. Even so, complaints from abortionists and their supporters that the administration was looking the other way when the bombs went off gained superficial justification from Mr. Webster's tortured interpretation of the FBI rulebook. Which made the president's words all the more welcome. With his clear and unequivocal statement last week, the president went a long way toward putting that canard to rest.

As more arrests are made, let us hope, would-be bombers will be driven back to the safety and civility of sidewalk picket lines and public debates, which is where and how this important issue ought to be resolved.

FORT WORTH STAR-TELEGRAM
Fort Worth, TX, January 4, 1985

Agents of the federal Bureau of Alcohol, Tobacco and Firearms had just arrested and charged two men in the Christmas Day bombing of abortion clinics in Pensacola, Fla., when another clinic in Washington, D.C., was damaged by a bomb.

Federal authorities counted 24 such bombings in 1984. The Washington incident, which blew out windows in other buildings near by, was the first of the new year.

The first man arrested in Florida indicated that he believed he was following God's law and attacking the clinics to save lives.

That's not the way to go about it.

Abortion is a touchy legal and moral problem.

Terrorist bombings are outside the law and outside morality. They are abhorrent.

Whatever the cause, whatever the principle involved, the bombings of these clinics must be stopped, the bombers caught and prosecuted.

Although federal authorities are correct that the primary enforcement responsibility in such bombings lies with the Bureau of Alcohol, Tobacco and Firearms, all appropriate federal agencies must become involved. The FBI has considerable manpower and investigative expertise that must be put to use. Indeed, it would help if President Reagan, whatever his personal attitude about abortion, would lend the authority of his office in opposition to these widespread bombings by assigning the FBI to concentrate on this problem in conjunction with ATF.

The opportunity is there to demonstrate that terrorism for any cause is a subject for massive effort by law enforcement.

When the first bomb went off, the issue ceased to be abortion and became public safety. The principle involved is the supremacy of law over violent imposition of will through terrorist activity.

Misguided fanatics must be shown that bombings are not the answer, before churches, or day-care centers or courthouses become the target of "principled" bombers who are out to save the world for their own private viewpoint of morality.

DAYTON DAILY NEWS
Dayton, OH, January 7, 1985

President Reagan finally condemned of bombing of abortion clinics in this country. He called the bombings the anarchist activities of a few. Hurrah for the President's decision to break his long and curious silence on this violence. He is right.

This is supposed to be the United States, not Iran or Northern Ireland.

Some people would prefer that the FBI handle the investigations. Currently the responsibility for finding the bombers remains with the Bureau of Alcohol, Tobacco and Firearms of the Treasury Department, with the FBI running fingerprint checks and psychological profiles of suspects.

If this arrangement does the job, fine. But it seems a bit odd that the FBI declined to spearhead the investigation because it said the attacks did not constitute terrorism. Terrorism is using force to intimidate. Bombing clinics in a number of cities as a way to stop or protest abortions seems intimidating enough.

Pittsburgh Post-Gazette
Pittsburgh, PA, January 4, 1985

After an indecent interval, President Reagan has lent his voice to the condemnation of violence against abortion clinics. Equally important, the president has ordered U.S. Attorney General William French Smith to ensure that all appropriate federal law-enforcement agencies cooperate in investigating what is becoming an epidemic of such attacks.

The latter assurance falls short of transferring prime responsibility for such investigations from the Bureau of Alcohol, Tobacco and Firearms to the Federal Bureau of Investigation. But White House spokesman Larry Speakes said that the FBI "is involved to a certain extent in the fact that they are monitoring the investigation, and I'm sure lending whatever support that they can that's appropriate."

That still represents a welcome correction of the insensitive posture struck by FBI Director William Webster, who commented a few weeks ago that abortion-clinic bombings were not a bureau priority because they did not conform to the official definition of "terrorism."

There is admittedly an element of symbolism in associating the FBI — the premier federal law-enforcement agency — with the investigation of the bombings, but symbolism is important in putting the federal government on record as deploring these acts of violence. President Reagan acknowledged as much in his tardy statement yesterday calling the bombings "anarchist activities" and promising that "I will do all in my power to assure that the guilty are brought to justice."

The president's comments are especially helpful because he is a powerful opponent of legalized abortion. At the least, his forthright condemnation should exorcise any lingering belief among anti-abortion extremists — a tiny fringe of the pro-life movement — that Mr. Reagan is even tacitly on their side.

The Miami Herald
Miami, FL, January 7, 1985

ANARCHY is a word not often heard in political discussions these days. When President Reagan used it in his welcome condemnation of abortion-clinic bombings, it sounded almost quaint, reminiscent of the infamous 1921 trial of Massachusetts anarchists Nicola Sacco and Bartolomeo Vanzetti. The two were executed, many believe wrongly, for armed robbery and murder.

Coming from a staunch conservative who campaigned to "get the Government off our backs," the word anarchy carries extra-strong meaning. While leftists seek to impose state control and direction throughout society, the anarchist denies the state's right to regulate *any* individual activity. The anarchist views the state as the source of evil. It therefore is extremely significant that even this conservative President condemns as anarchy the use of violence in supposed service of a Christian conscience.

President Reagan condemned "in the strongest terms those individuals who perpetrate these and all such violent, anarchist activities." He pledged to "do all in my power to assure that the guilty are brought to justice." And in fact, though the Administration refuses to bring the Justice Department's Federal Bureau of Investigation (FBI) into the investigations of 30 abortion-clinic bombings since May 1982, the Treasury Department's Bureau of Alcohol, Tobacco, and Firearms has made arrests in 12 of the 30 cases and secured convictions so far of five persons.

Mr. Reagan issued his strong condemnation only after criticism mounted of his Administration's attitude toward the rash of bombings. The President's personal disapproval of abortion is widely known. That fact, combined with the Administration's stubborn refusal to admit that the violence constitutes either terrorism or civil-rights violations and thus is FBI business, created the impression of a cavalier attitude toward the bombings. The President's strong condemnation helped dispel that damaging impression, which was fueling the ardor of anti-abortion zealots.

Abortion is not murder or homicide — those are legal terms, and the law is clear. People who oppose the legality of abortion are free to seek changes in the law. They are not free, however, to impose their own will on others through violence.

Whether such an imposition is called anarchy or terrorism, the result is the same. It abridges the most fundamental right of free people to go about their private business in conformity with laws adopted through the democratic process. The President's forthright condemnation of the supposedly Christian bombers is welcome indeed.

The Grand Rapids Press
Grand Rapids, MI, January 7, 1985

They call themselves pro-life, yet those individuals who perpetrated the two dozen terrorist acts against abortion clinics during the past year threaten to negate the positive efforts of anti-abortion forces across the country.

Few topics arouse stronger feelings or more heated exchanges than abortion. Whether pro or con, energies directed toward advancing either cause should be confined to rational activities.

More than 11 years ago, the U.S Supreme Court established the law of the land in its landmark Roe v. Wade decision, in which the court ruled that states may not prevent a woman from having an abortion during the first six months of pregnancy. That legal fiat heightened political activism on both sides of the abortion issue, since those opposed to the ruling must have a constitutional amendment to alter the high court's edict.

But the intensity of the dispute has never been felt as keenly as during recent weeks, when urban guerillas bombed three Pensacola, Fla., abortion clinics on Christmas Day and another clinic in Washington, D.C. on New Year's Day.

Most political groups have their fringe fanatics — those willing to go to destructive extremes in expressing their convictions. Quickly to mind come recollections of war protesters bombing research laboratories and trashing draft offices, and busing foes torching school buses. Such individuals seriously damage their cause; in this case, ironically, in the name of respecting life.

President Reagan has decried the violence, and properly so. He also has promised to do all within his power to bring the perpetrators to justice. But the president hasn't ordered the FBI to classify the bombings as terrorist acts, which has prevented the agency from placing the incidents among its top four priorities.

People who violently assail abortion clinics and their employees intend to further the pro-life cause. But they do just the opposite. They repel and offend the masses of people whose moral nerves they are trying to touch. Unless renounced and checked by responsible foes of abortion, these fringe kooks will discredit the entire pro-life effort. They could, in fact, be the death of it.

THE BLADE
Toledo, OH, January 9, 1985

PRESIDENT Reagan has finally spoken out against the bombings of some 30 abortion clinics around the nation, 25 in the past 12 months. But his belated response is not likely to lead to the federal law-enforcement action that is in order.

"I condemn, in the strongest terms, those individuals who perpetrate these and all such violent, anarchist activities," Mr. Reagan declared. Then he vowed to do all within his power to bring the bombers to justice.

But the President is not doing all he can. Although the FBI is sending an agent to act as a liaison with the Treasury Department's bureau of alcohol, tobacco, and firearms, which has jurisdiction in the bombings, Mr. Reagan failed to take the obvious step of ordering the FBI to take a more vigorous role in the investigation.

In this instance the President appears to be bowing to the vehement anti-abortion lobby. It may take a death or an injury in one of these explosions for the Federal Government — and the FBI in particular — to get off its duff and respond with real law-enforcement vigor.

One can imagine the furor that would have been unleashed had 30 schools been blasted apart. Abortion clinics deserve the same kind of attention, yet none is at hand. Suggesting that a double standard of justice is at work here is not far off the mark.

After a bombing recently in Washington, D.C., a caller claiming to be a representative of the Army of God said that the next incident would take place in Ohio. Law-enforcement officials in this state are alert to that possibility, but the most effective preventive step would be to call in the FBI.

That moment will not arrive until the White House responds more strongly to this pattern of domestic terrorism.

St. Petersburg Times
St. Petersburg, FL, January 8, 1985

The bomb that exploded outside a Washington abortion clinic on New Year's Day also shattered the silence from the White House. Two days later, President Reagan finally denounced the bombing and burning of abortion clinics across the nation. He used unusually harsh language, condemning the attacks as "violent, anarchist activities." He pledged to "do all in my power to see that the guilty are brought to justice."

The President's unequivocal statement was most welcome and needed, albeit overdue. For many months, Americans outraged over the escalating violence have urged Mr. Reagan to speak out against the attacks. His prolonged silence troubled those who felt his failure to condemn the violence indirectly encouraged it.

THE NEW YEAR'S Day blast followed the Christmas Day bombings of three abortion clinics in Pensacola, which followed 24 other attacks on clinics in 1984 alone. Many anti-abortion groups have denounced the bombings, realizing that their cause is not helped by fanatics who claim to be doing "God's work." It is particularly important for people who oppose abortion to take a strong stand against violent tactics aimed at terrorizing Americans who operate and use the clinics.

Mr. Reagan's own voice was needed to reassure American women and teen-age girls that the federal government would do all it could to protect their constitutional rights. However, the President did not order the FBI to take over primary responsibility for investigating the bombings. That task continues to rest with the Treasury Department's Bureau of Alcohol, Tobacco and Firearms (ATF).

ATF HAS BEEN doing a credible job. Twelve cases already have been closed, and all the bombers who have gone to trial have been convicted. Four people have been arrested in connection with the Christmas Day bombings in Pensacola. It is understandable, though, that many still believe the FBI should assume the leading role in the cases. As the nation's top law enforcement agency, the FBI would raise the stature of the probes and provide additional resources and expertise.

The President's continued moral leadership will be needed to break this ugly pattern of violence. The national debate over abortion cannot be resolved by blowing up buildings and endangering lives. It is imperative that the debate be conducted peacefully and with mutual respect for the sincerity of different beliefs.

The Oregonian
Portland, OR, January 8, 1985

Americans nationwide should join President Reagan in his condemnation of bombings of abortion clinics. Whatever their views on abortion, they, as has the president, should recognize this is a nation of laws, where differences are to be addressed by reason and debate, not by destruction.

No matter the intensity of belief, violence and anarchy have no place in a nation such as the United States, where people are guaranteed the right to free debate, to free elections, to representative lawmakers. Reagan, an ardent opponent of abortion, has properly used those guarantees to advance his views.

Unlawful acts of violence surely undermine those guarantees and, simultaneously, reduce chances of changing public policy within the democratic process.

There are people who feel strongly about many things happening on this planet: hunger, nuclear power plants and weapons, military installations, even taxes. If strong beliefs justify blowing up the property of someone who holds another position, this nation of varied peoples and perpectives will not long hold together.

The president's strong denunciation of the clinic bombings is welcome. His words — "I will do all in my power to assure that the guilty are brought to justice" — now can be measured against performance by federal law enforcement agencies in identifying, arresting and prosecuting the bombers who threaten far more than a few buildings.

THE PLAIN DEALER
Cleveland, OH, January 3, 1985

If 30 Exxon stations were bombed in protest of the environmental policies of oil corporations, no one would hesitate to call it terrorism and call in the FBI. If 30 Ford dealerships were bombed to highlight objections to the auto industry's employment practices, the result would be the same. Yet according to the administration, 30 bomb attacks on abortion clinics to protest the legal procedures practiced therein warrants neither the terrorism label nor the FBI's attentions.

The double standard that is suddenly apparent is easy to diagnose. First, the administration certainly agrees with the fundamental point of the bombers—that abortion is a sin—even if it does not condone random bombings as a means of getting the point across. Second, it is much easier for the administration to recognize terrorism when it comes from the left—as witness Central America. Last and least illegitimate, the FBI and the Bureau of Alcohol, Tobacco and Firearms could find no evidence of conspiracy, which is the government's debatable prerequisite for terrorist activity.

The government must no longer exclude the FBI and its formidable resources from the investigations. After the bombing Tuesday morning of an abortion clinic in Washington, D.C., an anonymous caller telephoned the Washington Times. The caller reportedly said:

This is the Army of God. We are responsible for last night's bombing. The bombing is a warning to abortionists everywhere, the bombings will not stop. This is also encouragement for John Goldsby, our brother in Florida, telling him to keep the faith. . . . the next bombing will be in Ohio. An Ohio abortion clinic will be bombed. . . .

That message, chilling in its bloody fanaticism, comes close to suggesting a national conspiracy, and in any event is evidence of a conspiracy to cross state lines with the intent to further destroy abortion clinics. Further, because it is a warning of future attacks, it is terrorism *prima facie:* it seeks to force politicial and social change through fear, destruction and, if need be, injury and death.

It now is evident that if the FBI remains aloof of the investigations, the administration must be saying, in so many words: "Gosh, this is a woeful state of affairs, but better them than us." That inescapable conclusion is as terrifying as the bombs and the maniacs that throw them.

More than a few walls and windows are at stake here. Innocent lives are being threatened, and with them the legitimate and legal methods of social change on which this nation is founded. Call it terrorism, and call in the FBI.

The Morning Union
Springfield, MA, January 8, 1985

None too soon, President Reagan has spoken out against the bomb-toting element that has been attacking abortion clinics around the country, ordering federal law enforcement agencies to cooperate in investigating the incidents.

The president's condemnation of the bombers carries added weight because of his well-known stand against legal abortions, and should help alleviate fear in such clinics in Massachusetts and elsewhere.

Administration silence during a year in which more than 20 clinics were attacked has been interpreted recently as support for the bombers' sentiments. Now Reagan has set things straight with his pledge for what one official called a "total federal effort" against the violence.

For all but the bombers, that's reassuring.

The Seattle Times
Seattle, WA, January 6, 1985

SINCE 1982, bombing and arson attacks against abortion clinics around the country have been a matter of concern that has deepened the past couple of years, as the violence grew.

Last Thursday, President Reagan issued a forthright statement deploring such acts and promising unequivocally that the administration now supports an all-out effort to halt a wave of life-threatening crimes perpetrated by misguided individuals in the name of protecting human life.

It was the president's first statement condemning the violence. Because Reagan is among those who oppose legal abortions, he is in a position to exercise persuasive moral leadership that ought not to be lost upon those who cannot perceive the line dividing legitimate protest and criminal behavior.

The president's statement was long overdue, but — no matter how belated — praiseworthy.

Post-Tribune
Gary, IN, January 9, 1985

It is redundant to say that the misguided people who bomb abortion clinics have flunked the moral standards test that they demand of those who run the clinics. They endanger society and hurt their cause — whatever it is.

Whether they are religious zealots who misread the Scriptures or frustrated crusaders, they are the kind of fanatics civilized society cannot accept.

Our opinions

There are dangers in the public's reaction to these acts of violence. One is that the bombings will stigmatize right-to-life groups that believe in using the system to settle such issues — lobbying, supporting candidates who agree with them, for example. That would be a grievous error.

The Rev. Jerry Falwell, the Moral Majority leader, helped clear the air by denouncing the clinic bombings.

Unfortunately, he clouded his remarks by predicting that there will be more bombings unless abortion laws are changed. "There are so many persons who see little progress in the pro-life effort and who feel they're doing God a service by doing such a terrible thing."

There is, of course, not a speck of godliness in setting off bombs. Falwell and others who respect civility must keep making that point. No law should be changed out of fear.

President Reagan broke his silence on the bombings by calling them "violent, anarchist activities."

But there remains a legacy of fear from these irrational attacks, and the danger of other, isolated bombings. Right-to-life groups, public safety officials and other leaders in communities that have such clinics should give the public firm, clear assurances that they abhor such violence and will expend extra efforts to prevent them. Those assurances would be redundant, of course, but under these circumstances might be helpful.

THE LOUISVILLE TIMES
Louisville, KY, January 8, 1985

We've been sparing in our praise for the Moral Majority's Jerry Falwell because of his zest for chipping away at the wall that's supposed to separate church and state.

But last week, Mr. Falwell — a leading foe of abortions who would like to see the Supreme Court's 1973 decision reversed — said something with which we can agree.

Speaking on the CBS Morning News, Mr. Falwell described recent bombings of abortion clinics around the nation as "terrorism" and condemned those responsible not only as "terrorists, they're criminals."

His comment followed Washington, D. C., Mayor Marion Barry's claim that the "Jerry Falwells of the world ought to condemn" the bombings. Another one occurred on New Year's Day at an abortion clinic in Mr. Barry's city.

Mr. Falwell's characterization flatly contradicted FBI director William H. Webster's recent claim that such attacks — of which there were 24 in 1984 — are not terrorism. Even President Reagan, who has been chided for failing to speak out against the attacks publicly, on Thursday was moved to call them "violent, anarchist activities."

Perhaps Mr. Falwell's decision to step forward prompted the stern words from the White House. The parson managed to champion law-and-order without going soft on his anti-abortion stand by attempting to explain how someone might perpetrate such a crime: "You can understand how a deranged person might do that kind of thing, but you can't condone it. You can understand when you realize that what's happening in the back of those abortion clinics is the mutilation, the destruction of 1½-million little babies."

Well, you can't blame Mr. Falwell for using the forum to issue yet another stinging rebuke of abortion. But his rebuke of people whose acts do constitute terrorism can only help in their speedy apprehension and prosecution.

Los Angeles Times
Los Angeles, CA, January 7, 1985

The bomb is the weapon of a coward afraid to test his ideas in open debate. In stern language President Reagan has condemned such cowardice in the spate of bombings at abortion clinics around the country over the last two years. He has directed all federal agencies to cooperate in the vigorous pursuit of those responsible.

The FBI says that there have been 30 bombings at clinics since May, 1982. Eight people have been arrested in connection with 12 of those violent acts; five have been convicted. Primary enforcement responsibility for crimes involving explosives lies with the Treasury Department's Bureau of Alcohol, Tobacco and Firearms. The President did not shift that responsibility, but the FBI has named a liaison official to ensure cooperation.

FBI Director William H. Webster has declined in the past to assume jurisdiction over the investigation, saying that the bombings do not constitute "terrorism." If the object of terrorism is to demoralize or intimate people through force, then these bombings have had exactly their desired effect. The bombings not only prevent some women from exercising their right to an abortion; they also restrict other women from seeking counseling on a range of family-planning options.

Reagan called the bombings "violent, anarchist activities." He is correct. Anarchy is lawlessness; anarchists seek the end of government. Democracy depends on the rule of laws consented to by the governed. Policy disagreements, even those as fundamental as the conflicts over abortion, are not resolved by fear and intimidation.

Ultimately the decision as to whether to bear a child and when to bear it is intensely personal and belongs in the private realm. It has unfortunately become a political issue through the question of abortion. The debate at least should be conducted in the forum of government free of influence by clandestine bombers.

The TENNESSEAN
Nashville, TN, January 5, 1985

PRESIDENT Reagan has spoken out against the bombings of legal abortion clinics as "anarchist activities" and ordered the Attorney General to make sure that all appropriate federal law enforcement agencies cooperate in the investigation of the attacks.

"I will do all in my power to assure that the guilty are brought to justice," the President said in a written statement.

Many people's reaction to Mr. Reagan's statement may be that it "was about time." The administration's seeming indifference to the series of 24 bombings over the past year have been blamed by some for giving the bombers comfort and encouraging what amounts to a reign of terror against legal establishments.

The failure of federal law-enforcement agencies such as the FBI and others to take a strong role in the investigation of the attacks could have been taken by some bombers as a sign that they had the tacit approval of the White House and had nothing to fear from the federal agencies.

Although it is late in coming, President Reagan's call for action against the clinic bombers is to be applauded. Regardless of what one may think about abortion, the settling of issues by bombings and other violence is not the American way and should not be tolerated.

THE MILWAUKEE JOURNAL
Milwaukee, WI, January 7, 1985

President Reagan's vigorous condemnation of those who have bombed abortion clinics in recent years was overdue, but welcome and necessary. As he pointed out, such bombings are "violent, anarchistic activities."

Reagan also said he would do "all in my power to assure that the guilty are brought to justice." Unfortunately, he refused to do one thing very much in his power and that he should do: order the FBI to take over the case.

The investigation is now being led by the Treasury Department's Bureau of Alcohol, Tobacco and Firearms. The White House says the bureau has solved 12 of 30 attacks on abortion clinics since 1982. That's a good record. But the ATF needs help, as shown by the fact that it has called on the FBI for fingerprint checks and similar assistance.

The FBI has nine times as many agents and more than six times as much money as the ATF. It also has far more prestige. The mere announcement that the FBI is entering the case could itself be a major deterrent to further terrorist attacks — a deterrent that would give needed weight to Reagan's dramatic denunciation of such terrorism.

Wisconsin State Journal
Madison, WI, January 9, 1985

Except in the most extreme cases, President Reagan is strongly opposed to abortion.

But Reagan showed last week that he is just as strongly opposed to violence — specifically, the recent rash of bombings of abortion and birth-control clinics around the country.

"I condemn, in the strongest terms, those individuals who perpetrate these and all such violent, anarchist activities," Reagan said. "As president of the United States, I will do all in my power to assure that the guilty are brought to justice."

(The president of the National Right to Life Committee, Dr. John Willke, concurred with Reagan's condemnation, saying his group has "consistently denounced this violence publicly and will continue to do so.")

Reagan carefully avoided use of the word "terrorism" in describing the bombings, by way of supporting FBI Director William Webster.

Webster has rejected an overall FBI role in investigating the bombings, claiming they are not terrorism (which falls under the FBI's jurisdiction) but the illegal use of explosives (which comes under the jurisdiction of the Treasury Department).

In past editorials, The Wisconsin State Journal has called the bombings acts of terrorism against the workers and patients at the clinics.

But the semantics and the assignment of an investigatory agency are far less important than Reagan's assurance that the federal government will aggressively investigate and prosecute these crimes.

Portland Press Herald
Portland, ME, January 2, 1985

A new year should bring the Federal Bureau of Investigation a new definition of terrorism, one that makes two dozen bombings of U.S. abortion clinics worth speedy, conclusive FBI investigation.

That argument grows stronger with the arrest of two Florida man charged with bombing three abortion clinics on Christmas Day. The object of such violence is clear: to intimidate persons from using and operating legal facilities.

But FBI Director William Webster says that isn't sufficient. The bombings, he says, don't fit the FBI's definition of terrorism. So let's come up with a new definition, one sufficient to require the FBI to do what is so clearly its job.

First we must define the "what": Terrorism must involve unlawful force or violence. Next comes the "who": the persons or property against whom it is directed. Then the "why" must be clearly spelled out: Force must be used to intimidate individuals or the government, with the intent of promoting social or political change.

Certainly a definition that made those points would cover the abortion clinic bombings. The bombings were violent and they were unlawful. They were directed against abortion clinic property. Their purpose: to intimidate persons from operating and using facilities which many Americans want to see made illegal.

OK. Let's formulate our definition: "Terrorism is defined as the unlawful use of force or violence against persons or property to intimidate or coerce a government, the civilian population or any segment thereof, in furtherance of political or social objectives."

That's fine. It's also the existing definition that's supposed to guide our FBI.

The Chattanooga Times
Chattanooga, TN, January 5, 1985

The only thing worse than a terrorist is a terrorist who fervently believes that his actions are divinely sanctioned, even ordered, by whatever god he professes to follow. That's the case in Pensacola, Fla., where four persons have been arrested in the bombings of three medical clinics that offer abortion services. Federal agents testified at a hearing where two of the defendants were denied bail that one of them, James T. Simmons, had said he had been instructed by God to carry out the bombings. Sure.

Two men have been charged in the bombings, and early this week agents of the Bureau of Alcohol, Tobacco and Firearms arrested the wife and fiancee of the two men and charged them as accessories. Fortunately, no one was inside the clinics when the bombs exploded, but the devices caused nearly $400,000 in damges. On New Year's Day, another clinic in Washington was bombed.

There is no disputing the sincerity of the defendants' belief that abortion is wrong. But that sincerity has become perverted into a self-righteous conviction by the Pensacola defendants, as well as the unknown bombers of clinics elsewhere in the nation, that they have been designated as God's instruments for shutting down the clinics.

U.S. Magistrate Robert Crongeyer correctly rebutted that conviction when, in rejecting Mr. Simmons' request for bail, he said: "Irrespective of the sincerity of the defendant's beliefs, these bombings are acts of terrorism, designed to create fear. That is simply not the way people express their viewpoints in this country." Exactly so, but judging from FBI's report that 30 bombing incidents have occurred at Planned Parenthood offices and abortion clinics, a radical element in this country believes precisely the opposite.

The FBI has adopted a narrow definition of "terrorism" in electing not to become involved in investigating the bombings — Director William Webster says the bombings do not signify an "attack on government" — but at least it is cooperating fully with the BATF, which is leading the federal investigation.

The bombings are the latest manifestation of the strong feelings that the subject of abortion has spawned. Abortion opponents have the right to press their arguments vigorously, but a resort to violence discredits their protests against practices they abhor.

The San Diego Union
San Diego, CA, January 4, 1985

Opponents of abortion should join President Reagan in decrying violence against abortion clinics across the nation. A New Year's Day bombing of a clinic in Washington, D.C., was the fourth bomb or arson attack in eight days and the 25th in less than a year, compared to four such incidents in all of 1983. The violent actions include an unsolved arson fire at an East San Diego abortion clinic last September.

Although there appears to be no pattern, most of the clinics that have been attacked had previously been targets of picketing and demonstrations.

Although no one has directly blamed them, the escalation of legitimate protest into violent action poses a dilemma for responsible opponents of abortion, who cannot ignore them, lest their silence be misconstrued as tacit approval.

This is precisely why the President, who adamantly opposes abortion, yesterday condemned the clinic bombings. Moreover, he has instructed the Treasury Department's Bureau of Alcohol, Tobacco, and Firearms to continue as the lead agency investigating the bombings. The ATF is the agency empowered by federal law to investigate bombings and has solved 12 of 30 attacks made on abortion clinics since May 1982.

Abortion is an extremely volatile and emotional issue, but violence is not the way to resolve a dispute over morality. The bombings must be stopped and the guilty brought to justice.

The Boston Globe
Boston, MA, January 4, 1985

True terrorism, says the FBI, must be politically motivated. Apart from the absurdity of not recognizing violent antiabortion activities as political, the FBI can hardly continue its ostrich-like stance in the face of the latest series of abortion-clinic bombings.

The rationale for the FBI's hands-off position has been that there is no evidence the bombings are the acts of an "organized" group that publicly takes credit for them. This time a group is organized, claiming credit and promising more of the same.

Just after midnight on New Year's Day, a Washington, D.C., clinic was bombed, and more bombings are in the works, according to a threat telephoned to The Washington Times. The Washington bombing, at the Hillcrest Women's Surgi-Center, is the third in two months within the District of Columbia and the eighth in two years – hardly the scenario of random violence.

On Christmas Day there were three bombings in Pensacola, Fla., bringing 1984's total to 24 abortion facilities that were bombed, burned or trashed.

So far, FBI Director William Webster has taken the view that such bombings are not "terrorist" acts and therefore neither the FBI's province nor its problem. Isolated explosions, explosive devices and arson are the domain of the federal Bureau of Alcohol, Tobacco and Firearms, says Assistant Treasury Secretary John Walker. The FBI concurs.

Added to the quickened pace of the bombings now, however, is the threat of continued attack. "This is the Army of God," said the caller, according to the Bureau of Alcohol, Tobacco and Firearms. "We are responsible for last night's bombing. The bombing is a warning to abortionists everywhere, the bombings will not stop. This is also encouragement for John Goldsby, our brother in Florida, telling him to keep the faith." The next bombing will be an Ohio abortion clinic, the caller warned, signing off with, "Happy New Year from the Army of God, East Coast division."

The modus operandi of the bombers must be clear to the FBI now: They are organized, they are political, their crimes are premeditated. If the FBI fails to move against the campaign of terror against abortion clinics that operate under full sanction of law, then the nation's top law enforcement agency is itself encouraging further lawlessness and violence.

Detroit Free Press
Detroit, MI, January 5, 1985

PRESIDENT Reagan has commendably, if belatedly, condemned the bombing of abortion clinics around the country. By his silence in the face of two dozen bombings in the last year, the president seemed to many people to be downplaying the seriousness of the incidents, especially since federal law enforcement agencies were sluggish in getting involved.

The last bombing was practically within earshot of the White House. If the attacks on the clinics continue, it is only a matter of time before those who claim to be acting to save lives end up taking them. The vigilante spirit of the bombers is as bad as the destruction they have caused: In the name of their own higher morality, they have been waging a violent campaign against people engaged in an activity that has repeatedly been declared lawful by the courts, and which is accepted as lawful by a majority of Americans.

The issue of abortion arouses strong feelings in some of its opponents. But they have campaigned for years in legislatures and in courts to outlaw abortion, and they have been unable to win either in the court of law or the court of public opinion.

No group — whether they are ban-the-bombers or right-to-lifers or nuclear activists or partisans of any other cause — is entitled to win by violence what they cannot win in the political or legal arena. It's a perversion of conscience to sneak around blowing up buildings and then argue, as one suspect in a clinic bombing did, that God made me do it.

Fanaticism and the rule of law are incompatible. The president's condemnation should help to encourage the investigation and prosecution of the bombers — and restore abortion as an issue to be settled by debate and discussion, not by a pipe bomb.

Part III: Abortion & Government Funding

While abortion foes have failed to push a constitutional amendment to ban abortions through Congress, they have been successful in getting Congress to prohibit federal financing of nearly all abortions. Under the Medicaid provisions of the Social Security Act, the federal and state governments share financing of the cost of medical care delivered to indigent recipients. In 1976, Congress passed the so-called Hyde Amendment, named for its sponsor Rep. Henry J. Hyde, stating that no federal Medicaid funds "shall be used to perform abortions except where the life of the mother would be endangered if the fetus were carried to term." This wording eliminated several categories of pregnancies—women with health disorders such as cancer or heart disease which would be seriously aggravated by a pregnancy, for instance, or those in whom the unwanted pregnancy could trigger severe mental disturbances—which would normally fall under the designation of "medically necessary" procedures that, under the language of the Medicaid act, the government is obligated to fund. But the amendment, immediately challenged, was upheld by the Supreme Court in 1980. The majority opinion, delivered by Justice Potter Stewart, stated: "By subsidizing the medical expenses of indigent women who carry their pregnancies to term while not subsidizing the comparable expenses of women who undergo abortions (except those whose lives are threatened), Congress has established incentives that make childbirth a more attractive alternative than abortion for persons eligible for Medicaid. These incentives bear a direct relationship to the legitimate congressional interest in protecting potential life. Nor is it irrational that Congress has authorized federal reimbursement for medically necessary services generally, but not for certain medically necessary abortions. Abortion is inherently different from other medical procedures, because no other procedure involves the purposeful termination of a potential life..." With the Supreme Court decision, the injunction placed on the Hyde Amendment was lifted. The rider, originally tacked on to the annual appropriations bill for the Departments of Labor and HEW (now HHS), has been reintroduced and passed by Congress each year since, though usually modified to include exceptions for women who have been the victims of rape or incest.

Opponents of abortion have also succeeded in implementing measures on the state and local levels to deny use of public funds for abortion. In three pivotal cases on this issue in 1977, the Supreme Court ruled, 6-3, that states and localities were not constitutionally required to fund elective—or not medically necessary—abortions for indigent women. The cases involved legislation in Pennsylvania, Connecticut and Missouri. In the Connecticut case, *Maher v. Roe,* the high court reversed a lower court ruling that had found the state's bar on Medicaid-funded elective abortions beyond the first three months of pregnancy in violation of a poor woman's right to equal protection of the laws. In three separate, sharply dissenting opinions, Justices William Brennan Jr., Harry Blackmun and Thurgood Marshall voiced perhaps the most frequently expressed objection of those who disagree with such funding restrictions—that they penalize poor women. In the words of Brennan's dissent: "The stark reality for too many, not just 'some,' indigent pregnant women is that indigency makes access to competent licensed physicians not merely 'difficult' but 'impossible'... *Roe v. Wade* and cases following it hold that an area of privacy invulnerable to the State's intrusion surrounds the decision of a pregnant woman whether or not to carry her pregnancy to term. The Connecticut scheme clearly impinges upon that area of privacy by bringing financial pressures on indigent women that force them to bear children they would not otherwise have." State and local governments continue to test the limits of the Supreme Court's interpretation of *Roe v. Wade* as it applies to Medicaid funding of abortions. In 1985, Colorado effected an amendment to the state constitution prohibiting the use of state money to fund abortions directly or indirectly, and many other states have either passed or proposed similarly restrictive measures. It remains to be seen how these individual measures will fare when challenged in the courts.

Federal Funding; Hyde Amendment Upheld

U.S. District Court Judge John F. Dooling of Brooklyn, N.Y. ruled in January 1980 that legislation restricting federal financing of abortions under Medicaid was unconstitutional. The ruling ordered government officials to authorize expenditure of federal Medicaid funds to help pay for "medically necessary abortions provided by duly certified providers." The decision by Judge Dooling defined medically necessary abortions as those "that are necessary in the professional judgement of the pregnant woman's attending physician, exercised in the light of all factors, physical, emotional, psychological, familial and the woman's age, relevant to the health-related well-being of the pregnant woman." The ruling in the three-year abortion case, the longest in the turbulent history of the abortion issue, struck down legislation known as the Hyde Amendment. The legislation, sponsored by Rep. Henry Hyde (R, Ill.), permitted federal Medicaid payments for abortions only in cases in which a woman's life was endangered or pregnancy had resulted from rape or incest that had been promptly reported.

The plaintiffs in the New York case had contended that the federal government's restrictions on abortion aid constituted discrimination on the basis of economic status, race and sex and also infringed on the rights of privacy, due process and equal protection under the law. The plaintiffs further argued that the federal statute abridged the constitutional separation of church and state by enacting into law the religious beliefs of those who regarded the fetus as a human being from the time of conception. Government attorneys on the other side argued that the fetus was a human being based on biological, not religious evidence—and that religious support for a belief did not by itself make a law supporting that belief unconstitutional. They also contended that a lack of financial means to exercise a right did not constitute a denial of that right. Public financing of abortions for low-income women eligible for Medicaid began nationally in 1973 with the legalization of abortion by the U.S. Supreme Court.

The Supreme Court announced in February 1980 that it would review the case, *Harris v. McRae*, before the end of the current term—and in the meantime lifted a stay on Judge Dooling's order so that it remained in effect. The Department of Health, Education and Welfare Feb. 19 began notifying states of the resumption of Medicaid financing of "medically necessary" abortions. But in its 5-4 decision June 30, the Supreme Court ruled that limits on the federal and state funding of abortions do not in fact violate the Constitution. The justices upheld the Hyde Amendment, handing down a decision that combined three Illinois cases with the *Harris v. McRae* case. The majority rejected the argument that the Hyde Amendment was unconstitutional because it discriminated against poor women. The poor were not specifically protected by the equal-protection clause of the Fourteenth Amendment, the decision stated. Allowing Medicaid funds to be used for childbirth, while restricting funds for abortions, was not discriminatory, it continued, but rather consistent with "the legitimate congressional interest in protecting potential life." The majority opinion, authored by Justice Potter Stewart, also rejected arguments that the Hyde Amendment represented a religious view and that it curtailed the freedom of choice established in the Supreme Court's 1973 decision legalizing abortions. "It simply does not follow that a woman's freedom of choice carries with it a constitutional entitlement to the financial resources to avail herself of the full range of protected choices," Stewart wrote. He added: "Although government may not place obstacles in the path of a woman's exercise of her freedom of choice, it need not remove those [obstacles] not of its own creation."

Dissenting justices said the ruling would have "a devastating impact on the lives and health of poor women" and would force "upon a needy minority [society's] own concepts of the socially desirable, the publicly acceptable and the morally sound." Those in the 'pro-choice' movement agree with them, pointing out that the ruling establishes a double standard by making it much more difficult for poor women to procure a safe, legal abortion—those who would be the least able to afford the costs of raising an unwanted child—than it is for women with larger incomes who can easily pay the doctor's fees for the procedure.

The Detroit News
Detroit, MI, April 24, 1980

Seven years after the U.S. Supreme Court declared abortion a constitutionally protected right, the issue of federal funding of elective abortions is once more before the court.

Observers on both sides of the debate agree that the upcoming decision promises to be the most important of its kind since the procedure became legal under Roe *vs.* Wade.

Two federal judges have declared the so-called Hyde Amendment, which prohibits federal funding for almost all abortions, unconstitutional. If these rulings are upheld, Washington will resume paying for an estimated 300,000 abortions a year.

Arguing for federal financing is a familiar group of "prochoice" organizations, many of which are committed to the principle that abortion is nothing more or less than a birth-control technique. Opposed is an equally familiar group of "prolife" organizations opposed to abortion in most, if not all, cases.

The positions of both sides are familiar to most Americans. To deny funds for this particular medical service is to discriminate against the poor, it is said. Abortion is the destruction of human life and, in a civilized society, must be discouraged and not condoned, it is argued.

The court is considered likely to decide the issue within the framework of the Constitution's equal protection clause. But the real underlying issue here, in our view, is the desirability of government *neutrality* toward a hotly-contested, and by no means resolved, moral question.

The Constitution protects freedom of expression, but does not mandate government support for pornography. The Constitution protects freedom of religion, but specifically prohibits support for any creed.

A majority of the Supreme Court in 1973 found in the Constitution's privacy guarantees a legal rationale for a woman's right to an abortion. But does this mean that the federal government must, in effect, promote abortion by subsidizing it?

Given the recent record of the courts, there is little reason to expect such an argument to prevail. This may be bad news for those who oppose abortion. But it may be even worse news, in the long run, for those who defend the practice.

In 1857, by a 6-3 margin, the court found that a slave named Dred Scott was not automatically freed when taken to a state which prohibited human bondage. The court also ruled that, under the Constitution, blacks could not be citizens and Congress could not bar slavery from the territories.

So radicalized was the tiny anti-slavery minority by the court's apparent willingness to extend — and even promote — the Peculiar Institution that abolitionists immediately charted a course which led inevitably to the 13th Amendment.

There are current portents that proabortionists might usefully ponder.

THE SAGINAW NEWS

Saginaw, Mich., February 24, 1980

"Choice" is a key word in the emotion-laden debate on abortion. Advocates of legalized abortion describe themselves as "pro-choice" to state the contrast with the opponents' adopted label of "pro-life."

But the U.S. Supreme Court last week had no fair choice but to uphold the legality of using federal Medicaid funds to pay for abortions for poor women, despite the dissent of three justices.

As long as the court's landmark 1973 decision legalizing abortion is the law of the land, access to its provisions should not be decided on the basis of personal wealth. The 1973 decision gives abortion status as a proper medical procedure. Aid to poor persons is readily available, as it morally should be, for other health-maintenance services. To remove abortion from the list of those services and in effect declare abortion is all right as long as you can pay for it, is to practice blatant discrimination against poor people.

The principle holds regardless of personal views on the entire abortion issue. Having set a precedent, the Supreme Court cannot lightly disregard it. The legalities apply as well on the state level, where we have several times defended Gov. Milliken's veto of anti-abortion aid legislation as mandatory in view of the law.

The court's ruling, however, hardly settles the matter. It upheld Medicaid for abortion only pending a full constitutional review of congressional action banning those payments. It's not out of the question that the court may take that opportunity to review once again the larger issue.

Whatever the outcome, it's disturbing, in our view, that the legality of abortion seems to be coming under increased abuse.

A significant and perhaps growing number of the more than 50,000 abortions performed annually in Michigan (about 800 in Saginaw County), and more than 1.4 million nationwide, are apparently attributable to simple "birth control."

That's almost as indefensible, at least from our moral point of view, as the reported increased use of abortion to eliminate a fetus determined to be the "wrong sex" by a new medical technique.

Under the law, no reason need be given for seeking an abortion in the first trimester of pregnancy. Restrictions are only slightly stronger, and subject to wide interpretation, on abortions during the second trimester.

We are not advocates of abortion. We are advocates of the rule of law. We recognize that seeking a legal abortion is an intensely personal matter for women.

We cannot help but wonder, however, if the original rational bases for legalized abortion are not being lost: As we saw them, protection of the mental, social and physical health of women, in accordance with their legal right to control of their bodies.

Pro-abortion, or "pro-choice" advocates argue that legal right carries no restrictions. And they are right. What we're talking about is a fading of the relationship of morality to that legal option when abortion is regarded in no way as a necessity, but as a convenience.

As a legal and constitutional matter, abortion remains resolved and, last week, reaffirmed. Beyond that, we enter the realm where no law can intervene, the one of personal morality and self-respect. In light of what we believe are disturbing trends, we can only ask all persons to conduct their own review of the uses, and abuses, of abortion.

The Boston Globe

Boston, Mass., February 27, 1980

William Baird surfaces with stunning, self-righteous regularity. Last week he hailed the Supreme Court order requiring the federal government to resume paying for all medically necessary abortions for Medicaid recipients as a "tremendous victory" and a "personal vindication." Baird has been a persistent champion of reproductive rights over the past 15 years and his contributions have been significant. But he, like others on both sides of the abortion question, can't seem to separate himself from the issue. He has invested so much of himself in the cause, he is so busy toting up wins and losses, that he frequently misses the point, raises the stakes and further confuses a complex and emotional subject.

Which is exactly why New York's Terence Cardinal Cooke's comments on the ruling were off the mark as well. Speaking in Washington on Saturday, the Roman Catholic cleric castigated the "handful of men" on the court for "interfering" in legislative affairs. He characterized the court-ordered use of public funds for abortions as "a blatant misuse of judicial power and an abuse of the democratic process." '

Obviously, quite the opposite is true. At this point it would be far more accurate to suggest that the recent Supreme Court ruling simply represents the next step in the lengthy proceedings that have moved up and down through state legislatures, Congress and the courts since abortion was legalized seven years ago. By a 6-to-3 vote, the high court lifted the stay that temporarily blocked enforcement of a New York federal court decision.

Last month Judge John Dooling found the Hyde Amendment unconstitutional and ordered the government to pay for abortions excluded by the legislation, which was passed in 1976. The Supreme Court's order means that poor women are once again, but temporarily, eligible for comprehensive Medicaid benefits denied by Congressional action. The court must still consider the merits of Dooling's 340-page opinion. It agreed to do so by consolidating the appeal with a narrower Illinois case accepted for review in November. Arguments are scheduled in April and a decision is expected by July.

Although the Supreme Court order may offer a glimmer of hope to those who concur with Judge Dooling's contention that a woman's decision to have an abortion is a fundamental right and prompt criticism from those who don't, it vindicates no one and is anything but a blatant misuse of judicial power. Ironically, Cardinal Cooke denounced the "handful of men" who must make judgements on abortion questions; pro-choice advocates haven't always been comfortable with this arrangement either. But for better or worse, that's the way the American law-making system works. There can't be any final resolution of the federal government's role in financing abortions — any victory, any defeat — until the court decides the cases on appeal.

The Des Moines Register

Des Moines, Iowa, February 21, 1980

In ordering the federal government to pay for abortions for women on welfare, the Supreme Court gave only a slight hint of how it may rule on the controversial Hyde Amendment. The brief order, issued without explanation, will apply to Medicaid abortions until the court has a chance to review lower-court opinions that have struck down the congressional restrictions imposed on welfare recipients.

In all likelihood, the order will incite anti-abortion groups to intensify their drives to elect congressional candidates pledged to a proposed constitutional amendment that would bar practically all abortions, for rich as well as poor. A heated-up attempt to make abortion a key issue of the fall election campaigns is predictable.

The court's order is consistent with its 1973 abortion decision, which upheld a woman's freedom of choice against restrictive state laws on abortions. But arguments about a woman's choice may be overshadowed in the court's thinking by a legislative body's right to decide how public funds are spent.

The Hyde Amendment forbids the use of Medicaid funds for abortions unless the woman's life is endangered or the pregnancy has been caused by rape or incest. The Burger court usually has been reluctant to intrude on legislative authority, especially the control of the public purse.

The Medicaid order, however, applies to all "medically necessary" abortions. This will broaden the options considerably for Medicaid recipients. Medically necessary abortions, as defined in several lower-court rulings, would include those recommended to prevent foreseeable risks to a woman's mental or physical health.

On that point, the court appears ready to return the abortion argument to the main theme of the 1973 decision: that a woman has a right to decide, in consultation with her physician, whether to terminate a pregnancy. A woman should not be deprived of that right because she accepts welfare payments. Neither should a government use public funds to force welfare recipients to abide by a particular moral teaching.

DESERET NEWS
Salt Lake City, Utah, February 21, 1980

Many Americans have a moral revulsion against abortion. They should not be forced to pay for what they consider to be unjustified killing.

Yet that's the position in which the taxpayers have been placed once again as a result of a ruling this week by the U.S. Supreme Court.

The high court agreed to rule this term on the constitutionality of the Hyde Amendment, by which Congress sharply restricted the use of federal funds to pay for the abortions of women on welfare.

Since a district court judge in New York ruled previously that the Hyde Amendment violates poor women's constitutional rights, a review by the Supreme Court was likely unavoidable.

But while the justices were waiting to hear the case and make up their minds, they could and should have kept the amendment in effect.

Instead, they put the U.S. Department of Health, Education, and Welfare in a position where it had no choice except to start spending federal funds again to finance abortions.

The least the Supreme Court should do now is to expedite the challenge to the Hyde Amendment instead of just letting the case take the normal, leisurely course.

The Hyde Amendment allows federal funding of abortions for the poor only when a woman's life is in danger and in cases where pregnancy resulted from rape or incest and was reported promptly.

Since this amendment was adopted, the number of federally funded abortions has decreased from 300,000 a year to less than 2,000. In Utah, the decrease has been from 200 a year to at or near zero.

This doesn't necessarily mean that poor women are no longer getting as many abortions as they used to — only that the taxpayers are no longer footing the bill.

In fact, abortion has become just about the most frequently performed surgical operation in the United States, second only to tonsillectomy.

This high rate of abortion comes at a time when the number of childless couples seeking to adopt far exceeds the available supply of adoptable children.

The two sets of circumstances strongly suggest that abortion is being resorted to not as a necessity but merely as a matter of convenience. Some convenience.

The fact that a woman has a qualified legal right to an abortion should not imply a corresponding legal right to a free abortion.

If the Supreme Court decides otherwise, there's no end to the demands that the poor could make on the taxpayers for no other reason than that they're poor.

The Cleveland Press
Cleveland, Ohio, February 22, 1980

Anatole France, the great French novelist, once ironically described "the majestic equality of the law" which forbids "the rich as well as the poor to sleep under bridges, to beg in the street, and to steal bread."

That is roughly how we feel about the abortion issue, which again is before the Supreme Court: if abortion is legal for well-to-do women, it ought to be available to poor women.

Six years ago, the high court ruled that government could not intrude in a woman's decision to end a pregnancy in its early stages. To do so would violate her constitutional rights to freedom and privacy.

The backlash to that decision led Congress to pass the Hyde Amendment, which bans Medicaid funds for abortions except when a women's life is endangered or if she is a victim of rape or incest.

Under the restrictive terms of the Hyde Amendment, federally financed abortions fell from about 300,000 in 1977 to fewer than 3,000 in 1978.

Last month, however, a federal judge in New York ruled the amendment unconstitutional. He said it violated both the equal protection guarantee of the Fifth Amendment and the religious freedom right of the First Amendment.

By a vote of 6-3, the Supreme Court now has ordered the federal government to resume paying for abortions for poor women, at least until it can rule on the New York decision and a similar pending case.

The high court has been ambivalent about publicly funded abortions, and there is no way of knowing how it will finally rule.

We hope it will be guided by equal treatment under the law. This humane society would not deny a poor person an expensive brain operation because he cannot pay for it. Similarly it should not withhold a medically necessary abortion from, say, an impoverished teen-ager.

If the court upholds the Hyde Amendment, it will be updating Anatole France's cruel irony: both rich and poor women have equal rights to high-priced abortions, but the poor cannot afford them.

The Hartford Courant
Hartford, Conn., February 21, 1980

Poor women are once again able to obtain Medicaid abortions, at least temporarily, without having to pass a morals test not given to other women receiving the same medical procedure.

The U.S. Supreme Court's 6-3 vote, in response to a decision by a New York federal district court judge, was surprising, in that a congressional decision to block such abortion funding was overturned in response to a ruling from one judge in one jurisdiction.

The decision by Congress was unfortunate, and the temporary action of the high court is proper, but the anti-abortion advocates may be rightfully stunned by the ease with which the abortion-funding mechanism has been restored.

A final ruling will come later in the Supreme Court term, when Judge John Dooling's New York ruling is heard on appeal. If the high court justices are inclined to face the substantive issue raised by Mr. Dooling head-on, the ruling will be the most important yet on the divisive subject.

The high court has already ruled on a narrow question of law, related to the Medicaid funding shutoff for abortions. The Constitution does not require states to pay for elective abortions.

But the New York judge's decision goes to the heart of the question: Can legislative action be used to impose a controversial and not-universally-accepted theological or moral restriction on the right of any woman to receive legal medical attention? Judge Dooley, in the most wise and courageous abortion decision to date, said no. Such restrictions are a matter of "moral judgment, and ultimately religious in nature," he said.

Millions of religious, compassionate Americans do not have moral objections to abortion. That is the practical truth that must guide policy strategy on the subject.

St. Petersburg Times
St. Petersburg, Fla., February 21, 1980

In the face of rising criticism from opponents of abortion, the U.S. Supreme Court remained courageously this week behind the right of a poor as well as a rich American woman to control her own body.

THE COURT'S 6-3 ruling allowed a federal judge's order to take effect immediately and caused the federal government again to pay for poor women's abortions — as was the case before the Hyde Amendment, the law at issue now, took effect. The justices let it be known that they will hear the case on its merits later this year, probably before summer.

An easier option would have been to acquiesce to the Carter administration's request to stay, or block, the federal judge's order until the justices have an opportunity to consider the case. That would have meant that abortions would continue to be denied poor women, a denial that U.S. District Judge John F. Dooling Jr. found unconstitutional last month for its discriminatory nature. After the Hyde Amendment took effect, only the well-to-do often had the practical right to a legal abortion because they could pay for it; the poor were forced either into illegal abortions or to have unwanted children, being deprived of their rights because they could not pay.

WE HOPE the court's choice of the two options can be read as a signal that it will adhere to the basics of its seven-year-old landmark ruling. The court declared at that time that all American women have a constitutional right to obtain abortions within the early months of pregnancy. It is the right that should now be restored to the poor along with the rich.

Los Angeles, CA, April 24, 1980

The U.S. Supreme Court is moving again on abortion and, as usual, a great deal is at stake. What the justices are now deliberating — after a two-and-one-half hour hearing Monday afternoon on two lower court rulings — is the issue of public funds for abortions. The justices' taking up whole the question of whether the government should pay for abortions was inevitable, because they've circled about it and considered small pieces of it in the past. Now the moment for a comprehensive ruling has arrived. Briefly, the chronology of laws and court decisions that have led up to the funding question now before the Court is as follows:

1973: The Supreme Court rules that the individual's right to privacy under the Constitution gives a woman the right to decide, with her doctor, whether to have an abortion during the first six months of pregnancy.

1976: Congress passes the Hyde Amendment, making illegal the use of Medicaid funds (federal benefits) for abortions except to save the mother's life or in cases of rape or incest. This prohibition has been reenacted by Congress each year since.

1977: The Supreme Court rules that the Constitution does not require the government to fund elective abortions.

1980: The Supreme Court accepts the appeals of two lower court rulings that challenge the constitutionality of the Hyde Amendment. In one, U.S. District Court Judge John Dooling of New York rules that the prohibition against the use of federal funds for nearly all abortions is unconstitutional under the equal-protection clause of the Constitution (the 14th Amendment) because it denies even medically necessary abortions to poor women. Dooling's definition of medical necessity is broad, including poverty as a possible defining factor. The Court orders the federal government to supply Medicaid funds for abortions under Dooling's order until it decides the case on appeal.

The other ruling, from a Chicago district court, not only challenges Hyde but raises the issue of whether the state of Illinois is required to fund medically necessary abortions by the provisions of Social Security law. This ruling is representative of similar orders in other states: In the 21 states that now fund abortions, 12 do so by court order and nine by state legislative mandate.

So, the Supreme Court is ready to clear up this legislative and judicial tangle. Because the justices are ruling on two different cases that challenge both state and federal bans on the use of public funds for abortions, the Court could rule sweepingly in the most permissive or most restrictive direction. We believe strongly that the Hyde Amendment and state fund cut-offs *do* violate the 14th Amendment, because the Supreme Court's pronouncement of a woman's right to obtain a medically necessary abortion, if the government then denies her the funds necessary to get one, is nothing but a broken promise.

But there's no way of knowing if the justices will take that view when they hand down their decision sometime in June. Three justices are known to oppose restrictions on abortions. Two are known to favor them, by leaving the matter up to Congress and the states to decide. That leaves four justices who could swing either way. We're hoping that they swing toward granting poor women the freedom of choice that other women already have. ∎

Los Angeles Times

Los Angeles, CA, April 23, 1980

The case of Harris v. McRae, now before the U.S. Supreme Court, turns on whether Congress is denying poor women equal protection under the law by cutting off virtually their only access to abortions by refusing to pay for them under the federally supported Medicaid program.

Medicaid pays for essential medical care for the poor. In 1976, Congress, under intense pressure from zealous antiabortion forces, passed an amendment deleting abortion from coverage except in limited cases. Also in 1976, Cora McRae was refused a Medicaid abortion. She sued, and a federal judge ordered the government to pay for the procedure. Meantime, the suit was continued as a nationwide class action for other poor women needing abortions. Since then, Congress has passed even more restrictive amendments.

By definition, Medicaid recipients are the poorest people in the United States. Their only source of medical care often is Medicaid.

According to a report on abortion by the Alan Guttmacher Institute, 90% of the women of reproductive age who are eligible for Medicaid receive aid to families with dependent children—that is, an average of $241 a month. The average cost of an abortion is $285.

As one brief filed by the proabortion side said, "The income level of indigent women is at that of subsistence; there is simply no money available to pay for an abortion. Where the physician cannot afford to work with no charge, and the women cannot afford to pay, safe medical abortion is not a realistic alternative."

The alternative is involuntary—and possibly unsafe—childbirth and an unwanted child, or an unsafe abortion. In 1977, the first year after the Medicaid cutoff, deaths from illegal abortions increased for the first time since 1972, the year before the landmark Roe v. Wade case that established a woman's right to an abortion.

The Supreme Court, which heard oral arguments in this case Monday, enters its deliberations knowing how politically charged the issue is. No matter the decision, the abortion controversy will not end. If the justices decide that cutting off money to poor women denies them equal protection of the law, that decision will only fuel the opponents' desire to push through a constitutional amendment outlawing all abortions. If the court rules that Congress may cut off this money, pressure will mount on states that have not already done so to do likewise.

The court said in 1973 that the decision to have an abortion is a private medical decision between a woman and her doctor—one in which the state cannot interfere, at least not until the last three months of pregnancy. All women, rich or poor, must have equal opportunity to exercise that right; poor women effectively lose that right if Medicaid financing remains cut off.

For the Supreme Court to say any less is for it to acknowledge that there is one law in this country for the rich, another for the poor. ☐

The Washington Post

Washington, DC, January 22, 1980

IT TOOK FEDERAL District Court Judge John Dooling 13 months to think through—and 642 pages to spell out—the reasons he ruled the Hyde Amendment banning Medicaid funding for abortions unconstitutional. The decision, issued on Jan. 15, marks the end of the longest (three years), broadest and most thorough legal debate in the history of the abortion controversy.

As have other courts, this one ruled against the denial of what it termed "medically necessary" abortions. More important was the court's redefinition of that phrase. "Medically necessary" abortions, wrote Judge Dooling, are those that the woman's physician believes are necessary "in the light of all factors, physical, emotional, psychological, familial . . . relevant to the health-related well-being of the pregnant woman." The ruling thereby subscribed to the argument that emotional and psychological factors play a much larger role in many forms of illness than has previously been recognized, and should be treated as components of health and ill health.

No one case, no matter how thorough, will end the controversy over abortion. National polls consistently show that a great majority of Americans—as high as 88 percent—believe abortions should be legal. Intensity of feeling on the other side of the issue, however, shows no sign of abating. At the Respect Life Leadership Conference held this past weekend in preparation for today's annual anti-abortion march on the Capitol, the director of a group called Committee for the Survival of a Free Congress said, "It doesn't matter what the majority of the American people think on a poll. . . . What matters is the perception members of Congress have about your issue and their future." In other words, the secret to influencing Congress is not how many people support a particular point of view, but how many are willing to make that one issue their *only* criterion in judging a congressman.

Thus, after more than a decade of intense debate, the abortion question is no closer to a national consensus. Frustration on both sides has diminished what mutual understanding and mutual respect ever did exist. The Senate and the House, for their part, continue a senseless yearly stalemate that succeeds only in delaying other important legislation until necessity finally forces a compromise.

In these conditions, neither side is going to "win." Congress and the rest of the country would do best to be satisfied with Judge Dooling's simple and sensible conclusion: "The irreconcilable conflict of deeply and widely held views on this issue of individual conscience excludes any legislative intervention except that which protects each individual's freedom of conscientious decision and conscientious nonparticipation."

THE MILWAUKEE JOURNAL
Milwaukee, WI, July 2, 1980

The US Supreme Court's latest ruling on abortion does a grave injustice to impoverished women.

The issue before the court was not so-called elective abortions. The court previously had ruled that government had no obligation to pay for non-therapeutic abortions for poor women — even though this created a double standard, with low-income women having less access to medically safe abortions than wealthier women.

No, this time the issue narrowed to *medically-necessary* abortions. Could the government provide medical care benefits for the poor under Medicaid and then single out medically-necessary abortions for nonpayment?

Five of the justices, to the dismay of their four colleagues, said yes. Justice Stewart argued for the majority that such a restriction, imposed by Congress through the harsh Hyde amendment, was not unlawful discrimination.

For one thing, Stewart said, abortion was different from other medical procedures because it "terminates a potential life." However, in rebuttal, it can be argued that a medically-necessary abortion may be as important to the *health* of the mother as any other basic form of medical care.

More disturbing was Stewart's curious argument that the Hyde amendment left poor women with "the same range of choice" regarding medically-necessary abortion as they would have had if Congress had never chosen to subsidize health care costs for the poor. The whole point is that Congress *did* decide to create Medicaid, thereby entitling poor people to equal access to basic medical care.

The perversity of the Hyde amendment is that it, in effect, says: A poor woman has equal access to basic health care — except when she exercises her constitutional right to a medically-necessary abortion. Then equal access constricts. As Justice Stevens declared in his dissent, that kind of denial is a "blatant violation of the sovereign's duty to govern impartially."

So where does society go from here? The Supreme Court has bucked the issue back to Congress and state legislatures. There is nothing in the decision that prevents lawmakers from doing what, at a minimum, should be done: include medically-necessary abortions in subsidized health care for the poor.

Abortion is admittedly an ugly answer to unwanted pregnancy. Better alternatives should be vigorously pushed — notably, widespread availability to contraception and extensive improvement of child-support programs to ease the hardship of raising children in poverty. However, unwanted pregnancy will continue to occur, often under distressful circumstances. The mother may be an indigent, poorly educated teenager; or a victim of rape or incest; or a woman facing grave medical risks if she carries the fetus to term.

Legislative bodies should have the courage to come to grips with these social realities in a reasonable and equitable manner. The Hyde amendment flunks that test.

The Miami Herald
Miami, FL, July 3, 1980

THE U.S. Supreme Court ruling on abortion on Monday did not ban the use of Federal funds for therapeutic abortions for Medicaid patients. It merely upheld the right of Congress to decide whether such procedures should be Federally funded or not.

The battle, then, must be joined in Congress and in the states through a concerted nationwide campaign to restore to poor women the same standard of medical care that other American women enjoy. The Hyde Amendment, which prohibits the use of Federal funds for abortions unless the mother's life is in immediate danger or the pregnancy resulted from a legally reported instance of incest or rape, should be repealed.

The affable Rep. Henry John Hyde, a Catholic Republican from Chicago's Irish neighborhoods, is a formidable foe. He is supported by a strong, nationwide network of one-issue campaigners who will endorse or oppose a congressional candidate on that single issue alone. They have been effective because their opponents in the pro-choice lobby tend to be more reasonable in assessing a candidate's overall promise. That reasonableness has permitted the vocal minority to prevail.

When the consequences of the anti-choice policy are being discussed, of course, the so-called pro-life lobby is conspicuous by its absence. Its spokesmen are not renowned for trying to educate the public regarding birth-control methods. Nor are they so vocal about providing Federal money to help care for the blind, retarded, crippled infants that can result when a woman contracts measles in early pregnancy. Nor do they express concern about the lifelong health problems that can result from an immature girl's giving birth at 13 or 14.

It's time for the enlightened majority of American voters, who in poll after poll indicate an understanding of the complexity of the subject, to make *their* wishes count. The Court has said that Congress and the states have the right to discriminate against the poor and intrude into the standards of medical practice that poor women receive. The organized medical profession should object, and strenuously, to the Hyde Amendment's usurpation of the doctor's prerogative to prescribe treatment for his patient.

Further, campaigning members of Congress should be forced to explain why they voted to cut off abortion funding when an abortion is so much cheaper for the taxpayer than the consequences of a full-term pregnancy. An indigent woman with continuing health problems, or a severely retarded or profoundly disabled infant, is enormously expensive to maintain.

The Court's 5-4 decision perched it on the narrowest possible balancing wire in upholding both the right to an abortion and the right to regulate standards of medical practice for the indigent. The Justices threw the issue back to Congress and to the states. That's where it now must be fought.

THE L.A. TIMES SYNDICATE

"In order to appreciate our opinion on the matter, you must understand that, never in its history, has a justice of the U.S. Supreme Court asked for, or received, a free abortion."

Arkansas Gazette.
Little Rock, AR, July 4, 1980

No issue in American politics is more bitterly divisive than the question of a woman's right to decide whether she will have an abortion. It is an issue that divides public opinion sharply, it divides the Congress, it divides the churches and it divides the United States Supreme Court. The public argument is often as anguished as it is bitter in the clash of rival values.

Now the Supreme Court has come forth with one of those cliff-hanging 5-to-4 decisions that decide a constitutional question for a few years but not necessarily for even a decade. The replacement of a single justice, or one justice's change of mind, can alter the outcome the next time around. New court tests will be on the way, certainly.

In this decision the Court has placed a new and severe restriction upon its landmark decision of 1973, when the right to have an abortion as a matter of individual choice was established under the law. The majority has upheld a provision in which Congress denied the use of federal welfare funds for abortions except in the case of rape or incest or saving the mother's life. The Court has held that the government does not have to pay for an abortion even if having the baby will be damaging to the mother's health or if the odds are heavy that the baby will be deformed. The narrow exceptions defined by Congress are the only ones to be allowed. In consequence, abortion funds will be cut off for an estimated 250,000 women annually.

In the majority opinion, Mr. Justice Potter Stewart engaged in gymnastics that would have stirred the envy of Baryshnikov as he sought to distinguish between abortion and other medical services in the welfare clinics. But no matter. On one point there is complete agreement: Abortion is established as the legal right of any woman who has the money to pay for it. Abortion is for the rich and the middle class but not for the poor. It is an unfair system, even more so than in the administration of justice, in which the courts will hire a lawyer for a defendant who can't afford one.

Everyone is agreed on the inequity, and so the anti-abortionists are mounting a campaign for a constitutional amendment forbidding abortion for anyone in any circumstances, however hideous the consequences. So it is that the question moves even deeper into the political arena in an election year. The anti-abortionist organizations, with the support of both the Roman Catholic Church and the Southern Baptist Convention, will take their single-issue politics into a presidential campaign that is badly cluttered already. There is evidence to suggest that the Republican best qualified for the vice presidential nomination, Senator Howard Baker of Tennessee, has been ruled out already because of two issues making him *persona non grata* with the far right, one of these being his position on abortion for welfare mothers.

Whatever the moral issues engaged in abortion, the social consequences of the Court's latest decision will be formidable. "Back-alley" abortions will increase even as tens of thousands more children will be added to the welfare rolls, increasing not merely cost to the government but the dimensions of the lowest strata in the American underclass. The rich get abortions and the desperately poor get children. Next time the fire.

THE ARIZONA REPUBLIC
Phoenix, AZ, July 1, 1980

CONGRESS and the state legislatures may refuse to authorize the use of tax money to pay for abortions for indigents, according to Monday's 5-4 decision by the U.S. Supreme Court.

This decision places abortion on demand in a different category from ordinary health services now held to be among constitutionally guaranteed rights.

While the highest court in the land was not considering the legality of abortions, the decision does lend support to the Right-To-Life movement.

The court may be feeling its way toward a middle ground in which a woman's right to do what she wishes with her own body can be modified by the right of an unborn child to live.

The decision may also be leaning toward the ultimate finding that individuals who are responsible for conception have a duty toward the child who did not ask to come into the world.

The decision ends four years of squabbling over whether Congress can withhold tax money to pay for abortions on demand.

In 1976, Congress passed the Hyde amendment limiting the use of federal money for abortion to cases of rape, incest or instances in which the life of the mother would be endangered. Subsequent congresses have upheld the Hyde amendment to Medicaid appropriation bills.

During the four years since 1976, the number of Medicaid-financed free abortions has fallen from 300,000 a year to fewer than 2,000.

Presumably, some 298,000 children owe their lives to the action originally sponsored by Rep. Harry Hyde, an Illinois Republican.

The Arizona Legislature has consistently refused to appropriate money for abortions, and its actions are now upheld.

Thirteen states are under some sort of a court threat to make them pay for abortions. Presumably these cases will now be dismissed. In 10 states local funds have been authorized to pay for abortions, and these states may continue to do so if they wish.

This newest decision will not entirely satisfy either the pro-abortionists or the anti-abortionists.

It does support the right to life at a time when the method of reproduction of the human species may be embarking on new and danger-filled paths.

SYRACUSE HERALD-JOURNAL
Syracuse, NY, July 3, 1980

Seven years ago the Supreme Court decided 7 to 2 that women could enter hospitals and undergo abortions within the first three months of their pregnancies and not go to jail.

According to a recent study, the court's legalization led 1.5 million women to abort their pregnancies in 1978.

More than a million paid for their own abortions. Medicaid paid for some 300,000 more.

Four years ago, Rep. Henry John Hyde decided to test anti-abortion feeling in the House by attaching an amendment to an appropriations bill, limiting federal funding. His amendment then as now limited federal financing of abortions to cases of rape or incest, if reported promptly, or to cases where the mother's life is endangered as confirmed by two doctors.

This is the appropriations bill "amendment" the court upheld.

The court ruled that freedom of choice doesn't carry "constitutional entitlement" to funds to use that freedom in getting an abortion.

* * *

Justice Potter Stewart put the reasoning in these words:

"Although government may not place obstacles in the path of a woman's exercise of her freedom of choice (such as putting her in jail), it need not remove those not of its own creation. Indigency falls in the latter category."

His comment carries a seed of logic.

In reality, the court didn't rule on the desirability of abortion as social engineering to hold down future welfare costs or as a choice taxing a woman's and, perhaps, a doctor's moral principles.

The court confined its attention to the right of Congress to tell executive departments how to allocate funds—an everyday legislative function except in cases that attract advocates and antagonists moved by deep philosophic, religious and social convictions.

Then activists file suits.

* * *

In advising us of the power of Congress to impose restrictions on spending, the court implied that "aid to dependent children" must be generous enough to give each indigent child a chance to live normally, well-fed and clothed, with shelter and schools.

This, we must bear with good cheer; otherwise the AID funds could go to abortion clinics around the country.

TULSA WORLD

Tulsa, Okla., July 2, 1980

THE U.S. Supreme Court has upheld the so-called Hyde Amendment which prohibits Federal funding of abortions for welfare clients. In so doing, the Court has reaffirmed — logically and correctly — the right of Congress to pass a bad law so long as the law does not violate the Constitution.

The Hyde Amendment is a bad law. It effectively denies the option of medical abortion to precisely those individuals who, as a rule, are most in need of abortions, i.e. poor people least able to deal with the tragic consequences of unwanted pregnancy.

But to say that a Congressional act is unwise or lacking in compassion is not to say it is unconstitutional.

The Supreme Court, in a landmark victory for individual freedom, ruled in 1973 that a woman has a Constitutional right to decide for herself whether to have an early-term abortion.

In challenging the Hyde Amendment, the advocates of free choice in matters of reproduction tried to stretch the 1973 decision. They contended that a woman not only has a right to decide the abortion question for herself, but if she is poor, she has a right to expect the Government to pay for the abortion.

It simply does not follow. It is one thing to say that a person has a right to something — free speech, freedom of religion, freedom not to reproduce. It is quite another to say other persons — the public — must be forced to pay for the exercise of those freedoms. The Court was right to make the distinction.

Unfortunately, the Court's logic will bring little relief to the thousands of teen-age children of deprived families who are victims of unwanted pregnancy, not infrequently the result of incest or rape.

Oklahoma, incidentally, is among the top 10 States in the rate of unintended pregnancies among teen-agers. More than 3,000 unmarried Oklahoma teen-agers had babies in 1977. At least 4,600 others were known to have had abortions.

The Governor's Committee on Children and Youth says childbirth by Oklahoma girls under age 15 is increasing at a rate of 31 percent annually.

Backers of the Hyde Amendment have contended, correctly we believe, that their law is not unconstitutional. But that doesn't make it right or wise or compassionate.

San Jose Mercury

San Jose, Calif., July 4, 1980

THE law, in its majestic equality," Anatole France observed, "forbids the rich as well as the poor to sleep under bridges, to steal bread, and to beg in the streets."

The French satirist would have appreciated the majestic equality of Monday's ruling by the U.S. Supreme Court. By a 5-4 majority, the court affirmed that the poor as well as the rich have an equal right to pay for their own abortions.

Specifically, the court upheld a four-year-old statute known as the Hyde Amendment that forbids use of federal funds to pay for abortions except in cases of promptly reported rape or incest, or when the mother is likely to die if the pregnancy is not terminated.

The majority — Chief Justice Warren Burger and Justices Potter Stewart, Byron White, Lewis Powell and William Rehnquist — argued that, while women have a constitutionally protected right to choose abortion, the government has no constitutionally prescribed duty to provide funds for abortion.

Moreover, the five justices asserted, there is no essential distinction between therapeutically necessary abortions and purely elective ones. Justice Stewart, writing for the majority, saw nothing irrational in the fact that "Congress has authorized federal reimbursement for medical services generally, but not for certain medically necessary abortions."

The majority's thinking is narrow, technical, legalistic, inhumane and wrong.

The premise that the government has no obligation to provide an abortion for everyone who wants one is plausible enough when used to justify denial of funds for elective abortions, as the court did in a 1977 decision. After all, a woman has the right to buy a facelift or a Ferrari, but that doesn't mean the government must pay the bill.

But the argument comes apart when it's stretched to rationalize the denial of medically necessary abortions. Therapeutic abortions — abortions required to prevent serious damage to the health of the mother — are as legitimate a medical procedure as appendectomies or gall bladder surgery. Withholding funds for one essential medical service while financing all others is so glaring an inconsistency that the majority's failure to see it is incomprehensible.

Justice William J. Brennan Jr. put it well in one of the four dissenting opinions: "Antipathy to abortion . . . has been permitted . . . to distort our nation's health care programs. As a means of delivering health services . . . the Hyde Amendment is completely irrational." Another dissenter, Justice John Paul Stevens, wrote that the Hyde Amendment constitutes "an unjustifiable, and indeed blatant, violation of the sovereign's duty to govern impartially."

Monday's ruling leaves Congress and the state legislatures free to approve financing of therapeutic or elective abortions if they choose. We can only hope our elected representatives have a clearer notion of equality than the Supreme Court does.

Minneapolis Tribune

Minneapolis, Minn., July 2, 1980

In 1973, the U.S. Supreme Court held that a woman's right to privacy included the right to choose to terminate a pregnancy by abortion. On Monday, a bare majority of that court added a qualification that will make the earlier decision meaningless for thousands of women each year: Woman have the right the court defined in 1973 — but only if they can pay for it.

The court's 5-to-4 decision upheld the Hyde amendment, which bars Medicaid funding for most abortions for women on welfare. That ban is constitutional, Justice Stewart's majority opinion said, even though the government will pay for virtually any other medically necessary services, including the cost of childbirth. That special treatment for one legal medical procedure does not violate a poor woman's rights to due process, Stewart wrote, because it leaves her "with at least the same range of choice in deciding whether to obtain a medically necessary abortion as she would have had if Congress had chosen to subsidize no health-care costs at all."

The callousness — or naivete — of that last remark is striking. "There is condescension in the court's holding that [a poor woman] may go elsewhere for her abortion; this is disingenuous and alarming," said Justice Blackmun's dissenting opinion. Justice Marshall's dissent pointed out just what choice the majority left most poor women needing abortions for medical reasons: ". . . they must resort to back-alley butchers, attempt to induce an abortion themselves by crude and dangerous methods, or suffer the serious medical consequences of attempting to bring the fetus to term."

Equally callous was the comment of Rep. Henry Hyde, the amendment's sponsor. The Illinois Republican agreed that the decision discriminated against the poor. No matter, however: "Poor women are discriminated against in anything that the non-poor" can afford to buy. That is true. But the humane purpose of Medicaid legislation was to assure that such harsh economic inequalities at least did not prevent the poor from obtaining necessary medical care. Monday's ruling permits an inhumane regression from the spirit behind that goal.

THE ATLANTA CONSTITUTION

Atlanta, Ga., July 2, 1980

The first thing to remember about the Supreme Court's "anti-abortion" ruling is that, in its larger constitutional sense, it really has nothing to do with abortions.

The court ruled repeatedly during the '70s — on somewhat arbitrary grounds it is true — that a woman's constitutional right to an abortion is absolute during the first three months of pregnancy and virtually absolute during the first six months.

But in its most recent decision the court dealt with another matter entirely: the right of the Congress, as an elected body, to establish guidelines for the expenditure of federal tax funds. In this case the question was whether Medicaid funds can be used to pay for abortions by the poor. The court said "no." But the issue might just as easily have turned on some other matter, such as the right of Congress to approve federally funded food stamp or welfare programs.

Still, the overtones of the decision are such that many people may assume that the court has completely reversed its previous stand. And the effect will be much the same as though it had done exactly that. More and more now the battleground on abortion will shift from the courts to the halls of Congress. In recent years the anti-abortion forces have gained great strength there as well as in the country at large, and seem to be growing more militant by the hour. The Hyde amendment which was the subject of this week's ruling is one result of that militance, and

there are sure to be other such acts now that the Supreme Court has upheld its constitutionality. Meantime, the sponsor, Rep. Henry Hyde of Illinois, now believes it will require only one more election — two at most — to give his followers the two-thirds majority they need in order to put Congress on record in favor of a constitutional amendment that, if ratified, would have the effect of undoing everything the high court has had to say on the subject.

But before that day comes there is apt to be many an inflamatory confrontation between the advocates of abortion and the "right-to-life" forces that have contributed so significantly to the strength of Republican presidential candidate Ronald Reagan.

But beyond all that is the question of whether the decision was the correct one. The court has protected abortion under the "right-to-privacy" nuances inherent in the language of the 14th Amendment. But that same amendment contains language guaranteeing each citizen "equal protection of the laws." And that is the provision that the court seems now to have breached, however tentatively. For it is hard to argue that if abortions are to be available to the well-to-do — and they are, because the well-to-do can afford to pay for them — they ought also to be available to the indigent, just as food stamps and free school lunches are available to those who cannot afford to pay for them on their own.

The Evening Bulletin

Philadelphia, Pa., July 2, 1980

Because of the U.S. Supreme Court's latest ruling on abortion, a woman who is poor can be advised by a doctor that she should not bear a child, yet have no choice but to risk a physical or emotional breakdown because she cannot afford an abortion.

The majority ruling of the sharply divided court shows no trace of compassion for the plight of impoverished women faced with going through with childbearing that could rob them of their health. The ability to pay for abortions is made the determining factor. We think that's tragically wrong.

Incredibly, the 5-to-4 Supreme Court majority in *Harris v. McRae* feels that because Congress isn't responsible for poverty, it has no obligation to provide federally funded abortions for women who are afflicted with poverty — regardless of dangers to their health. In so ruling, the court has done more than endorse the Hyde Amendment that denies federal financing for abortions except in cases of rape, incest or when a woman's life is threatened. Where the poor are concerned, this ruling virtually reverses the court's 1973 finding that women have a constitutional right to abortions during the first six months of pregnancy.

Rather than standing squarely behind that landmark decision, the Supreme Court's majority appears to be yielding to powerful anti-abortion groups and making poor women the victims of an untenable "compromise" on the issue. It has, in effect, approved a double standard of health care for women who can afford to pay for abortions, and those who can't.

In 1973, the Supreme Court held that, until a fetus becomes "viable," abortions are for a woman and her doctor to decide. "This," the court ruled in *Doe v. Bolton,* "allows the attending physician the room he needs to make his best medical judgment. And it is room that operates for the benefit, not the disadvantage, of the pregnant woman."

But now our highest court is saying that health conditions are practically irrelevant when the women involved are indigent. Poor women with blood problems, diabetes, advancing age, teenagers who, if they bear children before they are fully capable of doing so, might lose their reproductive capacity, can't expect the Federal Government, or the states, to pay for abortions. They have a right to them, true, but only if they have a checkbook, too.

We're sorry to see the Supreme Court retreating behind a doctrine that by extension, could throw into question the right of poor people to a minima standard of living simply because they *are* poor.

The News American

Baltimore, Md., July 6, 1980

The Supreme Court's latest variation on its 1973 declaration that first-trimester abortions are every woman's constitutional right says nothing quite so directly as this: Abortions are permissible, but childbirth is far preferable.

It is difficult to argue with that sentiment, judged all by itself. Abortion — whether one subscribes to the view that it is "murder," as so many people do, or a less morally freighted clinical procedure — is not a happy event. It is a decision any potential mother must weigh carefully, and it is the hard-hearted woman who does not find the decision an anguishing one to make, if make it she must. By contrast, the decision to bear a child is a happy event, an event rich in promise and wonder, even if the pregnancy is accidental or the consequences of childbirth worrisome or burdensome.

The Supreme Court — five of its nine members, in any case — has given that fine and noble sentiment the full force of law. It has said, in *Harris v. MacRae,* that with few exceptions the financial assistance state governments award to women choosing childbirth may not be shared by women choosing its alternative, abortion. Either choice is constitutionally protected, remember. But protection evidently has its limits, and the limits, baldly put, are purely economic: "Although government may not place obstacles in the path of a woman's

exercise of her freedom of choice it need not remove those not of its own creation. Indigency falls in the latter category."

The condescension of that remark speaks for itself. You may have an abortion if you can afford it; if not, well . . . you're on your own. The brethren are effectively washing their hands of a distasteful procedure: Whatever factors may compel a woman not to bear her child are of no interest to them; healthy babies are better, period. State help in delivering them into the world and caring for their mothers amount (quite properly, in the court's view) to "incentives that make childbirth a more attractive alternative than abortion." These incentives, the court concludes, "bear a direct relationship to the legitimate congressional interest in protecting potential life."

This last assertion raises troubling questions — troubling beyond the effect of the ruling itself. If there is a "legitimate congressional interest in protecting human life" — another assertion no one can dispute — then how does it square with the original ruling protecting a woman's right to an abortion? Are the congressional interest and the constitutional right in competition with one another? Is the Supreme Court saying there are some constitutional rights that enjoy government blessing and others that enjoy, well, something less?

Oregon Journal

Portland, Ore., July 2, 1980

The United States Supreme Court could not have expressed its disdain for women in any more painfully explicit manner than to have upheld the constitutionality of the Hyde Amendment, which prevents federal funding for abortions for indigent women.

Since the female is the only half of the population which can become pregnant, it follows that denying payment for "medically necessary abortions" is denying poor women proper medical treatment for a condition which may occur in most women.

Justice Potter Stewart, writing for the 5-4 majority, could hardly be more callous: " . . . the fact remains that the Hyde Amendment leaves an indigent woman with at least the same range of choice in deciding whether to obtain a medically necessary abortion as she would have had if Congress had chosen to subsidize no health care costs at all."

But Congress has chosen to subsidize health care costs for medically necessary procedures.

Let us suppose that the shoe were on the other foot. Let us imagine that there is an amendment denying to indigent male persons treatment for prostatitis. It's a painful inflammation of the prostate gland, more apt to afflict gentlemen of the age of the Supreme Court members than younger men. Miserable as it is, it is not by itself life-threatening.

It is obviously impossible to imagine such an amendment. Men, who run Congress, the Supreme Court, and quite a lot of other stuff, wouldn't stand for such discrimination on the grounds of ability to pay.

Now let us examine the sensitive and compassionate reasoning of Anne Higgins of the Ad Hoc Committee in Defense of Life. "No na-

tion can go on aborting its future at the rate of 1.4 million a year . . ." Welcome to the baby-factory, young girls (poor, of course) and women.

The Supreme Court has said that it prefers childbirth for the good of the nation to any personal wish of an individual woman. The woman may well have become pregnant through no wish of her own, but through the importuning of a man whose superior strength and dominance overcame her wishes.

If the government of 1980 says it has decided to prefer childbirth for the good of the nation, who can guarantee that in 1990, having conducted another census with frightening population statistics, it may not decide some other preference?

Might that government decide that persons over the age of 70, not employed in public government, were superfluous, and — for the good of the nation — should be tak-

en off Social Security, welfare and other public assistance?

Might that government decide to allow child-bearing only to persons receiving a genetic clearance?

Many governments, far more aware of world population problems than the U.S. Supreme Court or U.S. Rep. Henry Hyde, R-Ill., have taken strong measures to hold down the production of children — for the good of the nation.

Strong as those measures are, they still allow personal choice on the part of the man and woman who may be the producers of the children. Such nations also provide cheap and unlimited access to contraceptives and sex information.

There is one plain message from the Supreme Court — five members of it — that should be read to all of us. "Be a man if it's at all possible, and don't be poor under any circumstances." It's the American way.

The Dallas Morning News

Dallas, Texas, July 2, 1980

BY A precarious vote of 5 to 4, the U.S. Supreme Court has upheld the constitutionality of the "Hyde amendment," which bars the use of taxpayer money to finance most abortions.

Pro-abortionists are in anguish. The ban, they contend, discriminates against the poor and is based on a particular religious view of human life.

In fact, the high court has behaved laudably and prudently. It has placed responsibility for abortion policy — one aspect of it, at any rate — just where it belongs: with the people's elected officials.

Prior to the court's earthquake decision of Jan. 22, 1973, striking down state anti-abortion statutes, abortion was a moral issue, not a constitutional one. The states were free, as they always had been, to decide the issue for themselves: to allow the practice or to prohibit it strictly.

Then along came the court, proclaiming a new right it had discovered hidden way down in the folds of the Constitution — the right to end a pregnancy any time the mother wanted. There was a new moral consensus. Who said so? The judges did.

Their presumption was breathtaking. The people, speaking through their lawmakers, no longer might express themselves on a crucial moral question — liter-

ally a question of life or death. The court had spoken. End of discussion.

Yet not the end either; for serious people undertook to reassert what they took to be society's real moral consensus on abortion. Among other things, they persuaded Congress to enact the ban on abortions paid for by Medicaid funds.

A *right* to abortion at taxpayer expense? How could there be such a right? was the question put to Congress. Congress has said there should not be. Nor is there serious reason to question whether Congress has rightly read the national mood.

Lately support for no-strings-attached abortion would appear to be waning. Defectors from the abortion cause, such as Dr. Bernard Nathanson, who wrote a searing book on the question, have spoken their grave concerns about the kind of operation being performed. The Gallup Poll indicates that 73 percent of Americans think abortion should be illegal or available only under restricted circumstances.

Is a new consensus — or even the old consensus — emerging on abortion? That is more for lawmakers to say than for judges, as, up to a point, even the Supreme Court acknowledges in its Hyde amendment decision.

Richmond Times-Dispatch

Richmond, Va., July 8, 1980

A good deal of nonsensical criticism is being hurled at the U.S. Supreme Court because of its recent rulings on Medicaid funding of abortions. The criticism is misdirected. People who don't like the result of the ruling should be aiming their barbs at Congress.

The question at issue in the two cases was whether the Hyde Amendment to the Medicaid law, prohibiting the use of federal funds for most abortions, deprives poor women of their constitutional right to choose abortions.

The right to abortions (unlimited during the first trimester and subject to state restrictions during the second) was set forth by the Supreme Court in a 1973 case. The plaintiffs in the recent cases contended that the right was being abridged, as far as indigent women are concerned, in denying them Medicaid funds for abortions (except where the life of the mother is endangered or in cases of rape or incest). The plaintiffs argued that even though federal funds were not available, states were obligated to pay the costs of abortions for poor women, else these women could not exercise their right to choose abortions. It was even contended that the Hyde Amendment, since it coincides in general with Roman Catholic views on abortion, is a violation of the constitutional ban on the establishment of religion and denies non-Catholics the free exercise of their religion.

In its opinion, the five-member court majority dealt with all of the plaintiffs' arguments in detail, but the basic holding was summed up in the statement that while a woman has a right to choose an abortion, "it simply does not follow that a woman's freedom of choice carries

with it a constitutional entitlement to the financial resources to avail herself of the full range of protected choices." The indigency which may prevent a woman from getting an abortion is not an obstacle placed in her path by government and therefore government has no constitutional obligation to remove it, the court declared.

If the denial of Medicaid funds for abortions is bad policy, then those who don't like it should blame the lawmakers, not the judges whose duty it is to interpret the law in light of the Constitution. As the court put it:

"It is not the mission of this court or any other to decide whether the balance of competing interests reflected in the Hyde Amendment is wise social policy. If that were our mission, not every justice who has subscribed to the judgment of the court today could have done so. But we cannot, in the name of the Constitution, overturn duly enacted statutes simply 'because they may be unwise, improvident, or out of harmony with a particular school of thought.' Rather, 'when an issue involves policy choices as sensitive as those implicated here . . . , the appropriate forum for their resolution in a democracy is the legislature'." [The portions quoted by the court were from previous opinions.]

An example of the totally unjustified attacks on the court for its decision is found in a newspaper cartoon in which a justice is handing a coat hanger to a woman standing with three children, all forlorn and in rags. If the Hyde Amendment represents a coat hanger as a symbol of non-medical abortions, the cartoonist should have shown it being dispensed by a member of Congress.

CHARLESTON EVENING POST

Charleston, S.C., July 2, 1980

The U.S. Supreme Court, by a 5-4 vote, has upheld the constitutionality of the Hyde Amendment, sharply limiting the number of abortions funded for poor women through the Medicaid program. Henceforth, unless Congress decides otherwise, Medicaid will pay for abortions only in cases of promptly reported rape or incest, or when two doctors certify that childbirth would cause "severe and long-lasting physical health damage to the mother."

The court also made it clear that states would not be required to pay for abortions not funded by the federal government. The ruling does not change existing procedures in South Carolina, where the terms of the Hyde Amendment had been complied with even before the Supreme Court's action.

Few issues have aroused such passions in our country as abortion. Right-to-lifers point to an appalling slaughter of the unborn since the Supreme Court's landmark decision in 1973 legalizing abortion. An estimated one million legal abortions are performed in the United States every year, a third of them, prior to the Hyde Amendment, paid for by Medicaid. Why, the anti-abortionists ask, should they be forced to pay, through taxes, for something they find morally repugnant and violative of deeply held religious principles?

They have a point, but then so do the pacifists and the advocates of unilateral disarmament who protest the spending of *their* tax dollars on the implements of war.

Pro-abortion forces argue, persuasively, that without public aid, poor women desiring abortions will be forced to turn to the horrible coat-hanger abortion merchants, at great risk to their lives and welfare. They see denial of Medicaid abortions as grave social injustice. Why should the poor not have access to the relatively safe medical procedures enjoyed by those who can afford to pay?

Life, as President Jimmy Carter once said in an unguarded moment, is unfair — but why shouldn't a progressive society do what it can to make it less unfair?

It is, to be sure, a cruel moral dilemma. We cannot help but feel, though, that a society that encourages abortion — an act deemed criminal by most civilizations, including our own until but seven years ago — is not progressive, but decadent in just such a way as certain ancient civilizations that smiled on exposure of female infants unwanted by their parents.

Abortion should be a matter between a woman's conscience and her God, if she believes in one. It should not be a matter between her and her government. We applaud the Supreme Court for its latest ruling on this very difficult matter.

The Knickerbocker News

Albany, N.Y., July 3, 1980

The recent Supreme Court decision denying Medicaid funding to poor women wanting abortions is so full of contradictions and inconsistencies that we don't quite know what to make of it.

All women, the Supreme Court said seven years ago, have the right to choose abortion. No one can be forced into it, but none can be denied, either. Except, the court has now decided in upholding the Hyde Amendment, those women who are too poor to pay for the procedure themselves. *Those* women, the court decreed, must either find the money somewhere for legal or back-alley abortions, or bear unwanted children who will, in all likelihood, be supported by the state.

So what will be the result of the court's ruling? Many poor women will come up with the cash, skimping on food, rent, heat, the needs of their other children. More poor women will die and more will be left sterile under the filthy knives of abortion-mill quacks. More defective children will be born, and so will more unwanted children; unwanted children are too often neglected, ill-fed, abused. They too often become the human refuse of our society. They perpetuate the welfare state we all so loudly deplore.

And the effect of the Supreme Court's ruling on most of American womanhood? None. Those able to come up with a couple hundred dollars don't have to worry about it. The Supreme Court just made abortion difficult for the poor, not them.

A million and a half legal abortions are performed in this country every year; two-thirds are paid from private funds. Those will continue. Federal employees and their dependents will continue to receive abortion services paid for by their employer. Of the 300,000 abortions done under the Medicaid program, between 200,000 and 225,000 will still be performed, according to a study by the Guttmacher Institute — only the poor women receiving them will have begged, borrowed or stolen the money from somewhere to finance the medical procedure they consider so necessary.

Abortion is a right guaranteed under the Constitution, said the court, but the government doesn't have to pay for it. But the government has been forced to pay for other guaranteed rights — the right to counsel for an accused defendant, for one. Why is the right to abortion different?

The pro-life/pro-choice argument is emotional and fraught with political peril. It should not be fought over the bodies of poor women, which is what this particular Supreme Court decision appears to require.

The Hyde Amendment is so flagrantly discriminatory we simply can't comprehend the reasoning of the five justices who upheld it. They have left most American women with freedom of choice but poor women with no choice at all.

Wisconsin State Journal

Madison, Wisc., July 9, 1980

One certainty from last week's abortion decision by the U.S. Supreme Court is that it will result in fewer abortions in Wisconsin.

The high court ruled that federal and state governments are not required by the U.S. Constitution to finance Medicaid abortions except in limited cases. The court ruled on the "Hyde Amendment," named after Rep. Henry Hyde, R-Ill., who succeeded in winning support for a proposal allowing Medicaid payments for abortions only when the life of the mother is endangered and in cases of rape and incest.

Wisconsin's Medicaid abortion law, enacted in 1978 after a stricter bill was vetoed by Gov. Martin J. Schreiber, is somewhat more liberal. It permits Medicaid-paid abortions when the health of the mother is endangered. This must be certified by the physician before the abortion is performed in order for the physician to collect the Medicaid reimbursement.

Since the 1973 decision ruling most states' abortion laws unconstitutional, abortion has been one of the most divisive political issues in the United States. In Wisconsin, the issue aroused emotions in at least

three sessions of the Legislature as "right-to-life" advocates sought to cut off Medicaid financing of abortions and, having accomplished that, sought to petition Congress for a constitutional convention or constitutional amendment to outlaw all abortions.

Abortion should not be an alternative to birth control or a convenient way out of an unwanted pregnancy. That is why it is proper for state and federal governments to deny tax money (Medicaid) for elective abortions while financing abortions for medical reasons.

This Supreme Court decision does not reverse the 1973 vote to legalize abortions. They will continue to be available, but without tax subsidy. That also is proper.

But it would be improper and uncaring not to provide assistance to young women with unwanted pregnancies and to their babies, seeing that each get a chance to not only survive but to have as near an equal opportunity to a good life as possible.

Those who have fought for the "right to life" also should be willing to help finance the right to a good life.

The Providence Journal
Providence, RI, July 2, 1980

The United States Supreme Court has shut a door in the face of indigent women who seek to end a pregnancy by abortion. Its latest decision, upholding a federal law banning Medicaid payments for most abortions even when medically necessary, is cast on such narrow constitutional grounds that it fails utterly to address the hardship and inherent unfairness that such a holding is likely to bring.

In a succession of complex abortion cases since 1973, the Court has reiterated the rights of women to obtain early abortions — even though it also has affirmed governmental moves to abridge those rights. Now, by upholding the 1976 Hyde Amendment barring Medicaid financing of most abortions for poor wom-

---

Despite the Court's ruling, the right of women to choose whether to have an abortion continues to warrant protection

---

en, the Court has imposed on them another burden. Denied federal payment, many such women will find the abortion choice effectively foreclosed. Unless their state elects to pay for the procedure, most of them will be forced to bear the child against their will, even if the women's health is thereby jeopardized and even when the child would be born into extreme hardship.

The Supreme Court's five-member majority appears motivated in part by a desire to affirm a respect for human life, actual and potential. Such respect, fortunately, continues to command a high place in today's scheme of values. Abortions undertaken casually, as if scratching an itch, undermine such respect; and society does have a legitimate interest, as the Court argues, in trying to protect life. But bringing a fetus to term is not the only "life" at stake in such deliberations. Society also has an interest, it seems to us, in protecting the health (mental and physical) of pregnant women, in avoiding abnormal childbirth, and even in aiding women fearful of bearing a child in circumstances of acute poverty. By its decision on Monday, the Court failed to give these other interests the attention they deserve.

If the Court's majority opinion is assessed purely on constitutional grounds, at least one important and valid principle appears. Although government may not violate due process, the Court reasoned, it is not obliged to spend public funds to assure the access of every person to every

constitutionally protected right. "To hold otherwise," the Court accurately noted, "would mark a drastic change in our understanding of our Constitution."

Yet even this holding takes an extremely legalistic view of the abortion controversy. Congress set up the Medicaid program for the poor in 1965. By adopting the Hyde Amendment 11 years later, it exempted just one medical procedure — most abortions — from Medicaid coverage. Non-pregnant poor women may receive Medicaid care; so may pregnant poor women, so long as they are not seeking an abortion. Only those seeking abortions are excluded: they may obtain an abortion, sure, but not with Medicaid funds. To us, this seems callous, discriminatory and unfair.

Polls suggest that most Americans support the right of women, in most circumstances, to decide whether to have an abortion. Despite the Court's latest holding, this right continues to warrant protection. Until such time as Congress may rescind the Hyde Amendment, it will be the states' job to provide financing of some abortions for poor women. While they are at it, state governments could do more, educationally, to dispel the ignorance that has made abortion the explosive issue it is.

The Indianapolis Star
Indianapolis, IN, September 21, 1980

If the nation is lucky, one of the most bitter controversies of recent years, public funding of abortions, has been laid to rest.

The Supreme Court of the United States has refused to reconsider a June 30 ruling upholding the Hyde Amendment, which severely restricts federal payments for abortions for the poor.

That does not mean that the issue of abortion will fade from public or political forums. Far from it. But the court's action has clearly established that the so-called right to abortion does not carry with it the right to public funding.

That assumption of consequences, however, died hard. Despite the court's June finding, the Department of Health and Human Services continued to pay for about 1,000 Medicaid abortions a week though virtually all of them were ineligible under the law.

The argument of HHS officials was that a challenge to the finding was pending. Thus the agency gave the benefit of the doubt to dissenters, not to the highest court in the land or to the Congress. That, in itself, is a mighty strange way to run a government.

Aside from the controversial subject involved, there were two important aspects to the initial ruling and the refusal of rehearing and they deserve to be underscored.

First, it is the Congress, not federal agencies or executive fiat, that controls the public treasury. Second, though every citizen must have free access to the theater of freedom, in many cases he must buy his own ticket.

The Saginaw News
Saginaw, MI, July 2, 1980

The Supreme Court's ruling this week approving a congressional ban on federal funds for abortions is being hailed by "right-to-life" advocates. Most Americans probably would agree with that sentiment.

We might, too, because we're greatly disturbed by the extent to which abortion has become a means of birth control, or a matter of simple convenience. In our view, too-casual abortion contributes to decline in our moral regard and respect for all life.

But neither public opinions, nor ours, help write constitutional law. And the court's 5-4 decision doesn't make much sense in view of its landmark 1973 ruling legalizing abortion as a medical procedure without meaningful restrictions.

Even the anti-abortion movement can't claim much of a victory as long as the original ruling is left untouched.

The result of Monday's decision is a double standard for health care that can be resolved only if Michigan and other states put principle above personal opinion.

By approving the so-called Hyde amendment to the Medicaid law, the ruling means the medical procedure called abortion will be available only to those who can afford it, unless individual states agree to pay out of their own funds.

Justice Potter Stewart, writing for the majority, said a legitimate government objective is protecting "potential life" except in the "most urgent circumstances."

Fair enough — except that sounds like it could be an opinion banning abortions except, as the court this week conceded on the Medicaid question, when a woman's life is endangered or in cases of rape or incest.

If that is the Supreme Court's current view on abortion, then why didn't it simply overturn its 1973 decision rather than make financial ability the test of who can qualify for that ruling's legal options?

Michigan and Gov. Milliken now are in a dilemma because the court's ruling was permissive, not restrictive. Congress *may* restrict abortion funding; but states *may* choose to pay out of their own funds.

Milliken's proper assertion of fairness under the law has had much of the law pulled out from under it. The Legislature, reflecting public opinion, may this time override a Milliken veto of abortion-aid restrictions.

Unless the governor prevails, the Supreme Court has made medical equality in Michigan (and other states) a matter of wealth or poverty. Emotionally, many might agree. Legally, it is grossly unfair.

Newsday

Long Island, NY, July 6, 1980

The government didn't make poor women poor. Therefore the government isn't required to pay for their abortions—even if pregnancy jeopardizes their health, and even though the government would pay for carrying their babies to term and often for rearing them.

That's the tortuous reasoning applied by a five-member majority of the Supreme Court to the Hyde Amendment, which prohibits the use of federal funds for Medicaid-financed abortions unless the mother's life is at stake or the pregnancy is the result of promptly reported rape or incest.

The amendment's effect has been dramatic: Federally funded abortions dropped from 300,000 in 1977 to 2,000 in 1978. But that doesn't mean the government is saving money. It costs about eight times as much to have a baby as to have an abortion. And because federal aid to Medicaid pays for births but not for abortions, the ruling encourages poor women to bear children—or to patronize unskilled, unsanitary back-alley abortionists.

That's obviously not what the court intended in 1973 when it ruled that choosing to have an abortion is up to a woman and her physician. Without money to exercise that choice, it's really no choice at all.

The court didn't create the inequity; it merely sanctioned it. The double standard originated with Congress, which isn't likely to overturn the Hyde Amendment in an election year. That makes it all the more important for the states to assume responsibility for protecting the health of thousands of poor women. New York is doing so now. We hope state legislators have the compassion and courage to continue.

Sentinel Star

Orlando, FL, July 2, 1980

WHEN THE U.S. Supreme Court agreed last year to hear arguments on federal funding for abortions, the die was cast for what had to be a controversial decision regardless of the outcome.

In its 5-4 ruling this week, the court carried out that promise of controversy in deciding by the closest vote possible that the government has the right to restrict the use of Medicaid dollars for abortions.

Following the court's 1973 decision that abortion in the first three months of pregnancy was strictly a decision between a woman and her doctor, Medicaid paid for all abortions requested by poor women. In 1976, Congress passed the so-called Hyde amendment which limited abortions to cases of rape, incest, or where the life or health of the mother was endangered. Later those restrictions were further tightened to exclude the mother's health as a criterion.

The court was asked to rule on the constitutionality of the Hyde amendment: Had the Congress violated its duty to govern impartially? Was it impinging on the rights of poor women to terminate pregnancy?

Essentially, the court's majority ruled that Congress and the states violated no rights in restricting public money for abortion. It is a ruling that swung on close constitutional issues, and it is one that will be long debated.

But the highest court in the land has spoken, and the majority has clearly thrown the question of abortion funding back into the hands of Congress and the state legislatures.

The decision, however, should not be misconstrued. While the majority said that "federal subsidization is a question for Congress to answer, not a matter of constitutional entitlement," it did not endorse the Hyde amendment.

Instead, Justice Potter Stewart, in writing for the majority, made it clear that while the court might not like the restrictions placed by Congress, neither would it write social policy.

Indeed, that is where the question rests: Is it wise social policy to deny the money necessary for a poor woman to have an abortion, even if the abortion would mean the difference in her health?

There lies the terrible inconsistency of Congress and the Hyde amendment. Congress says that it is in the nation's best interests to protect the health of its people and to provide the money necessary to help those who cannot pay for that protection otherwise. The exception to that concern is where a pregnancy threatens a woman's health.

The Congress, however, will pay for prenatal care, for delivery of the child and for its support. In the first year of life, that adds up to about $1,800, while an abortion costs a maximum of about $200. The Hyde amendment takes away the freedom of the poor woman to choose which she wants.

Rep. Henry Hyde, R-Ill., for whom the amendment was named, says that his ultimate goal is a constitutional amendment to ban all abortions. If that is the case, he and his supporters should work for that instead of going through the back door to stop it for one class of women. The issue then would be clear, and it could pass or fail on its merits.

As it is now, a vocal and politically potent minority has convinced congressmen that "prochoice" is synonymous with "pro-abortion." It is not. There are many people in this country who personally find abortion an unacceptable alternative, but who believe just as strongly that it is a personal choice into which the government should not intrude.

That, in fact, is what the 1973 Supreme Court decision was all about: the right to make a decision without governmental interference. Undoubtedly, in balancing rights between the court's authority and the Congress' prerogatives, the court's latest ruling chips away at that right.

By definition, poor women who make the decision to have an abortion cannot afford legal abortions. They might be able to afford the back-alley butchers with coat hangers and death.

Or, with federal assistance that is available, they might deliver to the detriment of their health.

In either case, regardless of any constitutional hairsplitting, that is sorry social policy.

Rocky Mountain News

Denver, CO, July 2, 1980

THE Supreme Court has put itself in the position of saying, in effect, that women have a constitutional right to an abortion if they can afford it.

That stance — an awkward one, in our opinion — results from Monday's split decision upholding the Hyde Amendment that bans federal financing of most abortions.

The Hyde Amendment — named for its sponsor, Rep. Henry Hyde, R-Ill. — allows federal funds to be used for abortions only when the woman's life is endangered or when pregnancy results from rape and incest.

Since the Hyde Amendment was first attached to an appropriation bill four years ago, abortions financed through the federal Medicaid program have dropped from about 300,000 a year to fewer than 2,000.

Opponents of the Hyde Amendment argued that although the Supreme Court said in 1973 that a woman has a constitutional right to an abortion during the early stages of pregnancy, that right is effectively abridged for many poor women by the Hyde restrictions.

A federal district judge in New York agreed with the Hyde opponents in a decision last January. He held that the Hyde Amendment violated the U.S. Constitution's guarantees of free choice and free exercise of religion.

By a 5 to 4 decision, the Supreme Court overturned the lower court. The gist of the majority ruling is that while the Constitution guarantees many personal rights, it does not require expenditure of public funds to insure that poor people may exercise them.

The ruling will not end the argument over abortions, of course. Those who believe that a woman should have control of her own body will make greater efforts to have Congress remove the Hyde restrictions. Those who are against abortions in principle, whether affordable or not, will continue efforts to obtain an amendment to the Constitution to ban them.

About all that's settled by the Monday decision is that women who have the money can have abortions, while women who don't have the money can't.

THE PLAIN DEALER
Cleveland, OH, July 2, 1980

The Supreme Court's latest abortion decision is a bad one. It brutally rules out federal payment for an indigent woman's abortion. The same poor woman can have her whole obstetrical treatment paid for by Medicaid, but abortion? No.

It was a 5-4 vote. Associate Justice Potter Stewart's majority decision said: "Although government may not place obstacles in the path of a woman's exercise of her freedom of choice (of an abortion), it need not remove those not of its own creation. Indigency falls in the latter category."

That is a dry way of saying that poverty is none of the government's business. If you get pregnant and want or even need an abortion, it is up to you to scrape up the money for it.

It was the Hyde Amendment that was challenged. The amendment says government funds will be paid for abortions only if the pregnancy is due to promptly reported rape or incest or "where the life of the mother would be endangered if the fetus were carried to term."

There had been 250,000 to 300,000 abortions a year paid for by federal funds before the Hyde Amendment was enforced. Since late 1976 the number has shrunk to 2,000 a year.

What the Supreme Court's one-vote majority ignores is the damage it inflicts by making childbearing compulsory for the poor. Poor women will risk aborting themselves or getting dangerous back-street abortions, being unable to pay for proper care.

There will be thousands of unwanted children, unplanned for and unwelcome, living out the misery of a childhood in rejection. The social pathology this will produce will cost far more dollars than are saved by the Hyde Amendment, not to count the human pain involved.

We agree with the dissenting justices: with Justice William J. Brennan Jr. when he says "Antipathy to abortion . . . has been permitted to ride roughshod over a woman's constitutional right to terminate her pregnancy in the fashion she chooses;" and with Justice Harry A. Blackmun's words:

"Government punitively impresses upon a needy minority its own concepts of the socially desirable, the publicly acceptable and the morally sound."

This decision makes abortion not illegal but inaccessible to the poor alone. It only pretends even-handedness, but recalls to us Anatole France's aphorism:

"The law, in its majestic equality, forbids the rich as well as the poor to sleep under bridges, to beg in the streets and to steal bread."

THE LINCOLN STAR
Lincoln, NE, July 3, 1980

The U.S. Supreme Court's 5-4 ruling announced Monday upholding the Hyde Amendment limiting federal funding of abortions is another example of the fact that in a land of supposed equality, poor people are less equal than others.

In saying that, we are not arguing for abortion or against it, but only recognizing that abortion, under varying conditions throughout the states, is legal in this nation under a ruling of the same high court seven years ago. But as Dick Kurtenbach, executive director of the Nebraska Civil Liberties Union, says, "that right is really meaningless for poor women if they're not able to obtain the funds to have an abortion."

Perhaps this effective denial of rights is of no consequence to people who oppose abortion on moral or religious grounds. But it is of very real consequence to the hundreds of thousands of poor women who understand that rights in this country are accorded to those of privileged economic status, but not to them. The law provides funds for the medical needs of the disadvantaged and abortion, so the court has implied, is a medical need.

The Hyde Amendment bars Medicaid spending for abortions unless a woman's life would be endangered by childbirth, and in cases of promptly reported rape or incest. The court upheld the constitutionality of the amendment Monday and said further that the states did not have to fund certain types of abortions the federal government decides not to fund.

The decision was a highly significant victory for anti-abortion forces in the political realm. Spokesmen said it gave the pro-life movement a boost toward adoption of a constitutional amendment barring elective abortions for all. The author of the Hyde Amendment, Rep. Henry Hyde, R-Ill., praised the court for delivering a victory for "countless unborn children," but acknowledged how it will act to sharpen class distinctions by saying "the unborn of the rich are very much in jeopardy today."

That's not altogether correct. Hyde didn't go far enough. Many of the unborn of the poor are yet in jeopardy because abortion, self-induced or cheap and illegal, will remain an option for a significant share of those women. And for those children of the poor who are carried to term, many face unhappy lives in jeopardy, lives which most likely will be financed by the government — supported in part by those most insistent they not be forced to pay taxes for elective procedures.

Many of those celebrating the court decision do not, of course, know anything of the world of unwanted pregnancies, of poverty, hopelessness or of the countless factors that influence women, rich and poor, to seek abortion. To them, opposing abortion is an academic exercise.

Reality can be somewhat different. Coming to grips with unwanted or medically dangerous pregnancy causes agony, mental and physical.

In our own, admittedly arms-length view, abortion is repugnant, especially if used simply as a contraceptive measure when others have been ignored. But it is a procedure given legal sanction. And as that, it should not be easily available to only those who can afford it.

The Seattle Times
Seattle, WA, July 1, 1980

THE U.S. Supreme Court's decision, announced yesterday, to uphold the Hyde Amendment will add hot new sparks to the ongoing controversy over abortion.

The Hyde amendment restricts the spending of federal Medicaid dollars for abortions to those cases in which a woman's life would be threatened by childbirth, in cases of promptly reported rape or incest or when two doctors agree that childbirth would cause severe and long-lasting physical damage.

The court's decision makes no judgment on the specifics of the amendment. Instead, the justices focused on the legality of Congress' right to set conditions under which the government may pay for abortions. In the absence of such a judgment the Hyde amendment likely will spawn increasingly stringent anti-abortion funding legislation.

Despite the court's landmark 1973 ruling that abortions could not be forbidden, yesterday's decision was not surprising. The court has consistently and mistakenly sanctioned legislative obstacles to welfare clients having the same rights of choice as to abortion as do other women.

The ambivalence of the court was reflected in that 1973 decision. As Justice Harry A. Blackmun wrote in the majority opinion, the decision to end a pregnancy is best left to a woman and her doctor. Still, the justices persisted in setting forth conditions under which states might intervene in this decision-making process without violating what they viewed as a woman's right to privacy.

Now the court has gone even further along a perilous road. The new decision suggests that it is government's privilege to decide which rights poor women may exercise and which they may not. The right of choice, after all, is moot if one is powerless to act on one's choices.

Presumably welfare and its offshoots, such as Medicaid, exist out of the democratic belief that all people have the right to certain basics — including food, shelter and medical care — regardless of the ability to pay for these things. To declare that abortion is a right, then impose conditions on that right which assume that poor people are less equal than those who can pay for their choices is no right at all. Clearly, the court is saying that those who live under the thumb of government must abide by the moral values of others — for them the decision to end a pregnancy is between a woman and her government.

The question of abortion is not likely to be resolved permanently in the near future precisely because it is a question of moral values and intensely personal rights. A change in faces on the Supreme Court may, however, eventually change this unfortunate ruling. Meantime, the court is left with a curiously incompatible record on abortion.

Justice Blackmun understood this when be he wrote a dissenting opinion to a 1977 ruling on therapeutic abortions: "The court concedes the existence of a constitutional right to choose to have an abortion but denies the realization and enjoyment of that right. For the individual woman concerned, indigent and helpless, . . . the result is punitive and tragic. . ."

The Philadelphia Inquirer
Philadelphia, PA, July 2, 1980

Every woman in the United States has the right to freely choose whether or not to terminate her pregnancy — unless she is indigent. Every woman in the United States is equal in the eyes of the law — unless she is poor. So said the U.S. Supreme Court, ruling 5 to 4 Monday, that a woman's right to have an abortion is determined by her ability to pay.

Abortion is a moral, theological, legal and social issue. Its course through the courts and legislative halls of this land has been tortured and emotional, provoking bitterness and despair on all sides. The Supreme Court spoke clearly in its landmark 1973 decision: Abortion is a private matter between a woman and her physician. It is not an issue for the government. Depriving women of the right to terminate pregnancy is creating a barrier of inequality.

The court has spoken again, and with the decision has moved the law from its past role of neutrality on this controversial issue to a partisan one. Congress once again can deny Medicaid financing for abortions, even those determined to be medically necessary. Between 250,000 and 300,000 indigent women each year can be treated differently under the law.

Seven years ago, in the case of *Roe vs. Wade*, the court struck down the artificial distinction that separated abortion from other forms of medical care. With its ruling Monday, it has created a new distinction. Abortion is available to those who can afford it; those who cannot are to be comforted with the sop that the costs of bearing and raising children will be assumed by the government. It is the worst kind of Catch-22, and its victims are the nation's poor women.

The Supreme Court majority held that it is not the government's fault that a woman is poor and therefore is deprived of freedoms available to others. To rule otherwise, the majority said, would "mark a drastic change in our understanding of the Constitution." Such thinking flies in the face of dozens of other benefit programs, albeit less controversial ones, operating within the federal system.

In dissenting, four justices took their colleagues to task for ignoring the social and moral issues firmly tied to any abortion debate. "There truly is another world 'out there,' the existence of which the Court, I suspect, either chooses to ignore or fears to realize," said Justice Harry Blackmun.

The court has thrown the highly charged issue of abortion back to the Congress and the individual states, where, cool, rational thinking on this subject traditionally has not prevailed. Nevertheless, the court's basic decision that all women have the right to terminate pregnancy still stands. It is up to the Congress and the states to rectify this Catch-22 situation in which the court has made poor women unequal in the eyes of the law.

DESERET NEWS
Salt Lake City, UT, July 2, 1980

Both sides of the issue are over-reacting to this week's Supreme Court ruling that the government can limit the use of public funds to pay for abortions for the poor.

On the one hand, the ruling won't necessarily be a break for the taxpayers. Rather, to the extent that it does result in more births among the poor, the ruling can increase the welfare load.

To some extent, the ruling could also produce enforcement problems. Some poor women may now try to shop around for a doctor willing to claim that her pregnancy endangers the mother's life. Abortions for this reason can still be financed with public funds. So can pregnancies resulting from rape or incest — but only if the offense is promptly reported.

On the other hand, the ruling does not necessarily force the poor to resort to "back-alley butchers" or to remain forever poverty-stricken because of the expense of raising unwanted children they can't afford.

Those who insist that this is the case seem to have conveniently forgotten that there is such a thing as adoption. The number of childless couples seeking to adopt far exceeds the supply of children available for adoption. At the same time, abortion has become just about the most frequently performed surgical operation in the United States, second only to tonsillectomy. This situation suggests that abortion is being used not as a necessity but merely as a matter of convenience.

It's a convenience against which many Americans have a deep-seated moral revulsion. They should not be forced to pay for what they consider to be unjustified killing.

Nor could Congress be compelled by the courts to spend money for purposes to which it objects without violating an essential part of the Constitution — the part that keeps the branches of government separate and distinct.

With its ruling this week, the Supreme Court has merely struck a blow for common sense. But that isn't necessarily the last word on the subject. Rather, the battlefield over public funding for abortions now could easily switch from the courts back to Congress.

ARKANSAS DEMOCRAT
Little Rock, AR, July 6, 1980

The U.S. Supreme Court has all but ended taxpaid abortions – but only by a 5-4 decision, which shows you how narrowly in some cases our Constitution survives the scrutiny of its keepers.

But a bare majority did decide that "medically necessary" abortions for the poor are not a "right," underwritten by the taxpayers. In short, the Hyde Amendment, which permits taxpaid abortions only to save mother's lives or to avert the consequences of rape and incest, is constitutional.

Certainly. But that wasn't really the issue. The two federal district judges who tried to kill the amendment told Congress in effect that it must legislate public payment of "medically necessary" abortions. Federal courts can't tell Congress what to do. They can outlaw laws as unconstitutional but can't require specified legislative action.

But those judges were no worse than the high court's four dissenters. Talk about specious reasoning and arguments of expediency! The court moron, Associate Justice Thurgood Marshall, complained that there'll be "excess deaths" as poor women turn now to "unsafe means." Whose deaths is he talking about? The Justice William J. Brennan argued that the right to abortion is so indefeasible that it imposes corresponding duties on government. He mourned the loss of a right to terminate a pregnancy in any way the pregnant see fit.

Justice Potter Stewart answered Brennan precisely. "It simply does not follow that a women's freedom of choice (to have an abortion, as already guaranteed by the high court) carries with it a constitutional entitlement to the financial resources to avail herself of the full range of protected choices."

Exactly. People who lack the means to pay can't call on taxpayers to foot their abortions any more than they can call on government (meaning us) to buy the cars or color TVs they want and can't afford. Socialism works that way, but not rights.

Some of the dissenting judges, though, were disturbed by the thought of denying "medically necessary" abortions. But the Brooklyn judge who vacated the Hyde Amendment defined as medically necessary whatever reasons a doctor might prescribe – including "emotional needs." What kind of necessity is that? The majority of justices said no – that there's no distinction between "medically necessary" and "elective" abortions up to the point that danger-to-life is involved and that the Hyde Amendment takes care of that.

The big argument for free abortions, however, appeared in constitutional guise, and it was about as silly an argument as can be imagined. It was argued that since the Catholic Church bans abortion, any law that does the same sets up an "establishment of religion" – a sectarian religious doctrine that contravenes a constitutional right.

That's the same as saying that the Hyde Amendment is a Catholic canon, and the court gave the argument short shrift. The justices failed, however, to point out the irony of such an argument. The irony is that if the millions of people who have genuine religious objections to abortion were forced to subsidize them through taxes, government would be denying these millions the free practice of their religion. That's what the "Catholic" argument would have amounted to if the court had bought it.

Congress Continues to Set Medicaid Funding Limits, 1980-85

When the Supreme Court voted in 1980 to uphold the "Hyde amendment," by which Congress barred the use of federal funds for most abortions for poor women, it marked a turning point in the continuing abortion debate. (See pp. 100-113.) Congress followed suit, adding to the fiscal 1981 appropriations bill several amendments that barred all Medicaid abortions except those necessary to save the life of the mother, and permitted states to enact even tougher restrictions on Medicaid abortions than the federal law. The Senate, eager to avoid a battle over abortion, passed a final provision that allowed Medicaid abortions to save the mother's life and in cases of rape or incest, when the rape was reported within 72 hours. Following the Supreme Court decision, the Department of Labor, Health and Human Services (HHS) ordered an end to all Medicaid abortions except those allowed by the Hyde amendment. Instead of paying for some 300,000 abortions a year at a cost of $88 million, the department was expected to finance only about 2,000 abortions a year under the new law.

Since 1976, appropriations bills for the HHS have contained provisions barring the use of Medicaid funds for most abortions, except to save a mother's life. Funding was also allowed for abortions in cases of rape or incest or when two doctors determined that the woman would suffer serious, long-term physical problems if the pregnancy were carried to term. The Senate in May 1981 approved an amendment sponsored by Sen. Jesse Helms (R, N.C.) that placed even more stringent restrictions on federal funding of abortions. Already approved by the House, the amendment eliminated previous exceptions made for rape or incest and permitted federal aid only when the life of the mother was endangered. The new restrictions were passed as a rider on a supplemental appropriations bill for the remainder of that fiscal year, and remained in effect through September 1981. Since then, the Senate has tried to prohibit funds for cases involving rape or incest but those amendments have never survived.

In September 1983 the House voted for an amendment by Rep. Silvio O. Conte (R, Mass.), the ranking Republican on the Appropriations Committee, prohibiting the use of any Medicaid funds for abortions, regardless of the mother's health. That amendment, however, was killed in the Senate and was not contained in the bill's final form. Most recently, the Senate has passed a $105 billion fiscal '86 HHS appropriations bill that again includes language barring the use of funds for abortions unless the mother's life is endangered.

Los Angeles Times
Los Angeles, CA, September 30, 1980

Anti-abortion forces use every vehicle that they can think of to deny money to poor women for abortions. Just Monday they continued tightening restrictions on federal money for abortions through the congressional appropriations process. And their targeting of every plausible bill for an anti-abortion rider has placed these so-called "pro-life" groups in implausible opposition to a program designed to help poor, pregnant women have healthy babies.

At issue is a bill to expand the Child Health Assurance Program's medical coverage of pregnant women and children from poor families. The passage of that bill is stalled because Senate Majority Leader Robert C. Byrd (D-W.Va.) says he doesn't want the Senate's move toward election-year recess derailed by a debate on abortion. The issue is bound to come up, because before the House passed the measure last December it added one of those amendments that no Medicaid money could be spent for abortions unless the life of the woman would be endangered if she carried the pregnancy to term. While we appreciate the political realities that Byrd confronts, we point out that the main victims are children.

The House bill would expand Medicaid coverage for pregnant women, including those who are not eligible for aid to families with dependent children because their husbands are still living at home.

To deny aid to this group is to penalize intact families, which one would think were worth special efforts to preserve. The House bill also would set uniform financial standards across the country for determining children's eligibility for the screening and treatment program.

The Senate measure would not expand coverage for pregnant women as the House bill would, but Sen. Alan Cranston (D-Calif.) is sponsoring an amendment that would add prenatal care for women pregnant for the first time. The Senate bill would cost $22 million in the 1981 fiscal year. The Senate Finance Committee approved its version of the program in the summer of 1979, but its chairman, Sen. Russell B. Long (D-La.), blocked the bill from full Senate consideration until recently because he wanted its preventive approach incorporated in any national heath insurance plan emerging from Congress. None has, but now this bill probably will be lost in the rush to adjourn.

Cautious estimates say 1 million children could gain coverage if the Senate version goes through, and more if the House bill is adopted. Millions more children would benefit from improved services. Some 100,000 to 220,000 more women would receive prenatal care. We can't think of anything more pro-life than that. □

The Hartford Courant
Hartford, CT, January 7, 1980

Since the anti-abortion amendments regularly passed by the U.S. House of Representatives do not represent the will of the American people, and could not pass on their merits, the amendments tend to be tacked on to non-related legislation.

The inconvenience factor, and the importance of the major legislation in question, are used to impose abortion restrictions on poor women, by default.

The latest strategy of the anti-abortion forces has a saddening irony. The pro-life representatives have attached a new anti-abortion amendment to a bill designed to provide improved health care for poor children and pregnant mothers.

The amendment will delay action on the important legislation, for the Senate has fought such measures in the past.

The new House amendment is aimed at state courts. which in some cases, have overridden congressional efforts to severely restrict Medicaid abortion. Some state judges, seizing on the Medicaid language mandating "medically necessary" procedures, have quashed state regulations that would limit abortions to life-threatening situations, or in cases of rape and incest.

The House amendment would free states from that obligation for abortions.

In Connecticut, it is a federal judge, not a state judge, who has protected the rights of poor women. District Court Judge M. Joseph Blumenfeld has issued a restraining order preventing the state from imposing strict abortion restrictions.

This legal and political maneuvering should not cloud the basic cruelty that the House is attempting to inflict on the nation's poor women. The House is still standing firm on its original Medicaid amendment, which would limit funding for abortions to cases where the mother's life is endangered by pregnancy. House supporters of this amendment apparently have interpreted the American spirit of compassion to mean that women who become pregnant from rapes, or incest, had best be able to pay for the legal right of abortion.

Rep. Tim Lee Carter, a doctor from Kentucky who has neither the inclination nor political necessity to be labeled pro-abortion, went to the heart of the abortion fight during the recent floor debate. He told his colleagues that if their daughters were raped, "I believe you would take her right to a doctor . . . to stop the possibility of a pregnancy."

It is only the most poor and unsophisticated of women who fall victim to callous political restrictions on abortion. The Senate must once again fight to retain what little compassion remains in the guidelines for funding Medicaid abortions.

THE SACRAMENTO BEE
Sacramento, CA, February 15, 1980

It may take a body count to illustrate how wrong it is to prohibit federal financing of abortions for poor women. Some of the first figures compiled by the federal Center for Disease Control in Atlanta show that at least four poor women have died as a result of the cutoff of practically all federal funds for Medicaid abortions. In addition, investigators have identified eight other deaths resulting from illegal or self-induced abortions which, although not related directly to the termination of federal financing, can be fairly attributed to the general atmosphere fostered by the federal cutoff. Two of the eight were teen-agers who were afraid to tell their parents they were pregnant. If the teen-agers had known where and how to obtain a legal, safe abortion, it is reasonable to assume they would have done so. Instead of becoming healthy young women, they have become statistics in the campaign to prevent poor women from choosing whether or not to be mothers.

Members of the Center for Disease Control abortion surveillance team say a definite effect of the denial of federal funds has been a delay among poor women in obtaining abortions. This in turn increases the risk of medical complications related to terminating the pregnancy.

The CDC doctors had expected to find many more deaths linked to the cutoff of funds under Congress' Hyde Amendment which restricts federal payment for abortions to cases where the mother's life is in danger or the pregnancy results from rape or incest. The reason there are not more abortion-related deaths, the doctors say, is that the vast majority of women who would have received federally assisted abortions live in states that continue to pay for the medical procedures.

A federal judge ordered U.S. authorities to resume abortion funding today, but that ruling was stayed until it can be heard by the U.S. Supreme Court. We hope the high court will sustain the lower court ruling and declare that the Hyde amendment is not a normal exercise in congressional judgment about where to spend money, but an unwarranted intrusion by government in private decisions that should be left to a woman and her doctor.

The State
Columbia, SC, December 1, 1979

ONE of those emotion-charged issues crying out for deliberate and attentive treatment by government is that of government-paid abortions for the poor. Congress this year has certainly not taken an orderly approach to the subject.

Abortions in general, and publicly funded abortions specifically, make up one of those volatile issues that will just not go away. It is understandable, too, because people come to this controversy with deep religious, ethical, and political convictions.

For those most zealous against abortion, the question of funding is not really an issue. The strict right-to-lifers would prohibit abortions — period. Toward the other end of the spectrum, acceptance comes by degrees. Some would allow abortions only for the strictest of medical reasons. Others believe that, since abortions are available virtually on demand for those who can afford them, then the government ought to help those who cannot pay.

Since Congress first made abortion payments available under the Medicaid program several years ago, the anti-abortion lobby has hammered away at the issue. Three years ago, Congress narrowed the abortion benefit eligibility level to victims of incest and rape or in cases where the life and health of the mother is threatened. Even that is not enough for the anti-abortionists who want a constitutional amendment disallowing abortion rights for women.

This annual issue in Congress reached a point this fall where the lawmakers were attempting to deal with the controversy in the form of amendments to a resolution on the fiscal operations of the government. Eager lawmakers seized the resolution — a routine device allowing agencies to continue to operate in the absence of a completed budget bill — to tack on amendments further restricting Medicaid abortions. Thus, the simple resolution was bogged down for weeks.

It was foolish to strangle the continuing resolution with a highly volatile issue. Congress ought to deal with abortion as a single issue, out front, whether it be consideration of a constitutional amendment or a statute.

Now, the Supreme Court is getting involved again. The court has agreed to hear arguments on a case appealed from a district court judge who ruled unconstitutional a section of law restricting Medicaid payments to those in the health-endangered categories.

But, here again, even the Supreme Court might not meet the issue head on. The justices said they will first consider whether they have proper jurisdiction before getting into the substance of the case.

Paying for abortions for the indigent, and, indeed, the entire question of legalized abortions, might not be settled in the near future. Politically it is a no-win issue. But Congress is not helping matters with its haphazard approach.

The Courier-Journal

Louisville, KY, January 31, 1980

I would like to ask each one of you . . . what would you do if you had an 11-year-old daughter who was raped and became pregnant? Would you let that continue? You know that you would not. You would do something about it, and you would do something about it immediately. Let us face up to the proposition. Let us have a little grit and a little backbone.

THE ISSUE, of course, was abortion. But the person who spoke the words above was not what the Right-to-Lifers would call a pro-abortionist. What he was pleading for, in fact, was life.

At stake on the House floor, its prospects diminished by rigid anti-abortion amendments, was a crucial health program. It would provide decent medical attention for an estimated five million children (and 220,000 women about to bear children) who can't afford it and aren't presently eligible for government help.

The speaker was Kentucky Republican Tim Lee Carter, who will retire from the House this year after eight terms. He's a doctor and very much opposes abortion, as a general rule. Yet he recognizes that there are certain situations, particularly rape and incest, in which a woman's life can be ruined (and thus likely her child's, too) if she is denied medical help in time.

But most House members vote differently on even these situations. They have done so since the Supreme Court's 1973 ruling that states may not interfere with a woman's right to an abortion during the first three months of pregnancy and may impose only health regulations during the second three months. Every year, the House votes to forbid Medicaid financing of abortions except to save the life of the mother. In 1977 and 1978 (thanks to a compromise backed by Congressman Carter), it agreed to a further exception: when two doctors agree that continued pregnancy would result in severe and long-lasting damage to the mother's health. But even this was dropped last year.

The Senate, fortunately, has been less rigid. One can criticize its agreeing to severe limitations on tax-paid abortions. But at least it insists on extending such funding to cover cases of rape and incest, too. The Senate has managed to prevail in reconciling differences between the two houses. Presumably it will prevail again this time, if it passes the Child Health Assurance Program bill on which Representative Carter worked so long and hard.

In public, principles vanish

Any congressman, actually, can explain why the Senate wins on the rape/incest issue. Senators represent statewide constituencies. And House elections are so close together that campaigning to hold onto seats in that body never stops. So its members dread divisive, emotional issues that can enrage large blocs of single-issue voters. Abortion is such an issue.

Some congressmen privately admit that they don't agree with the single-minded "pro-life" forces, but fear to vote otherwise. Some of the latter won't even concede that a mother's life should have priority over that of a foetus, if only one can survive. (A "pro-life" bill before the 1980 Kentucky legislature embraces that view. It would forbid publicly financed abortions even to save the mother.) So these congressmen betray their own consciences, knowing that the Senate, its six-year terms better insulating members from emotional tides in the electorate, will repair at least the worst of the damage.

This doesn't do anything, of course, for the girl or woman — often desperate — who is poor but hasn't been raped and doesn't otherwise qualify for federal help. The way matters stand in this country, abortions (under the Supreme Court guidelines) are a constitutional right. But the poor must fend for themselves.

And the situation could get worse. Some states are under court orders to provide "medically necessary" health services, including abortion, from their own funds. But the Medicaid-extension bill discussed above was amended by the House to let states do as they please. And the pro-life forces rallied last week, in Washington and the state capitals, in behalf of their proposed constitutional amendment to outlaw abortions altogether.

The proposition isn't one-sided, of course. Many citizens saw fairness and wisdom in the Supreme Court decision. They knew of the horrors of clandestine abortions. They acknowledged the injustice of congressional curbs on the right of poor women to medical attention legally available to those with money. Above all, they supported a woman's right to reject one of life's ultimate cruelties: bringing into the world an unwanted child.

Those Americans haven't been as well organized or made as much noise as the "pro-lifers." But they have sensitivities, too, and they may be in a majority. It wouldn't take much to make them angry enough to do some shouting of their own.

Maybe they won't have to. The Supreme Court agreed in November to consider various lower-court findings that Congress is acting unconstitutionally in refusing federal funds to finance abortions for most women on welfare. And a U.S. district judge in New York ruled earlier this month, in a sweeping decision four years in the making, that the congressional restrictions violate individual rights of due process and of religious freedom. If upheld on appeal, this would vastly expand the original Supreme Court ruling based on the right of privacy.

Such a finding, of course, would be enormously divisive. The "pro-lifers" feel deeply that anyone defending abortion is — as a Kentucky lawmaker told the Frankfort Right to Life rally last week — "really pro-death." But it is our greatness as a nation that we put such store by individual rights, and that we recognize the need to respect differences of opinion.

Dr. Tim Lee Carter would be the last person anyone could fairly accuse of being pro-death. Yet he eloquently pleads that the abortion issue can have more than one dimension. Cannot the "pro-lifers" concede the same? Cannot they grant the possibility that others may be equally concerned about life but see the issue from a different perspective on what being human, and in a free America, is all about?

The Pittsburgh PRESS

Pittsburgh, PA, September 25, 1981

A government report on the impact of the abortion-restricting "Hyde Amendment" indicates it has had little effect on the number of abortions in the United States.

The congressionally passed amendment bans the use of federal funds to pay for abortions except to save a woman's life or prevent severe damage to her health or in pregnancies resulting from rape or incest.

According to the U.S. Centers for Disease Control, in the year after the amendment went into effect in August 1977 about 94 percent of the 300,000 Medicaid-eligible women who sought an abortion obtained one.

In about two-thirds of these cases the abortions were paid for by state Medicaid funds; the rest by private sources.

Thus, both the pro-abortionists, who predicted that the amendment would bring a new wave of illegal abortions, and the anti-abortionists, who hoped it would stem the tide of legal abortions, appear to have miscalculated its effect.

★ ★ ★

These figures, however, may be skewed by the fact that the vast majority of low-income women live in populous states like New York and California, which have continued to provide funds for medically indigent women.

Nine other states do so voluntarily. And four others, including Pennsylvania, continue to do so under court order.

In the 37 other states with varying restrictions, about one-fourth of the women seeking abortions had to forgo them for lack of funds.

Thus, if just one or two large states begin tightening the strings on paying for abortions the entire picture might change.

As it is, however, the Hyde Amendment hasn't been in force long enough to draw any firm conclusions about its likely impact on society.

TULSA WORLD

Tulsa, OK, November 3, 1981

WHAT has been the effect of the 1976 Hyde Amendment forbidding federally-financed abortions?

"Pro-choice" forces worried that it would force poor women to seek illegal abortions with a resulting rise in deaths from complications. "Pro-life" groups hoped women deprived of financing would carry to full term.

A study by Willard Cates of the Center for Disease Control, published in the Journal of the American Medical Association, indicates the Amendment had very little of either effect in a 2½-year period from August 1977 to February 1980.

The number of federally-financed abortions before Hyde was about 295,000 annually. The study showed an estimated 94 percent of poor women seeking an abortion had one anyway.

This was due largely to the fact that many states, particularly the large ones, provided funds for abortions for the poor. The study estimated that 85 percent of the number of women seeking aid for abortions were in states that provided it.

A number of conclusions can be drawn from the Cates study, depending, of course, on one's views on abortion, or more specifically, government-financed abortion.

But it seems clear that few of the predictions on both sides of the Hyde Amendment were borne out; that the entire matter is far more complicated than the simplistic arguments offered on both sides; and that regardless of how they are financed, upwards of 300,000 poor women a year are opting for abortion.

WORCESTER TELEGRAM.
Worcester, MA, September 7, 1981

When Congress passed the Hyde Amendment, which greatly restricted the use of federal Medicaid funds for abortions, fears were expressed that women with low incomes would be unfairly victimized.

The argument went that, merely because they were poor, they would be denied a medical service available to others.

It doesn't seem to have turned out that way.

According to a report by the National Centers for Disease Control in Atlanta, the law has had little effect. Most "medically indigent" women who want abortions manage to get them. Some of those abortions are financed by state funds, some by private philanthropies and some by clinic subsidies. Some low income women even manage to find the money on their own.

This finding should take a little of the heat out of the torrid abortion issue. It should help allay the fears of those who believe that Medicaid funding of abortions is essential to free choice.

Abortion raises a cluster of moral dilemmas. One of them is whether it is right to use taxpayer money for a procedure that is abhorrent to many taxpayers. The obverse of that is whether it is right to deny taxpayer money to poor women for a procedure that is freely available to women with the money to pay for it.

The new study does not answer either question. But it does indicate that withdrawing federal funding for abortions has not been as punitive as was feared.

The Dispatch
Columbus, OH, May 30, 1981

THE BILL passed by the Senate last week that would curtail federal funding for abortions is a piece of legislation that threatens to pit economic class against economic class.

It is an ill-conceived measure that skirts the major issue and denigrates the Constitution by sending undeniable signals to the poor that the rights of life, liberty and the pursuit of happiness belong only to those who can buy them.

If the Congress wants to ban abortions in this country, let it do so with the courage of its convictions and on the merits of its position. And let it do so without the inequities and contradictions inherent in the Senate bill.

The measure would allow federal funds to be used for abortions only in cases where the mother's life was threatened by the pregnancy. It prohibits the use of federal funds in cases of rape, incest and preference. Abortion itself remains a legal medical procedure.

This is the first time that such a measure has passed the Senate. The House has passed a similar bill, and the issue now goes to a joint committee that will seek compromises on differing aspects of the Senate and House bills. Final congressional approval of the restricted funding measure seems assured.

The abortion controversy has raged since 1973 when the Supreme Court ruled that abortions do not deprive the unborn of rights guaranteed by the Constitution. The court said it could not resolve the "difficult question" of when life begins.

Justice Harry Blackmun, writing for the majority, stated: "When those trained in the respective disciplines of medicine, philosophy and theology are unable to arrive at any consensus (as to when life begins), the judiciary, at this point in the development of man's knowledge, is not in a position to speculate as to the answer."

Four years later, the court ruled that states were not constitutionally required to finance elective abortion.

Some anti-abortionists saw an opportunity in the later decision to advance their cause. Money would be their weapon. But the strategy that evolved tried to straddle a huge philosophical chasm.

Take Sen. Jesse Helms, R-N.C., for instance. He is the sponsor of the bill the Senate just passed. Implicit in this bill is the notion that there are circumstances in which a fetus does not enjoy full constitutional rights and protections. According to this bill, the fetus's right to life is secondary to the mother's right to life.

But Helms is also the sponsor of another Senate bill, one that would define life as beginning at conception, would give a fetus full constitutional rights and protections, and would effectively ban abortions in the U.S.

Whether you agree with this bill or not, it advances the issue honestly. It can be debated on the basis of principle, not money, and can be applied to all, not just the poor.

This bill is the appropriate battleground for the pro-choice and right-to-life forces. And this is where the abortion issue should be fought.

The Wichita
Eagle-Beacon
Wichita, KS, May 23, 1981

The Senate vote prohibiting federal help to victims of rape or incest in obtaining abortions did not represent one of that body's finer hours. It is hard to believe 52 senators are that mean-spirited or that fanatically devoted to the premise that once male sperm is deposited in a female's body, it must be allowed to develop into a full-fledged child. And this is so, the Senate was saying, whether the potential mother is a frightened victim of a violent sexual attack or the 13-year-old daughter of the attacker.

No one likes to think about these things, but it's precisely what the Senate — and earlier, the House — should have been thinking about when they acted so callously. For their action has condemned countless numbers of innocent women and girls to pain and degradation, and perhaps even death at the hands of neophyte abortionists.

People of means, of course, don't have to worry about this. They can — and will — have abortions performed on loved ones who have been victimized by evil men. But for the poor among us, there is no such relief, so an act of violence reaps a double result: the anguish inflicted on the woman or child, and the unwanted child who in turn is brought into an unwelcoming world.

This was not an abortion issue, per se, for previous legislation already had restricted federal help for abortion to women whose lives were in danger and to victims of rape or incest. Is the next step now — if total abolition is the aim — to withdraw federal funding even in cases of women where carrying a child to term will claim the mother's life in the process?

A week ago, we would have said "of course not." Now we're not so sure. It will be interesting to hear what our senators and representatives think about that one.

As our readers know, we have struggled editorially with the issue of abortion, just as we imagine many thousands of others have struggled with it. There is a vast middle ground of opinion that cannot be claimed by either side, yet it's a middle ground that seldom is represented in public debate. Certainly it was not represented by the Senate majority on Thursday.

Human life is sacred. All life deserves reverence, for it represents the breath of God. But we cannot believe a merciful God would require one of his children — as the Congress now has done — to bear the fruits of a crime so horrible most mortals have trouble even imagining it

Roanoke Times & World-News

Roanoke, VA, October 14, 1981

THE CONSTITUTION, as interpreted by the Supreme Court, gives a woman the constitutional right to an abortion up to a certain point in fetal development.

It does not — and should not — require the government to subsidize that right.

That's why the Congress was quite right to cut off Medicaid funding for non-emergency abortions. That's why the federal government's top personnel officer had reason, if not the law, on his side when he tried to eliminate non-emergency abortion coverage from all 1982 federal-employee health-care plans.

The Supreme Court overruled the efforts of Donald J. Devine, director of the Office of Personnel Management, to anticipate the wishes of Congress in negotiating health-care packages for 1982.

Devine reasoned that both Congress and the Reagan administration had shown their intentions to end federal funding of abortions. He noted that the government paid $9 million last year to help finance 17,000 abortions through government insurance plans. The government pays 60 percent of the premium costs of its employee insurance.

The American Federation of Government Employees, which has 44,000 government workers in its health-benefits plan, sued. The court held that Devine's decision was based primarily on ideology and that he abused his authority.

That left the decision with the Congress. Congress still can remove from its insurance coverage any payments for non-emergency abortions. And it should.

The Supreme Court's interpretation of the Constitution requires that the state not interfere with a woman's decision to abort a fetus that has not yet developed enough to survive outside the womb.

That being the case, the state should remain neutral. If it can't forbid an abortion, neither should it use taxpayers' money to finance one, except where the mother's life and health are in jeopardy. If the employee unions insist upon full abortion coverage, let it be at the employee's option and let the employee pay the portion of the premium that would finance the coverage.

THE INDIANAPOLIS STAR

Indianapolis, IN, September 9, 1981

Scorn and praise aplenty have been heaped on the Hyde Amendment, which sharply restricts federal aid for abortions.

Opponents describe it as evil, discriminatory legislation that forces poor women to have unwanted children, pushes them into the clutches of back-alley abortionists or compels them to resort to dangerous drugs. Supporters, on the other hand, hail the measure as an effective way to curtail the abortion-on-demand phenomenon.

Apparently both are wrong. Since the amendment became effective in August 1977, legal abortions have continued apace in every income group.

The Center for Disease Control, which traced the effect of the amendment over a three year period, reported last week that despite the denial of federal funds, 95 percent of low-income women have abortions anyway.

They obtain them through various means: state or local aid, cut rates by clinics or doctors, charitable groups or by paying themselves.

The only dramatic change has been in federal bookkeeping. In fiscal 1977, before the Hyde Amendment, an estimated $87 million was distributed for combined federal-state funding for abortions. In fiscal 1978, after the law went into effect, only an estimated 4,000 abortions received federal aid.

Nine states still fund abortions voluntarily. Several others are under court order to do so. A few others fund abortions under certain conditions. Even where state funding is available, a fourth of eligible women used private funds.

At most, according to the CDC report, 5 percent of low-income women in any state have resorted to self-induced or non-physician abortions. To date, only one death is "directly attributable" and three "indirectly attributable" to lack of federal money.

So it would seem that neither the lamentations of the "pro-choicers" nor the promises of the "right-to-lifers" have been realized. The amendment has had only the most minor impact on poor women. It does, however, continue to uphold a critical constitutional principle: Congress, not government agencies or the courts, must determine who has access to the federal purse.

DAYTON DAILY NEWS

Dayton, OH, August 6, 1981

The rogue lightning of the anti-abortion militants has struck again, this time knocking down the right of private citizens to use their health insurance as they see fit.

The U.S. House has voted to bar government workers from using federal health insurance to pay for abortions except when the mother's life is in danger.

In this matter, government workers are every bit as private as the employees of, say, General Motors. Their health coverage, for which they pay 40 percent of the premium, is part of the compensation of their jobs. To deny them a lawful use of it is no more proper than to legislate restrictions on how they can spend their pay.

Private insurance is the new target of convenience for the anti-abortion movement, now that it has mauled poor women by denying them Medicaid for abortions. The movement has rammed state-employee insurance bans through the legislatures of Illinois, Massachusetts and Nebraska, and it is trying in Kentucky and North Dakota to enact bans on abortion coverage in all health insurance.

Poll after poll continues to show that a large and obviously hardy majority of Americans supports the Supreme Court ruling which left abortion decisions up to women and their physicians. Unable to persuade most Americans to imprison women who have abortions, the anti-abortion movement is using thumb-screw political pressure to twist lawmakers into taking away, bit by bit, citizens' access to a right which most want to keep.

The technique is clever — to build momentum and accumulate precedents by first taking away the rights of the politically weak. First it was "welfare mothers" (though in fact many covered by Medicaid are not on welfare: they are just grindingly poor) and now "government workers," another pariah class in current politics.

The ultimate objective is clear enough, however. It is to make all Americans abide by religious precepts which are believed only by some of us and are insisted on by even fewer.

The Oregonian

Portland, OR, October 20, 1981

A federal judge in Washington, D.C., has rightly thwarted an audacious attempt by the Reagan administration to eliminate medical coverage for therapeutic abortions from federal employees' health insurance plans.

U.S. District Judge Gerhard Gesell said that ideological, not statutory, considerations prompted Donald Devine, director of the U.S. Office of Personnel Management, to threaten cancellation of an insurance plan that covers 44,000 federal employees if the plan did not "voluntarily" drop abortion coverage. The threat came just a few days after Gesell ruled that Devine had exceeded his authority in ordering abortion benefits deleted from all 120 private insurance plans available to federal workers.

Devine claimed that because the House version of a temporary funding bill for his agency contained a rider, authored by Rep. John Ashbrook, R-Ohio, outlawing the use of federal funds for any non-emergency abortion purpose, he was prevented by Congress from expending federal funds either for the government's share of insurance premiums or for the costs of administering the insurance plans. The Senate version of the same resolution, however, specifically excluded the Ashbrook language.

In ruling on the legal challenge of Devine's policy brought by the American Federation of Government Employees, the judge no doubt based his charge of ideological bias on the fact that Devine was once an aide to Ashbrook and is a member of the board of directors of Life-PAC, a political action arm of the anti-abortion Right-to-Life movement.

Regardless of the prevailing political climate, the right of women to choose abortion still is protected by a 1973 U.S. Supreme Court decision. Although abortion foes have succeeded in making it difficult for welfare recipients to exercise that right through the Hyde Amendment and individual state policies that restrict or eliminate payments for abortions to poor women, it is presumptuous of the Reagan administration to try to bend the law to deny that right to government employees.

The Evening Bulletin

Philadelphia, PA, May 27, 1981

"We're not running this country by divine commandment or instructions from Sinai. We're running it by the Constitution. It's merely a matter of what is legal. Abortion is." — Sen. Lowell P. Weicker Jr. (R-Conn).

Yet, abortion foes have scored another legislative victory.

In granting its approval of a $12.8 billion supplemental appropriations bill, the Senate limited Medicaid funding for abortions for poor women to instances when the woman's life is endangered. Victims of rape or incest will no longer receive coverage.

There is no logic to the action. The Supreme Court ruled in 1973 that abortion is legal. Until the court's ruling is overturned, it is the law of the land.

By severely restricting the instances when a poor woman can get a Medicaid-funded abortion, we are saying that the law is there only for those who can afford it.

The medical expenses of childbirth are covered by Medicaid, yet abortion, a legal operation, is not.

To end Medicaid-funded abortions for victims of rape and incest sentences these women to back-alley quacks or forces them to carry to term the product of a rapist. Rape is a brutal violation of a woman's body. Its psychic scars can

be permanent. To refuse to aid a victim impregnated by such an attack shows a complete lack of compassion.

Sen. Jesse Helms (R-NC), the Senate's most visible opponent of abortion, said, "having the convictions that I do that abortions are the deliberate termination of human life, I don't see how we can vote to spend taxpayer dollars for this purpose."

Helms is entitled to his views. But he allows them to obstruct his view of the issue of legality of abortion, which the Senate was supposed to be dealing with. As an elected representative Helms is bound to uphold the laws of this nation, not ignore them because of personal beliefs.

He warned fellow conservatives that they could lose the backing of the "pro-life movement" if they did not support him. He said the outcome "will be attentively watched." Resorting to such threats only attempts to spread his myopia.

Yet, Helms's excessiveness is compounded by the Senate's hypocrisy. The Senate voted to forbid taxpayer-financed abortion funding to the nation's poor who are victims of rape or incest, yet refused to legislate against the use of federal-employe health-insurance funds for abortions — which the taxpayers also finance. The closer to home, it appears, the less ardent the anti-abortion cry.

The Des Moines Register

Des Moines, IA, May 30, 1981

Acting in the name of "life," 52 U.S. senators — including Iowans Roger Jepsen and Charles Grassley — passed the strongest anti-abortion provisions ever approved on Capitol Hill. The measure, approved by a vote of 52 to 43, would forbid federal payment for any abortion except where the life of the woman is in danger.

Unlike present law, the measure would not provide federal Medicaid money for women who have become pregnant as the result of promptly reported rape or incest.

The likely result is that poor women — including young teenagers who may have been criminally assaulted by their relatives — will find it harder to obtain safe abortions. The well-off, who don't have to rely on publicly supported health programs, will not be penalized.

Iowans are governed by a state law that permits the Iowa Department of Social Services to pay for abortions for women on welfare when their pregnancy endangers their life, when the fetus is deformed or when the pregnancy is the result of a

promptly reported rape or act of incest.

An official at the department said these payments will continue unless the state law is changed, but, because of the congressional action, Iowa no longer will be be reimbursed by Washington for abortions performed on the victims of rape and incest.

A leading backer of the new restrictions, Senator Jesse Helms (Rep., N.C.), said the issue is whether taxpayers should have to pay for "the deliberate taking of an innocent human life." He said there was a "set of instructions that came down from Mount Sinai" about that.

It is not clear that abortion is banned by the Ten Commandments, and it is even less clear that Helms speaks with the authority of Moses — or the wisdom of Solomon.

It would be a blessing if this country were run by Solomons. Instead, it is governed by lesser men and women. But even they could and should have displayed more humanity than they did when they pointed a dagger at the neediest of the nation's pregnant citizens.

Des Moines, IA, August 11, 1981

The House of Representatives voted the other day to chip away a bit more of the legal right of American women to undergo abortions. With all of Iowa's representatives going along, the House voted to forbid use of federal employees' health insurance to pay for abortions except when the mother's life is in danger.

A year ago, the same measure did not make it all the way through Congress, as it now appears likely to do. Then, the Iowa delegation split 4-1, with Representative Thomas Harkin (Dem.) opposed. A year ago, a vast majority of Americans thought abortion should be allowed under several conditions. Today, polls show, they still do. But times are changing because an impassioned minority is pressuring politicians to follow the minority's will.

In June, their victory was against the poor. About 10,000 women effectively lost their right to abortion in cases of rape or incest as the result of congressional action banning federal Medicaid payments for abortions unless the mother's life is at stake.

This time, the chip was bigger: Some 10 million people — 3 million federal workers plus their families — will be affected if the Senate and House agree on the bill. The chip was bigger, too, because it goes far beyond prohibiting the use of public money for abortions. It prohibits workers from using their own health insurance, paid 60 percent out of their own pockets, on a medical option they might choose.

The foes of choice on this issue are succeeding because they care deeply. The majority is losing

because it is less concerned. It will be interesting to see how far this chipping away will go before the majority cares enough to protest.

The poor were an easy target, no match for the anti-abortion people. The federal workers are more problematic, by virtue of their numbers and their access to policymakers. But it seems that the chipping will go on. The tide still is with abortion foes; they are still turning around votes like Harkin's.

One reason the Medicaid and health-insurance votes have succeeded while more sweeping anti-abortion legislation has failed so far is that these measures involve the use of public funds. Many people who believe that the government ought to stay out of this intimate decision feel qualms about financing abortion.

But there is no easy line to be drawn. In Iowa, for example, most abortions can be said to be underwritten by the public, since most hospitals receive some public subsidy.

The Supreme Court has ruled against state interference in the right of women to make their own decisions on abortion. It is wrong to infringe on that right just because a woman needs public assistance; it is wrong to deny federal employees the right to use their medical insurance for abortions in most circumstances.

Americans either have the right to abortions or they do not. Those who feel that abortion is murder are entitled to try to overturn the Supreme Court decision by constitutional amendment. But this chipping away satisfies no principle and hurts more people with each vote.

St. Louis Globe-Democrat

St. Louis, MO, September 26, 1981

The Reagan administration's refusal to finance abortions through federal employee health programs is consistent with the determination of Congress that taxpayer funds should not be used to destroy human life.

Last year, during the Carter administration, 17,000 abortions were performed through the Federal Employees Health Benefits program which taxpayers subsidize. The program covers 9 million civil servants, family members and retired government employees.

Donald J. Devine, director, has warned

federal employee health insurance carriers that any who provide non-emergency abortion benefits will be dropped from the program. This means that abortions will be permitted only when the life of the mother is at stake.

Taxpayer funds should not be used to finance the killing of unborn children at any level of government. The federal employee program has been a loophole that cried out to be closed. The Reagan administration has provided another "No" to outrageous abuse.

Newsday

Long Island, NY, June 2, 1981

Surely the campaign against abortion can't sink much lower.

Last month the Senate joined the House in refusing to spend federal Medicaid funds on abortions even for victims of rape or incest. At least until October, no federal money can be used to pay for an abortion unless the prospective mother's life would be endangered by bearing a child.

The ban was attached to a supplemental appropriations bill for the current fiscal year, which ends Sept. 30. Sen. Jesse Helms (R-N.C.) pushed through the amendment over the opposition of Republican Senate leaders, who generally would like to strip appropriations bills of such extraneous riders.

The vote was 52 to 43, and New York's senators were divided: Republican Alfonse D'Amato voted yes; Democrat Daniel P. Moynihan voted no. The amendment will cost New York money, since the state *does* permit Medicaid abortions and pays what would normally be the federal share.

It's bad enough to deny abortions to poor women when the affluent remain free to obtain them. But in a way it's even worse to falsify the argument against abortion for rape victims, as Helms did in the Senate debate. Even though the old law requires a rape to be reported within 72 hours to qualify for a Medicaid abortion, Helms called the rape question "a red herring whereby people come up four months later and say, 'Oh, by the way, I was raped four months ago.'"

Perhaps it's too much to expect the Senate to have some compassion for girls and women who become pregnant as a result rape or incest. But it's intolerable that these victims should be subjected to mockery and slander on the Senate floor.

The Kansas City Times

Kansas City, MO, May 23, 1981

Who can keep up with the laws controlling spending of federal money for abortion? Presently a woman of little income who is a victim of rape or incest can get Medicaid for an abortion, provided the crime is reported to authorities within three days. On Thursday, the U.S. Senate voted to shut that small loophole, even though it is a fact that rape and incest fall heaviest on women of little means. That would leave as eligible for federal aid only those abortions certified as necessary to save a woman's life.

Regardless of your position on abortion (and you may oppose it for yourself but support the right for others), take a moment to reflect if this is any way for the Congress of the United States to make laws governing the behavior of the citizens. Many talk at length about the sanctity of the process of governing, and the compelling need to keep government from becoming mired in the picky details of lawmaking. They say that a running feud over those details has the long-term effect of breaking down the trust of the citizens in those who govern them.

Several months ago, we praised a speech by Sen. John C. Danforth, R-Mo., about governing America in these times. Briefly, Danforth, who this week voted with the hard-right conservatives led by Sen. Jesse Helms, R-N.C., to deny abortions to poor women who are victims of rape or incest, made this comment: ", . . (We in Congress) don't set priorities at all, but instead spend an inordinate amount of our time and energy on other issues which are not central and about which there will never be a con sensus. These other issues include school prayer, busing, abortion, the Equal Rights Amendment and labor management relations.''

Bear in mind — and we're not singling out Danforth for criticism, though he does seem to have forgotten or ignored his own message — that the rider by Senator Helms to block federally funded abortions for poor women came up suddenly on the Senate floor and was attached to a supplemental appropriations bill for the current fiscal year. It was stampede legislation. Anyone who seriously studies Congress knows that Senator Helms is using fear and the quick-kill method of making public policy.

And anyone who understands the human condition at all — do the so-called conservatives? — also knows rape, incest and abortions will continue among the poor.

But let us return to Senator Danforth's words from his speech last December in St. Louis to the Anti-Defamation League of B'nai B'rith. He made an excellent point he should repeat to his colleagues — and recall himself:

"It is especially crucial at this time in our history that the political process not be relinquished to single-issue constituencies but be balanced by concerned citizens with broader perspectives. If federal officials are to focus on the problems of the economy, national defense and foreign policy, it is imperative that you and other Americans force that focus.''

THE SUN

Baltimore, MD, May 26, 1981

The political power of the anti-abortion lobby in Congress was never more evident than last week as the Senate cast aside warnings of intolerance and "religious moralism" and approved tight restrictions on Medicaid abortions for poor women. Yet even as anti-abortion attitudes in Congress grow more extreme, public attitudes are heading in the opposite direction.

Admittedly, public opinion toward abortion is sometimes ambiguous. Anti-abortionists cite a recent poll by Connecticut Mutual in which 65 percent of respondents agree that abortion is "morally wrong." But a recent CBS-New York *Times* poll showed that 67 percent of Democratic and 58 percent of Republican respondents said they believed in a woman's right to an abortion if her doctor agreed; in a Gallup poll last fall, 25 percent of respondents believed abortions should be legal in all circumstances, and 53 percent believed they should be legal in some.

One interpretation of the seeming conflicts in the polls is that while many Americans would not choose abortions for themselves or family members, they believe others should have that right. Another interpretation is that regardless of their personal feelings, most Americans believe (as did the Supreme Court in 1973) that the decision, during early pregnancy, should be a private one between a woman and her doctor.

Acceptance of the belief that most abortions should be legal is growing. Between 1975 and 1980, Gallup results indicate the percentage of Americans believing all abortions should be illegal declined from 22 to 18 percent; the percentage believing they should be legal under all circumstances increased from 21 to 25 percent. The recent referendum in Italy, in which that Catholic nation's liberal abortion law was upheld overwhelmingly, indicates the issue there is not drawn along sectarian lines. This is increasingly true here, too —though U.S. churchgoers, of all faiths, more often oppose abortions than non-churchgoers. Lower-income Americans also are more likely to oppose abortions.

The climate in Congress can be gauged not only by the deplorable Senate vote on Medicaid abortions, which denies to poor women medical care available legally to those with money, but also by the fact the "human life" bill, to define the beginning of life as the time of egg fertilization, has a chance at passage. Besides serious constitutional questions, there are immense practical problems: The bill might require states to outlaw birth control techniques—such as intra-uterine devices and hormones—now in widespread use and considered contraceptive, not abortive.

Along with many other Americans, we have moral reservations about abortions, especially abortions "on demand" used as an irresponsible means of birth control. But we have even stronger moral reservations about the "human life" bill, which not only seems to represent largely an extremist fringe of opinion but which also could outlaw birth control techniques that are responsible abortion alternatives.

Los Angeles Times
Los Angeles, CA, September 30, 1983

This June the Supreme Court reaffirmed the right of women to choose an abortion. Now Congress has reaffirmed its denial of that right to women who cannot afford to pay for the operation. A recent vote showed that there are still far too few members of the House of Representatives who are willing to stand up against anti-abortion forces.

At issue was the annual amendment to the health and human services appropriation barring any use of federal money for abortion. In recent years that restriction has been steadily tightened so that now it contains an exemption only if the life of the mother is threatened. This year even that exemption—which allows fewer than 1,000 federally financed abortions a year—was stricken in the House.

Ironically this total ban, which is not final, came about as a result of a parliamentary maneuver by groups that support federal payment for abortions for the poor. They wanted to force a vote to restore money for all abortions for poor women rather than go on arguing about conditions under which exemptions could be made. They got the vote but they lost, 184 to 231.

Pro-choice groups expect the Senate to restore the exemption for life-threatening cases; Rep. Silvio O. Conte (R-Mass.) has also pledged to try to do so when the measure reaches a conference committee. With this understanding, some of the groups that sought the up-or-down vote are able to see a bright side of the picture. It was the first direct vote on the issue as a whole since 1977, and showed that pro-choice forces had gained numerical strength. However, it also showed that 231 members of the House still are unwilling to stand up to anti-abortion groups.

The lesson in the vote is that anti-abortion forces continue to dominate legislators. Pro-choice groups estimate that they picked up about 26 votes with victories in the 1982 congressional elections. The campaign should continue in order to show lawmakers that pro-choice forces have strength at the voting polls as well as in public opinion polls.

One place to start would be with Rep. William E. Dannemeyer (R-Fullerton). He stated his moral opposition to abortion, and we have no quarrel with that. But he added that a country that was creating deficits should be aware of the financial consequences of abortion. "If we are going to pay off this debt, somebody has got to be born to pay the taxes to pay it off."

With that remark, Dannemeyer trivialized the rights of women. He lowered the level of debate, if that is possible. It is time to elect representatives with greater sensitivity on this issue and then end the debate. The Supreme Court was, after all, as clear and forceful as possible when it stated that "a woman has a fundamental right to make the highly personal choice whether or not to terminate her pregnancy." Economic status should not cloud that right.

OKLAHOMA CITY TIMES
Oklahoma City, OK, August 19, 1983

ADVOCATES of legalized abortion are laying the groundwork in Congress for an effort to overturn existing restrictions on federal funding for abortion.

The first step was a hearing in June on the "public health aspects" of unintended pregnancies. Next will come an attempt to repeal provisions in existing law that for 6½ years have barred the use of Medicaid funds for most abortions.

If the Equal Rights Amendment had been ratified, the abortion advocates probably would not have to go to all this trouble. Obviously, they are in no mood to wait on the new ERA and will push quickly for federal funding of abortions.

But testimony at a House subcommittee hearing last month on the new ERA is instructive, not only on the abortion issue, but on other moral questions that might be affected by it.

Grover Rees III, assistant professor of law at the University of Texas, told the subcommittee the federal courts probably would interpret the proposed federal ERA to require government funding of abortion. He said that under the ERA as now worded, the courts would apply to laws that distinguish on the basis of sex the same strict standard of review they now apply to laws that distinguish on the basis of race.

Under such "strict judicial scrutiny," Rees testified, the courts likely would declare unconstitutional any state or federal law that barred abortion funding, just as a law that excluded funding for sickle cell anemia, which afflicts mostly blacks, would currently be held unconstitutional.

THE DAILY OKLAHOMAN
Oklahoma City, OK, May 23, 1981

ABORTION is one of those explosive issues on which any comment on either side provokes hostile response, often of the knee-jerk variety.

However, the latest Senate action — an appropriations bill rider barring Medicaid funding of any abortion except when the woman's life is threatened — is subject to legitimate criticism in two specific areas.

As it stands, the measure heads for conference. And since the House had already passed a similar requirement, it would appear destined to become law.

What troubles many, including those opposed to abortion in principle and especially as a routine practice, is the Senate's

52-43 vote to deny federally funded abortions to women who become pregnant as a result of rape or incest.

These are among the most heinous offenses in our society, and the victims — often barely adolescent girls — should not be condemned to carry and bear offspring resulting from unwanted, brutal assaults on their bodies. Their physical health might not be at stake, but their mental health surely is.

If Congress in its wisdom sees fit to make an exception for the mother's health in this legislation, rape and incest should be accorded equal qualifying status.

The Seattle Times
Seattle, WA, September 29, 1983

IN THE U.S. House of Representatives, it was a point of order, a technical goof that resulted in an end to federal funding for abortions for any reason. For thousands of poor women, it was a little more freedom lost — a further devaluation of their worth in society.

The House last week approved spending legislation for the Departments of Labor, Education and Health and Human Services that denies money for abortions, including those when the mother's life is in danger.

As one woman representative pointed out to her colleagues after the vote, it means that the life of a fetus is more important than the life of the woman carrying it.

For the past seven years, the appropriations bills unfairly have limited federal funding for abortions to life-threatening situations. This year, because of some complicated technical rulings, even that category has been excluded.

Rep. Henry Hyde, R-Ill., one of the leading abortion foes in Congress and author of the anti-abortion Hyde Amendment, says he believes a House-Senate conference committee will restore the life-threatening clause before the bill is passed on to the president for signing.

Even if that is so, it will not be enough. To deny access to abortion (by withholding money) to women solely because they are poor is contrary to democratic principles. Money should not be the test of whether abortion is right or wrong.

As long as abortions are available upon demand to any women in this society, they must be available to poor women. Poverty should not make people weak, vulnerable and expendable to those who have the economic power to manipulate their lives.

Poor women should not be victimized by archaic and arrogant thinking such as was expressed by William Dannemeyer, R-Calif., who noted that abortions are reducing the number of taxpayers and "if ever we're going to pay off this debt, somebody is going to have to be born to pay it off."

The Record
Hackensack, NJ, June 6, 1985

Every year Congress gets into a tedious wrangle over whether federal funds may be used for abortions for the poor. Since 1976 Rep. Henry Hyde of Illinois has managed to attach a rider to the annual appropriations bill for the Department of Health and Human Services. The Hyde amendment bars states from paying for abortions with Washington's contribution to Medicaid, the federal-state insurance program for the poor. (Several states, including this one, provide abortions with their own funds.)

It's always a lengthy, contentious fight, and the outcome is always the same. Rep. Marge Roukema of Ridgewood, a pro-choice advocate, told us last week, wearily, that the Hyde amendment is certain to pass again this year. So now Sen. Orrin Hatch of Utah, a pro-lifer, is asking: Why rerun the debate every year? He wants to attach a permanent ban on abortions to Title VI of the 1964 Civil Rights Act.

But the Hatch proposal would cause more problems than it would solve. The civil-rights law bars discrimination in public accommodations and employment on the basis of race, sex, age, and handicap. It grew out of rulings that such discrimination is unconstitutional. The Supreme Court has repeatedly refused to include the unborn in this category. To legislate that fetuses have civil rights — in defiance of the courts, and with the public deeply divided on the question — would simply invite more disagreement and litigation.

Of course, Mr. Hatch is less concerned with the overburdened congressional calendar than with giving the executive branch a new excuse to restrict all abortions. Title VI now allows the government to cut off funds from an entire hospital if one unit or division of it illegally discriminates. Interpreted broadly, the Hatch amendment could bar any hospital that receives federal funds — and that's virtually all of them — from providing *privately* financed abortions.

As long as abortion is a volatile issue, Congress should state its intent each year, difficult and time-consuming as that may be. Opponents and proponents have even found some common ground during these debates and could do so again. It's likely this year, for example, that Congress will approve Medicaid payments for abortions involving victims of rape and incest. In the meantime, Senator Hatch cannot resolve the nation's abortion dilemma by fiat.

The Washington Times
Washington, DC, June 5, 1984

Desperate to remain on the offensive, pro-abortion forces have started a drive in Congress to repeal restrictions on abortion funding by Medicaid and federal insurance programs. It's a drive on paper only, because the legislation is being offered to the same House that repeatedly has passed the Hyde amendment restricting such funding. All the same, the House may need a reminder.

These lobbyists show, among other things, how shallow is their commitment to free choice. They would deny pro-lifers any choice at all in the allocation of their tax dollars to pay abortionists. This is a "pro-choice" position?

Within living memory, taking a life in the womb was looked upon with horror in Western society. The Supreme Court's 1973 decision capped a long drive to change that, completing abortion's transition from a crime to a right. Public funding of abortion takes the process a disagreeable step further.

Americans have lots of rights — free speech, for instance — that do not constitute a claim on the public purse. To assert that abortion is a "right" the public should be expected to fund, willy-nilly, is — well, preposterous. The evidence that fetal life is human and entitled to society's protection, though ignored by the court, is nonetheless compelling. The inevitable conclusion that abortion is homicide is scarcely a crank notion, as even many who nevertheless would permit some abortions will acknowledge.

Removing restrictions on publicly funded abortions would force many Americans, not just the pro-choice minority, to contribute to what they judge to be a monstrous wrong. The Hyde amendment should be retained.

THE ATLANTA CONSTITUTION
Atlanta, GA, October 2, 1984

Election-year pragmatism may at last accomplish what the forces of reason, persuasion and common decency could not: to spare a woman too poor to pay for an abortion the trauma and expense of bearing a child of rape or incest.

Wealthy women have never had to contemplate that ordeal. Abortion has always been available for a price, and the 1973 U.S. Supreme Court ruling legalizing abortion made it easier to find safe, therapeutic abortions.

But Congress voted six years later, under pressure from abortion foes, to treat poor women differently — and they've been treated differently, to the disgust of fair-minded people, ever since.

Under a rule that amounts to economic discrimination, the government has been banned since 1979 from using Medicaid funds to pay for abortions unless the mother's life was in danger.

And though the debate has been reopened several times since then, it's been stymied in the past by a determined anti-abortion vanguard, led by Sens. Jesse Helms (R-N.C.), Orrin Hatch (R-Utah), and lobbyists armed with such emotional "persuaders" as Mason jars containing aborted fetuses floating in formaldehyde.

This could be the year that rule is finally put to rest, thanks to the efforts of moderate Republicans like Connecticut's Lowell P. Weicker.

Weicker persuaded his Senate colleagues last week to attach a provision to a $95 billion appropriations bill broadening the conditions for Medicaid reimbursement.

Though Helms predicted ultimate defeat for the measure, which would make rape and incest victims eligible for Medicaid abortions, the conservative, two-term senator is in a bitter battle to retain his seat against a challenge from Gov. James B. Hunt.

As, Weicker said after the Senate sent the measure to a joint conference committee, "I don't think anybody wants to stand up in an election year and say that a woman should carry a baby to term when that pregnancy is the result of rape or incest."

The right to abortion has been favored by an overwhelming majority of Americans in every major public-opinion poll for more than a decade.

It was politics, pure and simple, that did the damage in 1979, and politics may indeed be its undoing. But where is it written that politicians must do the right thing for the right reason?

In this case, it will be more than enough to see right done, at last.

Court, Legislatives Battles Rage Over State Funding Of Abortions

In the years after *Roe v. Wade*, many states enacted legislation that restricted government funding of 'elective' abortions—those not necessary to save the life or protect the health of the woman. Many of these laws were struck down as a violation of the equal protection clause of the Fourteenth Amendment when they were challenged in the courts. (The obligation on any state to pay the pregnancy-related medical expenses of indigent women is not imposed by the Constitution. However, should a state decide to alleviate some of the hardships of poverty by providing medical care, constitutional limitations determine the way those funds may be apportioned.) According to a 1979 study by the Alan Guttmacher Institute, 18 states had by that year adopted the federal standard for funding abortions, as outlined in the Hyde Amendment. (See pp. 100-113.) Another 16 states funded abortion only to save the life of the woman, 10 states and the District of Columbia funded only medically necessary abortions and the remainder financed abortions under varying conditions.

The following court cases are typical of the many state funding battles discussed in the editorials on these pages:

■In 1979 the state of New Jersey was ordered by a state Superior Court judge to pay for medically necessary abortions for poor women. The ruling on a class action suit held that the state's ban on Medicaid payments for abortions unless the mother's life was threatened was in conflict with governing federal law.

■In 1981 the U.S. Supreme Court let stand a lower court order requiring the state of Arizona to honor its contract with the state branch of Planned Parenthood (*Arizona v. Planned Parenthood*). Under that contract, Arizona subsidized the organization with federal family planning funds. The state legislature had passed a budget amendment barring the transfer of such funds to organizations that performed abortions or abortion counseling.

■Later that year, the Massachusetts Supreme Court ruled that the state constitution required the state to pay for all "medically necessary" abortions for women on welfare, even if their lives were not in danger.

THE DENVER POST
Denver, CO, April 13, 1979

The Colorado Senate should defeat SB 438, by Sen. Sam Zakhem, R-Denver, before taking yet another step toward government control over the private lives of citizens.

Zakhem's bill would prohibit all state funding for abortions—a cost the state has borne for women receiving welfare assistance since the federal government cut off such payments in 1977.

Passing SB 438 wouldn't stop abortions in Colorado for the rich. It might indeed result in some of the very poor ending up with more unwanted children that they are unable to support without public assistance. But the basic point is not whether the resulting inequality of treatment is good or bad, but whether the government should substitute its judgment for that of the individual in such issues of conscience.

Abortion is a wrenchingly difficult thing for many Americans to accept. Others view it as simply another form of birth control, albeit one which extracts an excessive emotional toll on women, compared to the far-preferable family planning measures which prevent pregnancy in the first place.

With such disparate value judgments, it is virtually impossible for society to try to impose one set of such value judgments over the other. Whatever it may be to religious leaders or individuals, abortion to the state should simply be a medical question with the ultimate decision resting between the woman and her doctor.

As such, it should be funded as any other medical procedure. To do otherwise is to substitute the will of government over the free choice of the individual in a sphere of private conduct.

AKRON BEACON JOURNAL
Akron, OH, June 26, 1979

IF POLITICIANS could deal with all controversial issues simply by slipping an amendment into some other major bill, it would no doubt expedite the legislative body's work.

But it wouldn't, and it doesn't, serve the public interest.

That is just one of the things wrong with the amendment Sen. Harry Meshel (D-Youngstown) inserted in the final hours of the Senate Finance Committee's deliberation on the $16.3 billion budget bill for the next two years.

The amendment, adopted in a late night session without any public hearing, prohibits use of state funds for promoting or performing abortions unless two physicians sign statements saying that the operations are necessary to protect the mother's life.

The effect of the legislation would, of course, be to tighten the double standard that now exists. The U.S. Supreme Court in 1973 wisely decided that a woman's decision to have an abortion during the first three months of pregnancy is

Sen. Meshel

her constitutional right, and that it is a decision that should be reached between her and her physician.

With the right thus established under law, the only limiting factor becomes ability to pay for such medical service. For those who can afford their own medical care, there is no problem. For those who depend on public assistance, the legislation would set another standard.

It is a standard that runs contrary to federal law that allows abortions to be publicly funded if a doctor says it is necessary for the mother's physical or mental health or in cases of incest and rape.

Mr. Meshel's amendment does not concern itself with mental or physical health, incest or rape — just the possibility of the mother's death.

Having used the budget bill as a subterfuge to introduce this controversial proposal, Mr. Meshel refused to give his reasons for bypassing the democratic process, saying only that the amendment was sought by "several persuasions."

Some speculated that congressional aspirations motivated the senator. Whatever his reasons, he and other Senate leaders apparently promised pro-choice proponents in the legislature that the language of the amendment would be drastically changed in

the budget conference committee. That is where the bill with all its amendments is now.

With that assurance — if, indeed, it does exist — Democratic leaders smothered floor debate and pro- and anti-abortion groups in the Senate chambers left unheard.

Current law in Ohio allows abortions under terms similar to those provided under federal law — including protection of the mother's mental and physical health.

Sen. Meshel and his supporters, who do not even identify themselves, know that if the amendment stands, abortions will not end. But the state's poorest women will be denied access to an important aspect of safe, legal medical care.

That double standard of health care is wrong.

The lack of openness and absence of debate on such a critical issue is wrong in a democratic government.

And any attempt to build or destroy political careers on a single issue is unwise.

If the conference committee wants to do what is right, it will quickly remove any additional restrictions on abortion payments from the budget bill.

The Virginian-Pilot

Norfolk, VA, March 25, 1981

The law of the land is quite clear on the rights of a woman who becomes pregnant — in the case at hand, of the woman who is pregnant because of rape or incest or who is told by competent medical advisers that the fetus will be badly formed or otherwise seriously abnormal. If she acts within the first three months of pregnancy, and if she has about $200, she can obtain a medically safe abortion if she so chooses.

If she is on Medicaid, however, the fact itself suggests she does not have the $200. By virtue of Governor Dalton's veto of two abortion bills, this poor woman cannot obtain the effects of the law of the land which accrue to all other Virginia women who can obtain $200. The law of the land is the Supreme Court decision, *Roe v. Wade*, 1973.

The amount involved is small — a false economy excuse was once put forward against the bills. Private actions could swiftly raise the funds to take care of the few cases seemingly brought each year. But this minor action could illuminate the entire controversy which plagues the nation.

Who will give birth to the child involved? Who will love it, nurture it, bring it into a family? Who will make the child content with itself and not an enemy of society? It will not be those who urged Governor Dalton to veto the bills. It will not be those who constantly are pointing their fingers at the living while moralizing about the rights of the unborn.

As regular readers of this page well know, we believe the Supreme Court exceeded its rightful jurisdiction when it took over the abortion law authority of some 50 state legislatures. But *Roe v. Wade* is the law. We find very unsettling the spectacle of people who claim a higher morality while requiring decisions for which they do not bear the consequences.

How can such coldness to the rights of the born be squared with such passionate devotion to the rights of the unborn, whatever they may be? Such questions will persist long after the Dalton veto, for this issue, too, will not go away. In the end, it could well turn opinion against the opposition to abortion on major grounds. Extreme action, in our opinion, cooled off the initial sympathy for the Equal Rights Amendment (ERA). The Dalton veto is the kind of extremism that can do the same thing for the anti-abortion argument.

San Francisco Chronicle

San Francisco, CA, August 22, 1979

THE PRO'S AND ANTI'S are rallying at Sacramento for the annual showdown on the issue of state funding for abortions sought by women on the rolls of Medi-Cal.

The fight is, as usual, a bitter one, for emotions on the question run high and there is no doubt that many opponents of publicly-supported abortion are sincere in wanting, as taxpayers, to avoid any involvement in paying for a medical procedure that they disapprove of. Yet it is, of course, a fact that by a U. S. Supreme Court ruling in 1973 the decision to have — or not to have — an abortion is a private matter and that states may not prevent the woman's freedom to choose. What states *may* do is refuse to pay for a chosen abortion, but this, we submit, is unfairly to deprive the poor of that freedom of choice.

THERE WERE ABOUT 221,000 abortions performed in California last year, the State Department of Health Services estimates. Medi-Cal paid for less than half of these, the average cost being $330. More than half of Medi-Cal-financed abortions were obtained by white women, about one fourth by black women, and 16 percent by Hispanic women.

To oblige a woman unable to scrape up this fee to go through with an unwanted pregnancy, and bear an unwanted child, seems to us a hard-hearted denial of a very important personal right of decision that society should recognize and protect.

MEDI-CAL WAS ABLE to provide for more than 100,000 abortions last year notwithstanding that in 1978 the Legislature voted for crushing restrictions to limit the availability of this procedure. Such restrictions were taken to court and stayed from going into effect while the appeal was heard — the latest such stay having come just this month from the state Supreme Court.

The lawmakers should face this issue by settling it permanently. Assemblywoman Leona Egeland, D-Morgan Hill, is expected to offer legislation next week which will reverse the challenged restrictions by broadening abortion policy and, as she says, "take the state of California out of the business of compulsory pregnancy."

WE BELIEVE CONSIDERATIONS of fairness and equality compel the conclusion that the state should provide to the woman who is poor the same facilitated access to an abortion, if that is her free and medically advised choice, that the more affluent woman has by reason of her ability to pay the cost.

The Boston Globe

Boston, MA, June 15, 1979

The anti-abortion forces who pranced about, some with babies, in the State House on Tuesday while Gov. King signed into law the unfortunate bill prohibiting all public funding of abortions, except in cases where the expectant mother's life is at stake, were beneficiaries of a timid Legislature.

Last year the Legislature painstakingly arrived at the compromise position of prohibiting publicly funded elective abortions except in cases involving rape and incest and danger to the health of the woman. This year one of the major factors in the Legislature's willingness to approve the benighted piece of work which is now a state law was a desire to prevent anti-abortion people from holding hostage the fiscal 1980 budget, as they did the 1978 and 1979 budgets.

That is an abdication of legislative responsibility which could haunt them if other single-issue advocates become convinced that they too can use similar tactics in the future.

Apparently in the back of some legislators' minds was the strong possibility that some judge will take the heat and modify the new anti-abortion law to make it more humane when it is tested for constitutionality in court. The probability is good that some of these legislators are the same ones who complain bitterly about "judicial law-making."

Not only did the Legislature approve the bill restricting public funding of abortions — that was expected — they went further than they had to. Gov. King had stated that he would have been willing to sign a bill which allowed publicly funded abortions for cases involving rape and incest. That would have been a major concession on his part, since such an action would not have pleased those of his supporters who are principally attracted to him because of his anti-abortion stand.

In this case, the governor overestimated the mettle of the Legislature. It had been worn down by the abortion fights of previous years and legislative leaders had no taste this year for another prolonged bout of haggling over abortion rights while the budget hung in the balance and the end of the fiscal year bore down upon them.

Certainly, there were legislators who voted their consciences on abortion, but there were also a great many who caved in to the political threats of the most rigid of the anti-abortion advocates and passed the buck to the courts.

So now we have a law which not only prohibits Medicaid from paying for abortions for poor women, but one which also precludes all public employees, those who work for states, cities, towns, counties and school districts, from having abortions that would be paid for even partially by their group medical plans. The reason is that a portion of those benefits are financed with public money.

Women who want them and need them will continue to have abortions. Some will be able to afford them in medically sound environments. Others will, as they always have, get them where they can, at unnecessarily high health risks.

This victory for the anti-abortion proponents does not rest equitably on all the people of Massachusetts, nor is it based on logical considerations for the protection of assaulted women. It should be set aside as soon as possible.

The Detroit News

Detroit, MI, July 1, 1979

The Michigan Legislature and Gov. Milliken are engaged in their annual battle over state funding for abortions. The Legislature has once again attempted to limit the appropriation to $1 and the governor has applied his veto.

But there is a difference this year. An Ingham County Circuit judge has ruled that the governor has no right to a veto on this particular item. The judge reasoned that peculiarities in the law give the Legislature specific responsibility for setting abortion appropriations.

Whatever the outcome of the case on appeal, the struggle is certain to continue as long as public money is spent on abortion. Why? Because millions of Michigan residents believe that abortion is the taking of human life. And if they are unhappy with the procedure itself, they are even less happy that their tax dollars are paying for it.

The federal government already has banned the use of medicaid funds for most elective abortions. There are two major arguments for this policy. The first is that tax dollars should not be used for a medical procedure that is repugnant to many millions of Americans. The second is that the federal government cannot maintain its neutrality on abortion and at the same time provide millions of dollars to, in effect, promote it as a birth control technique.

The U.S. Supreme Court, which saw to it that the procedure was legalized in the first place, has ruled that the federal government has no obligation to fund abortions. It was this decision that set the stage for the struggle in Michigan and other industrial states where abortions continue to be funded with state tax dollars. (Michigan is spending an estimated $3.3 million a year on welfare abortions.)

Those who favor public funding for abortion typically argue that it is necessary to prevent unwanted children who would be a burden to themselves and society, and to guarantee indigent women the same access to abortion that other women have.

Often these arguments proceed along curious lines.

It has been noted, for example, that an unwanted child might be subject to abuse or an unhappy childhood. But surely this cannot be sufficient cause to prevent its birth. Abused and unwanted children have always numbered in the millions, regardless of abortion laws. It is just possible that child abuse has *increased* rather than declined with the rise of the abortion ethic. At any rate, have the determinists so prevailed in American thought that it must be *assumed* that an unhappy child cannot grow up to find happiness and love in adult life?

Others seek to quantify the results of denying poor women abortions. They compare the cost of social services needed to support poor children to the cost of the medical procedure. We will not dwell on the callousness of so utilitarian an approach to an important societal question. But we would point out that such measurements are a slander on poor families and, possibly, implicitly racist. On what basis do these social engineers assume that all poor families will *necessarily* remain poor or produce children who will not better their lot? Such an assumption not only betrays contempt for the poor, but also ignorance of American history and a tenuous grasp of reality.

Still others seek to portray the issue as involving equality under the law. Abortions are legal, they say, so the poor should be enabled to have them. This argument confuses the meaning of the words legality and subsidy, but that is not its worst weakness. The truth is that withholding public funding for abortion will not deny the poor access to the procedure. Many clinics dedicated to the proposition that abortions are "good" for the poor are offering them at reduced prices or even free of charge. In any event, the base price of a first trimester abortion can be as little as $100 — affordable even to the poorest woman in our time.

Nor are proponents of medicaid abortion able to provide any statistics that show poor women are actually having fewer abortions because of funding cutoffs. The statistics have been limited to how many abortions are funded from government sources.

The argument for public funding of abortions is largely a smokescreen. Those who favor abortion as a birth control technique want the official sanction that governmental funding provides. They want the government to *promote* abortion as a solution to population problems.

The federal government already has refused to collaborate. The Michigan Legislature has struggled mightily to follow, but the governor resists.

The Legislature's position should be vindicated in the courts. But if it isn't, the lawmakers have an obligation, mandated by the imperatives of humanity and reason, to return their bill to the governor and prepare to override his veto.

Roanoke Times & World-News
Roanoke, VA, March 25, 1981

The state should not fund abortions. To do so would put the government's imprimatur on a practice that raises moral questions of the most basic kind among a substantial proportion of Virginians. Governor John Dalton acted properly in vetoing a bill to provide Medicaid funds for abortions under certain conditions.

Let it be said that the conditions under which abortions would have been funded were extreme conditions: pregnancies resulting from rape or incest, or pregnancies involving fetuses that are likely to result in mentally or physically deformed offspring.

The Supreme Court has established the constitutional right to abortions up to a certain point in fetal development. That issue was not involved in the governor's decision.

The issue involved here is whether the state has an affirmative obligation to guarantee abortions to women who might otherwise not be able to afford them.

The answer should be no. It is one thing for the state to grant individuals the right to make certain moral decisions. It is quite another thing for the state to subsidize those decisions.

The question is not an easy one. Delegate J. Samuel Glasscock, D-Suffolk, eloquently poses the argument for state funding.

"The number of people involved was small, but the heartbreak is enormous," he said. "How the state of Virginia can stand by and let them suffer alone is absolutely beyond me. To be conservative is one thing; to be indifferent is something else."

There is no painless answer to Delegate Glasscock's concerns. The emotional suffering of women victimized by rape or incest must be balanced against the value of potential human life terminated. That is a resolution the victim must make. But once the state has consented to collaborate in the termination, a threshold has been crossed. It is not a terribly large step from the funding of abortions under extreme conditions to the funding of abortions under any constitutionally permissible condition.

Once the state has gone that far, it has devalued potential life to an extent that many would find disquieting.

Mr. Glasscock estimates that only about 10 rape or incest victims a year would have requested Medicaid funds. About 10 to 35 more women would have requested them to prevent the birth of a mentally or physically deformed child.

If the number is that small, state funding should not be necessary. Surely pro-abortion organizations have enough committed members to provide private, voluntary funding for anyone who makes the moral decision to seek an abortion. The state itself should not assume an affirmative role.

The Philadelphia Inquirer
Philadelphia, PA, June 9, 1981

Two legislators in Harrisburg, having won the fight last year to cut off nearly all state-paid abortions, intend to continue what one of them calls their "guerrilla war." They intend to introduce legislation which, among other things, would require that if pregnancy results from incest and a woman wants public funds for an abortion, she must have reported the offense to the law enforcement authorities within 72 hours of its occurrence and must identify the man involved.

Think about that. Here is a 12-year-old girl who is raped by her uncle or brother or even her father — and there are more of such cases than most people realize. And she is supposed to know enough about the facts of life and the facts of law that she will get on her bicycle and go to the district attorney or the nearest police station and say, "Please, sir, my father has raped me and I think I may get pregnant so will you kindly take me to an abortion clinic?" And suppose the uncle or the brother or the father denies he ever touched her. And suppose she can't prove anything. And suppose she has to go on living in the same house with that man.

The sheer cruelty of such a proviso boggles the mind, and it isn't all that Rep. Stephen F. Freind (R., Delaware) and Rep. Gregg L. Cunningham (R., Centre) are planning in their guerrilla warfare against women, in their right to choose, and doctors, in their responsibility to patients.

Meanwhile, in Washington, Congress has approved the most stringent restrictions ever placed on Medicaid abortions, agreeing to forbid funds for abortions except when necessary to save the life of the mother, but not in cases of rape or incest.

Does the American public share the view of the dogmatic right-to-lifers? Two national polls, just released, say exactly to the contrary. According to an Associated Press-NBC News poll, 75 percent of those questioned say the decision on abortion should be a matter between a woman and her doctor. According to a Washington Post-ABC News poll, 74 percent approve abortion on demand or in most circumstances, and 82 percent favor legal abortions in cases of rape or incest.

It is ironic that many who profess themselves eager to "get the government off the people's back" are so determined to get the government into people's most private decisions.

The Hartford Courant
Hartford, CT, August 24, 1981

Judge Robert Berdon has brought a much-needed sense of humanity back to an abortion debate that is becoming increasingly gruesome.

The Superior Court judge ordered the state to pay for an abortion needed by a New Haven welfare recipient who risked, according to her doctors, "great, substantial and immediate irreparable harm" without the operation. The doctors need to operate on her again to see if she has cancer of the cervix.

The problem is they cannot say her life would be in danger without the abortion, and that is one of the few ways the state will pay the Medicaid costs.

Judge Berdon noted in his decision that the attorneys for the woman had raised "very serious state constitutional challenges" to the restrictive state policy. He is considering making his ruling a class action, which would force the state to help other women in similar circumstances.

In this decision Judge Berdon picks up the banner the state General Assembly dropped earlier this year after the Appropriations Committee defeated by one vote a proposal requiring the state to pay Medicaid abortions. The state now pays only if the pregnancy is the result of incest or rape, or if the mother's life is in danger.

This, bizarrely enough, is becoming the moderate position at a time when Congress and the administration do not think even incest or rape are justification enough for Medicaid funding.

The real battle for abortion opponents is not over government payment for poor women's operations. It is over abortion itself. That fight has been lost. Abortion is legal.

At issue now is whether poor women should suffer unwanted pregnancies simply because they cannot pay for the available operation themselves. This is a question of fairness. Singling out abortion as a medical procedure whose costs the state will not assume for the poor is not fair.

The state's argument in the New Haven case that it cannot afford the payments pales in comparison, as Judge Berdon pointed out.

Besides, to the extent this is a consideration at all, it might not be even true. When the matter came before the legislature, the Office of Fiscal Analysis figured the state would save about $900,000 a year if it paid for Medicaid abortions, since it would not have to pay the more expensive delivery costs later.

But cost is not the issue. Even abortion is not the issue. Fairness is.

THE SAGINAW NEWS
Saginaw, MI, November 2, 1981

For the 10th time, Gov. Milliken has vetoed a bill to bar state-funded abortions for poor women. For the 10th time, the governor is right.

We want to make it very clear why we support Milliken's stand on this emotional issue. We do not advocate abortion. We believe the right of choice under the U.S. Supreme Court ruling of 1973 has been horribly abused. We are appalled by the use of abortion as an alternative birth-control method, or even a way to guarantee that a child will be of the desired gender.

The fact remains that abortion is a legal medical procedure. The fact also is that the state pays the legitimate medical expenses for poor persons. What the Legislature is trying to do is substitue a moral judgment for the requirements of the law.

Milliken stated the case clearly: "Once government decided to pay for medically necessary health services for the needy, it departs from its position of neutrality by deciding to fund or not to fund a particular health service."

The lawmakers should remember that they are bound by the law of the land — the Constitution. For the Legislature, especially, following the law cannot be a matter of personal opinion.

The veto was made as a matter of principle. But there is a practical side, too. If a veto override succeeds, many women who can't afford a safe abortion in a reputable clinic will simply turn elsewhere. They will risk their lives. That is ironic in view of the Legislature's own proposal to pay for abortions when necessary to save the mother's life.

Barbara Listing of Shepherd, leader of the anti-abortion group Right to Life of Michigan, accused Milliken of putting his own views above those of the people.

The power of "pro-life" groups certainly has an impact. In the past, Milliken has been only narrowly upheld. Opponents believe early 1982 may give them their best chance at the two-thirds majorities in both houses needed to override.

With two House members seeking other office Tuesday, and with Milliken's clout possibly lessened if he decides not to seek re-election, the vote is certain to be close.

We hope our legislators remember the real issue: Whether they are bound by the Constitution, or whether they can put their own views above those of the highest court in the land. This is not a referendum on abortion. It is a matter of law.

JUDGE ©1984 KANSAS CITY TIMES

THE HARD-TO-PLACE ADOPTION AGENCY

THOUSANDS OF RIGHT TO LIFERS PROTEST ABORTION

"FUNNY... YOU'D THINK WE'D BE SWAMPED!"

Oregon Journal

Portland, OR, May 7, 1981

In diversity there is strength, and in the diversity of the groups bringing suit to allow abortions to be paid for by Medicaid, there is a statement that should carry through all the way to Congress.

Petitioners in the suit number 39 organizations — not small single-issue groups, but ones which represent a varied and broad selection of the strata of society. Among them are: Central Pacific Conference of the United Church of Christ; First Unitarian Church; the Oregon-Idaho Annual Conference of the United Methodist Church, which is the board of the church and society; and the Presbytery of the Cascades of the United Presbyterian Church.

Support is coming from the American Federation of State, County and Municipal Employees, Local 2045; from Communication Workers of America; from the Coalition of Labor Union Women, Oregon Pioneer Chapter; Federally Employed Women, Mount Hood Chapter; National Association of Social Workers (Oregon Chapter); and Oregon Association for Women in Education.

Groups with a general membership, such as the American Association of University Women, Oregon State Division; and the YWCA are listed as petitioners.

Women's rights groups support the suit as well as at least six minority oriented action groups. The Oregon Nurses Association and the Oregon Society of Obstetricians and Gynecologists are also petitioners.

Their interest in this matter is that poor women shall be treated as fairly by their government as affluent ones. If funds are available for a woman for pregnancy care and childbearing, they must also be available to her if her choice is termination of the pregnancy.

The case in Oregon will be the fifth of its kind. Two are pending in New Jersey and Pennsylvania. Cases in Massachusetts and California have been successful in abolishing the restrictions on Medicaid abortion.

A recent study has shown that between 70 and 80 percent of all Americans believe legal abortion should be an option for all women.

To discriminate against a certain group because its members are poor and female is so un-American that one shudders to think of the political force that has brought about the need for this action at law. Noise and emotion may get attention — and they have. But they do not make right.

THE SUN

Baltimore, MD, March 11, 1981

It is going to be another nail-biter at the Maryland General Assembly. The outcome could hinge on the absence (or presence) of a single delegate, or the switch of just one person's mind. Hanging in the balance will be state payment for abortions for poor women.

The stage already has been set for this now-annual State House drama. Act One: A large contingent of anti-abortion ("pro-life") adherents rallies in Annapolis Monday night. They listen to emotionally charged speeches, then make their presence felt in the legislative halls. But lawmakers have seen this performance so often they take little notice of it.

Act Two: The Court of Appeals on Tuesday throws out a suit by anti-abortion advocates trying to stop the state from even considering if it should pay for such surgery for the poor. The unanimous decision of the state's highest court makes it crystal clear that it is up to the General Assembly to decide.

Act Three: This will take place late Thursday or Friday. The House of Delegates will vote on whether to tighten last year's budget language on abortions, which already has put a crimp in the number of such operations performed. State health officials are projecting only 4,600 Medicaid abortions in the current fiscal year, a drop of some 30 percent from last year. Anti-abortion advocates are certain to push hard for even stricter language. The matter probably will be decided by one or two votes.

The arguments on both sides have been presented so often there is little chance of a change of heart. It is interesting to note, though, that a poll by *The Sun* last fall detected a shift in public sentiment toward giving pregnant women the right to choose. But when it came to backing state-financed abortions, those polled reflected a split similar to that in the General Assembly: 43 percent supported the state financing, 40 percent were opposed.

If anything, *The Sun* feels that the present abortion language may be *too* restrictive. It has deterred some physicians from performing these operations for fear of violating the vaguely worded state law. Our consistent position has been that since Maryland has accepted as an obligation its role to provide medical care for the poor, it must accept its obligation to pay for procedures such as abortions which have been deemed medically necessary by a woman's physician. Especially in light of the Supreme Court's ruling that abortions are legal if a woman has the money to pay for it, equity and humanity dictate that the state continue to provide the same opportunity for poor women.

THE SACRAMENTO BEE
Sacramento, CA, March 24, 1981

There's no doubt that the California Supreme Court's 4-2 decision striking down legislative restrictions on Medi-Cal funds for abortions will generate a new attack on the court itself. Already the decision has been labeled "gruesome" by a pro-life liberal in the Legislature; already there is talk about legislative defiance and a constitutional amendment of some sort to reverse the court's ruling. In light of those possibilities and in light of the near-certainty that there will be new calls for the removal of certain justices, it's easy to wish that this issue hadn't gone to the Supreme Court at all.

The fact is that it did and that, under the circumstances, the court made the only decision that was both fair and, in our view, constitutionally defensible. Every woman in California has a guaranteed right to choose abortion in the early months of pregnancy. Every poor woman in California is entitled to general medical services under Medi-Cal, including the general range of obstetrical and gynecological services. It was, therefore, eminently proper for the court to rule that, as Justice Tobriner put it, "once the state furnishes medical care to poor women in general, it cannot withdraw part of that care solely because a woman exercises her constitutional right to have an abortion." It would have been just as unconstitutional for the Legislature to have provided for the reverse — paying for abortions but not for the normal delivery of children. Both condition availability of state funding on the willingness of an individual to waive a constitutionally protected right.

The principal argument against the decision — and the argument made by the court's two dissenters — is that policy on Medi-Cal funding, whether for abortions or anything else, is the prerogative of the Legislature, not the court. "We seriously err," wrote Justice Richardson, "when we continue, on misguided grounds, to usurp the lawmaking function of the California Legislature." Yet, in the absence of compelling reasons to the contrary, restrictions on abortion funding discriminate against one class of people just as surely as would a legislative ban on treatment for sickle-cell disease or on medical services for arteriosclerosis.

To argue that the state has a legitimate interest in protecting the lives of the unborn fetus is, in this instance, fatuous. The state does not intervene to restrict the constitutionally protected abortions of the thousands of women who can afford to pay for them; that kind of decision, the courts have held, is a private matter to be decided between a woman and her physician. There is thus neither justice nor social wisdom in intervening in the free choice of those who can't afford such abortions. To assert that the state should have a specially tender concern for the unborn fetuses of the poor is sophistry.

The Seattle Times
Seattle, WA, November 19, 1981

REGARDLESS of one's views on the always-complex abortion issue, wry amusement can be found at the contortions performed by politicians when that issue comes before them.

A fresh example was this week's action in Olympia as House members were confronted with legislation said by its sponsors to be a way of bringing the state's public-assistance standards into line with federal criteria. The state has continued to fund abortions for welfare clients even though federal aid for that purpose largely has been cut off.

Thus, the House voted first to suspend state payments for abortions for poor women. Although nobody could explain precisely why, the House decision was made by voice vote, even though recorded rollcalls are the rule on controversial issues.

Then the House turned around on a related issue and voted against public assistance for indigent women who decide against abortion in favor of carrying their pregnancies to term. This time there was a vote count — 49-47.

Pro-abortion people were quick to point out both the contradiction and also a measure of hypocrisy: Abortions still would be eligible for state funding in cases of rape or incest. Earlier, anti-abortion measures had been rejected both in the House Human Services Committee and by the full Senate.

The anti-abortion drive has been under way in Congress and state legislatures since the 1973 United States Supreme Court decision in favor of free choice. In this state, a voter-approved initiative legalizing abortion has been in effect since 1970.

While recognizing the sensitivity of the issue and the deeply held feelings on both sides, we do not believe that legislative decisions on the right to choose abortions should be rendered according to who can pay for them and who cannot.

The Des Moines Register
Des Moines, IA, May 19, 1981

"Tax money should not be used to pay for abortions," goes the argument of abortion critics. They succeeded in getting the Iowa Senate to prohibit free abortions for poor women at the University of Iowa's Early Termination of Pregnancy Clinic unless the mother's life is endangered.

The Iowa House heard the same argument, but it voted against imposing any restriction on abortions at the clinic. The House then switched and endorsed free abortions for the poor only if the mother's life is endangered, the fetus is deformed, mentally deficient or has a congenital illness, or if the pregnancy resulted from rape or incest reported within a specified time.

The tax-money argument for justifying restrictions seems to suggest that only the poor get subsidized abortions. Those who can afford it are charged from $140 to $469 for an outpatient abortion at the University of Iowa clinic. The cost assuredly would be more if the clinic were not part of a public institution. There is an element of public subsidy almost every time an abortion is performed in an Iowa hospital, most of which are tax-exempt.

If "tax money should not be used to pay for abortion," why pick on only the poorest of the poor and deny them access to abortion because of their poverty? Why not impose the same restrictions on every woman who has some part of the cost underwritten with public funds?

Such an effort would come perilously close to violating the Supreme Court's ruling against state interference with the right of women, in consultation with their physicians, to abortion. The upshot is that legislators concentrate their fire on poor women covered by such programs as Medicaid.

The upshot also is repeated wrangling and inequity. The Legislature should end it by recognizing that tax money unavoidably is involved in an overwhelming number of hospital-based medical procedures and that it is splitting hairs when it objects to one form of subsidy.

The Iowa House was on the right track when it voted at one point to give poor women the same right of access to abortion at the University of Iowa clinic as women with money. That's a position consistent with equity as well as with the oft-heard determination to get government to quit interfering in the lives of people.

The San Diego Union
San Diego, CA, March 24, 1981

The state Supreme Court has ruled that because women have a constitutional right to obtain abortions the state of California is required to pay for them under its Medi-Cal program providing health care for the poor. In so ruling, the court is deciding an issue of public policy that clearly should be determined by the Legislature.

The 4-2 decision by the state court last week stands in direct contrast to a decision by the U.S. Supreme Court last year involving the same issue. Once again, the state court has found language in the California Constitution to justify what prevailing interpretations of the U.S. Constitution do not abide.

Indeed, in a dissenting opinion Justice Frank K. Richardson finds it "bizarre" that the court's majority bases its decision on abortion financing under Medi-Cal on a 1972 amendment adding the right of privacy to the state Constitution. The connection is difficult to grasp — although the convoluted logic is what we have come to expect from the court's liberal majority.

If the state Supreme Court were deciding whether abortion should be permitted or not, a woman's right to make a private decision about carrying a child would be a point to raise. In fact, that point is usually raised in the long and continuing debate over abortion laws. But the issue before the California court did not concern a woman's right to seek an abortion but whether the state must provide such surgical service free to women covered by the Medi-Cal program, which provides health care to the poor.

The Legislature has voted to authorize Medi-Cal abortions only in cases where the mother's life is in danger, or when tests show a child would be born with genetic defects, or in cases of rape or incest. This was a simple matter of establishing policy for a public-financed health insurance program. The policy was challenged by pro-abortionists on grounds it denied to poor women a constitutional right enjoyed by women who can afford to pay for an abortion.

This is the issue that came before the U.S. Supreme Court after Congress imposed restrictions on the use of federal funds for abortion under the Medicaid program — restrictions similar to those voted by the California Legislature. The U.S. court ruled last year that Congress has the authority to impose such limits. The court did so without disturbing its own 1973 decision which established that laws forbidding abortion are an intrusion on a woman's right of privacy.

Whether or not one agrees with the 1973 decision permitting abortion on demand, one can appreciate the clarity of the 1980 decision on federal funding of abortions. The federal court sees the distinction between a woman's claim of a constitutional right to have an abortion, and the right of a lawmaking body to decide how the taxpayer's money is going to be spent.

The state Supreme Court refuses to make that distinction. It has grasped at the wispiest of constitutional threads to decree that Californians must finance abortions with their tax money even when a majority of their elected legislators have voted otherwise. This is an extraordinary invasion by the judiciary into the prerogatives of the legislative branch of the state government.

Richmond Times-Dispatch
Richmond, VA, February 17, 1982

Two bills sponsored by Del. J. Samuel Glasscock, D-Suffolk, are characterized by opponents as pro-abortion. They are not. They are pro-fairness.

These bills (H.B. 541 and 542) would permit indigent women to secure Medicaid funding for abortions when pregnancy had resulted from rape or incest, or when tests by a qualified physician showed that the fetus would be born with a "gross and totally incapacitating" physical deformity or mental deficiency.

This legislation would not require anyone to have an abortion. Instead, as Del. Glasscock remarked last week near the end of a hearing, it would provide that "very poor people in very difficult circumstances may have a choice" — the same medical option that victimized women with greater financial resources have readily and legally available to them.

The U. S. Supreme Court's 1973 *Roe vs. Wade* decision, which gave a woman and her physician a qualified right to decide to terminate a pregnancy in its early stages, has had effects that many persons who support Mr. Glasscock's bills would join Right-to-Lifers in decrying. Abortion as a handy and popular method of birth control is abhorrent. But for the estimated 20 women a year who would gain Medicaid funding under H.B. 541 and 542, carrying to full term a fetus that resulted from rape or incest, or that would be born in a hopelessly horrid condition, would be abhorrent, too.

Bills identical to this pair passed the General Assembly last year only because Charles S. Robb, then the lieutenant governor, cast the tie-breaking vote in their favor in the Senate. But then-Gov. John N. Dalton vetoed them. With their approval last week by a 2-1 margin in the House Committee on Health, Welfare and Institutions, and with the House of Delegates rejecting a series of crippling amendments yesterday, these bills have begun their legislative odyssey anew. As a matter of equity, the 1982 General Assembly should send them along for the new governor to sign.

THE ANN ARBOR NEWS
Ann Arbor, MI, February 18, 1982

AT 10 vetoes and counting, anti-abortion legislation in Michigan has remarkable staying power.

That is probably the most charitable thing to say about the endless hassle over state funding of Medicaid abortions for poor women.

Last week the forces of override fell short again. Just barely. And that means they'll be back when the times are more propitious. All that means is that Gov. Milliken will use his veto power again. It's getting awfully repetitious.

The same arguments are heard over and over again. Most likely, lawmakers don't even listen any more. Their minds are made up. Call the question, Mr. Speaker, and put it to a vote.

POOR WOMEN should have the right to choose abortion and have Medicaid funds pay for it. That's the position held by the governor and the pro-choicers.

The opposition argument is that although abortion is legal, state funds should not be used for a procedure which is morally objectionable to some taxpayers.

With elections looming, legislators will be strongly pressured to reconsider. Michigan Right-to-Life leaders already are targeting the weak and the vulnerable.

Termination of pregnancy is a health/medical matter between patient and physician. Abortion is a procedure to be carried out in a safe, sanitary environment by qualified, caring people.

The legality of abortion is the common ground on which both sides stand. Simple justice requires giving low-income women access to the same medical help that's available to women of greater financial means.

Is that so difficult to accept?

Detroit Free Press
Detroit, MI, January 23, 1984

A SCANT handful of votes in the Legislature will soon decide whether poor women in Michigan are entitled to the same availability of medical care as their well-off sisters. This time, House members are not going through the usual ritual to placate the anti-abortion groups in their districts. This time, the threat of a ban on Medicaid funding of abortions is real.

Anti-abortion forces in the House claim they are within a couple of votes of being able to override Gov. Blanchard's veto of the ban on Medicaid funding. If they succeed, it will be a case of poor judgment and political expedience overriding good medical science and equity.

The ban in question does not, after all, significantly restrict the availability of abortion — except for poor women who are Medicaid clients. For them, the proposed ban is particularly harsh, probably more harsh than many people with some reservations about abortion even realize or intend. The language under consideration flatly prohibits payment for abortions except when the life of the mother is threatened, a standard doctors have denounced as unworkable and one that ignores countless conditions during pregnancy that threaten serious, long-lasting harm short of death.

The ban falls with special cruelty on young girls, who are the most likely to suffer complications during pregnancy and the least likely to have the resources for care if Medicaid is denied them. Widespread outrage greeted the case of the Kalamazoo pre-teenager who was denied an abortion after being raped. What the House is contemplating is a ban that would condemn such girls — children, really — to the double penalty of sexual abuse and unwanted pregnancy.

Why the Legislature would want to take on the job of medical dictator, when it has performed so spectacularly badly on its real business in recent months, we can only speculate on. Abortion is a serious matter of conscience for many people; all the more reason for them to respect the conscience of others on so personal a matter.

Few issues that come before the Legislature affect personal beliefs and health and privacy and the right to equal treatment so directly. We hope that those legislators who are dubious or ambivalent about the wisdom of this piece of work will take the sensible route and reject it. It would help if they would hear some strong encouragement from the governor and women's rights advocates to do so.

The News American
Baltimore, MD, January 21, 1983

Today Gov. Harry Hughes, who has been consistent in his pro-choice stand on the abortion issue, is taking a step to restore consistency in women's freedom to obtain abortions in Maryland. Under the law any woman who can afford an abortion can get one. But poor women have a great deal of trouble getting abortions, and the governor is saying that the state law affecting Medicaid funding no longer should be stacked against women who cannot afford to pay.

Restrictive language determining the rules under which poor women could obtain Medicaid-paid abortions got into the law through the efforts of anti-abortion activists in 1981. The rules require that doctors applying for Medicaid reimbursement determine that the woman was a victim of rape *or* incest *or* that her life was in jeopardy because of her pregnancy — *or* that there is medical evidence that the mother's present and future mental health would be placed in serious danger if the pregnancy continued.

It is the mental health part the governor wants to change. Specifically, he wants to retore the law's pre-1981 language. Instead of the requirement of "medical evidence" he wants the words "reasonable degree of medical certainty" substituted, and he wants "present *and* future" changed to "present *or* future."

Since the anti-abortionists' language got into the law, the state health department has reported a 50 percent decline in the number of Medicaid abortions. This of course is what the anti-abortionists wanted. But it tends to confirm what pro-choice advocates feared — that doctors, because they are required to submit so much documentation proving that there is "medical evidence" of mental problems before they can be reimbursed, are refusing to perform the operations. For the same reason there are fewer clinics where Medicaid abortions are available; there were nine before 1981, and only one today.

The state's statistics show that not only has the number of Medicaid-funded abortions gone down, but the number of babies delivered through Medicaid funding has gone up — by 10 percent. That is an unusual increase, says John Folkemer, a state Medicaid official; he believes the 1981 restrictions are very likely the cause.

That may mean that there are more unwanted children as a result of the 1980 restrictions Gov. Hughes seeks to change. And it probably means that a lot of women, many of whom support their own families, paid for an abortion out of already meager earnings at the sacrifice of food and other needs.

This newspaper never has taken lightly the matter of abortion, or the controversy that always has surrounded it and always will. Nobody likes abortion. But the fact is that it is legal in this nation and this state — the law gives women the right to seek it. As long as it does, we will go on deploring the strategy of the anti-abortionists in singling out poor women, the only women they can get to, for punishment. It is for that reason we commend Gov. Hughes for submitting his proposal as part of the 1984 budget.

The Kansas City Times
Kansas City, MO, February 11, 1983

Attempts by anti-abortion advocates to severely restrict the right of a woman to have an abortion generally have been unsuccessful on the federal level. An obvious exception is the unfortunate congressional decision to outlaw use of public funds to pay for poor women's abortions.

The states and local governments have been more agreeable to approving restrictions. Perhaps that is why the latest attempt to bring government into that very personal decision is proposed in legislation before the Missouri General Assembly. Legislation backed by anti-abortion groups would prohibit private insurance companies from selling abortion coverage except as a more expensive rider which would have to be purchased separately. Undoubtedly the anti-abortionists hope to prevent women from terminating their pregnancies by making it more costly to get insurance coverage for this lawful procedure. It is the same absolutist attitude that insists on telling others exactly what they can do according to one's own beliefs. No woman has to get an abortion. No woman is compelled to, even if it might save her life. But this proposal would, in effect, make an abortion impossible for many because of cost. Many Americans have enough trouble affording basic insurance that includes pregnancy coverage. To add this additional cost would further discourage many women from seeking this medical procedure.

The proposal is highly unusual in attempting to legislate an insurance decision that belongs in the private sector. Until now that has been left to the insurors and to the individual or companies which purchase health insurance for their employees. It would set a poor precedent to begin delineating what could or could not be included by law. For instance, other health problems which affect one race, such as sickle cell anemia, could be excluded. Also policies issued elsewhere than Missouri could cover abortion procedures for those patients in Missouri, but Missouri residents would be denied the same coverage.

The current health care system, including insurance coverage, is designed to protect health, not endanger it. Yet women might be inclined to carry pregnancies to term when they would be endangering their health to do so. The state of Missouri would be making bad law for its residents and for the insurance industry if this is approved.

LOS ANGELES HERALD

Los Angeles, CA, July 28, 1985

Abortion is the least desirable form of birth control, one to be avoided whenever possible. At the same time, women have a legal right to choose abortion that cannot be denied. Yet opponents of legal abortion are mounting a campaign in California to restrict the ability of poor women — and only poor women — to make that choice. Last week, a Sacramento-based organization calling itself the Children's Fund started a petition campaign for a ballot measure that would bar the state from paying for abortions and use the money instead to benefit disabled or prematurely born children. The group wants to put the proposal to a statewide vote next year. Pro-choice activists fear the initiative would, in effect, be a referendum on abortion.

While Californians have shown time and again that they are none too selective in putting issues to a public vote, this particular campaign is likely to be worse than most. For one thing, abortion financing is an issue that has been pre-empted by the consistent rulings of the Supreme Court. If women have a legal right to choose abortion, it is no more proper to deny that right to the poor — through Medi-Cal restrictions — than it is to deny them any other legitimate medical procedure.

□

Nevertheless, it now appears that next year Californians will be subjected to a full-blown political battle over this most divisive and emotional of subjects. It is far from certain that the initiative, if approved, would actually accomplish anything, since it would certainly be challenged — and, almost as certainly, be overturned — in court. Nor is the campaign likely to accomplish much by way of public education; most voters have long made up their minds about abortion. Besides, the rhetoric in this kind of political campaign — on both sides — is usually calculated less to inform than to inflame. We urge the measure's backers to think twice about what they are doing and what its effects might be.

The Providence Journal

Providence, RI, February 23, 1985

Since Congress first passed the Hyde Amendment in 1976, barring the use of federal funds for abortions under the Medicaid program, except in emergencies, critics have argued that the law discriminated against poor women. An otherwise legal medical procedure was denied solely because of income level.

Nothing prevented the states from continuing to fund Medicaid abortions on their own, and some have done so. Others, including Rhode Island and Massachusetts, have excluded that service from other medical and health care services still offered. Last Wednesday the Massachusetts Supreme Judicial Court said, in effect, "enough." On a 6-to-1 vote, the court held that the Doyle-Flynn amendment of 1979 violated the state Constitution's guarantee of privacy and freedom of choice.

The majority ruled that the legislature has no obligation to "subsidize any of the costs associated with child bearing or with health care generally. However, once it chooses to enter the constitutionally protected area of choice, it must do so with genuine indifference." Since no limits were placed on the funding of child rearing or family care, the state "may not weight the options open to a pregnant woman by its allocation of public funds."

The decision differs pointedly with the U.S. Supreme Court's stand of last July.

That ruling upheld the constitutionality of the Hyde Amendment and instructed the states that they were not bound to fund abortions. But the Doyle-Flynn law was challenged under the state Constitution and failed to pass muster.

Whether this ruling will have any effect on the abortion controversy outside of the Bay State is in doubt. Certainly the logic of this latest decision is compelling — that equal protection of the laws and a woman's right to choose abortion as a matter of personal privacy inhibit the state's right to be selective in its Medicaid funding of services related to child bearing. But that issue has not been pressed in Rhode Island's courts.

It remains that poor women have become the principal scapegoats in the abortion struggle. Those with ample means may choose abortion at will. Those who are dependent on this state-federal program for the medically indigent, however, are sensitive to the state's compassion or lack thereof. Thus they become vulnerable to the anti-abortion forces whose will prevails where Medicaid abortions in Rhode Island are concerned.

There is a certain irony in the fact that the Massachusetts' Constitution is more protective of women's rights in this instance than is the U.S. Constitution. One more good reason for ratification of the Equal Rights Amendment.

The Washington Post

Washington, DC, August 7, 1985

TALK ABOUT taxation without representation. It's bad enough that residents of the District have no vote in Congress when decisions about their federal taxes are made. But now the House has actually voted to prevent the District from using *its own local revenues* for a purpose that is legal in every other jurisdiction in the country.

The 221-to-199 vote came during House consideration of the District's annual appropriations bill. The issue was the District government's policy of using local revenues—not federal funds but local income, sales, property and other taxes—to pay for abortions for indigent women. This same policy is in effect in 14 states, several of them under court order. Its purpose is to ensure that women who are poor are not denied access to an important medical service that can be freely purchased by upper- and middle-income women—a purpose clearly within the legitimate purview of state and local governments.

Rep. Christopher Smith of New Jersey, however, doesn't think that the District ought to have the same discretion in this matter that his own state has. On the House floor he said that the "home rule" issue is "baloney." After all, he argued, home rule or states rights were once invoked in defense of retaining slavery and segregation, and those defenses were properly rejected. Moreover, the federal government puts conditions on the use of its funds to pressure states to adopt environmental and many other regulatory controls, so why not use its power to prevent local funding of abortions?

The difference, of course, is that, in the first instance, the actions being defended were found to be in violation of the U.S. Constitution. Rep. Smith surely wishes that abortion were unconstitutional too, but the fact is that it is not. And when Congress uses its funding power to regulate activities that it deems undesirable, federal not local monies are involved and the rules are applied uniformly to all states and jurisdictions.

As for comparisons made by Rep. Robert Dornan of California to efforts by Congress to sanction China for allegedly condoning infanticide and coerced abortion, the difference again is that those activities are illegal both here and in China whereas voluntary abortions, within limits set by the Supreme Court, are not only legal but constitutionally protected.

People obviously disagree sharply about the desirability and morality of abortion under various circumstances. But in a democratic society, citizens of a locality, acting through their duly elected representatives, certainly ought to be able to choose to use their own taxes to make a constitutionally protected service available to the poor as well as the wealthy. Most members of the House understand that, and when the House meets in conference with the Senate—whose version of the bill does not include the anti-abortion amendment—presumably calmer heads will prevail. But as long as many members run in terror whenever the word "abortion" is mentioned, you can expect more nonsense to keep emerging from the House.

New U.S. Foreign Aid Stand Causes Furor at U.N. Parley

A White House draft statement began circulating within the Reagan Administration in June of 1984 which urged a change of United States policy regarding family planning assistance abroad. It called for the elimination of all such assistance for governments and organizations that support abortion, rather than simply barring the specific use of U.S. funds to pay for abortions abroad. White House spokesmen said President Reagan was determined to have Administration policy in this area reflect his own views on abortion. State Department officials, however, were reportedly concerned about the effect such a policy could have on U.S. relations with India and China, among other nations. At that time, the United States contributed about $240 million each year to population control programs around the globe; as much as $100 million of that amount went to developing countries and organizations that would not receive any assistance for such programs under the new policy. The Agency for International Development urged President Reagan to reconsider the proposal. The issue came to a head in August 1984, at the United Nations second International Conference on Population in Mexico City. The U.S. joined forces with the Vatican delegation to press their anti-abortion stance, which was expressed in a recommendation that abortion "in no case be promoted as a method of family planning." The recommendation was accepted by the conference Aug. 10. The strongest opponent of this measure was China, which argued that to promote economic development, women needed "the right to abortion, and this right must be respected." Though the conference was marked by much political squabbling, the parley did succeed in adopting a four-page declaration, approved by delegates from 149 countries, urging developed nations to provide aid to Third World family planning programs.

The United States also required the U.N. Fund for Population Activities to pledge that it was not involved in abortion or "coercive" family planning programs before the U.S. agreed Aug. 11 to release a $19 million appropriation that the Reagan Administration had threatened to cancel.

THE SUN
Baltimore, MD, July 9, 1984

If anti-abortion zealots in the Reagan administration have their way, a U.S. delegation will go to the International Population Conference in Mexico City less than a month from now and seriously weaken a long-standing U.S. commitment to assist family planning in the developing world.

The zealots' position is embodied in a draft policy statement, written in the White House, which calls population growth "an essential element in economic progress" and terms the family planning efforts of the last two decades an "overreaction." The real cause of population problems, the document says, is "governmental control of economies," and the solution — "the natural mechanism for slowing population growth in problem areas" — is free-enterprise capitalism.

The policy recommendations are ostensibly drawn to cut off U.S. assistance for abortions, which is already against U.S. law anyway. Actually, they go much farther. They could cut as much as $100 million from the $240 million the U.S. now contributes worldwide for family planning programs. Because the draft calls for denial of funds to "governments or private organizations that advocate abortion as an instrument of population control," it wouldn't just be the very few governments actively encouraging abortions that would lose funds. So would all governments that receive support from the International Planned Parenthood Federation or the United Nations Fund for Population Activities, should those organizations be judged to "advocate" abortion. Under this preposterous proposal, family planning funds for, say, the Dominican Republic could be reduced because the agency providing those funds had also helped Bangladesh, where abortions have been legalized.

This document is the work of ignorant ideologues. If it is adopted as official U.S. policy, it would be a major diplomatic embarrassment for the United States as well as a terrible policy decision.

Mexico, the conference host, may wonder why, if population growth is good for free-enterprise economies, the U.S. is so worried about illegal immigrants. Not many of the other governments at the conference will be thrilled at being lectured by the U.S. on how to organize their economies and what they may or may not do in family planning. All who understand the true nature of the population issue and who have seen an international consensus develop — not without struggle — during the last 20 years or so, will be disheartened.

The State Department and the Agency for International Development have both urged the White House not to adopt the draft statement as policy. For the sake of this country's reputation, as well as for humane policy considerations, we hope their advice is taken. The American policy of support for urgently needed worldwide family planning should be not weakened, but upheld.

Birmingham Post-Herald
Birmingham, AL, June 26, 1984

There is spreading concern about a Reagan administration proposal that would effectively end most U.S. aid to developing countries trying to control their population growth.

Present law already prohibits the use of U.S. funds to pay for foreign abortion services. But a White House position paper being prepared for a United Nations Population Conference in Mexico City in August would withhold all family-planning assistance to any country that supports abortion, even if U.S. funds are not involved.

The U.S. Agency for International Development, which presumably knows something about the needs of developing nations, is one of the latest voices to speak out against the proposal.

This reversal of U.S. policy, it warns, could be "extremely, and in our view, unnecessarily, controversial" at the Mexico City conference.

AID suggests as an alternative that the White House support a resolution calling for more family-planning programs that help women avoid abortions — "a position fully consistent with U.S. policy."

The State Department is also unhappy with the White House proposal. It has its own position paper, which affirms that U.S. assistance "will never be conditioned on a country's acceptance of any particular population policy."

Even if President Reagan's personal view on abortion were shared by the majority of Americans — which it is not — it would be insultingly arrogant of the United States to tell other countries what they may and may not do to limit their population growth, under threat of denial of U.S. assistance.

It is no less arrogant of anti-abortion groups to warn that they will punish the president politically if he backs off from the proposal.

Runaway population growth in the Third World is a serious problem that affects not only the countries experiencing it but ultimately the United States as well.

To moralistically undercut a government's efforts to control that growth through nonabortion programs because it also permits abortion would be tragically shortsighted. The end result would be a worse population problem and even greater recourse to abortion because other methods failed.

The Providence Journal
Providence, RI, July 5, 1985

The United States appears poised to weaken the United Nations Population Control Program. If true, this would be a blunder. Despite enormous obstacles, the U.N. program has registered real progress in curbing the birth rate in some Third World countries. The program needs more support, not less.

Supporters of the program are discouraged by the attitude of the Reagan administration, which has proposed to bar all U.S. contributions to any population-control programs that practice or advocate abortion. If the U.S. share were withheld on that basis, it would amount to $100 million, or almost half of this country's contribution. Such a reduction could seriously weaken the program.

The Wichita
Eagle-Beacon
Wichita, KS, July 8, 1985

Here are some things the Reagan administration should consider before it delivers its planned announcement to the 1984 International Conference on Population, in Mexico City next month, that the United States no longer will contribute to any international population control program that in any way involves or encourages the use of abortions:

• It will mean a reduction of about 40 percent, or $100 million, in the level of U.S. support of such programs — a kind of support five previous presidents have extended — at a time when the World Bank would like to see increased funding made affordable to developing nations' family planning programs that utilize contraception, not abortion. Poor countries now spend about $2 billion a year on population control, about $240 million of this coming from the United States and $300 million from other donors. The bank estimates another $945 million is needed.

• If present trends continue, the World Bank estimates, world population will more than double within the next 66 years, from 4.6 billion now to 10.3 billion in 2050, finally stabilizing about a century later — because Earth's limited earth can support only so many human lives — at 11 billion persons.

Most of that growth will take place in already overpopulated and impoverished developing countries, including India, which is expected eventually to become the world's most populous nation, surpassing even China. If present trends continue, the population of Bangladesh will increase from the present 93 million to 357 million by 2050.

• In the past two decades, the United States has been in the forefront of support for population control efforts that resulted in fertility rate reductions of 15 to 45 percent in such overcrowded nations as Indonesia, South Korea, Thailand, the Philippines, Colombia and Costa Rica. "This leadership," says the Population Institute, "has given hope to the poorest countries in the world that have gradually reached the inescapable conclusion that rampant population growth can severely retard and even cancel out economic development gains."

The Reagan administration may be right to deplore the use of officially advocated abortion programs as a brake on out-of-control population. But it would be wrong to restrict the use of American aid so inflexibly that more sensitive family planning programs also would be damaged.

Whatever may be the policy of individual countries or programs, abortion is only a small part of family-planning and other services designed to limit the population explosion that threatens economic progress in many of the developing countries. Most spending aimed at reducing high birth rates in those nations goes for contraceptive programs. Social programs, such as China's heavy emphasis on smaller families, also play a major part in averting uncontrolled growth.

The administration, however, is planning to send a new message to the U.N. Conference on Population in August. That message will argue that government programs are unnecessary to reduce births and that free-market economies, by promoting industrial growth, will tend to induce people to have fewer children. This would reverse a long-standing U.S. policy, which has recognized that developing countries cannot readily improve their economies when boosts in production are offset by the increase in hungry mouths.

India, which has a largely free-market economy, has made little headway in reducing its birth rate, which still stands at 2 percent a year. By contrast, China, where almost everything is under state control, has brought its rate down to 1.3 percent.

Critics of the Reagan administration are unkind enough to suggest that the new policy against organizations that condone abortion is politically motivated. Obviously, the administration's stance will draw approval from those Americans who lobby against abortion.

Yet even those vigorously opposed to abortion cannot fail to see the huge increases in population registered by most of the nations in Latin America, or the looming problems that the continent's poverty and unemployment present to this country. For social and religious reasons, Latin America has made less progress in curbing birth rates than almost any other region.

The proposed U.S. shift is unlikely to win much praise from developing nations trying to cope with their own numbing population worries. For the United States to ignore such concerns is simply short-sighted. Most babies in developing countries are born to the poorest families least able to cope with their needs. This growth, with its potential for added economic and social stress, may be enough to upset already delicately balanced economies and raise problems that the administration hasn't anticipated.

Population control is, at best, a slow process demanding patience, consistency and continuing resources. It would be unfortunate if the efforts of the U.N. and private agencies were undercut, even temporarily, by a self-defeating U.S. policy change.

Los Angeles Times
Los Angeles, CA, June 20, 1984

The global growth rate of the human species has slowed. Not by much—down a mere 0.3%—but at least the statistics are moving in the right direction. Yet the decrease in growth is hardly a sign to relax. There will still be 1.7 billion more people on Earth in the year 2000 than in 1984. And since the gap between rich and poor is expected to open even wider in the same period, putting 600 million more people below the world poverty line and even more just barely above it, the crisis created by the world's huge population will grow constantly more acute.

In this light the recent Reagan Administration draft statement on population control seems absurdly shortsighted. The draft seeks to redefine the U.S. stance toward global efforts to control overpopulation. In stark contrast to statistics that demonstrate the terrifying proportions of the problem, the paper attempts to dismiss overpopulation as the source of some of the developing world's greatest difficulties. It further concludes that population control is far from desirable and that all that the Third World needs is laissez-faire economics.

This conclusion is the most glaring fallacy in the document. On top of this general flaw in reasoning, the draft specifically calls for the ceasing of aid to any program abroad that includes abortion as a possible option, which could be interpreted as covering aid to the United Nations, the Fund for Population Activities, India, Bangladesh, Tunisia and many private assistance organizations. This is repugnant on two counts. Not only does it interfere with the right of women to choose for themselves whether to terminate their own pregnancies, but also it presumes to impose one set of debatable values on all needy nations, robbing them of the ability to determine their own moral priorities.

Policy-makers in the developing world have a difficult enough time in developing strategies to control their exploding populations, a task that has become a matter of life and death to them. If they choose to make abortion available to women who want to use it in the hope that this will assist them in their efforts, then they should be helped, not hindered. In this case that means continued U.S. financial support.

Fortunately, this ill-considered policy is still in the drafting stage. With the U.N. Conference on Population coming up in August, the government would be well advised to rethink its position and find constructive ways to contribute to the global struggle against overpopulation.

THE LOUISVILLE TIMES
Louisville, KY, June 26, 1984

When last we took up the Reagan administration's plan to restrict foreign aid to countries that in one way or another permitted abortion as a form of contraception, only $38 million was involved. In the last six weeks, however, this highly political initiative has exploded in a manner reminiscent of the world's population, which now stands at 4.75 billion and is expected to pass 11 billion by the year 2100 unless birth rates are sharply curbed.

The White House is now considering a policy that could trim a whopping $100 million from the $240 million that the United States plans to spend next year on population control activities abroad. While cutting $38 million would be short-sighted, to eliminate $100 million is folly in a world whose resource growth is unable to keep pace with the increase in population.

The administration proposal would deny family-planning aid to any nation that uses funds from any source — including aid from other countries — for abortions. This goes far beyond the short-sighted desire to eliminate, entirely, the $38-million U. S. contribution to the U. N. Fund for Population Activities, an organization whose efforts — in a small way — allegedly aid the Chinese government in requiring abortions for population control.

As was noted here previously, it is impossible to say whether a dime of that contribution has been diverted by the Chinese for mandatory abortions, which allegedly have been performed as part of the nation's population control effort. Congress has banned the spending of American aid for abortion, when used as a form of birth control, since 1974. That limitation is morally sound, and should continue.

But to impose that philosophy on countries that use our money entirely for birth control education and supplies simply because they sanction abortions is both naive and dangerous.

What's becoming increasingly clear is that zealots in the "pro-life" lobby who are hostile to abortion also dislike contraception. Some of them have considerable influence with the administration. The New York Times reports that others within the Reagan White House insist that economic growth that encourages the free market is the solution to the population crisis. Birth control, they contend, is not.

Hogwash! Population is controlled by avoiding pregnancy. And contraception is the sensible way to do that. What is more, the economic argument is full of holes, especially because the Western democracies' population growth slowed at the same time that contraception became widely available.

Of course, rationality really isn't the goal here. Indeed, reason rarely prevails when the Reagan administration takes up the social issues. In an election year it isn't really so surprising that topics with appeal for the single-issue, "pro-life" lobby are being exploited.

Despite the fact that most of Mr. Reagan's attempts to limit elective abortions at home have failed, anti-abortion stalwarts still consider him one of their own. All three of the leading Democratic candidates have endorsed the woman's right of choice.

But the danger of cutting back on already inadequate support for population control in underdeveloped nations is far too great.

Former Defense Secretary Robert S. McNamara warns in the current issue of Foreign Affairs that unless major efforts to restrict population growth are developed, the "penalty to the poor of the world, individuals and nations alike, will be enormous." He adds: "The ripple effects — political, economic and moral — will inevitably extend to the rich as well." That means us.

The Washington Post
Washington, DC, May 8, 1984

THE FORCES of the New Right are geared up for another attempt to disrupt U.S. aid for foreign nations' family planning programs. Amendments to be offered during the House debate on foreign aid this week will be forwarded under cover of the anti-abortion campaign. But since no U.S. foreign aid money flows directly or indirectly into either abortion or compulsory sterilization programs, sponsors of the amendments clearly have other goals in mind: to undermine all aid for population control measures and to embarrass their legislative opponents.

Since Sen. Jesse Helms succeeded in banning all U.S. aid for foreign countries' abortion programs a decade ago, the Agency for International Development has been careful to see that no U.S. funds flowed to such programs. Even a small and humanitarian research program to help women suffering from botched illegal abortions, a sadly frequent occurrence in developing countries, was ended to satisfy Sen. Helms and his friends.

Contrary to recent claims, moreover, the U.N. Fund for Population Activities, to which the United States contributes, provides neither direct nor general aid to what are said to be coercive population control programs in China. All U.N. aid is limited to specific projects—including population data development and reduction of infant and child mortality—that involve neither abortion nor compulsory sterilization.

Simple amendments to restrict government aid to abortion programs would thus have no practical effect. But amendments could seriously damage international family planning programs by preventing the flow of U.S. aid to major voluntary population organizations that, using private money, assist in foreign governments' abortion programs. These organizations carry out a major part of family planning efforts throughout the world. Although abortion-related activities are a very small part of their work, they, and the foreign governments to whose requests they respond, would rightly consider such a ban an unwarranted intrusion by the United States into the decisions of other governments.

The developing countries now face an explosion in population unprecedented in world history. Although the rate of growth has subsided slightly since its 1970 peak, the population base is now so large that record numbers are added to the world each year. Ninety percent of the 1 billion people who will be added to world population in the next 15 years will be born in developing countries. A new World Resources Institute study points out that those countries making the most progress in reducing birth and death rates have pursued both active birth control programs and economic and social policies that benefit the large majority of the population. It is strongly in this country's interest to help developing countries pursue both objectives.

Minneapolis Star and Tribune
Minneapolis, MN, June 30, 1984

The Reagan Administration makes a strong case that economic growth is the best solution for problems caused by overpopulation. Healthy economies can accommodate more people. Prosperity enhances prospects for survival, which in turn leads to lower birth rates. The White House proposed to include that valid message in a policy paper to be delivered at the United Nation's Conference on Population this August in Mexico City.

But the policy paper also contained another, more troubling message. Congress in 1974 banned the use of U.S. funds for abortion or abortion-related programs abroad. The White House proposal would have gone further, to cut off U.S. population-control aid to nations or agencies that provide abortion programs, even if no U.S. funds were used for those programs.

But the White House draft encountered resistance from the State Department, members of Congress and others opposed to making aid conditional on other nations' acceptance of U.S. population policies. Opponents of the policy cited the critical need for improved birth-control availability in areas such as drought-parched sub-Saharan Africa, where thousands of children are dying of hunger. Such areas also need help with longer-term efforts to improve agricultural output and encourage eco-

nomic development, but if present birthrates go unchecked, economic and social-development objectives will be difficult to achieve.

The State Department also expressed concern about the policy's effect on U.S. relations with nations such as India, China and Mexico that might be insulted by the doctrinaire tone. Apparently the concerns were heard. The department received permission to present a milder statement of U.S. policy last Monday at a meeting of the U.N. Fund for Population Activities. That version said the United States would continue to provide population-control funds as long as the money is not used for programs in nations where abortion is practiced as a means of birth control. The carefully drawn language apparently will allow continued U.S. assistance to population agencies that would have been ineligible under the earlier version.

The compromise balances the Reagan administration's concerns about abortion and the Third World's need for family-planning assistance. Anti-abortion advocates have made noises about seeking to restore the stronger language. But the compromise better reflects the humane course established by Congress 10 years ago. That is the best policy for the United States to bring to the world population conference in August.

Newsday
Long Island, NY, August 8, 1984

Unless today's population growth patterns change significantly, 6 billion people will inhabit the earth by the end of this century. That would be a calamity for a planet that hasn't figured out what to do with the 4.7 billion who are here now. Preventing this calamity is what this week's United Nations conference on world population in Mexico City is all about.

It's not going to be an easy task. Few human activities are as private or personal as sex, and few human instincts are as basic as procreation. But that only underlines the need for greater and more imaginative efforts to reduce the cultural pressures that encourage big families.

Fortunately, the political climate has changed dramatically since the first UN population conference 10 years ago, when many countries refused to recognize the economic, social and ecological threat of unchecked population growth and the improvements in the quality of life that smaller families bring. Now, many governments are asking for assistance in bringing down birth rates, which have continued to rise in Third World countries even as they have dropped sharply in the industrialized nations and China.

Yet in the United States, the Reagan administration is implying that the world has overreacted to the problem, and now Washington is trying to impose various restrictions on how funds may be used to control population.

Those who want the United States to halt family planning funds for programs that condone abortion should consider the consequences. Family planning could dramatically reduce the suffering that comes when parents have more children than they can feed and care for. To withhold U.S. money unless other funds are spent in accordance with U.S. wishes is both arrogant and shortsighted.

THE WALL STREET JOURNAL.
New York, NY, June 27, 1984

Reagan administration officials are fighting each other at the moment over the bland-sounding issue of population control. The United Nations is going to hold an International Conference on Population in Mexico City in August. Population-control officials in the bureaucracy have been preparing positions for the conference, but recently a bunch of White House staffers wrote a paper giving their own ideas about the subject. The bureaucrats went apoplectic over the White House views of abortion and of economic development. Underneath the obfuscation, the combatants are really fighting over competing visions of our future.

For years the U.S. has supported population control in the developing world. In fact, we spent a good deal of time preaching the idea to underdeveloped nations that weren't so sure that the thing wasn't just another fair-skinned imperialist plot. When "no growth" prophets in the West started predicting a world future of increasingly scarce material resources, the population-control advocates grew even more fervid. By the mid-1970s, the developed and underdeveloped worlds were preaching population control with an increasingly unified voice. The U.S. government's preparations for the Mexico City conference reflected this view of the world—that is, one under relentless resource pressures and needing population control to survive.

When the White House paper leaked to the public—through a dozen tiny holes—it was found to embody quite an opposite position. The paper agreed with the conventional idea that it would be a good thing for the world to head for some long-run population equilibrium. But "more people," it said plainly, "do not mean less growth." On the contrary, demographic growth brings misery only when a government louses up the economic mechanisms that can supply a people's needs. Conversely, population control is no substitute for tackling the real problems of economic development.

The State Department and the Agency for International Development wrote replies to the White House. They tried to say that they, too, were good pro-growth players on the Reagan team. They had never said that population control was the whole of economic development. They had always favored market mechanisms.

But, they made their attack—the kids in the White House were naïve to think the Third World could handle population growth as Europe had done in the 19th century. The staffers were imprudent to ignore the political dangers—ethnic tensions, urban riots—of Third World growth. And the staffers were extremists as well, for they proposed cutting off U.S. population aid from any program that included abortion. The dispute over abortion—whether the administration should cut off aid to offending governments, or to U.N. agencies, or to private organizations—seems to have occupied the attention so far.

On the broader issue, the bureaucrats say that they have been made into straw men. They are no birth-control freaks, they say, no coercive little old ladies scandalized by the licentious habits of foreigners, but only advocates of the sort of birth control availability that most reasonable people favor. And certainly it is true that few if any of the controllers have ever favored forcing people to have fewer children, and felt their cause damaged by the coercive extremes reported in China and India.

Yet this is not the whole truth. Population controllers have in fact helped spread the picture of a world that cannot be redeemed by growth but must be saved through vigorous bureaucratic planning. There is a connection between the desperate crisis they have described and the feeling by some governments that extreme measures are justified to meet it. By contrast, the White House paper asks that we make our policies from the assumption that growth is the key to our well-being, and that freedom is the key to growth.

No wonder there's a fight. The population combatants have gotten hold of the middle of the disputed territory in modern politics: the question of the capacity of free people to build their future and of the necessity for government action to make up for their weaknesses. We hope whoever has the final decision on Mexico City sees what he is dealing with.

Chicago Tribune
Chicago, IL, June 22, 1984

High moral principle does not always mix easily with foreign policy. The requirements of diplomacy in an imperfect world, armed with weapons of ultimate power, do not always square with the virtues as they are seen within the borders of a free and democratic country.

This was the trouble with President Carter's human rights campaign: not that it was ignoble, but that it was as stiff as a schoolmaster. And in this case the pupil was armed, dangerous and sovereign within its realm.

Now President Reagan wants to inject his own version of pure moral principle into foreign policy by eliminating U.S. aid to programs that practice or back abortion in population control. Specifically affected would be the United Nations Fund for Population Activities, some foreign governments and several private organizations.

The President's proposal will please the prolife faction of the Republican Party before this summer's convention. Perhaps after that, the issue will slide into the crowded oblivion of spent political gestures. But you can't say the basic impulse is a new one or that the President does not really mean it. The Reagan plan, which is contained in a draft proposal circulating within the administration, is consistent with anti-abortion positions the President has taken again and again over the years.

Abortion is controversial even in this society of public debate and political freedom. National policy has been set more by the Supreme Court than by political institutions, and it is constantly under righteous attack. In the international setting, a strict anti-abortion foreign policy makes no sense at all, no matter how noble the aim. If the limitation on foreign aid only applies to direct subsidies for abortion, this easily can be circumvented by any nation that wants to divert funds from elsewhere and make up for it with aid given for other purposes. If the moral proposition is really to bite, then there must be a total aid cutoff, which would make little sense in terms of the larger—and surpassingly important—issues of the international balance of power.

Moral considerations have a part in U.S. diplomacy. The public will not and should not tolerate a foreign policy that has no relation to the ethical values it is supposed to protect. But success in international relations requires that the United States not commit itself to a single-minded insistence that other nations follow the strict dictates of our own moral code, especially concerning matters such as abortion in which we ourselves have such a hard time deciding just what the rule ought to be.

The Houston Post

Houston, Texas, August 6, 1984

Beginning today and lasting the rest of this week in Mexico City, the year's most important international gathering will take place. It is the second United Nations International Conference on Population. It is convening under the clouds of a crisis.

The World Bank has estimated that the world's population, which totaled a little over 3 billion in 1960, has now risen to almost 4.8 billion. And global population might more than double to 10 billion by the middle of the next century. Almost all the growth would take place in the world's underdeveloped countries.

The report concluded that this population shock would severely undermine the ability of the developing nations to significantly raise their living standards, and might seriously retard their industrial growth altogether. If present trends continue, by the year 2000 the number living in abject poverty will increase from today's 780 million to 1.3 billion — and most will live in the Third World. Compounding this catastrophe, the number of adults in these countries entering the work force during this time will rise by 630 million people, while the industrialized nations will only have to create jobs for some 20 million.

What has been the United States' response to this? In past years the U.S. government has supported population control as fundamental in combating poverty and encouraging economic development in the Third World. Last year it spent over $300 million through the U.N. and private organizations toward that end.

But in June, in a total shift in policy, the Reagan administration (in an election-year concession to religious fundamentalists) announced that the United States would cease to fund organizations whose population programs included abortion — regardless of whether that particular program used U.S. contributions. This would cut $100 million from U.S. population-control expenditures.

Further, in *another* complete reversal, the U.S. delegation at the conference will advocate the de-emphasizing of population control entirely. They will claim that excessive population growth is not a cause of poverty in the Third World; rather, these countries' endemic underdevelopment is caused by their failure to follow good Reaganomic economic polices. This stand has shocked not only U.S. specialists in International Development; it also stands to make the United States the laughingstock of the conference. At a time when the world needs vision and foresight, all it gets is ignorance.

THE BLADE

Toledo, Ohio, August 12, 1984

PRESIDENT Reagan's envoy to the world population conference in Mexico City, James Buckley, carried a message that will not go down very well with delegates from the world's most populous nations.

"We take the view that population growth is neither good nor bad, it's neutral," Mr. Buckley said in an interview. "We will provide support for population programs as long as they are not coercive and are not being used to fund abortions."

Mr. Buckley and others who share his view are fond of pointing to South Korea as an example of a dynamic society that "through fewer government controls and free-market incentives, has been able to absorb growing populations and provide higher standards of living."

A far more instructive example would be Mexico City which is choking on pollution and unrestrained population growth. As Third World delegates pointed out, the South Korean economy is patterned rather successfully after the American model, and the country has a family-planning program that has slowed population growth and enabled the country's growing economy to improve the lot of most South Koreans.

It is ironic that the well-to-do Mr. Buckley can advocate a free-market economy for nations which are struggling desperately to bring all segments of their large populations above the subsistence level. After more than 30 years of Communist rule the living standard of mainland Chinese still remains quite low compared with some of its Asian neighbors like Taiwan, Japan and South Korea.

Political upheavals, some of which lasted for a decade, were one cause of this failure to match growth of other countries, but another important reason is the near-doubling of the population of China since 1949. That growth has largely canceled out productivity gains in agriculture, industry and other segments of the mainland economy.

Even if the Buckley formula made sense — which in light of world population trends in the poorest areas of the globe it does not — the United States and other developed countries would have to throw open their borders to larger amounts of commodities and manufactured goods from less developed countries and be prepared to give greater amounts in foreign aid.

The U.S. position at the world population conference is untenable. The President, speaking in this instance through Mr. Buckley, is entitled to his views on abortion and the population question, as wrong as they are. But the Reagan administration should not try to force those views on other nations trying to escape from dire poverty caused in large part by overpopulation.

Herald American
Syracuse, NY, July 8, 1984

If you thought the administration was heavy-handed in threatening to cut off highway aid to states that don't adopt a minimum drinking age of 21, get a load of what Washington wants to do abroad.

The Reagan team apparently is seeking to end aid to foreign population control programs that have abortion as an option. The plan is contained in a draft White House paper scheduled for presentation at an International Conference on Population in Mexico City next month.

The U.S. has, for 10 years, banned the use of foreign aid for abortion services. However, the new plan would go much further — cutting aid to countries and organizations that find other means of financing abortions.

The new twist is incredibly short-sighted. Few enough countries are doing anything to effectively combat overpopulation and accompanying poverty and malnutrition. Those that are don't need the U.S. undermining sincere efforts.

We can't buy the White House line that concern about world population growth is exaggerated. Rather, the new approach smells suspiciously like a sop to anti-abortionists. They backed the president heavily in 1980 and want to be in his corner again — if he'll hang tough on the abortion issue.

This is a way for the administration to do it without stirring up too much domestic ire.

Why, the Reagan team even has a "supply side" theory of population control:

The draft document says rapid population growth could help create jobs if "oppressive economic policies" were overturned in favor of free market policies.

These are the same guys who said we'd have a balanced budget by 1984.

Imagine the world's population if they're as far off on babies as they were on the deficit.

The Hartford Courant
Hartford, CT, July 15, 1984

The draft position paper prepared by Reagan administration officials for next month's World Population Conference in Mexico City is a puzzlement.

In the past, Mr. Reagan — as well as Secretary of State George P. Shultz and U.N. Ambassador Jeane J. Kirkpatrick — have contended that excessive population growth leads to poverty and famine. Pouring money into countries without trying to lower their population growth rates, Ms. Kirkpatrick has said, is like pouring money into a bucket with a hole in it.

Yet the position paper describes population growth as a "natural phenomenon" that might stimulate economic growth in developing countries as it has in this country, and suggests that the United States might cut its funding for population-control programs. The draft even said no American money would go to programs that permit abortion.

What gnomes in the White House could produce a position paper running contrary to previous statements by the president and some of his top officials, of the consistent stance taken by Congress and the past five administrations, and of the plain facts?

The World Bank report released last week says that the Earth's population could double to about 10 billion by the year 2050, miring many Third World nations in a continued state of poverty. Rapid population growth hampers development by reducing economic resources available for each individual, depleting natural resources and complicating national planning.

The population growth in the United States helped develop the nation economically because of the size of the continent and the richness of its resources. But it is absurd to suggest that a country like Bangladesh, which is the size of Wisconsin, would benefit from a projected population twice that of the United States today — about 450 million people by the year 2050.

The world population is growing at a rate of 82 million people a year, while development assistance from the industrialized countries, including the United States, has been dropping. Not only must economic assistance to Third World countries increase, but a greater proportion of that aid should be earmarked for family planning.

Such aid, mostly through education, has helped reduce fertility rates in some countries, notably Thailand, South Korea, the Philippines, Colombia and Costa Rica. Population-control efforts in China and India have had some startling success.

Not all means of limiting population growth are desirable, but without effective controls, more billions of people will be doomed to bleak lives — destabilizing and impoverishing the future for the entire world.

Sunday Journal-Star
Lincoln, NE, June 17, 1984

Those who read no further than the headline written about the United Nations' report last week that, for the first time in modern history, the pace of world population growth has slowed, may have taken away an awfully wrong impression.

The false impression would be that international overpopulation clouds are lifting. No, they are not. Definitely they are not. Those engulfing clouds are just slightly less dark at the moment. That is all.

Instead of the world's population rising from the current estimate of 4.76 billion people, to 6 billion in the late 1990s, the larger figure may not now come until the year 2000. But it will inexorably come. Make no mistake.

All should be able to share the satisfaction that the annual world population growth rate has declined from 2 percent to 1.7 percent in the last decade, and that the average number of children born to a female has dropped from 4.5 to 3.6.

The latter statistic is most encouraging. It demonstrates that worldwide birth control programs are having a pronouced ef-

fect. Keep in mind the figure provided by Dr. Luella Klein of Atlanta, Ga., the first woman president of the American College of Obstetricians and Gynecologists:

On the average, a fertile, sexually active woman using no contraception will face 14 births or 31 abortions during her reproductive lifetime.

Dr. Klein, not so incidentally, is critical of the U.S. media, especially television, for fleeing from the subject of contraception. There is, Dr. Klein charges, "a conspiracy of silence concerning pregnancy prevention in the media. Laxatives and vaginal and rectal products are widely advertised, but there is no one word about contraceptives. We need to abolish the taboos that prevent mentioning of birth control."

Contraceptive information and practices are critical if world population growth is to be further slowed. The benefits to all humankind from even a tiny moderation of the increasing competition for the resources of the world are so obvious as not to require a listing.

The Virginian-Pilot
Norfolk, VA, June 18, 1984

Thomas Malthus was author of the theory that world population tends to outstrip global food supply and that war, famine and pestilence forestall overpopulation. The gloomy projections by the 19th century political economist have made him spiritual father to generations of doomsayers.

His spirit, if not his projections, must have been enlivened by last week's news that "the growth rate of the human population has declined for the first time in human history," according to Rafael M. Salas, executive director of the United Nations Fund for Population Activities. His

State of World Population 1984 attributed the good news not to any natural apocalypse but rather to governmental planning. It all sounds so refreshingly optimist, upbeat, non-Malthusian.

Not so fast. The moral that Mr. Salas chooses to draw is not the good news that humanity is showing the skill and willingness to curtail its persistent problems but rather the bad news, as Mr. Salas puts it, "that we still have 80 million to 90 million more people a year to contend with." How in the world are we going to feed them all, he frets. Malthus would have loved him.

THE KANSAS CITY STAR
Kansas City, MO, June 22, 1984

This administration's position on family planning has been well defined by its actions over the past three and one-half years. The so-called "squeal rule" and cuts in federal funding are good examples of the withdrawal of federal support for birth control efforts.

Now President Reagan is attempting to transfer his antipathy to domestic family planning to other countries which receive U.S. dollars through the United Nations Fund for Population Activities and private organizations. Countries which practice abortion, or advocate it, would lose an estimated $100 million a year for family planning efforts under Mr. Reagan's proposal. Even those countries which receive private donations or other nations' help in paying for abortions would lose U.S. aid.

The outcome of this ill-conceived plan, which can be put into effect without congressional approval, will be lamentable. The president will be reversing the international population control policy which has existed in this country for eight administrations. Of greater importance to the U.S. is the effect it will have of increasing births in those countries which can least afford them—the overcrowded, resource-poor areas of the world where population control is the only hope of permanent improvement of their condition.

The U.S., which contributes to the United Nations fund with other countries, should not be writing the rules that go with that group effort to control population growth. In fact, each country receiving the aid should be able to instigate its own birth control program as it fits its citizen needs. China and India both have launched intensive efforts to improve economic and social conditions through massive birth control programs, but the programs are as different as the political philosophies of the governments which created them. It is not the role of the U.S. to march in and demand that some other philosophy govern their programs or this country will take its money and go home.

Abortion should not be viewed as a population control measure, we agree. But the loss of these millions of dollars will have a negative impact on every other aspect of family planning and birth control promoted to the citizens of these countries. It eventually will cost the U.S. more money in food, medical, and maternal and child health care if it is to help these countries keep pace with their growing numbers that will result. The ones who suffer from this short-sighted approach will be the mothers and children—the already-poor in the poorest countries of the world.

The Burlington Free Press
Burlington, VT, July 5, 1984

In a decision that defies logic, the Reagan administration would deny millions of dollars in aid to countries that use abortion in their mix of population control methods.

For overcrowded counties, which receive the funds through the U.N. Fund for Population Activities, the threat could not come at a worse time. Statistics released by the U.S. Census Bureau's Center for International Demographic Data indicate the population problem is an even greater threat than most experts realized.

Because there has been a dramatic decrease in the number of births in mainland China as the result of a draconian birth control program, the experts felt that the rate of population growth had slowed throughout the world.

Not so, says the Center for International Demographic Date. When mainland China is excluded, the center's figures indicate that the population of other overcrowded countries has increased over the last four years.

The Reagan administration's hard-line position rings of hypocrisy, for at the same time it argues for a pro-life position on abortion, it continues to pour millions of dollars in military aid to Central America where people are being killed by the benefactors of U.S. aid.

If the administration were sincere in its concern for human life, it might better direct the military aid into humanitarian efforts that would help the developing countries cope with the problems of uncontrolled population growth.

Absent that concern, it's not defensible for the administration to attempt to impose its anti-abortion philosophy on other nations.

Although Reagan supporters may be right when they deride population control because it's no panacea, they ignore the fact that it works. Population control can serve a world that cries out for stability.

Unless Reagan changes his mind on this policy, he will have to share the blame when in just a few years, the world has a thousand or a million more poor mouths it can't feed.

THE INDIANAPOLIS NEWS
Indianapolis, IN, July 7, 1984

The issue of population control in developing nations is causing a nasty White House struggle.

The conflict flared with the release of a position paper prepared for an August conference in Mexico on population matters.

The paper says that overpopulation is not the major source of Third World's problems; underproduction is the culprit, and that there is no reason the United States should be promoting morally questionable steps such as abortion and other stringent population control measures.

The delegation that prepared the paper and will be attending the conference wants to back words with deeds. They're willing to slash more than $100 million of the roughly $200 million of United Nations funds that go toward population control in the Third World.

The position paper undercuts one of the principles of American foreign policy over the past two decades.

The thesis under attack is that the world will soon be facing a severe population crunch. A rapidly expanding world population and steadily dwindling material resources will marry, population control proponents say, to produce mass starvation within a decade if stricter and more efficient population control methods aren't implemented.

To this, the administration delegation points to the vast, undeveloped lands in much of the Third World, particularly in Africa, and contends that the resources are available, but they aren't being developed.

Economic growth, not birth control, will stave off disaster in the coming years, they say.

The Reagan delegation does not deny that starvation and poverty in the Third World are serious problems that could upset the precarious balance in world affairs, perhaps causing bloodshed and famines.

The paper overlooks the fact, however, that without some short term success in bringing down birth rates, unbearable internal pressures will create instability on a grand scale.

How to avoid such potential explosions may be debatable, and the authors of the controversial paper may be contributing a balancing element to the debate. It is true that aggressive population control protagonists have tended to oversimplify the problems of the developing nations. Doubtless, development of Third World resources would ease many of the world's economic problems, but millions of helpless children could die while the mechanisms necessary for expanded development are put in place. All development takes time.

In the interim, present trends point to some progress in controlling the population explosion. Those trends must be encouraged, buying time for the economic development which will eventually come to pass.

the Charleston Gazette
Charleston, WV, November 18, 1984

THE United Nations is embarked upon a campaign throughout the Third World to curtail the population explosion. At the international organization's second World Population Conference, held in Mexico City this summer, delegates decided to beef up substantially family-planning programs.

But family-planning programs to curb population growth are doomed to fail, says Peter Huessy.

In a study published by *The Heritage Foundation* the natural resources specialist says couples in the Third World prefer having four to six children. They like large families.

The desire for a large family is what has to be altered, says Huessy. Family planning programs will be effective only when people want smaller families. "Drowning (people) in contraceptives . . . will not suddenly change decades of cultural tradition but will only waste money."

In Third World societies a large gap separates rich and poor. If the gap is to be narrowed the population explosion must be curbed — "a decisive decline in fertility over the next two decades is imperative," says Huessy.

Huessy believes that economic growth and enhanced economic opportunity — the old and ever-valid revolution of rising expectations — are crucial to convincing Third World husbands and wives to desire smaller families.

The director of U.N. family planning programs, Rafael Salas, has acknowledged that they don't succeed. In Third World nations showing a modest birth rate decrease, Salas admits, family planning merely reinforced an existing trend to a lowered fertility rate.

Third World families don't take maximum advantage of free services offered to prevent pregnancy because of a long tradition of large families. The assumption that couples who want large families are acting irrationally is wrong. Rather families are acting in accord with their own values, not the values of others.

These values must be revised if the world population explosion is to be halted and the doubling of the world's population every 35 years ended. That's correct: at today's rate the world's population doubles every 35 years.

BUFFALO EVENING NEWS
Buffalo, NY, June 25, 1984

AGAINST THE advice of its own international experts and common sense, the Reagan administration is seeking to cut off all family planning aid to countries that support or finance abortions.

At present, U.S. funds to finance abortion are barred by law, but the United States will assist governmental or private birth-control programs, even if the programs use other funds to finance abortions. Under the Reagan proposal, many developing countries would have their family planning funds cut off, with harmful effects on the worldwide effort to control the dangerously expanding world population.

The U.S. Agency for International Development has rightly urged the administration to reconsider the proposal, declaring that it would be unnecessarily controversial at a United Nations Population Conference in Mexico City this summer. The agency instead urged support for a resolution at the conference that would back family planning as a means of helping women avoid abortions.

Similarly, the State Department reportedly opposes the White House proposal, fearing that it would injure ties with the Third World nations generally. Some officials are said to feel that the document proposed by the White House would make the United States look foolish in Mexico City — and with good reason.

The draft policy statement now being circulated by the White House is a curious mixture of shrewd politics — appealing to Mr. Reagan's anti-abortion supporters — and vintage Reagan political ideology. It blames the world's problems of overpopulation on "government control of economies" that disrupts the "natural mechanism for slowing population growth."

It is sad to see simplistic reasoning swaying the administration's policy on this important issue. In contrast, Congress has recently been seeking to increase American assistance to family planning programs in underdeveloped countries. Such assistance should not be considered a handout to poor countries but an investment in a vital program that serves American interests by combatting hunger and poverty and encouraging stability throughout the world.

The development agency and the State Department have given President Reagan good advice, and he should heed it. Reducing American aid to international family planning programs would be a major step backward.

THE TENNESSEAN
Nashville, TN, June 19, 1984

THE world's annual population growth rate declined from 2% to 1.7% during the last decade, the first such decline in modern times, according to a United Nations report.

That should be good news to those worried about the population growth. But despite the decline in the rate, the world's population grew by 800 million during the decade and still is rising by a record 80 million to 90 million a year. Even a tiny growth rate applied to the world's current population of 4.76 billion adds a lot of people. And the problem is that much of the growth is occurring in poor countries that can ill afford the new mouths to feed. That means that hunger will increase in some parts of the world faster than others.

UN spokesmen emphasized that it would be a mistake to stop worrying about the population growth just because the rate is down.

Said one: "The growth rate of the human population has declined for the first time in human history. But at the same time, the number of people being added to the human population per year is bigger than at any time in history because the population base is larger."

The growth rate moved the world closer to stabilization and that is the current goal of those agencies concerned with the problem. The UN has projected that zero growth rate will be achieved in 2095. But at that time the world population is expected to be 10.5 billion, and if the forecasters are just a few tenths of a point off the total population growth could still be something to worry about. It seems there just aren't many bright spots in the future outlook for the world's population.

DAYTON DAILY NEWS
Dayton, OH, July 4, 1984

President Reagan has a right to his anti-abortion policy, but his effort to tell other countries what to do is gratuitous and could hurt more than help.

The administration plans to withhold all U.S. dollars from any population-control program that includes abortion.

The idea has horrified United Nations personnel and career diplomats at the U.S. State Department. And it has not been received too well by moderate Republicans like Sens. Charles Percy, Charles Mathias and Mark Hatfield.

It would dicate internal policies of foreign governments, particularly Third World countries such as India and China, that have enough problems without being forced to conform to U.S. whims in order to get U.S. dollars for population-control programs.

It already is a policy that no dollars are to be used to fund abortions. That is consistent with U.S. domestic policy. This new plan, however, would stop U.S. money from going to *any* population-control program that uses *any* kind of funds for abortions.

Mr. Reagan's feels birth control will come with economic development. After all, countries with high standards of living also have low birthrates. But Third World countries haven't been able to outrun their baby booms, and that helps perpetuate poverty.

Unless Mr. Reagan plans to pump megabucks to get these developing economies on their feet, he should stick with present U.S. policy on population-control programs.

Pittsburgh Post-Gazette
Pittsburgh, Pa., June 26, 1984

President Reagan is considering cutting off aid to international population-control programs that practice or advocate abortion, even if U.S. funds are not paying for the abortions. The president's imposition of his personal beliefs in this case, over the opposition of the State Department and the Agency for International Development, would be contrary to the spirit of American law and could have disastrous consequences.

The United States contributes $240 million annually to public and private population-control organizations, including the United Nations Fund for Population Activities. It is money well spent; in many Third World countries, rapid population growth continues to strain resources past the breaking point.

A White House proposal being circulated in the administration says in part that "the United States does not consider abortion an acceptable part of family-planning programs." But existing rules already ban the use of U.S. funds to pay for abortions abroad. Mr. Reagan apparently wants to go further than that by withholding funds that are put to other uses by population-control organizations, as punishment for advocating a procedure that is legal both in the United States and in the nations where these organizations do their work.

Ironically, this action might have the tragic consequence of causing more abortions to be performed, and under more dangerous conditions than those provided for by the United Nations Fund. By cutting off funding for birth control in overcrowded countries, the United States may force desperately poor mothers to abort children that they can't possibly support. Mr. Reagan should reconsider this unwise course of action.

The Miami Herald
Miami, Fla., June 25, 1984

IN SCORES of developing countries, runaway population growth combines with endemic poverty to thwart even the most conscientious plans for economic betterment. Now the Reagan Administration, in a decision based purely on its own right-wing ideology, is proposing to change U.S. aid rules to forbid assisting any country that uses abortion in its mix of population-control measures.

The Administration is circulating for interagency comments a draft proposal that could lop some $100 million from the $240 million annual U.S. contribution to international population-control efforts. The proposal would make ineligible for U.S. funds any nation whose birth-control programs practice or advocate abortion. The ban would apply even if the abortion programs were financed by private or other contributions and did not involve U.S. funds at all.

This proviso—ban abortion or lose all U.S. help for all your population-control efforts—is as repugnant when applied to other nations as its corollary is when applied within the United States itself. It denies women and their families the option of choice. Instead, it attempts to coerce them into using other family-planning measures that may not be as effective, may not suit their preferences, and indeed may only add to the pressures of too many births in countries unable to feed the extra mouths.

Current U.S. rules forbid American money to be used for other nations' abortion programs. That policy is questionable, but at least it's defensible. It's not defensible, however, for the Reagan Administration to attempt to impose its anti-abortion philosophy on other nations by denying them U.S. assistance if they make abortion available from other, non-U.S., funds. That's an interference with their rights of self-determination, and the United States should not put itself in that position. The proper way for Washington to try to reduce the use of abortion abroad would be to *increase* its support for every other kind of birth control so as to reduce the number of pregnancies subject to termination.

Groups that favor permitting abortion as one birth-control choice should implore individual members of Congress to stop this new rule before it starts.

The Record
Hackensack, N.J., June 26, 1984

The population of the United States doubles every 110 years. Now imagine what this country would be like if instead it doubled every 17 years — and every four years in cities like Newark and Camden. That's what is happening throughout the Third World. By the year 2000, there will be 1.7 billion more of us on earth. Most of the new people will live in impoverished countries. This population bomb threatens the food supply, overburdens natural resources, increases misery in the Third World, and undermines the quality of life for everyone.

About 20 years ago, a number of developing countries became alarmed at their rising populations and began a concerted effort to provide birth-control devices and information. The United States has been a generous partner in these efforts.

Now, however, the Reagan administration has invented an excuse for reducing U.S. involvement in population control. The White House says it is reviewing international family-planning efforts to make sure that no federal assistance goes to programs that are connected in any way with abortion. Such a ban could cut off more than half of all U.S. aid to such programs.

The prohibition is ridiculous. For one thing, the United States doesn't subsidize abortions now. Congress 10 years ago forbade the use of U.S. aid to pay for abortions and related services overseas, including counseling women to have them.

Second, the proposed guidelines are preposterously restrictive. They would even cut funding for groups that discuss abortion as an alternative to pregnancy at their conferences.

Finally, limiting family-planning resources would be counter to the aims of the Reagan administration and the best interests of developing nations. Less family-planning money means more unwanted pregnancies — and, eventually, more illegal abortions. Already, one in four pregnancies in the Third World ends in abortion. There's no question the number would increase if U.S. family-planning assistance were to dry up.

President Reagan hasn't managed to outlaw abortions in the United States, as he promised during his 1980 campaign. So now, just in time for his reelection campaign, he's latched onto an antiabortion policy aimed at women in the Third World. The president's gesture may please his right-to-life allies at home, but it threatens international efforts to deal with the population problem, which is accelerating at a frightening pace. It's a bad idea; he should forget it.

THE PLAIN DEALER
Cleveland, Ohio, June 22, 1984

The White House is passing around for review a policy paper that would eliminate family planning assistance to nations and international groups that support abortion. If you tried, you probably couldn't dream up a more egregious, more negative political ploy.

The United States currently provides roughly $240 million a year to population control programs. Since 1974, Washington has restricted those funds from being used for abortions or abortion-related activities. That is fair; the money comes from American citizens, and such expenditures risk violating the moral beliefs of many. Thus the money is made available—and spent—for other programs: contraceptive education, perhaps, or family counseling, or economic programs to diminish the need, found in many developing nations, for large rural families.

The new proposal, opposed by both the State Department and the Agency for International Development, would cut funding to any nation that uses any money, regardless of its source, in support of abortion. The State Department rightly fears that the policy will complicate relations with high-population countries such as India and China. AID fears that the policy would be needlessly controversial at the upcoming United Nations Population Conference in Mexico to be held only a week before the Republican convention in Dallas. The agency wisely encourages family planning assistance that helps "women avoid abortions."

The White House has yet to understand that international aid frequently is founded in altruism. That is the case with Washington's contribution to population control programs. The money is not an appropriate avenue for impressing personal moralities on other nations. If President Reagan wants to make peace with the conservative elements of his party, let him do so elsewhere. To curry partisan favor by attempting to manipulate the policies of other nations is moral imperialism: shameful and arrogant.

THE ATLANTA CONSTITUTION
Atlanta, GA, July 24, 1985

An administration attempt to impose its anti-abortion views on the desperately underfed and overpopulated nations of the Third World is headed for a showdown tomorrow. House-Senate conferees are scheduled to take up a measure that would dangerously extend the president's authority to cut off family-planning assistance abroad.

The administration could dictate how foreign governments must proceed with regard to abortion — a ploy with devastating implications abroad and for America's already-lagging credibility in much of the Third World.

There is simply no way to justify the imposition of domestic American politics that would add to the suffering of sickly and undernourished populations.

No U.S. funds have been used for abortion-related activities abroad since 1973, and the administration has all the assurance it needs that none will be. Even so, it has cut off more than $16 million in funds and supplies to the International Planned Parenthood Federation, the world's major provider of birth control in 100 developing countries. And it has persuaded the U.N. Fund for Population Activities to stipulate that no UNFPA funds will be used for abortion-related activities abroad, either.

These actions have eroded family planning efforts internationally — and have distorted them: The administration has increased U.S. aid to international groups that counsel sexual abstinence, rather than birth control, from $800,000 in 1981 to more than $7 million.

But going even farther, the White House has now persuaded the House it should be allowed to cut off family planning aid to nations or organizations that spend *their own money* on abortion-related activities. All that currently stands in the way is tomorrow's conference committee meeting, scheduled to reconcile the differences between a House foreign aid bill, supporting the president's position, and a Senate version, opposing it.

If anti-abortion forces succeed in bullying Senate conferees to go along with this unwise policy, they will have contributed in their small way to population explosions, food shortages and (a matter of bitter irony) a likely increase in abortions abroad as the number of unwanted pregnancies increases.

THE MILWAUKEE JOURNAL
Milwaukee, WI, March 19, 1985

The Reagan administration has a chronic case of tunnel vision on the subject of aiding population-control programs. Wisconsin Sen. Bob Kasten could (and should) help the Reagan gang shake the malady, but so far demurs.

In its zeal to ensure that no US government money gets spent for abortions anywhere in the world, the administration continues to deny aid to international population-control groups that so much as acknowledge the availability of abortion. The president and his aides seem curiously blind to the likelihood that their approach will backfire: If family-planning agencies are forced to reduce services, more pregnancies surely will result — and, tragically, more abortions.

Yet the Reaganites blunder on. In new rules that carry the sorry policy to its logistic and linguistic extreme, the US Agency for International Development proposes that any family-planning organization financed *even partly* by American dollars must ride herd on any groups it aids directly or indirectly. The AID document thus becomes a masterpiece of mumbo-jumbo in which "recipients" are ordered to ensure that "sub-recipients" refrain from promoting abortion and the "sub-recipients" in turn must monitor "sub-sub-recipients." Good grief.

Language quagmire aside, the policy is morally bankrupt. It threatens most foreign family-planning services, even those in nations grotesquely overpopulated and badly underequipped to ameliorate misery.

Moreover, because of the policy, AID has scuttled this year's $17 million grant to the International Planned Parenthood Foundation and held up $46 million intended for the United Nations population agency, ostensibly because AID wants assurances that no money will go to China, where some abortions are coerced.

So what is Bob Kasten's role? The Population Institute and the Population Crisis Committee, both based in Washington, view Wisconsin's Republican senator as wielding great clout in his chairmanship of the foreign operations subcommittee of the Senate Appropriations Committee. They contend that he could lobby the administration to rethink its policy. "One call from Bob Kasten would turn this money loose," says one population expert.

As Kasten's office replies, it's probably not so simple. But there's no harm in trying. How about it, senator? Just one call, a call that might spare the world needless abortions or the wretched alternative, more starving Ethiopians.

The Washington Times
Washington, DC, March 22, 1985

The Agency for International Development's efforts to soothe pro-lifers as to the nature of its population programs has hit a bumpy road. According to reports, top AID officials have been helping the United Nations Fund for Population Activities whitewash China's forced abortion policies.

The "population community" appears to assign to the word "voluntary" a sort of talismanic value, such that the mere utterance of it in connection with a policy is enough to silence critics. Never mind that the policy is about as voluntary as a transfer of $5 on a New York subway.

The claims of voluntarism inserted in UNFPA's report on China (thanks to the intervention of AID's Kathy Piepmeyer) are belied by Steven Mosher, whose reports on the horrors of China's population control program touched off a controversy at Stanford some time back.

Not to worry, says AID. It will appoint a "blue-ribbon" commission to go to China and find out What's Really Happening. It will even put pro-lifers on it.

Even if the commission membership is enirely pro-life, it easily may be misled. Mr. Mosher, at home with the Chinese language and culture, was a researcher who earned the grudging confidence of village authorities only after much time and effort. For him, village abortionists lowered their guard. Can a team of investigators from the U.S. government expect the same cooperation? It is unlikely.

The Kemp amendment to the current foreign aid appropriation prohibits U.S. aid to coercive population programs, but insiders say that AID now plans to define "program" as an actual coercive practice. Thus, taxpayers would continue to fund coercive population control as long as no American funds were directly traceable to the actual hauling away of kicking and screaming women.

AID is fulfilling neither the president's policy nor the intent of Congress. The administration should crack down.

Part IV: Abortion, Pregnancy & Family Planning

The battle over abortion is not between those who believe there should be abortions and those who believe they should be banned; there are no champions of abortion per se. Even the most radical of feminists have stated their preference for measures which prevent pregnancy over abortion, while defending the right of women to make their own choice about terminating a pregnancy once conception has already occurred. It would seem that even between the adherents of the most extreme 'pro-life' and 'pro-choice' viewpoints, common ground could be found in a mutual efffort to find more effective ways to prevent unwanted pregnancies and to channel financial support to those women who would carry their pregnancies to term if circumstances permitted. Some conservative groups do in fact offer free prenatal care for pregnant women as well as adoption services. But the Reagan Administration, far from allocating additional funds to birth-control research or economic assistance for single mothers, has consistently sought to cut federal family-planning programs. Many in the antiabortion or 'pro-life' movement also oppose such efforts to reduce the number of unplanned pregnancies. Groups such as the American Life Lobby and United Families of America oppose the basic family planning program, Title X, arguing that it does little to prevent unwanted pregnancies and actually encourages sexual promiscuity among adolescents.

In fact, although more than half of all abortions in the United States are performed on women in their twenties, much of the debate surrounding preventive measures has centered upon sex education and contraceptive use and their effect upon teenagers. The teenage pregnancy rate in the U.S. is certainly very high, and teenagers aged 15 to 19 do comprise nearly 30% of current abortion patients. But measures such as the Reagan Administration's proposed "squeal rule," which would require clinics to notify parents when teenagers receive birth control devices, seem to their opponents to defeat the primary goal of preventing unwanted pregnancies by making it more difficult for teenagers to obtain contraceptives.

Teen Pregnancy: Risks to Health, Cost to Nation

One of the issues that the abortion controversy has brought to the forefront is the high rate of teenage pregnancy throughout the United States. The Alan Guttmacher Institute, a private foundation, in 1985 released a report on the sexual habits and incidence of pregnancy among teenagers from 15-19 years old in the U.S. as compared to their peers in 36 other industrialized nations. The report stated that American teenagers as a whole had a pregnancy rate of 96 per 1,000, or a rate more than twice that of their counterparts in the other nations. One of the most disturbing statistics reported was the disproportionately high rate of pregnancies among black teenagers, which the study tallied at 163 per 1,000. This startlingly high figure, the report noted, contributes to a cycle of poverty in the black community, increasing both the rate of teenage unemployment and the numbers of female-headed families. The study also found that 60 of every 1,000 U.S. women had had an abortion by the age of 18. Of the five other countries studied in detail by the researchers—Canada, France, England, the Netherlands and Spain—France and Sweden trailed most closely behind the U.S., with 30 each.

Much of the difference in teen pregnancy rates between the U.S. and other countries, the report said, could be accounted for by the other countries' national programs of classroom sex education, and by government and private efforts to supply teenagers with low-cost contraceptives. The report questioned arguments that liberal sexual views or high welfare benefits resulted in increased pregnancy rates. It found that the average age for first sexual intercourse in the U.S.—just under 18—was roughly the same as in the five other countries highlighted in the study. The report also claimed that in most of the countries examined, "the overall level of support" given welfare recipients "appears to be more generous" than that received in the U.S.

Another 1985 study, conducted by the privately-financed Center for Population Options, revealed that teenage child-bearing cost the U.S. $16.6 billion that year in the form of welfare payments. In the next 20 years, the Center reported, welfare benefits would be given to the 385,000 children who were the firstborn of adolescents. According to government health statistics, some 1.1 million teenage girls become pregnant each year and 513,000 continue their pregnancies to birth.

The Charlotte Observer
Charlotte, NC, January 15, 1981

One of the more troubling aspects of the sexual revolution and the introduction of the pill has been the reversal of responsibility among sexually active men and women. Sex involves two people, and both ought to be responsible for protecting themselves and their partners from unwanted consequences.

In no segment of society is the failure to understand that message potentially more tragic than among teenagers: One study last year found that in metropolitan areas, nearly 50 percent of girls 15-19 have had premarital intercourse. Increasingly, girls are seeking counseling about birth control, but seldom do their male partners even come along, much less accept responsibility for avoiding conception or venereal disease.

Megan McKewan, the nurse practitioner at a drop-in teen clinic run by Charlotte's Planned Parenthood, touched on that troubling aspect of teenage pregnancy recently. "We'd like to reach out more to the men," she said. "We're just not sure how to do that."

One way to encourage men to practice birth control, says a study called "Men and Family Planning," released last month by the Worldwatch Institute, is to take contraceptive education out of clinics and *to* men and boys. Worldwatch cited an example of that approach here in Dillon County, S.C.

"In the mid-'70s, (Dillon County) had some of the highest rates of venereal disease and out-of-wedlock births in the state," Worldwatch said. "To combat this, the local health department decided to encourage more men to use contraceptives. Male health educators toured the county on motorcycles carrying pamphlets and condoms in their saddlebags. Wherever men congregated, the educators stopped to talk ... distributing contraceptives when appropriate, and making referrals for venereal disease."

The results were striking: Although out-of-wedlock births increased throughout South Carolina, the rate dropped in Dillon County, especially among nonwhites.

Perhaps Planned Parenthood ought to swap ideas with health educators in Dillon County.

The Kansas City Times
Kansas City, MO, June 13, 1981

Taking practical steps to attack the city's high infant mortality rate and very vulnerable teen-age mothers, major health centers here have joined to provide free pregnancy tests and maternal counseling. As many as 10,000 teens may be checked annually.

Children born to very young mothers are considered by medical professionals to be high-risk infants, with the young women's own incomplete growth and ignorance about proper personal nutrition and health care heightening chances of premature births. It is vitally important that these young mothers receive prenatal care as early as possible to reduce the odds against their babies. Problems of how to care for an infant, finances, housing, social responsibility and inadequate sexual information must be considered; guidance for the future is often needed, particularly concerning the teen's educational status. In Greater Kansas City, 2,500 girls 17 years old or younger became pregnant in 1979, and high school so interrupted may never be finished.

Sharing in the venture to do the tests are the Wayne Miner Neighborhood Health Center, Swope Parkway Comprehensive Health Center, the Kansas City Family Planning Clinic and Truman Medical Center. Adolescent Services Corp. administers the service which will include after-test referral to a private or public prenatal clinic or providing family planning information.

Considering the large number of teens who are already sexually active and the city's high infant mortality rate, the new service fills a gap in preventive health care that will be more than a paper cure, something young, unready and often frightened girls can use just by stepping inside the clinic door. It will be good help for them. And because of that, it is good for Kansas City.

Los Angeles Times
Los Angeles, CA, November 29, 1983

Four of ten girls who are now 14 years old will be pregnant before they are 20. For most of them it is not that they know nothing of birth control. It is rather that they believe that pregnancy happens to other people, not to them. Or that they will not admit in any public way that they are sexually active. Or that they feel that they cannot talk to their parents—who, they fear, will certainly find out if they visit a family-planning clinic. These are the young people who must be reached if the epidemic of teen-age pregnancies is to be curbed.

It is hard to describe to people who are not much more than children themselves the economic and emotional hardships that they impose on themselves by becoming parents before they are ready. Hard, for example, to persuade them that pregnancy often means giving up the dreams of education or even of getting a job or having a stable home life. But organizations like Planned Parenthood Federation of America are renewing efforts to counsel young men and young women about their family-planning options and the ways in which their decisions can alter their lives. Both boys and girls must be reached if there is to be hope that teen-agers will understand responsible sexuality.

Despite efforts to counsel both young men and women, there is no question that the heaviest burden is on the young women because they are the ones who get pregnant and all too often are the ones who must bring up the children on their own. Their prospects are dim: incomes of nearly 40% of all families headed by women—and that includes many teen-age mothers—fall below the poverty level. The figure is much higher for families headed by black women. Fewer than half of teen-age mothers finish high school, and their income is half that of women who give birth after age 20. There are no statistics that measure the problems that a single parent, inexperienced in life herself, will face in trying to raise a child alone.

Because young people often are better able to grasp the health risks of an early pregnancy than the economic ones, that is where the emphasis is often placed in counseling. What Planned Parenthood tells young people is that teen-age mothers are 92% more likely to be anemic and 23% more likely to suffer from complications that accompany premature birth than are mothers who give birth in their early 20s. Recent statistics also show that the maternal death rate among mothers under 15 is 2½ times that among women who give birth when they are 20 to 24. The children of teen-age mothers are at risk as well, with an infant death rate twice that of children whose mothers are in their 20s.

Dr. Shirley VanLieu, director of education and counseling for Planned Parenthood-Los Angeles, says that there are two approaches that should be more fully used in trying to reach young people:

The first is that parents can and should be the best sex educators. They can help teen-agers sort through the conflicting messages that society sends them about sexuality—that is, that they should "be free" and yet chaste or careful. To help parents learn what to tell their children and how best to tell them, Planned Parenthood is seeking to work with local churches and synagogues to organize discussion groups for the adults.

The second approach involves helping teen-agers who want to practice birth control but still believe that their parents will find out if they visit a family-planning clinic. While Planned Parenthood wants young people to talk to their parents, it is also stressing the confidentiality of any counseling. The damage of recent federal threats to impose "squeal rules" to inform parents when their children seek birth-control devices has yet to be totally undone.

The efforts to reduce teen-age pregnancy deserve the widest possible support because those pregnancies too often untrack lives for years, if not forever. It is a high price that need not be paid if guidance and understanding are readily available in the home and in the community.

SYRACUSE HERALD-JOURNAL
Syracuse, NY, June 10, 1981

The following chart mirrors the heart-breaking and heart-warming experiences of 1,541 teen-agers (15 to 19 years old) in Syracuse and 19 Onondaga County towns. The figures represent the number of pregnancies and abortions reported for that age group in 1979.

The totals are given in summary form, as well, for Central New York.

We should look at these numbers with compassion and, in many cases, with joy.

And we should look at them, not ignore them.

In the words of this newspaper's reporter, Jane Rhodes Lewis, the report, "Adolescent Pregnancy in Onondaga County," led the Community Health Information and Planning Services committee to field 23 proposals.

Specifically, the committee advised "all interested parties ... to encourage school

Teenage Pregnancies and Abortions in Central New York, 1979

Town or City	Pregnancies	Abortions	Abortion Percentage
Camillus	53	42	80.8%
Cicero	74	42	56.8
Clay	146	80	54.8
Dewitt	54	38	70.4
Elbridge	19	8	42.1
Fabius	6	3	50.0
Geddes	38	28	73.7
Lafayette	22	15	68.2
Lysander	45	16	35.6
Manlius	62	40	64.5
Marcellus	13	7	53.8
Onondaga	45	30	66.7
Otisco	1	0	0.0
Pompey	10	5	50.0
Salina	86	53	61.6
Skaneateles	6	3	50.0
Spafford	2	0	0.0
Syracuse	860	363	42.2
Tully	6	3	50.0
Van Buren	36	16	44.4
Onondaga County	1586	794	50.1
Central New York	4737	1903	40.2

Source: Onondaga County, data from Birth Records, compiled by Community Health and Planning Service.

Chart by Peter Allen

boards and administrators to provide comprehensive family education in elementary, middle and high schools."

CHIPS launched the task force because pregnancy between 10 and 19 years of age is happening far beyond that of previous years, say a decade ago.

CHIPS feels, and the committee verified, that information and instruction are lacking for the young people.

Agreed that this legal fact of life — and death — shouldn't be swept away by the wings of rumor, the trend alarms us as it alarms the health planners, school administrators and interested parents.

The CHIPS task force recommended more schooling about health, boy-girl relationships, offering of more advice and medical care plus day care, with a full-time director to ride herd on their "creation."

The community must respond, beyond a doubt, in and out of schools and social agencies.

That means offering continued schooling for the pregnant child, making certain medical care is at hand, providing not only advice but financial help when there's need.

Summaries of the report as published failed, however, to mention a prime resource which should be exploited first; namely, teen-agers' parents.

Teen-age pregnancy isn't fully and finally a community responsibility.

It's a responsibility first of the teens involved and secondly, both sets of parents.

We should tender information and counseling to parents BEFORE a child reaches dating age. They are the No. 1 source of strength and support — and if not, should be — among those in the schools and social agencies engaged also in helping teens grow up.

▽   ▽

If parents don't care, the community can't do much. But, the community, primarily schools, its churches, the social agencies, must try.

The task force debated also whether to advise teens to turn to their doctors for abortion advice as a means to ending their condition.

The task force concentrated on prevention rather than "responding to the pregnancy after the fact," reported Dr. Jessica Cohen, who advised the committee.

"The charge of the study was not to look at that particular issue, but services in general," she said. "We didn't want decisions based on the prevailing arguments over abortion."

Quite right.

As the statistical summary indicates, with 755 adolescents deciding to have their babies out of 1,541 reported pregnancies in 1979, the abortion word has gotten about in the city and the country, among all income levels.

The task force pointed us in the right direction and by "us," we mean the community, specifically, parents of the teen-agers involved.

The Chattanooga Times
Chattanooga, TN, March 27, 1983

The problem of teen-age pregnancies is one with broad ramifications in our society. It cannot be addressed effectively by "squealing" to young Susie's parents that their daughter has been given birth control pills or by political preachments about the breakdown of morality among the young. But it must be addressed, and Chattanooga Excel is sponsoring a program which offers a positive and constructive approach to this difficult issue.

Excel has organized a series of seminars on teen-age pregnancy for sophomores and juniors at Howard High School. By the middle of April, each student will have attended three seminars, two conducted by Family and Children's Services and a third by the Task Force for the Prevention of Handicapping Conditions. With films and lectures, the seminars will give students the unvarnished truth about the consequences of unwanted pregnancies, for both the teen-age mother and the teen-age father. The truth is not pretty

One out of every 10 teen-age girls in the United States becomes pregnant each year; in Tennessee it's worse: The figure is one in five. And while teen-agers account for one-third of all abortions performed in the United States, most of the adolescent girls who become pregnant have their babies; 96 percent keep them. As one Excel seminar leader stated recently, "When a child has a child we have two children in trouble." Dramatizing that statement is this statistic:

In Hamilton County in 1982, 29 babies were born to girls between the ages of 10 and 14.

Pregnancy is not only psychologically damaging to adolescents; it presents a significant health risk. Teen-age mothers die in childbirth twice as often as mothers in the 20 to 35 age range, and their babies are much more likely to have physical deficiencies. Infants born to teen-age mothers are two to three times more likely to die in the first year than are those born to mothers in the optimum childbearing years. Further, in part at least because teen-agers are not prepared for the responsibility of parenthood, there is a high rate of child abuse among adolescent mothers. And these child-mothers, who tend to drop out of school, become virtually locked into a lifetime pattern of poverty.

It is essential that the rising problem of teen-age pregnancies become a community priority for it affects us all — the adolescent mother, her child and the society which must grapple with their needs, the long-term problems which arise from children raising children and the effective condemnation of these families to the lowest rung of the economic ladder. The Chattanooga Urban League has slated this problem as a focus for future programs, and Chattanooga Excel has undertaken a commendable initiative to combat it. These and other efforts deserve full community support.

DAYTON DAILY NEWS
Dayton, OH, May 19, 1983

Teenage pregnancy is rarely a happy event. It is filled with loneliness, financial insecurity, and medical risks.

The problem is getting those facts across to teenagers inundated in the culture. The local Citizen's Task Force on Teenage Pregnancy hopes to make at least a dent of awareness with Teenage Pregnancy Awareness Week which ends Sunday.

In Montgomery County last year, 1,453 females under 20 years gave birth. Thirty-three of them were below 14. Planned Parenthood puts the average age for first sexual activity at 16.

For teenagers who become pregnant, the majority won't finish high school with their friends. Some will get diplomas at a later date when they find they can't get jobs without one.

That means a lot of those teenage mothers and their infants will need public assistance. That costs taxpayers. Last year in Montgomery County, the figure was $2,550 for prenatal checkups, delivery, and postpartum care plus $2,592 for the first year's public assistance for mother and child.

If teenagers aren't impressed by the fact that babies are expensive, the Task Force is hoping to make them aware of the health risks involved.

Local and national statistics show that the younger the mother, the greater the probability of a low birth-weight baby. And the smaller the newborn, the greater its health problems.

The same corollation is true for the expect-

The Citizen's Task Force on Teenage Pregnancy is waging a needed campaign to get facts across to teenagers.

ant teenager. The younger she is, the more her health is at risk — 2.5 times higher death risk than for woman over 20.

That is made worse by girls who won't admit they might be pregnant and put off getting medical care until late in the pregnancy.

The Task Force has set up a crisis hotline — 278-5846 — and is encouraging teenagers and parents alike to use it for help in dealing with a pregnancy or in preventing one. No judgments will be made. In fact, callers may remain anonymous. The Task Force simply wants teenagers to realize that there's more to sex than the act and that those choosing to be sexually active must realize the responsibilities they are assuming.

"YOU'RE ON YOUR OWN, KID, ONCE YOU'RE BORN!"

FORT WORTH STAR-TELEGRAM
Fort Worth, TX, May 9, 1983

Almost hidden in a Census Bureau report on child-bearing trends is a time bomb of enormous social impact.

The report finds that American women of child-bearing age are having an average of fewer than two children each, reflecting the increasingly higher educational level of women and their greater tendency to embark on careers outside the home.

But the report also found an enormous increase in child-bearing by unmarried women and in the number of women who were pregnant or had already given birth before marriage.

Such marriages, the report's author points out, are the most likely to end in divorce. Single parent households, whether the result of divorce or children born out of wedlock where no marriage is involved, and households in which a mother is most often the parent, are notable in poverty statistics. Indeed, such households stood out in the needs assessment report pinpointing poverty in Fort Worth last year.

Beyond any question of morality or sexual license is the question of what an increasing number of such households means for the nation's future in terms of societal problems such as unemployment, crime, perpetuation of an underclass and expensive welfare programs, etc.

America, even while more couples than before — particularly in the more educated segment of the population — are planning their families and having fewer children, may be thoughtlessly propagating itself into some problems that will cost dearly both in terms of dollars and human wastage.

AKRON BEACON JOURNAL
Akron, OH, January 23, 1984

NOT ONLY "bad" girls get pregnant. Certainly many of the more than 1.2 million teen-age pregnancies that occur each year in the United States involve "good" girls, placed in that condition by "good" boys.

For a complex variety of reasons, more and more of these pregnant teen-agers are deciding to keep their babies. They face tremendous social and economic handicaps as a result of that decision. Nonetheless, it is a choice that they are making in record numbers.

Arlene Pfeiffer, then, is hardly unique. This unwed mother, a Pennsylvania high-school senior, chose to keep her infant daughter and raise the child with her family's help.

What makes Ms. Pfeiffer special is that she is not keeping quiet while the local school board boots her out of the high school's National Honor Society. School officials deny that her pregnancy was the reason; they claim she has not maintained the leadership and character required for membership.

Ms. Pfeiffer, however, *has* maintained the 3.2 grade-point average required by the society, a feat in itself considering the profound changes in her life over the past year. She is a past president of the student government and ranks 14th out of a senior class of 164 students.

The decision to expose her life — many would say her mistake — to the nation could not have been easy for the teen-age mother. But since she has, we offer another opinion of this young woman.

While other teen-age girls are busy dreaming of the senior prom, Ms. Pfeiffer is taking care of the baby she brought into the world. She has accepted responsibility for her actions. And she is determined to finish school and build a life for her child.

Ms. Pfeiffer is hardly a disgrace to the National Honor Society. But she is a visible reminder of what occurs every year in nearly every high school in the country. Students get pregnant.

Teen-age fathers — even members of the National Honor Society — have the luxury of remaining invisible. They also can easily shrug off the unplanned consequences of teen-age sex.

It is sad that this western Pennsylvania school district chose to punish a young girl who fully accepts her role as a single parent and as an adult. Plug on, Arlene Pfeiffer, with or without your National Honor Society pin.

The Philadelphia Inquirer
Philadelphia, PA, August 29, 1984

In New Jersey, the head of the Family Planning Unit of the State Department of Health characterizes the problem as "an epidemic." The reference is to the alarming number of births among unmarried teenagers. In many areas of the state births among unwed teenage mothers far outstrip those among young married women.

In 1982, in Newark for example, there were 3,495 births out of wedlock, compared with 2,134 among the married. In Atlantic City, unwed mothers gave birth to 466 babies during the same period young married women gave life to 208. And in Camden there were 1,393 births out of wedlock and 685 births among teenage women with husbands. Trenton's figures reveal the same disturbing trend as 1,016 single teenagers gave birth compared with 795 for young married couples.

The growth of teenage pregnancies is hardly a phenomenon peculiar to New Jersey. The tragedy of kids having kids poses problems for Pennsylvania and every other state. Many of these little "families" wind up on public assistance, increasing the burden of taxpayers.

State health records indicate that of 98,225 births in New Jersey, 21,315 — or 21.7 percent — were born out of wedlock during 1982, the last year for which complete records are available. About 75 percent of all of the babies born to women 19 years old and younger were born to unwed mothers. Officials have been working to stem the tide but are hampered by a lack of funding and softening attitudes, toward young mothers without husbands.

Cutbacks in government funding of family planning agencies have denied medical contraceptive services and information to an estimated 186,000 women in New Jersey, most of whom are poor. These women are continually at risk of unwanted pregnancies. Officials indicate $1 million in federal funds in New Jersey has been lost to budget trimming.

It seems obvious that girls — and boys — should be made aware of the risks and consequences of early teenage pregnancies *before* they reach that age. To do that effectively would require a special effort and considerable coordination between the public schools and public and private social agencies to provide the essential information to the children — and their parents. It would be difficult, but it could be done with commitment and leadership from the top levels of the public and private sectors.

In the short run, funding cutbacks may save money. But over the long haul, government will have to pay enormous sums to support the products of a burgeoning birthrate among teenagers unprepared to care for themselves, let alone their children.

However, several states including New Jersey currently enjoy sizable budget surpluses. It would be wise to invest some of it in family planning assistance programs. In reducing teenage pregnancies, an ounce of prevention would be worth far more than a pound of cure.

The Record
Hackensack, NJ, November 6, 1984

Teen-age pregnancy remains one of the most vexing and far-reaching social problems in this country. Despite increasing public awareness and public and private birth-control counseling efforts, young people continue to have children at an alarming rate. Last year more than 1 million teen-age girls became pregnant, three quarters of them unintentionally.

What are the consequences of unwanted pregnancy? For some young people, it's fatal. The risk of death from pregnancy is 2½ times greater for teen-agers than for grown women. Children born to young teens — 15 and under — are twice as likely to die in infancy.

Half of all teen-age pregnancies end in abortion; more than one third of all abortions are performed on teen-age girls. Abortion can be painful, and can impose psychological burdens that will stay with these girls for life.

And of those teen-agers who carry their pregnancy to term, many end up living in poverty. Fewer than half of all teen-age mothers finish high school, meaning that many jobs will be closed to them forever. Six of every 10 mothers on welfare gave birth in their teens; 70 percent will eventually be single mothers.

There are ways to stop this epidemic. Sex education, distasteful as it may be to some adults, has proved an effective way to teach teen-agers the unhappy consequences of pregnancy. And birth-control counseling must be made widely available.

Finally, the government needs to do more. Title X of the Public Health Service Act underwrites the work of family-planning and counseling agencies like Planned Parenthood. But since 1981 the Reagan administration has steadily chopped away at the Title X budget, and it placed unreasonable strings on programs receiving federal funds. In its infamous "squeal rule," it insisted that parents be notified when their teen-agers got birth-control material from these clinics — an obvious discouragement to those seeking help. Happily, a federal court has nullified the squeal rule.

The Reagan administration has offered its own answer to the teen-age pregnancy problem — a $30-million adolescent family-life project. The idea is to minimize teen-age pregnancies by promoting abstinence through government publications and programs in the schools.

If this approach works, it can't be faulted. But it cannot take the place of support for family-planning clinics. That's why Title X remains our best hope. Money spent to prevent unwanted pregnancies is bread on the water: It comes back to us in the form of better-educated, healthier teens who have a better chance at becoming productive adults. What better investment can we make in the next generation?

THE MILWAUKEE JOURNAL
Milwaukee, WI, September 16, 1984

Statistics alone can scarcely convey the tragedy of teenage pregnancy, but there is a shocking force to the numbers: Nationally, more than 11 million young women between the ages of 13 and 19 become pregnant each year. Wisconsin has about 7,700 adolescent pregnancies annually. Here, as elsewhere, an estimated 30% to 40% end in abortion.

Wisconsin is launching a major new effort to break that sad cycle. Using two federal grants totaling more than $1.3 million, the state plans to underwrite programs designed to educate teens about the problems of unwed pregnancy and to prepare pregnant adolescents for jobs that will enable them to support their children. Schools, local governments and private, non-profit agencies have been invited to submit proposals for funding.

Some programs already exist, but they are often small and poorly funded. The state's help, which will extend for 2½ years, is especially welcome in that respect — and also because it is wisely targeted at high-risk youngsters: those between the ages of 10 and 18 who are living in low-income families with a history of early pregnancy.

The need for more effective programs is dramatized by the pattern of health problems, poverty and dependency that accompanies adolescent childbearing. Babies born to underage mothers are two times more likely to die within their first year than infants born to mothers in their 20s. Low birth weight (a major cause of infant mortality), birth injuries and mental retardation are also twice as prevalent among the youngest of these mothers. The reasons range from poor nutrition and the lack of good prenatal care to biological immaturity.

Studies show that early childbearing tends to frustrate educational opportunities. The majority of teenage parents never finish high school. Two-thirds of the families headed by mothers aged 14-25 live below the poverty level; nearly one-half of all federal payments in Aid to Families with Dependent Children go to households in which the woman gave birth for the first time as a teenager. In one month last spring, 1,125 of Wisconsin's 18,500 female welfare recipients between 14 and 19 were at least six months pregnant.

But the burden of prevention ought not fall exclusively on young women. We hope that some of the new initiative will focus on teaching young men — who are often overlooked — to shoulder their share of the responsibility in both preventing pregnancy and in parenting.

The time is long since past when the nation — or the state, for that matter — can afford to debate whether educators should even talk about pregnancy for fear it might encourage teenage sexual activity. Kids *are* sexually active, with as many as 8 of 10 men and 7 of 10 women having had intercourse before age 19, according to some national studies.

Parents have reason to be dismayed by adolescent sexual precocity. But wishing things were otherwise, in a society where jeans are sold for their sex appeal rather than durability, is not enough. The state is right to do all it can to prevent more children from having children.

THE LINCOLN STAR
Lincoln, NE, April 2, 1985

When you have a problem, you discuss it. The United States has a very large problem with teen-age pregnancies. Yet we refuse to discuss it or sex education or abortion without an often disturbing element of extremism clouding the issues.

A study of teen-age pregnancy in 37 nations by the Alan Guttmacher Institute has clearly outlined this problem for us, in terms we can no longer ignore. The United States has an alarmingly high pregnancy rate among teenagers aged 15 to 19 — 96 per 1,000. Of five countries selected for comparison because of their similarities to the United States in terms of values and industrial development, Great Britain came next with a teen pregnancy rate of 45 per 1,000.

Even when the rate excludes black teens, it still is nearly twice as high as Great Britain's. And the United States is the only country in which the rate was increasing. The United States, with a teen abortion rate higher than some countries' pregnancy rates, also was alone in its conservative attitude toward discussing sex and birth control.

The researchers partly blamed this on the peculiarly American notion that discussing sex education somehow encourages teen-age sex. Yet the local Planned Parenthood, when it surveyed teens aged 15-19 who visited the Lincoln clinic seeking birth control, found the vast majority already were sexually active.

TEENS IN the United States and the other five Western nations tended to become sexually active at about the same age and at about the same rate regardless of their society's attitude on premarital sex. Realistically, we may have no control over the sexual activities of our teen-agers, but we can put a lid on the skyrocketing pregnancy rate. Better to provide the facts — and the birth control — than to continue to let our children have children. A high teen pregnancy rate is more a health problem than a moral crisis. Its consequences for our society are long-term and negative.

But providing education is not enough. Contraceptives need to be available in the places teen-agers go, not hidden behind drug store counters nor locked away in doctor's offices.

Many European nations dispense birth control pills without the physical exam required in the United States. We might waive the exam for younger women, whose health risks from the pill are considerably fewer than for older women. In so doing we would drop the barrier the exam creates for some teens.

We have allowed the acceptability of sex on TV and in the theater, now we must show our children they have to take responsibility if they are sexually active.

ARKANSAS, which once claimed the nation's highest teen-age birth rate, learned the value of sex education after the Arkansas Family Planning Council began offering courses in junior and senior high schools in 1977. A study released a little over a year ago found its teen-age birth rate had dropped 10 percent overall, with the politically conservative northwest area, where the schools had resisted the classes, showing a slight rise.

In response to a Phil Donahue program on birth control ads we received the following from a Nebraska woman, "I was one of the few who was lucky enough to have a mom who trusted me. Mom accepted the fact that I was in high school, dating and could become pregnant if not well informed. We have a relationship not many mothers and daughters or mothers and sons are fortunate enough to have. We are best friends. She trusted me to do what is right for me. She told me about sex and birth control. She did not feel that by giving the information that it was a 'stamp of approval' to go ahead."

Discussing sex and its consequences no more gives that "stamp of approval" to children than ignoring the subject will make it go away.

Pittsburgh Post-Gazette
Pittsburgh, PA, June 23, 1984

Although some manage to carry the burden admirably, a teen-age girl who becomes pregnant usually has an extremely hard time coping with the difficult realities of being a parent. A teen-age boy who is equally responsible for the situation, however, more often escapes a permanent obligation.

Because of that double standard, the male's responsibility for personal sexual behavior tends to be underestimated among teen-agers. So a new National Urban League campaign to make black male adolescents aware of the responsibilities of fatherhood has an extremely important goal to achieve. Hopefully the cautions contained in broadcast messages aimed at the teen-age music market will be embraced by black and white teen-agers alike.

These messages, featuring popular singers James Ingram and Shalamar's Howard Hewitt, emphasize the negative consequences of being a teen-age parent. The campaign is spurred by growing concern over the shocking rate of infant mortality among black Americans, a statistic with an important relationship to teen-age pregnancies.

Because the occurrence of black infant mortality in Pittsburgh is extremely high, this community needs to make a committed effort to address that problem. And, because contemporary radio can only do so much, the schools, as always, also need to play an active role in helping sexually active adolescents to avoid teen-age pregnancies.

THE ATLANTA CONSTITUTION
Atlanta, GA, November 21, 1985

There is much to like in Wisconsin's new comprehensive package of laws aimed at treating the wrenching social malady of teen-age pregnancies. But, because it had to satisfy both the state's pro-life and pro-choice camps — a tricky requirement — it is a creature of compromise. In this case, too many cooks have spoiled the stew.

That is regrettable. The package, passed by the Legislature unanimously and signed into law last week, wisely appropriates funds for sex education in the schools, repeals restrictions on the advertising and sale of contraceptives and allocates $1 million for use in pregnancy counseling.

On the downside, however, is what is being called the grandparent-liability law, a misguided attempt to make teenagers communicate better with their parents and force parents to take a stronger role in teaching their children about sex and its consequences. The goal is laudable, but the approach is problematic.

The law makes parents financially responsible for the unwanted offspring produced by their teen-age children. The parents of both a boy and a girl who produce unwanted children will be equally responsible for the upbringing of the offspring. *Theoretically*, teenagers will be more careful because they will be fearful of placing such a heavy financial burden on their parents.

The reality may be quite different. Some rebellious teenagers could use the law as a means for getting back at their parents. And, worse, with parents facing liability, the pressure for pregnant teen-age girls to seek abortions is bound to increase.

Sure, it is difficult to put together a coherent, measured program to deal effectively with such a tough problem, especially when so many divergent groups have a hand in it. Yet it almost worked in this case. The grandparent liability law is a small part of the total package, and mars the whole, but the rest is a sober, innovative model for dealing with a problem whose deleterious effects are being felt by communities across this country.

Roanoke Times & World-News
Roanoke, VA, November 4, 1984

WASHINGTON Mayor Marion Barry decided to do something about the epidemic of teen-age pregnancies in his city. Last May he appointed a panel to investigate the problem. Recently the panel held a public hearing at a high-school auditorium that was filled with 800 teen-agers.

Among the most effective witnesses were teen-aged mothers, who told their peers what it was like to become pregnant and shoulder the responsibilities of motherhood.

"I had to learn the hard way," said Sherita Dreher, 18-year-old mother of a 2-year-old child. "My parent never taught me to use contraceptives."

That last remark illustrates the depth of the problem. It should not have been necessary for Sherita's parent to teach her about contraceptives. Sherita should have been taught that premarital sex is wrong and leads to trouble — especially for young girls who are not old enough to fend for themselves. The most effective contraceptive is an authoritative "No."

The promiscuous girl *should* be taught to use contraceptives — as a last resort to prevent unwanted pregnancy. But the surest form of birth control is abstinence — and abstinence is not an unreasonable thing to expect of teen-agers, provided the idea of sexual morality has been part of their upbringing since early childhood.

Joye Jackson, a 16-year-old mother of two, practiced birth control, but it didn't work.

"The first time I laid down I got pregnant," she told the hearing. "The second time I used an I.U.D. and still got pregnant."

Joye and Sherita apparently come from an environment that takes a morally neutral view of premarital sex.

"Most girls get pregnant so they can get a welfare check," said Joye. "I get $236 a month. What's that? I can't buy baby's milk or clothes to put on my back."

While the welfare-check motive applies primarily to the ghetto kids who are caught in the welfare cycle, the idea that sex is okay so long as you use contraceptives permeates middle-class society as well. Once the unwed girl who had lost her virginity was considered damaged goods. That may have been unfair to many a "nice girl" who was penalized excessively for one or two departures from the strait and narrow. But now many college girls are ashamed to admit they're virgins. The girl who wants to save herself for marriage is considered somehow old-fashioned or abnormal.

Popular entertainment — movies and television — look benignly and romantically upon fornication, fostering the impression that it's okay. Children from pre-teens upward imbibe this amorality from the tube and screen and see sex as a pleasurable and sophisticated form of relationship.

Barry's task force will launch an anti-pregnancy slogan contest in city schools as a way to increase awareness about the ills of pre-marital sex. The panel will also urge ministers to preach against premarital sex.

But the important task is to convince parents of their responsibility to supervise their children's reading, viewing and playing habits, and other activities that go into forming their moral perspectives.

Barry passes on some good advice to teen-aged girls: "Keep on saying 'no.' To those young men who don't want to hear no, tell them to 'get the heck out of here.'"

But the teen-aged girl will not say "no" unless she has benefited from a home environment in which the importance of sexual morality is stressed and pre-marital sex is looked upon as not only unwise but also wrong.

Our moral mentors have somehow allowed us to slip away from the attitude of pre-marital sex as morally offensive. Our teen-agers therefore are negotiating dangerous waters without a strong moral rudder to steer by. The result is appalling: 560,000 teen-age girls giving birth each year, with many others taking the morally repugnant path to the abortion clinic.

Children born to to teen-agers frequently are premature and are more likely to have serious health problems. The birth of out-of-wedlock children to indigent girls pushes up the cost of social welfare.

The girl must learn to say no. So must the parent when faced with questions concerning permissible reading, viewing and listening matter for teens and pre-teens. By the time the girl is asking for contraceptives it's a bit late to start preaching sermons on chastity.

THE TENNESSEAN
Nashville, TN, November 23, 1985

THIS week, *The Tennessean* is running a special series on an all too common topic — teenage pregnancy.

Two reporters, Ms. Renee Vaughn and Ms. Laura Milner, have spent the last few weeks interviewing health care professionals, educators, and community activists. They have examined the statistics on teenage pregnancy in Tennessee and in the United States, and reviewed the various agencies that provide information or help to pregnant teens. They have also talked with many of the young girls who make up those statistics.

Currently, 45 teens get pregnant every day in Tennessee. Half of those pregnancies end in abortion; 45% of the girls who give birth will be unwed, and 80% will drop out of school. It is not uncommon for 14- and 15-year-olds to get pregnant. Last year, four 11-year-old girls gave birth in Davidson County.

Those statistics are undoubtedly disconcerting to parents and educators, but they also should concern the public and public officials. After all, how many of those unwed teenage mothers or their babies are going to suffer health problems because of poor prenatal care and diet? How many of those uneducated mothers are going to depend on public assistance for housing, food, and other necessities? And how can an unwed, uneducated mother ever offer her children a chance for a better life?

The high numbers of pregnant teens might be surprising, given that today's young teenagers are generally considered to be the most sophisticated, best educated, most mature generation ever.

But for all their maturity — either real or imagined — they are still children. Many of them believe their peers more than their parents. Some just block out what they don't want to hear, and others literally don't know what they are doing. And while they might think that having sex is a grownup thing to do, they are often not grown up enough to face the consequences.

There are many agencies in Nashville that deal with teenage pregnancy on different levels — some by offering free or inexpensive pre-natal care, adoption counseling, birth control or abortion services. Every one of those services provides a necessary, valuable service to this community. Every pregnant teenager, her boyfriend, and their parents have some tough, personal questions to answer, and there is no absolute right and wrong for every situation.

Before teenagers can get the information they need to make responsible decisions, their parents and the public must first be responsible. Teenagers who have sexual relations with no thought about pregnancy are uninformed and careless. But parents and educators who ignore children's sexuality are being hopelessly naive. ◆

The Oregonian
Portland, OR,
December 26, 1985

The Wisconsin Legislature's pioneering effort to control the burgeoning problem of teen-age pregnancy has captured the imagination of other legislatures around the country. But wholesale adoption of similar legislation in other states would be premature.

Written by a committee evenly divided between opponents and supporters of abortion, Wisconsin's month-old Abortion Prevention and Family Responsibility Act provides for the tried and proven method of reducing the teen-age pregnancy rate: sex education and counseling in the public schools. More important, it also provides the money to pay for these programs. Recognizing that an unwanted teen-age pregnancy is an even greater social burden than termination of a pregnancy, the new law even provides for abortions without parental consent.

These provisions represent a pragmatic recognition that most parents cannot control the sexual activities of their teen-age children. At the same time, this law increases the incentive for parents to try to exercise control. The law increases the parental burden of responsibility by imposing upon them the legal obligation to support their minor child's child.

This so-called "grandparents liability clause" is the law's most innovative and most controversial provision. It may also be its most impractical. Well-intentioned supporters hope parents, faced with the financial consequences of a teen-age pregnancy, will take a more active role in reducing their teen-agers' sexual activity. Other provisions of the law, however, already concede that there is only so much a parent can do. If the grandparents liability clause is to reduce the teen-age pregnancy rate at all, it may do so through increased abortions rather than prevention.

And what about the pregnant teen-ager who doesn't want an abortion? The grandparents liability law puts her and her baby at greater risk. No longer will her income, or lack of income, be the sole determining factor for public assistance eligibility. Now, the incomes of her parents and her boyfriend's parents will also be taken into consideration. If the combined incomes are deemed sufficient to support a grandchild, the teen-age mother will not qualify for welfare.

That's fine for teen-age mothers whose parents can afford and are willing to accept their responsibility to deal with the consequences of their children's behavior. Teen-agers whose parents are willing but financially unable will also be protected.

But there always will be parents who are able but unwilling to provide support. It sadly is not uncommon for parents to throw an unwed, pregnant daughter out of their house. While the state goes through the lengthy process of extracting their legal dues from them, the teen-age mother and her baby may be cast adrift with no resources at all. The intended beneficiary of grandparents liability clause could end up being its unintended victim.

THE SAGINAW NEWS
Saginaw, MI, April 9, 1985

Nearly 10 percent of America's teen-agers are parents — children having children.

That's more than double the rate in England, France and Canada. It's almost triple the rate in supposedly sexually liberal Sweden.

And leaders in politics, education and religion are divided on the question of what to do about it.

"Some teens will insist on experimenting with sex," says the newspaper USA Today. "They need birth control advice. The alternative is an abortion or an unwanted baby."

European countries have lower teen pregnancy rates because birth control is readily available, asserts the Alan Guttmacher Institute, an organization which promotes family planning, but, as do we, postulates birth control as an alternative to abortions.

But the Rev. Jerry Falwell, who otherwise makes more sense than liberals often give him credit for, says education in birth control "is like offering a cookbook as a cure to people who are trying to lose weight."

In other words, says Falwell, more teens will engage in sex if they know how to prevent pregnancy.

We disagree. If a teen follows Falwell's advice and abstains for moral reasons, knowledge of birth control methods should make no difference.

That's why we support a "Plan A, Plan B" approach that mixes moral values with carefully designed programs of sex education.

Plan A should include efforts such as the new, statewide "Do Yourself A Favor, Save It For Later" campaign. Teens who control themselves — especially facing peer pressure and the sexual emphasis of modern entertainment and advertising — will be grateful later in life.

But for those who don't respond, Plan B — birth control advice — should serve as a backup to prevent unwanted pregnancies.

Teens often have stronger sexual urges than married adults who receive regular fulfillment. That's the way of nature. Those adults' message to teens should be: "Try to abstain, but if you fail, at least don't make a baby you don't want."

Falwell calls that "capitulation." We call it care and concern about the unavoidable facts of life.

Chicago Tribune
Chicago, IL, April 3, 1985

The same week the Alan Guttmacher Institute reported that the United States has the highest teenage pregnancy rate of all developed countries, "Us" magazine ran a cover story on single celebrity mothers and their "love babies." That single-mother trendiness helps point up some of the flaws in the teen pregnancy study.

There's no question about the magnitude of the problem. American 15- to 19-year-olds have a pregnancy rate of 96 per 1,000—more than twice that of any comparable country. The birth rate for younger girls is four times that of the next highest nation. And the U.S. abortion rate for teens is as high or higher than the combined abortion and birth rates in comparable nations.

But the conclusions the Guttmacher Institute draws from its statistics are open to argument. It says teenage pregnancy rates are lower in countries that are more open about sex, accept teenage sexual activity and provide more sex education and free or low-cost contraceptives than the U.S. It also sees a relationship between the high incidence of teen pregnancy and inequitable distribution of income in the U.S. and what it calls this country's "high degree of religiosity."

Other industrial nations make confidential, free (or virtually free) contraceptive services and free or subsidized abortion easily available to teens, the study points out. It argues that experience in these countries shows that young teens are not too immature to use birth control effectively, that welfare does not induce teens to have babies and that concern should be directed at reducing pregnancy, not lowering the level of teen sexual activity.

The institute recommends more openness about sex, family planning clinics associated with schools to provide free or low-cost contraceptives to all teens who want them, easing of restrictions on advertising nonprescription contraceptives, more encouragment for the use of the pill and more sex education.

The report notes that the United States is the only country where the incidence of teenage pregnancy has been increasing in recent years. But it conveniently neglects to mention that these years have also seen a spurt in sex education and easier availability of contraceptives and abortion—conditions that it claims reduce teen pregnancies. The increase in teen pregnancy has also occurred at a time when the "religiosity" of this country is declining.

The report fails to acknowledge that ignorance of contraception is not the only factor fueling the teenage pregnancy rate. A sort of single-mother chic is growing in the United States, not only among celebrities but also in some socio-economic and minority groups where many girls deliberately become pregnant—or at least do not consider a possible pregnancy enough of a problem to take contraception seriously.

What will trouble many parents and taxpayers, however, is the report's implications that this country should accept teenage sexual activity as a matter of fact, should not try to persuade even young adolescents to postpone sexual involvement and should supply contraceptives as readily as school books. The problem is much more complex than prescribing permissiveness-plus-the-pill and it can't be solved in isolation, without rethinking adult sexual values and behavior as well.

St. Paul Pioneer Press & Dispatch
St. Paul, MN, March 31, 1985

The most powerful emotion that emerges from even the briefest look at teen-age pregnancy in America has to be overwhelming sadness. Alarm, too? Yes, of course. But sadness most of all.

One phrase keeps surfacing — "children having children." Put a face on that. Then drape the child-mother in her most likely garment: the meager mantle of poverty that she may well wear for the rest of her life. And then hold on to that haunting image while looking hard at the statistics.

Statistics from a recent study by the Alan Guttmacher Institute in New York have broken into public awareness with sledgehammer impact. Some of the most stunning conclusions from that and other reports include these:

■ When the United States is compared with other developed nations, there is little difference in the rate of teen-age sexual activity; but both the pregnancy rate and the abortion rate are much higher for American girls than for those in England, Canada, France, Sweden or the Netherlands.

■ The greatest difference in birthrates between America and the other countries occurs in the youngest girls — those under 15. That is a devastating category in which to stand as the unquestioned, unhappy leader.

■ Census figures show that 50 percent of mothers under age 18 drop out of school; 30 percent are pregnant again within two years; many of them will never earn more than they did at age 16.

■ Nearly half of the federal AFDC budget goes to families that started with a mother in her teens.

■ A report from the Children's Defense Fund shows that teens are only half as likely as other mothers to get prenatal care, yet they are at greatest risk of low birthweight babies and maternal death. Good prenatal care costs about $600; the average cost to care for a baby with very low birthweight runs from $10,000 to $15,000.

Much can be done. None of it will be easy.

The first and most difficult task lies in the painful recognition that teens are sexually active, no matter how much distress that may cause their elders.

Shock and dismay won't help. Preaching won't help, either.

But there is still value in parents setting standards, and in being forthright and specific about how to say "no." There is also a point in helping teen-agers, boys and girls both, to take responsibility for their sexuality. There is a further point in revealing much more dramatically to teens the bleak consequences of unplanned adolescent pregnancy. There is a point in providing day care so that teen moms can stay in school. There is a final point — the most difficult — in making birth control more accessible to young people.

An excellent model program already exists in four St. Paul high schools: the Maternal and Infant Care/Adolescent Health Services Project. Clinics in the four schools offer broad health services for all students — as well as prenatal care and birth control counseling. The sweep of services, besides stressing overall health and wellness, means that no stigma is attached when a student walks into the clinic.

The project's most important goals are to prevent that first teen-age pregnancy; to avoid a second one if a first has occurred; to provide prenatal care as needed. Is it working? A single statistic is telling: The pregnancy rate has dropped 50 percent in those schools since the clinics opened, from 59 per thousand to 26 per thousand.

Some 70 percent of the students at the four schools use the clinics for one reason or another, all with signed consent forms from their parents. Setting up such a clinic in every junior and senior high school is an idea worthy of the most serious consideration.

Soul-searching adult responses of some kind are surely demanded by the pitiful image of the child-mother, robbed by crushing reality of any romantic notions she may once have held about bearing and bringing up her baby by herself.

TULSA WORLD
Tulsa, OK, March 30, 1985

A STUDY by the Alan Guttmacher Institute, which is allied with Planned Parenthood, ranks America first among six western nations in number of teen-age pregnancies and teen-age abortions.

Clearly, a strong, pragmatic approach to teen-age pregnancy is warranted, but will American parents support it?

The Guttmacher study clears up some myths about teen-age pregnancy in the U.S. First, the problem is not confined to the black population. True, black teenagers have higher pregnancy rates, but the rate among white teen-agers is far higher than for England, France, Canada, Sweden and Holland.

Second, the availability of welfare benefits does not correlate to pregnancy rates. In most of the other countries surveyed, single mothers receive greater welfare benefits than in the U.S.

What seems to account for the difference in pregnancy rates is the availability of birth control devices. Teenagers in Europe and Canada have greater access to birth control than in this country.

So one way to reduce teen-age pregnancy is to make birth control devices more readily available. But that idea will meet with strong resistence from those who argue that such a policy encourages sex.

That seems to leave an even more repugnant solution to the problem of teen-age pregnancy — abortion. That is the solution America is using now. The U.S. abortion rate for teen-agers is twice that of the other countries surveyed.

Clearly, our present "solution" is no solution at all.

THE LOUISVILLE TIMES
Louisville, KY, December 6, 1985

A photograph of a sad-eyed, pregnant teenager on the cover of *Time* magazine may not be the kind of publicity the girl and her hometown — Louisville — would normally want. Fifteen-year-old Angela Helton, however, deserves praise for having the courage to come forward, as does this community for receiving national attention for its successful education of "child" mothers.

Now the parent of a son, Angela is one of the million American teenagers, most of them unmarried, who get pregnant each year.

And the blonde, blue-eyed Angela is emblematic of the often ignored or unknown truth: The growing problem is hardly one for minorities alone. In fact, as the *Time* article noted, white American teenagers have nearly twice the pregnancy rate of their French and British counterparts and six times the Dutch rate. At the same time, European kids are just as sexually active.

Teenage pregnancy is clearly an *American* problem, and one that should alarm both advocates and opponents of readily available sex education and contraceptives. Ignorance and lack of caution are the cause of many of the pregnancies — and nearly half of them end in abortion.

For those that don't, there is the good chance that a life of missed opportunities, often leading to poverty, awaits both mother and offspring. But that need not be the case, if there were more programs, such as the one run by Jefferson County public schools, catering to teenage parents. Angela Helton and her family say *that's* the message they want *Time* readers to draw from her appearance in the publication.

It's a good one, offering the hope that counselors say is important if these same teenagers are to avoid another mistake.

Times-Colonist
Victoria, B.C., November 20, 1985

The statute passed by the state of Wisconsin recently endeavors to deal with a significant problem — teenage pregnancies — in a fundamentally unfair way.

The "grandparent liability law" makes the parents of teenagers who produce unplanned children financially responsible for them. The parents of both the teenage father and teenage mother are equally liable under this law, which was passed unanimously by the state legislature.

The idea is to wake up the parents of teenagers to their obligations. They either advise their children about sexual responsibility or they become financially responsible for the failure to do so.

One of the legislators offered this analogy to justify the law: "If a neighbor's son comes over to my home and breaks my window, his parents are liable — but if he pays a visit and my daughter gets pregnant, there's no liability at all."

Likely there are many parents who have failed to talk to their children about sexual responsibility — and to the extent this law pressures them to do so, it will have accomplished some good. But the law's assumption is that once talked to, all teenagers will become sexually responsible. That's nonsense. Some will; some won't. Even in those cases where parents have done their best, they will still be legally liable for their children's offspring — and that's not fair.

There is also a flaw in the analogy offered. If the neighbor's boy breaks a window, his parents are liable, but if he breaks into the house instead, then it is he who must face the consequences. That is because society wants young people held accountable for serious misbehavior — and unwanted pregnancy certainly qualifies.

Methods of helping young people understand their responsibilities (and helping parents to help them) are to be encouraged. But a law like this fails to acknowledge the numerous family situations which are beyond parental control.

DESERET NEWS
Salt Lake City, UT, April 1-2, 1985

When it comes to teen-age pregnancy, is it better to build a fence at the edge of the cliff or station an ambulance at the bottom of the precipice?

The debate seems to be heating up in Congress where Rep. Mickey Leland, D-Texas, and others are promoting a bill to provide money for services to pregnant teens. This "ambulance" group is opposing renewal of the Adolescent Family Life Act of 1981 that prohibits federal funds for abortion services and provides money for "fence-building" pilot projects to discourage teenage sex. The act stresses the importance of the family and adoption.

The administration supports renewal of the Family Life Act "fence." Dr. James Mason of the Public Health Service, former head of the Utah Department of Health, says the program is important in combatting the epidemic rate of teenage pregnancies.

But another piece of pending legislation, sponsored by Rep. Robert Garcia, D-N.Y., proposes "ambulance-type" protection — family planning services to teenagers, a euphemism for dissemination of birth control information and devices, plus restoration of Medicaid funding for abortion.

All of these proposals stem from the same problem — the alarming increase in teenage pregnancy in the U.S. In 1983, 514,000 babies were born to girls between the ages of 15 and 19. Nearly 10,000 babies were born to mothers under age 15.

Certainly, the problem must be dealt with. Doling out help to teenage mothers, however, is not going to stem the tide of pregnancies.

Just what concerns the federal government should have in assisting teen mothers is not clear. Welfare aid now is available to those who need it. Most school districts offer educational opportunities to those willing to accept them. Any other aid proposals from Washington ought to be carefully scrutinized to determine their necessity.

Psychologically, physically, morally, spiritually, and in every other way, the only fully acceptable answer is to strengthen the family and help teens find outlets other than sex for their abundant energies. Success will require the combined efforts of government, church, school and home.

The Cincinnati Post
*Cincinnati, OH,
December 20, 1985*

The National Urban League, concerned about the problem of teenage pregnancy in the black community, has come up with a unique approach—educating young black men on the pitfalls of teenage fatherhood.

The 'phantom fathers' often are overlooked by those attempting to curb illegitimate births among teenage children of all races. But the biological facts have not changed--every baby has a father.

Dewey C. Fuller, president of the Urban League of Cincinnati, believes now is the time to impress on young blacks that fathering a child is not macho—or even smart.

'Now we have to speak frankly to our young black males and tell them being a teenage father does not make you a man,' Fuller says. The national league's Male Responsibility Program will attempt to reach young black men through posters, newspaper and magazine ads, and radio commercials by popular singers.

The urban league program shows promise. If the league can cut down on teenage pregnancy by encouraging young black men to act responsibly toward the opposite sex, it will have made a major contribution toward alleviating a national problem.

Other organizations working with non-black teenagers should consider copying the league's model.

San Francisco Chronicle
San Francisco, CA, March 14, 1985

THE REPORT ON teenage pregnancy compiled by the Alan Guttmacher Institute of New York has produced — calmly and authoritatively — some dramatic findings. They are cause for concern. And they give the lie to those dogmatic types who would propel us back into the Victorian era.

America is not nearly as enlightened in the area of sex as some may think. Our teenagers become pregnant and give birth and have abortions at significantly higher rates than do adolescents in other industrialized countries. America is the only developing country where teenage pregancy has been increasing.

The study dashed any notion that high birth rates among young black women solely accounted for the discrepancy. If only figures from the white population were used, the U.S. would still be far ahead in teenage childbirths.

OTHER SIGNIFICANT findings included: Ready access to abortion services does not lead teenagers to have more abortions; availability of welfare is not a motive for parenthood, and greater availability of birth control and sex education does not lead to an increase in teenage pregnancy.

In the Netherlands, the country with the lowest rates of five closely-analyzed European nations, sex education in the schools is perfunctory. But clear, complete information about contraception is promulgated in the media, and mobile sex-education teams operate under auspices of a government-subsidized family-planning association.

In other words, sex education does not encourage licentiousness, or foster abortion. It does just the opposite. That is good reason to support population planning programs.

THE INSTITUTE'S ground-breaking report is welcome. It should bring constructive reality to a debate that in recent years has become overly strident and divisive.

THE PLAIN DEALER
Cleveland, OH, March 18, 1985

Why does the United States have a teen-age pregnancy rate twice that of comparable Western nations? According to conventional wisdom, the reasons are excessive permissiveness and sex education.

Research recently completed by the Alan Guttmacher Institute indicates that conventional wisdom is wrong. In-depth comparisons of the United States' rates with those of Sweden, the Netherlands, France, Canada, England and Wales, showed an enormous disparity. The United States reported 96 pregnancies per 1,000 19-year-olds; the next closest rate, found in England and Wales, was 45 per 1,000. The Netherlands has as few as 14 per 1,000.

Each of the nations displayed roughly equal figures for teen-age sexual activity, refuting excessive permissiveness as a nation-specific complaint. But why, then, the discrepancy? Broadly speaking, the study found that the other nations did not seek to prevent teen-age sex, as does the Reagan administration, but to limit pregnancy through comprehensive sex education programs and by making contraception and contraceptive counselling easily available.

Such programs are eminently reasonable. Teenage sexual activity is inevitable; teen-age sexual maturity is not. Sex education programs that cover the full range of sexuality—including both reproductive and emotional relationships—help match sexual maturity to sexual ability. Too often, it is ignorance that results in pregnancy.

Sexual responsibility, even among adults, is not enough, however. Thus the availability of contraceptives and contraceptive advice is crucial. Such assistance does not encourage sexual activity; it reinforces responsibility. It is futile to believe that, by making contraceptives difficult to obtain, teen-age pregnancies can be reduced. Such policies don't inhibit teen-agers, they inhibit caution.

That is especially so with younger teen-agers, who may be precocious enough to be sexually adventurous but not responsible enough to seek advice, education or contraception. The lack of consistently rigorous sex education courses is almost surely one reason why among American 14-year-olds, the pregnancy rate is four times as high as in any other nation.

There can be little doubt that teen-age sexual activity has risen over the years. It is an inescapable component of an increasingly sophisticated society and its changing sexual attitudes and taboos. To respond to that change with public policies based on retro-Forties realities, however, simply aggravates the problem.

The number of teen-age pregnancies among Americans is intolerably high and the solutions are perfectly obvious. Rigorous sex education programs, with contraceptive aid made available without stigma or threat, are responsible public policies that are long overdue.

Detroit Free Press
Detroit, MI, January 7, 1985

A RECENT Free Press story on teen motherhood painted a picture of how one family copes — a picture brightened by a beaming grandmother and loving relatives. The young, single mother, 17-year-old Norvena Dones, is on welfare, but she attends school and is making plans for her future. With continued strong family support, Norvena Dones may be able to make something of her life. But hundreds of thousands of other teenage mothers won't find it so easy to sidestep or surmount their mistakes.

For many of the estimated 1,800 girls in the Detroit public school system who are pregnant at any given time during the school year, family support is often missing. Some teen mothers are kicked out of home by their families. Others live with abusive, drunken or drug-addicted family members.

All too often, these young women lack any hope for the future, any sense that life holds options beyond poverty and childbearing. Like Norvena Dones' mother, Carmenlita Paul, who had her first child at the age of 14, they may feel that teen motherhood "is almost like a family tradition." Unlike Mrs. Paul, however, they may not have the strength to keep on striving for something better after years of lean times and deferred dreams.

Social service and juvenile justice workers see teenage pregnancy as the social problem that feeds and reinforces other problems. It is one of the main reasons that the proportion of black children in husband-wife families dropped from 64 percent in 1970 to 48.5 percent by 1978. It is, therefore, a major factor in increasing black poverty and welfare dependency.

And though child abuse occurs in every sector and economic class, there is some evidence that young, immature parents are more likely to abuse or neglect children simply because they don't know enough about parenting or about the sort of behavior to expect from infants.

Abused children, in turn, are likely to abuse others when they grow up. One study found that more than 90 percent of the inmates at San Quentin prison had been abused as children. The children of teen mothers are also more likely to have trouble in school, to become delinquent and to drop out.

The Michigan Department of Social Services has begun a program to develop strategies for preventing teen pregnancies, and the concept behind the program makes sense. The program, which is just now getting off the ground, focuses on having young girls counseled by their peers — girls their age who have already had babies.

It also will bring the parents of these girls together to talk about how to deal with the problem and will set up small group homes to help ease young mothers back into their communities. Television spots about teenage pregnancy will start appearing soon, and some state money will be used to implement community plans for attacking the problem.

The program, though it could help thousands, isn't the total answer. But it acknowledges that just teaching youngsters about birth control isn't the complete answer, either. Giving young women reasons to say "no," along with the self-esteem and support to do so, can be. Unlike Mrs. Paul and her daughter Norvena, many young, unwed mothers and their families don't manage to retain their optimism or their goals. They flounder around, lash out or sink — creating, in the process, problems with which all of society must somehow deal.

Las Vegas Review-Journal
Las Vegas, NV, March 15, 1985

A good deal of debate is being heard in this country about teen-age sex, contraceptives and abortion.

This is especially true in Nevada, with its relatively large Mormom and Catholic population, both religions with firm ideas about these issues.

Local interest has been intensified by a bill recently passed in the state Assembly that would require doctors to notify — but not require permission from — parents of girls under 18 who seek abortions, and the debate continues.

In light of the sometimes heated exchanges that have accompanied these issues, a study released this week by a respected research and educational organization revealed some information that might be useful to future discussion.

The overall picture is that American teen-agers become pregnant, give birth and have abortions at significantly higher rates than to do teen-agers in other industrialized nations.

Other findings:

— Easy access to abortions does not lead teen-agers to have more abortions.

— Greater availability of birth control and sex education does not lead to an increase in teen-age pregnancy.

— Welfare and other forms of support of young mothers is not a motive for parenthood.

The study involved 37 developed nations, but examined in detail teen-age sexual practices, pregnancy and abortion rates and public policy in six industrialized countries: the United States, the Netherlands, Sweden, England and Wales, Canada and France.

The study found that in the United States, black teen-agers had a higher pregnancy rate than white teen-agers — 163 pregnancies per 1,000 versus 83 per 1,000 for an overall rate of 96 per 1,000. But in other countries, the overall rate is much lower: 14 in the Netherlands, 35 in Sweden, 43 in France, 44 in Canada and 45 in England and Wales.

Why so low in these other countries?

The study concluded that countries with liberal attitudes toward sex, easy access to free or inexpensive contraceptives and family planning services and without parental consent, and with comprehensive progams in sex education had the lowest rates of teen-age pregnancy.

Why so high in the United States?

It's not that the level of teen-age sexual activity is higher here. The activity rates were roughly the same among all the industrialized countries.

The study observes that in the other countries the government, if it is involved at all in funding sex education, focuses on preganancy prevention, leaving the morality of the sex act up to family and the church.

In the United States, however, the study says, the government's role has been more to prevent sexual activity rather than encourage other methods of pregnancy prevention.

For abortion rates, the United States also ranks the highest of the countries studied. By the time they are 18 years old, 60 of every 1,000 women in the United States have had an abortion. In the Netherlands, the figure is 7 of every 1,000 (the lowest rate) and about 30 of every 1,000 in Sweden (the second highest rate).

So the assumption that low pregnancy rates reflect the frequent use of abortion is not indicated. Nor does it seem to be true that the reason the abortion rate is so high in this country is that abortions are more easily available. In fact, they are more easily available — in some instances free — or equally available in all the other countries.

Based on the study's findings, it is all too clear that the United States is doing something wrong when it comes to teen-age pregnancy and abortion. Our state and federal lawmakers — and particularly parents — would be well advised to look to the examples of these other industrialized nations for guidance.

Teen-age sex will not go away. But we can take steps to prevent the tragedy of unwanted pregnancy and abortion.

Parental Notification Rule Proposed, Debated, Dropped

Health and Human Services Secretary Richard Schweiker in February 1982 proposed a rule requiring that parents be notified when their teenage daughters received prescription birth control devices from federally funded clinics. The draft regulation, which was dubbed the "squeal rule" by critics, was released by HHS for a period of public comment. It would require clinics to notify parents within 10 days after giving birth control devices to girls below the age of 18. Birth control pills, intrauterine devices and diaphragms were included under the regulation. The rule, which stirred intense controversy, was not submitted for final approval to the Office of Management and Budget until January 1983, after HHS received more than 120,000 written reactions from the public. It was scheduled to take effect Feb. 25 of that year.

Margaret Heckler, who as a member of Congress had previously opposed parental notification, succeeded Richard Schweiker as Secretary of HHS in March 1983. In the confirmation hearings for her new cabinet post, however, she assured the Reagan Administration that she would pursue an appeal of a court decision blocking the "squeal rule."

The "squeal rule" had been issued in response to a 1981 congressional resolution that the government should "encourage family participation" in birth control planning for teenagers "to the extent practical." (Of the estimated 1.5 million teenagers who went to family planning clinics for contraceptives each year, forty-five percent of them were under the age of 18.) However, New York City Federal District Judge Henry F. Werker ruled February 14, 1983 that the regulation was invalid because it "contradicts and subverts the intention of Congress," which had also, in 1978, mandated federal support of teenage birth control programs in order to counter the "critical" problem of teenage pregnancy. And in July 1983 the U.S. District Court of Appeals for the District of Columbia also ruled that the proposed rule would "contravene congressional intent." The Reagan Administration had asked the federal appeals court to uphold the rule. But the three-judge panel found that "in enacting the [1981] amendment to encourage family participation, Congress most definitely did not intend to mandate family involvement." At this point the "squeal rule" was quietly dropped by the Administration as an issue.

The Philadelphia Inquirer
Philadelphia, PA, February 3, 1982

In the good old days, as some people remember them, there were "nice" girls and "bad" girls. Sometimes, even then, accidents would happen. A father would take out his shotgun and march a young fellow to the altar.

Actually, the good old days weren't quite like that, and, in any case, they are not about to return. The facts of life are these: Many teenagers are sexually active, and this is not a new thing. Ten years ago, a national survey revealed that nearly half of unmarried females had had sexual intercourse by the age of 19. That number is increasing. What should be done?

Well, you can preach to adolescents about continence, for whatever good that will do. You can also face the facts of life and teach young people about them, so that at least they'll know how to avoid pregnancy.

Secretary of Health and Human Services Richard S. Schweiker, however, doesn't think that's a federal responsibility. It is, he feels, a family responsibility. He doesn't think federal funds should be used for sex education programs. He also doesn't think Medicaid funds should be used to provide birth-control assistance.

And now HHS has come up with another idea that flouts the facts of life. The proposal is to require that family planning agencies receiving federal funds notify parents of teenagers under 18 who seek contraceptive devices or drugs.

Now these days, as in the good old days, most teenagers do not go to their parents for permission to practice birth control, for reasons that ought to be obvious. What would happen if this rule should be in effect? That ought to be obvious, too. As a public health official told the Washington Post, "They're not going to go to an agency that's obligated to squeal on them."

So what will they do? They'll take their chances. Accidents will happen. Girls will get pregnant, as four out of 10 teenager girls do now, and many of them will have abortions. They'll pay for them if they can afford to. If they can't and the government won't, they'll find a back-alley butcher, or try to do it themselves.

Mr. Schweiker says he is opposed to abortion. Why does he contemplate actions to encourage it?

Chicago Tribune
Chicago, IL, February 28, 1982

Unfortunately, Richard S. Schweiker, the secretary of Health and Human Services, hasn't been talked out of his misguided decision to insist that family planning services receiving federal funds must notify the parents of teenagers 17 or younger when they are given a prescription for contraceptive drugs or devices.

The dismaying proposal has been drafted into a federal regulation and published in the Federal Register. Unless public outcry is compelling before the comment period is over April 23, it will go into effect.

What Mr. Schweiker is trying to do is use the federal regulatory mechanism to distort a congressional amendment in ways Congress never intended. The result won't be the restoration of family togetherness and teenage sexual restraint that the Reagan administration apparently envisions; it is far more likely to be an increase in teenage pregnancy, abortion and single parenthood.

The legislation Mr. Schweiker is proposing to implement gives federal funding to family planning services and says such centers must encourage family participation "to the extent practicable." It also requires such clinics to provide services without regard to age or marital status.

Since Congress clearly intended to make birth control information and contraceptives easily available to teenagers, Mr. Schweiker seems to be trying to undercut it with the curious ploy of requiring the clinics to send written notification to parents within 10 working days *after* they have given a minor a prescription drug or device.

The proposed regulation also requires a family planning clinic to verify that the parents have received the notification and to keep files of the verifications. Without such confirmation, the clinic would not be permitted to provide the teen with any more contraceptives.

What about teenagers who say they are afraid to let their parents know they are sexually active? Well, the regulation would make an exception for them—but only if the director of the family planning center "determines that notification would result in physical harm to the minor." It can't be a vague fear or parental anger or discipline, the new rule emphasizes, but must be based on evidence as substantial as a history of child abuse. That would have to go into the files, too.

Mr. Schweiker has also found another stumbling block to put in the way of teens who want contraceptives. The regulation proposes to eliminate the current requirement that clinics consider just a teen's own resources in determining how much to charge for contraceptive services. That would mean much higher costs for most adolescents.

Mr. Schweiker may have the best of intentions about bringing families closer together, getting parents involved in a teen's decision to become sexually active and no longer letting the government seem to be conspiring with minors to get contraceptives behind parents' backs.

But he isn't going to reverse the recent sweeping changes in sexual morality and sexual activity with a federal regulation. Most teens who come to clinics for contraceptives are already sexually active and will no doubt continue to be sexually active, with or without effective birth control protection. If they are cut off from easy, inexpensive access to the most reliable contraceptives—those which require a prescription—for fear their parents will find out, they will resort to less effective methods available in drug stores or do without. There is no evidence whatsoever that they will turn to chastity.

The increasing incidence of premarital sex among teenagers has had devastating consequences in the rising incidence of abortion, high-risk pregnancy, single parenthood, disastrous early marriages, welfare costs.and stunted opportunities for education and careers. Mr. Schweiker cannot turn back the sweeping social tides of sexuality with a single federal regulation. What he will do, if the regulation goes into effect, is undermine the efforts of family planning services to help minors use their sexuality responsibly to minimize its potentially disastrous consequences.

Richmond Times-Dispatch

Richmond, Va., February 14, 1982

Under regulations proposed by the Reagan administration, federally funded clinics would have to notify the parents of teens to whom they give contraceptives. As Health and Human Services Secretary Richard S. Schweiker recently told grumblers: "Parents must give written permission before a child can go on a school trip.... It is paradoxical that [in] prescribing drugs and devices with potentially serious health consequences, federal policy has not recognized parental involvement." True enough. Yet even if the means of birth control were hazard-free, is it really the state's business to slip the Pill to minors?

Now the state does exactly that (note that the Reagan reform would involve parents *after* the dispensal occurred), even though such a policy overthrows the judgment of generations concerning minors' accountability to parents. In the contraception matter, federally-paid professionals routinely circumvent the traditional right of parents to exert a loving authority over their children, and seem to view mothers and fathers as potential "intruders" on a more intimate relationship between offspring and state. Outrageous.

Yet, two years from 1984 and counting, it should perhaps surprise no one when bureaus with delusions of omniscience view all citizens, including adults, as their "children" and seek, in the best paternal fashion, to prevent older children (i.e., Mom and Pop) from "bossing" younger ones. Contraception is these days only one of many fertile fields for Orwell scholars.

In Washington, of course, Big Brothers often masquerade as Big Hearts. For example, Rep. Henry A. Waxman, D-Calif., laments that the Reagan proposal would mean "more pregnancies among adolescents and more abortions" — ugly prospects, indeed. But Mr. Waxman overlooks "liberal" welfare policies that obviate the father's role, helping shatter the cohesiveness of poor American families, from whose ranks young, unwed mothers are now most apt to come. And when an activist Supreme Court legislated abortion-on-demand, there is little doubt that it obliquely encouraged the sort of conduct that has spawned so many of the clinics in question. It may be said of liberalism (without equating the two) what a Polish professor said of communism: It is a system that bravely confronts problems that don't exist under any other system.

Sen. Jeremiah Denton rightly observes that, while the Reagan proposal is a "long overdue step," the administration needs to take another one — sponsoring a bill that would require parental consent *before* a minor could obtain from a tax-funded clinic apparatus suggesting activities about which, for the best of reasons (such as an opportunity to impart moral guidance), parents have a right to know. Often when the state begins to operate *in loco parentis*, the operative word is *loco*.

TULSA WORLD

Tulsa, Okla., February 13, 1982

A PROPOSAL backed by the U.S. Department of Health and Human Services would require federally-funded family planning projects to notify the parents of teen-age girls who get birth control prescriptions.

Proponents of the regulation, including Health and Human Service Secretary Richard Schweiker, believe that notification will encourage parental involvement in the problem of teenagers and pre-marital sex.

The argument is only superficially appealing. The truth is, many young people pick up unwholesome sex attitudes from the street simply because their parents are unwilling or unable to provide the kind of guidance that would be useful. Notifying the parents in such a case might stop a young woman from obtaining birth control help, but it would not change her sex habits or attitudes.

It seems clear that strict enforcement of a such a regulation would merely frustrate the goal which family planning clinics seek to achieve — a lessening of the illegitimate birth rate among unmarried teen-agers.

Family planning professionals should be given the discretion to notify parents when there is an indication the parents might contribute some useful guidance. But making it a requirement in every case will be self-defeating.

The Kansas City Times

Kansas City, Mo., March 8, 1982

The Reagan administration is proposing a big step backward in family planning with its regulations requiring clinics to tell parents when their teen-agers get contraceptive devices.

Already about 75 percent of the 1.2 million teen-age pregnancies a year are unintentional, undoubtedly because the teen-agers did not take precautions to avoid pregnancy. Matters will only get worse if the proposed rules are adopted. More teen-age abortions are a predictable outcome, for one thing.

Proposed by Secretary Richard S. Schweiker of Health and Human Services, the new regulations would require federally subsidized family planning clinics to notify parents any time their children under 18 years receive birth control devices. The rules are scheduled to go into effect sometime after the period for public comment lapses in April.

County-run clinics in 60 Kansas counties and more than 120 publicly- and privately-run clinics in Missouri would have to go along or risk losing their federal Title 10 aid. That could mean an estimated loss next year of $900,000 in Kansas and $2.5 million in Missouri — something the clinics can ill afford because they already are expecting to get fewer federal dollars next year.

The toll in unwanted pregnancies, abortions and health risks to teen-age mothers would be much more serious if the rules are adopted and followed, however. Many adolescents will be reluctant to obtain family planning help if they know their parents will be told. The result for many will be sex without protection and a greater risk of becoming pregnant.

Family planning officials in Kansas estimate that the number of out-of-wedlock births for mothers ages 10 to 19 would surpass the 2,289 recorded in 1980 if teen-agers are scared away from the clinics. Likewise, they predict that the number of abortions would exceed the 2,546 reported for young women of those ages.

Neither Missouri nor Kansas now requires parental consent or notification when teens receive birth control devices, but leave that option to the family planning clinics. In Kansas, officials at many clinics already encourage teens to discuss their birth control questions with their parents.

Things should be left as they are. In families where there are good communications on sexuality, the rule would have little effect, anyway. In those cases, the kids talk to their parents.

But, sadly, the ones most affected by the proposed rules will be teen-agers who feel they cannot discuss sex with their parents, and cannot afford to go to the family doctor. Until now, they have been able to turn to family planning counselors at the clinics. For many of them, the proposed changes would close the last open door.

The Courier-Journal

Louisville, Ky., January 30, 1982

IN THE BEST of worlds, children tempted to engage in sex, drugs, shoplifting or other hazardous ventures would confide freely in their parents. The latter, in turn, would give marvelously mature and eagerly heeded advice about peer pressures, self-indulgence and other obstacles on the road to responsible adulthood.

Unfortunately, it's *not* the best of worlds — a truth that wouldn't need stating except that the Reagan administration appears to be on the verge of joining those well-intentioned dreamers who claim otherwise. The President's Cabinet reportedly is seriously studying a proposal that family planning centers receiving federal funds be required to inform the parents of any child obtaining birth-control materials.

The theory is that such a regulation would bring families together again. In some cases it would: the centers normally try to persuade troubled youngsters to confide in their parents. But long experience has shown that strict "help and tell" requirements mean more teen-age pregnancies, more back alley abortions, more venereal disease, more families on welfare, more desperation among young people with nowhere to turn.

Richard Schweiker, the Secretary of Health and Human Services, is the prime mover behind this dreadful idea, which was thoroughly explored last year during hearings on Senator Jeremiah Denton's "teen-age chastity centers" bill. These hearings considered such real-world evidence as a 1981 report by the Alan Guttmacher Institute on the problem of teen-age pregnancy. The report said that (1) most of the 1.5 million teen-agers who use birth control clinics don't go until well after their first sexual experience (and often after they suspect they are pregnant); and (2) the reason most of them don't go earlier is because they fear their parents might find out.

Because of various state laws, one-fifth of the nation's clinics already require parental permission before providing birth control aid to those under 15, the only exception being in the case of children who fear parental abuse if they are told. The Guttmacher report alarmingly estimates that if more clinics required parental notification, 113,000 teens a year would stop going for help.

But these youngsters wouldn't stop having sex: In most cases they'd simply turn to less effective means of preventing birth than the commonly-prescribed birth-control pill. The nation could then expect about 33,000 more unwanted births or abortions a year to add to the already spiraling numbers of illegitimacies, otherwise sidetracked lives and lifetimes on public welfare.

(By the end of the 1970s, according to the National Center for Health Statistics, babies born out of wedlock accounted for 17 percent of all births, versus 10.7 percent a decade earlier. Half of all Aid to Families with Dependent Children money goes to households in which the mother gave birth while still a teen-ager.)

Secretary Schweiker says he simply wants parents to know when their children are prescribed something that may entail a health risk. But if he were truly interested in the health of minors, he would take into consideration another statistic cited by the Guttmacher study: Pregnancy constitutes a health risk to teens five times that of using the pill, which has minimal side-effects in that age group.

What seems more likely is that the Secretary is simply responding to a conservative lobby that thinks the government has no right interfering in "family-type" decisions. Ironically, his proposed rule doesn't go far enough for those people, who would extend parental notification to clinic referral services as well. And it goes beyond congressional intent. Changes in the law last year encourage family participation but do not require it.

So, yes, it's right to encourage teens to talk with their parents before engaging in sex or seeking birth-control advice. But no law can enforce family communication. By making it harder for some children to get confidential help and counseling, the only thing this proposal could enforce is misery.

The Seattle Times

Seattle, Wash., March 7, 1982

WHEN it comes to sexuality involving adolescents, many parents today share deep unease that they have lost control in guiding their children's lives — a feeling that, as columnist Ellen Goodman has put it, "our parenthood role at times is reduced to picking up the pieces."

The depth of those concerns is not likely to be changed by the Reagan administration's naive and misdirected proposal to require notification of parents within 10 days when youngsters under 18 receive contraceptives from clinics supported in part with federal funds.

Rightly, it seems to us, the regulation has come under stiff attack not only from respected family planning groups such as Planned Parenthood but from the American College of Obstetricians and Gynecologists, the American Medical Association, and spokesmen for groups representing family physicians, pediatricians, and nurses.

Describing the proposal advanced by Health and Human Services Secretary Richard Schweiker as reflecting an "unrealistic 'father knows best' morality," Dr. George M. Ryan, Jr., president of the nation's gynecologists, said the rule would not stop teen-agers from having sex.

But such a policy, Dr. Ryan said, would discourage adolescents, especially those in poorer families, from seeking help. There's some evidence that publicity about the proposal already has caused thousands of teen-agers to shun clinics.

The end results: More unwanted pregnancies, more venereal disease, more abortions.

Young people plainly need guidance in handling the social responsibilities that go with sexual activity, counsel that often is available both within families and through skilled personnel at birth-control clinics. It is not available at the corner drugstore.

What the administration proposes, in effect, is to send parents a notice about something they probably know about already. Existing law encourages (but does not mandate) family participation when youngsters seek help from clinics.

It is ironic that an administration that wants to get government "off the backs" of the American people presses in this instance for federal intrusion into an intensely personal area.

AKRON BEACON JOURNAL

Akron, Ohio, February 26, 1982

THE IDEA that a family can be strengthened by federal fiat or that teen-age sexual activity can be curbed by violating a teen-age girl's privacy is nonsense.

But that apparently is what the New Right and President Reagan hope to accomplish with federal regulations published by the Department of Health and Human Services. Clinics that receive federal funds would be required to notify parents within 10 days after a daughter under 18 has been given birth control pills, a diaphragm or an intrauterine device.

Opponents, including several national medical groups and Planned Parenthood of America, say the new rule will lead to more teen-age pregnancies and abortions.

Supporters, including President Reagan, say parents have a right to know when their child is given a prescription drug or device — though the new rules would not require notice if a prescription drug is being used to treat a venereal disease.

HHS Secretary Richard S. Schweiker said, "The government should not construct a Berlin Wall between parents and children. We should also not assume teen-agers will risk becoming pregnant rather than let their parents know they are sexually active."

The regulations, though, would let parents know only when daughters are sexually active, since sons, however young, would normally get only non-prescription condoms at a clinic.

The arguments for the new regulations, besides being inconsistent and discriminatory, are fatuous.

Parents of teen-agers who are pushing this requirement must know that if they have not won the confidence and trust of their adolescent children, they are not likely to win it when a clinician calls to tell them their daughter is sexually active and wants help to avoid pregnancy.

Just the opposite is likely to occur. It is easy to imagine the anger parents and daughter might feel when such information is divulged, anger that would drive a deeper wedge between parent and child. Notice is not required if it "would result in physical harm to the minor by a parent or guardian." Disciplinary actions "of an unsubstantial nature" are acceptable.

With that kind of latitude in notification, the teen-ager may suffer far more than an unwanted pregnancy.

Health officials and statisticians have documented increasing sexual activity of teen-agers, increasing incidence of pregnancy among unmarried teen-age girls, and the desire for confidentiality on the part of those who seek help from family-planning clinics.

The administration has yielded to pressure from those who would impose their standards on all, regardless of the damage that may be done to young people. During the next 60 days, the HHS Department will receive comments on the proposals. Those who recognize the folly of "regulating" family solidarity should urge the administration to put the privacy of the family and the welfare of teen-agers ahead of political consideration.

RAPID CITY JOURNAL—

Rapid City, SD, February 28, 1983

A federal regulation that parents be notified after minors receive birth control pills or other contraceptive devices from federally- funded family planning centers is a classic case of theory bumping up against reality

The requirement, which has become known as the "squeal rule," was recommended by the Department of Health and Human Services on the theory it would promote communication between adolescents and parents. That's a worthy objective but there's a serious question that that will be the result.

Teen-age pregnancies cause tragedy and needless hardship. They result in large numbers of abortions or unwanted babies, many of whom will grow up in less than desirable conditions.

Ideally, it would be nice if parents and their youngsters could, and would, talk frankly about sex and contraceptives. But the ideal doesn't apply in most cases. Telling parents contraceptives have been prescribed for their child won't encourage communication, but it could discourage young women from asking for such contraceptives. The result may be a dramatic increase in teen-age pregnancies.

The choices facing the family planning centers if the regulation is adopted are not attractive. The centers can go along with the ruling and notify parents that their daughters have obtained prescription contraceptives. Or the centers can give up their federal dollars which could put many centers out of business.

The choices facing teen-age girls are equally unattractive. They can choose to receive the contraceptives and have their parents notified. For some that might not pose a problem, for many others it would. The alternative would be not to seek services from a family planning center and risk getting pregnant.

Of course there is the third alternative — refraining from sexual activity. However, surveys showing the level of sexual activity among teenagers and the number of teen-age pregnancies outside of marriage indicate young people continue to succumb to the sexual urge.

The notification rule, implementation of which is being held up by court challenges, threatens to reverse the progress that has been made in averting unwanted pregnancies.

It is regrettable that the federal government ever got into the business of family planning. However, now that it is, a regulation that would discourage young people from using the service would do more harm than good.

San Francisco Chronicle

San Francisco, CA, March 12, 1982

THE REAGAN ADMINISTRATION'S guardians of public health have incurred some bitter laughter now and then because of their absurd calls for chastity as an alternative to federal support for indigent women who want the freedom to choose whether or not to undergo abortion.

Now a new controversy has arisen and the administration's moralists are again in full cry against sexual activity among teenagers.

Since 1970, federal law has provided government funds to help finance family planning clinics. Medical supervisors are permitted to provide contraceptive pills and devices to adolescents who are sexually active.

For more than a decade this care has been given to youngsters without requiring parental consent. Now, however, comes the U.S. Department of Health and Human Services publishing in the Federal Register a proposal to require all federally-funded family planning agencies to notify parents within ten days whenever a minor is provided with a prescription for contraceptives.

The Department, of course, advances a not unreasonable proposition that parents have a right to know when their adolescent children are being given medical services. But that argument runs squarely against the certain knowledge that, for thousands upon thousands of sexually active teenagers, enforcing the rule will simply mean that they will stop seeking any birth control services at all.

THE RESULT WOULD BE predictable: Thousands more unplanned and unwanted pregnancies in adolescents too young to become stable parents, and thousands more abortions — legal or illegal. The result in human tragedy is uncountable.

It is curious that in their zeal to violate the privacy of young people whose sexual lives are already emancipated, the federal health guardians are violating at least three precedents:

First, in passing the original 1970 law, and in all its amendments ever since, Congress has insisted that the family planning agencies "encourage" young people to consult their parents but has specifically denied any intent to mandate such consultation. Second, The United States Supreme Court has already held unconstitutional a Utah law that required parental consent before minors could receive contraceptive services in that state. And third, a 1978 Federal law dealing with contraceptive services to minors clearly requires family planning agencies to "maintain the confidentiality" of all records on its youthful clients.

THE PLANNED PARENTHOOD Federation of America, the American Civil Liberties Union, and quite probably many other agencies will go to court to fight the federal government on this "unreasonable intrusiveness", to use George F. Will's words, into the privacy of medical practice. The American Medical Association has already spoken out realistically on behalf of young patients.

It is one thing to encourage, it is quite another to compel a closer and confiding relationship between adolescents and their parents.

We urge Secretary Schweicker of the Department of Health and Human Services to withdraw his pernicious proposal. It would be destructive to health, certainly cruel and inhuman in the consequences it would inflict on naive and unprotected teenage girls, and a defeat of the concept of government concern for young people.

SATURDAY OKLAHOMAN & TIMES

Oklahoma City, OK,
January 15, 1983

ONE of the first duties facing Margaret Heckler, President Reagan's nominee for Health and Human Services secretary, will be passing on a controversial new rule she fought while in Congress. Whether she tries to block it may tell something about how the department will be run under her jurisdiction.

Her predecessor, Richard Schweiker, announced his intention, just before resigning this week, to make final a regulation requiring federally funded clinics to notify parents or guardians when girls under 18 receive prescriptions for birth-control pills or devices.

It takes effect 30 days after publication in the Federal Register. But Planned Parenthood has filed suit in U.S. District Court to try to stop the government from enforcing it.

Although she opposes abortion, Mrs. Heckler generally was on the liberal side of most issues while she was a Republican representative from Massachusetts. Schweiker thinks she will hew to the middle-of-the-road philosophy he followed as head of the department.

The rule is a good one. The federal government has no business helping to undermine parental authority by subsidizing the dispensing of birth-control products to young girls on the sly. As long as an underage girl is living at home, she is subject to her parents' authority and their right to be informed about anything pertaining to her well-being should be considered paramount.

THE ⬛ SUN

Baltimore, Md., January 25, 1983

As a member of Congress, Margaret Heckler thought the proposed rule requiring the government to notify parents of teenagers seeking contraceptives was the wrong approach. By the time she is confirmed as secretary of Health and Human Services, the "squeal rule" apparently will be official. The departing secretary, Richard Schweiker, has pushed it through the regulatory process and Mrs. Heckler now must administer it.

But Mrs. Heckler was right in the first place. In a letter to Mr. Schweiker last April, she and 31 other representatives said teenage girls could be discouraged from using federal birth-control clinics if they knew that their parents would be informed. They cited a study that reached this conclusion and said the proposed rule could result in a higher rate of teen pregnancies. That would be a far cry from the protection the rule was designed to provide. It could hardly be the preference of parents who want to know what their daughters are doing. Mrs. Heckler has a clear record on this issue, but she also has much on her mind these days. She is about to take over the largest department in the federal government at one of its most trying times. She will administer government assistance programs under constant budget attack, and she will play an important role in the Social Security debate this year. The "squeal rule" may be considered a little matter by comparison. But Mrs. Heckler should have been given an opportunity to state her views as the official who would be charged with administering it.

Apparently, she was not. Mr. Schweiker gave his final approval to the rule and now the administration has ordered it printed in the *Federal Register*. Unless a court order blocks it, the rule becomes effective February 25. Other agency heads have been stuck with laws and rules they oppose. Now, Mrs. Heckler becomes the latest.

St. Louis *Review*

St. Louis, Mo., February 9, 1983

A highly controversial ruling was issued on Jan. 26 by the Department of Health and Human Services. This ruling requires government family planning clinics to notify parents when their minor children (17 or under) receive prescription contraceptives. The federal ruling has been backed by the United States Catholic Conference of Bishops.

On the other side 58 organizations, including the American Medical Association, the Salvation Army and the United Church of Christ, have criticized the measure. New York Attorney General Robert Abrams has filed a lawsuit against the rule.

What a formidable array of those ready to fight against parents' rights! All of these agencies and groups are concerned that this law will violate the minor child's right to privacy. They are also concerned that when young people realize that their parents will be notified many will avoid patronizing the clinic in seeking the contraceptives.

This opposition stand appears contradictory when we consider that no minor can receive medical assistance in any other set of circumstances without parental consent. A minor cannot even have her/his ears pierced without the permission of parents.

Medically, the side effects of many and indeed most contraceptives can be truly alarming. Parents are responsible before God and the law for the physical and spiritual well-being of their children. They are certainly responsible for medical expenses incurred by minor children who might suffer side effects from using the contraceptives.

Members of families, parents and children, need to be close to one another and trust one another. It is true that in some families there is little trust or caring between the members. Attacking such a rule takes for granted that there is no closeness between family members and to some degree says to young people "go ahead and play around, your parents have no right to know." We do not agree with that stance and support parents in their efforts to keep their families together and communicating. All things considered this is one of the most sensible rules to come out of Washington in quite a while.

THE SAGINAW NEWS
Saginaw, MI, March 1, 1983

Federal judges in two separate decisions have stayed a regulation that was to take effect last Friday, one derided as the "squeal rule," promoted as the family "togetherness" rule.

Those who believe that unwanted teenage pregnancies contribute nothing to family life, or to the health of society, should hope this regulation stays stayed.

Issued by the Department of Health and Human Services, the rule would force federally funded health clinics to notify parents within 10 days when they prescribe contraceptives for girls under 18.

In the sense of what ought to be, the rule is right. The government should not keep secrets between children and their parents.

What it ignores is that sexually active girls already are keeping such a secret. That's why they go to clinics which promise confidentiality. If there's no more privacy, there is sure to be more pregnancy, more abortion, more broken lives, more unwanted children and higher infant-mortality rates. None of that is remotely conducive to family happiness.

Neither the clinics' services nor this rule would be needed if parents and youngsters did talk to each other about the difficult decisions that adolescence demands. The evidence is that too many do not. A 1978 Stanford University survey found that more than a third of teen-age girls do not discuss sex with either parent. A better gauge is the sheer number of girls, more than 2,000 in Saginaw in 1981, 675,000 nationally, who visit the clinics.

The rule would be fine if it meant that all or most of those girls would stop risking pregnancy or start talking to their parents about it. Neither is about to happen.

The rule now is supposed to get a full court hearing. Margaret Heckler, the new HHS secretary who has so far remained silent on the subject, would serve health and teen-age humanity best if she just drops it before it goes that far.

The Orlando Sentinel
Orlando, FL, January 16, 1983

If the Senate approves Margaret Heckler to head Health and Human Services, one of her first jobs should be to clean up a department misstep. It is a proposal to require federally funded clinics to notify parents whose daughters under 18 seek prescription birth control.

Estimates suggest the regulation will affect about 530,000 teens each year. These are teens who already are sexually active. Thus the issue isn't teen sex, it is teen pregnancies. HHS Secretary Richard Schweiker says the rule would protect the health and safety of minors. More likely, it will keep many sexually active teens from using birth control. The result is more teen pregnancies and more abortions, hardly a better alternative.

Mrs. Heckler has opposed government funding for abortions and, if only for that reason, she should oppose this rule. The problems that keep parents and teens from communicating won't be solved by government mediation. Mrs. Heckler would make a good start by overruling this rule.

The Boston Globe
Boston, MA, February 6, 1983

The controversial "squeal law" requiring parental notification when minors receive prescription contraceptives from federally funded family planning clinics is scheduled to take effect March 1. Former Secretary of Health and Human Services Richard Schweiker's parting shot to teenaged girls was whisked through before Margaret Heckler's confirmation hearings. That way, the secretary-designate was presumably spared the embarrassment of defending a policy she didn't support.

In a letter last April, Heckler and other members of a Congressional women's caucus opposed the regulation and reminded HHS that Congress specifically intended the department to encourage, not mandate, parental involvement in family planning services. Now the regulation that mandates notification has been challenged in federal courts in New York and West Virginia where judges would be well advised to throw it out.

An affadavit filed in the West Virginia case is instructive. According to Dr. L. Clark Hansbarger, director of the West Virginia Department of Health, the regulation will increase abortions, pregnancies and medical complications among teenagers.

Until 1979, West Virginia state law required family planning clinics to inform parents whose teenagers received birth control. In the first year after a federal court invalidated that law, the number of minors using family planning services in West Virginia increased 63 percent. Nationally the increase was only 2 percent. In 1978, the West Virginia Health Department estimated that 16.8 percent of sexually active minors who needed family planning services received them. By 1982, 47 percent of the need was met.

Significantly, the birth rate for minors in West Virginia reached a seven-year low in 1981, representing a 12 percent decrease over 1980. Data from the Center for Disease Control indicate that the decrease is not due to abortion and that teen-aged pregnancies are less likely to end in abortion there than in the country as a whole.

Hansbarger's affadavit also claims the regulation would negatively affect the general health care received by minors whose visits to family planning providers are their only contact with the health care system. Generally, minors receive complete physicals when requesting birth control; often serious health problems are diagnosed as a result.

As national health care policy, Schweiker's regulation makes no sense. It increases paperwork requirements at health clinics where time would be better spent delivering services. It forces doctors and nurses to compromise themselves professionally. As a scare tactic that singles out young girls, the regulation hardly fosters family communication.

If the courts fail to throw it out, Margaret Heckler should do so after her confirmation. That way, she would be spared the embarrassment of upholding a policy that runs counter to her own convictions.

The Boston Herald
Boston, MA, January 18, 1983

Margaret Heckler made a rather smart and courageous move during her last year in Congress. She signed a letter, along with 32 of her congressional colleagues, protesting an administration plan to require that parents be told if their minor children were given prescription contraceptives at federally financed clinics.

The regulation was recently promulgated by outgoing Secretary of Health and Human Service Secretary Richard S. Schweiker, the man Heckler will replace following her Senate confirmation.

The April 23, 1982, letter signed by Heckler and the others said, "We fear that enactment of such a regulation would discourage many young people from utilizing these services and would result in a drastic increase in the number of teenage pregnancies."

Nothing has changed since April to make us change our minds about the regulation, and we certainly hope that Mrs. Heckler intends to stick by her guns, too.

While the intent of the regulation would appear to be to encourage communication between parent and child, no amount of government-imposed red tape will ever accomplish that, no matter how admirable a goal that may be.

The effect is also to unfairly discriminate against teenage girls. After all, the only contraceptives marketed for their male companions are sold over the counter, no prescription necessary, hence no letter home.

Now the Office of Management and Budget, which one would think has better things to do these days, is apparently intent on enforcing the rule before Mrs. Heckler even gets to her HHS office.

Such haste is unseemly in view of the transfer of power about to take place. It certainly wouldn't do any harm to hold off on implementation until Mrs. Heckler has a chance to review the policy.

Rockford Register Star
Rockford, IL, May 16, 1983

There are only a couple things wrong with the squeal law approved this week by an Illinois state Senate committee:

- It won't work.
- It's probably illegal.

The Senate committee voted 11-3 to support a state law requiring family planning clinics to notify parents when teen-agers request birth control services.

This has been a favorite proposal of groups that believe they can control teen-agers' morality if they only pass enough laws.

That is silly. Kids will do what kids will do. If they think mom and dad will be told, they'll just do it without taking any precautions against pregnancy.

Apart from that, where is the logic in proposing a bill virtually identical to one struck down by federal courts? Judges in three states have overturned such laws, saying the Reagan administration exceeded its authority when it decided parental notification was what Congress intended when it said federally funded clinics "shall encourage family participation, to the extent practical."

The issue now is in federal appeals court, where its future can be predicted by a comment made by one of the three judges hearing the appeal. "Do you really, honestly believe parental notification will discourage teen-agers?" the judge asked.

We all know the answer to that one.

DAYTON DAILY NEWS
Dayton, OH, February 7, 1983

Proselytizers of the "squeal rule" requiring federally-funded family planning clinics to notify parents of minors who receive contraceptives must be twitching behind their dogma, since kindred spirits in the Reagan Administration have been caught bearing false witness.

You'll remember the Department of Health and Human Services last year asked for comment on the proposed regulation. And all along, the administration said the reaction was balanced, pro and con. Now, the *Los Angeles Times* reports a confidential memo to HHS incoming secretary "acknowledges for the first time" that reaction was "largely" against the disclosure mandate. The administration, however, decided to ignore such matters and let the rule take effect Feb. 25.

That leaves the administration and a few fundamentalist conservatives pitted against just about every national association of experts in law, medicine, public health, social work and youth services. The administration thinks the rule will restore the sanctity of the family. People in the trenches know the new regulation's fallout will be more abortions (also an anathema to the radical right), teen pregnancies and unwed mothers and children on welfare.

Dayton's Planned Parenthood Association already has announced it has no intention of telling parents if their daughter receives a birth control device, citing invasion of privacy and breach of patient confidentiality. Other family planning centers are taking similar stands.

Punishment may come swiftly for the administration's self-serving fib. On Feb. 14, the Federal District Court of the District of Columbia will consider a request by Planned Parenthood and others to suspend the regulation until a full appeal can be heard.

In the meantime, the halo that anti-confidentiality disciples imagine hovering over their heads has slipped publicly. It may have landed around their necks. All the better to choke off more sanctimonious half-truths and misstatements.

Pittsburgh Post-Gazette
Pittsburgh, PA, February 19, 1983

The Reagan administration's so-called "squeal rule," under which federally financed clinics must notify parents if their daughters under age 18 receive contraceptives, has suffered a legal setback. In a victory for common sense, a federal judge in New York has issued a preliminary injunction barring the regulation from going into effect on Feb 25.

The legality of this ill-advised regulation awaits further scrutiny in courtrooms, and it was not immediately clear whether the injunction would apply beyond New York State. But the basis of U.S. District Judge Henry Werker's ruling gave hope that the regulation will never be enforced.

The judge noted that Congress had supplied funds to the clinics for the express purpose of combating the critical problem of teen-age pregnancy. The new rule contradicts and subverts the intent of Congress, the judge said, because "... common sense dictates but one conclusion: The deterrent effect of the regulations will cause increased adolescent pregnancies."

Common sense, of course, is not so common. Many of the supporters of this regulation actually believe that sexually mature teen-agers can be coerced into morality (when the evidence suggests that, deterred from visiting the clinics, adolescents will just take risks).

The regulation's supporters are quick to raise the smokescreen of family rights, but if they were truly honest most would have to admit that they are trying to impose their own religious views of sexual morality on teen-age girls. They hope that a bureaucratic ploy can succeed where fire and brimstone have failed.

Of course, the same people who are effectively trying to limit contraception are also against abortion. All in the name of helping the family, this dangerous thinking will cause a great deal of family grief and suffering, as well as put a patronizing government firmly into the bedroom.

The country cannot afford such cruel stupidity. In Pennsylvania alone, there were an estimated 15,306 women under age 18 who became pregnant in 1981 (the last year when figures were available.) That figure is shockingly high already. The last thing the society needs is an initiative to make it larger.

So, having lost a round in court, the Reagan administration should rethink its position and back off.

ALBUQUERQUE JOURNAL
Albuquerque, NM, February 16, 1983

Federal Judge Henry F. Werker of New York took what to us is the most sensible course this week when he temporarily prohibited the government from requiring clinics to tell parents when their teen-age daughters get birth control pills or devices. In the interest of society, that prohibition should be made permanent.

The judge noted that "Common sense dictates but one conclusion: the deterrent effect of the regulation will cause increased adolescent pregnancies."

The regulation by the Department of Health and Human Services was scheduled to become effective Feb. 25. Judge Werker ruled that the parental notice requirement is invalid because it contradicts and subverts the intent of Congress.

Rather than deterring sexual activity, and encouraging "family participation" in birth-control decisions as the department hopes, fear of parental knowledge would deter teen-age girls from seeking information to prevent pregnancy.

Thousands of teen pregnancies and abortions could result. The rule wouldn't stop youngsters from engaging in sexual activity.

A recent study concluded that the rule could cause 1,000 unwanted births and 1,000 abortions a month.

About 5,000 clinics nationwide would be covered by the regulation, if it is imposed. An estimated 400,000 teen-age girls could be affected.

The government received thousands of comments from groups opposing the rule, including agencies in 40 states and every major medical and family planning organization in the United States.

Ideally, children would communicate openly with their parents, would uphold high standards of behavior and would never engage in premarital sex, thus not requiring counseling or birth control devices. But we live in an imperfect world. The "squeal rule" would, we believe, compound that imperfection. It represents a bureaucratic flight from reality.

THE ATLANTA CONSTITUTION
Atlanta, GA, February 16, 1983

A federal judge reminded the White House Tuesday that reduced access to birth-control pills and information wasn't what Congress had in mind when it provided funds to combat "the problem of teenage pregnancy."

But that — and inevitably, increased teen-age pregnancies — would be the effect of the Reagan administration's "squeal rule," according to U.S. District Judge Henry F. Werker in New York, who enjoined the government from enforcing it until a trial is held.

Indeed, President Reagan and his staff seemed to need a reminder that it is Congress, and not the executive branch, that makes the laws — and that he has sworn to uphold them.

But it was only a temporary and perhaps a Pyrrhic victory for foes of the rule, which would require federally assisted clinics to notify the parents of teenage girls who receive birth-control pills or devices after Feb. 25. The administration has made no secret of its ambition to turn the clock back to that nostalgic, sepia-toned era when, as in Ronald Reagan's old movies, any explicit sexual activity was strictly out of sight. And it is mulling an appeal.

Still uncertain is whether two family-planning clinics and the state attorney general will be able to make a case for a permanent injunction in New York; whether the New York ruling stalls the rule in other states; and whether a federal judge in Washington will follow Werker's lead in a separate challenge by two national organizations: the Planned Parenthood Federation of America and the National Family Planning and Reproductive Health Association.

And there is probably no way of calculating the damage already done by the administration's widely publicized campaign to force parental notification. It's bound to erode the trust invested cautiously over the years in federally assisted clinics by two generations of teenagers, many of whom have repeatedly told pollsters that they who would sooner risk pregnancy than discuss their sexual activities with their parents.

But Werker's finding, that the so-called squeal rule "contradicts and subverts the intent of Congress," puts the ball squarely in the administration's court, where it belongs.

Werker found that the rule "would cause increased adolescent pregnancies," it is in "blatant disregard for one of the main purposes of Title X, and unless a trial on the merits discloses information that is drastically to the contrary, the regulations cannot be upheld."

Werker also observed that the rule would require doctors to violate patient confidentiality, and would mean that "many maladies including venereal disease will not be prevented, detected or treated."

Werker's decision injects a breath of reason in an increasingly ideological, administration-generated fog.

BUFFALO EVENING NEWS
Buffalo, NY, February 18, 1983

It is surely understandable why almost all parents would want to be informed when an unmarried daughter under 18 seeks prescription contraceptives from a family-planning clinic. Most parents would not want their daughter to become sexually active under these conditions, but in any event would want at least to be involved in the discussions about this matter and its many ramifications. Such parental concerns are logical and easily understood.

Thus, the pending new federal regulation that would require federally assisted family-planning clinics to notify parents when their minor unmarried daughter gets such prescriptive contraceptives was clearly developed with the best of intentions.

For all of that, however, we believe that the new regulation would do more harm than good in its actual consequences, and that Federal Judge Henry F. Werker reached a reasonable decision in suspending its implementation pending a trial of the contested issues.

Judge Werker found, for example, that the regulation requiring parental notification exceeded the 1981 law passed by Congress, which properly required family-planning clinics to encourage minors to consult with their parents but did not mandate notification by the clinics.

A revealing 1979-1980 study by the Alan Guttmacher Institute of 1,200 unmarried minors receiving contraceptives at family-planning clinics showed that 54 percent had already informed their parents. Another 22 percent said they would continue to attend the clinics if their parents were informed. The other 24 percent said they would not attend — but, significantly, only two percent said they would give up sexual relations.

In other words, the parental notification requirement, no matter how well intentioned, would be likely to keep thousands of teenagers out of the clinics but not away from sex. The probable consequences of that would be more teenage pregnancies and abortions. Additionally, in Judge Werker's opinion, it would mean that "many maladies, including venereal disease, will not be prevented, detected or treated."

All of this suggests why the Reagan administration, while correct in wanting to foster communication between parents and teenagers concerning sex, should reconsider the practical wisdom of mandatory notification

THE INDIANAPOLIS STAR
Indianapolis, IN, February 27, 1983

Your 14-year-old eighth grade daughter must have a signed permission slip from you before she is allowed to accompany her class downtown on a field trip — to the Statehouse, for instance, to watch state lawmakers in action.

But she can walk into a federally-subsidized agency and receive prescription drugs to prevent pregnancy without your even knowing about it, much less consenting to it. At least that's what a federal judge decided recently when he banned implementing "the squeal rule."

That harmless provision requires that a parent or guardian be informed *after the fact* that a minor has received birth control advice and drugs subsidized by tax funds. The "squeal" comes in when the parent is unaware the child is sexually active.

The tattle-tale aspect has believers and dispensers of the permissive society foaming at the mouth. They argue that the youngster's right to privacy is at stake and warn that squealing on them won't stop sexual activity but will result in more abortions and more illegitimate births.

They don't think it will promote teen-age continence or what folks used to call chastity. Even suggesting that possibility brings a smirk to their faces. On the other hand, neither can these self-appointed experts explain the irony in the fact that the more numerous and accessible sex counseling programs become, the higher abortion and illegitimacy rates soar.

The public forum appears obsessed with "squealing." A proposal in the Indiana Senate which would permit a physician to treat an unmarried pregnant girl without notifying her parents of her condition is officially labeled a "right to health" bill. But what's it called? The "no squeal" bill.

Both the federal and state issues are predicated on such notions as 1. the intimate life of a teenager is no business of the parent; 2. if the parent finds out about sexual activity, the minor is likely to be mistreated or abused and 3. objective, dispassionate third parties can best determine a minor's welfare.

In consequence, parental rights and responsibilities are discarded. Youth's right to do its own thing becomes inviolate. Family closeness and parental love are demeaned. A network of faceless sociologists and medical technologists are given custody of the future.

But who will pick up the pieces that slip through their sterile, mechanical fingers? Some robotized savior appointed from the bench?

The Morning News

Wilmington, DE, February 16, 1983

U.S. DISTRICT Judge Henry F. Werker wisely blocked the Reagan administration from enforcing an ill-thought and counterproductive regulation that would have required notification of parents whose children receive prescription contraceptives.

Appropriately dubbed the squeal rule, this notification requirement was to go into effect later this month. It would have affected all family planning services that get any federal money and would have required these agencies to notify within 10 days by registered mail the parents or guardians of any "unemancipated minor" getting prescription contraceptives.

The intent behind this regulation was noble: To improve communication between parents and children. Great. But who is so naive as to believe that family communication can be ordered by law? Besides, existing federal laws and regulations on family planning already specify that the counseling (as opposed to forced notification) of teen-agers include encouragement to consult with their parents.

A cogent reminder of how difficult such communication can be even in a supportive, good family situation is described by a young law student on this page. Ask if helpful discussion of anything as private and personal as sexual relations could take place in a bad home situation and the answer is obvious.

So what would a notification requirement achieve? It would violate patient-doctor confidentiality. It would discriminate against women, because prescription contraceptives apply only to them. It would differentiate between teen-agers getting contraceptives from private physicians where no parental notification is required and those getting contraceptives from federally supported agencies subject to the notification rule.

But that's not all. As Judge Werker pointed out, the most serious consequences of the regulations would be "increased adolescent pregnancies" and lack of treatment for "many maladies, including venereal diseases." What the promulgators of the squeal rule overlook is that the kind of counseling and contraceptive assistance available at organizations like Planned Parenthood involve medical examinations, explanations of the reproductive process, periodic checkups and more. All of that would be lost once the notification requirement would make it impossible for young women to seek on their own aid with sexual matters.

In the best of all worlds, with parents and children having harmonious, open relationships, with accord on ethics and sexual conduct, the notification requirement would work, though it would be superfluous. But in the real world, the notification requirement would cause more harm than good, as Judge Werker had the good sense to recognize.

THE PLAIN DEALER

Cleveland, OH, February 16, 1983

When a federal judge in New York ruled against the implementation of a new government regulation called — appropriately — the "squeal rule," it was as if a breath of sweet and rational air had gusted across the family-planning landscape. The rule would have forced all family-planning clinics that receive Title X federal funds to inform the parents of "unemancipated" minors that their children were seeking contraceptive help. That is obviously detrimental to the causes of health and family planning, to say nothing of the war against unwanted pregnancies.

We are not unsympathetic to the desires of most parents to know what their children are doing, especially when it comes to sex. And we are not unaware of the argument which states, essentially, that the uninhibited distribution of contraceptives to teen-agers may infringe on the rights of parental responsibility. Many parents are understandably concerned that the ready availability of contraception without accountability threatens the moral standards they try to set for their offspring.

The "squeal rule," however, will not promote accountability as much as irresponsibility. It will not deter teen-agers from sex, but rather deter them from contraceptives. It is clear that the rule would openly contribute thousands of unwanted teen-age pregnancies each year, and further help spread the vast assortment of health hazards that accompany the practice of uneducated, unprotected teen-age sex.

So, U.S. District Judge Henry F. Werker blocked the "squeal rule" regulation, calling it "ill-conceived and illegal." Although the real test will occur when challenges to the rule itself come before the courts, we are nevertheless optimistic that it will be permanently overturned.

It is not coincidental that the ignominious and ignoble "squeal rule" provides an argument in favor of sex education. The rule would surely perpetuate the stigmas surrounding teenage sex, thereby promoting both ignorance and recklessness.

The legitimate concerns of parents that the government is smothering their rights would be moot if high-quality sex education was universally available. Greater awareness of sexual responsibility will surely lead to more mature sexual attitudes and open little-used lines of communication so that children and parents can freely talk about sex without having the government hovering in the background, ready to point an accusatory finger of shame.

The Miami Herald

Miami, FL, July 14. 1983

THE REAGAN Administration's infamous "squeal rule" has gone to its just reward, rejected again by the unanimous, common-sense decision of a Federal appeals court. The three-judge panel was unequivocal in ruling that the lower court had been correct in blocking the Administration from forcing birth-control clinics to "squeal" to the parents of their teenage-girl patients.

If Congress had wanted a parental-notification requirement to be imposed on clinics that serve teenage girls, the two Federal courts agreed, Congress would have said so. Evidence was overwhelming, however, that Congress knew the difference between "encouraging" parental involvement and requiring notification.

Thus the punitive rule, which would have affected about 400,000 girls per year, is exposed for what it was. It was an attempt by then-Secretary of Health and Human Services (HHS) Richard Schweiker to erect a barrier between sexually active teenage girls and the public-service clinics that try to keep them out of the pregnancy-statistics columns.

Those columns have grown in recent years to frightening dimensions. By age 18, more than half of America's girls have had intercourse. Those encounters produce 1.2 million pregnancies per year. Forty per cent of all the women who turned 20 in the United States in 1982 had been pregnant at least once.

As a direct result of the teen pregnancy rate, which is rising fastest among girls aged 10 to 14, poverty in America has been increasingly an affliction of children living with a single mother. The odds that those children will suffer educational deficiencies, become criminal or dependent, or otherwise fail to contribute to society are stark and widely known.

Yet the Reagan HHS, in the grandfatherly pose of helping parents get closer to their children, tried to impose the wolfish snarl of the squeal rule. Never mind that few virgins seek help from birth-control clinics. Never mind that sexually active persons past puberty only rarely revert to voluntary celibacy. Never mind that some of the girls affected already had been pregnant. The HHS tried to inflict through the force of law the fantasy notion that every teenager in America enjoys the luxury of living with a sober, stable, concerned parent with whom she can discuss sex.

Not so, of course. Congress knows that, and it based the funding of birth-control clinics on its knowledge. Congress, as the courts have seen, adopted a "specific policy of confidentiality" because of its "overriding concern about the escalating teenage pregancy rate." The Administration exceeded its Constitutional authority when it unilaterally tried to make new law instead of administering the law that Congress wrote.

Even an Administration riddled with ideologs should not have required Federal-court action to interpret this law correctly. The nation, and the 400,000 young women potentially affected by the rejected rule, owe a debt of gratitude to the Congress and courts, which on this issue see so much more clearly than the President's men.

THE SACRAMENTO BEE
Sacramento, CA, July 18, 1983

Last week a federal appellate court in Washington affirmed a lower court ruling striking down the government's so-called "squeal rule." The rule, promulgated by former Secretary of Health and Human Services Richard Schweiker just before he left office earlier this year, would have required all federally funded clinics to notify parents when their teen-age daughters received contraceptives from such a clinic. The intent of Congress, said the court majority, was first and foremost to support rational family planning and prevent unwanted pregnancy, and while the law mentions the encouragement of "family participation" in such decisions, that was not its primary intent.

There is a sensitive moral issue here: Put most bluntly, should the government, in effect, collude with minors against their parents? Every good clinic already encourages teenagers to voluntarily discuss the matter with their parents. Yet as many medical and family-planning organizations have pointed out, if the clinics made it a practice of informing parents regardless of the wishes of the child, most teen-agers wouldn't go there at all and there would be even many more adolescent pregnancies than there are now.

The issue transcends the role of the clinic. The very fact that many teen-agers go to such clinics without informing their parents indicates that there are already serious problems in family participation and communication that no rule is likely to overcome; if anything, it's likely to exacerbate them no matter how well-intentioned the rule may be.

The teen-agers who go to family-planning clinics, unlike many of their peers, display the beginnings of some responsibility about their sex lives, however difficult their relations with their parents may be on this point. That responsibility ought to be encouraged by government, not stifled.

The Kansas City Times
Kansas City, MO, July 13, 1983

A three-judge U.S. Court of Appeals panel has turned thumbs down on the so-called "squeal rule" which requires family planning clinics to notify parents when their children are supplied contraceptives. The appeals court is the third to rule against the administration on this regulation — the two others were lower courts in New York and Washington — and that ought to settle it. It is time for the government to stop the waste of taxpayers' money in attempting to put into effect this order.

The appeals court said the Department of Health and Human Services regulation contradicts the intent of Congress, which has appropriated money to combat the problems of teenage pregnancy. The court said in effect that Congress, while encouraging family participation in this decision to the extent practical, did not want to discourage teen-agers from seeking contraceptives because they feared their privacy would be violated.

The squeal rule is not currently in effect, and clinics do not have to inform parents if teenagers visit them. Considering the reception it has received in the courts so far, the regulation may never become law.

That is good news for youths seeking more information about a subject they do not feel comfortable discussing with parents. It also is good news for a society coping with the financial, social and health consequences of thousands of unwed teen-age mothers and fathers. It is time the administration gave up this ill-conceived idea.

The Providence Journal
Providence, RI, July 12, 1983

Once again the courts have declared illegal a federal regulation that would have required family planning agencies to notify parents of girls under 18 who had been given birth control devices. Once again good sense has prevailed.

The "squeal rule," so named by its opponents, was proposed by the Department of Health and Human Services (HHS). It would do damage far beyond merely involving parents in a difficult situation. It would eliminate the confidentiality that family planning clinics need to help young women avoid unwanted pregnancies. And it would virtually force sexually active teenagers to ignore the risks in order to prevent interference at home. What that would do to teenage pregnancy statistics can only be imagined.

The U.S. Court of Appeals for the District of Columbia voted, 2 to 1, last Friday that the rule would violate the intent of Congress. Under the Public Health Service Act of 1970 Congress provided funds for family planning services. About 5,000 clinics receive these funds each year and assist some 600,000 teenagers under 18.

In concert with his opposition to legal abortion, President Reagan has been emphatic in promoting parental involvement in their children's sexuality. As long as such involvement remains voluntary it is all to the good. But once a teenager decides to make her own decisions, government violation of her privacy can only invite the most serious consequences.

The time to exert parental influence is early in a child's life. The purpose of sex education and guidance is to help prepare a young person for maturity. Clinics provide their services when this stage is passed and teenagers seek additional help.

Unwanted teenage pregnancies have become a national problem. Undoubtedly that problem would become far worse if the clinics' ability to assist young people were undermined. More unwed mothers and their children would become dependent on welfare; more young lives would be diverted from education, satisfying employment and a happy life.

The "squeal rule" represents a misguided effort to ignore the dynamics of teenage sexuality and revert to a simpler time before birth control had become an issue and when families supposedly solved all difficult problems without outside help.

The Des Moines Register
Des Moines, IA, December 16, 1983

Here's a common-sense victory on the family-planning front: The Reagan administration, after almost two years of trying to force parental notification before contraceptives can be prescribed for teen-agers, has finally given up.

The Reagan effort, greeted by hundreds of thousands of protests when it was issued in February 1982, was never enacted because of federal-court injunctions. The courts ruled against it, saying it went beyond the intent of Congress, which had said parents should be encouraged to become involved in their teen-agers' contraceptive decisions.

Indeed they should, and most family-planning agencies make strong efforts to involve them. But parental involvement is not the best course in every case. Making it a hard-and-fast requirement could only damage the effort to make family-planning readily available.

The Reagan administration's record on family planning makes it only too likely that damage was the intent. First the administration tried to turn funds for family-planning agencies from a specific grant to a block grant, in which the agencies would surely have lost out to less-controversial causes.

When Congress nixed that idea, Reagan wrote to Utah's Senator Orrin Hatch: "I regret that we do not have the votes to defeat the family-planning program. . . . Perhaps we can remedy some of the problems . . . administratively . . . ."

The ensuing "remedies" included guidelines requiring separation of family-planning and abortion functions, meaning higher costs for all concerned.

The next assault is likely to come in September, when the legislation authorizing federal spending on family planning expires. Family-planning opponents are expected then to attempt to include, in the legislation, parental-notification language similar to that in the now-defeated regulation.

Family-planning agencies can hardly rest easy with such an eager enemy. Still, at least one unwise chapter in this misguided attack has ended.

The Oregonian
Portland, OR, July 16, 1983

Last week, the U.S. Court of Appeals in the District of Columbia upheld a lower court order against enforcing the Reagan administration "squeal rule" on dispensing birth control devices. The decision should be seen as a statement about constitutional grants of power, not as a declaration on morality, birth control or parental authority.

Disregard of congressional intent by the Department of Health and Human Services, an executive agency, was cited as reason for the decision.

President Reagan should not appeal the matter further on that ground. If he feels he must persist in trying to inject his moral views into the law of the land, he should go back to Congress and get it to change its intent.

A Department of Health and Human Services order would have required federally funded family-planning clinics to notify parents when their teen-age daughters were given contraceptives. Opponents argued this would do little to curb teen-age sex but would increase the number of teen-age pregnancies by scaring away those who might have sought birth control information and help. Congress agreed.

The appeals court took note of this, calling the rule unlawful because it contravenes congressional intent, which "recognized the critical role played by the assurance of confidentiality in attracting adolescents to the clinics."

Last month, the Supreme Court rapped the knuckles of Congress for using the congressional veto to infringe on the rights of the executive branch. Now the court is reining in the executive branch.

These two rulings remind us that none of the three branches of federal government — executive, legislative or judicial — is to encroach on another's territory. The country will be triply well served if the judicial branch, which has drawn congressional disapproval on many occasions for decisions that congressmen contend are actually legislation by the courts, examines its own actions in this light.

Many things may have changed since the nation's founders framed the Constitution, but the government has the same separation of powers. Reagan properly was pulled up short for trying to upset the balance by misusing the executive branch's rule-making authority.

Detroit Free Press
Detroit, MI, July 12, 1983

A FEDERAL appeals court has struck down the "squeal rule," and for the time being, at least, that formidable barrier to providing family planning services for teenagers remains in abeyance.

The rule, proposed by Richard H. Schweiker, former secretary of Health and Human Services, would have required family planning clinics that receive federal funds to notify parents within 10 days if birth control devices were given to any client under 18. The rule would have affected about 5,000 clinics serving more than 600,000 women under the age of 18.

The rationale for the rule was that it would strengthen the family by alerting parents that daughters were sexually active. The practical effect was to deter such teens from seeking any help at all.

The heart of the argument is a chicken-and-egg controversy over whether the availability of contraceptive information encourages teenagers to be sexually active, or whether teenagers first become sexually involved and then seek birth control advice. Many family planners and counselors believe firmly it is the latter. Society sends frequent and blatant messages to young people about the acceptability of sex. Family planning clinics deal with the consequences, not the causes, of that.

Family ties surely do need to be strengthened; vulnerable teenagers need to be told that "no" is a perfectly acceptable, even desirable, word. But at the point that teens show up at family planning clinics, such observations are mostly after the fact. For most teenagers, the squeal rule was a deterrent not to sex, but to getting help. The court acted wisely in striking it down.

AKRON BEACON JOURNAL
Akron, OH, July 13, 1983

IT'S TIME for President Reagan to toss the "squeal rule" aside and get on with more pressing government business.

That, of course, would be the wise thing to do, now that a federal appeals court has said the Reagan administration can't force federally funded family planning clinics to notify parents of teen-age girls who receive birth control devices.

The panel of judges in Washington said the Department of Health and Human Services had no legal authority to require parental notification. Congress, they pointed out, did not mandate parental involvement when it approved federal money for family planning services.

The squeal rule was to have taken effect Feb. 25. It would have applied to 5,000 clinics which dispense birth control devices to unmarried girls under 18. Judges in New York and Washington blocked the rule from being enforced; now the appeals court has upheld the judges' orders.

The regulation was clearly aimed at tackling the growing epidemic of teen-age pregnancies. More than 1.2 million teen-age girls get pregnant each year, most accidentally. Many of the young women who decide to give birth will wind up on welfare.

In theory, the squeal rule was formulated to bring parents and children closer together; then, the entire family could cope sensibly with the issue of teen-age sexuality.

In reality, the rule would do nothing to lessen sexual intimacy among those too young to appreciate the consequences. It would merely frighten sexually active girls away from birth-control clinics, and the results would be more unwanted babies, more venereal disease.

Government decrees will not stop many young people from discovering sex before they are mature enough to handle it responsibly. Those teenagers wise enough to accept the responsibility should be able to get help without being afraid that their parents will find out.

Ultimately, the squeal rule won't help to build trust and respect among members of a family. That difficult but vital task falls to every parent and child, not the morality preachers in Washington.

The Chattanooga Times

Chattanooga, TN, December 5, 1983

The Reagan administration has wisely dropped its efforts to impose what became known as the "squeal rule" on birth control clinics receiving federal funds. The regulation would have required notification of parents when unmarried teen-agers received prescriptions for contraceptives or contraceptive devices. It would undoubtedly have had the effect of discouraging sexually active teen-agers from using birth control, thus adding to the tremendous national problem of teen-age pregnancies.

Parents should be involved in contraceptive decisions for their unmarried children, and Congress stipulated that such involvement should be encouraged by counselors at clinics receiving federal funds. The administration, however, overstepped the bounds of congressional intent by attempting to make notification of parents manadatory. It was on that basis that federal judges in Washington and New York ruled against the Reagan regulation. Solicitor General Rex Lee announced this week the government would not appeal those rulings to the Supreme Court.

This is not a question of the rightness or wrongness of pre-marital sexual activity among teen-agers. Government cannot successfully legislate or regulate what are essentially issues of moral standards. Surveys among youngsters clearly indicated that while mandatory parental notification would greatly reduce the number who use contraceptives, it would not change their sexual habits. Teen-age pregnancies, and the myriad problems they create for the mother, the child and society in general, could only have been expected to rise upon implementation of the "squeal rule."

Mr. Lee declined to explain what went into the decision to drop the government's appeal. We'd like to think the administration has come, albeit belatedly, to an understanding of the negative effects of the "squeal rule," but somehow that seems an overly optimistic view.

Chattanooga, TN, March 27, 1984

The Reagan administration has abandoned efforts to enforce a regulation requiring birth control clinics to notify parents of minors receiving perscription contraceptives, but the legal battle over the so-called "squeal rule" continues. This time the issue is who will pay legal fees incurred by the private groups which challenged the legality of the regulation in federal court. Under the Equal Access to Justice Act, parties who successfully sue the federal government may recover "reasonable" attorneys fees unless the government can show its position was "substantially justified." The Reagan administration maintains, of course, that it was justified, but the history of the "squeal rule" indicates otherwise.

The administration's chief attorney in the Department of Health and Human Services told the president in 1981 that the law would not allow the mandatory notification requirement. Mr. Reagan ignored this early advice and went full steam ahead; the rule became final last year. It sparked two lawsuits, both of which the government lost at the federal district court level. This judicial confirmation of the 1981 legal warning should have convinced Mr. Reagan he could not re-write the law by presidential fiat but it did not. The administration appealed the district court rulings and lost both.

The courts found that the "squeal rule" violated the intention of Congress and undermined the purpose of federal funding for birth control clinics, which is to reduce the number of adolescent pregnancies and abortions. Obviously, the parental notification rule would have discouraged many sexually active youngsters from seeking contraceptives, thereby contributing to the number of unwanted teenage preganancies. This was clear from the start, buttressed by the administration's own attorneys and by criticism from Congress.

The successful plaintiffs now seek reimbursement for legal fees totaling more than $290,000. That's a tremendous amount of money, but federal litigation is expensive. The government is never at a loss for funds to defend itself in court — even when it is in the wrong. And it was Mr. Reagan's stubborn intent to fight a losing battle that forced his opponents to their expense. That unreasonable intransigence should make his administration liable for reasonble attorneys fees, as provided by law. It will be up to the court to determine what is "reasonable."

FORT WORTH STAR-TELEGRAM
Fort Worth, TX, December 5 , 1983

In what amounts to a tacit acknowledgement of the wisdom of the cliche that says, "you can't win 'em all," the Reagan administration apparently has decided to surrender in its battle to force federally financed birth control clinics to clear it with parents before prescribing contraceptives to unmarried teen-agers.

That move on the part of the administration is as well-advised as the original move — immediately dubbed the "fink" rule — was ill-advised. Actually, it was worse than ill-advised. It was counterproductive, as are so many government programs that are spawned of good intentions but fall victim to shallow logic.

The restrictions were conceived by some of the more conservative advisers to the administration and were officially proposed by the Department of Health and Human Services in February 1982, while Richard Schweiker was still its director.

There was nothing wrong with the intent. People deeply concerned about what they perceived to be a breakdown in the American family structure deemed it morally offensive to furnish teen-agers with birth control information and/or devices without, first consulting their parents. And, morally, they were right. But, practically, they were wrong.

Teen-age pregnancies and venereal disease have been at an all-time high. The birth control clinics are trying to reverse that situation, and confidentiality is one of their best weapons. The major opposition to the government's proposal, voiced by clinic employees as soon as it was announced, was that its enforcement would tie their hands.

Application of the new rule would not cut down on sexual activity by teen-agers, but it would prevent them from contacting clinics and taking necessary precautions. The result, of course, would be higher pregnancy and VD rates.

The regulation has consistently lost when challenged in court, and last week, a Health and Human Services official said there were no plans to proceed to the Supreme Court. That is wise. Let's let the fink rule die a natural death.

Abortion Alternatives: Sex Ed, Adoption, Contraceptives

Encouraging alternatives to abortion has come to be as thorny an issue as the controversy over abortion itself. The possibilities range from preventing unwanted pregnancies to providing services for the children of those unwanted pregnancies that are carried to term. Opinion polls have shown that most people, including those who describe themselves as conservative, believe in the value of sex education. Usually, those parents who oppose sex education classes do so not because they object to the biological content of such instruction, but because they fear that along with this knowledge will be conveyed social attitudes different from their own. However, many school boards encourage or require sex education programs in order to counter the growing number of teenage pregnancies and abortions, hoping at least to eliminate simple ignorance as their cause.

Some parents and 'right-to-lifers' believe that the availability of contraceptives, as well as open classroom discussion of sexual matters, inevitably leads to promiscuity. Contraceptives are obviously the most widely used preventive measures against pregnancy—and the most effective, short of complete abstinence from sexual intercourse. But the Reagan Administration's efforts to promote "family values" through measures like the proposed "squeal rule" have seemingly been spent in a futile attempt to deny teenage sexuality, rather than to prevent the unwanted pregnancies that are often a result of the expression of that sexuality without benefit of contraception. (See pp. 154-165.) And, of course, the Catholic Church is adamantly opposed to the use of contraceptives even for married women.

At the other end of the spectrum is adoption. Funds for adoption counseling are included in some programs operated under Title X. (See pp. 172-177.) But in reality, most publicly funded programs do not extensively discuss the option of adoption with pregnant women. This is largely because adoption is the hardest course for a pregnant woman to take, requiring her to carry the unwanted fetus to term, with all the attendant physical and emotional difficulties, and then to turn the baby over to strangers.

The Charlotte Observer
Charlotte, NC, March 10, 1981

The anti-abortion movement in this country has taken a troubling new turn, steered by several key officials in the Reagan administration, including Richard Schweiker, Health and Human Services secretary, and Marjory Mecklenburg, his designee for adolescent pregnancy programs.

They're not only lobbying for the "human life amendment" — which would make abortion or birth control after conception tantamount to murder — but they've also begun arguing against federal support for education programs designed to help people *prevent* conception.

If their efforts are just part of the new administration's budget-cutting effort, it's false economy. Cutting money for sex education and distribution of contraceptives, and for abortion, only insures that more money will be needed for welfare and foster care.

But there's more than money involved. In effect, Mr. Schweiker, Mrs. Mecklenburg and others are not only demanding an end to tax-paid abortions; they're suggesting that women who become pregnant by mistake be required *by the Constitution* to bear their unwanted children. And they seem to be saying that a woman shouldn't have sex without the risk of unwanted pregnancy — almost as though unwanted pregnancy would be a proper punishment for her sin.

That attitude, despite its moralistic tone, is morally indefensible, because it victimizes the poor and the ignorant.

Among those who will suffer most are young girls, some as young as 12 and 13. Children are abysmally ignorant about sex, as the letter by Dr. Alex Sanchez, Jr. in today's Forum indicates. They learn about sex, as something carefree, from their friends, from television, and from the movies. They rarely hear about its dangers and responsibilities. And the results show up in record numbers of pregnant girls.

The anti-abortionists contend that children should learn how to "postpone sexual involvement" rather than how to use contraceptives, and they should learn that at home. Certainly they should, but unfortunately, most of them don't.

What makes the anti-abortion, anti-birth control movement particularly disturbing is that it comes at a time when many cities such as Charlotte are beginning to realize how many unwanted pregnancies occur within their limits each year. Agencies are beginning to put together programs which may, for the first time, start to combat the problem.

What they need is some encouragement, not discouragement, from public opinion shapers like Mr. Schweiker and Mrs. Mecklenburg.

The Star-Ledger
Newark, NJ, February 18, 1980

Reading, 'riting and 'rithmetic will be joined by a new required course if the State Board of Education presses ahead with its plan to require all schools in the state to conduct "family life" courses.

"Family life" is a code term for sex education, no more, no less. And the state would insist that a comprehensive program start with kindergarten and continue through high school, including lessons on sexual behavior and contraceptive techniques. Instruction would be offered in the "physical, mental, emotional, social, economic and psychological effects of interpersonal relationships."

Requiring sex education courses is justified by the board as a proper response to the increasing number of pregnancies among young students. It presupposes that ignorance is the villain, ignoring the possibility that "good" kids don't take contraceptive precautions because they don't intend to have intercourse, only to be caught up in an emotional situation. It's not that they don't know what to do, it's that they never expected to succumb.

* * *

There are other serious misgivings about teaching sex in school, including who will conduct the classes and what training will qualify them for the task. There is validity to the criticism that schools have enough to do trying to teach basics, and their record on this score leaves much to be desired.

One also must ask what the effect will be on impressionable youngsters of discussing sexual intimacies in a classroom setting. What happens to the privacy of the subject under such conditions?

The strongest objection to sex education in the schools, however, is the violence it does to the family structure. The school is not an acceptable surrogate parent. Social engineers already have gone too far in eroding parental authority — without providing an acceptable substitute.

* * *

No satisfactory relief can be expected from the Parents Right to Conscience Act which Gov. Brendan Byrne has signed into law. The measure permits children to be excused from sex education classes if parents or guardians sign a statement that they have moral or religious objections. Isolating youngsters from the pack is no answer, and it could be downright harmful, exposing sensitive students to peer-pressure ridicule.

There is an outside chance, however, that some enterprising parents may succeed in getting everyone to band together and sign their children out of the sex courses, thereby nullifying the state board's ruling.

Sex education may be a great idea for selling textbooks and teaching aids to school boards already straining to meet budget commitments. But it raises serious questions about societal relationships and should be resisted as a threat to family life as most families would like to live it.

Newsday

Long Island, NY, April 9, 1984

Suffolk County has the state's second highest rate of teenage pregnancy, but the county's lawmakers have been strangely reluctant to accept extra federal money for an existing program that counsels adolescents in the prevention of unplanned pregnancies.

Usually when more federal funding is available to pay for a local program, the Suffolk Legislature accepts it routinely. And that's how the legislature's health committee treated this $59,000 grant. But the full legislature voted 10-8 last month to send the proposal back to committee for a hearing.

Now that the hearing has been held and Health Commissioner David Harris has explained that the money would not be used to support abortion, the measure should be quickly approved.

The Right to Life Party, which lobbied for the hearing, used it to advocate abstention from intercourse as an alternative to contraceptive counseling. The trouble is, it's really not that much of an alternative. The county's health services department, which operates the program, already counsels abstention. But youngsters who are determined to ignore its advice need guidance on how to prevent unwanted pregnancies.

Over the past 10 years, the department estimates that adolescent births in the county have doubled. In 1981, 3,898 babies were born to women below the age of 19, and in 1982 the figure rose to 4,360. One of the mothers was 11 years old. The statistics don't divide the mothers into wed and unwed categories, but the department's 1982 estimate of births to unwed adolescents was 800.

"Nobody's trying to promote sexual activity," said a health department official. "What we're trying to do is make children understand that there is a relationship between sex and pregnancy."

The $59,000 is being funneled to Suffolk by the State Health Department, which is responsible for overall administration of the program. The money is from a federal maternal and child health program block grant.

In the 1982 gubernatorial election, the Right to Life Party drew less than 2 per cent of the total vote in Suffolk. That shouldn't be enough of a threat to prevent the county legislature from carrying out its responsibility.

The San Diego Union

San Diego, CA, April 7, 1984

National statistics show a decline in drug use among teens and figures suggest that teen-age premarital sexual activity is leveling off as well. Still, these social problems continue to plague most communities and San Diego is certainly no exception.

Last year, 2,168 area teens were arrested on drug charges. Of these, 261 were confirmed to be city school students. To date, 322 students have been apprehended for drug use this school year alone.

County health records show a significant percentage of VD cases among youngsters during the last several years. And, though the number of unwed mothers has dropped somewhat, it is well to remember that some 40 percent of all teen-age brides are pregnant.

What can be done to discourage young people from abusing their bodies? The city school district's social concerns advisory committee has recommended that the board of education require that drug and sex education units be part of mandated classes at the junior and senior high levels.

From 1967 to 1981, city students received a fairly detailed diet of classroom instruction and follow-up counseling from a team of 24 professionals who circulated among the system's schools. In the wake of budget cuts three years ago, however, sixth and eighth graders currently receive a smattering of hours in each area and only 63 percent of the 10th graders receive such instruction in an elective class that is part of the health and driver education program. Student counseling is almost non-existent because of recent staff reductions.

The committee doesn't think that this is sufficient instructional time and neither do we. At the same time, we doubt that the board will buy the committee's two-tier recommendation. Accordingly, we would suggest the city schools should concentrate their energies at the junior high level where these units will do the most good.

A one-semester course dealing with these two sensitive subjects could provide youngsters with the information and counseling they need. This way, the professionals would be better able to influence student behavior as well as impart cold facts. Surely such an approach would be preferable to the school system's present drug and sex education program that has been spread so thin as to be essentially meaningless.

The Idaho STATESMAN

Boise, ID, March 3, 1981

If recent advertisements in The Statesman are any indication, the battle over the abortion controversy is continuing full tilt. Ads from one side solicit support for some kind of human life amendment to the U.S. Constitution. Ads from the other side oppose such an amendment, charging it would infringe on Americans' right to privacy.

The rhetoric of this controversy has always been harsh. Right-to-lifers characterize their opponents as baby killers. Pro-abortionists castigate the right-to-lifers as fanatics who want to impose narrow-minded moral convictions on the rest of the population.

We suspect that neither characterization is really accurate. In fact, both sides appear to be motivated by the highest of considerations, a deep and abiding concern for their fellow humans. They simply have different beliefs and a corresponding difference in priorities.

Realistically, neither side is likely to change its mind. People who believe abortion is murder are going to continue to believe that. Likewise, those who want to reserve abortion as a last resort against unwanted pregnancy can be expected to cling tenaciously to that belief.

The point is that all these people — despite their philosophical differences — might do a lot of good by realizing there is a common ground on which they could cooperate to relieve human suffering now, while the political arguments rage on.

They could cooperate in at least two ways that would not compromise the beliefs of either side:

● By a renewed and joint effort to spread the word about birth control.

● By jointly encouraging adoption, as opposed to abortion, for pregnant women who are unwilling or unable to care for children. Abortion often is a dark and difficult experience for a woman, even if she believes it is acceptable. Adoption into a loving home is an alternative that can save the child and at the same time prevent the disruption of the lives of young men and women who are not able to assume the responsibility of parenthood.

Neither of these tactics will stop all abortions. Nor will they end the right-to-life movement's efforts to stop abortions through changes in the law.

What the tactics could do is save heartache for many. If such cooperation could stop one abortion or save one young couple from the trauma of parenthood at too early an age, then the small amount of compromise would be well worthwhile. The antagonists could continue their philosophical and political battle, but, meanwhile, lives would be saved.

The Philadelphia Inquirer
Philadelphia, PA, June 7, 1984

In Red Lion, Pa., parents, educators, students and concerned citizens are engaged in a roaring controversy about a health education class that includes such "volatile" subjects as premarital sex, prostitution, homosexuality and promiscuity.

Angered members of Red Lion Citizens for Decency, armed with 790 signatures, are demanding that the Board of Education fire Marlene Stein, a teacher with tenure, accused of "openly, directly and vehemently encouraging homosexuality, adulterous activity, premarital sex, prostitution, disrespect for parents and other types of activity...."

While Ms. Stein's teaching methods and class curriculum may appear to be at the heart of the controversy, her supporters argue that the commotion is really over many broader questions, including how much parental control should be asserted over curriculums in public schools.

Red Lion, located in an area sometimes referred to as Pennsylvania's Bible Belt, is only one of many communities of the country concerned about the lack of parental involvement in curriculum.

Clearly, parents should be involved in classroom subjects, but in a limited way. They also should be free to monitor all classes, especially those designed to provide information concerning sex.

The broad range of sex education for teenagers is needed more than ever. Teenage pregnancies are plentiful, homosexuality remains one of the most misunderstood of human situations and premarital problems among increasingly sexually active teenagers are on the rise.

Several educational organizations, including the National PTA, the National Education Association and the American Association of School Administrators, have expressed unhappiness with a Reagan administration plan to establish an office of Family Rights and Privacy in the U.S. Department of Education. They say such a program will be used to intimidate local school districts by meddling in curriculum disputes.

While family involvement in school affairs should be welcome, care must be taken to avoid the potential for abuse by religious, extremist, political and even radical groups who might infringe on the traditional rights of educators.

The best-qualified people to determine subject matter for public schools are still the professional teachers. Ms. Stein should not be made a scapegoat when broader issues are really at the center of the storm.

The Virginian-Pilot
Norfolk, VA, November 13, 1984

Suffolk parents are right to be alarmed by the rising number of teen pregnancies in the city. And the Teenage Pregnancy Committee of the Suffolk PTA Council is right to endorse a program of family-life education designed to curb early pregnancies and currently used in more than 60 state school districts. The sooner family-life instruction is added to the Suffolk schools' curriculum, the better for Suffolk youngsters.

The rising rate of teen pregnancies — children having children — constitutes a troubling national, as well as regional and local, phenomenon. Family-life education — for boys and girls alike, emphasizing constructive human relations — is one way in which society adds its voice to that of parents in trying to persuade young people of the merits of behaving responsibly toward one another during their school years and beyond.

There are no simple answers to preventing teen pregnancies. Some youngsters become sexually active early in their teen years. That such activity is often detrimental to their happiness and chances of leading fulfilling lives is amply and sorrowfully documented. Many youngsters who presumably know or should know about the hazards of premarital sexual intercourse become parents before they are self-supporting or capable of self-support. Everyone, including the parents-too-soon, pays for that.

Family-life education provides no guarantee against injudicious sexual behavior by unhappy, rebellious or manipulative young people. Learning is a weak bulwark against strong, if often transient, emotion. The forces that impel many young people to self-destructive behavior are usually complex: low self-esteem, poor communication within families, lack of motivation and a limited sense of the possibilities for self-development.

Nonetheless, a family-life curriculum in the Suffolk public schools could alter the course of some young lives for the better; could get across the message that teen pregnancy does not solve problems but multiplies them; that although becoming a mother may in some ways fill the emotional void felt by some young women, the long-term consequences for mothers and children are frequently undesirable.

A well-planned, well-executed family-life course of study makes that point as well as others. For those who become teen-age mothers anyway, the proposed Suffolk plan provides for home instruction in school subjects in the eighth and ninth months of pregnancy and for two weeks after a birth. That's sensible also. By furthering the education of young mothers, by encouraging young mothers to stay in school, the program could return to society dividends far greater than its modest cost to the taxpayers.

The Record
Hackensack, NJ, October 2, 1984

Here's an irony for you: Most parents believe that sex education belongs in the home, but fewer than 20 percent say they teach their children about sex. We have an idea that the subject comes up at more kitchen tables than that — but often the instruction is limited one word — "don't." To judge from the alarming rise in the number of teen-age pregnancies, that one word isn't enough.

New Jersey is one of a number of states that have tried to fill this information gap by requiring sex and family-life education in the public schools. By next year, all schools in this state must offer such programs. Many school districts — after debating recommendations from parents, teachers, and members of religious groups — have adopted curriculums on family planning and human sexuality.

The classroom is a better place to teach young people about sex than, say, the street corner. But the best place is still the home. Parents need to talk candidly about sex, because silence can also be a powerful teacher — of exactly the wrong lesson. Evading the topic just heightens curiosity about it.

Planned Parenthood, the family-planning organization, has declared October "National Family Sexuality Education Month." Through programs and community meetings, it will offer parents guidance on how to talk to their children about this sensitive subject. Planned Parenthood has enlisted help from other influential groups — the YMCA, the National Council of Churches, the Girls Clubs of America, and the National Education Association, among others.

No responsible parent can argue that sex education belongs in the home, then fail to provide it. But before parents teach their children about sex, they should be well prepared for the role — as much as any teacher on any subject. That's Planned Parenthood's mission, and a welcome one it is.

Hackensack, NJ, January 28, 1985

Considering the vehemence of their feelings, it isn't surprising that Right to Life organizations want "The Silent Scream" — a graphic videotape showing the abortion of a 12-week fetus — to become part of North Jersey's school curriculum.

The propriety of allowing public schools to become a platform for what is largely a religious issue is certainly debatable, but that's not our main concern. Nor do we want to delve into whether the intrinsic violence of any surgical procedure — from gall-bladder operation to abortion — is suitable fare for schoolchildren.

But if any North Jersey educator should make the highly questionable decision to allow this film into a school, it would be important to provide proper balance — by which we mean a videotape of equal length and vividness showing the fate of unwanted children.

"The Silent Scream" shows one side of the story — the horrors that can befall a tiny creature in the womb. Pictures of neglected and abused children — some of them abandoned or beaten or covered with cigarette burns — would show another.

In one case, the screams may be silent. In the other, they're very audible, but seldom heard by anyone who offers any help.

THE TENNESSEAN
Nashville, TN, January 23, 1984

STATE Sen. Douglas Henry is supporting a thorough and realistic program of family life education in the state schools. He is to be commended for his initiative in this delicate area.

According to the senator, there were 18,537 teenage pregnancies in Tennessee in 1981 and 5,375 of those pregnancies were terminated by abortion.

The senator has formed a task force of some knowledgeable professionals in the area of family planning and sex education. The group includes representatives of Planned Parenthood, Catholic Charities, Family and Children's Services, and several state departments.

Senator Henry presented the data compiled by the task force to a recent meeting of the state Board of Education. The board is now developing a long-range curriculum for health education, and Senator Henry wants family life education included in that program.

He is advocating a program that would go beyond instruction on sexual development. It would include counseling on prenatal care, adoption services, and responsible parenting as well as encouragement to teen-aged parents to return to school.

The highly personal and extremely sensitive nature of sex education has made it one of the most controversial curriculum areas. Many people still maintain that sex education is the responsibility of the family and the church, and is not a proper area of involvement for public schools. But the teenage pregnancy rate indicates that many families have not successfully shouldered that responsibility.

The program that Senator Henry advocates is realistic, thoughtful and sensitive. It could help many Tennessee youths receive accurate information that is vital to their physical and emotional development.

THE KANSAS CITY STAR
Kansas City, MO, April 2, 1984

What is it that possesses a certain kind of parent with the wish to keep their children as ignorant as they may have been? The theoretical answer may come from psychologists, but the practical aspects of the problem once again are in the hands of the Independence school board.

Some parents are objecting to books on sex in the teachers' reference library and in the private possession of a teacher. This theme is played frequently, for one generation of young people after another displays a persistent interest in and curiosity about sex. This continues to disturb and worry the type of adults who wish it would go away. It won't. After all these ages there is one certainty: Inflicting deliberate ignorance on children won't work. What they don't know *can* hurt them.

Parents have every right to raise questions about sex education or any other kind of schooling that concerns them. The school board has the responsibility to reject their head-in-the-sand view of the world that would penalize not only their own children but the children of others and the quality of Independence schools.

DAYTON DAILY NEWS
Dayton, OH, December 6, 1985

Baltimore school officials have evidence that sex counseling in schools can cut pregnancy rates among teen-age girls and help girls put off their first sexual experience. It's a program other metropolitan areas, including Dayton, should consider.

The Baltimore program was used in one junior high school and one high school. Two social workers, a nurse-midwife and a nurse practitioner were available as counselors. They were permitted to refer students to an outside family-planning clinic for contraceptive devices.

Apparently, many of the students did use the clinic. At those schools, the pregnancy rate for sexually active females dropped from 12.5 percent in 1981 to 11.5 percent four years later. At the same time, pregnancy rates were rising among Baltimore teen-agers in general.

In addition to a lower pregnancy rate, the girls at those two schools were delaying the start of sexual activity from an original 15 years, 7 months median age to 16 years, 2 months. That's not a spectacular change, but it suggests that if teens can talk openly about sexuality and get straightforward, non-judgmental answers, maybe they can make choices for them selves that are more responsible.

According to the clinic director, students were urged to say no, and if they weren't going to say that, they should use contraceptives.

More and more schools around the country, including Cleveland schools, have decided that the way to deal with teen pregnancies is to offer private sex counseling, even health clinics, on school premises.

This approach is controversial because many parents think sex should be discussed only at home in the context of religious beliefs, and if it is not discussed there, it shouldn't be discussed in school. Others fear frank discussions about sex will entice kids to try what they've learned. Meanwhile, a frightening number of our children are becoming parents.

the Charleston Gazette
Charleston, WV, April 5, 1984

TRAGICALLY, unmarried American teenage girls become pregnant and have babies with far greater frequency than their counterparts in most Western countries.

The sorry consequences — poverty, ruined education, lost careers, ill health, family disorder — are spelled out in the current *Gazette* series by reporter Patty Vandergrift.

Other nations do better. For instance, Ford Foundation researchers found that the pregnancy rate for 15- to 19-year-old girls is only 13 per thousand in Holland and 38 per thousand in Sweden — compared with 111 per thousand in the United States.

Does that mean Dutch and Swedish girls are more chaste?

Hardly. Instead, it means that most European youngsters enjoy the benefit of intelligent, matter-of-fact, general knowledge about how to cope with their sexuality and avoid harmful consequences.

America might gain ground if sex education were routine in public schools. But taboos remain deep-rooted and little progress is being made. Kanawha County hasn't recovered from the stormy days when sex education foes catapulted Alice Moore to the school board, then participated in the historic 1974 upheaval against "godless" textbooks.

Today, only one Kanawha County course, an elective for high school seniors, touches sex education. But it has good results: Youths at Herbert Hoover High School who experienced 24-hour-a-day, seven-day-a-week responsibility for make-believe babies decided they weren't ready for teenage pregnancy.

Since county school board members can be victims of hysterical, know-nothing, local outbreaks, the more insulated state Board of Education is the appropriate body to put sex education into West Virginia schools. If the board had courage enough to mandate C-average grades for student athletes, it should be equally brave in other fields.

Caution should be taken to reassure parents and church groups that sex education isn't X-rated. "Family life and human development" classes are just that: they deal with people's feelings, responsibility between people, biological changes of puberty, and finally with reproductive matters.

Maryland's well-established statewide program, outlined in today's chapter of the series, would be a good model for West Virginia. It begins in kindergarten with simple instruction in respecting feelings of others. It progresses as students progress. Parents may ask that their youngsters be excused — but few do.

West Virginia's statewide task force on teen pregnancy and the state Commission on Children and Youth each could play a role in establishing sex education in West Virginia. Their recommendations would be valuable to the state Board of Education.

Sexual development is a fact of teenage life. Ignorance and taboo hurt West Virginia youths — and the unintended babies they produce. Sensible classes in West Virginia schools are long overdue.

The Providence Journal

Providence, RI,
November 30, 1985

More than a million teenage pregnancies a year in the United States represents a social problem of staggering proportions. It has negative implications for the welfare system, for parents and grandparents of unwanted children, for delinquency, crime, drug abuse and numerous other major difficulties.

Researchers at Johns Hopkins University have demonstrated that the situation is not beyond control. In an experimental program conducted at two Baltimore public schools, they have shown that counseling and the availability of contraceptives does have an impact on the sexual activities of teenagers.

"This data is significant," said Janet B. Hardy, who oversaw the program started in 1981, "because it really refutes the claims of those who believe that the provision of contraceptives causes kids to become promiscuous." Over 2½ years of counseling, referral to a family planning clinic and dispensing of contraceptives, a 15 percent decline in pregnancy among sexually active girls was recorded. In contrast, among groups of students who received no such assistance, pregnancy increased 18 percent.

Further, the median age at which teenagers in the program became sexually active increased from 15 years, seven months to 16 years, two months after counseling.

With good reason, it appears that Americans are more concerned about this problem than was previously thought. A major study made public Nov. 4 found that 84 percent of the 1,253 adults 18 and over who responded considered the problem serious. Further, 64 percent of the parents questioned said they believed they had little or no control over their children's sexual activity and thought outside help from schools and television was needed. Seventy-eight percent said birth control information should be presented on television.

Clearly, parents, clergy, public policymakers, education and health officials and the media should collaborate on programs to impart a greater awareness to young people before the problems arise rather than afterwards. Faye Wattleton, president of Planned Parenthood, says case studies show that the average teenager engaged in sexual intercourse 11 months before the first exposure to birth control information.

If we expect children to be responsible without providing them with the information they need, adults in large part must accept responsibility for the consequences.

The Hartford Courant

Hartford, CT, April 9, 1985

The General Assembly's Education Committee acted courageously Monday in giving favorable readings to two legislative initiatives aimed at preventing teenage pregnancy.

By wide margins, proposals to require state-funded family life and sex education courses in Connecticut schools and to establish five model school-based health clinics were sent on to the Appropriations Committee.

Both bills are carefully considered and take the wishes of local authorities and parents into account. Moreover, the dimensions of the problem the measures seek to ameliorate should concern everyone. According to figures compiled by the legislation's co-sponsors, 10,000 teenagers become pregnant in Connecticut each year.

It's not just a city problem. Some rural towns and small cities have rates close to or worse than those of big cities. It's a problem that affects all groups. Non-white teens gave birth to 1,332 babies in 1982; white teens had 3,020 babies. And for every live birth to Connecticut teens, there are 1.2 abortions, mostly in the suburbs.

Besides its deleterious emotional effects on both boys and girls, adolescent pregnancy results in low birth weight and increased risk of death for infants; more physical, mental and emotional handicaps for babies who do survive infancy; and interrupted education and later inability to find or hold jobs for young mothers.

It's also expensive: The sponsors estimate the state spends $50 million annually in welfare and medical payments that directly stem from pregnancies among teenagers.

What's the solution? Teaching children not to have children is most basic.

To that end, the legislation proposes state-funded mandatory courses in family life and sex education in all 169 towns for grades kindergarten through 12. The other bill would create pilot health clinics for teens at risk of becoming pregnant or repeating pregnancy. The measures were recommended by the General Assembly's Task Force on Education To Prevent Adolescent Pregnancy.

Only about 70 towns and cities now have sex education programs in schools. Most of the curriculums are too little and too late to do any good. Under the proposed legislation, each town would set its own curriculum. Course materials on "family life, parenting, human sexuality, nutrition and decision-making" would be written by a community advisory council of parents, clergy, doctors, nurses and teachers.

The school-based clinic legislation is just as cautious. The five full-time pilot clinics would be for referral only, would not dispense contraceptives, would not be permitted to advocate termination of pregnancy and would be run with parent advisory boards.

A large body of literature supports the contention that sex education programs in schools and making contraceptives more easily available to teenagers helps prevent pregnancies, venereal disease and abortions and helps youngsters learn how to be better spouses and parents.

The measures provoked opposition because they involve sexuality, and the perception of state interference in what many feel should be a private matter. But what workable solutions do opponents suggest? The fact is that many teenagers are already sexually active and do get pregnant, give birth and have abortions.

The bills approved by the Education Committee deserve enactment by the Legislature.

THE SUN

Baltimore, MD, January 4, 1985

Most kinds of medical treatment offered the poor end up paying for themselves many times over, but few yield rewards on the scale of contraceptive programs. It costs about $80 a year to provide contraceptive services to a woman (teenager or adult) but society spends, on the average, more than $18,000 to help a single teenage mother raise a single child.

Indirect benefits are impressive, too. The Centers for Disease Control say treatments for sexually transmitted diseases in the United States cost $2 billion a year. The figure is far higher than necessary because poor people often wait too long before seeking help and end up with costly complications. Johns Hopkins and University of Maryland researchers say the rate of untreated sexually transmitted diseases among poor teenage girls in Baltimore is "appallingly high" — well over 30 percent for one kind of infection. A happy side effect of contraceptive services is that they also require medical examinations. These reveal the diseases, which can then be treated.

Another advantage — demonstrated in an East Baltimore pilot program for teenage girls and boys operated by Johns Hopkins — is that contraception programs reduce the number of abortions performed. Yet another: Too often the unwanted babies of poor mothers, especially teenage mothers, are poorly cared for and grow up to add to the welfare rolls or the crime rate.

Despite all the advantages, contraceptive services are so inadequate in Maryland that fewer than two-thirds of the poor women who need and want this sort of help can get it. Particularly hard hit by recent declines in federal funds are contraception education and outreach programs. Also harmed were rural family planning clinics, many of which have been forced to cut back the hours when they are open.

Governor Hughes will include money for contraceptive services for teenagers in his new "youth initiative" package to be presented to the General Assembly. He also plans to include some contraceptive services for adults under a women's initiative. Amounts have not been specified yet. Advocacy groups say the need is for at least $2.2 million. There are few better investments for the taxpayers to make.

The Chattanooga Times

Chattanooga, TN, January 24, 1986

We are seeing new calls for expanded sex education programs in high schools — and even junior high schools. Such programs are controversial, often because some opponents argue that they are mostly devoid of moral guidelines. Others charge that the classes actually result in increased sexual activity by teen-agers who have taken contraceptive precautions. The growing number of teen-age pregnancies, however, suggests that there is too little education in the consequences of sexual activity, not too much.

The state of Wisconsin has undertaken a novel approach to the problem of teen-age pregnancy that legislators, educators and, not least, thousands of parents in other states will be watching closely. The state recently passed a law under which the parents of an unmarried teen-ager who has a baby will be financially responsible for the child. The law's purpose is two-fold: to reduce the number of teen-age pregnancies, and to cut back the state's welfare rolls.

But if the law works, the chief beneficiaries will be the teen-age girls who don't get pregnant, especially those who have barely emerged from childhood. Nationwide, more than 60 percent of teen-age mothers require some form of public assistance. And that's just to help take care of the baby. Since many girls get pregnant before they finish high school, most have no marketable job skills, and thus no way to earn money to pay for food, medicine, clothing and other essentials for themselves and their child. Also, many are not emotionally mature, a factor that can cause them to become child abusers.

Children born to unwed teen-agers start with a disadvantage, both physically and socially. The danger is that they too will remain mired in poverty, and that girls born to teen-agers will themselves become mothers at an early age, thus continuing the cycle.

One attractive aspect of the Wisconsin law is that it could reverse a disturbing trend that has expanded over the past couple of decades. It involves the role society should play in discouraging premarital pregnancy at a time when moral codes regarding abstinence seem to be increasingly ignored. Many parents have abdicated their responsibilities, leaving it to the schools and social welfare agencies; that's one reason we're seeing more sentiment for sex education courses in schools.

But Wisconsin lawmakers sought to make clear to parents that disregarding their responsibilities could carry financial consequences. It's an intriguing approach to a nagging problem.

It is likely the law will have a clear impact on families that are able to make support payments, particularly the boys and their parents who traditionally have not borne much of the financial responsibility for teen-age pregnancies. Wisconsin is still drafting regulations on how the law will apply to welfare families, and there may be other unforeseen problems. Still, it will be interesting to see what effect the law has before it comes up for reconsideration in 1989.

If the law is effective, you can bet other states will adopt similar legislation. But in a broader sense, the chief beneficiaries within Wisconsin will not be just the taxpayers, or even the teen-agers' children who start life with a couple of strikes against them. Those who profit most from the law will be the teen-age boys and girls who elect not to become parents before they're finished being children themselves.

THE TENNESSEAN

Nashville, TN, January 15, 1986

BY law, every public school student in Tennessee must receive instruction on the proper method of display for the American flag and other patriotic symbols.

However, most of those students will not learn about their reproductive organs, or about veneral diseases, or pregnancy, or family planning.

Some of them may turn to their parents for information on sexuality. But many more will rely on the sources that the vast majority of American teens have used for decades — friends, restroom walls, television, and their own instincts.

The state Board of Education initiated a health education curriculum last year which includes segments on family life and sex education, but omits the more controversial topics of birth control and abortion. That curriculum, unlike instructions on how to fold a flag, is optional, and many school systems, including Nashville's, choose not to use it.

Like it or not, sex education is going to be a topic in the legislature this year. A legislative committee recently heard the testimony of the proponents and opponents of a state sex education curriculum. In an unusual but certainly welcomed twist of events, the participants who favored sex education were in the majority. Obviously, many Tennesseans now agree with Rep. Karen Williams, R-Memphis, and are "tired of this thing being swept under the rug."

Sex education discussions are sometimes laced generously with suppositions, horror stories, and biblical quotations. State officials, educators, and parents should remember that they are discussing young people's lives and they should base their decisions on facts, including the fact that 6,545 Tennessee girls between the ages of 10 and 17 were pregnant in 1984.

A pregnancy for a teenager is much more than a nine-month inconvenience. It can very well start a cycle of poverty and hopelessness for both the mother and the child. Commissioner Marguerite Sallee of the Department of Human Services reports that 80% of teenage mothers will not finish school. Two-thirds of them will receive some form of public assistance.

A meaningful sex education program would do more than reduce this state's teenage pregnancy rate. It could help teens achieve a healthy respect for all aspects of their physical growth. It could teach them the basics of genetics. It would give all Tennessee public school pupils something they need — the opportunity to make important personal decisions based on information instead of hearsay. Surely that would be more of a positive influence on their lives than a knowledge of flag etiquette.

A sex education course will in no way interfere or conflict with personal moral teachings that children receive at home or at church. Teaching young people about their bodies is not immoral. But turning a blind eye to thousands of teenagers is. ∎

THE MILWAUKEE JOURNAL
Milwaukee, WI, December 26, 1985

Stop down at your factory or office canteen, or check out the next rest room you visit, and you may get the impression that just about anything is available for purchase from vending machines. Anything, that is, except contraceptives.

Fine, you might say, but is it? While other states permit vending machine sale of one form of contraceptive, the condom, Wisconsin forbids the practice. Rep. Thomas Loftus (D-Sun Prairie) has introduced a sensible measure that would make such sales permissible.

Opponents like to argue that condom dispensers encourage a casual attitude toward sex, particularly among young people. Well, maybe. But recreational sex — even among the young — is a fact of life in America, condom machines or no.

Many teenagers are likely to engage in sex regardless of whether they have ready access to condoms or other contraceptives. Making condoms available by vending machine — in turn, making them easier to obtain and use — could have the welcome effect of diminishing the epidemic of teenage pregnancies.

Better yet, why not also sell over-the-counter birth control devices that women rely on — such as spermicides, foam and contraceptive sponges — in vending machines? The problem of unwanted pregnancy is so pressing that it should be attacked in every possible way, even the mechanical.

Reagan Supports Anti-Abortion Plan Linked to Family Planning Funds

Title X, the federal family planning program of the 1970 Public Health Services Act, has been the focus of antiabortion amendments since Ronald Reagan became president in 1981. The government's major family planning program, Title X authorizes funding for clinics that disseminate information on family planning and contraceptives; it provides funds to more than 5,000 family-planning clinics run by government and non-profit groups. No funds are used to perform abortions, although abortion counseling and referrals are permitted. In 1981, President Reagan was successful in cutting by almost one-fourth the money available for Title X. In the next three years, the Administration did not request any money expressly for the program but rather proposed to give states a "primary health care" block grant that could be used for a variety of purposes including family planning. Congress rejected the block grant and continued to provide earmarked funding, giving the program $142.5 million for fiscal 1985.

In November 1985 Rep. Jack Kemp (R, N.Y.) and Sen. Orrin Hatch (R, Utah) sponsored identical antiabortion amendments that would alter the guidelines of Title X. Kemp and Hatch proposed that clinics which received Title X funds be barred from informing pregnant women of the alternative of abortion or referring women to clinics and hospitals where abortions are performed. The amendment would deny Title X funds to any organization that performed such abortion counseling and referral services, even if it used its own non-federal funds to do so. The amendment stated that no federal funds "may be used to provide to any pregnant woman abortion procedures, counseling for abortion procedures or referral for abortion procedures, unless the life of the mother would be endangered by carrying the fetus to term." Opponents of the amendment claimed it would seriously undercut the federal family planning program, since medical ethics demand that patients be told about all their options; responsible health-care professionals, they argued, would refuse to work in clinics operating under such strictures. They also contended that the clinics have been instrumental in preventing unwanted pregnancies, many of which result in abortion. Adherents countered that the recipients of Title X funds have actually been promoting abortion, contrary to the intent of the program. By the end of 1985, the amendment had been dropped in committee debates in both houses of Congress.

THE KANSAS CITY STAR
*Kansas City, MO,
September 28, 1984*

The end-of-September deadline is nearing for Congress to reauthorize Title X family planning services for three more years. Although Congress can keep these programs going for another year under a continuing resolution, funding for them would not be increased. It is not good public policy to put these services, which do so much for adolescents and low-income persons with birth control assistance, on hold for another year.

A major hang-up is Utah Republican Sen. Orrin Hatch, who is insistent that the reauthorization legislation include language requiring parents to be notified when their teen-agers receive birth control services. The administration fought this battle once before, and lost in court. Now Mr. Hatch wants to make sure that is clearly in the law. What he will do, if successful, is discourage teen-agers from seeking protection from pregnancy when they already are sexually active.

Services made available because of Title X are among the most cost-effective government has to offer its citizens. Family planning helps to prevent unwanted pregnancies and illegitimacy, and that means a savings to the taxpayers in future public assistance for many of these children and their mothers. It also helps to prevent abortions, a fact that abortion foes haven't acknowledged since they generally are the ones who also oppose birth control aid.

The House-Senate conference committee which will work out Title X reauthorization likely will be stymied unless family planning opponents can be convinced to change their minds. Unless the Title X programs are continued, with higher levels of funding, the alarming number of teen-age pregnancies will continue to rise, along with the number of abortions. Is this what Congress really wants?

The Idaho STATESMAN
Boise, ID, September 15, 1981

The Reagan administration wants to return to the states the responsibility for providing family planning information to poor people. The administration's plan is to put the federal funds for this purpose into a block grant, which could be used by the states for family planning or a variety of other purposes.

We feel the administration plan guarantees that federal funds no longer would be spent for family planning in some states. Ultimately, society would be the loser.

There are two reasons for this stand. First, family planning is needed because it saves human suffering and money — tax money. Second, the job simply will not get done in some parts of the country if the decision is left up to the states.

The second reason involves the division of duties between states and the nation. There are certain needs that must be met by the federal government simply because people have to have the services and some states won't do the job.

If family planning is submerged in a block grant, pressure will mount for the states to spend the money on other programs. Many states, like Idaho, are strapped for cash because of the economic slump. Couple that fact with the controversial nature of family planning and it's likely that many state-level politicians will abandon the program for more popular causes.

That would be unfortunate, and not only for teen-age couples struggling with the problems sex can bring. The public would suffer, too.

A study by the Planned Parenthood Federation of America found that nine out of 10 of those enrolled in family planning clinics are of low or marginal income. A third are teen-agers. If these people don't receive birth control information, many will bear unwanted children and many of those children will end up on the welfare rolls.

The Planned Parenthood study concluded that for every tax dollar invested in family planning, at least two dollars are saved in government expenditures for health and welfare services during the next year. Such a savings alone is reason enough for the federal government to stay in the family planning business.

THE PLAIN DEALER
Cleveland, OH, November 1, 1985

Sens. Jesse Helms of North Carolina and Orrin Hatch of Utah, along with Rep. Jack Kemp of New York, are among Congress' more vociferous opponents of abortion. They are so doctrinaire that they fail to recognize when one of their knee-jerk responses to abortion actually would work against the very cause they promote. Such is the case with their proposed amendment to destroy the federal Title X family planning program.

None of the money spent on the program is used to recommend or perform abortions, a fact verified by a General Accounting Office study. But health clinics appropriately advise their clients as to all legal options, including abortion.

According to Helms et al., two things are wrong with that. First, they insist, family clinics promote abortion merely by advising patients of its availability. Second, some of the family planning money is used by organizations such as Planned Parenthood which, in separate facilities and with non-federal money, do recommend abortions and make abortion referrals. The proposed amendment would deny such organizations access to family planning money, and would do such things as reinstate the infamous "squeal rule" requiring parental notification before birth control services are provided to minors. The latter provision is sought despite the fact that previous "squeal rule" requirements were invalidated by a federal court.

The threat of the amendments has caused congressional leaders to withdraw funding for Title X from the 1986 fiscal year appropriations bills for the departments of labor, health and human Services and education. If the program is killed, 50,000 low-income women and teen-agers would be denied services in Northeast Ohio. Yvonne Bolitho, president of the Ohio Family Planning Association, estimates that 25,000 unwanted pregnancies would result, and with them, 12,000 abortions.

Helms and his crowd somehow can't make the connection between unwanted pregnancies and abortion. Their view, that ending birth control assistance also will end pre-marital sex, is a simplistic and costly approach. Teen-age mothers are less likely to complete school and are more likely to live a life of poverty, to depend on public support and to foster children who themselves become teen-age parents.

Title X money, distributed in the Cleveland area to institutions and organizations such as University Hospitals, the Hough Norwood Family Health Care Center, Mt. Sinai Medical Center and the Family Planning Association of Lake and Geauga counties, has enabled thousands of women to receive birth control assistance as well as medical care. Since Title X was signed into law by former President Nixon in 1970, it has been the centerpiece of the nation's efforts to minimize unwanted pregnancies and the need for abortion.

It merits continued support, not the kind of harrassment that's been coming from Helms, Hatch and Kemp.

"PROMOTE CONTRACEPTION?!!! ...WE OPPOSE ABORTION, BUT LET'S TRY TO AVOID GETTING RATIONAL ABOUT IT!"

THE ATLANTA CONSTITUTION
Atlanta, GA, June 14, 1984

Once again, Congress must step into the breach and save a worthwhile and needed federal program from the misguided wrecking ball of the Reagan administration. To its credit, the House already has voted overwhelmingly to extend the federally aided family-planning program for at least another year.

The administration remains curiously opposed to government aid for programs that help millions of women and teenagers make more informed decisions about their sexuality; programs that have helped to lower the incidences of unwanted pregnancies and abortions (which the administration professes to abhor).

The Reagan White House, grandstanding for the religious right and the anti-abortion lobby, fought the extension with uncommon zeal, and has vowed to continue the fight in the Senate. Recent history and common sense, however, are on the side of extension. The Senate, though somewhat less solidly than the House, has repeatedly rejected the administration's past efforts to savage family-planning programs. It should do so again.

The family-planning program not only must be extended, but should be expanded. Even though it serves millions of women and teenagers, supervised care still is not available to some 42 percent of the low-income women and 43 percent of the sexually active teenagers who need it. That, the administration's odd bias notwithstanding, must be changed.

The Chattanooga Times
Chattanooga, TN, November 7, 1985

Those who oppose abortion should logically be first in line to support family planning programs. If family planning services reduce the number of unwanted pregnancies which occur — and they do — it necessarily follows that these programs hold down the number of abortions performed. But abortion foes are again trying to weaken the mainstay of federal efforts to provide family planning services in this country, Title X of the Public Health Service Act. Congress should reject weakening amendments and reauthorize Title X as it is.

Title X funding cannot be used to perform abortions. Furthermore, Title X agencies, when counseling a woman with an unwanted pregnancy, are expressly prohibited from encouraging the woman to have an abortion. Clinics must ensure that all choices — prenatal care and delivery, either keeping the child or putting it up for adoption and abortion — are presented in a *nondirective* counseling session, one which does not steer the woman toward any alternative but gives her the information from which to make an informed decision. These restrictions are appropriate, and they are sufficient to satisfy public policy against the use of federal funds for abortion.

But for the avid anti-abortionists, they are not enough. Under one proposed amendment to Title X, counselors in clinics receiving federal funds would be prohibited from even mentioning the word abortion to a woman carrying a child she does not want or cannot provide for. Such a restriction is totally unwarranted and flies in the face of a fundamental principle of modern medical law and ethics: the patient's right to sufficient information on *all* alternatives so as to give "informed consent" to treatment.

Abortion is a legal medical procedure and cannot be written out of existence by writing into law a "gag rule" for pregnancy counselors. Ethical objections to such a gag rule could lead health care providers to drop family planning programs, which would clearly be counterproductive. Congress should reject this and other amendments aimed at weakening Title X.

The reason goes back to the purpose of the Title X program, which is to prevent unwanted pregnancies. It has been effective in fulfilling that purpose. Statistical analysis, based on the number of women served, the average frequency of pregnancy without access to contraceptives and the percentage of unwanted pregnancies normally terminated by abortion, suggest that in a single year more than 400,000 abortions are averted as a result of Title X services. Clearly it is devious to portray Title X as a program which promotes abortion, when its effect is, in fact, to greatly reduce the number of abortions.

The program should not be weakened or restricted, but expanded. Projections from the U.S. Department of Health and Human Services show that only 37 percent of U.S. women who need subsidized family planning services will receive them in this fiscal year. Many of those who will not be served are teen-agers, and Congress would do well to weigh the tremendous social, economic and public health costs of what is an epidemic of teenage pregnancy in this country.

Speaking in support of Title X last summer, Rep. Marilyn Lloyd pointed out one tragic element of those costs: "Pregnant teens," she said, "are seven to 10 times more likely to commit suicide than others." They and their children are also at more risk in terms of health problems and are much more likely to live their lives in poverty and dependence on public support. "What we must do," Rep. Lloyd said, "is prevent pregnancies, and to do that we must be realistic."

We couldn't agree more. The battle against abortion should not, realistically, be fought on Title X ground. This program should be recognized for what it is — a successful effort to help women avoid the unwanted pregnancies which sometimes result in abortions. Title X deserves the full support of Congress and should be reauthorized without amendment.

BUFFALO EVENING NEWS
Buffalo, NY, November 11, 1985

ABORTIONS TAKE place when women or girls are pregnant but don't want to be. It follows logically that one of the best ways to prevent abortion is by supporting family planning. Yet anti-abortion forces in Congress are now pushing legislation that would gut many of the family-planning programs the nation has been supporting.

Perhaps the most onerous of these attempts is an amendment being sponsored by a Western New York congressman, Rep. Jack Kemp, R-Hamburg, and by Sen. Orrin Hatch, R-Utah. The Kemp-Hatch amendment to Title X of the Public Health Services Act would cut off federal funds to any family-planning agency that so much as tells any client that abortion is a legal alternative that exists if she should become pregnant.

It is already the law that no federal funds can be used for abortions. But as agencies give their needy patients reproductive health advice, they often also answer questions and give information about alternatives for women who become pregnant when family-planning methods fail. These agencies typically offer pregnancy testing as well, and give counseling to pregnant women. Most of these agencies operate according to a code of medical ethics that simply would not allow them to deliberately keep their patients ignorant about any of their medical options, including abortion.

Significantly, the American Medical Association and 16 other medical and nursing orgnizations are among the many groups opposed to the Kemp-Hatch amendment. Dr. Harry Jonas of the American College of Obstetricians and Gynecologists says the amendment "would make it impossible for us to explain to our patients all of the information they have a right to know so they can make informed decisions about their own health care."

Rather than compromise their ethical and legal position, family-planning agencies would have to sacrifice their Title X funding if the Kemp-Hatch amendment were to be passed. Needy patients seeking contraceptive aid would have to be turned away.

The result, according to estimates made on the basis of past statistics, would be some 800,000 unwanted pregnancies per year. About 400,000 of the women involved could be expected to end those unwanted pregnancies by abortion. The cutoff of funds to agencies giving contraceptive help would produce more abortions, not fewer.

The family-planning programs now funded by Title X do not promote abortion; they help prevent it. Title X should be renewed, and renewed intact, without crippling amendments like the Kemp-Hatch proposal.

THE TENNESSEAN
Nashville, TN, November 10, 1985

WITH a whole array of amendments, pressure-tactics and other means, some in the Congress are trying to destroy the government's major family planning program, one that has existed since 1970 when it was signed into law by President Richard Nixon.

The program, Title X of the Public Health Services Act, provides funds to more than 5,000 family planning clinics, run by states, local health departments and private non-profit groups, that disseminate information on family planning and contraceptives.

But Title X provides a wide range of other preventive care, including pelvic and breast examinations, cancer screening and venereal disease testing.

In the 15 years since Title X was first passed, the federal family planning program has worked effectively and efficiently. It helped avert more than 800,000 unintended pregnancies — half among teen-agers — in 1981 alone. If these had occurred there would have been an estimated 282,000 additional births and 433,000 more abortions.

It is estimated that each dollar invested in family planning saves two dollars the following year in health and welfare costs associated with unintended births. The cost-benefit ratio is even higher for teen-agers: for every dollar invested, three dollars are saved the following year.

For the past 15 years, support in Congress for the national program has cut across party lines. Every president since Dwight Eisenhower has endorsed the concept as a vital social program. But now the attempt to eliminate Title X comes on the heels of a strategic shift by the anti-abortion movement and its point men in Congress, particularly Senators Orrin Hatch and Jesse Helms and their conterpart in the House, Rep. Jack Kemp. The aim is to destroy Title X.

Family planning clinics have always been prohibited from using Title X money for abortions. Congressionally-requested probes by the General Accounting Office and other agencies have reported that all clinics studied were operating in full compliance with the law.

But the strategy of the Title X opponents is to link it with abortions and to make any vote to save it as a "litmus test" of congressional members' stands on abortion. Many members of Congress who oppose abortion, but have supported Title X, have succumbed to this pressure.

It is bitterly ironic that the anti-abortion members of the Congress are intent on eliminating the one federally-funded program that reduces the need for abortion. The destruction of Title X will have expensive and tragic social consequences. It is hoped there are enough senators and congressmen who won't succumb to the pressures of the Title X opponents and will vote to keep the program alive and without crippling amendments. ◀

The Salt Lake Tribune
Salt Lake City, UT, November 4, 1985

No one *likes* or *favors* abortion. It's an abhorrent, tragic act. While many would forbid it in most cases, however, others see it as the lesser of two bad choices: ending a pregnancy or giving birth to countless complications for mother, infant and community.

Meanwhile, the U.S. Supreme Court has deemed abortion a constitutional right of women.

A 1984 Gallup Poll shows an almost even balance between attitudes about abortion in America. Only half the nation favored a ban on abortions (except for rape, incest and danger to the mother), leaving the remainder either opposed or undecided.

The two sides, unfortunately, seem unable or unwilling to coexist. The abortion abolitionists are not content to steer their own families and friends clear of abortions. They are so confident their position is correct that they refuse to tolerate any deviation from their rules.

Congress has responded by refusing to finance abortions. Such a policy makes it more difficult, but not impossible, for poor women to obtain affordable abortions. As long as private groups will pay for the procedure, federally subsidized birth control agencies can tell women where to procure safe services.

This is not good enough for those compelled to impose their own moralistic standards on the rest of the country. With leadership from Utah's Sen. Orrin Hatch, the so-called "pro-lifers" now are trying to circumvent the Supreme Court and to make Congress take an even stronger stand against abortion by amending Title 10 of the Public Health Service Act.

That program now provides $142.5 million worth of family planning services to Americans who otherwise could not afford them. Utahns receive about $500,000 from that fund through Planned Parenthood of Utah.

The proposed amendment would prevent subsidized clinics from telling women that abortions can be obtained and where. Consequently, other poor women will lose access to all types of contraception if these clinics continue to give women the last-resort option.

Suppressing abortion information will not eliminate pregnancy-related problems. There always will be some poor women or teen-agers who cannot afford the cost or stigma of an unplanned child and will resort to abortion, safe or not. Proposed congressional action would only contribute to their crisis.

LEXINGTON HERALD-LEADER
Lexington, KY, November 5, 1985

One thing you can say for the leaders of the anti-abortion movement in Congress: They're not afraid to follow an idea to absurdity.

Consider the efforts of three darlings of the national anti-abortion movement: Rep. Jack Kemp, R-N.Y., and Sens. Orrin Hatch, R-Utah, and Jesse Helms, R-N.C. These three gentlemen are now trying to kill a federal program that by any standard has reduced the number of abortions. And they're doing so in the name of stopping abortion.

The program in question provides federal aid to family planning clinics. Kemp and Hatch have authored a proposal that would prohibit family planning clinics from receiving federal funds unless the clinics promise not to mention abortion to their clients. Helms is pushing strongly for this and other measures aimed at family planning clinics.

In the minds of these lawmakers and of the Reagan administration, which supports the Kemp-Hatch proposal, such a prohibition is appropriate to prevent any ambiguity about the use of federal funds to promote abortion. In reality, the proposal would severely inhibit sensible birth control counseling. Conscientious counselors feel an obligation to apprise their clients of all legal methods of family planning, and abortion is one such method.

The fact is that federally financed planning clinics actually help decrease the need for abortions by offering women — particularly the young and the poor — free or low-cost counseling on birth control. The program has been in existence for 15 years. The Planned Parenthood Federation of the United States estimates that the counseling provided by federally assisted clinics helped prevent at least 433,000 abortions in 1981 alone.

You might think that would be enough to make the anti-abortion forces leave the family planning clinics alone. You'd be wrong, though. In addition to the Kemp-Hatch proposal, there are other proposals now floating around Congress that would further handicap the clinics. One of them would require parental consent for teen-agers seeking birth control counseling. Another would prohibit family planning clinics from operating in the same building or shopping center as an abortion clinic.

All of this has little to do with abortion. Instead, it is aimed at accomplishing a goal set at last year's National Right-to-Life Committee convention: Destroy the federal family planning program, either outright or through crippling amendments.

Congress should resist this attempt and move quickly to provide new funding for the program. The program will expire later this month unless Congress provides new funds. That's exactly what the lawmakers should do. And they can rightly and reasonably do so in the name of preventing abortion.

Newsday
Long Island, NY, November 6, 1985

Without pregnancy, there can be no abortion. So preventing unwanted pregnancies prevents abortions.

But apparently it's not that simple to Congress. Under pressure from anti-abortion groups, both the House and the Senate have voted not to include funds for the Title X family planning program in the health and human services appropriation for fiscal 1986. Unless Congress acts before Nov. 14, funding now provided under a continuing resolution will cease. And if Sen. Orrin Hatch (R-Utah) and Rep. Jack Kemp (R-Buffalo) succeed, a new amendment will prohibit federally funded family planning counselors from even mentioning that abortion is legal and can be obtained elsewhere.

That contravenes medical ethics, which requires that patients be made aware of their available options. Access to contraceptives may be further limited because many hospitals and clinics couldn't accept funds with such restrictions.

Title X, which dates back to 1970, provides federal aid to about 5,000 family planning clinics run by states, local health departments and private nonprofit groups. Spending federal funds to perform abortions has been prohibited for years, and a recent study by the General Accounting Office confirms that recipients are complying. But Congress is apparently so fearful of the anti-abortion movement that it's willing to drop the $142-million family planning program entirely to prevent counselors from even mentioning the legality and availability of abortions.

As it is, more than a million teenage girls become pregnant every year in this country. About half give birth. Many are poor and poorly educated, and they and their children often become wards of the state. Counseling abstinence, as many right-to-life groups propose in place of birth control, simply isn't enough.

Most parents seem to recognize this. In a poll conducted by Louis Harris & Associates for Planned Parenthood, 84 percent said they believed that they had little or no control over their teenagers' sexual activity and that some outside educational help was needed. Nearly 80 percent favored TV messages about birth control.

Teenagers in other western countries are about as sexually active as their American counterparts, yet their pregnancy rates are much lower, according to an extensive study by the Alan Guttmacher Institute. Judging from the appalling number of births and abortions among American girls, what's needed is more sex education and access to birth control, not less.

The anti-abortionists have already managed to cause great harm to U.S.-sponsored family planning programs abroad. This time their target is millions of mostly poor American girls and women — and their unwanted babies. For Congress to yield to such inhumane sentiments would be truly shameful.

Pittsburgh Post-Gazette
Pittsburgh, PA, November 4, 1985

Does the pro-life movement serve as a stalking horse for people who wish to impose their own moral or religious views on the rest of society? The latest attack on family planning in Congress has added some new weight to this old suspicion.

In the service of the "pro-life" cause, Republican Sens. Jesse Helms and Orrin Hatch and Rep. Jack Kemp are maneuvering to change the national family planning program under Title X of the Public Health Service Act, which must be restablished in Congress by Nov. 14.

Wait a minute. What does family planning have to do with abortion? Clearly, the program saves thousands upon thousands of unintended pregnancies every year. Moreover, Title X, as now written, flatly enjoins: "None of the funds appropriated under this title shall be used in programs where abortion is a method of family planning."

But this plain wording is not good enough for the champions of "pro-life." At least five amendments are being discussed, but the focus has fallen on a Kemp-Hatch proposal that would deny Title X funding "to any organization that provides to any pregnant woman abortion procedures, or referral for abortion procedures ... "

According to Rep. Kemp, "my amendment supports family planning by rebuilding the wall of separation between contraception and abortion." But according to simple common sense, attacking certain family-planning clinics will not reduce abortions. As Ellen Goodman pointed out in a recent column on this page, most hospitals, if it came to a choice, would probably choose to continue offering abortion services and forgo family-planning aid. In that case, of course, logic suggests that fewer contraceptive services would translate into *more* abortions. This is "pro-life"?

No, it is spite, not logic, that prompts this latest tinkering with Title X. Pro-lifers have a score to settle with such organizations as the Planned Parenthood Federation of America.

Congress should reauthorize Title X without regard to blind zealotry.

The Miami Herald
Miami, FL, November 3, 1985

FRESH from their success in gaining approval to fund organizations that counsel Third World couples about only one method of birth control — the unreliable rhythm method — the Reagan Administration and its supporters now are bent on sabotaging 4,000 responsible family-planning organizations in the United States.

U.S. Rep. Jack Kemp, Republican of New York, and Sen. Orrin Hatch, Republican of Utah, have sponsored an amendment that would deny Family Planning Program (FPP) money to hospitals and groups that advise poor women of their legal right to an abortion. The amendment also would strip Federal money from groups that use their .own money to perform abortions or to counsel women about them. The amendment would be attached to an emergency fiscal-1986 funding bill scheduled for discussion soon.

Federally funded clinics currently are required to inform women of a full range of family-planning options so that they may give their "informed consent" to their choice of methods. Indeed, in every situation requiring medical care, a patient is *owed* the fullest explanations before she assents to treatment. It's *her* body. The amendment also would place medical professionals in an untenable position by requiring them to conceal from pregnant women a legal medical option. What kind of medical practice is that?

It matters not that the General Accounting Office reports that groups, including the Planned Parenthood Federation, have followed FPP regulations and have not used one penny of that money to perform or promote abortions. Senator Hatch argues that Congress's true intent was that the annual $142-million FPP budget be used to help women prevent pregnancies, not terminate them.

What's really going on here is that the powerful anti-abortion lobby, failing to get legislation changed, now is doing everything it can to impede the exercise of free choice. Last month, with the Administration's approval, the Agency for International Development began funding organizations abroad that only tell women about "natural" birth control. Representative Kemp voted in subcommittee to fund one such group.

It's time for Congress to reaffirm its true intent and stand solidly behind the Family Planning Program as it always has been administered. Providing options for women in need, including the legal option to terminate a pregnancy, is the only responsible course to take. Anything less should be construed as political malpractice.

Washington, DC, November 12, 1985

Imagine this scenario: A family-planning clinic goes out of business. Now denied access to contraceptives, women clients become pregnant. Some of them get desperate and seek abortions. So the abortion rate climbs.

That tragedy could come true across the USA if Congress goes along this week with efforts to close the doors of public family-planning clinics.

Ironically, the anti-abortion activists in Congress are pressing for the change: Rep. Jack Kemp, R-N.Y., and Sen. Orrin Hatch, R-Utah, want to eliminate federal funds for every clinic that informs clients that abortion is an alternative to an unwanted pregnancy.

Under current law, not a single federal penny is spent to terminate a single pregnancy. But Kemp and Hatch — with the Reagan administration's blessing — want to distance the government even further from abortion, which was made legal in 1973 by the U.S. Supreme Court.

Sen. Jesse Helms, R-N.C., is so anxious to wash the government's hands of abortion that, until last week, he held hostage the appointment of a new U.S. ambassador to China to try to change Chinese abortion practices.

More than 4.5 million women a year turn to family-planning clinics for contraceptive counseling, pregnancy testing, breast exams, and screening for diseases. The 5,000 clinics hope to share $142.5 million in U.S. money this year.

If Kemp-Hatch passes, many clinics that counsel all options would be forced to go out of business. Family planning experts say that to remain mum about abortion would violate medical ethics by denying women the right to know all options.

Why do anti-abortion activists want to close down clinics that help *prevent* unwanted pregnancies?

Because some of them oppose *all* federal support for any form of birth control. They claim that making contraceptives readily available promotes promiscuity and leads to soaring rates of teen pregnancy.

That's crazy. How can anyone blame contraceptives for causing people to get pregnant?

For decades, our government has worked to give family planning services to those who could not afford them. It did this in the belief that a family that wants and plans for each of its children is less likely than others to experience poverty, child abuse, and addiction.

That logic remains sound.

Family planning should be *embraced*, not shunned, by people who oppose abortion. But to calm the sincere concern of many that abortion is being overused, counselors must make sure they suggest other valid options for women with unwanted pregnancies: Some learn to love unwanted children; others put them up for adoption.

Abortion foes must recognize that closing family planning clinics would not save the unborn. It would increase the demand for abortion. And that would be a tragedy.

The Hartford Courant
Hartford, CT, November 13, 1985

More than 4,000 clinics offer family planning services in the United States, mostly to poor women. The services include counseling and referrals in cases when women are considering abortion.

U.S. Rep. Jack F. Kemp of New York and Sen. Orrin G. Hatch of Utah want to erect, in Mr. Kemp's words, "a wall of separation between family planning and abortion." Mr. Hatch sees Title X of the Public Health Service Act, the prime source of funding, as "a multi-million-dollar assault on family rights and parental authority."

The two lawmakers, with the blessing of the Reagan administration, have proposed eliminating all federal funds — about $142 million in 1984 — now going to the clinics. We hope they will not succeed.

Federally funded family planning clinics do not recommend or provide abortions; they inform pregnant women that abortion is a legal medical alternative open to them, and make referrals only when asked. Teenagers may use the clinics for contraceptive information, but it's information not readily available to them elsewhere and knowledge that can prevent teenage pregnancy.

In either case, family planning clinics help women of all ages avoid the need for abortion by giving them knowledge of all their choices, the most elementary of which is contraception. The Planned Parenthood Federation of America estimates that family planning programs getting help from Title X prevent 800,000 unwanted pregnancies and about 435,000 abortions in an average year.

Such logic seems to elude abortion foes, as does the equally persuasive fact that helping to finance public family planning clinics saves the government millions each year in health and welfare costs that are incurred when poor, often malnourished, women have children they cannot afford.

Authority for Title X programs expires at midnight Thursday.

It should be renewed, with funding for all options, including a woman's constitutionally protected right to choose abortion.

THE MILWAUKEE JOURNAL
Milwaukee, WI, November 6, 1985

Let's suppose that for some reason you were bent on seeing more — not fewer — abortions performed in the United States. A good way to achieve that goal would be to deny federal aid to family planning clinics, which then would have to scale back services, presumably resulting in more unwanted pregnancies and therefore more abortions.

Incredible as it may seem, that is the very strategy being pursued by the people who squawk the loudest against abortion. Leading the attack in Congress are Rep. Jack Kemp of New York and Sen. Orrin Hatch of Utah, who are trying to amend the federal family-planning program to bar taxpayer money for health agencies that acknowledge abortion as among the options available to pregnant women.

Kemp and Hatch argue speciously that they want to erect "a wall of separation" between federally financed family planning and abortion. But the wall has long existed. By law, no agency receiving family planning aid from the federal government may perform or push abortions on its clients. However, an agency must counsel pregnant women who request such advice on all the doors open to them, including keeping their babies, giving them up for adoption or aborting them. It's Door No. 3 that Kemp and Hatch want to

close. The lawmakers imply that to let pregnant women know of the availability of abortion is to promote it, and they gain ammunition from the heavily publicized (albeit privately financed) campaign by Planned Parenthood and similar agencies to preserve a legal right to abortion.

Yet, government audits of family planning providers, undertaken specifically to prove that federal aid is being channeled improperly toward abortion counseling and lobbying, consistently have found scrupulous compliance with the law. No new regulations are needed, according to testimony before Congress. By the government's own measure, the "wall of separation" appears to be holding up nicely, indeed.

So what are Kemp and Hatch really up to? It's possible they are carrying water for a small but shrill minority who, because of personal opposition to contraception, want to end all government aid to family planning. These ideologues stubbornly refuse to accept that the upshot of such a foolish policy would be more abortions, a greater wrong than contraception to many.

Such a catastrophe awaits if the nation's family planning program is drastically amended or allowed to expire, as it will after Nov. 14 without congressional action. It deserves renewal, intact.

THE SACRAMENTO BEE
Sacramento, CA, November 4, 1985

Right-to-life groups, among them the Moral Majority, the American Life Lobby, and the National Right to Life Committee are mounting a new drive in Congress to kill the federal government's family-planning program. Key to the effort is legislation by Rep. Jack Kemp of New York and Sen. Orrin Hatch of Utah that would prohibit federal funding for any agency that provides information on abortion. The plea, painfully familiar by now, is that no one is against family planning, only the use of federal funds for abortions and abortion-related services.

It's a phony plea, in part because there is no way ethically to inform a client, male or female, of the full range of family-planning options without discussion of abortion, and in part because almost none of those involved in this campaign supports any form of family planning other than "natural family planning."

If they win this fight, they will inexorably

go on to the next one. That means no contraception other than rhythm. And while rhythm is a respectable personal — and moral — choice, as the sole option of a federal program it's absurd. It puts the government in the business of depriving individuals of legal choices and will inevitably lead to thousands of additional unwanted pregnancies, more abortions, legal or illegal, and more unwanted children.

Federally funded family-planning clinics are already prohibited by law from using those funds to perform abortions, a restriction they have carefully observed without impairing their counseling functions. But to now prohibit them from providing full and reliable information on the whole range of options is to turn the business of providing reliable information into a campaign of propaganda and manipulation for one religious or moral position. That's not medicine, it's not counseling and it's not honest.

THE LOUISVILLE TIMES
Louisville, KY, November 1, 1985

Rep. Jack Kemp of New York says he wants to erect a "wall of separation" between family planning and abortion. He has proposed a ban on abortion counseling and referrals by federally funded health agencies. Exceptions would be made only when a woman's life is threatened by pregnancy.

Mr. Kemp, and Sen. Orrin Hatch of Utah, have linked their scheme to continuation of Title X of the Public Health Service Act. Funding for the much-needed family planning program expires Nov. 14. Congressmen need to hear promptly from citizens who believe the change should be rejected and the program should be extended in its present form. (Addresses of senators and representatives from Kentucky and Indiana are in box at right).

Signed into law by President Nixon in 1970, Title X provides grants to public and nonprofit agencies to help them provide the full range of reproductive health services to women who might otherwise not have access to them. More than four million women have taken advantage of the services annually, and, it is estimated, more than 800,000 unplanned pregnancies have been averted by the program.

Under existing law and regulations, government funds may not be used to perform or encourage abortion, but in the event of unintended pregnancies women who visit federally supported clinics are given "non-directive counseling" outlining their choices.

So-called pro-family advocates don't like that. They would prefer that women be denied information about their options and rights.

If the Kemp-Hatch bill is passed, more than 4,000 clinics providing family-planning services at little or no cost to poor women would lose a large part of their income if they don't accept the restrictions. Doris Schneider, executive director of Planned Parenthood of Louisville, said her agency stands to lose one-fourth of its budget. But Planned Parenthood, she says, will not "compromise either our medical standards or ethical standards for Title X dollars."

It would, indeed, be unethical for a health-care provider not to advise a woman that abortion is her legal right. The anti-abortion forces may wish that weren't true, but they have not been able in the courts to abrogate that right.

In the meantime, through their assault on Title X they've shown a willingness to deprive millions of women of access to the health services they need. Nonsensically, they've jeopardized a program that is a proven success in helping *prevent* unintended pregnancies and, thereby, abortions.

Congress must repulse the attack — and quickly — so there is no interruption of this vital program.

Planned Parenthood the Target of Reagan Rhetoric, Budget Cuts

Planned Parenthood Federation of America and the International Planned Parenthood Federation have come under increasing fire from the Reagan Administration. These non-governmental organizations conduct research and monitor legislation on abortion, contraception and family planning, and the American arm of the organization accredits affiliated clinics nationwide which offer medical services and birth control and family planning information. The attack against Planned Parenthood has been waged on several fronts, the most vital being the Administration's efforts to cut government funding to both groups because of their involvement in abortion counseling; in some of the accredited clinics, abortions are also among the medical services provided.

The first move in this direction was the exclusion in 1983 of Planned Parenthood of America from the list of charities receiving funds from the annual federal employee charity drive. The drive, administered by the Combined Federal Campaign, enables federal workers to make donations to 150 different charities through one payroll deduction. The Office of Personnel Management said it based its rejection of Planned Parenthood on the organization's "failure to comply with financial and accounting standards required by OPM rules." But the next day a federal district judge reinstated Planned Parenthood in the list. U.S. District Court Judge Joyce H. Green noted OPM Director David Devine's publicly stated opposition to abortion and said the technical reasons he gave for rejecting Planned Parenthood were "pretextual." She said the OPM had shown no "substantial irregularities" in Planned Parenthood's accounting procedures. Planned Parenthood, with an annual budget of $170 million, had been included in the federal campaign for 14 years and in 1982 received $500,000 from the drive.

In June 1984 the Reagan Administration caused an uproar domestically and internationally when it announced that it was determined to cut off U.S. aid to international population programs that practiced or advocated abortion. (See pp. 178-182.) One of the organizations that would be most affected by the new policy—and may have been the real target of the Administration's announcement—was the International Planned Parenthood Federation. The agency stood to lose $11 million a year in U.S. aid (one-fifth of its budget) unless it changed its abortion policies.

The Idaho STATESMAN
Boise, ID, April 2, 1983

The most unsettling aspect of the controversy surrounding United Way and Planned Parenthood was the unethical way the anti-abortion movement went about imposing its moral judgment on the community.

In their fervor to oust Planned Parenthood from the United Way campaign, the anti-abortionists virtually took United Way hostage, threatening a boycott that could have curtailed funds not just for Planned Parenthood but for all the other United Way charities.

To achieve their end, the anti-abortionists apparently stood ready to sacrifice needy organizations and people throughout Ada County.

Their ploy worked. The United Way board decided it could not risk a bitter fight that might cut the flow of funds to charitable causes.

Caught in a no-win squeeze between the anti-abortionists and supporters of Planned Parenthood, the United Way board sought a compromise. If Planned Parenthood would agree never to allow abortions at its offices, United Way would continue funding for Planned Parenthood's other services, which include counseling and providing contraception.

Planned Parenthood's directors — to their credit — stood on principle. They said they would rather forgo the money than allow United Way to dictate Planned Parenthood policy.

In the end, the anti-abortionists won and the community lost. Though Planned Parenthood's policy on abortion is controversial, the value of its other programs in preventing venereal disease and unwanted pregnancies is obvious. Now, Planned Parenthood is locked out of the most effective fund-raising operation in the county.

No doubt, some supporters of Planned Parenthood are upset with United Way. That's understandable, but we hope they will not vent their anger by withholding contributions. Both United Way and Planned Parenthood still need community-wide support.

St. Louis Review
St. Louis, MO, October 17, 1980

Planned Parenthood is in the midst of a massive and costly drive to stop the pro-life movement and to improve its own image.

The pro-abortion organization will run television commercials of a so-called patriotic nature showing American families together. It will mention that these families enjoy "the good life" because they are limited in size and that the right to life movement would change this by its anti-abortion activities.

They envy the right to life movement its positive image and are trying to create one of their own by emphasizing the family.

Yet its advertising shows many contradictions. In its printed materials it says young people should come to Planned Parenthood for advice on family and sexual matters. What about the family? Parents are being ignored.

Films that the organization sponsors also depict youngsters going to Planned Parenthood counselors. Again what about the role of the family? Are most parents considered incapable of advice?

What about parental rights? Planned Parenthood seems to be following the pattern of some judicial decisions today which totally exclude parents from any say about their teenage children with regard to an abortion. Maybe it's legal, but is it pro-family?

It is difficult for us to imagine any pro-abortion organization being really pro-family. Planned Parenthood, of course, has its own unique idea of what the family should be. Again it advertises itself as a primary agency for social change with regard to the family.

The two main tools to reform the family according to its plan are abortion and birth control. We think the family is in trouble today and needs help but we don't think that abortion and birth control will be its salvation.

It is important that our Catholic parents see to it that their children are not exposed to Planned Parenthood propaganda either in the public schools or in any of the social or recreational agencies that push its films or pamphlets.

They don't present our ideal of a family!

Pittsburgh Post-Gazette
Pittsburgh, PA, September 17, 1984

Donald J. Devine, the appointed director of the Office of Personnel Management, objects to abortion, as do many members of the Reagan administration.

A shared point of view among high officials does not, however, give Mr. Devine the authority to impose his personal political beliefs upon lower-ranking members of the government. Yet Mr. Devine has overstepped the bounds that legally separate civil-service employees from the political whims of appointed government officials in an egregious fashion by deciding that the national Planned Parenthood organization will not receive donations from the 1983 charity drive of federal employees.

The ruling's effect upon Planned Parenthood, the social agency that pioneered family planning, will not be crippling, because the non-profit organization depends primarily upon tax-exempt private contributions and stands a good chance of reversing the rule in federal court.

The targeting of this particular agency does set a dangerous precedent, however, by usurping the right of federal employees to make personal contributions to social agencies chosen on a non-political basis.

Mr. Devine himself appeared to recognize the shaky ground upon which he stands by cloaking the decision in bureaucratic doubletalk. In a statement, OPM cited Planned Parenthood's "failure to comply with financial and accounting standards" and said its application was "not sufficiently candid and complete."

The decision to drop Planned Parenthood, after it has received voluntarily donated funds from federal employees for 14 years, also was based on hearings held earlier this month at which foes of abortion were invited to call for its elimination from the fund drive. Moreover, Mr. Devine, who made a public issue of his opposition to abortion, is already under a court order to avoid political and ideological choices in determining which agencies receive federal employee contributions.

With that order in mind, a spokesman said, Mr. Devine "did bend over backwards to insure that Planned Parenthood's rights were respected." But the vagueness of the objections upon which the decision was hung suggests instead that Mr. Devine bent over backwards to find a flimsy excuse for driving an ideological opponent from the funding campaign. The precedent ought to concern all Americans, lest political criteria be used in the future to justify ideological intervention into the lives of federal employees as it relates not only to abortion but also to any number of causes.

THE KANSAS CITY STAR
Kansas City, MO, December 6, 1984

International Planned Parenthood Federation is reducing its budget of $55 million by 30 percent. Americans at a meeting of donor countries could not tell the federation what money would be available. The administration in Washington has said it will not contribute to organizations that promote abortion and has threatened to withdraw its $17 million grant.

This sort of silliness will pacify fanatical anti-choicers in this country; it will also cause immense suffering among the poor of the world to whom abortion is an unaffordable alternative to a baby a year and the human misery that can bring. It is the thinking that makes Malthus triumphant in the Sahel. It is reflected in the enormous starving eyes of Ethiopian children and the dehydrated babies left to die in the sun on the outskirts of Rio.

It will, of course, cause many more abortions and many more deaths of women denied contraceptives who end up at the mercy of witch doctors.

The fundamental weakness of anti-choicers, along with their attempts to impose their belief on others (no one is forced to get an abortion), is that they talk incessantly of murder but do not do the one thing that could really reduce the number of abortions: Spread the word about and the means for contraception.

The Record
Hackensack, NJ, December 21, 1984

Unwittingly, President Reagan did more last week to promote abortions in the Third World than any previous president. His administration announced on Thursday that effective Jan. 1, Planned Parenthood Federation, the major international family planning agency, will lose all U.S. funding. That means a $17 million drop — about a sixth of its global outlay — in the 1985 budget of this internationally respected organization.

Mr. Reagan yanked federal support, a commitment that dates back to 1966, on the grounds that Planned Parenthood is funding abortions. It is not, but the agency does underwrite family-planning clinics around the globe, and some of them perform abortions. Most Third World nations have no prohibitions about the procedure. But Planned Parenthood, it should be noted, is not an advocate of abortions. Instead, the agency provides millions of women with birth-control information and other preventive programs and warns that abortion should be only a last resort in an unwanted pregnancy.

Now, with a big dip in the agency's budget, clinics throughout the Third World — in overcrowded countries such as India, Mexico, and Zaire — will have to close their doors. Women will not have access to any of their services, and of course, more pregnancies will result. There will be millions of unwanted births, and some of these women will seek out abortions which will turn out to be unsafe, as women in this country did before 1973. Many will die as a result.

The world's population, particularly in the developing nations, is growing at an alarming rate — and with the overcrowding comes poverty, hunger, poor health for millions upon millions of families. It's been hard enough convincing these women to rely on birth control to better plan their families. Planned Parenthood has a great track record in doing that. But now the Reagan administration is making family planning impossible for millions of the world's poorest women.

The Hartford Courant
Hartford, CT, September 24, 1984

Like other opponents of legalized abortion, Donald J. Devine has a right to make his views known and to lobby for changing the law.

But, as director of the Federal Office of Personnel Management, he should not have the right to penalize Planned Parenthood for holding a different view.

Dr. Devine ruled that Planned Parenthood would be dropped from the Combined Federal Campaign, a government charity drive that works much like the United Way. The family planning group received about $500,000 from the fund last year.

U.S. District Judge Joyce H. Green, however, overruled Dr. Devine. The judge noted that Dr. Devine's "candidly admitted bias" and the "substantial irregularities" in his handling of the case showed that his technical justification for disqualifying Planned Parenthood was merely "pretextual."

Dr. Devine argued that his abortion views were not a factor but that Planned Parenthood failed to meet new regulations which bar federal charity contributions to groups involved in political advocacy.

The new restrictions were prompted by President Reagan's executive order in March that said the fund drive should be limited to traditional charities. It is unclear why tougher rules were needed since the Internal Revenue Service already limits the political activities of organizations that seek tax exempt status.

If Dr. Devine wants to end legalized abortion, he should fight to change the law. Planned Parenthood is the wrong target.

St. Paul Pioneer Press & Dispatch
St. Paul, MN, December 23, 1984

International Planned Parenthood Federation is one of the most prominent family planning organizations in the world. About one-fourth of its $55 million budget comes from the U.S. government. Using unbalanced logic, the Reagan administration earlier this month decided to end that support.

The reason is quite simple. In the administration's view, no U.S. funds should go to any agencies that have any involvement with abortion. It makes no difference to the administration that none of the U.S. funds are used for abortions or that in the United States and in most countries abortions are legal.

Among the 120 countries where the IPPF operates, none of the affiliates perform abortions and only 12 provide abortion counseling. Some of those counseled are victims of illegal abortions. The 12 affiliates receive little U.S. money.

In its blinding zeal to fight abortion, the Reagan administration has decided to end all support for the IPPF. It matters not, apparently, that an overwhelming portion of IPPF activities are directed at educating parents about birth control, making birth control methods available and improving maternal care. All that counts is that in 12 countries, IPPF affiliates, in counseling pregnant women, discuss abortion as an option.

So, to punish 12 IPPF affiliates, the U.S. has decided not to provide any of the $17 million sought by the organization.

The message is that halting abortions takes precedence over everything, even more acceptable population control methods.

It is wrong for the Reagan administration to deal such a devastating blow to the vital and worthwhile work of the IPPF for the actions of 10 percent of its worldwide affiliates. It is wrong for the administration to seek greater success in banning abortions in other nations where the procedure is legal than the White House has achieved in this country. It is foolish for the administration not to see the consequences of its actions on population control efforts.

When the Congress returns in January, members should insist that U.S. aid to the IPPF be restored.

The Louisville Times
Louisville, KY, December 17, 1984

The greatest flaw in the Reagan administration's assault on international family planning is that it may very well promote more unwanted pregnancies and, perhaps, more abortions.

Nevertheless, it is in pursuit of an anti-abortion agenda that the White House has focused criticism on organizations such as the International Planned Parenthood Federation. If Mr. Reagan is serious about reducing the number of abortions, however, he has chosen the wrong target.

On Jan. 1, the U.S. will suspend its annual $17 million grant to the federation, an amount equalling 20 per cent of the group's budget. Precisely how that will affect the efforts to educate and equip Third World couples to plan their families with or without contraception has not been determined. But given Planned Parenthood's record of success, the impact, inevitably, will be substantial.

Contrary to the administration's claims, abortion is promoted by Planned Parenthood neither in the United States nor abroad. Indeed, the domestic organization has been wrongly accused not only of promoting, but of performing abortions — a lie that has damaged its reputation.

What has tarnished the international organization — at least in the eyes of U.S. abortion foes — is International Planned Parenthood's determination to continue its efforts even in places such as the People's Republic of China, where government-backed population control efforts have employed abortion.

As a condition for more American assistance, the Reagan administration required that Planned Parenthood suspend its efforts in such nations. But such a step would be costly. The nongovernment Population Crisis Committee predicts that elimination of U.S. funding could result in more than 2 million more unwanted pregnancies *annually* in underdeveloped countries. Inevitably, some of these women will turn in desperation to abortion.

In the United States and other developed countries, abortion as a substitute for contraception is bad policy. But discouraging contraception and other forms of family planning to stop abortion is self-defeating — and downright stupid.

The Washington Post
Washington, DC, December 14, 1984

THANKS TO A heedless decision by the Reagan administration, millions of needy people in the developing world will be denied family planning aid. This will occur because the Agency for International Development, under strong White House pressure, has cut off funds to the International Planned Parenthood Federation, the largest voluntary family-planning organization in the world.

The administration's decision to deny the IPPF the $17 million earmarked for it in this year's budget has no basis in any change in the law governing foreign population aid. For 11 years, that law has forbidden the use of U.S. aid for abortions. The IPPF insists it has scrupulously adhered to that law. It performs no abortions, does not advocate abortion as a method of birth control and, in distributing aid to independent national family-planning associations throughout the world, it is careful to warn that the U.S. allocation must not be used for abortions.

Less than 1 percent of all the money flowing through the IPPF is used for abortion-related services, and it is used by only 10 of the 119 participating nations. Moreover, the administration, which has administered the population program for the past four years, does not claim that the IPPF has violated the anti-abortion strictures. The administration simply decided last summer to reinterpret the law to please a group of extremists that wanted to change the pattern of family planning aid to developing countries.

The new interpretation was specifically rejected by the House in language incorporated into the appropriation bill passed by both houses this fall. It holds that no money can be given to the IPPF if any of that money flows to foreign family-planning agencies that, using *other* sources of money, provide abortion-related services.

Essentially this means that the United States, which is only one of 27 donor nations, is trying to dictate family-planning policies for all 119 member nations. Like the United States, many donor and recipient countries have legalized abortion. Adhering to a policy that would effectively prevent these sovereign countries from establishing rules for their own national organizations puts the IPPF—and the United States—in an untenable position.

Losing the American quarter-plus of its financing will mean that the IPPF—the single or major source of family planning aid to many Third World countries—will have to cancel or sharply cut back family planning and other public health programs in some of the poorest countries of Africa, Asia, Central America and South America. As a result, many desperately poor women will resort to self-inflicted or illegal abortions, which are still major birth-control methods in the less-developed world. This avoidable suffering will be in large part attributable to this decision, which contravenes congressional intent.

Los Angeles Times
Los Angeles, CA, December 17, 1984

President Reagan has kept his promise to the right-to-life movement. He has given the foes of abortion something to be immensely pleased about. American public support of the International Planned Parenthood Federation has been cut off. A strong lesson has been taught the world about the feelings of the American President concerning abortion—he doesn't like it—and the punishment for failing to conform to his wishes—no money.

In the flush of victory an officer of the National Right to Life Committee revealed the dimensions of ignorance and misinformation on which the decision was based. He called the federation "the largest and most effective promoter of abortion in Third World countries," saying further that the planned-parenthood group had lobbied to legalize abortion and promoted it as a means of birth control. If Reagan believed that, it is no wonder that he was upset about American taxpayers' money feeding such a monstrous operation.

The only trouble is that there is no truth to what the right-to-life committee spokesman said. The federation is the largest and most effective promoter of birth control in Third World countries, that is for sure, but it does not promote abortion, does not propose abortion as a birth-control method, and last year something less than 1% of its budget was used by affiliated organizations for abortion-related services. The U.S. government provided about 30% of the funds and contraceptives used by the federation last year. It was to have furnished $17 million for the year ahead.

The President has made his point at the expense of some of the most miserable people on Earth who now, with certainty, will be driven to increased reliance on abortion because of the deprivation of contraceptives. A fledgling program in Africa has been set back an estimated five years at the moment when that region is the most affected by out-of-control birthrates. New programs in 18 African nations will lose funding, and of necessity be postponed.

Speaking for Reagan, the administrator of the Agency for International Development has called on the planned-parenthood group to conform to the new rules devised by the Administration last summer, as if this problem were the fault of the agency. The federation wisely has resisted this calculated blackmail. It must know that a donor so sensitive to a political minority within its own borders can predictably be insensitive to the frustrated majority in poor nations beyond its frontiers.

What a cruel policy this is. What a callous way for the richest nation in the world to try to manipulate others.

LAS VEGAS REVIEW-JOURNAL

Las Vegas, NV, December 13, 1984

It's the 20th century, but you'd never know it the way some people behave.

They'd have us live in a fairyland where pregnancy, abortion and venereal disease do not exist.

They'd persist against educating our youth on birth control topics.

It would be one thing if parents taught their kids about such vital and natural biological matters. But too many parents don't, and the adolescents wind up in trouble through a lack of information, or just plain misinformation.

In Clark County last year there were 2,123 teen-age pregnancies. Of those, there were 1,308 births, 805 abortions and 10 fetal deaths. Clearly, the youth of Southern Nevada aren't getting the message.

But where can teen-agers go if they seek information on such subjects? They could turn to Planned Parenthood of Southern Nevada, a longstanding, non-profit family planning organization. They could, that is, if they knew about Planned Parenthood.

All but one of the Clark County School District's high school principals have banned Planned Parenthood advertisements in student newspapers, apparently because of pressure from a small but vocal minority of parents who object to them.

It's a ticklish situation, to say the least. The ads are about as innocuous as you can get, and are not the least bit offensive or lascivious. They merely state what services Planned Parenthood offers.

But there is another principle at stake here, and that is whether a newspaper — more precisely, a student newspaper published with taxpayer dollars — can be forced to print an advertisement.

The American Civil Liberties Union and Planned Parenthood Tuesday filed a lawsuit against the school district, alleging Planned Parenthood has been harmed by the "unconstitutional prior restraint upon the free speech rights" of the organization.

First Amendment case law is clear with regard to regular, privately owned newspapers such as this one. Newspaper publishers have the absolute right to reject any commercial speech —

advertisements — they want to, unless the rejection would violate some statute, such as the Sherman Act, or would breach a contract between the advertiser and the publisher.

The ACLU attorney, however, argued schools are a governmental agency and therefore cannot censor ads.

We doubt it. Case law seems equally clear on the right of student newspapers to reject advertising.

About the only leg Planned Parenthood appears to stand on is its assertion that the school district delegates censorship powers to the high school principals "without establishing narrow, objective and definite standards to guide their conduct."

Last year a school district committee toyed with adopting a policy that would ban all advertisements for birth control products or information, gambling aids, X- or R-rated movies, tobacco and liquor products, weapons, pornographic materials, drugs and drug paraphernalia.

But the policy was never put into force. So perhaps there is no clearcut, uniform policy guiding the high school principals. That might be necessary. If an ad policy is adopted, it would appear the Planned Parenthood suit would be moot.

A student newspaper — no matter if it is officially controlled by an adviser, a principal or the school district — must retain the right to reject any advertising it deems unfit. Otherwise massage parlor operators or escort services could solicit teen-agers for employment. No one is saying that would happen, but the potential for it would be there if student newspapers are forced to accept all advertising.

While we admire Planned Parenthood's desire and dedication to doing its job, and while we admire the service it is performing, the First Amendment has to take precedence.

The school district, however, should step firmly into the 20th century and specifically permit Planned Parenthood to advertise in student periodicals, and to help educate our obviously undereducated youth. The organization provides quality medical care and the kind of comprehensive sex education that is lacking in our schools. Planned Parenthood has never encouraged teen-agers to have sex, but it recognizes that they are intimately involved on their own, and therefore need guidance.

"SUPPORT BIRTH CONTROL ?!...ARE YOU NUTS ?!!"

Minneapolis Star and Tribune

Minneapolis, MN, December 24, 1984

Congress is often accused, justifiably, of dragging its feet on important matters. But 32 House members, including Minnesota Rep. Bill Frenzel, are acting quickly and commendably to challenge the Reagan administration's decision cutting off funding for the International Planned Parenthood Federation (IPPF).

In a letter to the Agency for International Development (AID), the House members criticized the decision and urged AID to work out an arrangement for further IPPF funding. AID announced recently that it would deny funds because 12 of the federation's 119 affiliates are involved in abortion programs — even though no U.S. aid is used.

The House members expressed confidence that the federation complies with a 10-year-old law prohibiting the use of U.S. money for abortion programs overseas. They also restated congressional intent that multilateral aid to private and voluntary organizations be encouraged, and that U.S. aid not be used to compromise the independence of private organizations or other governments.

In other words, the 32 said the Reagan administration should stop trying to use U.S. humanitarian programs to export its moral agenda overseas. The only result, they said, is to endanger the health of poor women and children in Third World nations and to undermine other development programs.

A Frenzel spokesman said that if the administration fails to provide aid for IPPF, several lawmakers have shown "a lot of interest" in congressional action to require funding. If that is necessary, we hope the full Congress can match the speed and conviction shown by Frenzel and his 31 colleagues.

LEXINGTON HERALD-LEADER
Lexington, KY, December 16, 1984

President Reagan has made his anti-abortion supporters happy by cutting off $17 million in aid to the International Planned Parenthood Federation. The irony is that by cutting off that aid at the beginning of next year, he is ensuring that more women in poor nations around the world will seek abortions.

The president made it clear some time ago that he planned to cut off the funds. The reason, he said, was that some of the nations that received family-planning funds through Planned Parenthood used the money for abortions.

The president's objection made little sense. In reality, only about 1 percent of the total funds went for abortions; the rest went for family planning, medical care and birth control. Nor did he make much sense with his proposal that the federation stipulate that its funds not be used for abortion. The federation — a non-profit, non-political international organization — is not in a position to prohibit sovereign governments from using the money as they see fit. The organization's leaders correctly protested that their making such a demand would merely cause them to lose their contacts with many governments.

So now the federation finds itself poorer by $17 million a year. That loss will translate into less family planning, less medical care, less access to methods of birth control in poor nations.

That in turn will translate into more pregnancies among women who cannot afford to have more children. And that will lead to more abortions, most of them performed in unsanitary rooms by untrained people.

Perhaps some zealots can take pleasure in knowing that they have managed to keep any of their tax dollars from supporting abortion. The rest of us, though, can only be dismayed to know that our government has decided to encourage overpopulation, risky medical procedures and — yes — more abortions simply to satisfy a minority's distorted notion of moral rectitude.

Roanoke Times & World-News
Roanoke, VA, April 24, 1984

PUBERTY. Masturbation. Penis. Testes. These are not words one uses in ordinary dinner conversation. But they shouldn't be considered taboo around the house either. They're part of the vocabulary one must use to communicate sexual information to young people. They appear in sex-education literature distributed by Planned Parenthood of Southwest Virginia.

Because the organization is actively involved in sex education, it draws support from the city of Roanoke. About $8,000 in federal revenue funds is funneled through the city treasury to Planned Parenthood each year. Because the organization deals openly and frankly with questions of sex, it offends many who believe that its literature can corrupt young minds. In fact, some citizens have asked the Roanoke City Council to discontinue funding for the organization because it distributes materials they regard as bordering on pornographic and it refers young girls to abortion clinics without notifying their parents.

For an organization devoted to combating sexual misunderstanding, Planned Parenthood is gravely misunderstood. Part of the problem lies in the nature of the subject matter with which it deals. Part lies in the nature of the national organization: It's a loose-knit collection of autonomous chapters. Some of them operate abortion clinics. The Southwest Virginia unit does not.

Planned Parenthood of Southwest Virginia is primarily concerned with preventing unwanted pregnancies. It distributes literature that discourages teen-age sexual activity. One of its leaflets is entitled "Teensex? It's okay to say NO WAY." It gives reasons for young people to refrain from intercourse. "If you need help," it advises, "Talk to people you trust and respect — at home, school, church or club."

When a young girl with an unwanted pregnancy comes to Planned Parenthood, the organization lays out her options. Those options include abortion. Planned Parenthood of Southwest Virginia insists that it does not encourage abortion. But if a girl chooses the abortion route, Planned Parenthood will tell her where she can obtain a legal one.

Federal courts have ruled that a girl has a right to choose an abortion without consulting her parents. Planned Parenthood encourages the girl to talk over her decision with parents or other mature advisers; but it does not itself advise the parents.

Does Planned Parenthood distribute materials that border on pornography?

City Council was given sample passages from a piece of literature obtained from Planned Parenthood. The literature is not for those who still undress in dark closets. It is written in a simple, light-hearted manner designed to make easy reading for teen-agers who don't like to read. Its illustrations are sometimes explicit, but not erotic.

And it does deal with masturbation without condemning the practice. In the booklet, "The Perils of Puberty," young girls are told: "If you feel sexual urges, for heaven's sake, admit it to yourself. If the feeling and the tension bother you, it is better to masturbate than to get into a relationship which is unreal, too soon, and sentimental. There is nothing 'sweet' or 'dear' about a pregnant 14-year-old. Masturbation cannot hurt you and will probably make you feel more relaxed."

In "The Problem with Puberty," boys are told: "It is not 'manly' or 'unmanly' to masturbate. Girls do it, too, and so do most adults from time to time. Some religions are against it, and some religions aren't. Almost 100 percent of all men do it at one time another; some before they're 6 and some after they're 60. It will not make hair grow on your hands, make you go crazy, give you pimples, wear out your penis, make you sterile, or make sex with women less rewarding. It is not a 'bad habit,' for you or for girls." The young man is advised that it's better to masturbate than to get a girl pregnant.

These booklets are not handed out indiscriminately to teens or preteens, says a Planned Parenthood spokesman. They are given to adults, who may then decide whether they want to pass them on to their children.

Planned Parenthood does not pass judgment on the morality or immorality of premarital sex. But it does provide the parent and child with plenty of good reasons for delaying sexual activity until the child has matured emotionally.

Planned Parenthood is not in the business of pushing religious viewpoints; so it remains neutral on moral questions. For those who insist that there's no such thing as moral neutrality, the books may offend. But on a subject as delicate as sex, there is no way to produce a set of guidelines that will please everyone.

The important thing is that Planned Parenthood attempts to provide factual information designed to discourage irresponsible sex and to curtail unwanted pregnancies. In a society obsessed with sex and bombarded with sexual messages, it makes its pitch in cool, factual style. And the dominant message is restraint.

It's hard to see pornographic content in this literature. It's hard to argue with the need for such literature among young people. Perhaps it's unnecessary among children reared in wholesome religious environments by parents who have definite standards and who know how to communicate them. It's the fortunate child who grows up in such a home. It's the rare one, too.

Index